SALEM HEALTH
PSYCHOLOGY
& MENTAL HEALTH

SALEM HEALTH

PSYCHOLOGY
& MENTAL HEALTH

Volume V

Sleep apnea — Zimbardo, Philip
Appendixes
Indexes

Editor

Nancy A. Piotrowski, Ph.D.
Capella University
University of California, Berkeley

LIBRARY

SALEM PRESS
Pasadena, California   Hackensack, New Jersey

Editor in Chief: Dawn P. Dawson

Editorial Director: Christina J. Moose	*Acquisitions Editor:* Mark Rehn
Developmental Editor: Tracy Irons-Georges	*Photo Editor:* Cynthia Breslin Beres
Project Editor: Rowena Wildin	*Research Supervisor:* Jeffry Jensen
Copy Editors: Constance Pollock	*Production Editor:* Joyce I. Buchea
Christopher Rager	*Design and Graphics:* James Hutson
Editorial Assistant: Brett S. Weisberg	*Layout:* William Zimmerman

Some of the updated and revised essays in this work originally appeared in *Magill's Encyclopedia of Social Science: Psychology,* edited by Nancy A. Piotrowski, Ph.D. (2003) and *Magill's Survey of Social Science: Psychology,* edited by Frank N. Magill (1993).

Library of Congress Cataloging-in-Publication Data

Salem health : psychology and mental health / editor, Nancy A. Piotrowski.
    p. cm.
Includes bibliographical references and index.
    ISBN 978-1-58765-556-2 (set : alk. paper) — ISBN 978-1-58765-557-9 (vol. 1 : alk. paper) —
ISBN 978-1-58765-558-6 (vol. 2 : alk. paper) — ISBN 978-1-58765-559-3 (vol. 3 : alk. paper) —
ISBN 978-1-58765-560-9 (vol. 4 : alk. paper) — ISBN 978-1-58765-561-6 (vol. 5 : alk. paper)
1. Psychology, Applied. 2. Medicine and psychology. I. Piotrowski, Nancy A.
BF636.S25 2010
150.3—dc22
    2009024237

First Printing

Contents

Complete List of Contents xci

Sleep apnea 1803
Smell and taste 1805
Social identity theory 1810
Social learning: Albert Bandura 1815
Social networks 1819
Social perception 1823
Social psychological models:
    Erich Fromm 1827
Social psychological models:
    Karen Horney 1831
Social schemata 1834
Social support and mental health 1838
Sociopaths 1842
Speech disorders 1845
Speech perception 1848
Spirituality and mental health 1852
Split-brain studies 1854
Sports psychology 1859
Stanford-Binet test 1864
Stanford prison experiment 1866
State-Trait Anxiety Inventory (STAI) 1869
Statistical significance tests 1870
Stepfamilies 1874
Stimulant medications 1877
Strategic family therapy 1880
Stress: Behavioral and psychological
    responses 1884
Stress: Physiological responses 1890
Stress-related diseases 1894
Stress: Theories 1898
Strong Interest Inventory (SII) 1902
Structuralism and functionalism 1904
Stuttering 1909
Substance Abuse and Mental Health
    Services Administration 1914
Substance use disorders 1915
Suicide 1920
Sullivan, Harry Stack 1925
Support groups 1926
Survey research: Questionnaires and
    interviews 1929
Synaptic transmission 1933
Synesthesia 1936

Systematic desensitization 1939
Systems theories 1943

Taste aversion 1945
Teaching methods 1949
Teenage suicide 1954
Teenagers' mental health 1959
Temperature 1963
Terrorism: Psychological causes and
    effects 1968
Testing: Historical perspectives 1971
Thematic Apperception Test (TAT) 1975
Thirst 1977
Thorndike, Edward L. 1979
Thought: Inferential 1980
Thought: Study and measurement 1984
Thyroid gland 1988
Tic disorders 1992
Time-out 1996
Tolman, Edward C. 1998
Touch and pressure 1999
Tourette's syndrome 2003
Transactional analysis 2007
Transtheoretical model 2011
Transvestism 2013
Type A behavior pattern 2015

Violence and sexuality in the media 2020
Violence by children and teenagers 2024
Violence: Psychological causes and
    effects 2027
Virtual reality 2030
Vision: Brightness and contrast 2034
Vision: Color 2038
Visual system 2041

Watson, John B. 2046
Wechsler Intelligence Scale for Children-
    Third Edition (WISC-III) 2047
Within-subject experimental designs 2050
Women's mental health 2054
Women's psychology: Carol Gilligan 2059
Women's psychology: Karen Horney 2064
Women's psychology: Sigmund Freud 2067
Work motivation 2072

Workforce reentry. 2076
Workplace issues and mental health 2078

Yalom, Irvin D. 2084

Zimbardo, Philip 2086

Appendixes
Glossary 2091
Bibliography. 2116
Web Site Directory 2133

Mediagraphy. 2142
Organizations and Support Groups 2156
Pharmaceutical List 2175
Biographical List of Psychologists 2187
Notable Court Cases 2196

Indexes
Category Index CVII
Personages Index CXXXI
Subject Index. CXLI

Complete List of Contents

Volume 1

Contents v
Publisher's Note vii
Introduction ix
Contributors. xiii
Complete List of Contents xxi

Ability tests. 1
Abnormality: Biomedical models 6
Abnormality: Legal models 11
Abnormality: Psychological models. 15
Achievement motivation. 21
Addictive personality and behaviors 25
ADHD. *See* Attention-deficit hyperactivity
     disorder
Adler, Alfred 29
Adlerian psychotherapy 30
Adolescence: Cognitive skills 35
Adolescence: Cross-cultural patterns 40
Adolescence: Sexuality 44
Adrenal gland 49
Advertising 52
Affiliation and friendship 56
Affiliation motive 61
African Americans and mental health 66
Ageism 69
Aggression 74
Aggression: Reduction and control. 77
Aging: Cognitive changes 81
Aging: Physical changes 87
Aging: Theories 91
Agoraphobia and panic disorders 96
Air rage 100
Alaskan natives. *See* Native Americans/
     Alaskan Natives and mental health
Albee, George W.. 102
Alcohol dependence and abuse 103
Allport, Gordon 107
Altruism, cooperation, and empathy 109
Alzheimer's disease. 114
American Indians. *See* Native Americans/
     Alaskan Natives and mental health
American Psychiatric Association 120

American Psychological Association. 123
Amnesia and fugue. 126
Analytic psychology: Jacques Lacan 130
Analytical psychology: Carl Jung. 134
Analytical psychotherapy. 138
Anger 142
Animal experimentation 145
Anorexia nervosa and bulimia nervosa 150
Antianxiety medications 156
Antidepressant medications 158
Antipsychotic medications 160
Antisocial personality disorder 161
Anxiety disorders 166
APA. *See* American Psychiatric Association,
     American Psychological Association
Aphasias. 171
Archetypes and the collective unconscious . . . 176
Archival data 180
Artificial intelligence 184
Asian Americans/Pacific Islanders and
     mental health 188
Asperger syndrome. 191
Assessment 195
Assisted living. 198
Attachment and bonding in infancy and
     childhood 201
Attention 205
Attention-deficit hyperactivity disorder 209
Attitude-behavior consistency 214
Attitude formation and change 218
Attraction theories 222
Attributional biases. 227
Autism. 230
Automaticity 234
Aversion, taste. *See* Taste aversion
Aversion therapy 238
Avoidant personality disorder 239

Bandura, Albert. 242
Battered woman syndrome. 243
Beck, Aaron T. 246
Beck Depression Inventory (BDI) 247

Bed-wetting 248
Behavior therapy 252
Behavioral assessment 257
Behavioral economics 261
Behavioral family therapy 265
Behaviorism. 269
Biases. See Attributional biases
Bilingualism. 273
Bilingualism and learning disabilities. 276
Binet, Alfred 278
Biofeedback and relaxation 279
Bipolar disorder 283
Biracial heritage and mental health. 288
Birth: Effects on physical development 290
Birth order and personality 295
Bisexual mental health. See Gay, lesbian,
    bisexual, and transgender mental health
Blacks. See African Americans and mental
    health
Blau, Theodore H. 298
Bobo doll experiment 299
Body dysmorphic disorder. 301
Bonding. See Attachment and bonding in
    infancy and childhood
Borderline personality disorder 304
Brain damage. 306
Brain structure 312
Breuer, Josef 318
Brief therapy 320
Bronfenbrenner, Urie 322
Bruner, Jerome 323
Bulimia nervosa. See Anorexia nervosa and
    bulimia nervosa
Bullying 324
Bystander intervention. 326

Caffeine and mental health 331
California Psychological Inventory (CPI). . . . 333

Cancer and mental health 335
Cannon, Walter Bradford 338
Career and personnel testing 339
Career Occupational Preference
    System (COPS) 344
Career selection, development, and
    change 346
Case study methodologies 351
Causal attribution 354
CDI. See Children's Depression Inventory
    (CDI)
Child abuse 358
Childhood disorders 363
Children's Depression Inventory (CDI) 369
Children's mental health 371
Circadian rhythms 376
Classical conditioning. See Pavlovian
    conditioning
Clinical interviewing, testing, and
    observation 381
Coaching 385
Codependency 388
Cognitive Abilities Test (CogAT) 391
Cognitive ability: Gender differences 392
Cognitive behavior therapy 396
Cognitive development: Jean Piaget. 401
Cognitive dissonance. 405
Cognitive maps 409
Cognitive psychology. 414
Cognitive social learning: Walter Mischel. . . . 420
Cognitive therapy. 423
Collective unconscious. See Archetypes and
    the collective unconscious
Collectivism. 427
College entrance examinations 431
Community psychology 434

Category Index III

Volume 2

Contents xxxvii
Complete List of Contents. xxxix

Comorbidity 439
Competency. See Incompetency
Competition. See Cooperation, competition, and
    negotiation

Complex experimental designs 442
Computer and Internet use and mental
    health 446
Computer models of cognition 448
Concept formation. 451
Conditioning 455
Conduct disorder. 461

Confidentiality 465
Consciousness 467
Consciousness: Altered states 471
Constructivist psychology 477
Consumer psychology 479
Conversion. *See* Hypochondriasis, conversion, and somatization
Cooperation. *See* Altruism, cooperation, and empathy
Cooperation, competition, and negotiation. 483
Cooperative learning. 487
Coping: Chronic illness 490
Coping: Social support. 495
Coping: Strategies 500
Coping: Terminal illness 504
COPS. *See* Career Occupational Preference System (COPS)
Couples therapy 508
CPI. *See* California Psychological Inventory (CPI)
Creativity and intelligence 514
Creativity: Assessment 517
Crisis intervention 520
Cross-cultural psychology 523
Crowd behavior. 525
Cultural competence. 529
Culture and diagnosis 531
Culture-bound syndromes 532

Dance therapy. *See* Music, dance, and theater therapy
Data, archival. *See* Archival data
Data description 535
Death and dying 541
Deception and lying 545
Decision making 547
Deductive reasoning 551
Defense mechanisms. 552
Defense reactions: Species-specific 555
Dementia 559
Denial 563
Depression 566
Depth and motion perception. 572
Desensitization, systematic. *See* Systematic desensitization
Development 576
Developmental disabilities. 580
Developmental methodologies 585
Developmental psychology. 589

Dewey, John. 593
Diagnosis 594
Diagnostic and Statistical Manual of Mental Disorders (DSM) 599
Dialectical behavioral therapy. 602
Disabilities, developmental. *See* Developmental disabilities
Disaster psychology. 604
Diseases, stress-related. *See* Stress-related diseases
Dissociative disorders. 609
Dissociative identity disorder. *See* Multiple personality
Divorce. *See* Separation and divorce
Dix, Dorothea. 613
Dollard, John. *See* Miller, Neal E., and John Dollard
Domestic violence 614
Down syndrome 619
Dreams 623
Drives 628
Drug therapies 631
DSM. See *Diagnostic and Statistical Manual of Mental Disorders* (DSM)
Dyslexia 636

Eating disorders 640
Ebbinghaus, Hermann 645
Ecological psychology 646
Economics, behavioral. *See* Behavioral economics
Educational psychology 649
Ego defense mechanisms 652
Ego psychology: Erik H. Erikson 658
Ego, superego, and id 664
Elder abuse 666
Elders' mental health 669
Elimination disorders 674
Ellis, Albert 676
Emotional expression 677
Emotional intelligence 681
Emotions 683
Empathy. *See* Altruism, cooperation, and empathy
Encoding 687
Endocrine system. 690
Endorphins 695
Enuresis. *See* Bed-wetting
Environmental factors and mental health . . . 699
Environmental psychology. 702

Environmental toxicology and mental
   health 707
Erikson, Erik H. 710
Ethology. 711
Evolutionary psychology 715
Exercise and mental health 719
Existential psychology 721
Experimental psychology 725
Experimentation: Ethics and participant
   rights 728
Experimentation: Independent, dependent,
   and control variables 733
Extroverts. *See* Introverts and extroverts
Eye movement desensitization and
   reprocessing 737
Eyewitness testimony 739
Eysenck, Hans 743

Facial feedback 745
Factitious disorders. 749
Family life: Adult issues 752
Family life: Children's issues. 756
Family systems theory 759
Family therapy, behavioral. *See* Behavioral
   family therapy
Family therapy, strategic. *See* Strategic family
   therapy
Farsightedness. *See* Nearsightedness and
   farsightedness
Father-child relationship. 762
Fear 766
Femininity. 770
Feminist psychotherapy 772
Fetishes 775
Field experimentation 777
Field theory: Kurt Lewin 781
Fields of specialization. *See* Psychology: Fields of
   specialization
Fight-or-flight response. 784
Forensic psychology 787
Forgetting and forgetfulness. 791
Forgiveness 795
Freud, Anna. 799

Freud, Sigmund 800
Freudian psychology 801
Friendship. *See* Affiliation and friendship
Fromm, Erich 806
Fugue. *See* Amnesia and fugue
Functionalism. *See* Structuralism and
   functionalism

Gambling 808
Games and mental health 810
GATB. *See* General Aptitude Test Battery
Gay, lesbian, bisexual, and transgender
   mental health 813
Gender differences. 817
Gender identity disorder. 820
Gender identity formation 824
Gender roles and gender role conflicts 827
General adaptation syndrome 830
General Aptitude Test Battery (GATB) 834
Generalized anxiety disorder 835
Genetics and mental health 838
Gesell, Arnold 842
Gestalt therapy 843
Giftedness. 847
Gilligan, Carol 851
Gonads 852
Grammar and speech 856
Grieving. 861
Group decision making 864
Group therapy 868
Groups 872
Guilt. 877

Habituation and sensitization 881
Hall, G. Stanley 885
Hallucinations 886
Hate crimes: Psychological causes and
   effects 890
Health insurance 892
Health maintenance organizations 894
Health psychology 895

Category Index. XXIX

Volume 3

Contents liii
Complete List of Contents lv

Hearing 901
Help-seeking 905
Helping 908
Hierarchy of needs 913
Hispanics. *See* Latinos and mental health
History. *See* Psychology: History
Histrionic personality disorder 916
Homelessness: Psychological causes and
    effects 918
Homosexuality 922
Hope and mental health 926
Hormones and behavior 928
Horney, Karen 934
Hospice 935
Hull, Clark L. 937
Human resource training and
    development 938
Humanistic psychology 942
Humanistic trait models: Gordon Allport . . . 946
Hunger 950
Hypnosis 955
Hypochondriasis, conversion, and
    somatization 960
Hypothesis development and testing 966
Hysteria 970

ICD. See *International Classification of*
    Diseases (ICD)
Id. *See* Ego, superego, and id
Identity crises 974
Implosion 978
Imprinting 980
Impulse control disorders 984
Impulses, inhibitory and excitatory. *See*
    Inhibitory and excitatory impulses
Incentive motivation 989
Incompetency 993
Individual psychology: Alfred Adler 996
Inductive reasoning 1001
Industrial and organizational
    psychology 1002
Inhibitory and excitatory impulses 1007
Insanity defense 1011
Insomnia 1013

Instinct theory 1018
Intelligence 1022
Intelligence, emotional. *See* Emotional
    intelligence
Intelligence quotient (IQ) 1027
Intelligence tests 1028
Intelligences, multiple. *See* Multiple
    intelligences
Interest inventories 1033
International Classification of Diseases
    (ICD) 1037
Internet psychology 1039
Internet use. *See* Computer and Internet
    use and mental health
Intervention 1043
Intimacy 1044
Introverts and extroverts 1047
IQ. *See* Intelligence quotient (IQ)

James, William 1050
Jealousy 1051
Johnson, Virginia E. *See* Masters, William H.,
    and Virginia E. Johnson
Jung, Carl 1054
Jungian psychology 1055
Juvenile delinquency 1059

Kelly, George A. 1063
Kinesthetic memory 1064
Kinsey, Alfred 1067
Kleptomania 1069
Kohlberg, Lawrence 1070
KOIS. *See* Kuder Occupational Interest
    Survey (KOIS)
Kraepelin, Emil 1071
Kübler-Ross, Elisabeth 1072
Kuder Occupational Interest Survey
    (KOIS) 1074

Lacan, Jacques 1076
Language 1077
Latinos and mental health 1085
Law and psychology 1088
Leadership 1092
Learned helplessness 1097
Learning 1100
Learning disorders 1106

Lesbian mental health. *See* Gay, lesbian, bisexual, and transgender mental health
Lewin, Kurt 1110
Linguistics 1111
Little Albert study 1117
Lobotomy 1119
Logic and reasoning 1121
Long-term memory 1126
Lorenz, Konrad 1130
Love 1131
Lying. *See* Deception and lying

Masculinity. 1137
Maslow, Abraham 1138
Masochism. *See* Sadism and masochism
Masters, William H., and Virginia E. Johnson 1139
May, Rollo 1141
MBTI. *See* Myers-Briggs Type Indicator (MBTI)
Media exposure and mental health 1142
Media psychology 1146
Meditation and relaxation 1152
Memories, repressed. *See* Repressed memories
Memory 1155
Memory: Animal research 1160
Memory: Empirical studies 1165
Memory: Physiology 1169
Memory: Sensory 1174
Memory storage 1180
Men's mental health 1184
Mental health parity 1189
Mental health practitioners. 1190
Mental illness: Historical concepts 1194
Mental retardation 1200
Midlife crisis 1205
Milgram experiment 1208
Miller, Neal E., and John Dollard 1210
Minnesota Multiphasic Personality Inventory (MMPI) 1211
Misbehavior 1213
Mischel, Walter 1218
MMPI. *See* Minnesota Multiphasic Personality Inventory (MMPI)
Modeling therapy. *See* Observational learning and modeling therapy
Mood disorders 1219
Mood stabilizer medications 1225
Moral development 1227

Mother-child relationship 1231
Motion perception. *See* Depth and motion perception
Motivation 1234
Motivation: Intrinsic and extrinsic 1238
Motivation, work. *See* Work motivation
Motor development 1240
Multicultural psychology 1244
Multiple intelligences 1246
Multiple personality 1250
Munchausen syndrome and Munchausen syndrome by proxy 1253
Murray, Henry A. 1256
Music, dance, and theater therapy 1257
Myers-Briggs Type Indicator (MBTI) 1261

Narcissistic personality disorder 1264
Narcolepsy 1266
National Institute of Mental Health 1270
Native Americans/Alaskan Natives and mental health 1271
Nearsightedness and farsightedness 1273
Needs, hierarchy of. *See* Hierarchy of needs
Negotiation. *See* Cooperation, competition, and negotiation
Nervous system 1277
Networks, social. *See* Social networks
Neurons 1280
Neuropsychology 1284
Neurotic disorders 1287
Neurotransmitters 1291
Nicotine dependence 1293
NIMH. *See* National Institute of Mental Health
Nonverbal communication 1295
Nutrition and mental health 1300

Obesity 1304
Observational learning and modeling therapy 1309
Observational methods 1314
Obsessive-compulsive disorder 1317
OCD. *See* Obsessive-compulsive disorder
Oedipus complex 1322
Operant conditioning therapies 1324
Optimal arousal theory 1328
Organizational behavior and consulting 1332
Organizational psychology. *See* Industrial and organizational psychology

Pacific Islanders. *See* Asian Americans/Pacific
Islanders and mental health
Pain 1335
Pain management. 1338
Panic attacks. 1343

Paranoia 1346
Paraphilias. *See* Sexual variants and paraphilias
Parental alienation syndrome 1349

Category Index LV

Volume 4

Contents lxxi
Complete List of Contents lxxiii

Parenting styles 1351
Parkinson's disease 1355
Passive aggression 1358
Pattern recognition 1360
Pattern vision 1364
Pavlov, Ivan Petrovich. 1367
Pavlovian conditioning 1368
Peabody Individual Achievement Test
(PIAT) 1373
Penis envy 1374
Perception. *See* Sensation and perception
Person-centered therapy 1377
Personal constructs: George A. Kelly 1382
Personality disorders 1385
Personality interviewing strategies 1391
Personality: Psychophysiological
measures 1394
Personality rating scales. 1399
Personality theory 1402
Personology: Henry A. Murray. 1406
Pervasive developmental disorders. 1410
Philosophy and psychology. 1415
Phobias 1418
Physical development: Environment
versus genetics 1423
Physical development, prenatal. *See* Prenatal
physical development
Piaget, Jean 1426
PIAT. *See* Peabody Individual Achievement
Test (PIAT)
Pinel, Philippe. 1428
Pituitary gland. 1429
Placebo effect 1433
Play therapy 1434
Positive psychology 1438
Postpartum depression 1441
Post-traumatic stress disorder 1443

Power 1448
Prejudice. 1452
Prejudice reduction. 1457
Prenatal physical development. 1461
Pressure. *See* Touch and pressure
Problem-solving stages 1467
Problem-solving strategies 1470
Profiling 1474
Projection 1477
Psychoanalysis 1481
Psychoanalytic psychology 1487
Psychoanalytic psychology and personality:
Sigmund Freud. 1491
Psychobiology 1495
Psychology: Definition 1500
Psychology: Fields of specialization 1504
Psychology: History 1509
Psychopathology 1517
Psychopharmacology 1523
Psychosexual development 1528
Psychosomatic disorders 1532
Psychosurgery 1537
Psychotherapy: Children 1541
Psychotherapy: Effectiveness 1546
Psychotherapy: Goals and techniques 1551
Psychotherapy: Historical approaches 1554
Psychotic disorders 1559
PTSD. *See* Post-traumatic stress disorder
Punishment 1563

Qualitative research. 1567
Quality of life 1570
Quasi-experimental designs 1572

Race and intelligence 1578
Racism 1583
Radical behaviorism: B. F. Skinner 1587
Rape and sexual assault. 1591
Rational emotive therapy 1595
Reactive attachment disorder 1600

Reality therapy 1603
Reasoning. *See* Logic and reasoning
Reasoning, deductive. *See* Deductive reasoning
Reasoning, inductive. *See* Inductive reasoning
Reflexes 1606
Reflexes in newborns 1610
Reinforcement 1613
Relaxation and biofeedback. *See* Biofeedback
    and relaxation
Relaxation and meditation. *See* Meditation
    and relaxation
Religion and psychology 1618
Religiosity: Measurement 1623
Repressed memories 1628
Research ethics 1630
Reticular formation 1634
Retirement. 1637
Risk assessment 1641
Road rage 1643
Rogers, Carl R. 1645
Rorschach, Hermann 1646
Rorschach inkblots 1647
Rosenhan experiment 1649
Rule-governed behavior 1650

S-R theory: Neal E. Miller and John
    Dollard 1655
SAD. *See* Seasonal affective disorder
Sadism and masochism 1659
SAMHSA. *See* Substance Abuse and Mental
    Health Services Administration
Sampling. 1662
Satir, Virginia 1666
Schemata, social. *See* Social schemata
Schizoid personality disorder. 1667
Schizophrenia: Background, types, and
    symptoms 1670
Schizophrenia: High-risk children 1675
Schizophrenia: Theoretical explanations . . . 1680
Schizotypal personality disorder 1685

Scientific methods 1688
Seasonal affective disorder 1694
Self 1699
Self-actualization 1704
Self-disclosure 1708
Self-efficacy 1712
Self-esteem. 1715
Self-help groups 1719
Self-perception theory 1721
Self-presentation 1725
Seligman, Martin E. P. 1730
Selye, Hans 1731
Sensation and perception 1732
Senses 1736
Sensitization. *See* Habituation and
    sensitization
Separation and divorce: Adult issues. 1740
Separation and divorce: Children's issues . . . 1743
Separation anxiety 1747
Sex hormones and motivation 1750
Sexism 1753
Sexual assault. *See* Rape and sexual assault
Sexual behavior patterns 1757
Sexual dysfunction 1761
Sexual harassment: Psychological causes
    and effects 1767
Sexual variants and paraphilias. 1770
Sexuality in the media. *See* Violence and
    sexuality in the media
Shock therapy 1775
Short-term memory 1779
Shyness. 1783
Sibling relationships 1785
Signal detection theory 1789
SII. *See* Strong Interest Inventory (SII)
Skinner, B. F. 1792
Skinner box 1793
Sleep 1796

Category Index LXXXI

Volume 5

Contents lxxxix
Complete List of Contents xci

Sleep apnea 1803
Smell and taste 1805

Smoking. *See* Nicotine dependence
Social identity theory 1810
Social learning: Albert Bandura 1815
Social networks 1819
Social perception 1823

Social psychological models:
Erich Fromm 1827
Social psychological models:
Karen Horney 1831
Social schemata 1834
Social support and mental health 1838
Sociopaths 1842
Somatization. See Hypochondriasis,
conversion, and somatization
Speech. See Grammar and speech
Speech disorders 1845
Speech perception 1848
Spirituality and mental health 1852
Split-brain studies 1854
Sports psychology 1859
STAI. See State-Trait Anxiety Inventory (STAI)
Stanford-Binet test 1864
Stanford prison experiment 1866
State-Trait Anxiety Inventory (STAI) 1869
Statistical significance tests 1870
Stepfamilies 1874
Stimulant medications 1877
Strategic family therapy. 1880
Stress: Behavioral and psychological
responses 1884
Stress: Physiological responses 1890
Stress-related diseases. 1894
Stress: Theories 1898
Strong Interest Inventory (SII). 1902
Structuralism and functionalism 1904
Stuttering 1909
Substance Abuse and Mental Health
Services Administration 1914
Substance use disorders. 1915
Suicide. 1920
Suicide, teenage. See Teenage suicide
Sullivan, Harry Stack 1925
Superego. See Ego, superego, and id
Support groups 1926
Survey research: Questionnaires and
interviews 1929
Synaptic transmission 1933
Synesthesia. 1936
Systematic desensitization 1939
Systems theories. 1943

Taste. See Smell and taste
Taste aversion 1945
TAT. See Thematic Apperception Test (TAT)
Teaching methods 1949

Teenage suicide 1954
Teenagers' mental health. 1959
Temperature. 1963
Terrorism: Psychological causes and
effects. 1968
Testing: Historical perspectives. 1971
Theater therapy. See Music, dance, and
theater therapy
Thematic Apperception Test (TAT) 1975
Thirst 1977
Thorndike, Edward L. 1979
Thought: Inferential 1980
Thought: Study and measurement. 1984
Thyroid gland 1988
Tic disorders. 1992
Time-out. 1996
Tolman, Edward C. 1998
Touch and pressure 1999
Tourette's syndrome 2003
Training and development. See Human
resource training and development
Transactional analysis. 2007
Transgender mental health. See Gay, lesbian,
bisexual, and transgender mental health
Transtheoretical model 2011
Transvestism 2013
Type A behavior pattern 2015

Violence and sexuality in the media 2020
Violence by children and teenagers 2024
Violence: Psychological causes and
effects. 2027
Virtual reality 2030
Vision: Brightness and contrast 2034
Vision: Color 2038
Visual system. 2041

Watson, John B. 2046
Wechsler Intelligence Scale for Children-
Third Edition (WISC-III) 2047
WISC-III. See Wechsler Intelligence Scale for
Children-Third Edition (WISC-III)
Within-subject experimental designs 2050
Women's mental health. 2054
Women's psychology: Carol Gilligan 2059
Women's psychology: Karen Horney. 2064
Women's psychology: Sigmund Freud 2067
Work motivation. 2072
Workforce reentry. 2076
Workplace issues and mental health 2078

Yalom, Irvin D. 2084

Zimbardo, Philip 2086

Appendixes
Glossary 2091
Bibliography. 2116
Web Site Directory 2133
Mediagraphy. 2142

Organizations and Support Groups 2156
Pharmaceutical List 2175
Biographical List of Psychologists 2187
Notable Court Cases 2196

Indexes
Category Index CVII
Personages Index CXXXI
Subject Index CXLI

SALEM HEALTH
PSYCHOLOGY
& MENTAL HEALTH

Sleep apnea

DATE: 1970's forward
TYPE OF PSYCHOLOGY: Biological bases of behavior; stress
FIELD OF STUDY: Sleep

Sleep apnea is a condition in which many episodes of apnea (the absence of breathing) occur, interfering with the quality of sleep. People with sleep apnea are often chronically fatigued. Treatments for sleep apnea include continuous positive airway pressure, mandibular devices, and surgical procedures.

KEY CONCEPTS
- continuous positive airway pressure (CPAP)
- electroencephalogram (EEG)
- genioglossal tubercle advancement
- mandibular devices
- polysomnograph
- somnoplasty
- tracheostomy
- uvulopalatopharyngoplasty

INTRODUCTION

Sleep apnea is a condition that is characterized by frequent periods of ceasing to breathe during sleep. There are two types of sleep apnea: obstructive sleep apnea and central sleep apnea. The most common type is obstructive sleep apnea, which is caused by the repeated collapse of the upper airway during sleep, leading to periods of apnea. Central sleep apnea is caused by a problem in the brain. All people have occasional episodes of sleep apnea. Pathological sleep apnea occurs when these episodes exceed ten per hour and the oxygen saturation of the blood drops below normal for the person's age. Normal oxygen saturation is 96 to 100 percent. When the level of apneas exceeds ten per hour and the oxygen saturation drops below normal, the person is awakened or the level of sleep decreases. People with sleep apnea tend to awaken frequently during the night and to snore and sputter during sleep. They complain of being tired all the time and are likely to fall asleep during the day. Research has demonstrated that people with sleep apnea are at increased risk of developing heart failure, having a heart attack or a stroke, and of developing depression. They are also more likely to fall asleep while driving.

People diagnosed with sleep apnea can find this condition to be troubling. Although continuous positive airway pressure (CPAP) is very effective at treating obstructive sleep apnea, it is not always easy to adapt to it. Many patients struggle to get comfortable with CPAP therapy, and it can take months or years for many patients to adapt to it. Some patients never do become comfortable using CPAP, particularly if they have claustrophobia or if they do not like wearing a face or nasal mask. Poor compliance is a big issue with treatment for sleep apnea.

POSSIBLE CAUSES

There are no definitive answers as to what actually causes obstructive sleep apnea. It is thought that people with sleep apnea have a smaller upper airway than normal because of anatomical variations, obesity, chronic lung disease, or chronic sinus disease. Central sleep apnea may be caused by decreased blood levels of carbon dioxide, particularly in people with increased sensitivity, such as those with chronic obstructive pulmonary disease (COPD) or patients with chronic heart failure.

Sleep apnea can occur in people of all ages, including children. However, it is most common in obese men. Recently, it was discovered that postmenopausal women, even if they are not obese, are at increased risk of developing sleep apnea. It is also more common in people with respiratory and sinus conditions.

DIAGNOSIS

Sleep apnea is diagnosed by having the patient undergo a sleep study, which is called a polysomnograph. For the sleep study, the patient spends the night at a sleep center, being monitored by a sleep technician. Typically, a sleep technician is a specially trained respiratory therapist. During the sleep study, the patient's brain waves are monitored by an electroencephalogram (EEG). The patient's heart rate and rhythm, eye movements, oxygen saturation (blood oxygen content), breathing, snoring, sleep position, and leg movements are also monitored. For the EEG, electrodes attached to wires are placed on a number of sites on the patient's head. Electrodes are placed on the patient's chest to measure heart rate and rhythm. To monitor leg movement and eye movement, electrodes are placed on the patient's lower leg and next to the eyes. A strap is placed around the patient's chest to monitor the

DSM-IV-TR Criteria for Sleep Apnea

BREATHING-RELATED SLEEP DISORDER
(DSM CODE 780.57)

Sleep disruption, leading to excessive sleepiness or insomnia, judged to be due to sleep-related breathing condition (such as obstructive or central sleep apnea syndrome or central alveolar hypoventilation syndrome)

Disturbance not better accounted for by another mental disorder and not due to direct physiological effects of a substance or another general medical condition (other than a breathing-related disorder)

person's respiratory rate. A tiny microphone is placed near the mouth to monitor snoring. Finally, a tape attached to a wire with a red light is placed on one of the patient's fingers to monitor oxygen saturation. In addition, there is a video camera in the control room that allows the sleep technician to watch for movement and body position during sleep.

All this equipment provides a visual record of what happens during sleep. The EEG allows the determination of the levels of sleep that are achieved and how long they last. The printout correlates all the factors being monitored to the brain waves. A specially trained sleep doctor interprets all these data and assesses whether there are periods of apnea, if they exceed the normal limit, and what happens when they occur.

TREATMENT OPTIONS

The treatment of choice for sleep apnea is CPAP, which provides pressurized air to the upper airway during sleep to keep the airway open. There are a variety of masks and machines available. Generally, the apparatus consists of an air compressor and a nasal or facial mask. The most common masks cover the nose, although full face masks are available. Some CPAP machines provide a continuous flow of air under pressure, while others monitor the patient's breathing and apply pressurized air only when the patient needs it. CPAP machines can be equipped with a humidifier so that dry air is not forced into the nose, which can lead to nosebleeds.

A variety of oral mandibular (of the lower jaw) devices can be made for the sleep apnea patient. These devices push the tongue forward in an at-

tempt to keep the airway open. There are many such devices that can be tried by the patient. However, these devices can be uncomfortable, and they may not be effective in eliminating sleep apnea.

Several surgical procedures can be performed for sleep apnea. If the patient has nasal polyps or nasal obstruction, surgery can be performed to open the nasal passages. This is usually performed by a sinus endoscopy. Another procedure strives to widen the pharynx. It is called a uvulopalatopharyngoplasty (UPPP). The purpose of this procedure is to remove extra tissue from the upper palate and uvula, as well as to remove the tonsils and adenoids if they are enlarged. The procedure can also be performed using a laser.

Surgery can be performed on the lower jaw. Sometimes, a small portion of the tongue is also removed. The rationale for this surgery is that the muscles that assist in keeping the upper airway open are attached to the lower jaw. There are three procedures that can be performed on the lower jaw. One procedure, a genioglossal tubercle advancement, involves moving part of the chin, in the area where the tongue is attached, to move the tongue forward. The second procedure involves using bone chips placed in the jaw to lengthen a very short jaw. The third procedure is usually performed on people with a facial deformity; it includes the UPPP and a genioglossal tubercle advancement, and it may also include enlarging the lower jaw. Jaw surgery is helpful only for certain individuals, and it requires wiring the jaw closed for several weeks after surgery.

Another surgical procedure for sleep apnea is the somnoplasty. This procedure entails the use of microwaves to stiffen and eliminate some of the deep tissue in the pharynx.

The original surgical procedure for treating sleep apnea is the tracheostomy. This procedure involves making a permanent hole in the cricoid cartilage of the neck. At night, the person breathes through the tracheostomy and bypasses the narrowing of the pharynx. During the day, a cap is placed over the opening so that water cannot enter the lungs. This surgical procedure is quite radical and is disfiguring.

The only surgical procedure that has proven to be effective is the tracheostomy. All the other surgical procedures produce inconsistent results in research studies. For persons with severe sleep apnea, a surgical procedure might only decrease the severity of the sleep apnea, and therefore, the person might still need CPAP. Another drawback to these surgical procedures is that they can be quite painful afterward while tissue is healing.

For the obese patient, whose sleep apnea is caused by increased fat tissue in the pharynx, weight loss can sometimes improve or eliminate sleep apnea. However, weight loss is not a solution for all people with sleep apnea, and sleep apnea can occur in persons who are thin, as well as those who are obese.

History of Treatment

Sleep apnea was first identified in the mid-1970's. At that time, only tracheostomy was available to treat it. CPAP was developed by Colin Sullivan from Sydney, Australia, and was first tested in 1980. Originally, sleep apnea was thought to be relatively rare, but later it was found to affect roughly 4 percent of adult men and 2 percent of adult women.

Sources for Further Study

American Sleep Apnea Association. http://www .sleepapnea.org. Organization offers information on the problem and its treatment.

Chokroverty, Sudhansu. *Questions and Answers About Sleep Apnea.* Sudbury, Mass.: Jones and Bartlett, 2009. A popular work about sleep apnea that describes its symptoms, diagnosis, and treatment.

Johnson, T. Scott, William A. Broughton, and Jerry Halberstadt. *Sleep Apnea: The Phantom of the Night.* Onset, Mass.: New Technology Publishing, 2003. Provides a comprehensive overview of sleep apnea and its causes, as well as the treatments for sleep apnea, with particular emphasis on CPAP, which is the treatment of choice for sleep apnea.

Jordan, Amy S., David P. White, and Robert B. Fogel. "Recent Advances in Understanding the Pathogenesis of Obstructive Sleep Apnea." *Current Opinions in Pulmonary Medicine* 9, no. 6 (2003): 459-464. This article reviews the research that has been performed regarding the cause of sleep apnea. It includes the theories that have been put forth regarding causes for this condition.

Rauch, Megan. "Making CPAP Work." *Respiratory Therapy Magazine* (June 4, 2003). Discusses how CPAP is customized to each person and how to assist patients in adapting to CPAP.

Yaggi, H. Klar, et al. "Obstructive Sleep Apnea as a Risk Factor for Stroke and Death." *New England Journal of Medicine* 353 (November 10, 2005): 2034-2041. This article discusses an observational research study performed to determine the likelihood of stroke and death in untreated sleep apnea.

Christine M. Carroll

See also: Depression; Insomnia; Sleep.

Smell and taste

Type of psychology: Sensation and perception
Fields of study: Auditory, chemical, cutaneous, and body senses

The senses of taste and smell, which are closely related, depend on sensory receptors known as chemoreceptors. These receptors detect molecules of various kinds and respond by generating nerve impulses. Chemoreception is believed to depend on proteins in receptor cell membranes that can recognize and combine with molecules from the environment.

Key concepts
- adaptation
- chemoreceptors
- olfactory sensory neurons
- papillae
- taste buds

Introduction

The senses of taste and smell, which are closely related, depend on a type of sensory receptor cell known as a chemoreceptor. This receptor detects molecules of various kinds and responds on contact with them by generating nerve impulses. Although the basis for the detection is incompletely understood, chemoreceptor cells are believed to contain proteins in their surface membranes that are able to recognize and combine with various kinds of molecules. Combination with a recognized molecule causes the protein to open an ion channel in the surface membrane. The resulting ion flow creates an electrical change in the membrane that triggers generation of a nerve impulse by the chemoreceptor cell.

Taste

Chemoreceptors for taste occur primarily on the upper surface of the tongue. A comparatively few taste receptors are also located on the roof of the mouth, particularly on the soft palate, and in the throat. The taste receptors in these locations are parts of taste buds, which are small, pear-shaped bundles of modified epithelial cells. Molecules from the exterior environment reach the taste receptor cells through a small pore at the top of a taste bud. Altogether, there are about ten thousand taste buds on the tongue and throat. The taste buds of the tongue, which are only 30 to 40 micrometers in diameter and thus microscopic, are embedded in the surfaces of small, moundlike outgrowths called papillae. The papillae give the surface of the tongue its rough or furry texture.

Taste receptor cells occur in taste buds along with other cells that play a purely supportive structural role. Individual taste receptor cells are elongated and bear thin, fingerlike extensions at their tips that protrude through the pore of a taste bud. Combination with chemicals from the environment, which must dissolve in the saliva of the mouth to reach the taste buds, probably occurs in the membranes of the fingerlike processes at the tips of the

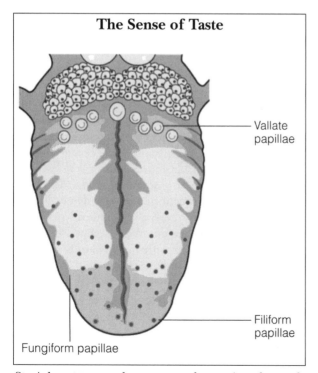

The Sense of Taste

Vallate papillae

Filiform papillae

Fungiform papillae

Special receptors on the tongue send nerve impulses to the brain that are registered as the various tastes of bitter, sweet, salty, and sour. (Hans & Cassidy, Inc.)

taste receptor cells. The opposite end of the taste receptor cells makes connections with sensory nerves serving the taste buds.

Each taste receptor cell probably has membrane proteins that can combine with a variety of molecules from the environment; however, individual taste cells, depending on their location on the tongue, typically combine more readily with some molecular types than with others. Taste cells with a preponderance of membrane proteins recognizing and combining with organic molecules, such as carbohydrates, alcohols, and amino acids, are crowded near the tip of the tongue. Combination of these taste receptors with organic molecules gives rise to nerve impulses that are interpreted in the brain as a sweet taste. Just behind the tip of the tongue is a region containing taste receptor cells that combine most readily with inorganic salts; combination with these substances gives rise to nerve impulses that are interpreted in the brain as a salty taste.

Farther to the rear of the tongue, particularly along the sides, are taste receptor cells that combine most readily with the hydrogen ions released by acids; this combination is perceived as a sour taste. The rear of the tongue contains taste receptor cells that combine most readily with a wide variety of organic and inorganic molecules, particularly long-chain organic molecules containing nitrogen and a group of organic substances called alkaloids. All the alkaloids, including molecules such as quinine, caffeine, morphine, and strychnine, give rise to a bitter taste. People tend to reject substances stimulating the bitter taste receptors at the rear of the tongue. This may have a survival value, because many bitter substances, including alkaloids produced by a variety of plants, are strongly poisonous. Many of the organic molecules with a bitter taste differ from those with a sweet taste by only minor chemical groups. A few substances, such as pepper, primarily stimulate pain rather than taste receptors when present in foods. Trigeminal nerves in the nose and mouth also contribute a generalized chemical sensitivity sometimes referred to as chemesthesis. Trigeminal response describes the fizzy tingle from carbonated beverages, the pungency of mustard or horseradish, and the irritant response to hot peppers or raw onions.

The distribution on the tongue of regions of strongest taste does not mean that the taste receptor cells in these areas are limited to detecting only

The Sense of Smell

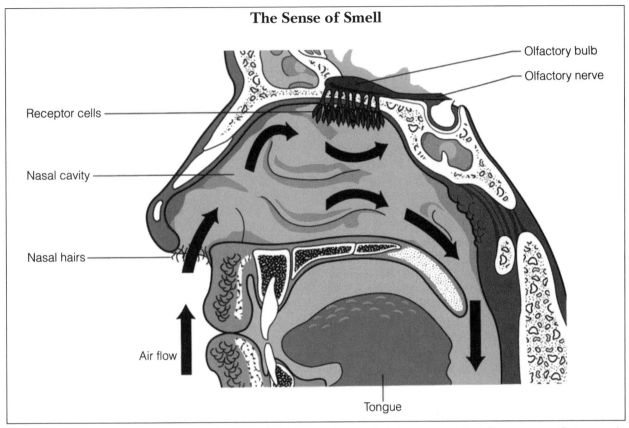

Receptors in the nasal cavity interact with odor molecules to send nerve impulses through the olfactory nerve that are registered as various smells. (Hans & Cassidy, Inc.)

sweet, salty, sour, or bitter substances; all regions of the tongue can detect molecules of each type to at least some extent. Four pairs of nerves innervate the tongue, making the sense of taste difficult to degrade substantially even during disease or the aging process.

Traditionally, the wide range of different flavors that humans can differentiate, which easily amounts to thousands, was considered to be the result of subtle combinations of four primary flavors: sweet, salty, sour, and bitter. More recently, umami was identified as a distinct taste. Often described as "savory," umami is present in foods such as meat, cheese, and mushrooms as well as in the additive monosodium glutamate (MSG). There are indications that the picture may be even more complex than this. Other taste categories that have been proposed include metallic and astringent. Persons can be "taste-blind" for certain very specific, single molecules, such as the chemical phenylthiocarbamide (PTC). The abil-

ity to taste this substance, which has a bitter flavor, is hereditary; some persons can taste PTC, and some cannot. The pattern of inheritance suggests that a membrane protein able to combine with PTC is present in some persons and not in others. Persons taste-blind for PTC do not have the specific membrane protein and cannot respond to the presence of the chemical even though other bitter flavors can be detected. It is possible that there are a wide variety of specific membrane proteins like the one responsible for detecting PTC distributed in the surface membranes of the taste receptor cells of the tongue. On the other hand, there are also "supertasters" of PTC who are hypersensitive to the taste.

SMELL

The chemoreceptors responsible for the other chemical sense, the sense of smell, are located within the head at the roof of the nasal cavity. The receptor cells detecting odors, called olfactory cells, are distributed among supportive cells in a double patch of tissue totaling about 5 square centimeters in area. Although limited to this area, the olfactory region contains between ten and one hundred million olfactory cells in the average person. Unlike taste receptor cells, olfactory receptor cells are nerve cells, often called olfactory sensory neurons.

Each olfactory cell bears between ten and twenty fine, fibrous extensions, or cilia, that protrude into a layer of mucus that covers the olfactory area. The membranes of the extensions contain the protein molecules that recognize and combine with chemicals to trigger a nerve impulse by an olfactory cell. To reach the fibrous extensions, molecules detected as odors must dissolve in the mucous solution covering the olfactory region.

The olfactory sensory neurons have a long arm, or dendrite, that extends to the surface of the nasal passage and ends in a knoblike swelling. From these knobs protrude ten to thirty fine hairs, or cilia. The cilia reach through a layer of mucus. The olfactory sensory neurons have another arm, or axon, which extends through the bony shelf of the cranium into the region of the brain called the olfactory bulb. Short axons terminate in globular structures called glomeruli. Additional neurons in the glomeruli send axons through the olfactory tract into the central nervous system.

Efforts to identify primary odors equivalent to sweet, salty, sour, bitter, and umami flavors have been largely unsuccessful. Studies of the genetic coding for the olfactory receptor proteins suggest that as many as one hundred to one thousand primary olfactory sensations exist. Similar to taste-blindness for PTC, discrete odor blindness has been identified for more than fifty substances.

ADAPTATION

The chemoreceptors responsible for the senses of taste and smell typically adapt rapidly to continued stimulation by the same molecules. In adaptation, a receptor cell generates nerve impulses most rapidly when first stimulated; with continued stimulation at the same intensity, the frequency of nerve impulses drops steadily until a baseline of a relatively few impulses per second is reached. Adaptation for the senses of taste and smell also involves complex interactions in the brain, because discernment of tastes and smells continues to diminish even after chemoreceptors reach their baselines.

For the sense of taste, adaptation is reflected in the fact that the first bite of food, for example, has the most intensely perceived taste. As stimulation by the same food continues, the intensity of the taste and a person's perception of the flavor steadily decrease. If a second food is tasted, the initial intensity of its taste is high, but again intensity drops off with continued stimulation. If the first food is retasted, however, its flavor will again seem stronger. This effect occurs because adaptation of the receptors detecting the initial taste lessens during the period during which the second food is tasted. If sufficient time passes before the first food is retasted, the flavor will appear to be almost as strong as its first taste. For this reason, one gains greater appreciation of a meal if foods are alternated rather than eaten and finished separately.

Taste receptor cells have a life expectancy of about ten days. As they degenerate, they are constantly replaced by new taste cells that continually differentiate from tissue at the sides of taste buds. As humans reach middle age, the rate of replacement drops off, so that the total number of taste receptor cells declines steadily after the age of about forty-five. This may account for the fact that, as people get older, nothing ever seems to taste as good as it did in childhood. Smoking also decreases the sensitivity of taste receptor cells and thereby decreases a person's appreciation and appetite for foods.

Olfactory cells also adapt rapidly to the continued presence of the same molecules; they slow or stop generating nerve impulses if the concentration of the odoriferous substances is maintained. This response is also reflected in common experience. When engaged in an odor-generating activity such as cooking or interior painting, a person is strongly aware of the odors generated by the activity only initially. After exposure for more than a few minutes, the person's perception of the odor lessens and eventually disappears almost completely. If the person leaves the odoriferous room for a few minutes, however, allowing the olfactory receptors and brain centers to lose their adaptation, the person is usually surprised at the strength of the odor if he or she returns to the room.

The region at the top of the nasal cavity containing the olfactory cells lies outside the main stream of air entering the lungs through the mouth and nose. As a result, the molecules dissolving in the mucous layer covering the olfactory cells are carried to this region only by side eddies of the airflow through the nose. Flow to the olfactory region is greatly improved by sniffing, a response used by all air-breathing vertebrates as a way to increase the turbulence in the nasal passages and thereby to intensify odors from the environment. Head colds interfere with people's sense of smell through congestion and blockage of the nasal cavity, which impedes airflow to the olfactory region.

Although humans are not nearly as sensitive to odors as are many other animals, their ability to detect some substances by smell is still remarkable, particularly in the case of smells generated by putrefaction. Some of the mercaptans, for example, which are generated in decaying flesh, can be detected in concentrations in air as small as 0.0000000002 milligram per milliliter. One of these substances, methyl mercaptan, is mixed in low concentration in natural gas. The presence of this mercaptan allows people to detect natural gas, which otherwise would be odorless, by smell.

HISTORY, GENETICS, AND RESPONSES
The idea that taste and smell receptors operate by recognizing specific molecular types is an old one, dating back to the first century B.C.E., when Titus Lucretius Carus proposed that the sense of smell depends on recognition of atomic shapes. Definitive experimental demonstration of this mechanism for the sense of smell, however, was not obtained until 1991, when Linda Buck and Richard Axel finally isolated members of a large family of membrane proteins that can actually do what Lucretius proposed: They recognize and bind specific molecular types and trigger responses by olfactory cells. Axel and Buck have obtained indications that there are hundreds of different proteins in the family responsible for molecular recognition in the sense of smell.

One of the many interesting features of the family is that, as with the sense of taste, many people inherit a deficiency in one or more of the membrane proteins and are congenitally unable to detect a particular odor. There are in fact many thousands of different odors to which persons may be insensitive, which directly supports the idea that the family of membrane proteins responsible for detecting individual molecular types is very large indeed. Another interesting feature of the mechanism is that there are many odors for which people must be "educated." People cannot recognize them on first en-

counter but later learn to discern them. This indicates that membrane proteins recognizing previously unknown molecules may be induced; that is, they may be newly synthesized and placed in olfactory cell membranes in response to encountering a new chemical in the environment. People can also smell, and often taste, artificial substances never before encountered by humans or indeed any other animal. Thus, the chemoreceptors have membrane proteins capable of recognizing molecules not encountered in animal evolution.

Both taste and smell receptors are linked through nerve connections to regions of the brain stem that control visceral responses, as well as to the areas of the cerebral cortex registering conscious sensations. As a result, different odors and tastes may give rise to a host of involuntary responses, such as salivation, appetite, thirst, pleasure, excitement, sexual arousal, nausea, or even vomiting, as well as to consciously perceived sensations. The odor of a once-enjoyed food may make someone ill in the future if the person became sick after eating the food; previously unobjectionable or even pleasant odors and tastes may become unpleasant and nauseating to women during pregnancy. The odor of other foods, such as some of the ranker cheeses, may be repulsive at first experience but later become appetizing as a person learns to enjoy them. The degree to which many substances are perceived as pleasant or unpleasant is also related to their concentration. Many substances perceived as pleasantly sweet in low concentration, for example, taste bitter and unpleasant at higher concentrations.

SOURCES FOR FURTHER STUDY
Firestein, Stuart. "How the Olfactory System Makes Sense of Scents." *Nature* 413 (September, 2001): 211-218. The author provides a review of the anatomical organization of the sensory neurons and how signal transduction works. Although fairly sophisticated with biochemistry explanations, the summaries are easily understood by the high school reader.

Guyton, Arthur C., and John E. Hall. *Textbook of Medical Physiology.* 11th ed. Philadelphia: Elsevier Saunders, 2006. The chapter "The Chemical Senses: Taste and Smell" presents information on the sensation of taste and the sense of smell, as well as on receptors, nerve transmission, and responses. Intended for college and medical students, but easily understood by readers at the high school level.

Herz, Rachel. *The Scent of Desire: Discovering Our Enigmatic Sense of Smell.* New York: Harper Perennial, 2008. Using scientific research, the author relates in accessible language how the sense of smell affects one's psychology, emotions, physical being, and sex life.

Hummel, Thomas, and Antje Welge-Lüssen, eds. *Taste and Smell: An Update.* New York: Karger, 2006. Discusses the anatomy and physiology of smell and taste as well as their disorders and dysfunctions.

Lawless, Harry T., and Hildegarde Heymann. *Sensory Evaluation of Food: Principles and Practices.* Gaithersburg, Md.: Aspen, 1999. Chapter 2, "Physiological and Psychological Foundations of Sensory Function," presents the physiology of taste and sensory interactions, as well as information on sensory testing and psychological methods. Intended for college students, but easily understood by readers at the high school level.

Lindemann, Bernd. "Receptors and Transduction in Taste." *Nature* 413 (September, 2001). The author presents information on receptor functioning for taste, as well as additional information on umami and taste interactions. Although fairly explicit in its biochemistry, the summary and descriptions are clear enough to be understood by nonscientists.

Stephen L. Wolfe;
updated by Karen Chapman-Novakofski

SEE ALSO: Hearing; Sensation and perception; Signal detection theory; Taste aversion; Touch and pressure; Vision: Brightness and contrast; Vision: Color; Visual system.

Social identity theory

TYPE OF PSYCHOLOGY: Social psychology
FIELD OF STUDY: Prejudice and discrimination

Social identity theory examines the relationship between group membership and self-esteem. It has provided insights into intergroup conflict, ethnocentrism, cultural affirmation, and self-hatred, predicting both individual and group responses to an unfavorable self-concept.

KEY CONCEPTS
- distinctiveness
- in-group bias
- minimal group situation
- personal identity
- self-image
- social categorization
- social change approach
- social comparison
- social mobility

INTRODUCTION

Social identity theory maintains that all individuals are motivated to achieve and maintain a positive self-concept. A person's self-concept derives from two principal sources: personal identity and social identity. Personal identity includes one's individual traits, achievements, and qualities. Social identity includes the group affiliations that are recognized as being part of the self, such as one's image of oneself as a Protestant, a blue-collar worker, or a conservative. Some individuals emphasize the personal aspects in their quest for a favorable self-image, while others emphasize their social identities. Social identity theory focuses on the latter. It attempts to explain when and how individuals transform their group affiliations to secure a favorable self-concept.

Psychologist Henri Tajfel introduced social identity theory in 1978. The theory maintains that a person's social identity emerges from the natural process of social categorization. People categorize, or classify, themselves and other people by many criteria, including occupation, religious affiliation, political orientation, ethnicity, economic class, and gender. An individual automatically identifies with some categories and rejects others. This creates a distinction between "in-groups," with which one identifies, and "out-groups," with which one does not identify. A person who identifies himself or herself as a Democrat, for example, would consider other Democrats members of the in-group and would view Republicans as members of the out-group. Individuals inevitably compare their groups with other groups; the goal of the comparisons is to establish the superiority of one's own group, or the group's positive distinctiveness, on some level, such as affluence, cultural heritage, or spirituality. If the comparison shows that the individual's group memberships are positive and valuable, then the social identities become an important part of the self. If, however, one's group appears inferior, then one's self-image acquires negative distinctiveness. The individual is then motivated to acquire a more satisfactory self-concept.

Enhancing Self-Concept

Tajfel and John Turner proposed three strategies that can be used to enhance one's self-concept: "exit," "pass," and "voice." The first two strategies represent attempts to validate the self. Both involve rejecting or distancing oneself from the devalued group to improve identity; both presume the existence of social mobility—an individual-based strategy for image enhancement whereby a person "exits" an inferior group or "passes" as a member of a more prestigious group. Exit involves simply leaving the group. This response is possible only within flexible social systems that permit individual mobility. Although individuals cannot usually shed affiliations such as race or gender, they can openly discard other affiliations, such as "Buick owner" or "public school advocate." If dissatisfied with an automobile, one trades it in for another; if unhappy with the public school system, one may exit and move one's children into a private school. Pass, a more private response, occurs when individuals with unfavorable group memberships are not recognized by others as belonging to that group. A Jew may pass as a Gentile, for example, or a fair-skinned black person may pass as a Caucasian. Typically in such cases, the objective features that link the individual to the devalued group are absent or unnoticeable.

Voice, the final strategy for identity improvement, is a collective response: Group members act together to alter the group's image and elevate its social value. Also called the "social change" approach, it is common in rigid social systems in which individual movement away from the disparaged group is impossible. It also occurs when psychological forces such as cultural and personal values bind the individual to the group. Members of such physically identifiable groups as women, blacks, or Asians might adopt the social change strategy, for example, as might such cultural or religious group members as Irish Catholics or Orthodox Jews.

Voice is a complex response. Simply recognizing that social mobility is blocked for members of one's own group is insufficient to prompt social change activity. Two additional perceptions of the overall social structure are important: its stability and its legitimacy. Stability is concerned with how fixed or secure the social hierarchy seems. Theoretically, no group is completely secure in its relative superiority; even groups that historically have been considered superior must work to maintain their favored position. If members of a denigrated group believe that alternatives to the current social hierarchy are possible, then they are encouraged to reassess their own value. Legitimacy, in contrast, involves the bases for a group's negative distinctiveness. If a group believes that its social inferiority is attributable to illegitimate causes, such as discrimination in hiring practices or educational opportunities, group members will be more likely to challenge their inferior position.

Social Creativity and Direct Competition

Voice challenges to negative distinctiveness take two general forms: social creativity and direct competition. Social creativity involves altering or redefining the elements of comparison. The group's social positions and resources, however, need not be altered. In one approach, a group may simply limit the groups with which it compares itself, focusing on groups that are similar. A group of factory workers may choose to compare itself with warehouse workers or postal employees rather than with a group of advertising executives. This approach increases the chances that the outcome of the comparison will be favorable to one's own group. The group might also identify a new area of comparison, such as bilingual fluency, in its effort to enhance group distinctiveness.

Finally, the group might recast some of its denigrated attributes so that its value is reassessed. A new appreciation for group history and culture often emerges from this process. The Civil Rights movement, an important force for social change in the 1960's, caused this to occur. In the context of that movement, the label "Negro" was replaced by "black," which was recast by African Americans to symbolize group pride. Under the slogan "Black is beautiful," the natural look became more valued than the traditional European American model. African Americans were less likely to lighten or straighten their hair or to use makeup to make their skin appear lighter.

Direct competition, in contrast, involves altering the group's social position. It is often an institutional response; consequently, it encourages competition among groups. Displaced groups target institutions and policies, demanding resources in an effort to empower the group politically and economically. In the 1960's, for example, black students demonstrated for curricular changes at colleges and universities. They demanded greater relevance in existing courses and the development of Black Studies programs to highlight the group's social and political contributions. In the 1970's, the women's movement demanded economic and political changes, including equal pay for equal work, and greater individual rights for women, such as abortion rights and institutionalized child care.

IN-GROUP BIAS

Social identity theory has been used to explain several intergroup processes. Among them are the phenomenon known as in-group bias (observed in laboratory experiments) and the actions of some subordinate groups to challenge their relative inferiority through collective (voice) approaches. The response of African Americans in the 1950's and 1960's to negative perceptions of their group illustrates the latter process.

In-group bias is the tendency to favor one's own group over other groups. In laboratory experiments, young subjects were put in groups according to simple and fairly arbitrary criteria, such as the type of artwork they preferred. The goal was to establish a "minimal group situation": an artificial social order in which subjects could be easily differentiated but which was free of any already existing conflicts. Once categorized, subjects were asked to perform one of several tasks, such as distributing money, assigning points, evaluating the different groups, or interpreting group members' behavior. In all the tasks, subjects repeatedly showed a preference for their own groups. They gave to in-group members significantly more points and money than they gave to out-group members—despite a lack of previous interaction among the subjects. When describing in-group members, they attributed altruistic behavior to the person's innate virtuous and admirable qualities rather than to outside causes. When describing out-group members, however, they reversed the pattern, attributing altruistic behavior to situational factors and hostile behavior to personal character. Thus, even without any history of competition, ideological differences, or hostility over scarce resources, sub-

jects consistently demonstrated a preference for their in-group.

Social identity theory predicts this pattern. The powerful need to achieve a positive self-image motivates a person to establish the value of his or her group memberships. Since groups strongly contribute to an individual's self-image, the individual works to enhance the group's image. Group successes are, by extension, the individual's successes. Daily life offers many examples of group allegiance, ranging from identification with one's country to support of one's hometown baseball team. Experiments in social identity suggest that ethnocentrism, or the belief in the superiority of one's own ethnic group, serves important psychological needs.

STUDY OF NEGATIVE GROUP SELF-IMAGE

Social identity theory also explains why some subordinate groups challenge their relative inferiority through rebellion or social change while others do not. The theory predicts that individuals who are objectively bound to negatively distinct groups—by gender or skin color, for example—will have fewer options for self-enhancement. Because they are driven by the powerful need to obtain a worthy self-image, however, they are unlikely to engage in self-hatred by accepting the denigrated image imposed on them by others. Instead, they will engage in some form of voice, the collective approach to image improvement.

Psychologists studying social identity do not directly explore the historical background of a group's negative self-image. Rather, they perform laboratory experiments and field studies designed to determine individuals' actual perceptions of groups—how individuals identify groups and whether they see them as having a positive or a negative image. Social psychologists also attempt to measure the changes that occur in group self-image over time; they can then infer that social or political movements have affected that image. Studies involving African American children—for whom the essential identifying element, race, is a physical one—provide an example.

In the landmark 1954 Supreme Court decision *Brown v. Board of Education*, which mandated school desegregation, social scientists presented evidence that educational segregation produced feelings of inferiority in black children. Support was drawn in part from a 1947 study by Kenneth and Mamie

Clark, in which they compared the preferences of black and white children between the ages of three and seven for dolls with either dark or fair skin tones. Approximately 60 percent of the black children said that the fair-skinned doll was the "nicer" doll, the "nicer color" doll, or the doll they "preferred to play with." The dark-skinned doll, by contrast, "looked bad." Based on a combination of this negative self-image and the fact that African Americans are objectively bound to their group by their race, social identity theory would predict collective action for social change.

COLLECTIVE ACTIVITY AND POSITIVE SELF-IDENTITY

The Civil Rights movement embodied that collective, or voice, activity, and it offered blacks a new context within which to evaluate black identity. Results from studies performed in the 1970's suggest that, indeed, there was a significant rise in black self-esteem during that period. A replication of the Clarks' study by other researchers showed a clear preference for the dark-skinned doll among black children. Later analyses of comparable doll studies showed that such preferences were most common among young subjects from areas with large black populations and active black pride movements.

A positive self-image may also emerge when social and cultural themes and historical events are reinterpreted within a group. A group's cultural image may be emphasized; its music, art, and language then become valued. To continue using the African American example, in the twentieth century, black music, which once had been the music of the oppressed—work songs and spirituals—evolved into a music that communicated ethnic identity in a new way. Blues and jazz became a focus of group pride; jazz, in particular, become renowned worldwide. The acceptance of jazz as a valuable art form by people of many races and nationalities illustrates another frequent outcome of activity for generating a positive self-concept: It often initiates a response from the larger society that improves the group's relative position in that society.

PERSONAL AND INTELLECTUAL ORIGINS

Social identity theory evolved from a series of experiments conducted in England at the University of Bristol in the 1970's. Originated by social psychologist Tajfel, the theory represents the collaborative

efforts of Michael Billig, John Turner, and several other European associates over a decade-long period.

Like many social science theories, social identity theory has both personal and intellectual origins. Tajfel's own identity as a European Jew who survived World War II contributed significantly to his desire to understand conflicts between groups. His early work in the psychology of prejudice and his personal distrust of reductionist or oversimplified models of psychological processes laid the foundation for the theory. Other concepts, including stereotypes, values, ethnocentrism, and the social psychology of minorities, became incorporated into the theory; these themes contributed to the attractiveness of the theory in Europe, a region recognized for its religious, linguistic, and social diversity and for the conflicts this diversity has caused.

RELATED GROUP RESEARCH

Group processes have long been emphasized in American social psychology, but the main thrusts have varied over the years. Kurt Lewin's work in the late 1940's, for example, focused on leadership in small groups; research in the mid-1950's examined the relationship of intergroup contact to prejudice and discrimination. In the late 1950's, Muzafer Sherif studied intergroup relations in socially created groups that he and his colleagues observed in real-life settings for extended periods of time. In the 1960's, however, internal conflicts in the field of social psychology led to the development of two distinct subdisciplines: sociological social psychology and psychological social psychology. Intergroup relations began to seem too sociological a topic for psychologists to study. This split, coupled with a renewed emphasis on studying individual cognitive processes, resulted in the displacement of intergroup studies in American social psychology in the 1970's.

Social identity theory revived American research on intergroup relations in the early to mid-1980's. Following more than a decade of political and social turmoil in the United States, social psychologists were looking for better ways to understand conflict between groups. They began to ask new questions and to adopt a wider variety of methodologies, including surveys and field studies. Race, class, and gender were recognized as critical psychological variables. The "group member," an individual with a sociocultural history that affected social behavior, became accepted as a respectable research subject. Social identity theory provided both theorists and researchers with a broad paradigm from which to investigate intergroup conflict, group identification, ethnocentrism, hostility, and social change strategies.

The three central psychological processes—motivation, emotion, and cognition—are incorporated into social identity theory in a logical and sophisticated manner. Earlier social psychological theories usually emphasized one or two of those processes. Both comprehensive and complex, the theory offers a way of understanding a wide range of psychological topics.

SOURCES FOR FURTHER STUDY

Brown, Rupert. "Intergroup Relations." In *Introduction to Social Psychology*, edited by Miles Hewstone, Wolfgang Stroebe, Jean-Paul Codol, and G. Stephenson. New York: Basil Blackwell, 1988. Brown summarizes intergroup relations literature in this accessible chapter in a social psychology textbook. Locates social identity theory in the broader context of intergroup relations and explains important terms clearly, providing excellent examples; can be understood by the college or high school student.

Capozza, Dora, and Rupert Brown, eds. *Social Identity Processes: Trends in Theory and Research*. Thousand Oaks, Calif.: Sage Publications, 2000. Explores social identity theory from multiple angles. A comprehensive source.

Eagly, Alice H., Reuben M. Baron, and V. Lee Hamilton, eds. *The Social Psychology of Group Identity and Social Conflict: Theory, Application, and Practice*. Washington, D.C.: American Psychological Association, 2004. Examines conflict between social groups, including prejudice and violence.

Ellemers, Naomi, Russell Spears, and Bertjan Doosje, eds. *Social Identity*. New York: Blackwell, 2000. A collection of essays on contemporary social identity research, covering theoretical issues and empirical research, including perceptions of self and others, communication between groups, and behavioral consequences of social identity issues.

Jenkins, Richard. *Social Identity*. 3d ed. New York: Routledge, 2008. This text provides a comprehensive overview of theories of identity and offers chapters on self-image and public image, belonging, identification, and organizations. Suitable for advanced undergraduates and postgraduates.

Messick, David M., and Diane M. Mackie. "Intergroup Relations." In *Annual Review of Psychology*. Vol. 40. Stanford, Calif.: Annual Reviews, 1989. Reviews intergroup relations theory and research from a cognitive perspective. Categorization, ingroup and out-group effects, and intergroup bias are emphasized. Tajfel's social identity theory dominates the section on intergroup bias; his work is examined and critiqued. Variants of social identity theory are discussed.

Rhodewalt, Frederick, ed. *Personality and Social Behavior*. New York: Psychology Press, 2008. A collection of essays on how personality develops in relation to one's situation. Identity with a group plays an integral role in this process.

Tajfel, Henri. *Human Groups and Social Categories*. Cambridge, England: Cambridge University Press, 1981. An easy-to-read account of Tajfel's conceptualization of intergroup conflict, accessible to college students. This book incorporates his early work on prejudice, essays on social perception and categorization, stereotypes, children's images of insiders and outsiders, and social identity theory. Includes both theory and research, emphasizing descriptions of the former. Tajfel provides an extensive bibliography.

_____, ed. *Differentiation Between Social Groups: Studies in the Social Psychology of Intergroup Relations*. London: Academic Press, 1978. Presents the work of the team of European social psychologists that conceptualized and formalized social identity theory. Thorough and detailed, it is important to those who wish to replicate key experiments or to understand the empirical and theoretical foundations of the theory.

Tajfel, Henri, and John Turner. "The Social Identity Theory of Intergroup Behavior." In *Social Psychology of Intergroup Relations*, edited by Stephen Worchel and William G. Austin. 2d ed. Chicago: Nelson-Hall, 1986. An excellent summary of social identity theory. This chapter focuses on the origin and importance of the theory, including intergroup competition and conflict. It offers examples of the concepts and attempts to answer practical questions.

Turner, John C., et al. *Rediscovering the Social Group: A Self-Categorization Theory*. New York: Basil Blackwell, 1988. Turner's book argues for the group as an important social phenomenon and articulates assumptions made about the relationship between the individual and the group in social identity theory. Provides the reader with a valuable backdrop for understanding many of Tajfel's predictions in a readable blend of theoretical and empirical work.

Jaclyn Rodriguez

SEE ALSO: African Americans and mental health; Aggression; Asian Americans/Pacific Islanders and mental health; Attributional biases; Causal attribution; Gay, lesbian, bisexual, and transgender mental health; Groups; Latinos and mental health; Native Americans/Native Alaskans and mental health; Prejudice; Racism; Religion and psychology; Self-esteem; Social perception; Social schemata.

Social learning
Albert Bandura

TYPE OF PSYCHOLOGY: Personality
FIELDS OF STUDY: Behavioral and cognitive models; cognitive learning

Bandura's social learning theory, later called social cognitive theory, provides a theoretical framework for understanding and explaining human behavior; the theory embraces an interactional model of causation and accords central roles to cognitive, vicarious, and self-regulatory processes.

KEY CONCEPTS
• determinism
• model
• observational learning
• outcome expectancies
• reciprocal determinism
• reinforcement
• self-efficacy

INTRODUCTION
Social learning theory, later amplified as social cognitive theory by its founder, social psychologist Albert Bandura, provides a unified theoretical framework for analyzing the psychological processes that govern human behavior. Its goal is to explain how behavior develops, how it is maintained, and through what processes it can be modified. It seeks to accomplish this task by identifying the determinants of human action and the mechanisms through which they operate.

Bandura lays out the conceptual framework of his approach in his book *Social Learning Theory* (1977). His theory is based on a model of reciprocal determinism. This means that Bandura rejects both the humanist and existentialist position viewing people as free agents and the behaviorist position viewing behavior as controlled by the environment. Rather, external determinants of behavior (such as rewards and punishments) and internal determinants (such as thoughts, expectations, and beliefs) are considered part of a system of interlocking determinants that influence not only behavior but also the various other parts of the system. In other words, each part of the system—behavior, cognition, and environmental influences—affects each of the other parts. People are neither free agents nor passive reactors to external pressures. Instead, through self-regulatory processes, they have the ability to exercise some measure of control over their own actions. They can affect their behavior by setting goals, arranging environmental inducements, generating cognitive strategies, evaluating goal attainment, and mediating consequences for their actions. Bandura accepts that these self-regulatory functions initially are learned as the result of external rewards and punishments. Their external origin, however, does not invalidate the fact that, once internalized, they in part determine behavior.

COGNITIVE MEDIATING FACTORS
As self-regulation results from symbolic processing of information, Bandura in his theorizing assigns an increasingly prominent role to cognition. This is reflected in his book *Social Foundations of Thought and Action: A Social Cognitive Theory* (1986), in which he no longer refers to his approach as social learning but as social cognitive theory. People, unlike lower animals, use verbal and nonverbal symbols (language and images) to process information and preserve experiences in the form of cognitive representations. This encoded information serves as a guide for future behavior. Without the ability to use symbols, people would have to solve problems by enacting various alternative solutions until, by trial and

error, they learned which ones resulted in rewards or punishments. Through their cognitive abilities, however, people can think through different options, imagine possible outcomes, and guide their behavior by anticipated consequences. Symbolic capabilities provide people with a powerful tool to regulate their own behavior in the absence of external reinforcements and punishments.

According to Bandura, the most central of all mechanisms of self-regulation is self-efficacy, defined as the belief that one has the ability, with one's actions, to bring about a certain outcome. Self-efficacy beliefs function as determinants of behavior by influencing motivation, thought processes, and emotions in ways that may be self-aiding or self-hindering. Specifically, self-efficacy appraisals determine the goals that people set for themselves, whether they anticipate and visualize scenarios of success or failure, whether they embark on a course of action, how much effort they expend, and how long they persist in the face of obstacles. Self-efficacy expectations are different from outcome expectations. Outcome expectancies are beliefs that a given behavior will result in a certain outcome, while self-efficacy refers to the belief in one's ability to bring about this outcome. To put it simply, people may believe that something can happen, but whether they embark on a course of action depends on their perceived ability to make it happen.

RELEVANCE TO OBSERVATION AND MODELING

Perhaps the most important contribution of social learning theory to the understanding of human behavior is the concept of vicarious, or observational, learning, also termed "learning through modeling." Before the advent of social learning theory, many psychologists assigned a crucial role to the process of reinforcement in learning. They postulated that without performing responses that are followed by reinforcement or punishment, a person cannot learn. In contrast, Bandura asserted that much of social behavior is not learned from the consequences of trial and error but is acquired through symbolic modeling. People watch what other people do and what happens to them as a result of their actions. From such observations, they form ideas of how to perform new behaviors, and later this information guides their actions.

Symbolic modeling is of great significance for human learning because of its enormous efficiency in transmitting information. Whereas trial-and-error learning requires the gradual shaping of the behavior of individuals through repetition and reinforcement, in observational learning, a single model can teach complex behaviors simultaneously to any number of people. According to Bandura, some elaborate and specifically human behavior patterns, such as language, might even be impossible to learn if it were not for symbolic modeling. For example, it seems unlikely that children learn to talk as a result of their parents' reinforcing each correct utterance they emit. Rather, children probably hear and watch other members of their verbal community talk and then imitate their behavior. In a similar vein, complex behaviors such as driving a car or flying a plane are not acquired by trial and error. Instead, prospective drivers or pilots follow the verbal rules of an instructor until they master the task.

In summary, Bandura's social learning theory explains human action in terms of the interplay among behavior, cognition, and environmental influences. The theory places particular emphasis on cognitive mediating factors such as self-efficacy beliefs and outcome expectancies. Its greatest contribution to a general theory of human learning has been its emphasis on learning by observation or modeling. Observational learning has achieved the status of a third learning principle, next to classical and operant conditioning.

STUDIES OF LEARNING AND PERFORMANCE

From its inception, social learning theory has served as a useful framework for the understanding of both normal and abnormal human behavior. A major contribution that has important implications for the modification of human behavior is the theory's distinction between learning and performance. In a now-classic series of experiments, Bandura and his associates teased apart the roles of observation and reinforcement in learning and were able to demonstrate that people learn through mere observation.

In a study on aggression, an adult model hit and kicked a life-size inflated clown doll (a "Bobo" doll), with children watching the attack in person or on a television screen. Other children watched the model perform some innocuous behavior. Later, the children were allowed to play in the room with the Bobo doll. All children who had witnessed the aggression, either in person or on television, viciously attacked the doll, while those who had observed the model's innocuous behavior did not display aggression toward the doll. Moreover, it was clearly shown that the children modeled their aggressive behaviors after the adult. Those who had observed the adult sit on the doll and hit its face, or kick the doll, or use a hammer to pound it imitated exactly these behaviors. Thus, the study accomplished its purpose by demonstrating that observational learning occurs in the absence of direct reinforcement.

In a related experiment, Bandura showed that expected consequences, while not relevant for learning, play a role in performance. A group of children watched a film of an adult model behaving aggressively toward a Bobo doll and being punished, while another group observed the same behavior with the person being rewarded. When the children subsequently were allowed to play with the Bobo doll, those who had watched the model being punished displayed fewer aggressive behaviors toward the doll than those who had seen the model being rewarded. When the experimenter then offered a reward to the children for imitating the model, however, all children, regardless of the consequences they had observed, attacked the Bobo doll. This showed that all children had learned the aggressive behavior from the model but that observing the model being punished served as an inhibiting factor until it was removed by the promise of a reward. Again, this study showed that children learn without reinforcement, simply by observing how others behave. Whether they then engage in the behavior, however, depends on the consequences that they expect will result from their actions.

DISINHIBITORY EFFECTS

Models not only teach people novel ways of thinking and behaving but also can strengthen or weaken inhibitions. Seeing models punished may inhibit similar behavior in observers, while seeing models carry out feared or forbidden actions without negative consequences may reduce their inhibitions.

The most striking demonstrations of the disinhibitory effects of observational learning come from therapeutic interventions based on modeling principles. Bandura, in his book *Principles of Behavior Modification* (1969), shows how social learning theory can provide a conceptual framework for the modification of a wide range of maladaptive behaviors. For example, a large number of laboratory studies of subjects with a severe phobia of snakes showed that phobic individuals can overcome their fear of reptiles when fearless adult models demonstrate how to handle a snake and directly assist subjects in coping successfully with whatever they dread.

SELF-EFFICACY MECHANISM

In later elaborations, the scope of social learning theory was amplified to include self-efficacy theory. Self-efficacy is now considered the principal mechanism of behavior change, in that all successful interventions are assumed to operate by strengthening a person's self-perceived efficacy to cope with difficulties.

How can self-efficacy be strengthened? Research indicates that it is influenced by four sources of information. The most important influence comes from performance attainments, with successes heightening and failures lowering perceived self-efficacy. Thus, having people enact and master a difficult task most powerfully increases their efficacy percepts. A second influence comes from vicarious experiences. Exposing people to models works because seeing people similar to oneself successfully perform a difficult task raises one's own efficacy expectations. Verbal persuasion is a third way of influencing self-efficacy. Convincing people that they have the ability to perform a task can encourage them to try harder, which indeed may lead to successful performance. Finally, teaching people coping strategies to lower emotional arousal can also increase self-efficacy. If subsequently they approach a task more calmly, then their likelihood of succeeding at it may increase.

Bandura and his associates conducted a series of studies to test the idea that vastly different modes of influence all improve coping behavior by strengthening self-perceived efficacy. Severe snake phobics received interventions based on enactive, vicarious, cognitive, or emotive treatment (a method of personality change that incorporates cognitive, emotional, and behavioral strategies, designed to help resist tendencies to be irrational, suggestible, and conforming) modalities. The results confirmed that the degree to which people changed their behavior toward the reptiles was closely associated with increases in self-judged efficacy, regardless of the method of intervention. It is now widely accepted among social learning theorists that all effective therapies ultimately work by strengthening people's self-perceptions of efficacy.

THEORETICAL INFLUENCES

Social learning theory was born into a climate in which two competing and diametrically opposed schools of thought dominated psychology. On one hand, psychologists who advocated psychodynamic theories postulated that human behavior is governed by motivational forces operating in the form of largely unconscious needs, drives, and impulses. These impulse theories tended to give circular explanations, attributing behavior to inner causes that were inferred from the very behavior they were supposed to cause. They also tended to provide explanations after the fact, rather than predicting events, and had very limited empirical support.

On the other hand, there were various types of behavior theory that shifted the focus of the causal analysis from hypothetical internal determinants of behavior to external, publicly observable causes. Behaviorists were able to show that actions commonly attributed to inner causes could be produced, eliminated, and reinstated by manipulating the antecedent (stimulus) and consequent (reinforcing) conditions of the person's external environment. This led to the proposition that people's behavior is caused by factors residing in the environment.

Social learning theory presents a theory of human behavior that to some extent incorporates both viewpoints. According to Bandura, people are neither driven by inner forces nor buffeted by environmental stimuli; instead, psychological functioning is best explained in terms of a continuous reciprocal interaction of internal and external causes. This assumption, termed reciprocal determinism, became one of the dominant viewpoints in psychology.

An initial exposition of social learning theory is presented in Bandura and Richard H. Walters's text *Social Learning and Personality Development* (1963). This formulation drew heavily on the procedures and principles of operant and classical conditioning. In his later book, *Principles of Behavior Modification*, Bandura places much greater emphasis on symbolic events and self-regulatory processes. He argues that complex human behavior cannot be satisfactorily explained by the narrow set of learning principles that behaviorists had derived from animal studies. He incorporates principles derived from developmental, social, and cognitive psychology into social learning theory.

EVOLUTION OF THEORETICAL DEVELOPMENT

During the 1970's, psychology had grown increasingly cognitive. This development is reflected in Bandura's 1977 book *Social Learning Theory*, which presents self-efficacy theory as the central mechanism through which people control their own behavior. Over the following decade, the influence of cognitive psychology on Bandura's work grew stronger. In his 1986 book *Social Foundations of Thought and Action*, he finally disavows his roots in learning theory and renames his approach "social cognitive theory." This theory accords central roles to cognitive, vicarious, self-reflective, and self-regulatory processes.

Social learning/social cognitive theory became the dominant conceptual approach within the field of behavior therapy. It has provided the conceptual framework for numerous interventions for a wide variety of psychological disorders and probably will remain popular for a long time. In recognition of his work, Bandura was honored with the Award for Distinguished Scientific Contributions to Psychology from the American Psychological Foundation in 1980.

SOURCES FOR FURTHER STUDY

Akers, Ronald. *Social Learning and Social Structure: A General Theory of Crime and Deviance.* Somerset, N.J.: Transaction, 2009. Uses research on social learning theory to predict crime and delinquency.

Bandura, Albert. *Principles of Behavior Modification.* New York: Holt, Rinehart and Winston, 1969. Presents an overview of basic psychological principles governing human behavior within the conceptual framework of social learning. Reviews theoretical and empirical advances in the field of social learning, placing special emphasis on self-regulation and on symbolic and vicarious processes. Applies these principles to the conceptualization and modification of a number of common behavior disorders such as alcoholism, phobias, and sexual deviancy.

_____. *Social Foundations of Thought and Action: A Social Cognitive Theory.* Englewood Cliffs, N.J.: Prentice-Hall, 1986. Presents a comprehensive coverage of the tenets of current social cognitive theory. Besides addressing general issues of human nature and causality, it provides an impressive in-depth analysis of all important aspects of human functioning, including motivational, cognitive, and self-regulatory processes.

_____. *Social Learning Theory.* Englewood Cliffs, N.J.: Prentice-Hall, 1977. Lays out Bandura's theory and presents a concise overview of its theoretical and experimental contributions to the field of social learning. Redefines many of the traditional concepts of learning theory and emphasizes the importance of cognitive processes in human learning.

Evans, Richard I. *Albert Bandura, the Man and His Ideas—A Dialogue.* New York: Praeger, 1989. An edited version of an interview with Bandura. Easy to read, presenting Bandura's thoughts on the major aspects of his work in a very accessible form. The spontaneity of the discussion between Evans and Bandura gives a glimpse of Bandura as a person.

Feist, Jess, and Gregory J. Feist. *Theories of Personality.* 7th ed. Boston: McGraw-Hill Higher Education, 2009. Chapter 16 contains an excellent summary of Bandura's work. Gives an easy-to-read overview of his philosophical position (reciprocal determinism), discusses his theory (including observational learning and self-regulatory processes), and presents a summary of relevant research conducted within the framework of social cognitive theory. An ideal starting point for anyone who would like to become familiar with Bandura's work.

Zimmerman, Barry J., and Dale H. Schunk, eds. *Educational Psychology: A Century of Contributions.* Mahwah, N.J.: Lawrence Erlbaum, 2003. Describes Bandura's contributions to theory, research, and practice as well as his legacy and impact on psychology.

Edelgard Wulfert

SEE ALSO: Aggression; Bandura, Albert; Bobo doll experiment; Cognitive behavior therapy; Cognitive social learning: Walter Mischel; Learning; Mischel, Walter; Observational learning and modeling therapies; Phobias; Self-efficacy.

Social networks

TYPE OF PSYCHOLOGY: Psychological methodologies; social psychology; stress
FIELDS OF STUDY: Coping; depression; stress and illness

A social network is the total set of people with whom a person interacts and from whom a person can potentially receive help in time of need. The positive consequences of having good social networks have been rigorously studied and have been shown to relate to a range of health outcomes and psychological well-being.

KEY CONCEPTS
- health outcomes
- perceived integration
- role-based measures
- social integration
- social participation

INTRODUCTION

In almost every culture in the world, men and women live embedded within a network of other people. Young infants are surrounded by caregivers; toddlers, growing children, and adolescents have their peers; and young, middle-aged, and older adults have varying numbers of friends and relatives with whom they interact. Trained research psychologists and laypeople alike have recognized that the presence of others—friends, family, and sometimes even strangers—can be very comforting. A large body of research has focused on how the number and quality of one's interactions with other people influence psychological and physiological health and well-being.

Within formal network theorizing, the term "network" refers to the ties that connect a specific set of entities, be they people, groups, or organizations. Social networks can be described as the sum total of an individual's connections with others. They encompass the different contacts a person may have in one or more distinct social groups (people who are seen on a regular basis for business or pleasure); the types of roles a person plays (mother, coach); the number of friends, family, and relatives a person has; and even the different types of activities in which a person participates (such as attending weekly softball games, where the team becomes part of the network). In psychological writing on the topic of social relationships, a clear distinction is made between social networks, also referred to as structural social support, and functional social support (processes by which people give resources, information, or help to promote emotional or physical well-being). Although social networks can and do serve important functions, such as providing a person with emotional social support or tangible resources in times of need, research on social networks focuses more on the health benefits that are gained from the participation in one or more distinct social groups (the structure of, and stable pattern that exists between, one's ties). This approach and understanding of social networks makes possible the use of more direct measurements of connections, such as how many people an individual speaks to in a week. The underlying assumption in much of this work is that others can influence how people think, feel, and behave through interactions that may not be explicitly intended to exchange help or support.

HISTORICAL BEGINNINGS

Sociologists were the first to write on and study the psychological relevance of social ties or social integration. The French sociologist Émile Durkheim conducted the earliest study of the influence of social networks in 1897. He contended that the breakdown in family, community, and work ties that occurred when workers migrated to industrial areas would be bad for psychological well-being. Durkheim wanted to see if there was any relationship between the number of social ties that a person had and their likelihood of committing suicide. He identified people who had taken their own lives and looked into their social relationships, collecting information from those who knew them and local public records. He found that suicide was most common among individuals who were not married and lacked ties with the community and the church. Some years later, the American sociologist Robert Faris tested if being culturally isolated had anything to do with the development of mental illness. His paper, published in the *American Journal of Sociology* in 1934, emphasized the importance of social contacts and showed that socially isolated individuals were more at risk for developing schizophrenia.

One of the most important studies on the role of social networks was conducted in the late 1970's by the American social epidemiologists Lisa Berkman

and Leonard Syme. Whereas the work of Durkheim and Faris was correlational in nature, in that they looked at cases of suicide and schizophrenia and worked backward to assess the factors that were associated with the outcome, Berkman and Syme conducted a nine-year longitudinal study. They first measured the social ties of close to seven thousand residents of Alameda County in California. They asked the participants in the study what hobbies they had, what groups they attended on a regular basis, if they were members of clubs, if they went to church, and other questions that tapped into their connections with others. Nine years later, they assessed how many of the people were still alive. They found that the people who were more socially integrated at the beginning of the study (had more social connections) lived longer than their counterparts who had fewer social connections. Having social contacts enabled women to live an average of 2.8 years longer and men to live an average of 2.3 years longer. These effects were not caused by differences in education, income level, health status at the beginning of the study, or the practice of health habits. This result was not a fluke. Similar results were found in other large studies conducted since that time.

HEALTH BENEFITS OF SOCIAL NETWORKS

Having good social connections has many benefits. Along with being associated with longer life, having good social networks has been related to a large number of positive health outcomes. Socially integrated people have been found to be less likely to have heart attacks; tend to recover faster from colds and other illnesses; are more likely to survive breast cancer; cope better with stress; are more likely to eat better, exercise, and be physically active; and are less likely to start smoking and have a slightly easier time quitting if they do. In perhaps one of the most impressive demonstrations of the health-buffering ability of social networks, American psychologist Sheldon Cohen exposed a large group of consenting volunteers to a cold virus (delivered via a nasal spray). The participants who reported having more social support and higher quality social networks were less likely to develop upper respiratory illnesses. Cohen randomly sampled his participants such that anyone in the general population had an equal chance of being in his study, allowing generalization of his results and assurance that there was nothing else influencing his findings.

Good social networks are especially important for healthy aging. Many studies have shown that having a close confidant or intimate social partner is associated with increased longevity. Increased social network size is associated with a reduced risk of mortality. This is an important finding, as research shows that the networks of the elderly often shrink with age, as a result of both death and changes in activities that reduce social contact. Therefore, a large number of studies have investigated whether support from one source, such as a friend, can substitute and compensate for support from another, such as a spouse. Results on this issue have been mixed. Some studies show that friends and relatives can make up for less support from spouses or children, while others suggest that this may not always be the case. One clear conclusion is that studies of social support should assess support from many different sources.

One aspect of the health benefits of social networks needs special attention. Because Durkheim's early work showing that people who were married were better off psychologically, many psychologists and studies proclaimed that just being married is enough. This oversimplifies the issue and is inaccurate. The fact seems to be that the benefits of being married vary for each sex. Whereas being married is very important for the well-being of men, it is not always the case for women. For women, having a close female confidant seems to be the critical element for well-being. This sex difference extends over many forms of social support. In general, women have been found to be better at creating social networks and keeping them alive and functioning, to

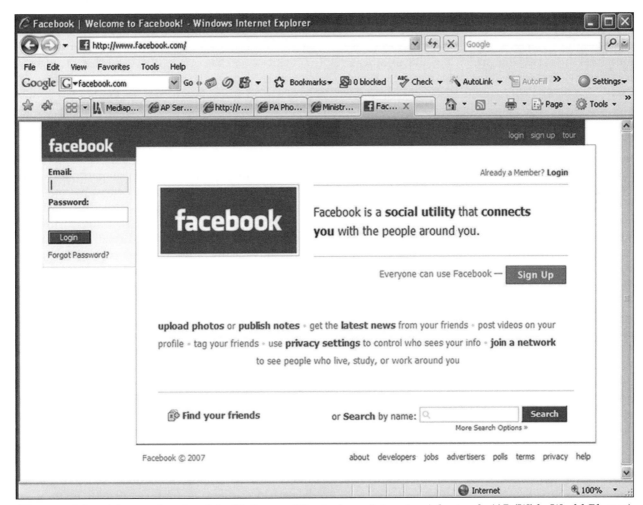

Many people's social networks expanded with the use of Facebook, an Internet social network. (AP/Wide World Photos)

benefit the most from networks, and to give and receive more functional forms of social support from networks than do men.

MEASUREMENT

Social networks can be measured in many different ways. To make them easier to understand and study, psychologists separate social networks into different components. The first main distinction can be made between the behavioral component of networks and the mental component of interacting with networks. The behavioral component consists of measurements of active participation in a wide range of activities (often a direct count of items such as the number of social groups to which people belong or the number of people they talk to on the telephone each week) and is perhaps the most common approach to studying social networks. Behavioral components are further subdivided into measurements of recognized social positions or social identities, termed role-based measures, and measures that assess the frequency and number of social activities, termed social participation measures. The mental component of social networks refers to how people think about their networks and what resources they believe they have. This category of measures, commonly called perceived integration measures, focuses purely on the perceptions of the individual, regardless of whether the perceptions are an accurate reflection of reality. Although this may seem like a problematic issue—how an individual's perceptions of something can be measured other than by using that individual's own report—psychologists have found that even believing that one has many people to whom to turn in case of need has many benefits.

One of the first researchers to study actively how roles influence social networks was the American psychologist Margaret Thoits. Using data collected from a large study of the community in New Haven, Connecticut, she constructed a tool assessing participation in eight key social roles: parent, spouse, worker, friend, neighbor, student, church member, and group member. Consistent with earlier work on this topic, she found that people who possessed more roles experienced less stress and had fewer psychological problems. Extensions of her work have added additional roles such as lover, son or daughter, son-in-law or daughter-in-law, relative, hobbyist, athlete, and stepparent.

Building on this work, Cohen created the Social Network Index (SNI), a popularly used measure of social networks that assesses participation in twelve types of social relationships similar to those used by Thoits. Participation in a relationship is defined as talking to the person on the telephone or in person at least once every two weeks. The total number of persons communicated with thus provides a measure of network size.

Social participation measures assess how often individuals interact with others regardless of the number of roles that they may have. This work focuses both on the type of activities (going to church versus going to a party) as well as the number of activities (how many times things are done in general). For example, Swedish researchers developed a questionnaire, the Welin Activity Scale, that assesses the degree to which people participate in three main categories of activities: social activities, home activities, and outside home activities. Respondents estimate how often they engage in thirty-four different activities over the course of a year, using three main response options (never, occasionally, and often). A twelve-year study conducted in Gothenburg, Sweden, with this scale showed that people with higher scores on this measure of social participation were less likely to die from heart problems.

The American psychologist James House developed a similar measure of social participation in 1982. House and colleagues assessed participation in four main categories of social activity: intimate social relationships, formal organizational involvements outside work, active and relatively social leisure, and passive and relatively social leisure. Together, these measures of social participation help assess the extent to which social participation contributes to well-being.

Perceived integration measures often provide the most direct ways to capture the psychological benefits of networks. Believing that others will help one in time of need can provide a sense of security and comfort. Very often, perceptions actually map onto reality when members of an individual's social networks help the individual cope with stressors and supply needed tangible resources such as money, materials, or information. Perceived integration has been measured in a variety of different ways, most commonly by asking individuals to think about whom they could turn to if they needed help.

It is important to note that researchers are not

certain whether the effects of social support on health represent a slope (where a person is less likely to die the more social connections they have) or a ceiling (where social networks are very important for people with few or no connections, but not as important for people with many connections). Some answers to this problem can be found by looking at how social support changes over time.

THEORETICAL APPROACHES TO SOCIAL NETWORK CHANGE

Two main theoretical frameworks have been proposed to predict and account for age-related changes in social networks. The American psychologist Toni Antonucci proposed that people are motivated to maintain their social network sizes as they age. Calling her theory the social convoy model, Antonucci suggested that although there may be many changes in the composition of the networks, people are thought to sift through their relationships, retaining those they value most. According to American psychologist Laura Cartensen's socioemotional selectivity theory, people prune their social networks to maintain a desired emotional state depending on the extent to which time is perceived as limited. Correspondingly, whereas the sizes of older adults' social networks are smaller than those for younger adults, the numbers of close relationships are comparable. Both theories have been well supported and indicate that it is not the size of the network (structure) but the quality of transactions (perceived and received social support that may vary in function) that is critical. Even though networks may sometimes decrease in size, the quality of support may in fact increase.

SOURCES FOR FURTHER STUDY

Cohen, Sheldon, Lynn G. Underwood, and Benjamin H. Gottlieb, eds. *Social Support Measurement and Intervention: A Guide for Health and Social Scientists.* New York: Oxford University Press, 2000. Provides a comprehensive review of the social support literature, highlighting many different theoretical approaches, surveying main research findings, and providing in-depth coverage of the main ways of measuring and using social networks. The contributors in this book represent the major contemporary researchers of social networks.

Levy, Judith A., and Bernice A. Pescosolido, eds. *Social Networks and Health.* New York: JAI, Elsevier Science, 2002. A collection of essays that examine the interactions between social networks and health, looking at where social networks originate, how they are activated, and how they can be measured.

Parks, Malcolm R. *Personal Relationships and Personal Networks.* Mahwah, N.J.: Lawrence Erlbaum, 2007. Examines how personal relationships form and progress, and how they interact with social networks.

Silverman, Philip, et al. *Social Networks of Older Adults: A Comparative Study of Americans and Taiwanese.* Youngstown, N.Y.: Cambria Press, 2008. A comparison of older adults in two cultures that looks at the social networks they form, the values that they reflect, and the health benefits.

Uchino, Bert N., John T. Cacioppo, and Janice K. Kiecolt-Glaser. "The Relationship Between Social Support and Physiological Processes: A Review with Emphasis on Underlying Mechanisms and Implications for Health." *Psychological Bulletin* 119, no. 3 (1996): 488-531. In this review, the authors examine more than eighty-one studies and describe the evidence linking social support to physiological processes. Social support and social networks were reliably related to beneficial effects on aspects of the cardiovascular, endocrine, and immune systems.

Regan A. R. Gurung

SEE ALSO: Affiliation and friendship; Affiliation motive; Altruism, cooperation, and empathy; Coping: Social support; Health psychology; Helping; Social perception; Social support and mental health; Support groups.

Social perception

TYPE OF PSYCHOLOGY: Social psychology
FIELDS OF STUDY: Interpersonal relations; social perception and cognition

Social perception deals with how people think about and make sense of other people—how they form impressions, draw conclusions, and try to explain other people's behavior. Sometimes called social cognition or the study of "naïve psychology," social perception focuses on factors that influence the ways in which people understand other people and on how people process, organize, and recall information about others.

KEY CONCEPTS
- actor-observer bias
- causal attribution
- correspondence bias
- disposition
- fundamental attribution error
- primacy effect
- priming
- schema (*pl.* schemata)
- self-fulfilling prophecy

INTRODUCTION

Social perception deals with two general classes of cognitive-perceptual processes through which people process, organize, and recall information about others. Those that deal with how people form impressions of other people's personalities (called person perception) form the first class. The second class includes those processes that deal with how people use this information to draw conclusions about other people's motivations, intentions, and emotions to explain and predict their behavior (called attribution processes). This importance of social perception in social psychology is revealed in the fact that people's impressions and judgments about others, whether accurate or not, can have profound effects on their own and others' behavior.

People are naturally motivated to understand and predict the behavior of those around them. Being able to predict and understand the social world gives people a sense of mastery and control over their environment. Psychologists who study social perception have shown that people try to make sense of their social worlds by determining whether other people's behavior is produced by a disposition—some internal quality or trait unique to a person—or by something in the situation or environment. The process of making such determinations, which is called causal attribution, was developed by social psychologists Fritz Heider, Edward Jones, Keith Davis, and Harold Kelley in the late 1950's and early 1960's.

According to these attribution theorists, when people decide that a person's behavior reflects a disposition (when, for example, someone decides that a person is friendly because he acted friendly), people have made an internal or dispositional attribu-

tion. In contrast, when people decide that a person's behavior was caused by something in the situation—he acted in a friendly way to make someone like him—they have made an external or situational attribution. The attributions people make for others' behaviors carry considerable influence in the impressions they form of them and in how they will behave toward them in the future.

INACCURACIES AND BIASES

People's impressions and attributions are not always accurate. For example, in many situations, people seem to be inclined to believe that other people's behavior is caused by dispositional factors. At the same time, they believe that their own behavior is the product of situational causes. This tendency has been called the actor-observer bias. Moreover, when people try to explain the causes of other people's behavior, especially behavior that is clearly and obviously caused by situational factors (factors such as a coin flip, a dice roll, or some other situational inducement), they tend to underestimate situational influences and overestimate the role of dispositional causes. This tendency is referred to as correspondence bias, or the fundamental attribution error. In other words, people prefer to explain other people's behavior in terms of their traits or personalities rather than in terms of situational factors, even when situational factors actually caused the behavior.

In addition to these biases, social psychologists have examined other ways in which people's impressions of others and inferences about the causes of their behavior can be inaccurate or biased. In their work, for example, psychologists Daniel Kahneman and Amos Tversky have described a number of simple but efficient thinking strategies, or rules of thumb, called heuristics. The availability heuristic is the tendency to explain behaviors on the basis of causes that are easily or quickly brought to mind. Similarly, the representativeness heuristic is the tendency to believe that a person who possesses characteristics that are associated with a social group probably belongs to that group. Although heuristics make social thinking more efficient and yield reasonable results most of the time, they can sometimes lead to significant judgment errors.

INFLUENCE OF SCHEMATA AND PRIMACY EFFECT

Bias can also arise in social perception in a number of other ways. Because of the enormous amount of social information that people must process at any given moment, they have developed various ways of organizing, categorizing, and simplifying this information and the expectations they have about various people, objects, and events. These organizational structures are called schemata. For example, schemata that organize information about people's membership in different categories or groups are called stereotypes or prototypes. Schemata that organize information about how traits go together in forming a person's personality are called implicit personality theories (IPTs). Although schemata, like heuristics, help make social thinking more efficient and yield reasonable results most of the time, they can also sometimes lead to significant judgment errors, such as prejudice and discrimination.

Finally, social perception can be influenced by a variety of factors of which people are unaware but that can exert tremendous influence on their thinking. Social psychologist Solomon Asch was the first to describe the primacy effect in impression formation. The primacy effect is the tendency for things that are seen or received first to have a greater impact on people's thinking than things that come later. Many other things in the environment can prime people, or make them "ready," to see, interpret, or remember things that they might not otherwise have seen, thought about, or remembered. Priming occurs when something in the environment makes certain things easier to bring to mind.

During the 1970's and 1980's, social psychologists made numerous alterations and extensions of the existing theories of attribution and impression formation to keep pace with the field's growing emphasis on mental (cognitive) and emotional (affective) processes. These changes focused primarily on incorporating work from cognitive psychology on memory processes, the use of schemata, and the interplay of emotion, motivation, and cognition.

STEREOTYPE AND CONFLICT RESEARCH

Social psychologists have argued that many social problems have their roots in social perception processes. Because social perception biases can sometimes result in inaccurate perceptions, misunderstandings, conflict between people and groups, and other negative consequences, social psychologists have spent much time and effort trying to understand them. Their hope is that by understanding such biases they will be able to suggest solutions for

them. In a number of experiments, social psychologists have attempted to understand the social perception processes that may lead to stereotyping, which can result in prejudice and discrimination.

For example, one explanation for why stereotypes are so hard to change once they have been formed is the self-fulfilling prophecy. Self-fulfilling prophecies occur when people have possibly inaccurate beliefs about others (such as stereotypes) and act on those beliefs, bringing about the conditions necessary to make those beliefs come true. In other words, when people expect something to be true about another person (especially a negative thing), they frequently look for and find what they expect to see. At other times, they actually bring out the negative (or positive) qualities they expect to be present. In a classic 1968 study by social psychologists Robert Rosenthal and Lenore Jacobson, for example, children whose teachers expected them to show a delayed but substantial increase in their intelligence (on the basis of a fictitious intelligence test) actually scored higher on a legitimate intelligence quotient (IQ) test administered at the end of the school year. Presumably, the teachers' expectations of those students caused them to treat those students in ways that actually helped them perform better. Similarly, social psychologists Rebecca Curtis and Kim Miller have shown that when people think someone they meet likes them, they act in ways that lead that person to like them. If, however, people think a person dislikes them, they act in ways that actually make that person dislike them.

The behaviors that produce self-fulfilling prophecies can be subtle. For example, in 1974, social psychologists Carl Word, Mark Zanna, and Joel Cooper demonstrated that the subtle behaviors of interviewers during job interviews can make applicants believe that they performed either poorly or very well. These feelings, in turn, can lead to actual good or poor performance on the part of the applicants. What was most striking about this study, however, was that the factor that led to the subtle negative or positive behaviors was the interviewers' stereotypes of the applicants' racial group membership. Black applicants received little eye contact from interviewers and were not engaged in conversation; the behaviors displayed by interviewers in the presence of white applicants were exactly the opposite. Not surprisingly, black applicants were seen as less qualified and were less likely to be hired. Clearly, subtle behaviors produced by racial stereotypes can have major consequences for the targets of those stereotypes.

PRIMACY EFFECT IN ACADEMIC SETTINGS

The relevance of social perception processes to everyday life is not restricted to stereotyping, although stereotyping is indeed an important concern. In academic settings, for example, situational factors can lead teachers to form impressions of students that have little bearing on their actual abilities. Social psychologist Jones and his colleagues examined the way in which primacy effects operate in academic settings. Two groups of subjects saw a student perform on a test. One group saw the student start out strong and then begin to do poorly. The other group saw the student start out poorly and then begin to improve. For both groups, the student's performance on the test was identical, and the student received the same score. The group that saw the student start out strong and then falter thought the student was brighter than the student who started out poorly and then improved. Clearly, first impressions matter.

CORRESPONDENCE BIAS

Finally, research on the correspondence bias (fundamental attribution error) makes it clear that people must be very careful when trying to understand what other people are like. In many situations, the demands of people's occupations or their family roles force them to do things with which they may not actually agree. Substantial research has shown that observers will probably think these people have personalities that are consistent with their behaviors. Lawyers, who must defend people who may have broken the law; debaters, who must argue convincingly for or against a particular point of view; and actors, who must play parts that they did not write, are all vulnerable to being judged on the basis of their behavior. Unless the observer is particularly sensitive to the fact that when these people are doing their jobs, their behaviors do not reveal anything about their true personalities, the observer may actually (and incorrectly) believe that they do.

INFLUENTIAL RESEARCH AND THEORIES

The study of social perception has multiple origins that can be traced back to a number of influential researchers and theorists. It was one of the first topics to be emphasized when the modern study of social psychology began during World War II. Later perspectives on social perception processes can be traced to the early work of Asch, a social psychologist who emigrated to the United States before the war. His work yielded important demonstrations of primacy effects in impression formation.

Also important to the development of an understanding of social perception was the work of Heider, another German émigré, who came to the United States as World War II was ending in Europe. Heider's influential book *The Psychology of Interpersonal Relations* (1958) arguably started the cognitive approach to social perception processes. In many circles, it is still regarded as a watershed of ideas and insights on person perception and attribution.

Perhaps the most important historical development leading up to the modern study of social perception, however, was the work of Jerome Bruner and other "new look" cognitive psychologists. Following World War II, a number of psychologists broke with the then-traditional behaviorist/learning theory perspective and applied a Gestalt perspective to human perception. They emphasized the subjective nature of perception and interpretation and argued that both cognition (thinking) and situational context are important in determining "what" it is that a person perceives. Using ambiguous figures, for example, they demonstrated that the same object can be described in many different ways depending on the context in which it is seen.

THEORETICAL COMMONALITIES

Although their perspectives differ, theorists on social perception share some common themes. First, they all acknowledged that social perception is inherently subjective; the most important aspect of understanding people is not what is "true" in an objective sense, but rather what is believed to be true. Second, they acknowledged that people think about other people and want to understand why people do the things they do. Finally, they believed that some general principles govern the ways in which people approach social perception and judgment, and they set out to demonstrate these principles scientifically.

SOURCES FOR FURTHER STUDY

Alicke, Mark D., David A. Dunning, and Joachim I. Krueger, eds. *The Self in Social Judgment.* New York: Psychology Press, 2005. The group of essays begins with the history of social judgment; looks at main themes, such as the presumption of self-superiority; and examines research approaches.

Deaux, Kay, and Gina Philogene, eds. *Representations of the Social: Bridging Theoretical Traditions.* Malden, Mass.: Blackwell, 2001. A concise collection of papers by well-known experts on social perception, intended as a textbook for undergraduates.

Forgas, Joseph P., ed. *Affect in Social Thinking and Behavior.* New York: Psychology Press, 2006. An examination of how emotions affect relationships and people's perceptions of others and their social interactions.

Gilbert, Daniel T., ed. *The Selected Works of Edward E. Jones.* Hoboken, N.J.: Wiley, 2004. A collection of works by Jones, one of the leading social psychologists of the twentieth century, who laid the foundation for attribution theory.

Strack, Fritz, and Jens Forster, eds. *Social Cognition: The Basis of Human Interaction.* New York: Psychology Press, 2009. An examination of social perception and social psychology and their importance in human relations.

Teiford, Jenifer B., ed. *Social Perception: Twenty-first Century Issues and Challenges.* New York: Nova Science Publishers, 2008. A collection of essays examining social perception and the issues surrounding it.

John H. Fleming

SEE ALSO: Attributional biases; Causal attribution; Emotions; Memory; Motivation; Prejudice; Racism; Self-presentation; Social schemata.

Social psychological models
Erich Fromm

TYPE OF PSYCHOLOGY: Personality
FIELDS OF STUDY: Humanistic-phenomenological models; psychodynamic and neoanalytic models

Erich Fromm studied the effects of political, economic, and religious institutions on human personality. Fromm's work provides powerful insight into the causes of human unhappiness and psychopathology as well as ideas about how individuals and social institutions could change to maximize mental health and happiness.

KEY CONCEPTS
- dynamic adaptation
- escape from freedom
- freedom from external constraints
- freedom to maximize potential
- mental health
- personality
- productive love
- productive work

INTRODUCTION

The approach of Erich Fromm to the study of human personality starts from an evolutionary perspective. Specifically, Fromm maintained that humans, like all other living creatures, are motivated to survive and that survival requires adaptation to their physical surroundings. Humans are, however, unique in that they substantially alter their physical surroundings through the creation and maintenance of cultural institutions. Consequently, Fromm believed that human adaptation occurs primarily in response to the demands of political, economic, and religious institutions.

Fromm made a distinction between adaptations to physical and social surroundings that have no enduring impact on personality (static adaptation—for example, an American learning to drive on the left side of the road in England) and adaptation that does have an enduring impact on personality (dynamic adaptation—for example, a child who becomes humble and submissive in response to a brutally domineering, egomaniacal parent). Fromm consequently defined personality as the manner in which individuals dynamically adapt to their physical and social surroundings to survive and reduce anxiety.

Human adaptation includes the reduction of anxiety for two reasons. First, because humans are born in a profoundly immature and helplessly dependent state, they are especially prone to anxiety, which, although unpleasant, is useful to the extent that it results in signs of distress (such as crying), which alert others and elicit their assistance. Second, infants eventually mature into fully self-conscious human beings who, although no longer helpless and dependent, recognize their ultimate mortality and essential isolation from all other living creatures.

Fromm believed that humans have five basic inorganic needs (as opposed to organic needs associated with physical survival) resulting from the anxi-

Erich Fromm. (Library of Congress)

ety associated with human immaturity at birth and eventual self-consciousness. The need for relatedness refers to the innate desire to acquire and maintain social relationships. The need for transcendence suggests that human beings have an inherent drive to become creative individuals. The need for rootedness consists of a sense of belonging to a social group. The need for identity is the need to be a unique individual. The need for a frame of orientation refers to a stable and consistent way of perceiving the world.

FREEDOM AND INDIVIDUAL POTENTIAL

Mental health for Fromm consists of realizing one's own unique individual potential, and it requires two kinds of freedom that are primarily dependent on the structure of a society's political, economic, and religious institutions. Freedom from external constraints refers to practical concerns such as freedom from imprisonment, hunger, and homelessness. This is how many people commonly conceive of the notion of freedom. For Fromm, freedom from exter-

nal constraints is necessary but not sufficient for optimal mental health, which also requires the freedom to maximize one's individual potential.

Freedom to maximize individual potential entails productive love and productive work. Productive love consists of interpersonal relationships based on mutual trust, respect, and cooperation. Productive work refers to daily activities that allow for creative expression and provide self-esteem. Fromm hypothesized that people become anxious and insecure if their need for transcendence is thwarted by a lack of productive work and love. Many people, he believed, respond to anxiety and insecurity by what he termed an escape from freedom: the unconscious adoption of personality traits that reduce anxiety and insecurity at the expense of individual identity.

PERSONALITY TYPES AND FREEDOM ESCAPE

Fromm described five personality types representing an escape from freedom. Authoritarian people reduce anxiety and insecurity by fusing themselves with another person or a religious, political, or economic institution. Fromm distinguished between sadistic and masochistic authoritarians: The sadistic type needs to dominate (and often hurt and humiliate) others, while the masochistic type needs to submit to the authority of others. The sadist and the masochist are similar in that they share a dependence on each other. Fromm used the people in Nazi Germany (masochists) under Adolf Hitler (a sadist) to illustrate the authoritarian personality type.

Destructive people reduce anxiety and insecurity by destroying other people or things. Fromm suggested that ideally people derive satisfaction and security from constructive endeavors, but he noted that some people lack the skill and motivation to create and therefore engage in destructive behavior as an impoverished substitute for constructive activities.

Withdrawn people reduce anxiety and insecurity by willingly or unwillingly refusing to participate in a socially prescribed conception of reality; instead, they withdraw into their own idiosyncratic versions of reality. In one social conception, for example, many devout Christians believe that God created the earth in six days, that Christ was born approximately two thousand years ago, and that he has not yet returned to Earth. The withdrawn individual might singularly believe that Earth was hatched from the egg of a giant bird a few years ago and that Christ had been seen eating a hamburger yesterday. Psychiatrists and clinicians would generally characterize these withdrawn people as psychotic or schizophrenic.

Self-inflated people reduce anxiety and insecurity by unconsciously adopting glorified images of themselves as superhuman individuals who are vastly superior to others. They are arrogant, strive to succeed at the expense of others, are unable to accept constructive criticism, and avoid experiences that might disconfirm their false conceptions of themselves.

Finally, Fromm characterized American society in the 1940's as peopled by automaton conformists, who reduce anxiety and insecurity by unconsciously adopting the thoughts and feelings demanded of them by their culture. They are then no longer anxious and insecure, because they are like everyone else around them. According to Fromm, automaton conformists are taught to distrust and repress their own thoughts and feelings during childhood through impoverished and demoralizing educational and socializing experiences. The result is the acquisition of pseudothoughts and pseudofeelings, which people believe to be their own but which are actually socially infused. For example, Fromm contended that most Americans vote the same way that their parents do, although very few would claim that parental preference was the cause of their political preferences. Rather, most American voters would claim that their decisions are the result of a thorough and rational consideration of genuine issues (a pseudothought) instead of a mindless conformity to parental influence (a genuine thought—or, in this case, a nonthought).

IMPACT OF HISTORICAL CONSTRAINTS

In *Escape from Freedom* (1941), Fromm applied his theory of personality to a historical account of personality types by a consideration of how political, economic, and religious changes in Western Europe from the Middle Ages to the twentieth century affected "freedom from" and "freedom to." Fromm argued that the feudal political system of the Middle Ages engendered very little freedom from external constraints. Specifically, there was limited physical

mobility; the average person died in the same place that he or she was born, and many people were indentured servants who could not leave their feudal lord even if they had somewhere to go. Additionally, there was no choice of occupation: A man's job was generally inherited from his father.

Despite the lack of freedom from external constraints, however, economic and religious institutions provided circumstances that fostered freedom to maximize individual potential through productive work and productive love. Economically, individual craftsmanship was the primary means by which goods were produced. Although this was time-consuming and inefficient by modern standards, craftspeople were responsible for the design and production of entire products. A shoemaker would choose the design and materials, make the shoes, and sell the shoes. A finished pair of shoes thus represented a tangible manifestation of the creative energies of the producer, thus providing productive work.

Additionally, the crafts were regulated by the guild system, which controlled access to apprenticeships and materials and set wages and prices to guarantee maximum employment and a fair profit to the craftspeople. The guilds encouraged relatively cooperative behavior between craftspeople and consequently engendered productive love. Productive love was also sustained by the moral precepts of the then-dominant Roman Catholic church, which stressed the essential goodness of humankind, the idea that human beings had free will to choose their behavior on Earth and hence influence their ultimate fate after death, the need to be responsible for the welfare of others, and the sinfulness of extracting excessive profits from commerce and accumulating money beyond that which is necessary to exist comfortably.

The dissolution of the feudal system and the consequent transition to parliamentary democracy and capitalism provided the average individual with a historically unprecedented amount of freedom from external constraints. Physical mobility increased dramatically as the descendants of serfs were able to migrate freely to cities to seek employment of their choosing; however, according to Fromm, increased freedom from external constraints was acquired at the expense of the circumstances necessary for freedom to maximize individual potential through productive work and productive love.

IMPACT OF CAPITALISM

Capitalism shifted the focus of commerce from small towns to large cities and stimulated the development of fast and efficient means of production, but assembly-line production methods divested the worker of opportunities for creative expression. The assembly-line worker has no control over the design of a product, does not engage in the entire production of the product, and has nothing to do with the sale and distribution of the product. Workers in a modern automobile factory might put on hubcaps or install radios for eight hours each day as cars roll by on the assembly line. They have no control over the process of production and no opportunity for creative expression, given the monotonous and repetitive activities of their jobs.

In addition to the loss of opportunities to engage in productive work, the inherent competitiveness of capitalism undermined the relatively cooperative interpersonal relationships engendered by the guild system, transforming the stable small-town economic order into a frenzied free-for-all in which people compete with their neighbors for the resources necessary to survive, hence dramatically reducing opportunities for people to acquire and maintain productive love. Additionally, these economic changes were supported by the newly dominant Protestant churches (represented by the teachings of John Calvin and Martin Luther), which stressed the inherent evilness of humankind, the lack of free will, and the notion of predetermination—the idea that God has already decided before a person's birth if that individual is to be consigned to heaven or hell after death. Despite the absence of free will and the idea that an individual's fate was predetermined, Protestant theologians claimed that people could get a sense of God's intentions by their material success on Earth, thus encouraging people to work very hard to accumulate as much as possible (the so-called Protestant work ethic) as an indication that God's countenance is shining on them.

CALL TO EMBRACE POSITIVE FREEDOM

In summary, Fromm argued that the average person in Western industrial democracies has freedom from external constraints but lacks opportunities to maximize individual potential through productive love and productive work; the result is pervasive feelings of anxiety and insecurity. Most people respond to this anxiety and insecurity by unconsciously adopting personality traits that reduce anxiety and insecurity, but at the expense of their individuality, which Fromm referred to as an escape from freedom. For Fromm, psychopathology is the general result of the loss of individuality associated with an escape from freedom. The specific manifestation of psychopathology depends on the innate characteristics of the individual in conjunction with the demands of the person's social environment.

Fromm argued that while escaping from freedom is a typical response to anxiety and insecurity, it is not an inevitable one. Instead, he urged people to embrace positive freedom through the pursuit of productive love and work, which he claimed would require both individual and social change. Individually, Fromm advocated a life of spontaneous exuberance made possible by love and being loved. He described the play of children and the behavior of artists as illustrations of this kind of lifestyle. Socially, Fromm believed strongly that the fundamental tenets of democracy should be retained but that capitalism in its present form must be modified to ensure every person's right to live, to distribute resources more equitably, and to provide opportunities to engage in productive work.

THEORETICAL INFLUENCES

Fromm's ideas reflect the scientific traditions of his time as well as his extensive training in history and philosophy, in addition to his psychological background. Fromm is considered a neo-Freudian (along with Karen Horney, Harry Stack Sullivan, and others) because of his acceptance of some of Freud's basic ideas (specifically, the role of unconsciously motivated behaviors in human affairs and the notion that anxiety-producing inclinations are repressed or prevented from entering conscious awareness) while rejecting Freud's reliance on the role of biological instincts (sex and aggression) for understanding human behavior. Instead, the neo-Freudians were explicitly concerned with the influence of the social environment on personality development.

Additionally, Fromm was very much influenced by Charles Darwin's theory of evolution, by existential philosophy, and by the economic and social psychological ideas of Karl Marx. Fromm's use of adaptation in the service of survival to define personality is derived from basic evolutionary theory. His analysis of the sources of human anxiety, especially the awareness of death and perception of isolation and aloneness, is extracted from existential philosophy. The notion that human happiness requires productive love and work and that capitalism is antithetical to mental health was originally proposed by Marx. Fromm's work has never received the attention that it deserves in the United States because of his open affinity for some of Marx's ideas and his insistence that economic change is utterly necessary to ameliorate the unhappiness and mental illness that pervade American society. Nevertheless, his ideas are vitally important from both a theoretical and practical perspective.

SOURCES FOR FURTHER STUDY

Anderson, Kevin, and Richard Quinney, eds. *Erich Fromm and Critical Criminology: Beyond the Punitive Society.* Urbana: University of Illinois Press, 2000. Contains a chapter on Fromm and his life as well as two essays by Fromm, but focuses on alienation and crime and the psychology of the criminal.

Fromm, Erich. *Beyond the Chains of Illusion: My Encounter with Marx and Freud.* New York: Continuum, 2001. Fromm discusses his views of Marxism, capitalism, and psychology in relation to the works of Karl Marx and Sigmund Freud.

_____. *Escape from Freedom.* 1941. Reprint. New York: Henry Holt, 1995. Fromm's early seminal work, in which his basic theory about the relationship between political, economic, and religious institutions and personality development was originally articulated. All of Fromm's later books are extensions of ideas expressed here.

Funk, Rainer. *Erich Fromm: His Life and Ideas—An Illustrated Biography.* New York: Continuum, 2000. A biography of Fromm that tells the story of his life and discusses his ideas.

Wilde, Lawrence. *Erich Fromm and the Quest for Solidarity.* New York: Palgrave Macmillan, 2004. Argues that Fromm's humanistic ethics provide a framework for examining alienation in affluent societies.

Sheldon Solomon

SEE ALSO: Freud, Sigmund; Fromm, Erich; Horney, Karen; Humanistic psychology; Psychoanalytic psychology and personality: Sigmund Freud; Self; Self-esteem; Social psychological models: Karen Horney; Sullivan, Harry Stack; Workplace issues and mental health.

Social psychological models
Karen Horney

TYPE OF PSYCHOLOGY: Personality
FIELDS OF STUDY: Personality theory; psychodynamic and neoanalytic models; psychodynamic therapies

Karen Horney's social psychoanalytic theory focuses on how human relationships and cultural conditions influence personality formation; the theory describes how basic anxiety, resulting from childhood experiences, contributes to the development of three neurotic, compulsive, rigid personality styles: moving toward others, moving away from others, and moving against others. Normal personality is characterized by flexibility and balance among interpersonal styles.

KEY CONCEPTS
- basic anxiety
- externalization
- idealized self
- neurosis
- neurotic trends
- search for glory
- self-realization
- tyranny of the should

INTRODUCTION

Karen Horney spent the major part of her career explaining how personality patterns, especially neurotic patterns, are formed, how they operate, and how they can be changed to increase individual potential. In contrast to Sigmund Freud's view that people are guided by instincts and the pleasure principle, Horney proposed that people act out desires to achieve safety and satisfaction in social relationships. She was optimistic about the possibility for human growth and believed that, under conditions of acceptance and care, people move toward self-realization, or the development of their full potential. She wrote almost exclusively, however, about personality problems and methods for solving them.

ROLE OF CULTURE

Horney believed that it is impossible to understand individuals or the mechanisms of neurosis (inflexible behaviors and reactions, or discrepancies between one's potential and one's achievements) apart from the cultural context in which they exist. Neurosis varies across cultures, as well as within the same culture, and it is influenced by socioeconomic class, gender, and historical period. For example, in *The Neurotic Personality of Our Time* (1937), Horney noted that a person who refuses to accept a salary increase in a Western culture might be seen as neurotic, whereas in a Pueblo Indian culture, this person might be seen as entirely normal.

The neurotic person experiences culturally determined problems in an exaggerated form. In Western culture, competitiveness shapes many neurotic problems because it decreases opportunities for cooperation, fosters a climate of mistrust and hostility, undermines self-esteem, increases isolation, and encourages people to be more concerned with how they appear to others than with fulfilling personal possibilities. It fosters the overvaluing of external success, encourages people to develop grandiose images of superiority, and leads to intensified needs for approval and affection as well as to the distortion of love. Moreover, the ideal of external success is contradicted by the ideal of humility, which leads to further internal conflict and, in many cases, neurosis.

ROLE OF THE FAMILY

Cultural patterns are replicated and transmitted primarily in family environments. Ideally, a family provides the warmth and nurturance that prepares children to face the world with confidence. When parents have struggled unsuccessfully with the culture, however, they create the conditions that lead to inadequate parenting. In its most extreme form, the competitiveness of the larger culture leads to child abuse, but it can also lead to parents' preoccupation with their own needs, an inability to love and nurture effectively, or a tendency to treat children as extensions of themselves. Rivalry, overprotectiveness, irritability, partiality, and erratic behavior are other manifestations of parental problems.

Within this negative environment, children experience fear and anger, but they also feel weak and helpless beside more powerful adults. They recognize that expressing hostility directly might be dangerous and result in parental reprisals or loss of love. As a result, children repress legitimate anger, banishing it to the unconscious. By using the defense mechanism of reaction formation, they develop emotions toward parents that are the opposite of anger, and they experience feared parents as objects of admiration. Children unconsciously turn their inner fears and anger against themselves and lose touch with their real selves. As a result, they develop basic anxiety, or the feeling of being alone and defenseless in a world that seems hostile.

DEFENSE AND COPING STRATEGIES

To cope with basic anxiety, individuals use additional defensive strategies or neurotic trends to cope with the world. These involve three primary patterns of behavior: moving away from others, moving toward others, and moving against others. In addition, neurotic individuals develop an idealized self, an unrealistic, flattering distortion of the self-image that encourages people to set unattainable standards, shrink from reality, and compulsively search for glory (compulsive and insatiable efforts to fulfill the demands of the idealized self) rather than accept themselves as they are.

Horney wrote about these in rich detail in *Our Inner Conflicts: A Constructive Theory of Neurosis* (1945). The person who moves toward others believes: "If I love you or give in, you will not hurt me." The person who moves against others believes: "If I have power, you will not hurt me." The person who moves away from others thinks: "If I am independent or withdraw from you, you will not hurt me."

The person who moves toward others has chosen a dependent or compliant pattern of coping. The person experiences strong needs for approval, belonging, and affection, and strives to live up to the expectations of others through behavior that is overconsiderate and submissive. This person sees love as the only worthwhile goal in life and represses all competitive, hostile, angry aspects of the self. The moving-against type, who has adopted an aggressive, tough, exploitive style, believes that others are hostile, that life is a struggle, and that the only way to survive is to win and to control others. This person sees herself or himself as strong and determined, and represses all feelings of affection for fear of losing power over others. Finally, the moving-away type, who has adopted a style of detachment and isolation, sees himself or herself as self-sufficient, private, and superior to others. This person represses all emotion and avoids any desire or activity that would result in dependency on others.

The interpersonal patterns that Horney discussed are no longer known as neurotic styles, but as personality disorders. Many of the behaviors that she described can be seen in descriptions of diagnostic categories that appear in the American Psychiatric Association's *Diagnostic and Statistical Manual of Mental Disorders: DSM-IV-TR* (rev. 4th ed., 2000), such as dependent personality disorder, narcissistic personality disorder, and obsessive-compulsive personality disorder. Like Horney's original criteria, these categories describe inflexible and maladaptive patterns of behavior and thinking that are displayed in various environments and result in emotional distress or impaired functioning.

USE OF PSYCHOANALYSIS
In her practice of psychoanalysis, Horney used free association and dream analysis to bring unconscious material to light. In contrast to Freud's more passive involvement with patients, she believed that the psychoanalyst should play an active role not only in interpreting behavior but also in inquiring about current behaviors that maintain unproductive patterns, suggesting alternatives, and helping people mobilize energy to change.

Horney also made psychoanalysis more accessible to the general population. She suggested that, by examining themselves according to the principles outlined in her book *Self-Analysis* (1942), people could increase self-understanding and gain freedom from internal issues that limit their potential. Her suggestions indicate that people should choose a problem that they could clearly identify, engage in informal free association about the issue, reflect on and tentatively interpret the experience, and make specific, simple choices about altering problematic behavior patterns. Complex, long-standing issues, however, should be dealt with in formal psychoanalysis.

INFLUENCES
Horney was one of the first individuals to criticize Freud's psychology of women. In contrast to Freudian instinct theory, she proposed a version of psychoanalysis that emphasized the role that social relationships and culture play in human development. She questioned the usefulness of Freud's division of the personality into the regions of the id, ego, and superego, and viewed the ego as a more constructive, forward-moving force within the person.

Horney's work was enriched by her contact with psychoanalysts Harry Stack Sullivan, Clara Thompson, and Erich Fromm, who also emphasized the role of interpersonal relationships and sociocultural factors and were members at Horney's American Institute of Psychoanalysis when it was first established. Horney's work also resembled Alfred Adler's personality theory. Her concepts of the search for glory and idealized self are similar to Adler's concepts of superiority striving and the superiority complex. Furthermore, Adler's ruling type resembles the moving-against personality, his getting type is similar to the moving-toward personality, and his avoiding type is closely related to the moving-away personality.

CONTRIBUTIONS TO THE FIELD
Horney anticipated many later developments within cognitive, humanistic, and feminist personality theory and psychotherapy. Abraham Maslow, who was inspired by Horney, built his concept of self-actualization on Horney's optimistic belief that individuals can move toward self-realization. Carl R. Rogers's assumptions that problems are based on distortions of real experience and discrepancies between the ideal and real selves are related to Horney's beliefs that unhealthy behavior results from denial of the real self as well as from conflict between the idealized and real selves. In the field of cognitive psychotherapy, Albert Ellis's descriptions of the mechanisms of neurosis resemble Horney's statements. He borrowed the phrase "tyranny of the should" from Horney and placed strong emphasis on how "shoulds" influence irrational, distorted thinking patterns. Finally, Horney's notion that problems are shaped by cultural patterns is echoed in the work of feminist psychotherapists, who believe that individual problems are often the consequence of external, social problems.

SOURCES FOR FURTHER STUDY
Hitchcock, Susan Tyler. *Karen Horney: Pioneer of Feminine Psychology.* Philadelphia: Chelsea House, 2005. An examination of Horney's life, especially in her work on women's psychology, which was in opposition to Freud's theories.
Paris, Bernard J. *Karen Horney: A Psychoanalyst's Search for Self-Understanding.* New Haven, Conn.: Yale University Press, 1996. Traces the relationship between Horney's personal life and develop-

ment of her thought; includes extensive bibliography.

_____, ed. *The Unknown Karen Horney: Essays on Gender, Culture, and Psychoanalysis.* New Haven, Conn.: Yale University Press, 2000. A collection of essays that look at the work and theories of Horney, especially with regard to culture and women.

Quinn, Susan. *A Mind of Her Own: The Life of Karen Horney.* Reprint. New York: Other Press, 2003. Readable, honest, fascinating biography of Horney's life; provides insights into personal factors that influenced Horney's theoretical and clinical work.

Solomon, Irving. *Karen Horney and Character Disorder: A Guide for the Modern Practitioner.* New York: Springer, 2006. An examination of Horney's basic tenets and how they are applied in dealing with character disorders in clinical practice.

Carolyn Zerbe Enns

SEE ALSO: Adler, Alfred; Antisocial personality disorder; Avoidant personality disorder; Borderline personality disorder; Defense mechanisms; Ego defense mechanisms; Freudian psychology; Histrionic personality disorder; Horney, Karen; Individual psychology: Alfred Adler; Narcissistic personality disorder; Psychoanalysis; Psychoanalytic psychology and personality: Sigmund Freud; Self-actualization; Social psychological models: Erich Fromm; Sullivan, Harry Stack; Women's psychology: Karen Horney; Women's psychology: Sigmund Freud.

Social schemata

TYPE OF PSYCHOLOGY: Social psychology
FIELD OF STUDY: Social perception and cognition

Social schemata are certain clusters of information that people have stored in their memories; each cluster concerns a person, group of persons, or social event. Having such clusters of information already stored in memory can help people understand their social world yet can also lead people to have a biased perception of it.

KEY CONCEPTS
- cognition
- cognitive processes
- relational scheme
- schema (*pl.* schemata)
- script
- self-fulfilling prophecy
- self-schemata
- social cognition
- stereotype

INTRODUCTION

Life would be very complicated if people did not have the ability to store things in memory or to organize the information that did get stored; people would have to relearn information over and over. Because of memories of past experiences, people do not have to relearn what an apple is, for example, or what to do with it each time they come in contact with one.

A well-organized memory system also helps people make educated guesses. People are able to conclude that, because of an apple's texture, it will not make a satisfactory baseball. People are able to make educated guesses because the human brain has the ability to categorize objects and to generalize from past experiences to new experiences. Indeed, social psychologists believe that the brain has not only the ability to categorize but also the tendency to do so. For example, a very young city child who is taken to the zoo may point to a goat and say, "Doggy!"

The brain's memory system categorizes objects, people, and events by connecting different pieces of related information together. Social psychologists call this collection of related information a schema. The young child knows that "doggies," for example, have fur, four legs, and wet noses. Somehow, the brain links these pieces of information together. In the child's mind, there is an idea of the typical characteristics an object must have for it to be a "doggy."

TYPES OF SOCIAL SCHEMATA

All people have many schemata, covering the entire range of topics about which a given person knows things. Some of these topics are social in nature; some are not. If the content of a schema concerns a person, group of people, or social event, the schema is called a social schema. One type of social schema is a script. A script is a schema about a social event, such as a "good party" or "going to class." Another type of social schema is a stereotype, which is a schema about a group of people. If a person were to list, for example, everything that individual could think of regarding "criminals," including personal opinions or experiences, that person would have listed the contents of his or her "criminal" stereotype.

A third type of social schema is a self-schema. Each of a person's many self-schemata combine to make up the person's overall self-concept, and the self-schema most salient at any given moment is called the working self-concept. A person might, for example, have a self-schema regarding himself or herself as a student, another one as a man or woman, and yet another regarding his or her athletic abilities. Each self-schema might have many, or few, pieces of information. A person's self-schema as a student, for example, might include information about where the individual goes to school, the classes being taken, the level of enjoyment of student life, memories of the first day in kindergarten, or memorable books. Some of these pieces of information might also be included in other schemata; the information stored in the "student" self-schema might also be stored in a script about school, for example.

Another type of social schema is the relational schema. Relational schemata are cognitive structures that exist within an interpersonal, interdependent context. Relational schemata are truly social psychological in nature, as they reflect people's views about themselves and others, not in an isolated context but in the context of others. Relational schemata contain three aspects. First is the self-schema in relation to another person, or how the self is experienced in interaction with another. A good example of this relational self-schema is the distinct self-schema a person has when interacting with a parent or romantic partner. The second component of relational schemata is a partner or particular other schema within the context of an interaction or relationship. For instance, a person holds a distinct schema of a parent, unique to his or her particular parent/child relationship. Finally, relational schemata also include an interpersonal script composed of expectations about how the relationship will and should transpire based on past experiences within the relationship. These three components of relational schemata interact to influence expectations and behavior. As a result, a person having a relational schema with a parent would have a specific self-schema when interacting with the parent ("When I'm with Mom I feel incompetent"), a specific schema of the parent within the interaction

("When Mom is with me, she is very critical"), and finally, an interpersonal script specific to the parent-child relationship ("If I bring up school, Mom will start yelling at me").

SOCIAL SCHEMATA AS MENTAL SHORTCUTS

Schemata, whether they are self-schemata, scripts, stereotypes, relational schemata, or other types of schemata, help people organize and understand new events. They function as shortcuts to help people navigate through both their physical and social worlds. Just as a person's schema for an apple helps the individual recognize and know what to do with an apple, a person's social schemata help the individual function in social situations. For example, most high school juniors know what to do in a new classroom without having to be told because their "classroom" schema, created during previous semesters, already holds information about how to behave in class. Schemata, then, help people simplify the world; they do not constantly have to relearn information about events, concepts, objects, or people.

To understand how social schemata help people simplify the world, social psychologists study the cognitive processes that schemata affect. This area of study is called social cognition. Cognitive processes are thinking processes, such as paying attention, that enable the brain to perceive events. Research has shown that schemata affect what people pay attention to, what they store in permanent memory and then later recall, how they interpret events, and even how people behave (although "behaving" is not considered a cognitive process).

IMPACT ON MEMORY AND INTERPRETATION

Research in social cognition shows that having a schema makes it more likely that a person will pay attention to events that are relevant to the schema than to events that are irrelevant. Schemata also make it more likely that a person will store in permanent memory and later recall new information that confirms the beliefs that person already has in his or her schemata.

An interesting study illuminating this tendency had research participants view a videotape of a woman eating dinner with her husband. Half of the participants had previously learned that this woman was a librarian, while the other half had been told that the woman was a waitress. The researchers found that when they later asked participants to recall what they had seen on the videotape, those who had been told the woman was a librarian recalled more information consistent with the "librarian schema," such as the fact that the woman wore glasses or that she played the piano. Those participants who had been told the woman was a waitress recalled more information consistent with a "waitress schema," for instance, that the woman had a bowling ball in the room or that there were no bookshelves.

There are exceptions to this general rule. When a schema is either very new or very well established, inconsistent information becomes more important and is often more likely to be recalled than when a schema is only moderately established. For example, if one is just getting to know a new person or if the person is one's best friend, information inconsistent with one's schema is more likely to stand out.

Schemata also affect how people interpret events. When people have a schema for an event or person, they are likely to interpret that event or the person's behavior in a way that is consistent with the beliefs already held in the schema. For example, researchers found that when participants were exposed to either a list of words designed to bring to mind a schema of an adventurous person (brave, courageous, daring) or to invoke the schema of a reckless person (foolish, careless), their later judgments of a paragraph they read about a fictional person named Donald, who loved to go white-water rafting and skydiving, were influenced. Specifically, participants whose adventurous schema had been activated judged Donald positively, while those whose reckless schema had been activated judged Donald negatively.

Finally, people tend to act in ways that are consistent with the schemata they hold in memory, and their actions can affect the actions of others in such a way as to confirm the original beliefs. All these cognitive memory biases result in confirmation of the beliefs that are already held; thus, these biases often produce self-fulfilling prophecies.

The Negative Impact

Although social schemata can facilitate people's understanding of their social world, they also can bias people's perceptions. Often, people are not accurate recorders of the world around them; rather, their own beliefs and expectations, clustered and stored as schemata, distort their perceptions of so-

cial events. Such distortions help answer the social psychological question, Why are stereotypes so difficult to change?

If a person has a schema, a stereotype, about criminals and then meets a man who is introduced as a criminal, perceptions of this person can be biased by the schema. Because schemata affect what people notice, this person will be more likely to notice things about this man that are consistent with his or her schema than things that are irrelevant. Perhaps the person believes that criminals use foul language but has no expectations regarding the type of listening skills a criminal might have. In this case, the person might be more likely to notice when the criminal swears than to notice his empathic listening skills. Then, because schemata affect what is stored in and recalled from memory, the person might be more likely to put into memory, and later remember, the criminal's swearing. Even if the person did notice his good listening skills, he or she would be less likely to store that in memory, or to recall it later, than to store information about his swearing.

On the other hand, if a person believes that criminals are not very empathic, he or she might be especially likely to notice this new acquaintance's empathic listening skills. It is unlikely, though, that a person would change his or her schema to fit this new information; what is more likely is that he or she would interpret this information in such a way as to make it fit the stereotype—for example, consider this one criminal to be the exception to the rule, or conclude he developed his listening skills as a con to get out of jail more quickly.

Finally, a person very well might treat a criminal in a way that fits his or her beliefs about him. For example, a person who believes criminals lie might express doubt over things he says. The criminal might then respond to these doubts by acting defensively, which might then confirm the other person's belief that criminals act aggressively or that they have reasons to feel guilty. The criminal also might respond to doubting comments by actually lying. He might have the attitude, "If you expect me to lie, I might as well." What has happened, in this case, is this: A person's beliefs have affected his or her behavior, which in turn has affected the criminal's behavior, and the criminal's behavior now confirms the person's stereotype. This chain of events is one of the problems created by schemata. Very often, negative beliefs make it more likely that a person will find or produce confirmation for these beliefs.

These biases in information processing also can apply to how people perceive themselves, and thus explain why it can be difficult to change a negative self-concept. If a woman sees herself as incompetent, for example, she is likely to notice when her own behavior or thoughts are less than adequate, to store those examples in memory, and to recall such examples from memory. Furthermore, if she engages in an activity and her performance is up for interpretation, she will be more likely to evaluate that performance as incompetent than as competent. Finally, if she believes she is incompetent, this can lead her actually to act that way. For example, her belief may lead her to feel nervous when it is time to perform, and her nervousness might then lead her to perform less competently than she otherwise might have. This provides her with more proof of her own incompetence, another self-fulfilling prophecy.

History of Research
Research in social cognition, the area of social psychology that focuses on social schemata, evolved as a hybrid from two areas of psychology: social psychology and cognitive psychology. In 1924, Floyd Allport published a book titled *Social Psychology*; this early text was the first to assert that an individual's behavior is affected by the presence and actions of other individuals. In the 1950's, though, Kurt Lewin asserted that an individual is more influenced by his or her perceptions of other individuals than by what the other individuals actually are doing. For many years after, a popular subfield in social psychology was person perception. Researchers studying person perception discovered many factors that influence people's judgments and impressions of others. For example, researchers showed that individuals are more influenced by unpleasant than by pleasant information when forming an impression of a stranger. Person perception research focused on how individuals perceive others, rather than on how individuals are influenced by others, and such research provided one of the main foundations for the field of social cognition.

The second main foundation was research on cognitive processes. In the 1980's, researchers studying person perception realized they could better understand why people perceive others as they do by

learning more about cognitive psychology. Cognitive psychology was first developed to explain how individuals learn—for example, to explain the relationship between a child's ability to pay attention, put information into memory, and recall information, and the child's ability to learn information from a textbook. As cognitive psychologists created techniques for studying these cognitive processes, researchers studying person perception realized that the same processes that affect a schoolchild's ability to learn textbook material also might affect how individuals learn about other individuals. As these new cognitive research techniques began answering many questions in the field of person perception, that field branched into a second field, the field called social cognition.

Practical Applications of Research
In the 1970's and 1980's, Aaron T. Beck demonstrated that individuals who are depressed have a self-schema for depression and also a hopeless schema about the world in general. Beck's work has been extremely influential in the understanding of depression. Because of his work, one of the major approaches to treating depression is to help the depressed individual change his or her thoughts and cognitive processes.

Understanding that schemata can bias people's thinking can help people resist such biases. Resisting the biases can help people change parts of their self-concepts, their stereotypes of others, or even their schemata about their loved ones. If a person sees his or her roommate as messy, for example, that individual might be especially likely to notice and remember the roommate's messy behaviors and may respond by cleaning up after the roommate, nagging, or joining the roommate in being messy. The roommate might then rebel against all these responses by becoming even more messy, resulting in a downward spiral. If the person's roommate also is his or her spouse, this can lead to marital problems. Not all self-fulfilling prophecies have these types of unpleasant consequences, but to stop the cycle of those that do, people need to search actively for evidence that disconfirms their schemata.

One of the earliest contributions from the field of social cognition and social schemata research was a better understanding of interracial problems. Before their understanding of social schemata, social psychologists had been interested in discovering the factors that lead to unpleasant feelings toward other racial groups and the conditions that would eliminate such feelings. Research on social schemata helped explain unpleasant intergroup relations by showing that thoughts, that is, schemata, can be resistant to change for reasons that have nothing to do with unpleasant feelings toward a group; the biases in attention, storing information in memory, recalling information, and interpreting events can occur even when unpleasant feelings are not present. Just as a young child's brain perceives a goat to be a "doggy," an adult's brain also tends to perceive new events in ways that fit information already held in memory.

Social psychologists came to understand that cognitive processes also affect many other psychological phenomena that formerly were explained by emotional processes alone. For example, social schemata contribute to psychologists' understanding of why crime victims do not always receive help, why bullies initiate fights, and why some teenagers are so angry with their parents.

Social schemata, studied by social psychologists, have such far-reaching effects that researchers in areas of psychology other than social psychology also study them. For example, personality psychologists study how social schemata affect self-concept, and clinical psychologists study how social schemata can inhibit or facilitate therapy sessions. Social schemata themselves may simplify people's understanding of social events, but the study of schemata has greatly enriched the understanding of the social perceiver.

SOURCES FOR FURTHER STUDY

Burns, David D. *Feeling Good Together: The Secret of Making Troubled Relationships Work.* New York: Broadway Books, 2008. This self-help book by a colleague of Aaron T. Beck shows how beliefs and expectations can influence a couple's feelings toward themselves and others. He helps people identify what they want out of a relationship and how to deal with conflict.

Lassen, Maureen Kirby. *Why Are We Still Fighting? How to End Your Schema Wars and Start Connecting with the People You Love.* Oakland, Calif.: New Harbinger, 2000. This book, written by a clinical psychologist in private practice, applies scientific research on social schemata to a relationship context. It suggests various ways to identify and change unconscious self and other schemata to help resolve conflicts and improve relationships.

Rison, Lawrence P., et al., ed. *Cognitive Schemas and Core Beliefs in Psychological Problems: A Scientist-Practitioner Guide.* Washington, D.C.: American Psychological Association, 2007. Looks at what schemata are and how they affect disorders such as depression, obsessive-compulsive disorder, eating disorders, and post-traumatic stress disorder.

Saltz, Gail. *Becoming Real: Defeating the Stories We Tell Ourselves That Hold Us Back.* New York: Riverhead Books, 2004. The *Today* show psychiatrist explains how the stories people told themselves as children to understand the world can linger on and prevent them from living a full life.

Strack, Fritz, and Jens Forster, eds. *Social Cognition: The Basis of Human Interaction.* New York: Psychology Press, 2009. An examination of social perception and social psychology and their importance in human relations.

Julie A. Felender; updated by Michelle Murphy

SEE ALSO: Attributional biases; Causal attribution; Cognitive psychology; Prejudice; Prejudice reduction; Racism; Social perception.

Social support and mental health

DATE: 1980's forward
TYPE OF PSYCHOLOGY: Social psychology
FIELDS OF STUDY: Social motives; social perception and cognition

Social support is the perception or experience that a person is esteemed and part of a social network characterized by mutual obligation and helping behaviors. Support can involve either instrumental helping behaviors or attention to emotion through expressing empathy or bolstering self-esteem. The presence of supportive others may diminish the effects of stress and the risk of developing certain mental illnesses such as depression.

KEY CONCEPTS
- emotional social support
- instrumental social support
- main effect model

- need to belong
- perceived available social support
- stress-buffering model

INTRODUCTION

Social support is a pervasive phenomenon spanning people's relationships throughout their lives. In everyday life, particularly in times of distress, people convey a need for support from relatives, friends, partners, coworkers, or other members of their social community. This powerful inclination to seek and provide support is thought to have adaptive evolutionary significance because interdependency may enhance the likelihood of survival, especially when under threat of predation. The human response to seek the presence of others in the aftermath of natural disasters or other trauma testifies to the need for and benefits of social affiliation. Research suggests that social support is sought to such an extent because it is an effective method of coping with stressors and may protect against potential adverse mental health consequences.

A primary psychological need to belong may underlie the tendency to turn to others under demanding circumstances. In support of this possibility, aside from fostering adjustment to stressful and demanding events, a sufficient quantity and quality of support are essential for optimal functioning in daily life. It is important that social contact is regular, positive, and meaningful, and that interaction is perceived as having the potential for disclosure of private and sensitive feelings. The need to belong may compel people to provide this kind of emotional support or more tangible assistance to those with whom they have formed interpersonal attachments. Indeed, the theoretical literature has proposed several types of social support in a bid to form a taxonomy of support and to detail the situations in which various types of social support are most effective.

INSTRUMENTAL AND EMOTIONAL SOCIAL SUPPORT

The numerous ways that supportive people can help others have been categorized broadly as either instrumental or emotional in focus. Instrumental support involves the provision of direct, pragmatic assistance aimed at solving problems. This can be by passing on information to facilitate better understanding of a stressful event, by helping to remove obstacles or counteract losses and harm, or by providing goods or financial assistance. Instrumental assistance can reduce the impact of a stressor by promoting effective coping strategies through the distribution of information and by facilitating protective action through the supply of tangible resources. Emotional support, in contrast, is aimed at the person instead of the objective problem or stressor. It may include helping the person escape from negative emotions and feel better, conveying warmth and affection, reaffirming a commitment to a nurturing relationship, talking about emotions, listening to what the suffering person wants to say, and in general encouraging the other person to feel loved, cared for, and valued.

Evidence within the social support literature is mixed as to whether instrumental or emotional support is more important for mental health. In 1999, Chockalingam Viswesvaran and colleagues conducted a meta-analysis of social support studies focusing on work situations and found emotional support to be more predictive of good outcomes following stressful experiences. Instrumental support may have a closer relationship with physical health, as demonstrated by Viveca Östberg and Carin Lennartsson, who found economic support to be more predictive than emotional support of good physical health. Emotional support may potentially capture the essence of social support more completely than instrumental support, insofar as it contributes to feeling worthwhile, competent, and esteemed as a member of a group. However, substantial overlap is typically observed in the measurement of both types of support. This may reflect the emotional meaning of instrumental support and how certain emotions facilitate action. For example, information may relieve emotional concerns such as worry and anxiety, and positive emotion may promote problem-solving behavior.

Therefore, although a taxonomy of social support strategies is useful, the distinction between types is by no means absolute, and instrumental and emotional support may interact. As is apparent in the definition of social support, it is important to recognize that it is not enough that support is in place, but rather that the perception or experience of that assistance is required for effects to occur.

EXPERIENCE OF SOCIAL SUPPORT

Considerable reassurance can be found in simply knowing that one is cared for and that support is available from others in times of distress. Implicit social support refers to the emotional comfort derived from social networks without explicit discussion of problems or stressful events. The perception of social support is the comfort of implicit social support combined with the belief that others can be relied on to provide care and solace when needed. This perception has been shown not to coincide exactly with the actual amount of instrumental or emotional support that one receives. In fact, perceived available social support can be beneficial in reducing stress even if support is not actually used. Sheldon Cohen and S. Leonard Syme in 1985, and several researchers since, have provided evidence that beliefs about the availability of social support are more closely related to mental health than received support. The critical importance of subjective perceptions of social support opens up the question as to what psychological factors may condition how support is viewed.

The extent to which a person feels affective concern from others may be substantially related to factors such as personality, attachment style, and various needs and goals. For instance, Nancy Collins and Brooke Feeney in 2004 showed the construal of supportive interaction to vary as a function of the participant's attachment style. Insecure attachment is characterized by a diminished expectation that others will be emotionally available and responsive when needed. Such anxious or avoidant people rated messages sent by an assigned partner in a stressful task as less supportive than did securely attached people. The divergence between the support that insecurely attached people feel they need and the support they perceive to be available has been linked to early experiences with parents or other attachment figures. Such experiences are thought to negatively influence both the construal of social support and the cultivation of supportive relation-

Social support, such as can be gained from fellow mah-jong players, is important for the health of older people. (©Robert Lerich/Dreamstime.com)

ships by enhancing the salience of potential rejection and stimulating avoidance behaviors.

The urge to approach rather than avoid others has been linked to positive emotion, which functions to broaden momentary thought-action repertoires and build personal resources. In the context of social support, considering the well-being of others and having compassionate goals has been shown to build support over time. Jennifer Crocker and Amy Canevello in 2008 demonstrated compassionate goals to increase perceived social support, connectedness, and trust over a ten-week period in first-semester college students. Goals are thought to condition the development of one's support system. This occurs positively when the focus of the relational goal is on supporting others and responding to their needs rather than obtaining something for the self (for example, promoting a desired self-image through one's relationships). In this way, responsiveness is reciprocated even though this is not the primary goal of support offered out of compassion.

PROTECTIVE ROLE OF SOCIAL SUPPORT

In 1995, Roy Baumeister and Mark Leary proposed that humans have a fundamental need to belong, and that a sufficient quantity of stable interpersonal relationships characterized by affective concern is essential for optimal levels of well-being in daily life. Integration in a social network characterized by mutual obligation and the perception that one is loved and cared for can have ameliorative effects on mental health through promoting a stream of positive feelings, a sense of stability, and a perception that one has a worthwhile role in the community. Evidence supporting the beneficial effects of social integration has been detailed by Sheldon Cohen and Thomas A. Wills, who describe a main effect model of social support. In this model, social integration can enhance well-being without improving the capacity for coping with stressful events. However, the authors show that another form of social support, perceived available support, protects against the effects of stressful events, thus mitigating the relationship between stressors and the development of mental illness. This stress-buffering model has led to the proposition that deficits in social support enhance the risk for depression, alcoholism, anxiety, and psychosomatic symptoms. Michael Windle in 1992 showed that parental social support, but not peer support, had beneficial stress protective effects.

Similarly, Eric Stice and colleagues, in a 2004 prospective study, demonstrated that deficits in parental but not peer support were related to a worsening of depressive symptoms over time and an increased likelihood of the onset of major depression.

As well as the source of social support, there is evidence to suggest that the type and degree of explicitness of support are important factors in determining the effect of the support provided. Stephanie Brown and colleagues in 2003 found that providing social support to others can be more beneficial to health and well-being than receiving support, and can even reduce the risk of mortality. Actively supporting others may reinforce existing relationships, provide a sense of meaning, and fortify the belief that one is esteemed and matters to others. Explicit acts of support may have potential costs to the recipient, such as leading to perceptions of being a burden, and feelings of stress, guilt, and indebtedness. Support may be most effective when responsiveness is subtle and the receiver is unaware of the explicit action of the support network. For example, when stressful decisions are being made regarding college course selection, job changes, or resolving interpersonal problems, explicit advice from multiple and potentially conflicting sources can interfere with decision making and cause additional stress. Less visible emotional support may reduce the distress associated with major life changes or threatening situations. It is also imperative that there is a suitable match between the support provider and the type of support provided. During times of stress, emotional support may be best received from an intimate partner or one's immediate family, whereas information and advice may be more welcomed from an expert.

SOURCES FOR FURTHER STUDY

Baumeister, Roy F., and Mark R. Leary. "The Need to Belong: Desire for Interpersonal Attachments as a Fundamental Human Motivation." *Psychological Bulletin* 117, no. 3 (1995): 497-529. The authors present a detailed review of evidence suggesting that humans possess a fundamental motive to seek out and maintain interpersonal relationships.

Brown, Stephanie, Randolph M. Nesse, Amiram D. Vinokur, and Dylan M. Smith. "Providing Social Support May Be More Beneficial than Receiving It: Results from a Prospective Study of Mortality."

Psychological Science 14, no. 4 (2003): 320-327. In this example of research indicating how receiving social support may not always be beneficial, the authors succinctly present evidence of situations in which receiving support can be harmful.

Cohen, Sheldon, and Thomas A. Wills. "Stress, Social Support, and the Buffering Hypothesis." *Psychological Bulletin* 98, no. 2 (1985): 310-357. Summarizes evidence indicating that the association between social support and mental health may be due to a direct or main effect of social support on well-being or an indirect stress-buffering effect of support.

Stice, Eric, Jennifer Ragan, and Patrick Randall. "Prospective Relations Between Social Support and Depression: Differential Direction of Effects for Parent and Peer Support." *Journal of Abnormal Psychology* 113, no. 1 (2004): 155-159. Addresses the issue of the protective effects of different sources of social support in the progression of depression.

Taylor, Shelley. "Social Support." In *Foundations of Health Psychology*, edited by Howard S. Friedman and Roxane C. Silver. New York: Oxford University Press, 2006. Provides a very readable overview of the recent literature on social support with a focus on health implications and cultural differences.

Michael Daly and Roy F. Baumeister

SEE ALSO: Coping: Strategies; Self-help groups; Social networks; Social perception; Stress: Behavioral and psychological responses; Support groups.

Sociopaths

TYPE OF PSYCHOLOGY: Personality; psychopathology
FIELDS OF STUDY: Aggression; interpersonal relations; personality assessment; personality disorders

Sociopathy is a condition that describes a constellation of interpersonal, emotional, and behavioral functioning that is marked by deceit, lack of guilt and empathy, and callous disregard for the welfare of others. Contrary to popular conception, sociopaths are not necessarily violent, nor is there good evidence that they are untreatable.

KEY CONCEPTS
- antisocial personality disorder
- mask of normalcy
- personality disorder
- psychopathy
- sociopathy

INTRODUCTION

Sociopathy is a clinical condition marked by a pattern of disturbed interpersonal, emotional, and behavioral functioning. It is characterized by remorselessness, manipulativeness, lack of concern for the welfare of others, deceit, shallow emotional experience, and poor impulse control. Sociopaths tend to be superficially charming and often make a good first impression on others. Nevertheless, they are typically egocentric, dishonest, and irresponsible, often without apparent motivation. They tend to be callous, externalize blame, and fail to learn from negative consequences. Many authors use the term "sociopathy" interchangeably with "psychopathy."

HISTORY

Georgia psychiatrist Hervey Cleckley's classic book *The Mask of Sanity* (1941) was the first to delineate the core features of the syndrome. Cleckley described sociopathy as characterized by a mask of normalcy that conceals a pernicious mental disorder, and he listed sixteen criteria as essential features of this condition. Among these criteria are the presence of superficial charm, the absence of delusions and nervousness, a lack of remorse and shame, irresponsibility, and untruthfulness.

Cleckley depicted sociopaths as appearing to be relatively normal. They are not psychotic (out of touch with reality); rather, in the words of nineteenth century British physician James Cowles Prichard, they are "morally insane," meaning they have a core deficit in conscience. Sociopaths' personality characteristics, such as poor impulse control and callousness, render many of them prone to violence. Nevertheless, the view that all sociopaths engage in violent behavior—or that all violent people are sociopaths—is a misconception. As an attractive and intelligent young man, Theodore "Ted" Bundy, the prolific U.S. serial killer of the 1970's, fit the profile of a typical sociopath. However, the fact that Bundy was violent does not mean he was sociopathic. Instead, his charm, callousness, deceit, and lack of empathy and guilt are what mark him as

People described serial killer and sociopath Ted Bundy as charming and handsome. However, he called himself "the most cold-blooded sonofabitch you'll ever meet." (AP/Wide World Photos)

is the major cause of sociopathy remains controversial.

PREVALENCE OF THE CONDITION

Although sociopaths make up an estimated 1 percent of the general population, they are overrepresented in prisons, with around 25 percent of incarcerated men meeting research criteria for the condition. Most individuals who meet the criteria for sociopathy are men, although the causes of this gender difference remain unknown. Sociopathy appears to be a cross-cultural phenomenon. Research by Harvard University anthropologist Jane Murphy has shown that conditions similar or identical to sociopathy appear to be present in remote regions of Alaska and Nigeria that have had scant exposure to Western culture.

a bona fide sociopath. Indeed, some authors have suggested that sociopathic characteristics may be expressed in a variety of ways, with a few individuals being extremely violent, others moderately violent, and still others even entirely nonviolent. Moreover, at least some sociopaths may be drawn to socially adaptive occupations, like politics, business, and contact sports, although systematic research on this conjecture is lacking.

Cleckley's rich clinical descriptions catalyzed research on sociopathy. In 1957, University of Minnesota psychologist David Lykken demonstrated that sociopaths showed diminished responses to a buzzer that was paired repeatedly with an electric shock. Based on this finding, Lykken proposed that the core deficit of sociopaths is fearlessness. This lack of fear, he proposed, gives rise to the other features of the disorder, such as lack of guilt and poor impulse control, which depend on at least a modicum of fear for adequate socialization. As a consequence, psychopaths often display a failure of passive avoidance learning—learning to inhibit responses that lead to punishment. The finding that sociopaths are relatively fearless has since been replicated in a host of studies, although the hypothesis that fearlessness

RELATION TO ANTISOCIAL PERSONALITY DISORDER

The American Psychiatric Association's *Diagnostic and Statistical Manual of Mental Disorders: DSM-IV-TR* (rev. 4th ed., 2000) contains the diagnosis of antisocial personality disorder (ASPD), a condition that shares many characteristics with sociopathy. The two are not synonymous, however, as antisocial personality disorder designates a persistent pattern of antisocial and criminal infractions. Therefore, its diagnosis emphasizes behavioral indicators, whereas sociopathy emphasizes core personality traits. Some sociopaths are guiltless, dishonest, manipulative, and egocentric, but display little or no history of criminal behavior.

Lykken posited that psychopathy and sociopathy are two distinct kinds of antisocial personality disorder, with the former primarily deriving from temperamental and biological differences and the latter primarily from negative sociological influences, such as poor parenting and exposure to delinquent peer groups. According to Lykken, both conditions predispose toward antisocial behavior and callous disregard of others, but stem from different causes.

Nevertheless, many or most researchers use the terms psychopathy and sociopathy interchangeably.

ASSESSMENT OF SOCIOPATHY

The most widely used assessment tool for sociopathy is University of British Columbia psychologist Robert Hare's Psychopathy Checklist-Revised (PCL-R). The PCL-R consists of twenty items derived in part from the Cleckley criteria. Each item is scored zero to two, based on a standardized clinical interview and criminal files. The PCL-R has been widely used in criminal populations, as scores above thirty are strong predictors of recidivism and violence.

The PCL-R, however, can be unwieldy to administer, requiring comprehensive interviews and file review. Further, the PCL-R may not be suited for detecting psychopathy among noninstitutional populations, in which some individuals may exhibit the key personality features of sociopathy while refraining from criminal behavior or avoiding detection by the legal system. Although the high levels of sociopathic traits in prison samples are expedient for research purposes, exclusive reliance on criminal samples may result in a failure to detect important characteristics that buffer some sociopaths against criminal behavior, such as adequate impulse control or intelligence. Promising attempts have been made to detect the core personality characteristics of sociopathy using self- or peer-rating scales. With the aim of constructing a measure of sociopathic personality traits in noninstitutional populations, Emory University psychologist Scott Lilienfeld developed the Psychopathic Personality Inventory (PPI). The PPI-R and several other self-report measures show promising but preliminary validity for the assessment of sociopathy.

RESPONSE TO TREATMENT

Traditionally, sociopaths have been viewed as nonresponsive to treatment. Indeed, sociopaths are often viewed as incurable and therefore in need of control rather than treatment. Sociopaths' emotional detachment and manipulativeness may often impede psychotherapy. However, this widespread clinical conviction may perpetuate the paucity of interventions aimed at curtailing sociopaths' antisocial behavior. Jennifer Skeem of the University of California, Irvine, has found that sociopaths are as likely as nonsociopaths to respond to violence reduction interventions. More research directed toward understanding the development, nature, and causes of sociopathy, and the conditions under which sociopaths may respond to interventions, is essential before sociopathy can be effectively controlled in society.

SOURCES FOR FURTHER STUDY

Blair, R. J. R., Derek Mitchell, and Karina Blair. *The Psychopath: Emotion and the Brain.* Malden, Mass.: Blackwell, 2005. The authors present a comprehensive summary of recent research on the cognitive, emotional, and neurological correlates of sociopathy, with special attention to the manifestations of sociopathy throughout the life span.

Cleckley, Hervey. *The Mask of Sanity.* 5th ed. Augusta, Ga.: Emily S. Cleckley, 1988. In the seminal text on psychopathy, Cleckley offers rich case summaries to depict the sociopath. His diverse and fascinating descriptions are united by his assertion that sociopathy is, at its core, a disorder of emotion, and that this deficit explains the perplexing corpus of behavior displayed by his patients.

Hare, Robert D. *Without Conscience: The Disturbing World of the Psychopaths Among Us.* New York: Guilford Press, 1999. Hare argues that psychopathy is distinct from antisocial personality disorder and notes that psychopaths disregard the distinction between right and wrong. He paints a vivid portrait of the psychopath that is palatable to the lay reader.

Lykken, David T. *The Antisocial Personalities.* Hillsdale, N.J.: Lawrence Erlbaum, 1995. An incisive analysis of sociopathy and related disorders that combines scientific evidence with keen clinical insights. Lykken's engaging style offers a highly readable text to the scholar and educated layperson alike.

Patrick, Christopher J., ed. *Handbook of Psychopathy.* New York: Guilford Press, 2006. A comprehensive assemblage of information on the etiology, assessment, and treatment of psychopathy. This is an indispensable volume for researchers, practitioners, and students interested in theory and research on sociopathy.

Kristin E. Landfield and Scott O. Lilienfeld

SEE ALSO: Aggression: Reduction and control; Antisocial personality disorder; Deception and lying; Emotions; Fear; Impulse control disorders; Intimacy; Personality disorders; Psychopathology.

Speech disorders

Type of psychology: Language
Fields of study: Behavioral therapies; infancy and childhood; organic disorders

Speech disorders may have an organic or learned origin, and they often affect a person's ability to communicate efficiently. Having a speech disorder may cause a person to avoid talking with others and to experience low self-esteem.

Key concepts
- communication
- self-esteem
- social interaction
- speech
- vocal folds

Introduction

The ability to communicate is one of the most basic human characteristics. Communication is essential to learning, working, and perhaps most important, social interaction. Normal communication involves hearing sounds, interpreting and organizing sounds, and making meaningful sounds. The ear takes in sounds, changes them into electrical impulses, and relays these impulses to the brain. The brain interprets the impulses, assigns meaning, and prepares a response. This response is then coded into the precisely coordinated changes in muscles, breath, vocal folds, tongue, jaw, lips, and so on that produce understandable speech.

Between 5 and 10 percent of Americans experience speech or language difficulties, often referred to as speech disorders. For these individuals, a breakdown occurs in one of the processes of normal communication. People with speech disorders may exhibit one or more of the following problems: They may be difficult to understand, use and produce words incorrectly, consistently use incorrect grammar, be unable to hear appropriately or to understand others, consistently speak too loudly, demonstrate a hesitating speech pattern, or simply be unable to speak. Speech disorders can be categorized as one of three disorder types: disorders of articulation, of fluency, or of voice. Articulation disorders are difficulties in the formation and stringing together of sounds to produce words. Fluency disorders, commonly referred to as stuttering, are inter-ruptions in the flow or rhythm of speech. Finally, voice disorders are characterized by deviations in a person's voice quality, pitch, or loudness.

Types of Speech Disorders

Articulation disorders are the most common types of speech errors in children. Articulation errors may take the form of substitutions, omissions, or distortions of sounds. An example of a substitution would be the substitution of the *w* sound for the *r* sound, as in "wabbit" for "rabbit." Substitutions are the most common form of articulation errors. An example of an omission would be if the *d* sound was left out of the word "bed," as in "be_." Finally, sounds can also be distorted, as in "shleep" for "sleep."

Stuttering is defined as an interruption in the flow or rhythm of speech. Stuttering can be characterized by hesitations, interjections, repetitions, or prolongations of a sound, syllable, word, or phrase. "I wa-wa-want that" is an example of a part-word repetition, while "I, I, I want that" is an example of a whole-word repetition. When a word or group of words such as "uh," "you know," "well," or "oh" is inserted into an utterance, it is termed an interjection. "I want uh, uh, you know, uh, that" is an example of a sentence containing interjections. There may also be secondary behaviors associated with stuttering. People may use secondary behaviors to extricate themselves from a stuttering incident. Stutterers may blink their eyes, turn their heads, tap their legs, look away, or perform some other interruptive behavior to stop the stuttering. In therapy, secondary behaviors are very difficult to extinguish.

Although articulation disorders and stuttering are often seen in children, voice disorders are common among adults. Voice disorders are categorized into disorders of pitch, intensity, nasality, and quality. A person with a voice disorder of pitch may have a vocal pitch that is too high. A person may speak too softly and thus exhibit a voice disorder of intensity. Still others may sound as though they talk through their nose (hypernasality) or always have a cold (hyponasality). The most common voice disorder is a disorder of quality. Examples of disorders of vocal quality include a voice that sounds hoarse, breathy, harsh, or rough. This type of voice disorder may be caused by vocal abuse, or an overusage of the voice, and might be found among singers, actors, or other individuals who abuse or overuse their voices. If the vocal abuse continues, vocal nodules (like calluses) may appear on the vocal folds. Vocal nodules may be surgically removed, and a person may be put on an extended period of vocal rest.

Speech disorders may be caused by a variety of factors. They may result from physical problems, health problems, or other problems. Physical problems such as cleft lip and palate; misaligned teeth; difficulty in controlling movements of the tongue; injury to the head, neck, or spinal cord; poor hearing; mental retardation; and cerebral palsy can contribute to poor articulation. The exact causes of stuttering are not known; however, a variety of factors are thought to be involved, including learning problems, emotional difficulties, biological defects, and neurological problems. Problems with voice quality can be caused by too much strain on the vocal folds (for example, yelling too much or clearing the throat too often), hearing loss, inflammation or growths on the vocal folds (vocal nodules), or emotional problems.

SPEECH AND COMMUNICATION

Speaking, hearing, and understanding are essential to human communication. A disorder in one or more of these abilities can interfere with people's capacity to communicate. Impaired communication can influence all aspects of a person's life, creating many problems. Behavioral effects resulting from the speech disorder can be found in both children and adults. Children with speech disorders can experience difficulties in learning and find it hard to establish relationships with others. Speech disorders in adults can adversely affect social interactions and often create emotional problems, which may interfere with their ability to earn a living. Speech disorders can interfere with people's relationships, independence, well-being, and ability to learn. People who have trouble communicating thoughts and ideas may have trouble relating to others, possibly resulting in depression and isolation. Furthermore, job opportunities are often limited for people who cannot communicate effectively. Thus, they may have trouble leading independent, satisfying lives. Emotional problems may develop in people who exhibit speech disorders as a result of embarrassment, rejection, or poor self-image. Finally, learning is difficult and frustrating for people with speech disorders. As a consequence, their performance and progress at school and on the job can suffer.

When trying to communicate with others, individuals with speech disorders may experience other negative behavioral effects as a result of the disorder. These effects include frustration, anxiety, guilt, and hostility. The emotional experience of speech-disordered people is often a result of their experiences in trying to communicate with others. Both the listener and the speech-disordered person react to the disordered person's attempts to communicate. In addition, the listener's

---

DSM-IV-TR Criteria for Speech Disorders

PHONOLOGICAL DISORDER (DSM CODE 315.39)

Failure to use developmentally expected speech sounds appropriate for age and dialect

Examples include errors in sound production, use, representation, or organization (substitutions of one sound for another, omissions of sounds such as final consonants)

Speech sound production difficulties interfere with academic or occupational achievement or with social communication

If mental retardation, speech-motor or sensory deficit, or environmental deprivation is present, speech difficulties exceed those usually associated with these problems

STUTTERING (DSM CODE 307.0)

Disturbance in the normal fluency and time patterning of speech inappropriate for age

Characterized by frequent occurrences of one or more of the following:
- sound and syllable repetitions
- sound prolongations
- interjections
- broken words (such as pauses within a word)
- audible or silent blocking (filled or unfilled pauses in speech)
- circumlocutions (word substitutions to avoid problematic words)
- words produced with an excess of physical tension
- monosyllabic whole-word repetitions

Fluency disturbance interferes with academic or occupational achievement or with social communication

If speech-motor or sensory deficit is present, speech difficulties exceed those usually associated with these problems

reactions may influence the disordered individual. These reactions may include embarrassment, guilt, frustration, and anger and may cause the disordered individual to experience a sense of helplessness that can subsequently lower the person's sense of self-worth. Many speech-disordered people respond to their problem by being overly aggressive, by denying its existence, by projecting reactions in listeners, or by feeling anxious or timid.

TREATMENT AND PREVENTION

Treatment of speech disorders attempts to eliminate or minimize the disorder and related problems. Many professionals may be involved in providing therapy, special equipment, or surgery. In therapy, specialists teach clients more effective ways of communicating. They may also help families learn to communicate with the disordered individual. Therapy may also include dealing with the negative behavioral effects of having a speech disorder, such as frustration, anxiety, and a feeling of low self-worth. In some cases, surgery can correct structural problems that may be causing speech disorders, such as cleft palate or misaligned teeth. For children with articulation disorders, therapy begins with training for awareness of the misarticulations, then learning of the correct sound productions. For people who exhibit voice disorders, therapy is designed to find the cause of the disorder, eliminate or correct the cause, and retrain them to use their voices correctly. Therapy for stutterers takes many forms. Some are self-proclaimed "cures," while others help individuals live with their stuttering. Still other types of therapy help stutterers overcome their fear of communicating, or help them develop a more normal breathing pattern.

Though there are many ways to treat speech disorders, disorder prevention is even more important. Certain things can be done to help prevent many speech disorders. All the methods focus on preventing speech disorders in childhood. Children should be encouraged to talk, but they should not be pushed into speaking. Pushing a child may cause that child to associate anxiety or frustration with communicating. Infants do not simply start talking; they need to experiment with their voice, lips, and tongue. This experimentation is often called babbling, and it should not be discouraged. Later on, caregivers can slowly introduce words and help with correct pronunciation. When talking with young children, caregivers should talk slowly and naturally, avoiding "baby talk" and gibberish. Children will have difficulty distinguishing between the baby-talk word (for example, "baba") and the real word ("bottle"). Having children point to and name things in picture books and in real-world surroundings allows them to put labels (words) on the objects in their environment. Increases in the number of labels a child has learned can subsequently increase the number of topics about which the child can communicate. It is most important to listen to what the child is trying to say rather than to how the child is saying it. Such prevention strategies will encourage positive behavioral effects regarding the act of communicating. These positive effects include feelings of self-efficiency, independence, and a positive self-image.

SPEECH-LANGUAGE PATHOLOGY

Early identification of a speech disorder improves the chances for successful treatment, and early treatment can help prevent a speech disorder from developing into a lifelong handicap. Professionals who identify, evaluate, and treat communication disorders in individuals have preparations in the field of speech-language pathology. A speech-language pathologist is a professional who has been educated in the study of human communication, its development, and its disorders. By evaluating the speech and language skills of children and adults, the speech-language pathologist determines if communication problems exist and decides on the most appropriate way of treating these problems.

Speech-language pathology services are provided in many public and private schools, community clinics, hospitals, rehabilitation centers, private practices, health departments, colleges and universities, and state and federal governmental agencies. There are more than fourteen hundred clinical facilities and hundreds of full-time private practitioners providing speech services to people throughout the United States. Service facilities exist in many cities in every state. A speech-language pathologist will have a master's or doctoral degree and should hold a Certificate of Clinical Competence (CCC) from the American Speech-Language-Hearing Association or a license from his or her state.

Responsibilities of a speech-language pathologist include evaluation and diagnosis, therapy, and referral to other specialists involved with speech disorders. By gathering background information and by direct observation and testing, the speech-language pathologist can determine the extent of the disorder as well as a probable cause. The speech-language pathologist chooses an appropriate treatment to correct or lessen the communication problem and attempts to help the patient and family understand the problem. When other treatment is needed to correct the problem, the patient is referred to another specialist. Audiologists, special educators, psychologists, social workers, neurologists, pediatricians, otolaryngologists (also known as ear, nose, and throat specialists), and other medical and dental specialists may be involved in the diagnosis and treatment of a speech disorder. For example, psychologists may be best suited to treat the emotional or behavioral aspects of having a speech disorder (such as anxiety, frustration, anger, and denial). Otolaryngologists are often involved in the diagnosis of voice disorders. Audiologists determine whether an individual's hearing is affecting or causing a speech disorder.

Speech disorders can affect anyone at any time. The chances are good that everyone at one time has either had, or known someone with, a speech disorder. Because communication is so overwhelmingly a part of life, disordered speech is not something to take lightly. With good prevention, early identification, and early treatment, lifelong difficulties with communication can be prevented.

SOURCES FOR FURTHER STUDY

Haynes, William O., and Rebekah H. Pindzola. *Diagnosis and Evaluation in Speech Pathology*. 7th ed. Boston: Allyn & Bacon, 2008. Focuses on the assessment of speech disorders, whether to determine etiology, the extent of the problem, or the best therapy. Covers fluency, aphasia, and stuttering.

Hegde, M. N. *Introduction to Communicative Disorders*. 3d ed. Austin, Tex.: Pro-Ed, 2001. A look at the anatomy and physiology of speech and the various disorders, which are described in detail.

Luterman, David M. *Counseling Persons with Communication Disorders and Their Families*. 5th ed. Austin, Tex.: Pro-Ed, 2008. Luterman addresses the emotions of people with speech disorders and discusses how to counsel these patients and their families.

McNeil, Malcolm R., ed. *Clinical Management of Sensorimotor Speech Disorders*. 2d ed. New York: Thieme, 2009. This work focuses on the diagnosis and treatment of speech disorders in clinics.

Shames, George H., and Norma B. Anderson, eds. *Human Communication Disorders*. Boston: Allyn & Bacon, 2002. This general text covers a wide range of communication disorders. Includes a section on speech-language pathology as a profession. Also includes sections on cleft palate, aphasia, and cerebral palsy.

Jennifer A. Sanders Wann and Daniel L. Wann

SEE ALSO: Aphasias; Bilingualism and learning disabilities; Grammar and speech; Language; Speech perception; Stuttering.

Speech perception

TYPE OF PSYCHOLOGY: Sensation and perception
FIELD OF STUDY: Auditory, chemical, cutaneous, and body senses

Speech perception involves a set of enigmatic phenomena, and no completely acceptable theory explaining all of its aspects has been developed. During speech perception, people rapidly extract meanings from a complex spoken signal in the face of many apparently insurmountable obstacles.

KEY CONCEPTS
- acoustic
- articulation
- formant
- motor neurons
- phonetic

INTRODUCTION

The perception of human speech signals involves a variety of phenomena that initially appear trivial but are actually exceedingly complex. The basic phenomena are the ability to perceive the same speech message correctly when it is presented by various speakers or by the same speaker performing under different conditions (the phenomenon of perceptual constancy); differences in the perceptual processing of speech and nonspeech sounds; the ability to discriminate well among sounds from different speech sound categories, but only poorly among sounds from within the same speech sound category (categorical perception of speech); and the problems presented by the signal's immediate speech sound (phonetic) context for the correct identification of the signal (the phenomenon of context-sensitive cues).

Each phenomenon is so complex primarily because of the nature of the speech signal. A spoken language is perceived by a native listener as a sequence of discrete units, commonly called words. The physical nature of the typical speech signal, however, is more accurately described as a continuous, complex acoustic wave. In this signal, not only the sounds associated with consecutive syllables but also the sounds of consecutive world often overlap considerably.

The ultimate goal of speech perception research is the development of a theory that explains the various phenomena associated with the perception of the human speech signal. To achieve this goal, researchers need two basic types of information: a detailed description of the speech signal, to test whether any acoustic cues exist that could be used by listeners; and accurate measurements of the acts of speech perception, to test hypotheses related to the different theories of speech perception.

CONSONANT AND VOWEL DISTINCTIONS

When describing the speech signal for a given language, researchers have noted that the signal is composed of a set of basic units called phonemes, which are considered to be the smallest units of speech. The phonemes can be thought of (though this analogy is imprecise) as corresponding somewhat to the letters in a written word. For example, American English is said to contain twenty-five consonant phonemes and seventeen vowel phonemes. The distinction between consonant and vowel speech sounds is based on the degree to which the vocal tract is closed. Consonants are generated with partial or complete closure of the vocal tract during some point of their production. Vowels are created with the vocal tract in a more open state.

Consonants are produced by closing or nearly closing the vocal tract, so they contain relatively little acoustic energy. Because of the dynamic changes occurring in the shape of the resonant cavities of the vocal tract during consonant production, the consonants are difficult to specify exactly in terms of acoustic patterns. Consonants commonly contain bursts of noise, rapid changes of frequencies, or

even brief periods of silence, which all may take place within twenty-thousandths of a second.

Vowels have less complex acoustical characteristics, primarily because they are produced with the vocal tract open and do not change its shape so dramatically. They are of relatively long duration and tend to have more constant acoustical features than consonants. The most important features of vowel sounds are their formants, which are narrow ranges of sound frequencies that become enhanced during vowel production. The formants result from basic physical characteristics of the vocal tract, chief among these being its shape for a particular vowel, which cause most of the vocal frequencies to become suppressed, while only a few narrow bands of frequencies (the formants) are reinforced. Formants are numbered in increasing order from the lowest- to the highest-frequency band. The relative-frequency relationships among the formants of a vowel sound characterize that vowel.

Experiments show that the vowel sounds in English speech can be distinguished from one another by reference to the frequency values of formants one and two. For any given vowel sound, however, there is a range of frequencies that typically occurs for the formants, depending on the person speaking and the conditions under which the individual speaks. There is even some overlap between the ranges for some vowels.

Vowels and consonants can be further subdivided according to the articulatory features that characterize production of the sound. Articulatory features include the location of the greatest constriction in the vocal tract, the degree of rounding of the lips, the place of articulation (that is, where in the vocal tract the sound tends to be primarily produced, such as the lips or in the nasal cavity), and the manner of articulation (for example, voiced means the vocal folds vibrate, and voiceless means the vocal folds do not vibrate). These factors are important because of their possible use by a listener during the process of speech perception.

The nervous system can be viewed as consisting of two main subdivisions: transmission systems and integrative systems. For speech perception, the transmission systems both transmit and process the nervous signals that are produced by acoustic stimulation of the sensory structures for hearing. The integrative systems further process the incoming signals from the transmission systems by combining and comparing them with previously stored information. Both systems are actively involved in the processes of speech perception. Much research has been done concerning the exact mechanisms of signal processing in the nervous system and how they enable listeners to analyze complex acoustic speech signals to extract their meaning.

THEORETICAL APPROACHES

Theories of speech perception can be described in several ways. One way of categorizing the theories labels them as being either top down or bottom up. Top-down theories state that a listener perceives a speech signal based on a series of ongoing hypotheses. The hypotheses evolve at a rather high level of complexity (the top) and are formed as a result of such things as the listener's knowledge of the situation or the predictability of the further occurrence of certain words in a partially completed sequence. Bottom-up theories take the position that perception is guided simply by reference to the incoming acoustic signal and its acoustic cues. The listener then combines phonemes to derive the words, and the words to produce sentences, thereby proceeding from the simplest elements (the bottom) up toward progressively more complex levels.

A contrasting description is that of active versus passive theories. Active theories state that the listener actively generates hypotheses about the meaning of the incoming speech signal based on various types of information available both in the signal and in its overall context (for example, what has already been said). The listener is said to be using more than simply acoustic cues to give meaning to what has been heard. Passive theories state that the listener automatically (passively) interprets the speech signal based on the acoustic cues that are discerned.

PERCEPTUAL CONSTANCY AND PROCESSING

Often, major differences in acoustic waves are produced by different speakers (or the same speaker performing under different conditions) even when speaking the same speech message. Nevertheless, native listeners typically have little trouble understanding the message. This phenomenon, known as perceptual constancy, is probably the most complex problem in the field of speech perception.

Variations in the rate of speaking, the pitch of the voice, the accent of the speaker, the loudness of signal, the absence of particular frequency compo-

nents (for example, when the signal is heard over a telephone), and other factors are handled with amazing speed and ability by the typical listener. Many variations result in drastic changes or even total elimination of many acoustic cues normally present in the signal.

There is experimental evidence to support the hypothesis that when speech occurs at a higher-than-normal rate, the listener uses both syllable and vowel durations as triggers to adjust the usual stored acoustic cues toward shorter and faster values. This automatic adjustment permits accurate speech perception even when the speaking rate approaches four hundred words per minute.

Another difficult task is to explain the ease with which a listener can understand speech produced by different persons. The largest variations in vocal tract size (especially length) and shape occur between children and adults. Even among adults, significant differences are found, the average woman's vocal tract being nearly 15 percent shorter than that of the average man. These differences introduce quite drastic shifts in formant frequencies and other frequency-dependent acoustic cues. Nevertheless, experiments show that even very young children generally have no difficulty understanding the speech of complete strangers, which indicates that the nervous system is able to compensate automatically even before much speech perception experience has been garnered.

Studies of human perceptual processing using speech and nonspeech sounds as stimuli provide evidence for differences in the way people deal with these two categories of sounds. The implication is that specialized speech-processing mechanisms exist in the human nervous system. A major difference is a person's ability to process speech signals at a higher rate than nonspeech signals. Experiments show that phonetic segment information can be perceived as speech at rates as high as thirty segments per second (normal conversation rates transmit about ten segments per second). The rate of perception for comparable nonspeech signals, however, is only about four sounds per second.

CATEGORICAL PERCEPTION OF SPEECH

The phenomenon of categorical perception of speech refers to the fact that people discriminate quite well among sounds from different speech sound categories (for example, a /b/ as opposed to a /p/ sound, as might occur in the two words "big" and "pig"); however, people's discrimination of different acoustic examples of sounds from within the same speech sound category (for example, variations of the /b/ sound) is not as good. One theory to explain categorical perception proposes that the auditory system is composed of nerve cells or groups of nerve cells that function as feature detectors that respond whenever a particular acoustic feature is present in a signal. In the example of the sounds /b/ and /p/ from the spoken words "big" and "pig," according to this theory, there are feature detectors that respond specifically to one or the other of these two consonants, but not to both of them, because of the different acoustic features that they each possess. One problem for proponents of the theory is to describe the particular features to which the detectors respond. Another problem is the number of different feature detectors a person might have or need. For example, is one detector for the consonant /b/ sufficient, or are there multiple /b/ detectors that permit a person to perceive /b/ correctly regardless of the speaker or the context in which the /b/ is spoken (and the consequent variations in the acoustic patterns for the /b/ that are produced)?

CONTEXT-SENSITIVE CUES

Although variations in the immediate speech sound (phonetic) context often result in major changes in the acoustic signature of a phoneme (the phenomenon of context-sensitive cues), a person's ability to identify the phoneme is remarkable. People can recognize phonemes even though the variations found in the acoustic signatures of a given phoneme when spoken by even a single speaker but in different contexts (for example, for /d/ in the syllables "di," "de," "da," "do," and "du") make it difficult to specify any characteristic acoustic features of the phoneme.

Research shows that many acoustic cues (such as short periods of silence, formant changes, or noise bursts) interact with one another in determining a person's perception of phonemes. Thus, there is no unique cue indicating the occurrence of a particular phoneme in a signal because the cues depend on the context of the phoneme. Even the same acoustic cue can indicate different phonemes, according to the context. A complete theory of speech perception would have to account for all these phenomena, as well as others not mentioned.

RESEARCH QUESTIONS

Speech sounds represent meanings in a language, and a listener extracts the meanings from a speech signal. What has remained unclear is how the nervous system performs this decoding. One hypothesis is that there are sensory mechanisms that are specialized to decode speech signals. This idea is suggested by the experimental results that indicate differences in the processing of speech and nonspeech signals. An alternative hypothesis is that special speech-processing mechanisms exist at a higher level, operating on the outputs of generalized auditory sensory mechanisms.

In the 1960's, the study of speech perception developed rapidly and three major theories were developed. These motivated a wealth of research projects, assisted by advances in electronic instrumentation, and have formed a basis for the development of later theories. All three theories specify an interaction between the sensory representation of the incoming speech signal and the neuromotor commands (that is, the pattern of signals that the nervous system would have to generate to activate the muscles for speaking) that would be involved in the production of that same signal. Two of the main theories are the motor theory and the auditory model of speech perception.

MOTOR THEORY

The first and probably most influential of the theories is Alvin M. Liberman's motor theory of speech perception. Briefly stated, the motor theory maintains that a listener decodes the incoming speech signal by reference to the neuromotor commands that would be required to produce it. The process of speech perception therefore involves a sort of reverse process to that of speech production, in which a speaker has a message to send and generates appropriate neuromotor commands to enable the articulatory muscles to produce the speech signal. According to the motor theory of speech perception, the listener has an internal neural pattern, generated by the incoming speech signal's effects on the sensory apparatus. This pattern can be "followed back" to the neuromotor commands that would be necessary to produce an acoustic signal like the one that has just produced the internal (sensory) neural pattern. At this point, the listener recognizes the speech signal, and perception occurs by the listener's associating the neuromotor commands with the meanings they would encode if the listener were to produce such commands when speaking.

Among the problems facing the motor theory, a major one has been to explain how infants are able to perceive surprisingly small differences in speech signals before they are able to produce these same signals, since it would seem that they do not possess the necessary neuromotor commands. Another problem has been the inability for the supporters of the theory to explain how the "following back" from the incoming signal's generated neural activity patterns to the appropriate neuromotor commands.

AUDITORY MODEL

At the other end of the theoretical spectrum from the motor theory, Gunnar Fant's auditory model of speech perception places greater emphasis on an auditory analysis of the speech signal. This theory proposes that the speech signal is first analyzed by the nervous system so that distinctive acoustic features get extracted or represented in the activity patterns of the nervous system. Then these features are combined into the phonemes and syllables that the listener can recognize. Much as in the motor theory, this recognition depends on the listener possessing basic knowledge about the articulatory processes involved in speech production—in particular, the distinctive phonetic features possible in the language being heard.

In contrast to the motor theory, Fant's model supposes an ability of the listener's auditory system to pick out distinctive acoustic features from the phonetic segments being heard. The auditory model, therefore, separates the auditory and articulatory functions more distinctly than the motor theory does.

One of the problems of the auditory model is that distinctive acoustic features of phonetic segments are difficult to specify unambiguously. Supporters of the model argue that the important features are more complex than the relatively simple ones normally proposed and represent characteristic relationships between various parts of the signal.

SOURCES FOR FURTHER STUDY

Behrman, Alison. *Speech and Voice Science*. San Diego, Calif.: Plural, 2007. The author looks at the production and perception of vowels and consonants as well as various speech perception theories.

Jekosch, Ute. *Voice and Speech Quality Perception: Assessment and Evaluation*. New York: Springer, 2005. Examines how listeners perceive speech and voice quality and how to model these processes. Uses engineering and humanities to address measurement and other issues.

Pisoni, David B., and Robert E. Remez, eds. *The Handbook of Speech Perception*. Malden, Mass.: Blackwell, 2005. Contains sections on sensing speech, perception of linguistic and indexical properties, and speech perception by special listeners.

Tatham, Mark, and Katherine Morton. *Speech Production and Perception*. New York: Palgrave Macmillan, 2006. Provides the framework for a fully explanatory theory of speech production integrating with speech perception. Emphasizes the difference between static models and dynamic models.

Warren, Richard M. *Auditory Perception: An Analysis and Synthesis*. 3d ed. New York: Cambridge University Press, 2008. This textbook examines the mechanics of auditory perception and also looks at how speech is perceived.

John V. Urbas

SEE ALSO: Aphasias; Bilingualism; Brain structure; Hearing; Language; Linguistics; Split-brain studies.

Spirituality and mental health

TYPE OF PSYCHOLOGY: Psychopathology
FIELDS OF STUDY: Anxiety disorders; depression; substance-related issues

Research suggests that spirituality, variously defined, is favorably related to multiple aspects of mental health. In particular, spirituality is related to less psychopathology and higher levels of psychological well-being.

KEY CONCEPTS
- anxiety
- depression
- mental health
- religion
- spirituality
- substance abuse

INTRODUCTION

Both spirituality and mental health have multiple dimensions, making summary statements about their connection complex. Spirituality may involve traditional religiousness (such as attendance at religious services or congregational support), a sense of transcendence or connection with the divine, or behaviors such as meditation and prayer. Mental health may range from psychopathology, such as depression, anxiety, and substance abuse, to positive mental states, such as happiness and life satisfaction.

Research findings generally indicate that spirituality is correlated with better mental health, although causality has not been shown. Most of this research has specifically examined the religiousness-mental health link. Harold Koenig, Michael Mc-Cullough, and David Larson conducted a major review of 850 studies on this topic in 2001. They found that higher levels of spirituality generally related to less psychopathology and higher levels of psychological well-being.

Spirituality has been shown to be modestly associated with lower levels of clinical depression, depressive symptoms, and negative mood states. In addition, many dimensions of spirituality appear to protect against suicidal behavior or ideation. These effects seem to be stronger for spirituality related to service attendance and integration in spiritual communities. In addition, spirituality is related to lower levels of a range of anxiety disorders, including phobias, panic disorder, and generalized anxiety disorder, and to lower levels of anxious mood in general population samples. In particular, individuals who have higher levels of social connections through their spirituality and who use spiritual coping methods or find comfort in their beliefs are less inclined to anxiety and anxiety disorders.

There is little evidence that spirituality is related to schizophrenia or obsessive-compulsive disorder, but the delusions of those diagnosed with the former and the obsessions and compulsions of those diagnosed with the latter often contain spiritual, particularly religious, elements.

Spirituality consistently relates to less abuse of or dependence on alcohol and other drugs, including marijuana, heroin, and nicotine. The fact that use or abuse of intoxicating substances is forbidden by certain religious groups makes usage low among the followers of these groups. Those who use more religious coping, feel a stronger connection to the transcendent, or have a more active private spiritual life, including prayer and meditation, are less likely to use or be dependent on alcohol and other drugs.

Myriad studies have demonstrated that spirituality is favorably correlated with positive mental health and psychological well-being, including measures such as life and relationship satisfaction, happiness, and higher morale. These findings have been demonstrated for a number of aspects of spirituality, including service attendance, a sense of connection to the transcendent, spiritual beliefs, and the use of spiritual coping in the context of stressful events.

Many dimensions of spirituality are related to mental health. These relationships are, for the most part, modest in strength but are found consistently in numerous studies conducted in samples diverse in race, ethnicity, socioeconomic status, gender, age, and religious affiliation. A caveat to these findings, however, is that research shows associations but has not demonstrated causal relationships between spirituality and mental health. Based on these positive links, psychotherapies are being developed and implemented to assist clients in drawing on their spiritual resources.

However, some experts note that religion and spirituality are not always conducive to good mental health. A study in the December, 2007, issue of the *American Journal of Psychiatry* found that 21 percent of psychiatrists thought that religion had equally negative and positive effects on mental health. Some 82 percent found that religion or spirituality could cause guilt, anxiety, or other negative emotions that increased patients' suffering. Other studies have linked religion with failure to comply with treatment or fatalistic attitudes toward illness. Other studies have linked religion with the use of extensive medical procedures to prolong life, hoping for a medical miracle. Excessive religiosity also has been linked to adverse mental health effects, both on the individual and on the person's children.

PATHWAYS OF INFLUENCE

The pathways through which spirituality may influence mental health are diverse and include the promotion of healthier lifestyles and positive psychological states, the reduction of stress, and the provision of social support, meaning, and resources that aid in more adaptive coping in stressful situations.

Many individuals derive a sense of meaning or purpose in their lives through their spirituality. This sense of meaning provides direction and grounding and also seems to help buffer against the stresses of life, thus protecting against psychopathology. Some types of spirituality also directly promote taking better care of one's physical and mental health by engaging in a lifestyle that incorporates preventive health care behaviors, a healthful diet, and regular exercise. Such a lifestyle leads to more robust physical and mental health. In addition, spirituality can help bring about positive psychological states that promote mental health; these include gratitude, hope, optimism, awe, forgiveness, and being at peace.

Spirituality offers many positive social aspects, which can provide support, a sense of value and belonging, integration into a social network, and the comfort of a shared belief system. These aspects of social support provide strong protection against psychopathology, especially depression.

Spirituality can foster particular beliefs that allow more benign interpretations of potentially stressful events, lessening the impact of minor and major life stressors. In addition, spirituality provides a range of coping behaviors, including engaging in prayer and relying on the religious community for support. These coping resources have been shown to lower distress and promote better mental health.

Sources for Further Study

Curlin, Farr A., et al. "Religion, Spirituality, and Medicine: Psychiatrists' and Other Physicians' Differing Observations, Interpretations, and Clinical Approaches." *American Journal of Psychiatry* 164 (2007): 1825-1831. Although the psychiatrists in this study generally found that spirituality had a positive effect on their patients, they also noted its negative effects.

Hackney, C. H., and G. S. Sanders. "Religiosity and Mental Health: A Meta-analysis of Recent Studies." *Journal for the Scientific Study of Religion* 42 (2003): 43-55. A meta-analysis was conducted to see whether different definitions of spirituality might affect the sometimes contradictory findings of studies looking into a link between mental health and religiosity.

Koenig, H. G., M. McCullough, and D. B. Larson. *Handbook of Religion and Health: A Century of Research Reviewed.* New York: Oxford University Press, 2001. Examines the relationship between religion and health in various studies. Looks at clinical applications and makes suggestions for further research.

Miller, L., and B. S. Kelley. "Relationships of Religiosity and Spirituality with Mental Health and Psychopathology." In *Handbook of the Psychology of Religion and Spirituality,* edited by R. F. Paloutzian and C. L. Park. New York: Guilford Press, 2005. Looks favorably on the link between religion and mental health.

Schumacher, John F., ed. *Religion and Mental Health.* New York: Oxford University Press, 1992. A collection of essays that examine the controversial findings on religion and mental health from the points of view of a wide range of experts. Touches on negative and positive aspects.

Crystal L. Park

See also: Religion and psychology; Religiosity: Measurement; Social support and mental health.

Split-brain studies

Type of psychology: Biological bases of behavior
Fields of study: Cognitive processes; nervous system

Split-brain studies provide insight into cognitive asymmetries in hemispheric functioning following surgery to sever the major interconnecting fiber tracts that allow communication between the cerebral hemispheres. Knowledge of hemispheric asymmetries is useful for understanding the organization and information-processing abilities of the human brain.

Key concepts
- cerebral commissures
- cerebral hemispheres
- commissurotomy
- dichotic listening
- dyslexia
- expressive aphasia
- hemispheric asymmetries
- laterality
- receptive aphasia
- tachistoscope

INTRODUCTION

The study of laterality, or the specialized asymmetric functions throughout the body, is not a new and novel field, as might be suggested by the popularization of "left brain-right brain" dichotomies. Lateralization of functions in the brain, sometimes referred to as hemispheric asymmetries, was demonstrated in 1861 by Paul Broca, a well-known physician at the time. He found that patients suffering from damage to certain regions of the left cerebral hemisphere exhibited more frequent speech and language disorders than did those with right cerebral hemisphere damage. Based on these findings, Broca correctly reasoned that the left hemisphere is specialized for speech and language in the vast majority of people. However, these results were quickly transformed into an overly simplistic dichotomization of cerebral functioning in which the left hemisphere was conceptualized as the dominant hemisphere and the right hemisphere as a rather minor, perhaps even unimportant, hemisphere. From split-brain studies performed since 1940, it has become obvious that the right hemisphere is essential for normal visuospatial functioning.

COMMISSUROTOMY EFFECTS

Split-brain surgery, sometimes referred to as commissurotomy, was first performed on a human patient by the neurosurgeon William Van Wagenen in 1940 to reduce the severity of life-threatening epileptic seizures. Other early commissurotomies were performed by two neurosurgeons, Philip Vogel and Joseph Bogen. The rationale for commissurotomies is rather simple: By severing the cerebral commissures, the major interconnecting fiber bundles that allow communication between the cerebral hemispheres, surgeons can prevent epileptic seizures from spreading beyond their focal hemisphere. Commissurotomies are performed only as a last resort, after traditional drug therapy fails to control seizure activity.

Surprising as it may seem, commissurotomy patients show few long-term alterations in behavior. All subjects suffer from acute disconnection syndrome, in which they are mute and partially paralyzed on the left side of the body for an interval ranging from a few days to a few weeks. Otherwise, commissurotomy patients exhibit relatively normal behavior. Moreover, the severity and frequency of seizure activity decline, sometimes quite dramatically, in response to this surgical procedure.

HEMISPHERIC ASYMMETRIES IN INFORMATION PROCESSING

On closer examination with a tachistoscope (an experimental apparatus for presenting visual information very briefly to the right or left visual field, sometimes called a T-scope) of split-brain patients, however, hemispheric asymmetries in information processing are evident. These asymmetries are investigated in T-scope or divided visual field studies. The split-brain patient is required to fixate on a central point, while visual stimulation is presented to the right or left visual field. Assuming that the patient is fixated on the central point, stimulation in the right visual field is projected to the left hemisphere, and left visual field stimulation to the right hemisphere. Once the information is available to the left or right hemisphere of a split-brain patient, it is not able to cross the cerebral commissures, principally the corpus callosum, because those fibers have been partially or completely severed.

The pioneering studies of the divided visual field in split-brain patients are described in *The Bisected Brain* (1970) by Michael Gazzaniga, who was a coprincipal investigator with Roger Sperry in those studies. In one of their investigations, pictures of common objects were presented to either the right visual field or the left visual field of split-brain patients. All patients were able to identify the information verbally when it was presented in the right visual field (left hemisphere), but not in the left visual field (right hemisphere). These results suggested specialization for verbal tasks in the left cerebral hemisphere but did not address functioning in the right cerebral hemisphere.

To assess the psychological functions of the right cerebral hemisphere, the researchers repeated the procedure described in the previous experiment, except that subjects were asked to reach under a curtain with their left or right hand to select the object from among several alternatives (rather than verbally identifying the picture of the object). Subjects were able to perform this task competently with their left hand, which is controlled primarily by the right cerebral hemisphere. Therefore, stimulation presented to the left visual field is projected to the right cerebral hemisphere, which controls the left hand. The opposite is true for stimulation presented to the right visual field. Correct identification of objects with the left hand indicated right cerebral hemisphere involvement in recognition of nonverbal stimuli.

Support for the superiority of the right hemisphere on visuospatial tasks came from a study in which split-brain patients were required to assemble patterned blocks into particular designs. Even though all patients were right-handed, they were much better at this task with the left hand, presumably because the right cerebral hemisphere controls that hand. Yet another test of the abilities of the left cerebral hemisphere was performed by requesting subjects to copy pictures of line drawings. Again, despite being right-handed, all subjects performed better with the left hand. Their left-handed efforts were rather clumsy, but the spatial dimensions of the line drawings were proportionally correct. Overall, split-brain studies seem to indicate left-hemisphere superiority on verbal tasks and right-hemisphere superiority on nonverbal, visuospatial tasks.

Further proposals for differences between the right and left hemispheres have been suggested from split-brain research. For example, it now appears that the left hemisphere is specialized for verbal tasks, but only as a consequence of its analytical, logical, information-processing style—of which language is one manifestation. Similarly, the right hemisphere is specialized for visuospatial tasks because of its synthetic, holistic manner of processing information. Support for these hemispheric asymmetries was derived from a 1974 study conducted by Jere Levy in which split-brain patients were given ambiguous instructions; they were simply to match similar pictorial stimuli. These pictures could be matched either by their functions, such as a cake on a plate matched with either a spoon or a fork, or by their appearance, such as a cake on a plate matched with a hat with a brim. When the pictures were presented to the right visual field (left hemisphere), matching was accomplished by function, while pictures projected in the left visual field (right hemisphere) were matched according to appearance. Matching by function was construed to involve logical, analytical information processing; matching by appearance was interpreted as involving holistic, synthetic information processing.

Most of the basic findings on hemispheric asymmetries in split-brain patients have been extended to normal subjects whose cerebral commissures are intact, with the exception that right-hemisphere superiority for visuospatial tasks seems to be slightly weaker in normal subjects. Investigations with normal subjects require measurement of reaction time, because information projected to one visual field can quickly and easily transfer to the opposite hemisphere.

REAL-WORLD PHENOMENA

When generalizing basic laboratory research findings to real-world situations, it is important to note that information transfer across the cerebral commissures is nearly instantaneous in normal subjects. In addition, the real-world environment provides prolonged visual stimulation, which is typically scanned with continuous eye movements. In these situations, environmental stimulation is available to both cerebral hemispheres. Therefore, one must be cautious not to overstate the case for a relationship between hemispheric asymmetries and real-world phenomena. The two cerebral hemispheres do work in combination as a unified brain in normal subjects. Even in split-brain patients, the prolonged availability of environmental stimulation and continuous eye scanning movements result, for the most part, in unified overt behavior. Behavioral, perceptual, and motor differences in split-brain patients are evident only with highly specialized and artificial laboratory testing with such instruments as the tachistoscope. Generalizations, then, from divided visual field studies of asymmetry to everyday situations require actual research evidence rather than the speculation that is popular among some segments of both the scientific and lay community.

STUTTERING RESEARCH

Stuttering is one real-world phenomenon for which laterality research has practical implications. There is some evidence that stutterers are bilaterally represented for speech and language to a greater extent than are nonstutterers. In one investigation, R. K. Jones, a neurosurgeon, was presented with four stutterers who had blood clots or tumors located near the normal speech center in the left hemisphere. Because of concern that removal of the blood clots or tumors would produce muteness in his patients by damaging the speech center, Jones performed the Wada test to determine where the speech center was located in each patient. This test involves the injection of an anesthetic agent, sodium amobarbital, into the right or left carotid artery. The carotid arteries provide the frontal regions of the brain, where the speech center is located, with oxygenated blood. The sodium amobarbital anesthetizes the particular hemisphere into whose carotid artery the drug is injected. If speech is disrupted by this procedure, either the speech center is located in the opposite hemisphere or the patient is bilaterally represented for speech. Additional testing of the opposite hemisphere will reveal whether the patient is bilaterally represented.

Using this procedure, Jones found that all four stutterers possessed bilateral speech representation. After the surgery, all four patients stopped stuttering and began to speak normally. These findings raise the question as to why stuttering is related to bilateralization of speech functions. One explanation is that stuttering occurs in these patients because, unlike normal people, they have a speech center in one hemisphere that is competitive with the speech center in the opposite hemisphere. Neural impulses from the two speech centers arrive out of synchrony at the muscles that control speech, which produces stuttering. What are the practical implications of these findings? It is quite obvious that producing irreparable damage to the brain for the sole purpose of eliminating a speech disorder, such as stuttering, would be highly unethical at current levels of medical technology and knowledge about the brain. Additional research on the hemispheric basis of stuttering will need to be conducted, and technological advances will be required before stuttering can be eliminated in bilaterally represented patients by means of neurosurgery; however, findings such as these may be increasingly useful in future applications of laterality research.

DYSLEXIA RESEARCH

Yet another phenomenon linked with laterality research is dyslexia, a disorder of reading that is not associated with sensory impairment, retardation, or emotional disturbances. In 1937, a physician by the name of Samuel T. Orton was the first to propose a link between hemispheric asymmetries and dyslexia. He observed mirror-image reversals of letters and words in reading and writing among children with reading problems. Orton also noted that many of these children exhibited unstable hand preferences, often accomplishing tasks normally reserved for a preferred hand with either hand on a given occasion. To account for these observations, Orton proposed that these children were insufficiently

lateralized for speech and language functions. In other words, neither hemisphere was specialized for speech and language.

Evidence to support the hypothesis that dyslexia is attributable to incomplete lateralization was generated in 1970 by E. B. Zurif and G. Carson, who compared the performance of fourteen normal readers in the fourth grade with fourteen dyslexic fourth graders on a dichotic listening task. Dichotic listening involves presenting simultaneous, competing verbal stimuli of differing content to each ear through headphones. The subjects' task is to identify the words, letters, or digits presented to each ear. Since the right ear primarily transmits auditory input to the left hemisphere, and the left ear to the right hemisphere, detectable differences in the processing of verbal stimulation can be used to suggest hemispheric asymmetries. In the foregoing study, presentation of a dichotic digits task showed a significant right-ear (left-hemisphere) advantage for the normal children and a weak, insignificant left-ear (right-hemisphere) advantage for the dyslexic children. Failure to find a significant hemispheric advantage in processing dichotically presented verbal stimulation suggests that dyslexic children may, indeed, be incompletely lateralized for speech and language. Before practical applications of this finding are realized, further explorations on the development of hemispheric asymmetries will be necessary to determine whether lateralization of functions can be influenced by environmental manipulation. Only if such modifications are possible can the development of incomplete lateralization be altered in dyslexics.

EARLY ROOTS OF RESEARCH

Modern research on hemispheric asymmetries has its origins in a short paper read at an 1836 medical conference in Montpellier, France. Marc Dax, an obscure country physician, reported that aphasia (any loss of the ability to use or understand language) is related to left-hemisphere brain damage and concluded that each hemisphere is specialized for different function. Unfortunately, the paper received little attention and Dax died the following year, never knowing that he had anticipated one of the most exciting and productive research fields to emerge in the twentieth century. Because Dax's paper was not widely known, credit for the discovery of hemispheric asymmetries was incorrectly given to

Broca, who presented a similar paper in 1861 to a meeting of the Society of Anthropology in Paris. Broca does deserve some of the credit for the discovery of hemispheric asymmetries in that he suggested an exact area of the left frontal lobe that produces an expressive aphasia when damaged. Furthermore, Broca presented a much more impressive case for left-hemisphere lateralization of speech and language; his paper was received with enthusiasm and controversy.

In 1868, British neurologist John Hughlings Jackson proposed the idea of a "leading" hemisphere, which preceded the modern concept of "cerebral dominance," the idea that one hemisphere is dominant for psychological functions over the other hemisphere. By 1870, Carl Wernicke, a German neurologist, had presented evidence that a specific region of the temporal lobe in the left cerebral hemisphere is essential for comprehending language and, when damaged, produces a receptive aphasia. In combination, these findings led to a widely held position that one hemisphere, usually the left, is dominant for verbal tasks and other higher functions, while the opposite hemisphere, usually the right, possesses no special function or only minor, limited functions. Even though the term "cerebral dominance" is still used today, it is generally recognized that there are no "major" or "minor" hemispheres; they are simply specialized for different tasks and information-processing styles.

The strongest early evidence for a specific function mediated primarily by the right hemisphere came from widespread assessment of brain-damaged patients on spatial relationship tests. After testing more than two hundred brain-damaged patients, T. Weisenberg and K. E. McBride concluded in 1935 that the right hemisphere is specialized for spatial relationships. These results refuted the notion of a single dominant hemisphere for all psychological functions.

Modern contributions made by Sperry, Gazzaniga, and their colleagues have been, perhaps, most instrumental in establishing the functions of the cerebral hemispheres. Their results, as well as those of neuropsychologists, have been incorporated into such areas as biological psychology, cognition, and perception. Biological psychologists are concerned with establishing the functions of various brain structures in normal subjects, including the cerebral hemispheres. Neuropsychologists contribute to laterality research by specifying the cognitive, motor, and behavioral deficits that arise following brain damage to a specific region in the cerebral cortex. Laterality research also provides information about hemispheric specialization for cognitive and perceptual processes.

Future explorations on laterality will continue to examine performance for specific tasks and information-processing strategies in each hemisphere, but with greater emphasis on localizing functions to specific brain structures. In addition, more effort will be expended on developing practical applications of laterality research in clinical and educational settings.

SOURCES FOR FURTHER STUDY

Bakker, Lars N., ed. *Brain Mapping Research Developments.* New York: Nova Biomedical Books, 2008. Deals with research into mapping the areas of the brain responsible for various functions; covers asymmetry.

Davidson, Richard J., and Kenneth Hugdahl, eds. *Brain Asymmetry.* Cambridge, Mass.: MIT Press, 1996. Twenty-three essays on the phylogenetic antecedents and anatomical bases; perceptual, cognitive, and motor lateralization; attention and learning; central-autonomic integration; emotional lateralization; interhemispheric interaction; ontogeny; and developmental disabilities; and psychopathology of brain asymmetry.

Hellige, Joseph B. *Hemispheric Asymmetry: What's Right and What's Left.* Cambridge, Mass.: Harvard University Press, 1993. Discusses the evolution and function of brain asymmetry in humans. Split-brain studies are referenced throughout.

Hugdahl, Kenneth, and Richard J. Davidson, eds. *The Asymmetrical Brain.* Cambridge, Mass.: MIT Press, 2003. An examination of the hemispheres of the brain and their respective functions.

Springer, Sally P., and Georg Deutsch. *Left Brain, Right Brain.* 5th ed. New York: W. H. Freeman, 1997. A comprehensive introductory book on laterality that addresses research with split-brain and normal subjects in considerable detail and provides thorough coverage of potential practical applications of laterality research.

Richard P. Atkinson

SEE ALSO: Aphasias; Brain structure; Speech disorders; Speech perception; Stuttering.

Sports psychology

TYPE OF PSYCHOLOGY: Cognition; emotion; learning; motivation; personality; social psychology; stress

FIELDS OF STUDY: Aggression; aging; attitudes and behavior; behavioral therapies; cognitive therapies; humanistic therapies; motivation theory; psychodynamic therapies; social motives

Involvement in sports as a participant or spectator serves similar psychological functions for individuals: Both help people create and maintain a positive self-concept, allow them to feel a sense of membership in social groups, and provide pleasant stimulation.

KEY CONCEPTS
- attribution
- eustress
- motivation
- participant
- self-esteem
- social identity
- spectator

INTRODUCTION

Sports psychology, also called sport psychology, is the study of the relationship between psychological or mental factors and sports participation and appreciation. Practitioners study both the ways in which athletes' psychology affects their sports performance and the ways in which fans' identification with a team affects their well-being. For athletes, sports psychology involves the understanding of skills such as relaxation, visualization, concentration, and goal setting. Sports psychology assumes that people's motivational level is a critical determinant of their involvement in sports, either as participants or spectators. Involvement in sports by both participants and spectators is a result of similar motivational factors: the desire to maintain a positive self-concept, the need to affiliate with or belong to meaningful social groups, and the need for positive levels of stress.

POSITIVE SELF-CONCEPT

As illustrated by the work of social psychologists such as Henri Tajfel, John Turner, and Jennifer Crocker, who have tested aspects of social identity theory, humans have a tendency to maintain a positive view of themselves. Therefore, evaluations that people make of the groups to which they belong have consequences for their social identity. For many people, the goal of feeling positive about themselves can be accomplished, at least in part, through involvement with athletics—either actively as participants or passively as spectators.

For the athlete, self-esteem begins to play an important motivational role in early childhood. Children tend to choose activities in which they are successful, allowing them to feel proud of their accomplishments. Those children who find success in athletic games begin to prefer them to other recreational or intellectual activities. In short, those with the most skill (presumably a genetic predisposition) tend to show the most enthusiasm for sports participation. Success and its subsequent self-esteem benefits fuel their desire to continue or increase their participation in athletics.

When studying the motivation of children, it is important to distinguish between intrinsic motivation and extrinsic motivation. When an individual is intrinsically motivated to complete a task, that person is moved by internal factors such as feelings of competence or an interest in the task itself. Persons who are extrinsically motivated are driven by external rewards, such as money, trophies, or praise from coaches and parents. Ideally, children should become involved in sports for intrinsic reasons, and most do become involved as a result of such motives. When intrinsically motivated children are given external rewards for their performance, however, the result can be a reduced overall motivation to participate in sports; that is, they tend to become less interested. The findings on the intrinsic-extrinsic motivational dichotomy have been used to help people who are trying to establish youth sports leagues. In the early stages of a league, intrinsic motives should be emphasized. Increases in extrinsic motivation via rewards and trophies will probably result in a reduction of intrinsic motivation and decrease of interest in the activity. In fact, simply having children come to expect their parents' praise can reduce intrinsic motivation. Unexpected praise and rewards are less likely to reduce intrinsic motivation. In general, it is probably best to take a hands-off approach to children's athletic games.

Coaches often try to increase the motivation of athletes as a means of increasing their performance; however, increasing the player's motivation is only one method of enhancing performance. Another popular technique, referred to as using mental imagery (what many call visualization), involves having the athlete mentally rehearse game situations. Before shooting a free throw, a basketball player might form a mental image of lining up his or her body correctly with the basket, bending at the knees when ready to release the ball, and following through with the fingertips and wrist after release. For example, L. Verdelle Clark had varsity and junior varsity high school basketball players practice their free-throw shooting through both mental imagery and physical practice. The results indicated that mental practice was almost as effective as physical practice.

SELF-ESTEEM

The desire to maintain positive levels of self-esteem continues to be a primary motivational force for both adolescent and adult athletes. Participation in athletics allows them the opportunity to feel good about themselves by helping fulfill their need for achievement and status. Successful athletic performance provides them with a feeling of accomplishment and mastery.

Self-esteem also serves as a motivational force for sports spectators. Although spectators do not personally accomplish performance goals, they can experience feelings of satisfaction and accomplishment along with their team's members. Sports fans report elation following their team's victory and sor-

Runners compete in the Badwater Ultramarathon, a 135-mile, nonstop run from Badwater in Death Valley to Mount Whitney Trailhead that takes place in the heat of July. To be successful, participants must prepare psychologically as well as physically. (AP/Wide World Photos)

row after their team's defeat, with levels of intensity similar to those of the players. The success of a fan's favorite team produces feelings of pride and increased self-esteem in the fan. Thus, spectators can improve their self-concept without any special athletic skills.

Nyla Branscombe and Daniel Wann performed a series of studies showing that spectators may experience increases in self-esteem even if their favorite team is not of championship caliber, as team identification provides a buffer from the feelings of isolation and alienation inimical to a society that values mobility. In general, fans of the local team, regardless of the success of that team, tend to have higher self-esteem, experience fewer negative emotions, and report greater life satisfaction than do persons who are not fans of the team. Such high self-esteem seems to be caused by the social support gained through interactions with other fans.

The desire to affiliate with and belong to certain groups also motivates sports participants. As adolescents begin to detach themselves from their families, social groups involving their peers become increasingly important, and a primary source of peer-group membership is belonging to a sports teams. Membership on such teams permits adolescents to be accepted by their peers, extends their social network, gives them a sense of belonging, and helps establish their social identity. Adults also may satisfy their need for affiliation and belonging by playing in recreational sports leagues.

POSITIVE STRESS

Another factor shown to motivate both athletes and spectators is a desire for positive levels of stress. Unlike the negative stress that often accompanies academic or work endeavors, positive stress, called eustress, is reflective of people's desire to find stimulation in life. For both participants and spectators, an athletic event involving their chosen team can be very stimulating. Hearts begin to race, people may feel nervous, and in general, the event can be quite arousing—much like a roller-coaster ride. This stimulation is actively sought by many people, and involvement in sports is an easy way to obtain it.

ATTRIBUTION

The motivational forces described earlier help to explain a wide variety of the behaviors exhibited by athletic participants and spectators. For example, the importance of maintaining a positive self-concept has been used to explain players' and fans' self-serving attributions—the explanations that people give when explaining why certain events occur. Attributions can be either external (the "A" grade attributable to luck or easy questions) or internal (the "A" on a test attributable to intelligence or intensive studying). Because of the desire for a positive self-concept, people tend to use external attributions to explain their failures (thereby protecting their self-concept) while forming internal attributions concerning their successes (thereby enhancing their self-concept). This self-serving attributional bias can be found in many areas, including athletics. Research has demonstrated that when a participant or a spectator's team has failed a competition, people tend to form external attributions as a means of explaining the defeat. For example, when asked to explain why they lost, athletes often blame the officials, bad luck, or the opponents' dirty play. They do not perceive the failure to be internal (attributable to a lack of skill or ability on their part); hence, their self-concept is protected. Conversely, when victorious, athletes tend to assign internal causes for their success. That is, when the contest was won, they state that it was attributable to their skill rather than to luck.

This pattern of self-serving attributions is also found among sports spectators. When their favorite team is successful, sports fans tend to give internal attributions similar to those of the players. When their team loses, spectators choose external attributions to explain the defeat. This bias, used most frequently by highly allegiant or identified fans, is driven by a desire to maintain the belief that the groups with which they are associated are good. Spectators can increase their self-esteem through a related process, called "basking in reflected glory" by Robert Cialdini and his colleagues. Cialdini found that spectators enhance their self-esteem by increasing their association with successful teams and protect their self-esteem by decreasing their association with failing teams. In one study, students at a large university were telephoned and asked to describe the most recent game of the university's football team. When the team had won, people tended to give statements such as "We won" or "We were victorious." When the team had lost, however, the typical reply was "They lost" or "They were defeated." In a second study, the day after their college

Human-Animal Athletic Dynamics

Sports psychology does not apply only to humans. Some athletes who interact with animals for sport use psychological techniques to enhance performances. Sports psychologists help human-animal athletic teams. Horse and dog trainers learn about their emotions and animal behavior to communicate effectively with their four-legged partners. Humans mentally practice how to focus themselves and their animals on tasks to be performed such as penning calves, jumping obstacles, or completing an obedience trial.

The relationship between humans and animals is crucial for success. Competitions can cause both people and animals to feel anxious and vulnerable to distractions. While preparing for competition, people can consult with sports psychologists in an effort to control the person's and animal's emotions, including fear and nervousness. Sports psychologists aid human athletes to utilize their emotional energy by comprehending negative thoughts and feelings instead of ignoring them. People are encouraged to condition themselves men-

tally to have positive emotions which calm them and their animals. Sports psychologists design training exercises to develop people's strategy skills and guide them to be aware of how arousal affects their animal partners.

Animals can detect and react to humans' physiological changes, such as tense muscles and increased heart rate caused by emotional stress. As a result, the team performs poorly. Mental preparation and practice to think positively and be relaxed and confident enable more consistent performances by both human and animal. A combination of physical and mental practice helps human-animal pairs to achieve coordination and a sense of timing and finesse which makes their performances seem effortless. Sports psychology helps athletes from Olympians to weekend enthusiasts achieve compatibility with their animals for competition and companionship.

Elizabeth D. Schafer

team played, more students wore clothing that identified their university affiliation following a victory compared with after a defeat. The most allegiant fans, however, tended to continue showing support for their team even when it lost over long periods of time.

MOTIVATION RESEARCH

The topic of motivation is one of the major areas of emphasis within the discipline of sports psychology, and it has attracted considerable research and theoretical attention. Since the 1990's, sports psychologists have been increasingly researching sports participation and spectatorship. Increased interest in the factors underlying the motivation of sports participants and spectators has been driven by the fact that sports are among the most popular leisure-time activities. Satisfaction with leisure-time activities greatly influences other areas of an individual's life, such as school or work.

Understanding the motivations of sport spectators and participants is important for several reasons. First, most individuals begin their involvement with sports at a young age, usually by early adolescence. Because of the impact of peer relations on the psychological development of youth, insight

into these relationships is important, and some comprehension can be gained by studying athletic team formation and cohesion. Second, because self-esteem plays such a critical role in determining whether individuals will become involved in sports, the positive emotional impact of athletics may be used for therapeutic purposes. Third, professional sports is a very big business with many millions of dollars at stake. If an individual's performance could be increased by increasing motivation, the result could be quite profitable for team owners and the professional involved.

DEVELOPMENT OF THE FIELD

Sports psychology is a relatively young specialty area within psychology. Pioneers, such as Coleman R. Griffith of the University of Illinois's Athletic Research Laboratory, expressed interest in sports psychology in the early twentieth century. Griffith published *Psychology of Coaching* (1926) and *Psychology of Athletics* (1928). The field, however, did not develop at that time. In fact, most of the national and international professional organizations designed to examine issues in sports psychology were founded no earlier than the 1970's, and it was not until 1986 that the American Psychological Association (APA) recognized sports psychology as a separate academic division. Organizations promoting professionalism include the North American Society for the Psychology of Sport and Physical Activity and the International Society of Sport Psychology.

Sports psychologists can receive certification from the Association for the Advancement of Applied Sport Psychology or by completing continuing education courses offered by the American Board of Sport Psychology. Individual sports psychologists train athletes differently and use various treatment methods. Some analyze how social environments influence the behavior of athletes, while others focus on cognitive aspects, such as how mental processes shape athletic behavior. Others focus on psychophysiology, which correlates how brain chemistry affects behavior. The concept of motor development interests many sports psychologists. In addition to traditional forms of counseling, sports psychologists use biofeedback, hypnosis, and neurofeedback. Certified sports psychologists can register with the United States Olympic Committee and National Collegiate Athletic Association to assist elite and student athletes in fine-tuning their performances and developing coping and psychological skills to deal with demanding, high-profile lives.

SPECIALITIES AND APPLICATIONS

As psychologists develop specialties within the field to explore both familiar and emerging concerns, sports psychology research has expanded. Research topics include self-determination theory, emotional intelligence, and mood states, especially how anxiety and catastrophe theory can affect athletes. Technological developments offer sports psychologists new tools such as real-time online surveying and the ability to study athletic performance via virtual reality. The Internet provides sports psychology resources for experts, athletes, and related personnel worldwide to network and share insights to advance research on universal issues.

Some sports psychologists focus on individual athletes, while others study the dynamics of teams and how members communicate to achieve effective cohesiveness. Investigators collect data concerning athletes' perceptions of sports psychology and subsequent acceptance of or resistance to such efforts to improve their performances.

Sports psychologists and physicians study athletes' psychological responses to injuries and ill-

nesses, particularly those medical conditions that halt high-profile athletic careers. They also examine psychological factors involved in rehabilitation and how athletes endure pain, deal with their temporary inability to compete, and commit to physical therapy. Health professionals are also interested in learning more about athletes who engage in substance abuse, have eating disorders, or develop mental illnesses.

Many therapists address aging-related concerns, especially as professional athletes attempt to lengthen their careers and amateur athletes seek recreational exercise during retirement. Some researchers evaluate how athletes' age, gender, and ethnicity affect development of the psychological skills that aid athletic performances. They also study how grief and terrorism affect athletes and how exercise is psychologically beneficial to casual exercisers.

Some sports psychologists apply techniques used for athletes to situations outside sports. As consultants to corporations, sports psychologists can improve employees' performance by teaching them cognitive restructuring and visualization methods to cope with stressful situations such as presentations. Private patients benefit from learning to focus on process instead of outcome and to relax with breathing methods to achieve better job performances both on and off athletic fields.

SOURCES FOR FURTHER STUDY

Jarvis, Matt. *Sport Psychology: A Student's Handbook.* Rev. ed. New York: Routledge, 2006. An updated volume in the Routledge Modular Psychology series that differentiates between academic and applied sports psychology. Discusses such research topics as attitude, memory and learning, anxiety and stress, types of participation, and the process of skill acquisition, describing how such knowledge can benefit athletes ranging from ballerinas to football players.

Lane, Andrew M., ed. *Mood and Human Performance: Conceptual, Measurement, and Applied Issues.* New York: Nova Science Publishers, 2007. Collection of scholarly essays by diverse hands that deal with trends in sports psychology, such as mood states and emotional intelligence.

Moran, Aidan P. *Sport and Exercise Psychology: A Critical Introduction.* New York: Routledge, 2004. An academic text that is accessible to the layperson, this collection of theoretical discourses, combined with real-world sport examples, will serve as a good primer in the field.

Silva, John M., III, and Diane E. Stevens, eds. *Psychological Foundations of Sport.* 2d ed. Boston: Allyn & Bacon, 2002. Discusses how the psychological dynamics of sports influence athletes, coaches, and spectators. The book's significant sections address gender, aggression, teamwork, confidence, and youth athletes.

Singer, Robert N., Heather A. Hausenblas, and Christopher M. Janelle, eds. *Handbook of Sport Psychology.* 2d ed. New York: John Wiley & Sons, 2001. A comprehensive collection that incorporates both theoretical and practical sports psychology information for mental health professionals, athletes of all competency levels, and coaches to condition minds in addition to bodies. Subjects, activities, and exercises include psychological skill development for managing pain, increasing self-confidence, and gauging improvement.

Taylor, Jim, and Gregory S. Wilson, eds. *Applying Sport Psychology: Four Perspectives.* Champaign, Ill.: Human Kinetics, 2005. Renowned researchers and consultants discuss goal setting, mental imagery, routines, team cohesion, and the coach-athlete relationship. Each chapter takes the form of a discourse between four experts in the field.

Van Raalte, Judy L., and Britton W. Brewer, eds. *Exploring Sport and Exercise Psychology.* 2d ed. Washington, D.C.: American Psychological Association, 2002. The editors, psychology associate professors and coaches at Springfield College, compile a guide of insights from experts explaining how to become a sports psychologist, how to improve athletes' physical and mental health, and how to apply interventions such as intensity regulation and modeling.

Wann, Daniel L. *Sport Fans: The Psychology and Social Impact of Spectators.* New York: Routledge, 2001. Focusing on the role played by spectators, emphasizes that sports tend to benefit fans' mental health.

Weinberg, Robert S., and Daniel Gould. *Foundations of Sport and Exercise Psychology.* 4th ed. Champaign, Ill.: Human Kinetics, 2007. A basic text that explains fundamental psychological aspects that can be appropriated for therapy, coaching, sports medicine, and exercise education.

Williams, Jean M., ed. *Applied Sport Psychology: Personal Growth to Peak Performance.* 5th ed. Boston: McGraw-Hill, 2006. Thoroughly presents both basic and advanced information to assist students and coaches in sports and exercise psychology. Authors explain why intervention is necessary in sports psychology and how to achieve desired behavioral changes.

Nyla R. Branscombe and Daniel L. Wann;
updated by Elizabeth D. Schafer;
updated by Anthony J. Fonseca

SEE ALSO: Achievement motivation; Affiliation motive; Aggression: Reduction and control; Attributional biases; Coaching; Crowd behavior; Exercise and mental health; Groups; Motivation; Motivation: Intrinsic and extrinsic; Self-esteem.

Stanford-Binet test

DATE: 1910 forward
TYPE OF PSYCHOLOGY: Intelligence and intelligence testing; learning
FIELDS OF STUDY: Ability tests; general issues in intelligence; intelligence assessment

The Stanford-Binet test represented the first widespread method for evaluation of intelligence. Later, the score on the test was adapted into the concept of an intelligence quotient (IQ).

KEY CONCEPTS
- Binet-Simon
- intelligence quotient (IQ)
- mental age
- Wechsler scale

INTRODUCTION

The origin of the idea that intelligence could be tested can be found as early as the 1860's, following the publication of British naturalist Charles Darwin's work *On the Origin of Species by Means of Natural Selection* (1859). Among the concepts addressed in this book, and in his later *The Descent of Man* (1871), was the idea that the intelligence of animals, including man, could be understood and measured through scientific investigation.

Sir Francis Galton, a British scientist and explorer, who was also Darwin's cousin, was among the first to adopt Darwin's ideas for testing. Galton maintained a laboratory in London, England, where visitors could undergo assorted physical or sensory tests. A subject could be observed on the basis of, for instance, ability to interpret musical pitch. Galton believed such physical or sensory abilities reflected intelligence.

THE BINET-SIMON TEST

In 1904, the Commission for the Education of Retarded Children was established in Paris, France, for the purpose of developing a test that could accurately measure levels of intelligence. The concern was that children were being labeled as retarded not on the basis of mental capacity but because of behavioral problems. An intelligence test could be used to avoid such incorrect labeling.

Alfred Binet believed that what was recognized as intelligence actually represented a combination of factors, including both knowledge gained from school and knowledge obtained from general observations and interactions with others. The Stanford-Binet test represented the first attempt at determining the mental age of a subject as a means of separating retarded children from those who were normal. The basis of such testing consisted of a series of mental tasks of increasing difficulty. Children of various ages were assumed to have a certain level of knowledge in dealing with such tasks. The number of correct responses to these questions resulted in the assignment of a certain "mental age" to the child.

As originally developed in 1905 by Binet and his colleague Théodore Simon, the test, known as the Binet-Simon test, consisted of thirty tasks that ranged from manual dexterity to the ability to remember general facts or concepts. Binet initially screened fifty children considered of average intelligence and developed a series of norms, now called the 1905 scale. Children were tested in this manner and received a score reflecting what Binet and Simon considered their mental age.

TERMAN'S REFINEMENTS

In 1912, psychologist William Stern adapted Binet's work by calculating what became known as the intelligence quotient, or IQ. The IQ score was calculated by dividing the mental age by the chronological age and multiplying by 100. For example, a mental age

of ten and a chronological age of ten resulted in an IQ of 100, considered average. A mental age of twelve in a child of ten would result in an IQ of 120, considered somewhat above average.

Experience with administration of the test to thousands of children over many decades has demonstrated that the distribution of scores resembles a symmetrical pattern, a normal distribution or bell-shaped curve. Most children (approximately two-thirds) fall within the middle of the curve, with the remaining children distributed more or less equally in higher or lower ranges.

The test as originally devised by Binet consisted primarily of verbal reasoning, reflecting the purpose of the test as a means to separate retarded children from normal counterparts. In 1916, Lewis Terman of Stanford University increased the length of the test and extended the range of age among the children who served as subjects. The result was the normal distribution of scores that is now characteristic of the results. What now became known as the Stanford-Binet test replaced its predecessor, the Binet-Simon. Terman's adaptation has undergone several revisions in the ensuing decades.

The most recent version of the Stanford-Binet test, developed in 1985, consists of both verbal and nonverbal items. The verbal portion involves asking the child to explain or define the use of specific objects. The nonverbal portion contains questions that attempt to examine concepts such as quantitative and abstract reasoning, and memory.

SOURCES FOR FURTHER STUDY

Binet, Alfred, and Théodore Simon. *The Development of Intelligence in Children.* 1916. Reprint. Manchester, N.H.: Ayer, 1983. Reprint of the original articles by Binet on the subject.

Gould, Stephen Jay. *The Mismeasure of Man.* Rev. ed. New York: W. W. Norton, 2008. A highly controversial book by one of the most forceful proponents of evolution. Gould traces the use and, in great depth, abuse of intelligence testing.

Hernnstein, Richard, and Charles Murray. *The Bell Curve.* New York: Simon & Schuster, 1996. The authors address the question of whether the genetics and heritability of intelligence can be reflected both in IQ and in subsequent social success. The authors' conclusions resulted in significant discussion and controversy about the topic.

Minton, Henry L. *Lewis M. Terman: Pioneer in Educational Testing*. New York: New York University Press, 1990. Biography of the man most noted for adaptation of the modern Stanford-Binet test.

Naglieri, Jack A., and Sam Goldstein, eds. *Practitioner's Guide to Assessing Intelligence and Achievement*. Hoboken, N.J.: Wiley, 2009. Looks at questions of assessment in general and by specific tests, including the assessment of intellectual strengths and weaknesses with the Stanford-Binet test.

Richard Adler

SEE ALSO: Ability tests; Assessment; Career and personnel testing; Cognitive Abilities Test (CogAT); College entrance examinations; General Aptitude Test Battery (GATB); Intelligence; Intelligence quotient (IQ); Intelligence tests; Peabody Individual Achievement Test (PIAT); Race and intelligence; Testing: Historical perspectives; Wechsler Intelligence Scale for Children-Third Edition (WISC-III).

Stanford prison experiment

DATE: 1970's
TYPE OF PSYCHOLOGY: Social psychology
FIELDS OF STUDY: Aggression; social motives

Designed and led by renowned psychologist Philip Zimbardo, the Stanford prison experiment is a case study that illustrates the overriding power of the situation to transform good people into authoritarians and sadists. The study illuminates the dark side of human nature, which lurks closely beneath the surface and can emerge under the right set of circumstances.

KEY CONCEPTS
- bystander effect
- dehumanization
- deindividualization
- simulation research
- situational influences

INTRODUCTION

In 1971, a prison was constructed in the basement of Stanford University's psychology building. The makeshift prison was to provide a realistic setting for examining the effects of simulated confinement on prisoners and guards. The Stanford prison experiment, designed and led by Philip Zimbardo, a renowned psychologist and professor emeritus at Stanford University, is a case study that demonstrates how the power of a situation can transform those who are generally regarded as good people into authoritarians and sadists. It highlighted the ability of human nature's dark side to emerge under certain circumstances.

Truly a classic study in psychology, the Stanford prison experiment is one of the best known and most widely cited experiments in the discipline. The investigation has been discussed in most introductory psychology courses since the early 1970's. Videos or still photos of the experiment have been featured in television documentaries and newsmagazines, are shown to students in undergraduate classes, and even appear on the Internet. The study, along with Stanley Milgram's obedience to authority experiment, has become very widely known outside the realm of psychology.

PRISON SIMULATION

To bring realism to the experiment, the study began with televised, dramatized arrests of the student participants by the Palo Alto Police Department. Arrests were followed by a real-life booking process: handcuffing, fingerprinting, and photographing (mug shots), as well as the conducting of strip searches and the assignment of numbers to the detainees, which gave the students a new identity. The study even involved fictitious parole board hearings, administered by an actual former prison inmate, in which students pled for their release. The experiment ended abruptly and unexpectedly after six days instead of the scheduled fourteen because of the emotional suffering of the prisoners and the escalating abusiveness of the guards, which took the form of sleep deprivation, sexual humiliation, physical abuse, solitary confinement, incessant prisoner counts, and mindless activities. Half of the student prisoners had to be released from the study because of psychological strain.

PARTICIPANTS

Before being selected for the study, participants were thoroughly assessed for mental illness, medical disabilities, and personality or character problems. The participants were twenty-four healthy undergraduates with no hint of severe emotional problems or predilections toward violence or any other untoward behaviors. Not only were the experiment guards and prisoners free of significant emotional problems as they began the experience, they were also randomly assigned, by a coin toss, to their respective roles for a two-week study of authority and social influence. Yet, the behaviors of the inmates and guards in the ersatz prison belied their scores on the personality tests.

TRANSFORMATIONS

The students became guards and inmates through a simple change of uniform. The prison-based conversion was facilitated by two complementary processes: deindividualization and dehumanization. Deindividualization allowed the guards to hide behind uniforms, badges, ranks, and titles. The detention officers in the experiment donned mirrored sunglasses, wore khaki uniforms, carried batons and whistles, and insisted on being addressed as "Mr. Corrections Officer," all of which fueled the sadistic behaviors they directed toward the inmates.

When the student-guards entered the basement of Stanford University's psychology building, they not only put on a new set of clothes but also assumed the mantle of authority. In the experiment, the inmates wore flimsy gowns, which were undignified and demeaning. They were forced to cover their hair with nylon stocking caps, which further eroded their identities. Inmates were stamped with insulting names as part of a ritualized depersonalization and demoralization process. They were punished by the guards' ordering them to sleep on the floor; having them perform exhausting exercises and mindless, repetitive activities; restricting their use of the bathroom facilities; locking them in a solitary confinement closet; and forcing them to engage in simulated homoerotic behaviors. The research participant-inmates were no longer individual students, but a collective caricature of prison dwellers.

The student-inmates became abjectly submissive young men whose dialogues and interactions were scripted by the surroundings that dictated their behaviors, self-perceptions, and even their thoughts about others in the situation. The roles ossified as the research unfolded and eventually unraveled. The experiment showed that even a brief period of confinement in a contrived prison environment can precipitate short-term mental health problems in a sample of seemingly healthy young men.

In the experiment, Zimbardo maintained enough distance from the guards and gave them loose rules of engagement with prisoners (keep order, permit no one to escape, and commit no acts of violence) so that they enumerated their own set of regulations, which were applied arbitrarily and often with the sole intention of controlling and tormenting the inmates. In addition, the tacit approval of the abuse by the warden and prison superintendent (Zimbardo) most certainly encouraged more abuse. In submerging himself in the role of prison superintendent/principal investigator, Zimbardo lost his perspective and reasonable judgment. He wore dark glasses while running the prison, and he was blind to the escalating abuse even though he reviewed the audio and videotapes that recorded each day of confinement.

The bystander effect operated in the experiment as the "good" guards permitted the most sadistic ones to define appropriate actions. Not wanting to be chastened by fellow guards, the more humanitarian ones did nothing while the dominant ones meted out their punishments and degradations. Therefore, the silence of the good guards allowed the bad ones to act with impunity. The guards who were exceptionally physically imposing and harsh, particularly during the night shift, created a natural hierarchy of leaders and followers, setting the stage and atmosphere for the guards to imitate and revel in the sadistic treatment of inmates.

The guards at Stanford University prison probably feared losing face in front of their compatriots, being superseded by a superior officer or alpha guard, or offering unwanted assistance. As the situation was highly ambiguous, the guards monitored and mimicked the reactions of others in the prison; their motivation was to ascertain and follow acceptable standards of behavior. As no one lodged complaints about inmate mistreatment at the prison facility, the abuse continued and escalated. The inaction of others, especially the leadership, led the "good" guards to conclude that the situation must be acceptable, which is an example of pluralistic ignorance and social proof.

Conditions in the Stanford University prison acutely deteriorated following an escape attempt and an uprising of the prisoners in protest of their shoddy treatment and harsh conditions. The uprising was followed by more mistreatment and violence against the inmates. The prison guards and leadership took precautions to thwart future out-breaks of dissension, which they believed demanded stricter rules and a further crackdown on inmates' rights and privileges, thus beginning the slippery slide down the slope of abuse and mistreatment. Echoing the times, some of the inmates organized a group to present their demands and rally for justice; one went on a hunger strike. These activities were to no real avail and served mostly to justify the progressively harsher treatment issued by the guards.

TERMINATION OF THE STUDY

At Stanford University prison, Susan Maslach, a young assistant professor from the University of California, Berkeley, was helping Zimbardo with the student prisoners. After listening to her complaints about the cruelty of the study, he terminated the research and debriefed the participants to educate them about the experience and to forestall future mental health problems.

LATER STUDIES

Decades after the original study, Thomas Carnahan and Sam McFarland tested to see if the researchers investigated whether students who selectively volunteer for a study of prison life might possess characteristics that predispose them to act abusively. To recruit subjects for the study, the investigators posted a news-paper advertisement that was virtually identical to the one used in the Stanford prison experiment. One advertisement included the term "prison life" while the other did not. Those who volunteered for the "prison study" scored significantly higher on measures of aggressiveness and authoritarianism, which are directly related to the propensity toward aggressive abuse, and lower on empathy and altruism, which are inversely related to the propensity toward aggressive abuse. These results challenge the conclusions of the Stanford prison experiment, which suggested that behavior is determined entirely by the situation rather the person in the situation or the interaction between the person and the situation.

SOURCES FOR FURTHER STUDY

Banuazizi, Ali, and Siamak Movahedi. "Interpersonal Dynamics in a Simulated Prison: A Methodological Analysis." *American Psychologist* 30, no. 10 (1975): 152-160. The authors provide a critical analysis of the methodology employed in the Stanford prison experiment. The article argues that the subjects entered the study with powerful stereotypic beliefs about how prisoners and guards behave, which dictated their interactions with one another and caused them to adopt roles that were reinforced by the subtle (and not so subtle) cues of Zimbardo and his research team.

Carnahan, Thomas, and Sam McFarland. "Revisiting the Stanford Prison Experience: Could Participant Self-Selection Have Led to Cruelty?" *Personality and Social Psychology Bulletin* 33, no. 5 (2007): 603-614. The study that challenged the Stanford prison experiment conclusions by looking at the role of volunteer self-selection in the results.

Haney, C., W. C. Banks, and Philip G. Zimbardo. "Interpersonal Dynamics in a Simulated Prison." *International Journal of Criminology and Penology* 1, no. 1 (1973): 69-97. This paper presents the implementation and basic findings of the Stanford prison experiment and focuses on the practical implications of the study for correctional administrators and officers. In particular, the article discusses the aspects of the prison environment that can cause both detention officers and prisoners to behave pathologically. The article enumerates a series of remedies and reforms to alleviate the oppressive conditions in prisons.

_____. "Study of Prisoner and Guards in a Simulated Prison." *Naval Research Reviews* 9, no. 2 (1973): 1-17. This article is required reading for anyone interested in the Stanford prison experiment. The paper describes the original background, methodology, results, and conclusions of the study as written by the primary members of the research team.

Zimbardo, Philip G. *The Lucifer Effect: Understating How Good People Turn Evil.* New York: Random House, 2007. A multilayered and compelling treatise about the malleability of human nature and the utter rapidity with which it can change from civility to malevolence. At the heart of the book is a painstaking chronology of the Stanford prison experiment, a case study that illustrates the overriding power of the situation to transform good citizens into evildoers. The book's most valuable contributions are the parallels the author draws between the Stanford prison experiment and the Abu Ghraib atrocities, which underscore the timelessness of the insights generated in Zimbardo's laboratory.

Arthur J. Lurigio

See also: Aggression: Reduction and control; Depersonalization; Experimental psychology; Experimentation: Ethics and subject rights; Group decision making; Milgram experiment; Zimbardo, Philip.

State-Trait Anxiety Inventory (STAI)

Date: 1970 forward
Type of psychology: Personality; psychopathology
Fields of study: Anxiety disorders; personality assessment

The State-Trait Anxiety Inventory, developed in 1970, was the most widely used questionnaire to measure anxiety in the late twentieth century. The brief twenty-item inventory is widely used in clinical and research settings.

Key concepts
- anxiety
- psychological inventories
- reliability
- state anxiety
- trait anxiety

Introduction

The State-Trait Anxiety Inventory (STAI) is a very widely used measure of anxiety. It was developed by American psychologist Charles Spielberger, who first produced it in collaboration with Richard L. Gorsuch, Robert Lushene, Peter R. Vagg, and Gerald A. Jacobs in 1970. It is copyrighted by Consulting Psychologists Press.

The State-Trait Anxiety Inventory consists of twenty items about a person's feelings of anxiousness (such as "I am presently worrying over possible misfortunes") that are answered on a four-point scale ranging from 1 ("Not at all") to 4 ("Very much so"). Some of the items are worded positively ("I feel calm"); others are worded negatively ("I am tense"). The positive items are reverse-scored, so that higher scores indicate more anxiety. The inventory has two forms: state form and trait form. In the state form (also called Y-1), the items are about feelings at the present time; in the trait form (also called Y-2), the items are about general feelings

overall. The STAI has cut-off scores; a score over this point indicates clinically relevant anxiety symptoms. The original form of the STAI was called Form X.

The STAI has been revised so that it can be used with many different kinds of people. Test forms include a children's version with twenty items that the child rates on a three-point scale, a short version with only six items, and a version for parents to complete about their children with the usual twenty items and six additional items. There are versions in many different languages, including Arabic, Amharic, Chinese, Czech, Dutch, French, German, Hindi, Italian, Japanese, Norwegian, Polish, Portuguese, Spanish, and Thai.

Uses

The STAI has clinical uses: It can be administered before and after therapy or before and after medication for anxiety. For example, in one report, a woman had distressing a vocal tic, which meant that she involuntarily made repeated sounds and words and coughed. A vocal tic is similar to stuttering. She received therapy that included awareness training, a review of situations and of how inconvenient the habit was, relaxation training, the learning of competing responses, and social support. The therapist measured whether she improved by videotaping her and counting the number of vocal tics and having her complete the STAI to measure her anxiety. She improved in having fewer vocal tics and less anxiety.

The STAI is widely used in research with both adults and children. In a citation analysis of six commonly used measures of anxiety, it ranked first. It is so widely used because it is a reliable and valid research instrument. One type of reliability is test-retest reliability, which means that people typically describe themselves the same way on the STAI from one time to another. Another type of reliability is internal consistency, which means that all the STAI questions are measuring the same thing. In terms of validity, the STAI is correlated with other measures of anxiety. Also, people who describe themselves as anxious or who are diagnosed with anxiety disorders score higher on the STAI than people who describe themselves as calm or who are not diagnosed with anxiety disorders. For research purposes, questionnaires must be reliable and valid to be useful, and the STAI meets both criteria.

An example of a research project using the STAI with adults was a study of 147 cancer patients (mean age 57.6 years). They completed the STAI and interviews before and after discussions with their cancer physician. Patients who did not like their physician's communication style had higher anxiety following the discussion. Further, after the discussion, patients' anxiety levels remained low, even among those patients with unfavorable examination results, when the patients liked their physician's communication style.

An example of a research project using the STAI with children is a study of ninety children with spina bifida who attended a one-week summer camp. They completed the STAI before and after camp. By the end of the camp, their anxiety was lower than it had been at the beginning.

SOURCES FOR FURTHER STUDY

Antony, Martin M., and Murray B. Stein, eds. *Oxford Handbook of Anxiety and Related Disorders.* New York: Oxford University Press, 2009. Contains a chapter on anxiety assessments and a wealth of other information about anxiety disorders.

Briery, Brandon G., and Brian Rabian. "Psychosocial Changes Associated with Participation in a Pediatric Summer Camp." *Journal of Pediatric Psychology* 24, no. 2 (1999): 183-190. This study is a good example of research using the State-Trait Anxiety Inventory for Children.

Fuata, Patricia, and Rosalyn A. Griffiths. "Cognitive Behavioural Treatment of a Vocal Tic." *Behavior Change* 9, no. 1 (1992): 14-18. This article describes how the State-Trait Anxiety Inventory might be used in a clinical situation.

McDowell, Ian. *Measuring Health: A Guide to Rating Scales and Questionnaires.* 3d ed. New York: Oxford University Press, 2006. This textbook on health assessments contains a chapter on anxiety measures, including the State-Trait Anxiety Inventory.

Takayama, Tomoko, Yoshihiko Yamazaki, and Noriyuki Katsumata. "Relationship Between Outpatients' Perceptions of Physicians' Communication Styles and Patients' Anxiety Levels in a Japanese Oncology Setting." *Social Science and Medicine* 53, no. 10 (2001): 1335-1350. This study is a good example of research using the State-Trait Anxiety Inventory with adults.

Lillian M. Range

SEE ALSO: Anxiety disorders; Beck Depression Inventory (BDI); California Psychological Inventory (CPI); Children's Depression Inventory (CDI); Clinical interviewing, testing, and observation; Depression; Diagnosis; Minnesota Multiphasic Personality Inventory (MMPI); Personality: Psychophysiological measures; Personality interviewing strategies; Personality rating scales; Thematic Apperception Test (TAT).

Statistical significance tests

TYPE OF PSYCHOLOGY: Psychological methodologies
FIELD OF STUDY: Methodological issues

Statistical significance tests are techniques that help assess the importance of research findings; they are crucial in helping determine what inferences can be drawn from the data gathered from a psychological study.

KEY CONCEPTS
- mean
- normal distribution
- null hypothesis
- probability
- significance level
- standard deviation
- t-test

INTRODUCTION

Psychological researchers make extensive use of statistical methods in the analysis of data gathered in their research. Statistical methods serve two primary functions: descriptive, to provide a summary of large sets of data so that the important features are readily apparent, and inferential, to evaluate the extent to which the data support the hypothesis being studied as well as the extent to which the findings can be generalized to the population as a whole. It is this second function that makes use of statistical significance tests.

Researchers may employ these tests either to ascertain whether there is a significant difference in the performance of different groups being studied or to determine whether different variables (characteristics) of subjects have a strong relationship to one another. For example, in conducting an experiment to test the effect of a particular treatment on behavior, the experimenter would be interested in testing the differences in performance between the treatment group and a control group. Another researcher might be interested in looking at the strength of the relationship between two variables—such as scores on the SAT Reasoning Test and college grade-point average. In both cases, statistical significance tests would be employed to find out whether the difference between groups or the strength of the relationship between variables was statistically significant.

LAWS OF PROBABILITY

The term "statistically significant" has a specific meaning based on the outcome of certain statistical procedures. Statistical significance tests have their basis in the laws of probability, specifically in the law of large numbers and conditional probability. Primarily, the law of large numbers states that as the number of events with a certain probabilistic outcome increases, the frequencies of occurrence that are observed should come closer and closer to matching the frequencies that would be expected based on the probabilities associated with those events. For example, with a coin flip, the probability associated with "heads" is .50 (50 percent), as is the probability associated with "tails." If a person flipped a coin ten times, it would not be too startling if he or she got eight heads; if the coin were flipped ten thousand times, however, the observed frequencies of heads and tails would be about 50 percent each. Thus, with large numbers of probabilistic events, the expected outcomes can be predicted with great precision.

Conditional probability refers to the probability of a second event, given that a certain first event has occurred. For example, if someone has already pulled one ace from a deck of cards, what is the probability of pulling a second ace on that person's next attempt (without replacing the first card)? The probability of pulling the first ace was four (the number of aces in the deck) out of fifty-two (the number of cards in the deck). The second draw has a conditional probability created by what happened on the first pick. Because an ace was drawn first, there are now three left in the deck, and since the card was not replaced, there are now fifty-one cards left in the deck. Therefore, the probability of pulling the second ace would be three out of fifty-one.

ESTABLISHING AND TESTING HYPOTHESES

Armed with these two concepts, it is now possible to understand how statistical significance tests work. Researchers are always investigating hypothetical relationships between variables through experiments or other methodologies. These hypotheses can be about how strongly related two variables are or about differences between the average performance between groups—for example, an experimental and a control group. One possible hypothesis is that the variables have no relationship, or that the groups are not different in their performance. This is referred to as the null hypothesis, and it plays an important role in establishing statistical significance. A second possible hypothesis is that there is a relationship between variables, or that there is a difference between the mean (the average value of a group of scores) performances of groups. This is referred to as the alternative hypothesis, and it is the hypothesis truly of interest to the researcher. Although it is not possible to test this hypothesis directly, it is possible to test the null hypothesis. Because these hypotheses are both mutually exclusive and exhaustive (only one can be true, but one must be true), if it can be shown from the data gathered that the null hypothesis is highly unlikely, then researchers are willing to accept the alternative hypothesis.

This works through a conditional probability strategy. First, the researcher assumes that the null hypothesis is true. Then the researcher looks at the data gathered during the research and asks the question, "How likely is it that we would have gotten this particular sample data if the null hypothesis were true?" In other words, researchers evaluate the probability of the data given the null hypothesis. If they find, after evaluation, that the data would be very unlikely if the null hypothesis were true, then they are able to reject the null hypothesis and accept the alternative hypothesis. In such a case, it can be said that the results were statistically significant.

Arbitrarily, the standard for statistical significance is usually a conditional probability of less than .05 (5 percent). This probability value required to reject the null hypothesis is referred to as the significance level. This criterion is set at a stringent level because science tends to be conservative; it does not want to reject old ideas and accept new ones too easily. The significance level actually represents the probability of making a certain type of error—of rejecting the null hypothesis when it is in fact true.

The lower the significance level, the higher the confidence that the data obtained would be very unlikely if the null hypothesis were true and the observed effects are reliable.

EVALUATION OF CONDITIONAL PROBABILITY

Statistical significance tests are the procedures that allow researchers to evaluate the conditional probability of the data, given the null hypothesis. The data from a study are used to compute a test statistic. This is a number whose size reflects the degree to which the data differ from what would be expected if the null hypothesis were true. Some commonly encountered test statistics are the t-ratio, the F-ratio, and the critical (Z) ratio. The probability associated with the test statistic can be established by consulting published tables, which give the probability of obtaining a particular value of the test statistic if the null hypothesis is true. The null hypothesis is rejected if the probability associated with the test statistic is less than a predetermined "critical" value (usually .05). If the probability turns out to be greater than the critical value, then one would fail to reject the null hypothesis; however, that does not mean that the null hypothesis is true. It could simply be that the research design was not powerful enough (for example, the sample size may have been too small, like flipping the coin only ten times) to detect real effects that were there, like a microscope that lacks sufficient power to observe a small object that is nevertheless present.

DIFFERENCES IN SIGNIFICANCE

There is sometimes a difference between statistical significance and practical significance. The size of most test statistics can be increased simply by increasing the number of subjects in the sample that is studied. If samples are large enough, any effect will be statistically significant no matter how small that effect may be. Statistical significance tests tell researchers how reliable an effect is, but not whether that effect has any practical significance. For example, a researcher might be investigating the effectiveness of two diet plans and using groups of one thousand subjects for each diet. On analyzing the data, the researcher finds that subjects following diet A have a significantly greater weight loss than subjects following diet B. This is practically significant. If, however, the average difference between the two groups was only one-tenth of a pound, this difference would be statistically significant, but it would have no practical significance whatsoever.

T-TEST

Statistical significance tests provide a measure of how likely it is that the results of a particular research study came about by chance. They accomplish this by putting a precise value on the confidence or probability that rerunning the same study would produce similar or stronger results. A specific test, the t-test, can provide an example of how this works in practice. The t-test is used to test the significance of the difference between the mean performance of two groups on some measure of behavior. It is one of the most widely used tests of significance in psychological research.

Suppose a professor of psychology is interested in whether the more "serious" students tend to choose the early morning sections of classes. To test this hypothesis, the professor compares the performance on the final examination of two sections of an introductory psychology course, one that met at 8:00 A.M., and one that met at 2:00 P.M. In this example, the null hypothesis would state that there is no difference in the average examination scores for the two groups. The alternative hypothesis would state that the average score for the morning group will be higher. In calculating the mean scores for each of the two groups, the professor finds that the early morning class had an average score of 82, while the afternoon class had an average score of 77. Before reaching any conclusion, however, the professor would have to find out how likely it is that this difference could be attributable to chance, so a t-test would be employed.

INFLUENTIAL FACTORS

There are three factors that influence a test of significance such as the t-test. One is the size of the difference between the means. In general, the larger the measured difference, the more likely that the difference reflects an actual difference in performance and not chance factors. A second factor is the size of the sample, or the number of measurements being tested. In general, differences based on large numbers of observations are more likely to be significant than the same differences based on fewer observations (as in the coin-flipping example). This is true because with larger samples, random factors within a group (such as the presence of a "hot-shot" student, or some students who were particularly sleepy on exam day) tend to be canceled out across groups. The third factor that influences a measure of statistical significance is the variability of the data, or how spread out the scores are from one another. If there is considerable variability in the scores, then the difference (variability) in the group means is more likely to be attributable to chance. The variability in the scores is usually measured by a statistic called the standard deviation, which could loosely be thought of as the average distance of a typical score from the mean of the group. As the standard deviation of the groups gets smaller, the size of the measure of statistical significance will get larger.

Knowing these three things—the size of the difference of the two groups, the number of scores for each group, and the standard deviations of the test scores of the two groups—the professor can calculate a t-statistic and then draw conclusions. With a difference of mean test scores of five points, fifty students in each class, and standard deviations of 3.5 in the first class and 2.2 in the second, the value of t would be 1.71. To determine whether this t is significant, the professor would go to a published statistical table that contains the minimum values for significance of the t statistic based on the number of subjects in the calculation (more technically, the degrees of freedom, which is the total number of subjects minus the number of groups—in this case, 100 minus 2, or 98). If the computed value of t is larger than the critical value published in the table, the professor can reject the null hypothesis and conclude that the performance of the early morning class was significantly better than that of the afternoon class.

COMPLEX DESIGNS

Many research studies in psychology involve more complex designs than simple comparisons between two groups. They may contain three or more groups and evaluate the effects of more than one treatment or condition. This more complex evaluation of statistical significance is usually carried out through a procedure known as the analysis of variance (or F-test). Like the t-test, the F-test is calculated based on the size of the group differences, the sizes of the groups, and the standard deviation of the groups.

Other tests of statistical significance are available, and the choice of the appropriate technique is de-

termined by such factors as the kind of scale on which the data are measured, the number of groups, and whether one is interested in assessing a difference in performance or the relationship between subject characteristics. One should bear in mind, however, that statistical significance tests are only tools and that numbers can be deceptive. Even the best statistical analysis means nothing if a research study is designed poorly.

EVOLUTION OF PRACTICE

Tests of statistical significance have been important in psychological research since the early 1900's. Pioneers such as Sir Francis Galton, Karl Pearson, and Sir Ronald A. Fisher were instrumental in both developing and popularizing these methods. Galton was one of the first to recognize the importance of the normal distribution (the bell-shaped curve) for organizing psychological data. The properties of the normal distribution are the basis for many of the probabilistic judgments underlying inferential statistics. Pearson, strongly influenced by Galton's work, was able to develop the chi-squared goodness-of-fit test around 1900. This was the first test that enabled the determination of the probability of discrepancies between the observed number of occurrences of categories of phenomena and what would be expected by chance.

It was the publication of Fisher's book *Statistical Methods for Research Workers* in 1925, however, that popularized the method of hypothesis testing and the use of statistical significance tests. Through his book, Fisher was able to establish the 0.05 level of significance as the standard for scientific research. Fisher's second book, *The Design of Experiments* (1935), brought his theory of hypothesis testing to a wider audience, and he believed that he had developed the "perfectly rigorous" method of inductive inference. Among Fisher's accomplishments was the development of the method of analysis of variance for use with complex experimental designs (the F-test was named for Fisher). Before Fisher's work, the evaluation of whether the results of research were "significant" was based either on a simple "eyeballing" of the data or on an informal comparison of mean differences with standard deviations. Through the efforts of Fisher and some of his followers, hypothesis testing using statistical significance tests soon became an indispensable part of most scientific research. In particular, between 1940 and 1955, statistical methods became institutionalized in psychology during a period that has been called the inference revolution. Many researchers believed that these techniques provided scientific legitimacy to the study of otherwise abstract psychological constructs.

PROBLEMS WITH APPROACH

Some problems, however, have arisen with the statistical revolution in psychological research. For example, many researchers routinely misinterpret the meaning of rejecting the null hypothesis. Employing statistical significance tests can only tell the probability of the data, given the null hypothesis. It cannot tell the probability of a hypothesis (either the null or the alternative), given the data. These are two different conditional probabilities. Yet many researchers, and even some textbooks in psychology, claim that the level of significance specifies the probability that the null hypothesis is correct or the probability that the alternative hypothesis is wrong. Often the quality of research is measured by the level of significance, and researchers are often reluctant to submit, and journal editors reluctant to publish, research reports in which there was a failure to reject the null hypothesis. This tendency has led over the years to the publication of many statistically significant research results that have no practical significance and to the withholding by researchers of reports of worthwhile studies (that might have had practical significance) because of a failure to reject the null hypothesis.

Statistical significance tests are valuable techniques for the analysis of research results, but they must be applied correctly and analyzed properly to serve their intended function.

SOURCES FOR FURTHER STUDY

Aron, Arthur, Elaine N. Aron, and Elliot J. Coups. *Statistics for Psychology*. 5th ed. Upper Saddle River, N.J.: Pearson Prentice Hall, 2009. This textbook covers all aspects of statistics for psychology, including significance tests.

Howell, David C. *Fundamental Statistics for the Behavioral Sciences*. 6th ed. Belmont, Calif.: Thomson/Wadsworth, 2008. An excellent text designed for an introductory statistics course in the behavioral sciences. It emphasizes the logic of statistical procedures rather than their mathematical derivation.

Morrison, Denton E., and Ramon E. Henkel, eds. *The Significance Test Controversy: A Reader*. New Brunswick, N.J.: AldineTransaction, 2006. A collection of essays that discuss controversies surrounding the use of significance tests, including that valid research is sometimes thrown out, and attention is paid to statistically significant but useless results.

Rowntree, Derek. *Statistics Without Tears: A Primer for Non-mathematicians*. Boston: Pearson/A & B, 2004. An excellent introduction to the main concepts and terminology of statistics. Concepts are presented through words and diagrams rather than by means of formulas and equations.

Ziliak Stephen T., and Deirdre N. McCloskey. *The Cult of Statistical Significance: How the Standard Error Costs Us Jobs, Justice, and Lives*. Ann Arbor: University of Michigan Press, 2008. Ziliak and McCloskey criticize the widespread use of statistical significance, claiming that the tests to measure it are often in error and have replaced analytical thinking.

Oliver W. Hill, Jr.

SEE ALSO: Data description; Hypothesis development and testing; Qualitative research; Sampling; Scientific methods; Survey research: Questionnaires and interviews.

Stepfamilies

TYPE OF PSYCHOLOGY: Developmental psychology; social psychology

FIELDS OF STUDY: Adolescence; coping; infancy and childhood; interpersonal relations; stress and illness

Stepfamilies, created when adults with children marry, remarry, or cohabit, constitute a family form that differs in several ways from the nuclear family. Children in stepfamilies may evidence different levels of social adjustment than children in nuclear families, and there are several perspectives to understand these differences.

KEY CONCEPTS

- child abuse
- developmental stages
- effects on stepchildren
- family system perspective

- family stress perspectives
- nuclear families
- parenting
- stepparent/parent involvement or style rationales

INTRODUCTION

Social scientists have coined a number of terms for the new social unit that is created when adults with children marry, remarry, or cohabit and form a new family: stepfamilies, blended families, binuclear families, remarried families, subsequent families, and reconstituted families. Historically, there has been some social stigma attached to these terms, and some scholars believe that any structure other than the nuclear family is deficient. Other scholars note the increasing number of stepfamilies and the challenges faced by stepfamilies as they suggest constructive and therapeutic means to assist them.

According to the U.S. Bureau of the Census, nearly one-half of marriages each year in the United States involve a remarriage for one or both parties. Slightly more than half of all divorces involve children under the age of eighteen. Approximately 75 percent of divorced people remarry, on average within four years of the divorce, with 30 percent remarried within one year. The result is that approximately 15 percent of children live with a parent and a stepparent, and about one child in three will live with a stepparent at some point before age nineteen. Patterns of marriage, divorce, and remarriage vary by race, ethnicity, and gender. For example, African Americans and Latinos remarry at lower rates than whites. Some groups are more likely to cohabit than remarry after divorce, but this still introduces a new partner into the family dynamic. Stepfamilies also include never-married parents who later marry a person who is not the child's biological parent. Finally, approximately half of all women in remarriages give birth to at least one child in the new relationship. Because of the variety of means of formation of these families, they are not a homogenous group; tremendous variations exist among stepfamilies.

EXPLANATORY MODELS

According to a review of the literature conducted by Marilyn Coleman, Lawrence H. Ganong, and Mark A. Fine of the University of Missouri, the primary models for understanding stepfamily issues and effects on children include family stress perspectives

and stepparent/parent involvement or style rationales. Other scholars note the importance of the developmental stages of the stepfamily and the entire family system perspective.

Family stress models focus on the changes and transitions faced by stepfamilies, such as moving into a different home, learning new rules and routines, and adapting to new family members. These challenges may increase levels of distress, reduce parenting competencies, or result in more conflict in stepfamilies than in nuclear families. The age of children in stepfamilies may affect the amount of conflict, because studies show that adolescent stepchildren report more conflict with stepparents than adolescents in nuclear families.

Stepparent/parent involvement or style models suggest that biological parents and stepparents may have less time and energy to devote to interactions with stepfamily children because they need to devote those resources to building the new marital relationship or to their children from prior relationships. This is illustrated in the fact that the parents in stepfamilies spend less time with their children on schoolwork and school activities than parents in nuclear families, sometimes resulting in lower academic achievement and behavior problems. Research consistently finds that stepparents interact with their stepchildren less than the biological parents do, and that stepparents are more disengaged and show less affection to stepchildren. The role of genetic relationship to children is understood to affect parenting style, but it is also a major explanation for the fact that children who reside in a household with an adult who is not their biological parent are more at risk for physical and sexual abuse than children who live in a nuclear household. However, research does not show clearly that the stepparent always commits the abuse; it may be committed by another adult, such as a step-grandparent. It is clear that the same types of authoritative parenting processes, such as warmth and control, which are positive in other types of families, are effective styles in stepfamilies.

Fine and Lawrence A. Kurdek note that stepfamilies evolve through several developmental stages: dating and courtship with the eventual spouse, cohabitation (more likely in remarriage situations, but may not occur), early remarriage (the first two years), middle remarriage (two to five years), and late remarriage (over five years). They suggest that premarital relations between the adults who will marry establish the foundation and procedures for later definition of roles and relationships in the stepfamily. The early stage often focuses on management of the transitions and stress of remarriage, while the middle stage concentrates on relationship issues and achieving family consensus about roles.

The family system perspective views the stepfamily as an interactive system in which all members mutually influence each other regarding emotions, relations, and behavior. The system is understood to include people who do not live in the stepfamily household, such as the noncustodial biological parent, the new spouse of the noncustodial parent, or siblings who live with the other parent. This perspective recognizes real-life implications of the complex factors influencing stepfamily relations.

EFFECTS ON STEPCHILDREN

Research on children in stepfamilies has demonstrated a number of differences between them and children in first-marriage families. In academics, stepchildren on average had lower grades, lower scores on achievement tests, lower school attendance, higher drop-out rates, and greater likelihood to receive a General Education Degree (GED) rather than to graduate from high school. Regarding conduct, stepchildren were more likely to have problems with drugs and alcohol, to have sexual relations or conceive a child outside of marriage, and to be arrested. In emotional adjustment, stepchildren on average evidence more emotional problems. However, it is important to recognize that the differences found in the research were relatively small. Many stepchildren do not have conduct or emotional problems, and they do well in school. More research is needed to determine what factors lead to success and positive adjustment.

Psychologist James H. Bray at Baylor College of Medicine conducted research with stepchildren at three periods after remarriage: six months, two and a half years, and five to seven years. He found that children often experience a period of calm and apparent adjustment to the divorce and remarriage prior to a new eruption of problems during adolescence. He suggests that the adolescent task of achieving autonomy and individuality may be complicated by the absence of one biological parent. Many adolescents in stepfamilies experience a renewed interest in their noncustodial parent and about 20 percent of adolescents changed residence from their mother's to their father's home. These findings may indicate that it is especially difficult to create a stepfamily when one or more children are adolescents. Bray notes that young children accept stepparents more rapidly than do adolescents.

Sociologist Jean Giles-Sims researched the literature on child abuse in stepfamilies and found that a higher percentage of stepchildren than children from nuclear families are included in severe cases of abuse that have been reported and confirmed. She warns against the assumption that all stepchildren are at risk, however, and notes that further research must be conducted to determine the specific factors that contribute to the likelihood of abuse in some stepfamilies.

PARENTING IN STEPFAMILIES

Researchers report that parenting in stepfamilies is difficult and stressful. Certain conditions improve the interaction with biological children and stepchildren in the stepfamily. First, it is important to recognize the developmental stage of the stepfamily and the children. At the beginning of stepfamily formation, even positive, normally successful parenting behaviors may be rejected by stepchildren. Emily B. Visher and John S. Visher, founders of the Stepfamily Association of America, recommend that stepparents build a friendly relationship with stepchildren before focusing on discipline. After a positive, nurturing relationship is established over several months, discipline is more likely to be accepted and respected. However, Bray notes that children and stepparents may define friendly affection differently. Children in stepfamilies report that they prefer praise and compliments to hugs and embraces as signs of affection.

Biological parents may have a difficult time with child discipline by the stepparent, even when the biological parent has encouraged the stepparent to be involved. Loyalty to one's own children may create a reaction to discipline from the new spouse. Visher and Visher suggest that the biological parent may need to be the primary disciplinarian initially, but that both adults do need to support each other's authority in the household. However, stepparenting that is too strict or lacking in warmth is consistently connected with more behavior problems and poorer social adjustment in children, no matter how long the remarriage has been in place.

OTHER ISSUES

Several other issues are noted in the literature on stepfamilies as common occurrences. Difficulties between the former spouses (biological parents) after one or both have remarried may complicate the functioning of the stepfamily. Visitation with the noncustodial parent or lack of consistent visitation may cause tensions and loyalty problems for children. Child support payments or lack of payment of prescribed child support can cause conflict with the former spouse or marital tension in the new relationship.

Stepsibling relationships may also complicate stepfamily life. Problems may occur if there is too much conflict between stepbrothers and stepsisters, or if adolescent stepsiblings experience sexual attraction or engage in sexual behavior toward each other.

Finally, the lack of clear role definitions for stepfamily members in American society appears to complicate the formation and conduct of stepfamilies. The most common difficulty is the attempt to superimpose roles and understandings from the nuclear onto the stepfamily. Clinicians such as the Vishers suggest that open discussion and dialog about expectations are important in stepfamilies to avoid misperceptions and missed expectations.

SOURCES FOR FURTHER STUDY

Coleman, Marilyn, Lawrence H. Ganong, and Mark A. Fine. "Reinvestigating Remarriage: Another Decade of Progress." *Journal of Marriage and the Family* 62 (2000): 1288-1307. This article provides a review of research during the 1990's on stepfamilies. It summarizes key ideas and trends and provides a thorough reference list.

Ganong, Lawrence H., and Marilyn Coleman. *Stepfamily Relationships: Development, Dynamics, and Interventions.* New York: Kluwer Academic/Plenum Publishers, 2004. A comprehensive, multidisciplinary text that examines the variety of relationships within step-households as well as between households, focusing on internal family dynamics while maintaining a cultural and historical viewpoint. Includes minority and gay and lesbian stepfamilies in its discussion.

Lofas, Jeannette. *Family Rules: Helping Stepfamilies and Single Parents Build Happy Homes.* New York: Kensington Books, 1998. A practical guide to forming stepfamilies and single-parent families that looks at family life within a nontraditional structure.

Pryor, Jan, ed. *The International Handbook of Stepfamilies: Policy and Practice in Legal, Research, and Clinical Environments.* Hoboken, N.J.: Wiley, 2008. This international perspective on stepfamilies looks at the internal dynamics, outside influences, and clinical and legal issues.

Stewart, Susan D. *Brave New Stepfamilies: Diverse Paths Toward Stepfamily Living.* Thousand Oaks: Sage Publications, 2007. An examination of the demographics that created stepfamilies, their various forms, and relationshps among their members. Includes stepfamilies created by cohabitation and gay and lesbian stepfamilies.

Mark Stanton

SEE ALSO: Family life: Adult issues; Family life: Children's issues; Father-child relationship; Mother-child relationship; Parental alienation syndrome; Parenting styles; Separation and divorce: Adult issues; Separation and divorce: Children's issues; Sibling relationships.

Stimulant medications

DATE: 1960's forward

TYPE OF PSYCHOLOGY: Biological bases of behavior; cognition; developmental psychology; emotion; learning; psychopathology

FIELDS OF STUDY: Adolescence; adulthood; attitudes and behavior; biological influences on learning; biological treatments; childhood and adolescent disorders; cognitive learning; cognitive processes

Stimulant medications are one of two classes of medications used in the treatment of attentional disorders (the other is antidepressants). They work by stimulating the parts of the brain that inhibit perceived incoming stimuli and process outgoing stimuli, in effect, slowing the brain so that focus, attention, and mood reactivity are improved.

KEY CONCEPTS

- attention-deficit hyperactivity disorder (ADHD)
- controlled substance
- executive mental functions
- hyperactivity
- impulsivity

INTRODUCTION

In 1937, Rhode Island psychiatrist Charles Bradley first used stimulant medication in controlling behavioral disturbances in children with brain injuries. Stimulants, which are controlled substances (drugs listed on the U.S. Government's Schedule of Controlled Substances and that have abuse potential), are now used to treat a range of conditions including cancer-related fatigue, cocaine abuse, geriatric anorexia, geriatric failure to thrive, narcolepsy, prescription drug abuse, sleep-disordered chronic obstructive pulmonary disease (COPD), and Tourette's syndrome. Their primary use is for treating attention-deficit hyperactivity disorder (ADHD/ADD). In the 1960's, multiple placebo-controlled trials showed that two stimulants, methylphenidate

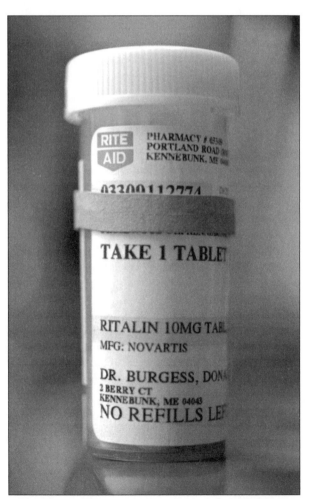

Ritalin is commonly used to treat attention-deficit hyperactivity disorder. (AP/Wide World Photos)

(later marketed in varying formulations as Concerta, Daytrana, Metadate, Methylin, and Ritalin), and dextroamphetamine (later marketed in varying formulations as Adderall and Dexedrine) were able to successfully control impulsivity, inattention, and hyperactivity in children suspected of having a condition then called "minimal brain dysfunction." Use of stimulants increased sharply from the late 1980's until the mid-1990's with steady increase afterward until 2002, after which use has remained stable. Of the 4.4 million children between the ages of four and seventeen diagnosed with ADHD in the United States, 2.5 million (56 percent) are prescribed a stimulant medication to help treat the condition. Though it is well established that ADD is chronic, with symptoms becoming problematic by age nine and continuing throughout adulthood, actual use of the medication often does not go beyond the first year it is prescribed, and a majority stop taking it all together by midadolescence—even though symptoms persist. Often, at the same time that the prescribed use of stimulants tapers off, illicit use of stimulants grows among secondary and college-age students. As many as one in four college students admits to having taken prescription stimulant medications illicitly for either academic or recreational purposes. Only alcohol and marijuana are more widely used.

CLINICAL USE

The term "stimulant" is counterintuitive, especially as people with ADHD are generally seen as being overstimulated. The action of this class of medication, however, is in its stimulating the parts of the brain that are involved with inhibition, control, and delay. These inhibitory circuits are underactive in people with ADHD. They have difficulty controlling how much and how fast external stimuli enters the brain, and therefore their attention shifts quickly to the next perceived stimulus, making it hard to stay on track. In ADHD, the brain is constantly, almost randomly, shifting tracks so that the person finds it hard to sustain focus and see tasks, thoughts, and even conversations through to the end. Massachusetts psychiatrist Edward Hallowell compares the action of stimulant medications in the brains of persons with ADHD to applying (stimulating) the brakes on a car, allowing the driver to be in control of the vehicle. In treating ADHD, stimulants work about 80 percent of the time, and they work well in about 80 percent of those people. So, roughly six out of ten people will experience major benefit from trying a stimulant medication, although stimulant medication alone should not be the sole treatment for ADHD. Mental focus and mental executive functions (the cognitive brain functions responsible for sequential reasoning, ordering and prioritization of information, planning, and tracking intellectual stimuli) improve without added effort. Planning, organizing, sequencing, and tracking are made much easier.

In addition to improved mental focus, people with ADHD who receive stimulant medications generally experience improved occupational, educational, and social performance. People experience greater self-satisfaction with their work and interactions and receive less negative feedback and reactions from others. Stimulants make these people easier to talk to and work with; interactions require less effort on everyone's part. People with ADHD are less irritating to others and become less irritable themselves. Ironic as it may seem, stimulants produce patience and greater interactive calm with greater productivity—again, all with less effort than previously. Most patients taking prescription stimulants report that they are more centered and more productive while feeling more relaxed and less intense. Despite these benefits, people should not take stimulant medications until they feel comfortable doing so.

For reasons that remain elusive, some people who do not respond well to a stimulant such as Ritalin can respond well to a different one such as Adderall. It is common for patients to have to try two or more medications (or different formulations of the same one) before they find the one that works best for them.

Because compliance (taking medication as prescribed) drops off as the number of doses per day increases, most patients are put on a long-acting version of a stimulant. The medications that carry the designation LA (long-acting) or XR (extended release) are consumed whole, with the effect sometimes occurring within the first twenty minutes. The outer shell dissolves, releasing stimulant into the bloodstream. The inner portion of the capsule slowly releases more stimulant as it continues to dissolve. These longer-lasting stimulants remain neuron-active from eight to twelve hours, with different individuals metabolizing the medication at different rates.

Side Effects

Most patients using stimulants experience a decrease in hunger, although these medications should not be used for weight control. For this reason, they should be taken while eating or right after a meal. Concerns about this class of medication stunting growth have grown out of anecdotal accounts of children, usually taking Ritalin, who stopped eating and consequently lost weight and stopped growing. A couple of studies have shown actual differences in children's weight and body mass. Following an at-breakfast or right-after-breakfast regimen avoids this potential.

Uncommonly, stimulants can produce tension, anxiety, and temper outbursts. These side effects often spontaneously remit but should be addressed by the prescribing health care provider who will usually be a pediatrician, family physician, or psychiatrist.

The beneficial effects of improved attention and focus are harmful for getting to sleep. For this reason, those patients with a typical day-night schedule should not take a longer-lasting stimulant after noon.

Another side effect can occur when the medicines reach the end of their effective half-life: rebound. As the benefits wear off, some people experience a re-emergence of symptoms, a rebound. They can even experience greater inattention, irritability, or restlessness than usual. Nearly all these patients can avoid, or at least lessen, rebound through the use of longer-acting stimulants. When these medicines are used and rebound does occur, it occurs less intensely and lasts for a shorter time.

Conclusion

Stimulant medications are the first line, though not the only, therapy for treating ADHD. They have been shown to increase intelligence quotient (IQ); improve academic, social, and job performance; reduce absenteeism, and for the vast majority of patients, improve their sense of self-mastery, interpersonal connectedness, and quality of life.

Sources for Further Study

Hallowell, Edward M., and John J. Ratey. *Delivered from Distraction: Getting the Most Out of Life with Attention Deficit Disorder.* New York: Ballantine, 2005. The sequel to the psychiatrist-authors' *Driven to Distraction* (1995), this is a clear, lucid, well-researched, balanced, and most of all, hopeful work on ADHD that is useful for adults with

ADHD or parents of children with the disorder. Presents the benefits and risks of stimulant medications with clear descriptions of how they work.

Ratey, John J. *A User's Guide to the Brain: Perception, Attention, and the Four Theaters of the Brain.* New York: Random House, 2002. This professor of psychiatry at Harvard describes the structure and chemistry of the brain, how it responds to the conscious use of its owner, and why stimulants work in the brain the way they do.

Richardson, Wendy. *AD/HD and Stimulant Medication Abuse.* Pottstown, Pa.: Attention Deficit Disorder Association, 2005. Presents factual and clinical considerations in the growing use of stimulants as recreational and addictive drugs.

Watkins, Carol. *Stimulant Medication and ADHD.* Baltimore: Northern County Psychiatric Associates, 2004. Helpful fact sheet presenting a thorough overview of the role stimulants can play in managing ADHD.

Paul Moglia, Saima Ahmed,
and Muhammad Usman Majeed

SEE ALSO: Attention-deficit hyperactivity disorder; Caffeine and mental health; Childhood disorders; Psychopharmacology; Substance use disorders.

Strategic family therapy

TYPE OF PSYCHOLOGY: Psychotherapy
FIELD OF STUDY: Group and family therapies

Strategic theory and interventions have been highly influential in the founding of modern family therapy. Strategic family therapy focuses on influencing family members by carefully planned interventions and the issuance of directives for resolving problems. At times, these directives may appear to be in direct opposition to the goals of treatment (an approach referred to as paradox). Strategic therapy is one of the most widely studied, taught, and emulated approaches to treating family (and individual) dysfunction.

KEY CONCEPTS
- agoraphobia
- double bind
- paradoxical intervention
- reframing
- restraining strategies
- symptom prescription

INTRODUCTION

Families engage in complex interactional sequences that involve both verbal and nonverbal (for example, gestures, posture, intonation, volume) patterns of communication. Family members continually send and receive complicated messages. Strategic family approaches are designed to alter psychological difficulties that emerge from problematic interactions between individuals. Specifically, strategic therapists view individual problems (for example, depression, anxiety) as manifestations of disturbances in the family. Psychological symptoms are seen as the consequences of misguided attempts at changing an existing disturbance. For example, concerned family members may attempt to "protect" an agoraphobic patient from anxiety by rearranging activities and outings so that the patient is never left alone; unfortunately, these efforts serve only to foster greater dependency, teach avoidant behaviors, and maintain agoraphobic symptoms. From a strategic viewpoint, symptoms are regarded as communicative in nature. That is, symptoms have distinct meanings within families and usually appear when a family member feels trapped and cannot break out of the situation via nonsymptomatic ways.

COMMUNICATION MODELS

The strategic model views all behavior as an attempt to communicate. In fact, it is impossible not to communicate, just as it is impossible not to act. For example, adolescents who run away from home send a message to their parents; similarly, the parents communicate different messages in terms of how they react. Frequently, the intended message behind these nonverbal forms of communication is difficult for family members to discern. Moreover, when contradictions appear between verbal and nonverbal messages, communication can become incongruent and clouded by mixed messages.

Gregory Bateson, who was trained as an anthropologist and developed much of the early theory behind strategic approaches, worked with other theorists to develop the double-bind theory of schizophrenia. A double-bind message is a particularly problematic form of mixed communication that occurs when a family member sends two messages, requests, or commands that are logically inconsistent, contradictory, or impossible. For example, problems arise when messages at the content level ("I love you" or "Stay close to me") conflict with nonverbal messages at another level ("I despise you" or "Keep your distance"). Eventually, it is argued, a child who is continually exposed to this mixed style of communication, that is, a "no-win" dilemma, may feel angry, helpless, and fearful, and may respond by withdrawing.

Since Bateson's early work in communication theory and therapy, the strategic approach has undergone considerable revision. At least three divisions of strategic family therapy are frequently cited: the original interactional view of the Mental Research Institute (MRI) of Palo Alto, California; the strategic approach advocated by therapists Jay Haley and Cloe Madanes, and the Milan systemic family therapy model. There is considerable overlap among these approaches, and the therapy tactics are generally similar.

FAMILY THERAPY TYPES

The MRI interactional family therapy approach shares a common theoretical foundation with the other strategic approaches. In addition to Bateson, some of the prominent therapists who have been associated with the institute at one time or another are Don Jackson, Haley, Virginia Satir, and Paul Watzlawick. As modified by Watzlawick's writings, including *The Invented Reality* (1984), the MRI model emphasizes that patients' attempts to solve problems often maintain or exacerbate difficulties. Problems may arise when the family either overreacts or underreacts to events. For example, ordinary life difficulties or transitions (for example, a child beginning school, an adult dealing with new work assignments) may be associated with family overreactions. Similarly, significant problems may be treated as no particular problem. The failure to handle such events in a constructive manner within the family system eventually leads to the problem taking on proportions and characteristics that may seem to have little similarity to the original difficulty. During family therapy, the MRI approach employs a step-by-step progression of suggested strategies toward the elimination of a symptom. Paradoxical procedures represent a mainstay of the MRI approach.

Haley and Madanes's approach to strategic family therapy argues that change occurs through the process of the family carrying out assignments (to be completed outside therapy) issued by the therapist. As described in Madanes's *Strategic Family Therapy* (1981), strategic therapists attempt to design a therapeutic strategy for each specific problem. Instead of "suggesting" strategies, as in the MRI approach, therapists issue directives that are designed deliberately to shift the organization of the family to resolve the presenting problem. Problems are viewed as serving a function in the family and always involve at least two or three individuals. As detailed in Haley's *Leaving Home: The Therapy of Disturbed Young People* (1980) and *Ordeal Therapy: Unusual Ways to Change Behavior* (1984), treatment includes intense involvement, carefully planned interventions designed to reach clear goals, frequent use of therapist-generated directives or assignments, and paradoxical procedures.

The Milan systemic family therapy model is easily distinguished from other strategic approaches because of its unique spacing of therapeutic sessions and innovative team approach to treatment. The original work of therapists Mara Selvini-Palazzoli, Luigi Boscolo, Gianfranco Cecchin, and Guiliana Prata has been described as "long brief" family therapy and was used to treat a wide variety of severe problems such as anorexia and schizophrenia. The first detailed description of the Milan group's approach was written by the four founding therapists and called *Paradox and Counterparadox: A New Model in the Therapy of the Family in Schizophrenic Transition* (1978). The original Milan approach incorporated monthly sessions for approximately one year. The unusual spacing of sessions was originally scheduled because many of the families seen in treatment traveled hundreds of miles by train to receive therapy. Later, however, the Milan group decided that many of their interventions, including paradox, required considerable time to work. Thus, they continued the long brief model. Another distinguishing factor of the Milan group was its use of therapist-observer teams who watched treatment sessions from behind a two-way mirror. From time to time, the therapist observers would request that the family therapist interrupt the session to confer about the treatment process. Following this discussion, the family therapist would rejoin the session and initiate interventions, including paradox, as discussed by the team of therapist observers who remained behind the mirror. In 1980, the four originators of the Milan group divided into two smaller groups (Boscolo and Cecchin; Selvini-Palazzoli and Prata). Shortly thereafter, Selvini-Palazzoli and Prata continued pursuing family research separately. The work of Boscolo and Cecchin is described in *Milan Systemic Family Therapy* (1987), while Selvini-Palazzoli's work is presented in *Family Games* (1989), which she wrote with several new colleagues.

THE IMPORTANCE OF FAMILY

Haley argued that conventional mental health approaches were not providing effective treatment. Based on his work with schizophrenics, he observed that patients typically would improve during their hospitalizations, return home, and then quickly suffer relapses. He also suggested that if the patient did improve while away from the hospital, then a family crisis would often ensue, resulting in the patient's eventual rehospitalization. Thus, effective treatment from a strategic framework often required family members to weather crises and alter family patterns of communication so that constructive change could occur.

Related to Haley's work with hospitalized patients was his treatment of "disturbed" young adults who exhibited bizarre behavior, continually took illegal drugs, or both. In *Leaving Home: The Therapy of Disturbed Young People* (1997), Haley suggests that it is best to assume that the problem is not an individual problem, but a problem of the family and the young person separating from each other. That is, young adults typically leave home as they succeed in work, school, or career and form other intimate relationships. Some families, however, become unstable, dysfunctional, or distressed as the son or daughter attempts to leave. To regain family stability, the young adult may fail in attempts to leave home (often via abnormal behavior). Furthermore, if the family organization does not shift, then the young adult may be destined to fail over and over again.

Haley's approach to treating such cases includes several stages of strategic therapy. First, the entire family attends the initial interview, and the parents are put in charge of solving their child's problems. During treatment, the parents are told that they are the best therapists for their child's problems. Because the family is assumed to be in conflict (as shown by the patient's problems), requiring the

family to take charge and become active in the treatment of the identified patient allows for greater opportunities to intervene around the conflict. In particular, it is assumed that the hierarchy of the family is in confusion and that the parents must take an active role in shifting the family's organization. Also, all family members are encouraged to adopt a position in which they expect the identified patient's problems to become normal.

As the identified patient improves, the family will often experience a crisis and become unstable again. A relapse of the identified patient would follow the usual sequence for the family and return stability (and familiarity) to the system. Unfortunately, a relapse would only serve to perpetuate the dysfunction. Therefore, the therapist may further assist the family by dealing with concerns such as parental conflicts and fears, or attempt to assist the young adult by providing opportunities away from therapy sessions that foster continued growth. Eventually, termination is planned, based on the belief that treatment does not require the resolution of all family problems, but instead those centered on the young adult.

PARADOXICAL PROCEDURES

Strategic therapists share a common belief in the utility of paradoxical procedures. In fact, the history of modern paradoxical psychotherapy is frequently credited as beginning with the MRI group, although paradoxical techniques have been discussed by various theorists from other orientations. Paradox refers to a contradiction or an apparent inconsistency that defies logical deduction. That is, strategic paradox is employed as a means of altering behavior through the use of strategies in apparent opposition to treatment goals. The need for paradoxical procedures is based on the assumption that families are very resistant to change and frequently attempt to disrupt the therapist's effort to help them. Thus, if the therapist suggests common therapeutic tactics (for example, communication homework, parenting suggestions), then the family may resist (for example, may "forget" to do the homework, sabotaging the exercise) and fail to improve. On the other hand, if the therapist tells the family to do what they are already doing, then the family may resist by getting better.

A variety of explanations have been offered to explain the manner in which paradox works. In *Change:*

Principles of Problem Formation and Problem Resolution (1974), written by Watzlawick and his colleagues, paradox is described as producing a special type of change among family members. That is, there are two levels of change: first-order and second-order change. First-order change is change within a family system (for example, a parent increasing punishment as the child's behavior becomes more disruptive). First-order change is typically conducted in a step-by-step fashion and involves the uses of problem-solving strategies. On the other hand, second-order change refers to changing the family system itself, and it typically occurs in a sudden and radical manner. The therapist attempts to change the system by unexpected, illogical, or abrupt methods. Paradoxical procedures are designed to effect second-order change. A paradoxical approach might be to encourage the child to act out every time he or she believes that the parents are about to have a fight. In such a case, the family system may be transformed by family members receiving important feedback about the manner in which they operate, by increased understanding of one another's impact on the system, and by efforts to discard "old family rules" by initiating new procedures for effective family living.

Several different classes of paradoxical interventions are highlighted in Gerald Weeks and Luciano L'Abate's book *Paradoxical Psychotherapy: Theory and Practice with Individuals, Couples, and Families* (1982). These include reframing, prescribing the symptom, and restraining.

REFRAMING, RESTRAINING, AND RELAPSING

Reframing refers to providing an alternative meaning or viewpoint to explain an event. A common example of reframing is Tom Sawyer, who described the boredom of whitewashing a fence as pleasurable and collected cash from his peers for the opportunity to assist him. Reframing provides a new framework from which to evaluate interactions (for example, "Mom is smothering" versus "Mom is caring and concerned").

Prescribing the symptom refers to encouraging or instructing patients to engage in the behavior that is to be eliminated or altered. Symptom prescription is the most common form of paradox in the family therapy literature. Following the presentation of an appropriate rationale to the family (for example, to gain more assessment information), the therapist offers a paradoxical instruction to the family, typically as part of the week's homework. For example, a child who frequently throws temper tantrums may be specifically instructed to engage in tantrums, but only in certain locations at scheduled times. Another common use of paradox involves symptom prescription for insomniacs. A patient with onset insomnia (difficulty falling asleep) may be encouraged to remain awake to become more aware of his or her thoughts and feelings before falling asleep. As might be guessed, anxiety is often associated with onset insomnia, and such an intervention serves to decrease anxiety about failing to fall asleep by introducing the idea that the patient is supposed to stay awake. Frequently, patients describe difficulty completing the homework because they "keep falling asleep too quickly."

Restraining strategies include attempts to discourage, restrain, or even deny the possibility of change; the therapist might say, "Go slow," "The situation appears hopeless," or "Don't change." The basis for restraining strategies is the belief that many patients may not wish to change. Why would patients seek treatment and spend money toward that end if they do not wish to improve? All change involves risk, and with risk comes danger or uncertainty. Moreover, the future may be less predictable following change. In fact, it is possible to conceive of most recurring patterns of family dysfunction or individual difficulties as a heavy overcoat. At times, the heavy overcoat serves a useful purpose by protecting one from harsh weather. As time passes, however, the overcoat becomes uncomfortable as the weather becomes warmer. Still, many people dread taking off the overcoat because they are used to it, it has become familiar, and the future seems uncertain without it. From the patient's viewpoint, discomfort may be more acceptable than change (and the uncertainty it brings).

Perhaps the most common restraining strategy is predicting a relapse. In predicting a relapse, the patient is told that a previous problem or symptom will reappear. By so doing, the therapist is in a no-lose situation. If the problem reappears, then it was predicted successfully by the therapist, is understood by the therapist, and can be dealt with by the therapist and patient. If the problem does not reappear, then the problem is being effectively controlled by the patient.

THEORETICAL EVOLUTION

Strategic approaches, based on communication theories, developed from research conducted at the Mental Research Institute in the 1950's. In contrast to psychodynamic approaches, which emphasize the importance of past history, trauma, and inner conflicts, strategic therapies highlight the importance of the "here and now" and view psychological difficulties as emerging from problematic interactions between individuals (family members or married partners). Moreover, strategic therapists tend to follow a brief model of treatment, in contrast to many individual and family therapy approaches.

The effectiveness of family therapy approaches, including strategic approaches, is difficult to measure. Although there has been a clear increase in research evaluating the efficacy of family interventions since about 1980, the results are less than clear because of difficulties with research methodologies and diverse research populations. For example, psychodynamic therapists prefer to use case studies rather than experimental designs to determine effectiveness. Strategic therapists have conducted only a handful of research studies, but these results are encouraging. A structural-strategic approach developed by psychologist M. Duncan Stanton has demonstrated effectiveness in the treatment of drug abuse. Also, the Milan approach has been found to be effective for a variety of problems identified by families who participated in a three-year research program. Further research is warranted, however, before definitive conclusions about the empirical effectiveness of strategic approaches can be reached.

SOURCES FOR FURTHER STUDY

Goldenberg, Herbert, and Irene Goldenberg. *Family Therapy: An Overview*. 7th ed. Belmont, Calif.: Thomson Brooks/Cole, 2008. An updated review of the major family therapy approaches, including strategic family therapy. Also provides a background on family development, and highlights issues in family therapy research and training.

Haley, Jay, and Madeleine Richeport-Haley. *Directive Family Therapy*. New York: Haworth Press, 2007. Haley was one of the foremost theorists and therapists in strategic approaches. This work contains chapters on the many stages of life, from birth, raising kids, leaving home, couples, and retirement and aging.

Lebow, Jay L., ed. *Handbook of Clinical Family Therapy*. Hoboken, N.J.: John Wiley, 2005. Each chapter examines specific problems, the theoretical and practical elements of the treatment approach, recommended intervention strategies, special considerations, supporting research, and clinical examples.

Madanes, Cloe. *Strategic Family Therapy*. 1981. Reprint. San Francisco: Jossey-Bass, 1991. Provides an overview of strategic family therapy from one of the primary therapists in the field. Describes the philosophy and common approaches employed by strategic therapists in the treatment of a variety of presenting problems.

Weeks, Gerald R., ed. *Promoting Change Through Paradoxical Therapy*. Rev. ed. New York: Brunner/Mazel, 1991. Provides an overview of paradoxical approaches and details a variety of considerations in using paradox in treatment.

Gregory L. Wilson

SEE ALSO: Behavioral family therapy; Couples therapy; Family life: Adult issues; Family life: Children's issues; Observational learning and modeling therapies; Parenting styles; Play therapy; Psychotherapy: Children; Satir, Virginia; Separation and divorce: Adult issues; Separation and divorce: Children's issues.

Stress
Behavioral and psychological responses

TYPE OF PSYCHOLOGY: Stress
FIELDS OF STUDY: Coping; critical issues in stress; stress and illness

Stress is an adaptive reaction to circumstances that are perceived as threatening. It motivates people and can enhance performance. Learning to cope with adversity is an important aspect of normal psychological development, but exposure to chronic stress can have severe negative consequences if effective coping mechanisms are not learned.

KEY CONCEPTS
- circumplex model
- coping strategies
- daily hassles

- phobias
- state anxiety
- trait anxiety

INTRODUCTION

The term "stress" is used to designate how human beings respond when they confront circumstances that they view as dangerous or threatening and that tax their coping capability. Stressful events (stressors) elicit a wide range of responses in humans. They not only bring about immediate physiological changes but also affect people's emotional state, the use of their intellectual abilities, their efficiency at solving problems, and their social behavior. When experiencing stress, people take steps to do something about the stressors eliciting the stress and to manage the emotional upset they are producing. These maneuvers are called coping responses. Coping is a key concept in the study of the stress process. Stress management intervention techniques are designed to teach people appropriate ways to cope with the stressors that they encounter in their everyday lives.

ANXIETY AND PHOBIAS

The emotional state most directly affected by stress is anxiety. In fact, the term "state anxiety" is often used interchangeably with the terms "fear" and "stress" to denote a transitory emotional reaction to a dangerous situation. Stress, fear, and state anxiety are distinguished from trait anxiety, which is conceptualized as a relatively stable personality disposition or trait. According to psychologist Charles Spielberger, people high in trait or "chronic" anxiety interpret more situations as dangerous or threatening than do people who are low in trait anxiety, and they respond to them with more intense stress (state anxiety) reactions. Instruments that measure trait anxiety ask people to characterize how they usually feel, and therefore they measure how people characteristically respond to situations. Measures of trait anxiety (such as the trait anxiety scale of the State-Trait Anxiety Inventory) are especially useful in predicting whether people will experience high levels of stress in situations involving threats to self-esteem or threat of failure at evaluative tasks.

The two-dimensional circumplex model has been adopted for illustrating how emotion relates to stress. The activation-deactivation dimension of the circumplex relates to how much the emotion invokes a sense of alertness, energy, and mobilization, in contrast to the deactivation end of the continuum that connotes drowsiness and lethargy. The second dimension of the circumplex relates to the degree of

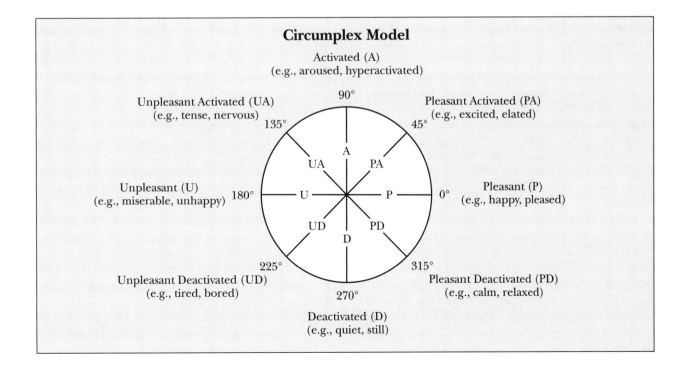

Circumplex Model

Activated (A)
(e.g., aroused, hyperactivated)

Unpleasant Activated (UA)
(e.g., tense, nervous)

Pleasant Activated (PA)
(e.g., excited, elated)

Unpleasant (U)
(e.g., miserable, unhappy)

Pleasant (P)
(e.g., happy, pleased)

Unpleasant Deactivated (UD)
(e.g., tired, bored)

Pleasant Deactivated (PD)
(e.g., calm, relaxed)

Deactivated (D)
(e.g., quiet, still)

pleasantness or unpleasantness associated with the emotion. For example, perceived stress and anxiety relate to unpleasant activation. In contrast, serenity is associated with deactivation and positive affect. Richard Lazarus has argued that the relational meaning of a stressful event determines the particular emotion associated with the event. For example, the relational meaning of anger is "a demeaning offense against me and mine." The relational meaning of anxiety is "facing an uncertain or existential threat." The relational meaning of fright is "facing an immediate, concrete, and overwhelming physical danger." Coping alters the emotion by either changing reality (problem-focused coping) or changing the interpretation of the event (emotion-focused coping).

Common phobias or fears of specific situations, however, especially when the perceived threat has a strong physical component, are not related to individual differences in general trait anxiety level. Measures of general trait anxiety are therefore not good predictors of people's stress levels when they are confronted by snakes, an impending surgical operation, or the threat of electric shock. Such fears can be reliably predicted only by scales designed to evaluate proneness to experience fear in these particular situations.

Seemingly minor events that are a constant source of irritation can be very stressful, as can more focalized events that require major and sometimes sudden readjustments. Psychologists Lazarus and Susan Folkman have dubbed these minor events "daily hassles." The media focus attention on disasters such as plane crashes, earthquakes, and epidemics that suddenly disrupt the lives of many people, or on particularly gruesome crimes or other occurrences that are likely to attract attention. For most people, however, much of the stress of daily life results from having to deal with ongoing problems pertaining to jobs, personal relationships, and everyday living circumstances.

People often have no actual experience of harm or unpleasantness regarding things that they come to fear. For example, most people are at least somewhat uneasy about flying on airplanes or about the prospect of having a nuclear power plant located near them, though few people have personally experienced harm caused by these things. Although people tend to pride themselves on how logical they are, they are often not very rational in appraising how dangerous or risky different events actually are. For example, there is great public concern about the safety of nuclear reactors, though they in fact have caused very few deaths. The same general public that smokes billions of cigarettes (a proved carcinogen and risk factor for heart disease), which cause more than 400,000 deaths per year, also supported banning an artificial sweetener because of a minuscule chance that it might cause cancer.

POSITIVE STRESS

People tend to think of stress as being uniformly negative—something to be avoided or at least minimized as much as possible. Psychologists Carolyn Aldwin and Daniel Stokols point out, however, that studies using both animals and humans have indicated that exposure to stress also has beneficial effects. Being handled is stressful for rats, but rats handled as infants are less fearful, are more exploratory, are faster learners, and have more robust immune systems later in life. In humans, physical stature as adults is greater in cultures that expose children to stress (for example, circumcision, scarification, and sleeping apart from parents) than in those that are careful to prevent stress exposure—even when nutrition, climate, and other relevant variables are taken into account. Although failure experiences in dealing with stressful circumstances can inhibit future ability to function under stress, success experiences enable learning of important coping and problem-solving skills that are then used to deal effectively with future stressful encounters. Such success experiences also promote a positive self-concept and induce a generalized sense of self-efficacy that in turn enhances persistence in coping with future stressors.

Psychologists Stephen M. Auerbach and Sandra E. Gramling note that stress is a normal, adaptive reaction to threat. It signals danger and prepares people to take defensive action. Over time, individuals learn which coping strategies are successful for them in particular situations. This is part of the normal process of personal growth and maturation. Stress can, however, cause psychological problems if the demands posed by stressors overwhelm a person's coping capabilities. If a sense of being overwhelmed and unable to control events persists over a period of time, a person's stress signaling system ceases to work in an adaptive way. The person then misreads and overinterprets the actual degree of threat posed by situations, makes poor decisions as to what coping strategies to use, and realizes that he or she is coping inefficiently; a cycle of increasing distress and ineffective coping may result. Some people who have experienced high-level stress for extended periods or who are attempting to deal with the aftereffects of traumatic stressors may become extremely socially withdrawn and show other signs of severe emotional dysfunction.

In severe cases in which these symptoms persist for over a month, a psychological condition known as post-traumatic stress disorder (PTSD) may develop. Common symptoms of PTSD include reliving the traumatic event, avoiding anything that reminds the person of the event, insomnia, nightmares, wariness, poor concentration, chronic irritability resulting in angry or aggressive outbursts, and a numbing of emotions. The symptom of numbing of emotions has been referred to as alexithymia, a condition in which people lack the ability to define and express their emotions to themselves and others. James W. Pennebaker believes that although alexithymics cannot express their emotions, their emotions are still present in an unconscious cycle of rumination; this suppression and rumination of negative thoughts is associated with increased psychological and physiological arousal. That is, it takes a lot of work to inhibit one's emotions.

Although anxiety is the most common emotion associated with stress, chronic stress may induce chronic negative emotions such as hostility and depression. Chronic hostility and depression have been shown to have damaging effects on social relationships and physical health. The known physical costs of chronic stress include poor immune functioning, not engaging in health-promoting activities (such as exercise and following the advice of a physician), and a shortened life expectancy.

When people are faced with a stressful circumstance that overwhelms their coping mechanisms, they may react with depression and a sense of defeat and hopelessness. According to Martin E. P. Seligman, learned helplessness is the result of a person coming to believe that events are uncontrollable or hopeless, and it often results in depression.

ASSESSING AND MEASURING STRESS
The fact that stress has both positive and negative effects can be exemplified in many ways. Interpersonally, stress brings out the "worst" and the "best"

in people. A greater incidence of negative social behaviors, including less altruism and cooperation and more aggression, has generally been observed in stressful circumstances. Psychologist Kent Bailey points out that, in addition to any learning influences, this may result from the fact that stress signals real or imagined threats to survival and is therefore a potent elicitor of regressive, self-serving survival behaviors. The highly publicized murder of Kitty Genovese in Queens, New York, in 1964, which was witnessed by thirty-eight people (from the safety of their apartments) who ignored her pleas for help, exemplifies this tendency, as does the behavior during World War II of many Europeans who either did not stand up for the Jews and other minorities who were oppressed by the Nazis or conveniently turned their heads. Everyone has heard, however, of selfless acts of individual heroism being performed by seemingly ordinary people who in emergency situations rose to the occasion and risked their own lives to save others. After the terrorist attack on the World Trade Center on September 11, 2001, firefighters continued to help victims and fight fires after more than two hundred of their fellow firefighters had been killed in the buildings' collapse. In addition, in stressful circumstances in which cooperation and altruism have survival value for all concerned, as in the wake of a natural disaster, helping-oriented activities and resource sharing are among the most common short-term reactions.

Stress may enhance as well as hinder performance. For example, the classic view of the relationship between stress and performance is represented in the Yerkes-Dodson inverted-U model, which posits that both low and high levels of arousal decrease performance, whereas intermediate levels enhance performance. Although this model has not been unequivocally validated, it seems to be at least partially correct, and its correctness may depend on the circumstances. On one hand, psychologists Gary Evans and Sheldon Cohen concluded that, in learning and performance tasks, high levels of stress result in reduced levels of working-memory capacity and clearly interfere with performance of tasks that require rapid detection, sustained attention, or attention to multiple sources of input. On the other hand, psychologist Spielberger found that in less complex tasks, as learning progresses, high stress levels may facilitate performance.

Psychologist Irving Janis examined the relationship between preoperative stress in surgical patients and how well they coped with the rigors of the postoperative convalescent period. He found that patients with moderate preoperative fear levels adjusted better after surgery than those with low or high preoperative fear. He reasoned that patients with moderate fear levels realistically appraised the situation, determined how they would deal with the stressful aspects of the recovery period, and thus were better able to tolerate those stressors. Patients low in preoperative fear engaged in unrealistic denial and thus were unprepared for the demands of the postoperative period, whereas those high in preoperative fear became overanxious and carried their inappropriately high stress levels over into the recovery period, in which that stress continued to inhibit them from realistically dealing with the demands of the situation. Janis further found that giving people information about what to expect before the surgery reduced their levels of fear and stress and allowed them to recover from surgery more quickly.

BENEFITS OF CONTROL

Research by Judith Rodin and others has shown that interventions designed to increase the predictability of and perceived control over a stressful event can have dramatic effects on stress and health. In one control-enhancing intervention study, nursing home residents were told by the hospital administrator to take responsibility for themselves, were asked to decide what activities to participate in, and were told what decisions were their responsibility to make. Patients who received the control-enhancing intervention reported being happier in the nursing home, and the death rate was half of that among nursing home residents who were told that it was the staff's responsibility to care for them. Rodin's research has been replicated by other researchers. More intensive stress reduction interventions have even been shown to increase survival rates among patients with breast cancer.

The negative effect of unrealistically low fear levels is also exemplified in the description by psychologists Walter Fenz and Seymour Epstein of two first-time sky divers who surprised everyone with their apparent total lack of concern during training and on the morning of their first jump. Their reactions changed dramatically, however, once they entered the aircraft. "One began vomiting, and the other developed a coarse tremor. Both pleaded for the air-

craft to be turned back. On leaving, they stated that they were giving up jumping."

Janis's investigation was particularly influential because it drew attention to the question of how psychologists can work with people to help them cope with impending stressful events, especially those (such as surgery) that they are committed to confronting and over which they have little control. Findings by psychologists Thomas Strentz and Auerbach indicate that in such situations it may be more useful to teach people emotion-focused coping strategies (those designed to minimize stress and physiological arousal directly) than problem-focused strategies (those designed to change the stressful situation itself). In a study with volunteers who were abducted and held hostage for four days in a stressful simulation, they found that hostages who were taught to use emotion-focused coping techniques (such as deep breathing, muscular relaxation, and directed fantasy) adjusted better and experienced lower stress levels than those who were taught problem-focused techniques (such as nonverbal communication, how to interact with captors, and how to gather intelligence).

In a series of studies, Pennebaker and others have found that writing for just twenty minutes a day for three or four consecutive days about the most stressful experience one has ever experienced has widespread beneficial effects that may last for several months. In a series of studies, he found that his writing task improved immune functioning, reduced illness and perceived stress, and even improved students' grade-point averages. He believes that his writing task may help people to release their inhibited emotions about past stressful events. This release of emotions decreases physiological arousal and psychological anxiety associated with repressing negative past events.

ADAPTIVE AND MALADAPTIVE FUNCTIONS

Stress has many important adaptive functions. The experience of stress and learning how to cope with adversity are essential aspects of normal growth and development. Coping strategies learned in particular situations must be generalized appropriately to new situations. Exposure to chronic stress that cannot be coped with effectively can have severe negative consequences. Work by pioneering stress researchers such as Hans Selye brought attention to the physiological changes produced by exposure to chronic stress, which contribute to diseases such as peptic ulcers, high blood pressure, and cardiovascular disorders. Subsequent research by psychiatrists Thomas Holmes and Richard Rahe and their colleagues indicated that exposure to a relatively large number of stressful life events is associated with the onset of other diseases, such as cancer and psychiatric disorders, which are less directly a function of arousal in specific physiological systems.

Studies by these researchers have led psychologists to try to understand how best to teach people to manage and cope with stress. Learning to cope with stress is a complex matter because, as Lazarus has emphasized, the stressfulness of given events is determined by how they are cognitively appraised, and this can vary considerably among individuals. Further, the source of stress may be in the past, the present, or the future. The prospect of an impending threatening encounter (such as a school exam) may evoke high-level stress, but people also experience stress when reflecting on past unpleasant or humiliating experiences or when dealing with an immediate, ongoing danger. Sometimes, people deal with past, present, and future stressors simultaneously.

It is important to distinguish among present, past, and future stressors, because psychological and behavioral responses to them differ, and different kinds of coping strategies are effective in dealing with them. For example, for stressors that may never occur but are so aversive that people want to avoid them if at all possible (for example, cancer or injury in an automobile accident), people engage in preventive coping behavior (they stop smoking, or they wear seat belts) even though they are not currently experiencing a high level of anxiety. In this kind of situation, an individual's anxiety level sometimes needs to be heightened to motivate coping behavior.

When known stressors are about to affect people (for example, a surgical operation the next morning), it is important for them to moderate their anxiety level so that they can function effectively when actually confronting the stressor. The situation is much different when they are trying to deal with a significant stressor (such as sexual assault, death of a loved one, or a war experience) that has already occurred but continues to cause emotional distress. Important aspects of coping with such stressors include conceptualizing one's response to the situation as normal and rational rather than "crazy" or inadequate, and reinstating the belief that one is in control of one's life and environment rather than subject to the whims of circumstance.

Sources for Further Study

Auerbach, Stephen M., and Sandra E. Gramling. *Stress Management: Psychological Foundations.* Upper Saddle River, N.J.: Prentice Hall, 1998. Examines what stress is and details effective coping strategies based on psychological theories.

Davis, Martha, Elizabeth Eshelman, and Matthew McKay. *The Relaxation and Stress Reduction Workbook.* 6th ed. Oakland, Calif.: New Harbinger, 2008. An overview of techniques used to reduce stress. Sections include body awareness, progressive relaxation, visualization, biofeedback, coping skills training, job stress management, and assertiveness training.

Greenberg, Jerrold S. *Comprehensive Stress Management.* 11th ed. New York: McGraw-Hill, 2009. Looks at what stress is and how it affects people, and contains numerous chapters on stress-reduction methods.

Janis, Irving Lester. *Stress and Frustration.* New York: Harcourt Brace Jovanovich, 1971. Describes some of Janis's early investigations evaluating relationships between stress and behavior. The focus is on his pioneering study evaluating the relationship between preoperative stress levels in surgical patients and their ability to adapt to the rigors of the postoperative convalescent period.

Monat, Alan, Richard S. Lazarus, and Gretchen Reevy, eds. *The Praeger Handbook on Stress and Coping.* Westport, Conn.: Praeger, 2007. In this manual on stress and coping strategies, Lazarus describes the link between emotion and stress in a section on the concept of stress. Other sections cover stress and illness (heart disease, gastrointestinal disorders, and depression) and post-traumatic stress (terrorism and violence).

Pennebaker, James W. *Opening Up: The Healing Power of Expressing Emotions.* Rev. ed. New York: Guilford Press, 1997. Presents evidence that personal self-disclosure not only benefits emotional health but also boosts physical health.

_____. *Writing to Heal: A Guided Journal for Recovering from Trauma and Emotional Upheaval.* Oakland, Calif.: New Harbinger, 2004. Explains how writing about problems can improve one's physical and psychological health.

Stephen M. Auerbach; updated by Todd Miller

SEE ALSO: Anxiety disorders; Biofeedback and relaxation; Bystander intervention; Coping: Strategies; Emotions; Fear; General adaptation syndrome; Learned helplessness; Meditation and relaxation; Phobias; Post-traumatic stress disorder; Seligman, Martin E. P.; Selye, Hans; State-Trait Anxiety Inventory (STAI); Stress: Physiological responses; Stress-related diseases; Type A behavior pattern.

Stress
Physiological responses

TYPE OF PSYCHOLOGY: Stress
FIELDS OF STUDY: Biology of stress; critical issues in stress; stress and illness

The human body contains a number of regulatory mechanisms that allow it to adapt to changing conditions. Stressful events produce characteristic physiological changes that are meant to enhance the likelihood of survival. Because these changes sometimes present a threat to health rather than serving a protective function, researchers seek to determine relations between stressors, their physiological effects, and subsequent health.

KEY CONCEPTS
- fight-or-flight response
- general adaptation syndrome
- homeostasis
- parasympathetic nervous system
- stress response
- stressor
- sympathetic nervous system

INTRODUCTION

Although the term "stress" is commonly used by the general population to refer to various responses to events that individuals find taxing, the concept involves much more. For centuries, scientific thinkers and philosophers have been interested in learning more about the interactions between the environment (stressful events), emotions, and the body. Much is now known about this interaction, although there is still much left to discover. In the late twentieth century and beyond, much was learned about how stressful events affect the activity of the body (or physiology); for example, it has been established that these physiological responses to stressors sometimes increase the risk of development or exacerbate a number of diseases. To best understand the body's response to stressful events (or stressors), the general sequence of events and the specific responses of various organ systems must be considered.

Almost all bodily responses are mediated at least partially by the central nervous system: the brain and spinal cord. The brain takes in and analyzes information from the external environment as well as from the internal environment (the rest of the body), and it acts to regulate the activities of the body to optimize adaptation or survival. When the brain detects a threat, a sequence of events occurs to prepare the body to fight or to flee the threat. Walter Bradford Cannon, in the early twentieth century, was the first to describe this fight-or-flight response of the body. It is characterized by generalized physiological activation. Heart rate, blood pressure, and respiration increase to enhance the amount of oxygen available to the tissues. The distribution of blood flow changes to optimize efficiency of the tissues most needed to fight or flee: Blood flow to the muscles, brain, and skin increases, while it decreases in the stomach and other organs less important for immediate survival. Increased sweating and muscle tension help regulate the body's temperature and enhance movement if action is needed. Levels of blood glucose and insulin also increase to provide added energy sources, and immune function is depressed. Brain activity increases, resulting in enhanced sensitivity to incoming information and faster reactions to this information.

Taken together, these physiological changes serve to protect the organism and to prepare it to take action to survive threat. They occur quite rapidly and are controlled by the brain through a series of neurological and hormonal events. When the brain detects a threat (or stressor), it sends its activating message to the rest of the body through two primary channels, the sympathetic nervous system (SNS) and the pituitary-adrenal axis. The sympathetic nervous system is a branch of the nervous system that has multiple, diffuse neural connections to the rest of the body. It relays activating messages to the heart, liver, muscles, and other organs that produce the physiological changes already described. The sympathetic nervous system also stimulates the adrenal gland to secrete two hormones, epinephrine and norepinephrine (formerly called adrenaline and nor-adrenaline), into the bloodstream. Epinephrine and norepinephrine further activate the heart, blood vessels, lungs, sweat glands, and other tissues.

Also, the brain sends an activating message through its hypothalamus to the pituitary gland, at the base of the brain. This message causes the pituitary to release hormones into the bloodstream that circulate to the peripheral tissues and activate them. The primary "stress" hormone that the pituitary gland releases is adrenocorticotropic hormone (ACTH), which in turn acts on the adrenal gland to cause the release of the hormone cortisol. The actions of cortisol on other organs cause increases in blood glucose and insulin, among many other reactions.

In addition to isolating these primary stress mechanisms, research has demonstrated that the body secretes naturally occurring opiates—endorphins and enkephalins—in response to stress. Receptors for these opiates are found throughout the body and brain. Although their function is not entirely clear, some research suggests that they serve to buffer the effects of stressful events by counteracting the effects of the sympathetic nervous system and stress hormones.

GENERAL ADAPTATION SYNDROME

The human body contains a very sophisticated series of mechanisms that have evolved to enhance survival. When stressors and the subsequent physiological changes that are adaptive in the short run are chronic, however, they may produce long-term health risks. This idea was first discussed in detail in the mid-twentieth century by physiologist Hans Selye, who coined the term "general adaptation syndrome" to describe the body's physiological responses to stressors and the mechanisms by which these responses might result in disease.

Selye's general adaptation syndrome involves three stages of physiological response: alarm, resistance, and exhaustion. During the alarm stage, the organism detects a stressor and responds with sympathetic nervous system and hormonal activation. The second stage, resistance, is characterized by the body's efforts to neutralize the effects of the stressor. Such attempts are meant to return the body to a state of homeostasis, or balance. (The concept of homeostasis, or the tendency of the body to seek

to achieve an optimal, adaptive level of activity, was developed earlier by Cannon.) Finally, if the resistance stage is prolonged, exhaustion occurs, which can result in illness. Selye referred to such illnesses as diseases of adaptation. In this category of diseases, he included hypertension, cardiovascular disease, kidney disease, peptic ulcer, hyperthyroidism, and asthma.

Selye's general adaptation syndrome has received considerable attention as a useful framework within which to study the effects of stressors on health, but there are several problems with his theory. First, it assumes that all stressors produce characteristic, widespread physiological changes that differ only in intensity and duration. There is compelling evidence, however, that different types of stressors can produce very different patterns of neural and hormonal responses. For example, some stressors produce increases in heart rate, while others can actually cause heart rate deceleration. Thus, Selye's assumption of a nonspecific stress response must be questioned.

Also, Selye's theory does not take into account individual differences in the pattern of response to threat. Research during the later twentieth century demonstrated that individuals vary widely in their physiological responses to identical stressors. Such differences may result from genetic or environmental influences. For example, some studies have demonstrated that normotensive offspring of hypertensive parents are more cardiovascularly responsive to brief stressors than individuals with normotensive parents. Although the genes responsible for hypertension might have been passed on from the hypertensive parents, these children might also have different socialization or learning histories that contribute to their exaggerated cardiovascular reactivity to stressors. Whatever the mechanism, this research highlights the fact that individuals and organ systems vary in the degree to which they respond to stress.

STRESS AND ILLNESS

Coinciding with the scientific community's growing acknowledgment that stressful events have direct physiological effects, much interest has developed in understanding the relations between these events and the development or maintenance of specific diseases. Probably the greatest amount of research has focused on the link between stress and heart disease, the primary cause of death in the United States. Much empirical work also has focused on gastrointestinal disorders, diabetes, and pain (for example, headache and arthritis). Researchers are beginning to develop an understanding of the links between stress and immune function. Such work has implications for the study of infectious disease (such as flu and mononucleosis), cancer, and acquired immunodeficiency syndrome (AIDS).

A number of types of research paradigms have been employed to study the effects of stressors on health and illness. Longitudinal studies have identified a number of environmental stressors that contribute to the development or exacerbation of disease. For example, one study of more than four thousand residents of Alameda County, California, spanning two decades, showed that a number of environmental stressors such as social isolation were significant predictors of mortality from all causes. Other longitudinal investigations have linked stressful contexts such as loud noise, crowding, and low socioeconomic status with the onset or exacerbation of disease.

A major drawback of such longitudinal research is that no clear conclusions can be made about the exact mechanism or mechanisms by which the stressor affected health. Although it is possible, in the Alameda County study, that the relationship between social isolation and disease was mediated by the sympathetic nervous system/hormonal mechanisms already discussed, individuals who are isolated also may be less likely to engage in health care behaviors such as eating healthy diets, exercising, and maintaining preventive health care. Thus, other research paradigms have been used to try to clarify the causal mechanisms by which stressors may influence particular diseases. For example, many scientists use laboratory stress procedures to investigate the influence of brief, standardized stressors on physiology. This type of research has the advantage of being more easily controlled. That is, the researcher can manipulate one or a small number of variables (for example, noise) in the laboratory and measure the physiological effects. These effects are then thought to mimic the physiological effects of such a variable in the natural environment.

This research primarily is conducted to ask basic questions about the relations between stressors, physiology, and subsequent health. The findings also have implications, however, for prevention and in-

tervention. If a particular stressor is identified that increases risk of a particular disease, prevention efforts could be developed to target the populations exposed to this stressor. Prevention strategies might involve either modifying the stressor, teaching people ways to manage more effectively their responses to it, or both.

During the last two or three decades, applied researchers have attempted to develop intervention strategies aimed at controlling the body's physiological responses to stress. This work has suggested that a number of stress management strategies can actually attenuate physiological responsivity. Most strategies teach the individual some form of relaxation (such as deep muscle relaxation, biofeedback, hypnosis, or meditation), and most of this work has focused on populations already diagnosed with a stress-related disease, such as hypertension, diabetes, or ulcer. The techniques are thought to produce their effects by two possible mechanisms: lowering basal physiological activation (or changing the level at which homeostasis is achieved) and providing a strategy for more effectively responding to acute stressors to attenuate their physiological effects. Research has not proceeded far enough to make any statements about the relative importance of these mechanisms. Indeed, it is not clear whether either mechanism is active in many of the successful intervention studies. Although research does indicate that relaxation strategies often improve symptoms of stress-related illnesses, the causal mechanisms of such techniques remain to be clarified.

THE MIND-BODY CONNECTION

The notion that the mind and body are connected has been considered since the writings of ancient Greece. Hippocrates described four bodily humors (fluids) that he associated with differing behavioral and psychological characteristics. Thus, the road was paved for scientific thinkers to consider the interrelations between environment, psychological state, and physiological state (that is, health and illness). Such considerations developed most rapidly in the twentieth century, when advancements in scientific methodology permitted a more rigorous examination of the relationships among these variables.

In the early twentieth century, Cannon was the first to document and discuss the fight-or-flight response to threatening events. He also reasoned that the response was adaptive, unless prolonged or repeated. In the 1940's, two physicians published observations consistent with Cannon's of an ulcer patient who had a gastric fistula, enabling the doctors to observe directly the contents of the stomach. They reported that stomach acids and bleeding increased when the patient was anxious or angry, thus documenting the relations between stress, emotion, and physiology. Shortly after this work was published, Selye began reporting his experiments on the effects of cold and fatigue on the physiology of rats. These physical stressors produced enlarged adrenal glands, small thymus and lymph glands (involved in immune system functioning), and increased ulcer formation.

Psychiatrists took this information, along with the writings of Sigmund Freud, to mean that certain disease states might be associated with particular personality types. Efforts to demonstrate the relationship between specific personality types and physical disease endpoints culminated in the development of a field known as psychosomatic medicine. Research, however, does not support the basic tenet of this field, that a given disease is linked with specific personality traits; thus, psychosomatic medicine has not received much support from the scientific community. The work of clinicians and researchers in psychosomatic medicine paved the way for late twentieth century conceptualizations of the relations between stress and physiology. Most important, biopsychosocial models that view people's health status in the context of the interaction between their biological vulnerability, psychological characteristics, and socio-occupational environment have been developed for a number of physical diseases.

Future research into individual differences in stress responses will further clarify the mechanisms by which stress exerts its effects on physiology. Once these mechanisms are identified, intervention strategies for use with patients or for prevention programs for at-risk individuals can be identified and implemented. Clarification of the role of the endogenous opiates in the stress response, for example, represents an important dimension in developing new strategies to enhance individual coping with stressors. Further investigation of the influence of stressors on immune function should also open new doors for prevention and intervention.

Much remains to be learned about why individuals differ in their responses to stress. Research in this area will seek to determine the influence of genes, environment, and behavior on the individual, elucidating the important differences between stress-tolerant and stress-intolerant individuals. Such work will provide a better understanding of the basic mechanisms by which stressors have their effects, and should lead to exciting new prevention and intervention strategies that will enhance health and improve the quality of life.

SOURCES FOR FURTHER STUDY

Brannon, Linda, and Jess Feist. *Health Psychology: An Introduction to Behavior and Health.* 7th ed. Belmont, Calif.: Wadsworth Cengage Learning, 2009. Written for undergraduate students. A very readable overview of the field of health psychology. Provides the reader with chapters on stress and health, and various stress-related diseases.

Craig, Kenneth D., and Stephen M. Weiss, eds. *Health Enhancement, Disease Prevention, and Early Intervention: Biobehavioral Perspectives.* New York: Springer, 1990. Includes, among other chapters of interest, an excellent chapter by Neal Miller (the "father of biofeedback") on how the brain affects the health of the body.

Fink, George, et al., eds. *Encyclopedia of Stress.* 2d ed. 4 vols. Boston: Academic Press, 2007. This multivolume set looks at stress from all aspects, including its physiological effects.

Karren, Keith J., et al. *Mind/Body Health: The Effects of Attitudes, Emotions, and Relationships.* 4th ed. San Francisco: Pearson/Benjamin Cummings, 2009. Argues that there is a disease-prone personality and looks at the general connection between stress and disease.

Selye, Hans. *The Stress of Life.* Rev. ed. New York: McGraw-Hill, 1978. A classic work on stress, first published in 1956. A thoroughly readable account of Selye's work and thinking about stress and health.

Sher, Leo, ed. *Psychological Factors and Cardiovascular Disorders: The Role of Stress and Psychosocial Influences.* New York: Nova Science, 2009. Examines the link between stress and other psychological factors and heart disease.

Virginia L. Goetsch and Kevin T. Larkin

SEE ALSO: Anxiety disorders; Biofeedback and relaxation; Cannon, Walter Bradford; Emotions; Endocrine system; Fight-or-flight response; General adaptation syndrome; Meditation and relaxation;

Nervous system; Psychosomatic disorders; Selye, Hans; Stress: Behavioral and psychological responses; Stress-related diseases; Stress: Theories; Type A behavior pattern.

Stress-related diseases

TYPE OF PSYCHOLOGY: Stress
FIELD OF STUDY: Stress and illness

As a person experiences stress, physical responses occur that have been associated with a host of physical diseases. Understanding the stress-disease relationship, including how to control and lower stress levels, is important in maintaining health.

KEY CONCEPTS
- biofeedback
- endorphin
- general adaptation syndrome
- locus of control
- psychoneuroimmunology
- relaxation response
- stressor
- Type A personality
- Type B personality

INTRODUCTION

The term "stress," as it is used in the field of psychology, may be defined as the physical or psychological disturbance an individual experiences as a result of what that individual perceives to be an adverse or challenging circumstance. Four observations concerning this definition of stress should be made. First, stress is what the individual experiences, not the circumstance causing the stress (the stressor). Second, individuals differ in what they perceive to be stressful. What may be very stressful for one individual may not be at all stressful for another. Hans Selye, the researcher who did more than anyone else to make the medical community and the general population aware of the concept and consequences of stress, once noted that, for him, spending the day on the beach doing nothing would be extremely stressful. This difference in people's perceptions is behind the familiar concept that events do not cause stress. Instead, stress comes from a person's perception or interpretation of events.

Third, stress occurs in response to circumstances that are seen as negative, but stress may also arise from challenging circumstances, even positive ones. The well-known Social Readjustment Rating Scale developed by Thomas Holmes and Richard Rahe includes both positive and negative life events. A negative event, such as the death of a spouse, is clearly stressful; however, marriage, generally viewed as a positive life event, can also be stressful. Fourth, stressors can lead to stress-related disturbances that are psychological, physiological, or both. The psychological response is rather unpredictable. A given stressor may result in one individual responding with anger, another with depression, and another with a new determination to succeed.

GENERAL ADAPTATION SYNDROME

The physiological response is more predictable. Beginning in the 1930's, Selye began studying the human response to stressors. Eventually he identified what he termed the general adaptation syndrome to describe the typical pattern of physical responses. Selye divided the general adaptation syndrome into three stages: alarm, resistance, and exhaustion.

The first stage begins when an individual becomes frightened, anxious, or even merely concerned. The body immediately undergoes numerous physical changes to cope with the stressor. Metabolism speeds up. Heart and respiration rates increase. The hormones epinephrine, norepinephrine, and cortisol are secreted. Sugar is released from the liver. The muscles tense. Blood shifts from the internal organs to the skeletal musculature. These and a host of other changes are aimed at helping the body cope, but the price paid for this heightened state of arousal typically includes symptoms such as headache, upset stomach, sleeplessness, fatigue, diarrhea, and loss of appetite. The body's increase in alertness and energy is accompanied by a lowered state of resistance to illness.

Obviously, people cannot remain in the alarm stage for long. If the stressor is not removed, the body enters the resistance stage—a stage that may last from minutes to days or longer. During this stage, the body seeks to adapt to the stressor. The physical changes that occurred during the alarm stage subside. Resistance to illness is actually increased to above-normal levels. Because the body is still experiencing stress, however, remaining in this stage for a long period will eventually lead to physical and psychological exhaustion—the exhaustion stage.

Selye has noted that over the course of life, most people go through the first two stages many, many times. Such is necessary to adapt to the demands and challenges of life. The real danger is found in not eliminating the stressor. During the exhaustion stage, the body is very vulnerable to disease and in extreme cases may suffer collapse and death. Although later research has found subtle differences in the stress response, depending on the stressor involved, the basic findings of Selye have continued to be supported. In addition to the direct physiological effects of stress on the body, indirect effects may also lead to illness. For example, stress may cause or exacerbate behavioral risk factors such as smoking, alcohol use, and overeating.

Heart Disease and Immune Effects

Specific illnesses can also be caused or promoted by stress. For many years Americans have been aware of the relationship between stress and heart disease. The biochemical changes associated with stress lead to higher blood pressure, an increased heart rate, and a release of fat into the bloodstream. If the fat is completely consumed by the muscles through physical activity (for example, defending oneself from an attacker), no serious health consequences follow. If, however, a person experiences stress without engaging in physical activity (a more common scenario in Western culture), the fat is simply deposited on the walls of the blood vessels. As these fatty deposits accumulate, life is threatened.

The work of two cardiologists, Meyer Friedman and Ray Rosenman, is of particular importance to a discussion of heart disease and stress. Friedman and Rosenman demonstrated, based originally on personal observation and subsequently on clinical research, that there is a personality type that is particularly prone to heart disease. The personality type that is at the greatest risk was found to be one which is highly stressed—impatient, hostile, hard-driving, and competitive. They termed this a Type A personality. The low-risk person, the Type B personality, is more patient, easygoing, and relaxed.

Numerous studies have examined health based on the Type A-Type B concept. Virtually all have supported Friedman and Rosenman's conclusions. One major report, however, did not; subsequent analysis of that report and other research generally

has indicated that the aspects of the Type A personality that are threatening to one's health are primarily the hostility, cynicism, and impatience, not the desire to achieve.

A newer area of research that is even more fundamental to understanding how stress is related to disease involves the immune system. As the physiological changes associated with stress occur, the immune system is suppressed. The immune system has two primary functions: to identify and destroy hazardous foreign materials called antigens (these include bacteria, viruses, parasites, and fungi) and to identify and destroy the body's own cells that have undergone changes associated with malignancy. Thus, if the immune system is suppressed, the body is less able to detect and defend against a host of diseases. An example of this effect again involves research with laboratory rats. One such investigation involved placing tumor cells in the bodies of rats. Some of the rats were then exposed to an abundance of stress. Those that were given this treatment were less resistant to the cancer. Their tumors were larger, and they developed sooner than those found in the "low-stress" rats.

The recent growth of the field of psychoneuroimmunology focuses specifically on the chemical bases of communication between mind and body. Research in this area provides evidence that the body's immune system can be influenced by psychological factors that produce stress. One study, for example, showed that during students' examination periods, the levels of students' antibodies that fight infections were lowest. Thus they were most vulnerable to illness at that most stressful time. Health centers confirm that students tend to report more illness during examination times.

As research continues, the number of specific diseases that can be linked to stress grows. A partial listing of stress-related diseases and disorders for which recent research is available would include acne, asthma, cancers (many types), colds, coronary thrombosis, diabetes mellitus, gastric ulcers, herpes simplex (types 1 and 2), human immunodeficiency virus (HIV) infection, hyperlipidemia, hypertension, infertility, irritable bowel syndrome (IBS), migraine headache, mononucleosis syndrome, rheumatoid arthritis, streptococcal infection, stroke, systemic lupus erythematosus, and tuberculosis.

Research has shown that stress may also play a role in depression, sleep disturbances, ovulation, and brain atrophy associated with Alzheimer's disease. Stress as a cause of stomach ulcers has been essentially negated, with the discovery that these ulcers are generally caused by the bacterium *Helicobacter pylori*, which can be treated with antibiotics. However, stress may still play a role in decreasing the mucous lining of the stomach, which makes it more vulnerable to ulcer formation. Some experts feel that there is no illness that is not in some way influenced by stress.

Few, if any, of these physical problems are caused solely by stress. Many other factors influence risk, including genetic composition, gender, race, environmental conditions, and nutritional state. Nevertheless, stress is frequently an important factor in determining initial resistance as well as the subsequent course of a given disease.

STRESS REDUCTION AND COPING

Some individuals appear to live with many stressors yet generally avoid physical and psychological illness. Understanding why is important, because it can provide insight as to what the average person can and should do to lower stress levels. Dispositional factors (optimistic versus pessimistic, easygoing versus hard-driving, friendly versus hostile) are probably most important in determining a person's stress level. The Type A-Type B research is an example of research demonstrating the influence of dispositional factors.

Research with twins has found that temperament is largely inborn; however, any individual can choose to be more optimistic, generous, and patient. Norman Cousins is often cited as an example of a person who decided to change his outlook and mental state to preserve his life. He had read Selye's *The Stress of Life* (1956), which describes how negative emotions can cause physical stress and subsequent disease. Cousins, who had a rare and painful illness from which he was told he would most likely never recover, decided that if negative emotions could harm one's health, then positive emotions could possibly return one's health.

As Cousins describes his experience in *Anatomy of an Illness as Perceived by the Patient* (1979), he left his

Studies show that stress, and the accompanying health risks, can be lessened through contact with pets. (©Lyn Baxter/Dreamstime.com)

hospital room for a more pleasant environment, began trading massive doses of drugs for massive doses of vitamin C and a steady diet of television comedies and laughter, and decided to stop worrying. To the surprise of his medical team, his recovery began at once. Though this now-classic example is only anecdotal, the research on disposition and stress would support the assumption that Cousins's decision to change his mental state and stop worrying—not his avoidance of traditional medical care—was a truly important influence.

A related area of research has investigated how psychological hardiness helps people resist stress. Studies by Suzanne Kobasa and her colleagues examined business executives who all had an obvious abundance of stressors in their lives. In comparing those hardy individuals who handled the stressors well with the nonhardy individuals, the researchers found that the two groups differed in three important but basic ways.

The first was commitment. Stress-resistant executives typically possessed a clear sense of values. They had clear goals and a commitment to those goals. Less hardy executives were more likely to feel alienation. The second was challenge. The hardy executives welcomed challenges and viewed change rather than stability as the norm in life. Their less healthy counterparts viewed change with alarm. The third factor was control. The hardy executives felt more in control of their lives. This aspect of Kobasa's research overlaps with research conducted since the 1960's involving a concept known as the locus of control. People with an internal locus of control are those individuals who believe they are influential rather than powerless in controlling the direction of their lives. This area of research has also found that such a belief lowers stress.

Many studies have been conducted to examine the relationship between physical fitness and mental health. What has emerged from this heavily researched area is a clear conclusion: Exercise can lower stress levels. Though regular, sustained aerobic exercise is generally advocated, research has found that even something as simple as a daily ten-minute walk can have measurable beneficial effects. During exercise, there is a release of chemical substances, including neurotransmitters called endorphins. Endorphins act to decrease pain and produce feelings of well-being, somewhat like an opiate. Exposure to stress has been shown to increase the level of endorphins in the body. For example, studies were conducted with runners, one group using naloxone, a substance that blocks the effects of opiates, and the other group a placebo that had no effect on the body. After strenuous runs, those taking the placebo reported feelings of euphoria, sometimes known as runners' high. Those taking naloxone reported no such feelings. During exercise, the body releases other chemicals, including dopamine, which is thought to act as an antidepressant. Thus there is abundant evidence of the stress-reducing benefits of exercise.

Another approach to reducing stress involves learning to evoke a physical relaxation response, a term coined by Harvard Medical School cardiologist Herbert Benson. Benson became intrigued by the ability of some people who practice meditation to lower their blood pressure, heart rate, and oxygen consumption voluntarily. He discovered that the process is not at all mystical and can be easily taught. The process involves getting comfortable, closing the eyes, breathing deeply, relaxing muscles, and relaxing the mind by focusing on a simple word or phrase.

Others are helped by using an electronic device that closely monitors subtle physiological changes. By observing these changes (typically on a monitor), a person can, for example, learn to slow down a heart rate. This is known as biofeedback training. Many other techniques and suggestions arising from research as well as common sense can lower stress. A strong social support system has been found to be very important; disciplining oneself not to violate one's own value system is essential. Even having a pet that needs love and attention has been found to lower stress.

RESEARCH AND THE FUTURE

A general recognition that a relationship exists between mind and body is at least as old as the biblical Old Testament writings. Proverbs 17:22 reads, "A cheerful heart is good medicine,/ but a crushed spirit dries up the bones." Hippocrates, generally considered the father of medicine, sought to understand how the body could heal itself and what factors could slow or prevent this process. He clearly perceived a relationship between physical health and what is now termed stress, though his understanding was shallow.

Several physiologists of the nineteenth century made contributions; however, it was not until the twentieth century that the classic studies of American physiologist Walter Bradford Cannon proved the link scientifically. Cannon and his student Philip Bard began their analysis of stress and physiological arousal to disprove the idea espoused by others, that emotion follows physiological arousal.

Cannon found a variety of stressors that led to the release of the hormones adrenaline and noradrenaline (or, properly now, epinephrine and norepinephrine). Heat, cold, oxygen deprivation, and fright all led to hormonal changes as well as a number of additional physiological adaptations. Cannon was excited about this discovery and impressed with the body's remarkable ability to react to stressors. All these changes were aimed at preparing the body for what Cannon termed the fight-or-flight response. It was Selye's task to build on Cannon's work. His description of the reaction subsequently termed the general adaptation syndrome first appeared in a scientific journal in 1936. As knowledge of the stress concept began to spread, interest by the public as well as the research community increased.

Literally tens of thousands of stress research studies conducted throughout the world were completed during the last half of the twentieth century. Of particular importance was the discovery by three American scientists that the brain produces morphinelike antistress substances. The discovery of these substances, named endorphins, won the 1977 Nobel Prize for the scientists involved and opened a whole new area of research.

Research has shown that the brain itself produces neuropeptides, or brain message transmitters, that may also be produced by macrophages—white blood cells that attack viruses and bacteria. Because some forms of stress-reduction such as relaxation also seem to result in production of neuropeptides, if the brain could be caused to produce more of these substances, the immune system could be strengthened. The hope remains that someday an endorphin-type drug could be used to counter some of the unhealthy effects of stress, ensuring better health and longer lives. Better health and longer lives are available even today, however, for all people who are willing to make lifestyle changes based on current knowledge.

Sources for Further Study

Greenberg, Jerrold S. *Comprehensive Stress Management.* 11th ed. New York: McGraw-Hill, 2009. This is an excellent source that includes numerous self-tests, explains the scientific foundations of stress, and offers methods and techniques used to reduce stress in a variety of life situations.

Kahn, Ada P., ed. *The Encyclopedia of Stress and Stress-Related Diseases.* 2d ed. New York: Facts On File, 2005. Covers all aspects of stress and the diseases that have been connected to it.

Kendall-Tackett, Kathleen, ed. *The Psychoneuroimmunology of Chronic Disease: Exploring the Links Between Inflammation, Stress, and Illness.* Washington, D.C.: American Psychological Association, 2010. Examines the relationship among stress, inflammation, and disease, particularly chronic disease.

Romas, John A., and Manoj Sharma. *Practical Stress Management: A Comprehensive Workbook for Managing Change and Promoting Health.* 5th ed. San Francisco: Pearson Benjamin Cummings, 2010. This handbook contains techniques for handling stress that can be used by people in their daily lives.

Sapolsky, Robert M. *Why Zebras Don't Get Ulcers: The Acclaimed Guide to Stress, Stress-Related Diseases, and Coping.* Rev. ed. New York: Holt, 2004. A somewhat humorous approach to a discussion of stress and its effects on the human body. Contains some coping strategies.

Selye, Hans. *The Stress of Life.* Rev. ed. New York: McGraw-Hill, 1978. Originally published in 1956, this is the most influential book ever written about stress. It focuses on the relationship between a stressful life and subsequent illness.

Timothy S. Rampey;
updated by Martha Oehmke Loustaunau

See also: Anxiety disorders; Biofeedback and relaxation; Cannon, Walter Bradford; Emotions; Endocrine system; Endorphins; Exercise and mental health; Fear; General adaptation syndrome; Meditation and relaxation; Nervous system; Selye, Hans; Stress: Behavioral and psychological responses; Stress: Physiological responses; Type A behavior pattern.

Stress
Theories

Type of psychology: Stress
Field of study: Critical issues in stress

Stress generally involves emotional and physiological responses to circumstances that an individual views as threatening. Most theories of stress claim that stress involves the interaction between problems people face and their resources for dealing with them. A wide range of theories emphasize physiological responses, environmental circumstances, cognitions, personal coping skills, personal characteristics, or some combination of these factors.

Key concepts
- biological theories of stress
- coping
- fight-or-flight response
- general adaptation syndrome
- interactionist approach to stress
- psychological theories of stress
- stress appraisal
- tend-and-befriend response
- Type A personality
- Type B personality

INTRODUCTION

Researchers are trying to answer questions regarding how thoughts and feelings can be translated to changes in the body and whether prolonged stress alters health in life-threatening ways. These questions are new versions of much older ones that for centuries have addressed the dichotomy between mind and body. Unlike most areas within psychology, the study of stress did not begin until well into the twentieth century. Theories of stress began to play an important role as the potential relationships between stress and illness were systematically investigated.

BIOLOGICAL THEORIES OF STRESS

The first important theorist who attempted to account for stress was Walter Bradford Cannon. He claimed that the sympathetic nervous system is activated by signals from the brain when a person is exposed to an emotionally arousing stimulus. This produces a series of physiological reactions that includes increases in heart rate, blood pressure, and respiration. This fight-or-flight response prepares the person for potential vigorous physical activity. According to Cannon, the confrontation with an arousing stimulus produces both the feelings and physiological reactions that are associated with stress. Although the contributions of Cannon were important, they did not take into consideration the role played by psychological and behavioral factors in the overall stress response.

The work of Cannon paved the way for the efforts of the most renowned stress theorist, Hans Selye, who has claimed that stress is nonspecifically induced and can be caused by diverse stimuli. It does not matter if the event is a major disaster, an uncooperative colleague, or a disobedient child. The important point to remember is that if the event is stressful for a person, the person's bodily reaction remains the same. Selye has labeled the body's response to stress the general adaptation syndrome. This process occurs in three stages. Stage one is the alarm reaction, during which the body activates to handle the perceived danger at hand. This activation resembles Cannon's fight-or-flight response. Blood is diverted to the skeletal muscles to prepare them for action. The second phase of the general adaptation syndrome is the resistance stage. During this stage, the person either adapts to or resists the source of stress. The longer this stage lasts, the greater is the danger to the person. If the individual accepts the source of stress as a necessary part of life, the stressor may persist indefinitely. The person then gradually becomes more susceptible to a wide range of stress-related problems and diseases including fatigue, headaches, hypertension, certain forms of cancer, and cardiovascular disease. These are but a few of the physical problems that are potentially related to stress. The third stage is the exhaustion stage. This demonstrates the finite nature of the body's ability to battle or adapt to stress. If the stressor is extremely intense and persists over a long period of time, the exhaustion stage sets in and the risk of emotional and physical problems increases. In Selye's system, the precise nature of the source of the stress is unimportant. The reaction is hypothesized to be the same in the face of physiological and psychological stressors.

INTERACTIONIST APPROACH TO STRESS

Cannon and Selye clearly focus on stress as a person's biological response to a wide range of stimuli. Selye emphasizes the nonspecific nature of the stress response. This position has been criticized by John Mason, who maintains that while the general adaptation syndrome does exist, responses differ according to the stimuli. He views stress as dependent on emotional responses to situations. It is the nature of a person's emotional response that will play an important role in the probability that stress will lead to disease. People who are not psychologically aware of the existence of a potentially stressful event are least likely to experience a stress response. Mason believes that Selye's approach is too simplistic and does not provide ample opportunities to explain why some people develop stress-related disorders and others do not.

In 2000, Shelley Taylor and her colleagues proposed that, although fight-or-flight may characterize the primary physiological responses to stress for both men and women, behaviorally women's responses are more marked by a pattern of "tend and befriend." Tending, or the nurturing activities that protect the self and offspring, promotes safety and reduces distress; befriending is the creation and maintenance of social networks that may aid in this process. The brain-behavior mechanism that underlies the tend-and-befriend pattern appears to draw on the attachment-caregiving system. Evidence from animal and human studies suggests that the neuropeptide oxytocin, in conjunction with female reproductive hormones and endogenous opioid peptide mechanisms, may be at its core of this previously unexplored stress regulatory system.

PSYCHOLOGICAL THEORIES OF STRESS

The theories of Cannon and Selye emphasize biological factors, while Mason's theory is typically described as an interactionist approach to stress. The psychological approach to stress is best represented by the work of Richard Lazarus. He claims that the key to a stress response cannot be found in either the nature of a specific stressful event or people's psychological responses to that event. Rather, the most important factors are cognitive ones. Lazarus believes that it is people's perception of an event that is crucial. This involves a combination of people's perceptions regarding the potential danger of an event and their ability to cope with it. Stress will occur in those circumstances in which people perceive that they do not have the ability or resources needed to cope with the situation.

Clearly, an important factor within the stress equation provided by Lazarus is appraisal of the situation. Along with his colleague Susan Folkman, Lazarus has described three types of appraisal of a potentially stressful situation. The first to occur is the primary appraisal. When people are exposed to a new event such as a spouse returning to work, the situation can be judged as irrelevant, positive, or potentially stressful. The key to the stress is the people's appraisal of the situation, rather than the situation itself. Next in the appraisal process is the secondary appraisal. It is at this point that people determine their ability to control, handle, or cope with the new situation. During this process, people examine potential options for dealing with an event, that is, their ability to make use of one or more of these options and a consideration of the success potential of each option, or whether they are likely to be successful in making this option work for themselves. The final type of appraisal is reappraisal. During this process, people reevaluate the stressful potential of a situation based on access to new thoughts and information. This can lead to an increase or decrease in stress. For example, the man who might have been mildly stressed by his wife's return to work may experience a decrease in stress as the family finances improve and he learns that many domestic tasks which he must now perform

are less noxious than he originally thought. On the other hand, his stress may increase if he determines that he has less free time and that the cost of babysitters has removed the potential for financial improvement associated with his wife's return to work outside the home.

An alternative to the appraisal-based conception of stress and coping developed by Lazarus and Folkman is the resource-based approach to the stress process first proposed by S. E. Hobfoll in the late 1980's. Resources were defined as those things that people value or that act as a means to obtaining that which they value and include social, personal, object, and condition resources. The conservation of resource theory has been applied, for example, to assess the impact of resource losses and gains that occur in women's lives. One study found that resource losses better predicted postpartum anger and depression than resource gains (in the opposite direction).

Whether they support a biological, interactionist, or psychological approach to stress, all theorists agree that stress has the capability of increasing the risk of suffering various forms of illness. In addition, many theorists believe that important relationships exist between stress, personality, and susceptibility to disease.

FACTORS AFFECTING RESPONSE TO STRESS

Potentially stressful events occur in everyone's life. Many people, however, never develop stress-related symptoms and illnesses. This may result in part from issues pertaining to lifestyle and personality. One interesting approach to this problem has been provided by Suzanne Kobasa. She found that several personality factors are helpful in people's efforts to avoid illness in the face of stress. These factors are control, commitment, and challenge. When faced with difficult events, people can view the situation either as hopeless or as one over which they have a degree of control. In a situation in which a man is notified that the factory in which he works is going to close in three years, it is normal initially to treat the news with shock and disappointment, but it is the worker's long-term response that is critical. On one hand, he can continue to report for work during the next three years and commiserate with his colleagues. He can make the statement that the factory is going to close and there is nothing he can do about it. This response is likely to lead to gradual increases in stress and susceptibility to illness. On the other hand, he could take control of the situation by looking for other work, entering a job retraining program, or returning to school on a part-time basis. This approach is likely to decrease his risk of stress-related illness.

The second factor, commitment, involves people's dedication to and involvement with other people, activities, institutions, and themselves. Some people have nowhere to turn in the presence of a stressful event. They have no friends, family ties have been severed, and they are loners who have no goal in life other than to wake up the next morning. These individuals will find it extremely difficult to cope with a stressful event such as the death of a parent or loss of a job. They may feel that they have nowhere to turn in the face of adversity; they lack the social supports that help one cope with stressful situations. These people are highly susceptible to those illnesses that are associated with stress. Conversely, people with many friends, strong family ties, and a sense of purpose in life will be better able to cope with significant stress.

The final factor, challenge, relates to people's view of changes in their life. For example, a secretary who is transferred from one department at work to another, and who views this change as presenting interesting and new challenges, is likely to remain healthy. However, if she views the new position as a threat that should be avoided at all costs, she is likely to become ill. The three factors of control, commitment, and challenge make up an overall factor known as hardiness. The person who maintains high levels of these three factors has a high level of hardiness and is not a likely candidate for stress-related illnesses.

PERSONALITY TYPES

Perhaps the most talked-about and researched personality factor that has been related to stress is the Type A personality. Type A people are always on the go and are extremely driven. They walk fast, talk fast, are impatient with others, and are easily angered. Type A people are workaholics who measure life in numbers. They are concerned about money earned and saved, hours worked, praise received, and clients served. They always have a sense of time urgency. Type B people are just the opposite. They are relaxed and easygoing, and never seem in a hurry to do anything.

Research on the topic of the Type A personality, spearheaded by Meyer Friedman and Ray Rosenman, has traditionally maintained that the Type A personality is associated with increased stress and, more important, an increased risk of heart disease. This finding has been supported in at least forty research studies. For many years, the notion that Type A behavior was a risk factor for heart disease was taken for granted by many health professionals; however, several studies have failed to support this relationship. Researchers have attempted to account for these discrepancies. The mystery appears to have been solved in that it has been discovered that not all Type A behaviors are associated with increased risk of heart disease. The key factors appear to be anger and hostility. Those Type A people who are angry and hostile are likely to convert potentially stressful situations into disease. The best advice that can be given to the typical Type A angry person is to learn to respond to situations without anger. This does not mean that anger that is felt should be held inside. Rather, the person should learn to respond to situations with feelings and emotions other than anger.

Evidence increasingly indicates that stress can influence the immune response, the body's defense against many types of illness. Research with animals has demonstrated the direct impact of various stressors on the immune system and, consequently, on infectious, malignant, and autoimmune diseases. Human studies also suggest that stress can adversely affect the body's immune response.

People must learn to cope with situations in ways that do not lead to increased stress and increased risk of disease. The good news is that many such strategies have proved to be very effective in helping people deal with those potentially stressful situations that seem to occur in the lives of everyone. The work of pioneers such as Cannon and Selye and more recent research by Rosenman and Friedman, Lazarus, and Taylor has opened up many new avenues of research related to stress and stress management. The potential role of stress in a wide range of diseases including cancer is being explored. It can be anticipated that the future will bring to light many new and unexpected relationships between stress and health.

SOURCES FOR FURTHER STUDY

Fink, George, et al., eds. *Encyclopedia of Stress.* 2d ed. 4 vols. Boston: Academic Press, 2007. A compilation of the latest information on stressors, stress responses, and the disorders that can result. These volumes cover a wide range of stress-related topics, from stress in the workplace and post-traumatic stress disorder to stress-related diseases and approaches to treatment.

Greenberg, Jerrold S. *Comprehensive Stress Management.* 11th ed. New York: McGraw-Hill, 2009. Looks at the scientific concept of stress and methods and techniques to reduce stress.

Kahn, Ada P., ed. *The Encyclopedia of Stress and Stress-related Diseases.* 2d ed. New York: Facts On File, 2005. This encyclopedia of stress, while covering all aspects, focuses on diseases caused or made worse by stress.

Lazarus, Richard S., and Susan Folkman. *Stress, Appraisal, and Coping.* New York: Springer, 2006. Provides a thorough analysis of Lazarus's views on stress. Includes his comments on the three types of appraisal and approaches to coping with stress.

Lovallo, William R. *Stress and Health: Biological and Psychological Interactions.* 2d ed. Thousand Oaks, Calif.: Sage Publications, 2005. This book examines the biological links between thoughts and feelings and the potential health changes that can result from stress. Also discusses how individual differences in physiology and in perceptions and evaluations of events can have physical and long-term health consequences.

Selye, Hans. *The Stress of Life.* Rev. ed. New York: McGraw-Hill, 1978. The classic book, originally published in 1956, in the field. Includes Selye's original analysis of stress and his development of the general adaptation syndrome. Also includes a thorough analysis of the proposed relationships between stress and various forms of disease.

Lawrence A. Fehr; updated by Allyson Washburn

SEE ALSO: Cannon, Walter Bradford; Emotions; General adaptation syndrome; Selye, Hans; Stress: Behavioral and psychological responses; Stress: Physiological responses; Stress-related diseases; Type A behavior pattern.

Strong Interest Inventory (SII)

DATE: 1974 forward

TYPE OF PSYCHOLOGY: Intelligence and intelligence testing

FIELDS OF STUDY: Ability tests; intelligence assessment

The Strong Interest Inventory (SII) is one of the most empirically sound interest surveys. The survey is relatively easy to administer and requires at least a sixth-grade reading level and a computer for scoring. There are twenty-three basic occupational scales, and the results are mainly applicable for use by people who are oriented toward professional, semiprofessional, or managerial occupations that attract college students.

KEY CONCEPTS
- assessment
- Holland reporting system
- interest inventory
- job choice
- occupational testing

INTRODUCTION

The Strong Interest Inventory (SII), which replaced the well-known Strong-Campbell Interest Inventory in 1985, was developed based on several decades of compiling empirical data. The empirical nature of the studies developed by E. K. Strong, Jr., is grounded in his observation of the specific interest patterns of workers in the occupational groups and careers he studied. He suggested that an individual who has interests that are similar to those of persons working in a given occupation is more likely to find satisfaction in that particular occupation than is a person who does not have common interests with those workers.

The SII contains 325 test items that measure a respondent's interests in a wide range of occupations, occupational activities, hobbies, leisure activities, school subjects, and types of people. Most test takers can complete the interest inventory in about thirty minutes; the reading level is sixth grade. The survey is appropriate for use by people with an approximate age range of thirteen years through adulthood. The SII has been translated into several foreign languages for administration.

The scores can also be converted to a common

reporting system developed by John L. Holland relating to a general occupational grouping or a job choice. The Holland system consists of six concepts arranged in a hexagon indicating relative positioning. The nomenclature for the Holland system consists of Realistic (R), Investigative (I), Artistic (A), Social (S), Enterprising (E), and Conventional (C) (also referred to as the R-I-A-S-E-C sequence).

TECHNICAL ASPECTS

The SII has been well researched in relation to other inventories by Strong and others. The stability of the SII is well documented, and reliability and validity studies suggest that the SII is well suited for career development, counseling, and review. The strength of the SII is the variety of data generated on an interpretive report. This is useful in providing information that is usually not found on interest inventory profiles.

Interpreting the SII develops from a review of the general occupational theme scores. These provide three phases of review from the scores: first, a general overview of interest patterns; second, specific basic interest scores; and third, interests in specific occupations or jobs. The SII profiles are structured around Holland's six occupational styles. Each of the six themes is reported and indicates whether the interest level is considered very low, low, average, high, or very high.

The basic interest scales focus on subdivisions of the six occupational themes from which career groups or clusters of occupations can be derived. Ten administrative indices are reported on the SII, including an infrequent response index, an academic comfort scale indicating the degree to which a person likes academic work, and an introversion-extroversion (IE) index indicating whether a person likes working with people or things. To make maximum use of the information on the SII profile, a systematic evaluation by a professional who can develop a complete evaluation of the responses is recommended.

CRITIQUE

Needs and interests have been found to be closely related. The relationship between needs, occupational interests, and personality identification has been demonstrated carefully. Holland's research has also demonstrated that inner-directed and other-directed personalities differ in their occupational interests, as do people who are decided and undecided. The relative importance of interests to vocational decisions has also been extensively studied. Certain occupations evidently satisfy specific needs, and these needs are related to interests. With respect to career maturity, high scores on the SII correspond to other career inventory scores.

To make maximum use of the information on the SII profile, a systematic evaluation is recommended. For these purposes, an SII summary evaluation is devised from the total number of responses. Several steps are outlined for evaluation of SII scores along with the available interpretations. Comparing the interests of African Americans, Latinos, Asian Americans, and Native Americans, it was found that Holland's theory of six occupational groupings adequately represents the interests of these groups.

For individuals to enter an appropriate career, they must begin to identify specific interests and relative importance of those interests. Some individuals will need little guidance in making career choices; others will need to guidance of a survey instrument such as the SII. Millions of people have received important information from it to use in decision making. Caution is always expressed by the authors of these inventories that no decision should be made solely on the basis of the results determined by one inventory alone. The SII is one of eighty interest inventories in use.

SOURCES FOR FURTHER STUDY

Herr, E. L., Stanley H. Cramer, and Spencer G. Niles. *Career Guidance and Counseling Through the Life Span: Systematic Approaches.* 6th ed. Boston.: Pearson/Allyn & Bacon, 2004. An overview of career counseling and guidance needs and resources for people from elementary school through adulthood.

Maddox, Teddy, ed. *Tests: A Comprehensive Reference for Assessments in Psychology, Education, and Business.* 6th ed. Austin, Tex.: Pro-Ed, 2007. Contains information on psychological, educational, and vocational tests and their uses.

Osborn, Debra, and V. G. Zunker. *Using Assessment Results for Career Development.* 7th ed. Belmont, Calif.: Thomson Higher Education, 2006. A workbook for career counselors, focused on what assessment results mean in practical terms for their clients.

Power, P. W. *A Guide to Vocational Assessment.* 4th ed.

Austin, Tex.: Pro-Ed, 2006. Useful guide for those both administering and creating vocational assessment tools.

Sharf, R. S. *Applying Career Development Theory to Counseling.* 5th ed. Belmont, Calif.: Brooks/Cole, Cengage Learning, 2009. Covers theory and practice, with numerous case examples.

Daniel L. Yazak

SEE ALSO: Ability tests; Assessment; Career and personnel testing; Career Occupational Preference System (COPS); College entrance examinations; General Aptitude Test Battery (GATB); Human resource training and development; Interest inventories; Kuder Occupational Interest Survey (KOIS); Testing: Historical perspectives.

Structuralism and functionalism

DATE: 1879-1913
TYPE OF PSYCHOLOGY: Origin and definition of psychology
FIELDS OF STUDY: General constructs and issues; thought

Structuralism and functionalism represent early schools of thought in psychology. The structuralists were devoted to discovering the elements of consciousness, and the functionalists believed that psychology should focus on understanding how consciousness is useful or functional.

KEY CONCEPTS
- applied psychology
- evolution
- imageless thought
- introspection
- stimulus error
- stream of consciousness
- voluntarism

INTRODUCTION

Structuralism and functionalism were two of the earliest schools of thought in psychology. To understand these early perspectives, it is important to consider the sociohistorical context in which they developed. Psychology as an independent scientific

discipline was founded in 1879 by German scholar Wilhelm Wundt at the University of Leipzig. Wundt was a medically trained physiologist appointed to the department of philosophy at Leipzig. In 1879, he established the first-ever laboratory devoted solely to the experimental study of psychological issues. The German *Zeitgeist* was conducive to this development. For example, the education reform movement encouraged the development of university research and promoted academic freedom. Furthermore, German scholars at the time accepted a broader definition of science compared with their counterparts in many other European countries.

Wundt defined psychology as the scientific study of conscious experience and organized it into two broad areas: experimental psychology (the study of sensation and perception, reaction time, attention, and feelings) and *Völkerpsychologie* (cultural psychology, which included the study of language, myth, and custom). Wundt made an important distinction between immediate and mediate experiences. Mediate experiences involve an interpretation of sensory input ("I see an apple"), whereas an immediate experience consists of pure and unbiased sensory experiences ("I see a roundish, red object"). Wundt emphasized the process of organizing and synthesizing the elemental components of consciousness (the immediate experiences) into higher-level thoughts. Because this process of apperception was considered to be an act of will or volition, he often referred to his system as voluntarism.

One of Wundt's students, Edward Titchener, an Englishman who earned his doctoral degree under Wundt in 1892, ascended to prominence by establishing the structural school of thought in psychology as a professor at Cornell University. Functionalism soon arose as a school of thought that opposed structuralism.

Titchener, it should be noted, considered structuralism to be a refined extension of and largely compatible with Wundt's work. Because Titchener was the main translator of Wundt's work into English and was widely considered to be a loyal and accurate representative of Wundt's system, the term "structuralism" at the time was used as a label for both Titchener's and Wundt's work. This interpretative error, which is still propagated in some textbooks, was not fully realized until the mid-1970's, when scholars started to examine Wundt's original work in detail. There are some important differences between Titchener's structuralism and Wundt's system of voluntarism. First, Titchener rejected the idea of a branch of cultural psychology. Second, structural psychology neglected the study of apperception and focused almost exclusively on the identification of the elements of consciousness. Finally, in a structuralist framework, the elements of consciousness themselves were of utmost importance; mediate and immediate experiences were considered the same event simply viewed from different vantage points. There was no need for a volitional process.

STRUCTURALISM

For Titchener, psychology was the study of consciousness. Whereas physics was said to be concerned with assessing environmental events from an objective, external standard, psychology was concerned with examining how humans experience such events subjectively. For example, an hour spent listening to a boring speech and an hour spent playing an enjoyable game last exactly the same length of time— 3,600 seconds—but, psychologically, the second event goes by more quickly.

In structuralism, consciousness is defined as the sum total of experiences at any given moment, and the mind is defined as the sum of experiences over the course of a lifetime. To understand consciousness and thus the mind, psychology, according to structuralism, must be concerned with three primary questions: First, what are the most basic elements of consciousness? Just as chemists break down physical substances into their elemental components, psychologists should identify the basic components of consciousness. Second, how are the elements associated with one another? That is, in what ways do they combine to produce complex experiences? Third, according to Titchener, what underlying physiological conditions are associated with the elements? Most of Titchener's work was devoted to the first goal of identifying the basic elements of consciousness. The primary methodology used toward this end was systematic experimental introspection.

INTROSPECTION

A primary goal for structuralism was to identify the basic elements of consciousness. Titchener reasoned that any science requires an observation of its subject matter, and psychology was no different. As detailed in Titchener's classic work, *Experimental Psychology: A Manual of Laboratory Practice* (4 vols., 1901-1905), introspection involved the systematic analysis and reporting of conscious experiences by highly trained researchers. Such individuals were trained to report on the most basic of sensory experiences and to avoid the stimulus error of reporting perceptual interpretations. For example, to report seeing "an apple" or having "a headache" would be a stimulus error. It would be more accurate, psychologically, to report seeing a "roundish, red object" or experiencing a "throbbing sensation of moderate intensity in the lower right part of the head." This methodology was used by Wundt, but Wundt emphasized quantitative judgments (such as size, weight, duration, or intensity), whereas in Titchener's system, descriptive reports were emphasized.

Titchener concluded that there were three basic elements of consciousness: sensations, images, and feelings. Sensations were the most fundamental and were the building blocks of all perceptions. In his *An Outline of Psychology* (1896), Titchener listed more than forty-four thousand elementary sensations, including approximately thirty-two thousand visual, twelve thousand auditory, and four taste sensations. It was held that these indivisible sensations could be combined in any number of ways to produce unique perceptions and ideas. Images are the building blocks for ideas and reflect previous sensory experiences. It is possible to have an image of an apple only because of past experiences with a particular combination of sensations. All feelings were viewed as reducible to experiencing a degree of pleasantness or unpleasantness. (In contrast, Wundt postulated two other dimensions: strain/relaxation and excitement/calmness.) A feeling, when combined with certain sensations, can give rise to a complex emotional state, such as love, joy, disgust, or fear.

Later in his career, Titchener asserted that each element of consciousness could be characterized with regard to five basic dimensions: quality, intensity, protensity (duration), attensity (clearness), and extensity (space). Quality refers to the differentiation of sensations (an apple may be red or green; the water may be hot or cold). Intensity refers to the strength or magnitude of the quality (the extent to which the apple is red or the water is cold). Protensity refers to the duration or length of a sensory experience. Attensity refers to the clarity or vividness of the experience and reflects the process of attention (sensations are clearer when they are the focus of attention). Some sensations, especially visual and tactile ones, can also be characterized in terms of extensity (that is, they take up a certain amount of space). Feelings were characterized only in terms of quality, intensity, and protensity. Titchener believed that feelings dissipated when they were the subject of focused attention and therefore could not be experienced with great clarity.

EVALUATION

Structuralism faded away after Titchener's death in 1927. However, the basic tenets of structuralism had been under attack for years. First, there were serious problems with introspection as a scientific methodology. The results of such studies were frequently unreliable and there was no way of objectively verifying the content of someone's consciousness. The controversy over imageless thought was important. One group of researchers, most notably a former follower of Wundt, Oswald Külpe, at the University of Würzburg, concluded, using introspection methodology, that some thoughts occurred in the absence of any mentalistic sensations or images. This was completely at odds with structuralism, and researchers loyal to the structuralist position were not able to replicate the findings. On the other hand, researchers sympathetic to the Würzburg school were able to replicate the findings. Obviously, a theoretical bias was driving the results. It was widely concluded that introspection was lacking the objectivity needed to sustain a scientific discipline. Other methodologies were discouraged by structuralists in part because of the limited scope of psychology they practiced. In essence, structural psychology was limited to the study of the elements of consciousness in the healthy adult human. There was no place for the use of nonhuman animals as subjects, no child psychology, and no concern with the psychology of physical or mental illness. In addition, Titchener was against applied research, that is, conducting research to help resolve practical problems. He felt that this would detract from the objectivity of the study, and that academic researchers should be devoted to advancement of pure knowledge. Finally, structuralism was criticized for focusing almost exclusively on the elements of consciousness without taking into serious consideration the idea that consciousness is experienced as a unified whole, and that this whole is different from the sum of the elements.

In the twenty-first century, two major contributions of structuralism are recognized. The first is the strong emphasis that Titchener and his followers placed on rigorous laboratory research as the basis for psychology. Although other methods are used by contemporary psychologists (such as case studies and field research), the emphasis on experimentation in practice and training remains dominant. Second, structuralism provided a well-defined school of thought and set of ideas that others could debate and oppose, with the ultimate result being the development of new and different schools of thought. The most prominent opposition to structuralism was functionalism.

FUNCTIONALISM

Unlike structuralism, functionalism was not a formal school of psychological thought. Rather, it was a label (originally used by Titchener) applied to a general set of assumptions regarding the providence of psychology, and a loosely connected set of principles regarding the psychology of consciousness. In many respects, functionalism was defined in terms of its opposition or contrast to structuralism. For example, functionalists believed that psychology should focus on the functions of mental life (in contrast to the structuralist focus on elemental components); be concerned with using psychology for practical solutions to problems (structuralists were, at best, indifferent to this concern); study not only healthy adult humans (the main focus of attention of structuralists) but also nonhuman animals, children, and unhealthy individuals; employ a wide range of methodologies to investigate psychological issues (structuralists relied almost totally on introspection); and examine individual differences, rather than being solely concerned, like the structuralists, with the establishment of universal (nomothetic) principles.

Although structuralism was imported to the United States by a British scholar (Titchener) who received his psychological training in Germany (under Wundt), functionalism had a distinctly American flair. The American *Zeitgeist* at the time emphasized pragmatism and individuality. Such qualities made American psychologists especially receptive to the revolutionary work of Charles Darwin on evolution and its subsequent application (as "social Darwinism") by anthropologist Herbert Spencer to education, business, government, and other social institutions. Other important developments that influenced functionalism include work by Sir Francis Galton on individual differences in mental abilities and the work on animal psychology by George Romanes and C. Lloyd Morgan.

WILLIAM JAMES

William James is considered the most important direct precursor of functional psychology in the United States, and one of the most eminent psychologists ever to have lived. James earned his medical degree from Harvard University in 1869 and subsequently became keenly interested in psychology. Despite his severe bouts with depression and other ailments, he accepted a post at Harvard in 1872 to teach physiology. Shortly thereafter, in 1875, James taught the first psychology course offered in the United States, "The Relations Between Physiology and Psychology," and initiated a classroom demonstration laboratory.

James published the two-volume *The Principles of Psychology* in 1890. This work was immediately a great success and is now widely regarded as the most important text in the history of modern psychology. Given the expansiveness of his work—more than thirteen hundred pages arranged in twenty-eight chapters—it is impossible to summarize fully, but it includes such topics as the scope of psychology, functions of the brain, habit, methods of psychology, memory, the consciousness of self, sensation, perception, reasoning, instinct, emotions, will, and hypnotism. James presented ideas that became central to functionalism. For example, in the chapter "The Stream of Consciousness," James criticized the postulate of structural psychology that sensations constitute the simplest mental elements and must therefore be the major focus of psychological inquiry. In contrast, James argued that conscious thought is experienced as a flowing and continuous stream, not as a collection of frozen elements. In critiquing introspection, the methodology championed by the structuralists, James asserted,

> The rush of the thought is so headlong that it almost always brings us up at the conclusion before we can arrest it . . . The attempt at introspective analysis in these cases is in fact like seizing a spinning top to catch its motion, or trying to turn up the gas quickly enough to see how darkness looks.

With this new, expansive conceptualization of consciousness, James helped pave the way for psycholo-

gists interested in broadening the scope and methods of psychology. What was to emerge was the school of functionalism, with prominent camps at the University of Chicago and Columbia University.

THE CHICAGO SCHOOL

The Chicago school of functionalism is represented by the works of American scholars John Dewey, James Rowland Angell, and Harvey A. Carr. Functionalism was launched in 1896 with Dewey's *Psychological Review* article, "The Reflex Arc Concept in Psychology." Dewey argued against reducing reflexive behaviors to discontinuous elements of sensory stimuli, neural activity, and motor responses. In the same way that James attacked elementalism and reductionism in the analysis of consciousness, Dewey argued that it was inaccurate and artificial to do so with behavior. Influenced by Darwin's evolutionary theory of natural selection, Dewey asserted that reflexes should not be analyzed in terms of their component parts, but rather in terms of how they are functional for the organism—that is, how they help an organism adapt to the environment.

Angell crystalized the functional school in his 1907 *Psychological Review* paper, "The Province of Functional Psychology." In this work, three characteristics of functionalism were identified: Functional psychology is interested in discerning and portraying the typical operations of consciousness under actual life conditions, as opposed to analyzing and describing the elementary units of consciousness. Functional psychology is concerned with discovering the basic utilities of consciousness, that is, how mental processes help organisms adapt to their surroundings and survive. Functional psychology recognizes and insists on the essential significance of the mind-body relationship for any just and comprehensive appreciation of mental life itself.

Carr's 1925 textbook *Psychology: A Study of Mental Activity* presents the most polished version of functionalism. As the title suggests, Carr identified such processes as memory, perception, feelings, imagination, judgment, and will as the topics for psychology. Such psychological processes were considered functional in that they help organisms gain information about the world, retain and organize that information, and then retrieve the information to make judgments about how to react to current situations. In other words, these processes were viewed as useful to organisms as they adapt their environments.

THE COLUMBIA SCHOOL

Another major camp of functionalism was at Columbia University and included such notable psychologists as James McKeen Cattell, Robert S. Woodworth, and Edward L. Thorndike.

In line with the functionalist's embrace of applied psychology and the study of individual differences, Cattell laid the foundation for the psychological testing movement that would become massive in the 1920's and beyond. Under the influence of Galton, Cattell stressed the statistical analysis of large data sets and the measurement of mental abilities. He developed the order of merit methodology, in which participants rank-order a set of stimuli (for instance, the relative appeal of pictures or the relative eminence of a group of scientists) from which average ranks are calculated.

Woodworth is best known for his emphasis on motivation in what he called dynamic psychology. In this system, Woodworth acknowledged the importance of considering environmental stimuli and overt responses but emphasized the necessity of understanding the organism (perceptions, needs, or desires), representing therefore an early stimulus-organism-response (S-O-R) approach to psychology.

Thorndike represented a bridge from functionalism to behaviorism, a new school of thought that was led by John B. Watson and emerged around 1913. Thorndike was notable for his use of nonhuman subjects, a position consistent with Darwin's emphasis on the continuity among organisms. He is also famous for his puzzle box research with cats, which led to his law of effect, which states that when an association is followed by a satisfying state of affairs, that association is strengthened. This early operant conditioning research was later expanded on by the famous behaviorist psychologist B. F. Skinner.

EVALUATION

Functionalism paved the way for the development of applied psychology, including psychological testing, clinical psychology, school psychology, and industrial-organizational psychology. Functionalism also facilitated the use of psychological research with a wide variety of subjects beyond the healthy male adult, including infants, children, the mentally ill, and nonhuman animals. Finally, functional psychologists used a wide variety of methods beyond that of introspection, including field studies, questionnaires, mental tests, and behavioral observations.

These developments were responsible, in part, for the United States becoming the world center for psychological study by 1920. The term "functional psychology" faded from usage as it became clear that, by default, being simply a psychologist in the United States meant being a functional psychologist. The shift in psychological thought instigated by functionalism set the stage for the next major evolutionary phase in American psychology, behaviorism.

SOURCES FOR FURTHER STUDY

Benjamin, Ludy T., Jr. "The Psychology Laboratory at the Turn of the Twentieth Century." *American Psychologist* 55 (2000): 318-321. This is a nontechnical and brief introduction to laboratory research in psychology from 1879 to 1900. The author discusses the importance of the laboratory for establishing psychology as a scientific discipline separate from philosophy.

Boring, Edwin G. *A History of Experimental Psychology.* 2d ed. New York: Appleton-Century-Crofts, 1950. This is the classic text on the history of psychology, written by one of Titchener's students.

Hergenhahn, B. R. *An Introduction to the History of Psychology.* 6th ed. Belmont, Calif.: Wadsworth/Cengage Learning, 2009. An excellent standard textbook on the history of psychology. Includes in-depth chapters on structuralism and functionalism.

Leys, R., and R. B. Evans. *Defining American Psychology: The Correspondence Between Adolf Meyer and Edward Bradford Titchener.* Baltimore: Johns Hopkins University Press, 1990. Adolf Meyer was a highly influential psychiatrist who exchanged a series of letters with Titchener in 1909 and again in 1918. This book represents an interesting firsthand look at how the new science of psychology was being discussed and situated among other disciplines.

Viegas, Jennifer. *William James: American Philosopher, Psychologist, and Theologian.* New York: Rosen, 2006. A biography of James that looks at his work in psychology as well as in religion and philosophy.

Jay W. Jackson

SEE ALSO: Behaviorism; Dewey, John; James, William; Mental illness: Historical concepts; Psychoanalytic psychology; Psychology: Definition; Psychology: History; Psychotherapy: Historical approaches; Skinner, B. F.; Thorndike, Edward L.; Watson, John B.

Stuttering

TYPE OF PSYCHOLOGY: Language; psychopathology; stress

FIELDS OF STUDY: Adolescence; adulthood; childhood and adolescent disorders

Stuttering is the most common speech disorder among adolescents and adults, and it has profound consequences for self-esteem. It usually begins in early childhood, as a result of both biological influences and learning processes. Modern therapy often focuses on treatments addressing behavioral aspects of stuttering.

KEY CONCEPTS
- communication environment
- desensitization techniques
- distraction techniques
- learning theory
- neurosis
- psychotherapy
- speech disrupters
- stuttering
- verbal disfluencies

INTRODUCTION

All people sometimes hesitate when they speak or repeat the starting sound or syllable of a word when they are nervous. These are examples of normal verbal disfluencies. Stutterers are different from normal speakers primarily because of the frequency of their problem, not because their speech problem is by itself unusual. Stuttering is a disorder involving the timing and rhythms of speech, not of articulation. Thus, it is quite different from other common speech defects. It is also the most common speech problem to affect teens or adults.

Stuttering is a universal phenomenon, impacting people of every society and language group on earth. It is approximately four times as common in boys as in girls. The disorder typically begins in the preschool years (almost always before age six) and, unless outgrown by adolescence, becomes progressively more pronounced. Some stutterers also exhibit cluttering, nonsensically vocalizing sounds. As the speaking problem worsens, the stutterer is likely to show other, related behavior problems such as nervous twitches or slapping oneself when trying to stop stuttering. Furthermore, a stutterer's self-esteem usually suffers; teens, especially, are self-conscious about this speech problem, which can lead to avoidance of speaking or to more pronounced social withdrawal.

POSSIBLE CAUSES

There are several possible causes of stuttering. Scientists do not seek to designate one as absolute; for different stutterers, different causes may apply. In addition, in any individual case, more than one cause may be relevant. For example, stuttering tends to run in families, suggesting a genetic contribution. This contribution may make an individual more likely to develop the stuttering problem, given the circumstances. About the only cause of stuttering that has been ruled out is imitation. No evidence exists that stuttering develops from a child's exposure to another stutterer.

A variety of physical differences between stutterers and nonstutterers have been investigated, with all aspects of the mouth and airways involved in speech production taken into account. When searching for a possible cause of stuttering, hearing problems should be considered, although stuttering is actually less common among the deaf. Nevertheless, partial hearing losses can influence confidence in learning to speak, and, in fact, the onset of the stuttering problem often corresponds with the earliest use of sentences. In the treatment of any speech defect, screening for hearing problems is an important preliminary step. Brain damage can also lead to neurogenic stuttering, although this trauma is not the usual cause of speech disfluencies.

While stress aggravates stuttering, it is not usually the cause of the speech disorder. Most stuttering problems develop gradually; parents of a stutterer typically cannot pinpoint when the problem began. Extremely stressful events have, however, been known to be direct causes of stuttering.

Most stuttering probably develops gradually during the time when children are beginning to speak in sentences and engage in conversation. Everyone shows verbal disfluencies; young children are even more likely to do so. Wendell Johnson argues that the difference between stuttering and nonstuttering preschoolers is not in the children, but in the perceptions of their parents. By overreacting to normal disfluencies, parents may impair a young child's self-confidence, instigating a vicious cycle: Low self-confidence creates more disfluency, which further lowers self-confidence. The cycle continues until the child is, in fact, a "stutterer."

The difficulty with this line of reasoning is that it imposes an unfair burden of guilt on the parents. In effect, concerned parents are accused of causing the problem by expressing their concern. While parental behavior may contribute to stuttering, most experts believe that the genetic evidence and the preponderance of boys among stutterers suggest a physical contribution as well. Moreover, treatment of speech disorders is most effective when begun early, and the social impact of stuttering makes early treatment even more critical; thus, parents of stutterers may not know whether they will do more harm by calling attention to the problem or by ignoring it.

TREATMENT APPROACHES

The best advice to parents is to be patient but watchful. First, parents should remember that all speakers show disfluencies, which are impacted by stress. The child learning to speak may require patience from the adult listener. Parents should not pressure a child who is attempting to express what, to the child, may be a complex idea. Parents should not finish a child's sentences. If a child's stuttering problem does not disappear with time, if it appears without obvious stressful circumstances, or if accompanying nervous behaviors develop, the parent should seek help. Patience and lack of pressure are extremely important with a diagnosed stutterer. The most helpful roles for the parent at this point are to provide unconditional emotional support and to cooperate with the therapist.

Many approaches to the treatment of stuttering emphasize controlling the problem rather than eliminating it. Stutterers are often advised to slow down their speaking and simply to stop and take a deep breath if stuttering begins. They may be advised to sigh before any speech attempt. Therapy is also concerned with self-esteem problems and with the social avoidance of stutterers, treating these as results, not causes, of stuttering.

Stutterers often develop their own control techniques. Some find, for example, that singing is easier than talking and take advantage of this to modify the pitch of their speech when a problem occurs. The best advice may be to do whatever works for any individual.

The decision whether or not to treat stuttering is complicated by the similarity of speech between early stutterers and nonstutterers and by the resulting difficulty in pinpointing the origin of the problem. Edward G. Conture has pointed out that therapists deal both with parents who are overconcerned about normal disfluency and with parents who are underconcerned about a real problem. Moreover, Conture has noted, the nature of treatment depends considerably on the age of the stutterer.

Young stutterers offer the best hope for treatment, before the complications created by social stigma occur or worsen. On the other hand, young stutterers present greater problems in diagnosis, as well as a need to counsel parents who are themselves experiencing stress related to the stuttering. For example, parents of stutterers frequently have great difficulty looking at their child when the child stutters. They feel their child's pain, but their own pained response may not be helpful. Additionally, young children may not understand instructions for speech exercises or may lack the patience to practice techniques. Teens are better able to cooperate with the activities of speech therapy, which involve following directions and practice. On the other hand, they may be uncooperative for a number of reasons: past negative therapy experience, fear of peer reactions to speech therapy, and normal adolescent resistance to adults.

Adult stutterers have the least likelihood of overcoming the problem but are highly motivated (although they also may have had bad experiences with past therapy efforts) and have the freedom to structure their own environments. The adult's freedom from parent and peer pressure can make psychotherapy for self-esteem problems more successful than it is for children and adolescents. On the other hand, the adult continues to face a tremendous social stigma, which can even take the form of job discrimination. Moreover, by this time in a stutterer's life, stuttering has become part of the person's identity, making change difficult.

SPEECH THERAPY

Specific speech therapy techniques are varied. Distraction techniques aim to divert the stutterer from the speech problem. The theoretical basis for this technique is that self-consciousness about speech aggravates stuttering. In one example of this type of therapy the stutterer crawls on the floor while speaking. These techniques often provide only temporary success because the general use of such methods in real-life situations is unlikely.

Desensitization techniques focus on training the stutterer to deal with situations that provoke stuttering. This requires analyzing all situations that produce stuttering. After a stress-free therapy environment is created, the "speech disrupters" are reintroduced one at a time, with the aim of strengthening the individual's tolerance for disruption.

Therapy is most effective for children when parents are involved, especially in terms of promoting self-esteem. Parents may require counseling also, both to deal with their own frustrations and to understand the impact of their and others' reactions on the stuttering child. In addition, parents are the most important members of the child's communication environment. The parents' roles, not only in their responses to the child's speech but also in their own manner of speaking with the child, largely structure that environment. For example, studies show that a child's stuttering diminishes when parents slow down their speech to a stuttering child.

An individual's self-esteem is central to effective therapy. Psychotherapy frequently deals with the psychological damage created by the stigma of stuttering. There are also numerous books on stuttering, many with a focus on self-help. Several authors advise stutterers of the needs, first, to increase their self-confidence and, second, to refrain from avoiding social interaction. For example, Johnson specifically emphasizes concentrating on one's "normal" speech instead of on one's stuttering. The idea is that the stutterer's preoccupation with stuttering has served to maintain and worsen the problem.

A common tactic in the self-help literature is to cite notable stutterers, including Moses, Aristotle, Thomas Jefferson, Winston Churchill, Charles Darwin, Annie Glenn, John Stossel, and Marilyn Monroe. Many significant stutterers have been known for their writing, and some have sufficiently coped to become public speakers, news reporters, or actors. This success may inspire a stutterer, enhancing a stutterer's self-esteem. Self-confidence is the common thread among all treatments, whether self-help, speech therapy, psychotherapy, or unconditional parental support.

CONTEMPORARY THEORIES

Descriptions of stuttering treatments can be found throughout history. Charles Van Riper listed several of the prescientific approaches, some dating to ancient Greece and Rome, including speaking with pebbles in the mouth (an ancient use of a distraction technique), exorcism, hot substances applied to the tongue, and bloodletting. At the beginning of the modern era, techniques included tongue exercises and surgery that deformed the tongue.

In the late nineteenth century, stuttering was described as a neurosis, or disorder caused by anxiety. Twentieth century psychoanalysts expanded on this theme in their treatment of stutterers. Through the first half of the twentieth century, the psychoanalytic view dominated theories and treatments of stuttering. According to this view, stuttering results from an unconscious conflict between the desire to speak and a preference to remain silent. The obvious tension experienced by stutterers, as well as their avoidance of speaking, supported this interpretation. The *Diagnostic and Statistical Manual of Mental Disorders* has included stuttering as a communications disorder.

Although some therapists remain influenced by psychoanalytic views, most contemporary therapists

---

DSM-IV-TR Criteria for Stuttering (DSM code 307.0)

Disturbance, inappropriate for age, in the normal fluency and time patterning of speech

Characterized by frequent occurrences of one or more of the following:
- sound and syllable repetitions
- sound prolongations
- interjections
- broken words (such as pauses within a word)
- audible or silent blocking (filled or unfilled pauses in speech)
- circumlocutions (word substitutions to avoid problematic words)
- words produced with an excess of physical tension
- monosyllabic whole-word repetitions

Fluency disturbance interferes with academic or occupational achievement or with social communication

If speech-motor or sensory deficit is present, speech difficulties exceed those usually associated with these problems view the tension between wanting to speak and wanting to remain silent to be a result, not a cause, of stuttering. These therapists were more influenced by learning theory than psychoanalysis. For them, stuttering is considered the result of a process of learned reactions to specific environmental influences. Johnson's research on the similarities between preschool stutterers and nonstutterers, along with the differences among the perceptions of those same children's parents, strongly supports this interpretation. Most theorists and therapists also accept the role of genetic disposition in determining those likely to develop a stuttering disorder. In this view, therapy focuses on a stutterer's relearning and on control of the communication environment, especially the speech and reactions of the parents. Psychotherapy remains important not because psychological problems are seen as the cause of stuttering but because they appear to result from stuttering— from social stigma and frustrations in communicating with others.

The shift in professional views of stuttering may be attributed to the growing role in research of people who themselves have or have had a stuttering problem. Van Riper was such an individual, and he devoted his entire career to research and treatment of stuttering. The value of his personal experience is found in his own solution: He became fluent when he stopped trying to hide his problem. Stuttering is a learned speech problem, with tremendous emotional consequences; stutterers are simply normal people coping with this problem.

SCIENTIFIC AND TECHNOLOGICAL ADVANCES

In the early twenty-first century, researchers used advanced imaging technologies such as magnetic resonance imaging (MRI) to achieve greater comprehension of brain anatomy and activity associated with stuttering. Investigators discussed their findings in professional journals and public media; those examining neurophysiological aspects detected that brain areas stutterers used to process their speech differed from the speech locations in brains of normal speakers. Scientists assessed gray-matter volume, left inferior frontal gyrus, and bilateral temporal regions associated with speech functions and white matter tracts linked to facial and larynx motor functions. Mark Onslow and his Australian Stuttering Research Centre colleagues noted stutterers' brains often contained more gyri and matter volume in

speech parts of their brains than nonstutters. Other studies revealed that neuron connection flaws occurred in stutterers, and researchers hypothesized about whether the poor connections caused or were the result of stuttering. Aware that brain functioning affected speech, some therapists enhanced treatments to focus on physiological not psychological, intellectual, or social factors.

This knowledge of stutterers' brain functioning aided comprehension of other physical difficulties which many stutterers experienced, such as the inability to move their fingers quickly in rhythmic sequences needed to play some instruments. Scientists aware of brain activity in stutterers determined that the areas in brains associated with muscle control functions in tongues and other speech-related anatomy were adjacent to brain sites tied to finger movement.

Speech professionals considered that stuttering could be connected to mental stresses and traumas, emphasizing that more research would enhance comprehension of psychogenic stuttering. Researchers began studying the roles of anxiety and other psychological issues in stutterers' lives. Onslow and his colleagues determined that 60 percent of stutterers who were clinical trial participants admitted they had social phobia. Ross G. Menzies led a study of thirty-two adults who stuttered to evaluate how receiving speech restructuring treatment only or experiencing both cognitive-based therapy to address social phobia and speech restructuring treatment impacted the subjects' psychological health and stuttering. Some researchers evaluated groups of stutterers with psychological tests, such as the Minnesota Multiphasic Personality Inventory. Studies also considered how emotions in children influenced their speaking abilities and how stuttering provoked emotional abuse from peers.

Because of advances in communication technology, people who stuttered gained access to new therapeutic tools and methods. In 2008, the Hollins Communication Research Institute (HCRI) in Roanoke, Virginia, introduced its Hollins Fluency Program (HFP): Advanced Speech Reconstruction for Stuttering, which used computing and electronics technology to evaluate, readjust, and monitor a stutterer's speaking behavior to attain fluency. Ronald L. Webster, who founded HCRI, emphasized that HFP assisted people with varying forms and intensities of stuttering. During twelve days of therapy, HFP teaches stutterers how to stop muscle movements in their mouths, throats, and lungs associated with stuttering and practice alternative muscle behavior for fluent speaking. Clients interact with a computer program to study how to achieve specific movements of muscles for desired speech. A biofeedback component immediately assesses if clients have attained correct muscle motion while speaking. Approximately 93 percent of stutterers undergoing HFP achieved their desired results.

In January, 2009, the HCRI extended its therapy possibilities by developing an iPhone application to assess people's speaking behavior, in which stutterers carry iPhones while talking to family, friends, and people they encounter in public places. The iPhone application performs evaluations and presents feedback which had been restricted previously to the HCRI clinic computers. The mobility of the iPhone provides clients consistent assistance in environments where they most frequently speak instead of in artificial clinical surroundings.

SOURCES FOR FURTHER STUDY

Chang, Soo-Eun, et al. "Brain Anatomy Differences in Childhood Stuttering." *NeuroImage* 39 (2008): 1333-1344. Reports how imaging techniques assessed brain areas associated with speech and facial motor functions in three groups of children—fluent speakers, stutterers, and recovered stutterers—comparing data with imaging results in adults and emphasizing the importance of neuroplasticity in brain development.

Conture, Edward G. *Stuttering: Its Nature, Diagnosis, and Treatment.* Boston: Allyn & Bacon, 2001. A basic text aimed at speech therapy students. Emphasis on evaluation and treatment, highlighting important treatment differences related to the age of the stutterer. Includes numerous clinical examples and a complete case study in an appendix.

Davis, Stephen, Peter Howell, and Frances Cooke. "Sociodynamic Relationships Between Children Who Stutter and Their Non-Stuttering Classmates." *Journal of Child Psychology and Psychiatry* 43, no. 7 (2002): 939-947. Studied group of 403 children, ages eight through fourteen, of whom 16 stuttered, to observe how nonstutterers interact with stutterers. Discusses behavioral categories that the children used to describe their peers.

Guitar, Barry. *Stuttering: An Integrated Approach to Its Nature and Treatment.* 3d ed. Philadelphia: Lippincott Williams & Wilkins, 2006. Discusses basic stuttering information and addresses neurological diseases, emotional and psychological issues, trauma, brain imaging, neurogenic and psychogenic stuttering, and cluttering. Each chapter concludes with study questions and suggested projects. Tables, figures, bibliography.

Karrass, Jan, et al. "Relation of Emotional Reactivity and Regulation to Childhood Stuttering." *Journal of Communication Disorders* 39, no. 6 (November/December, 2006): 402-423. Researchers tested preschoolers who stuttered and a group who did not to assess how emotional issues might interfere with speech development. In addition to two laboratory-based speech tests of preschoolers, parents of the children tested responded to a survey about their children's emotional reactions and control.

Menzies, Ross G., et al. "An Experimental Clinical Trial of a Cognitive-Behavior Therapy Package for Chronic Stuttering." *Journal of Speech, Language, and Hearing Research* 51, no. 6 (December, 2008): 1451-1464. Evaluated the effect of singular and combined forms of cognitive behavior and speech restructuring therapies to aid stutterers with speaking problems and social anxieties twelve months after assistance from those therapies concluded.

Packman, Ann, Chris Code, and Mark Onslow. "On the Cause of Stuttering: Integrating Theory with Brain and Behavioral Research." *Journal of Neurolinguistics* 20, no. 5 (September, 2007): 353-362. Explains development of authors' syllable initiation theory to hypothesize about possible causation of stuttering, noting precedents investigating both healthy and damaged brain activity associated with speech.

Treon, Martin, Karen Blaesing, and Lloyd Dempster. "MMPI-2/A Assessed Personality Differences in People Who Do, and Do Not, Stutter." *Social Behavior and Personality: An International Journal* 34, no. 3 (April, 2006): 271-294. Study of sixty stutterers and sixty nonstutterers who were tested with the Minnesota Multiphasic Personality Inventory MMPI-2 and MMPI-A to detect any tendencies for psychological conditions sometimes associated with stuttering.

Nancy E. Macdonald; updated by Elizabeth D. Schafer

SEE ALSO: Language; Linguistics; Self-esteem; Speech disorders; Tic disorders.

Substance Abuse and Mental Health Services Administration

DATE: Founded in 1992

TYPE OF PSYCHOLOGY: Psychopathology; stress

FIELDS OF STUDY: Adulthood; coping; critical issues in stress; depression; models of abnormality; personality disorders; schizophrenias; stress and illness; substance-related issues

The Substance Abuse and Mental Health Services Administration is an agency of the U.S. Department of Health and Human Services. It was established by an act of Congress in October, 1992, under Public Law 102-321 to create services that would focus attention on improving the lives of individuals at risk for mental illness and substance use disorders.

KEY CONCEPTS

- addiction
- co-occurring disorders
- early intervention
- mental illness
- substance abuse

INTRODUCTION

As a subsidiary of the U.S. Department of Health and Human Services (HHS), the Substance Abuse and Mental Health Services Administration (SAMHSA) operates on the premise that all people (regardless of age, race, or background) who have or are at risk for mental health or substance use disorders (or co-occurring disorders), should be able to live a fulfilling and meaningful life. Therefore, they are entitled to an education, a career, a place to live, and satisfying relationships with family and friends. According to SAMHSA's *Results from the 2007 National Survey on Drug Use and Health: National Findings* (2008), there were nearly 47 million adolescents and adults in the United States in 2007 with mental health problems or substance use disorders. SAMHSA provides financing to states for programs aimed at prevention of or early intervention in co-occurring disorders. It also funds treatment programs and recovery support services for people with either mental health, substance use, or co-occurring disorders.

STRUCTURE

SAMHSA is subdivided into three major centers, which are instrumental in fulfilling the goals of the agency. The Center for Mental Health Services (CMHS) is the center charged with improving prevention and treatment of mental health services for all citizens of the United States. It is within its purview to oversee the application of scientifically established findings and evidence-based practice to the prevention and treatment of mental disorders. CMHS integrates these findings into programs aimed at detection, intervention, treatment, and support of children, adolescents, and adults with mental illness.

The Center for Substance Abuse Prevention (CSAP) is the agency charged with the dissemination of information aimed at prevention of illegal drug use, as well as of underage alcohol and tobacco use. It is a leader in the development of national policies and programs aimed at prevention of illegal substance use. According to CSAP, its aim is to help the states create healthy environments in which their citizens will have good quality of life.

The Center for Substance Abuse Treatment (CSAT) is the center charged with integrating the application of scientifically established findings and evidence-based practices to programs aimed at prevention and recovery within the substance abuse community. It works to foster the development of high-quality treatment and recovery services for people with alcohol or drug problems while providing support for their family and their communities.

PROGRAMS AND SERVICES PROVIDED

SAMHSA maintains a number of Web sites and databases to provide information on the prevention and treatment of mental illness and substance use disorders. One such site is SAMHSA's Health Information Network (SHIN). SHIN consists of the National Clearinghouse for Alcohol and Drug Information and the National Mental Health Information Center. The National Clearinghouse for Alcohol and Drug Information provides a very large number of resources featuring information about substance abuse prevention and treatment. The National Mental Health Information Center provides resources related to mental illness prevention, treatment, and recovery. Additionally, SAMHSA provides a wide variety of publications (both online and in print form) that deal with prevention and treatment of mental illness and substance abuse. These publications range from brochures to newsletters and books dealing with these topics and are generally available for free from the agency. Among the best known of these publications are the Treatment Improvement Protocols (best practice guidelines for treating substance abuse known as TIPs) and the Technical Assistance Publications (competencies for individuals involved in the treatment of substance abuse, known as TAPs). One of the agency's most used and useful publications is the *National Directory of Drug and Alcohol Abuse Treatment Programs* (published annually). SAMHSA also serves as a funding source for grants available from its three centers.

SOURCES FOR FURTHER STUDY

Aldworth, J., et al. *2004 National Survey on Drug Use and Health: Serious Psychological Distress Report.* Rockville, Md.: SAMHSA, 2005. This working paper reviews the tools that SAMHSA uses to identify seriously disturbed adults and provides an overview of the individuals so categorized.

Coomba, R. H. *Handbook of Addictive Disorders: A Practical Guide to Diagnosis and Treatment.* Hoboken, N.J.: John Wiley & Sons, 2004. This compendium of works describes types of addictive behavior ranging from drug and alcohol addiction through sex, gambling, and work addictions. It describes symptomatology, diagnosis, and treatment of these disorders, relying on and citing SAMHSA for much of its information.

De Jong, J., and N. Reatig. "SAMHSA Philosophy and Statement of Ethical Principles." *Ethics and Behavior* 8, no. 4 (1998): 339-343. This article highlights the ethical principles underlying SAMHSA's existence. It spells out the protocol by which the agency operates and gives an overview of its mission and goals, along with the types of programs in which it participates.

Jahn Moses, D., M. Kresky-Wolff, E. Bassuk, and P. Brounstein. "Special Issue: Homelessness and Mental Illness—Perspectives on Prevention." *The Journal of Primary Prevention* 28, nos. 3/4 (2007): 187-400. This special issue of the journal, consisting of fifteen articles, supported by SAMHSA, attempts to raise awareness about effective homelessness prevention and available intervention programs.

Substance Abuse and Mental Health Services Administration. *National Directory of Drug and Alcohol Abuse Treatment Programs.* Rockville, Md.: Author, 2008. This SAMHSA publication, which is updated on a regular basis, provides information on all the alcohol and drug treatment programs located in the United States. It describes the types of facilities available, types of patients treated, and levels of care for all the drug and alcohol treatment programs in the United States.

Robin Kamienny Montvilo

SEE ALSO: Addictive personality and behaviors; Alcohol dependence and abuse; Codependency; Elders' mental health; Men's mental health; Substance use disorders; Teenagers' mental health; Women's mental health.

Substance use disorders

TYPE OF PSYCHOLOGY: Biological bases of behavior; motivation; psychopathology; stress

FIELDS OF STUDY: Biological treatments; coping; critical issues in stress; motivation theory; nervous system; stress and illness; substance-related issues

Substance use disorders include the formal medical diagnoses of substance abuse and substance dependence for many types of drugs of abuse, including alcohol and prescription drugs. These disorders are characterized by recurrent problems in everyday life and physical or emotional distress and impairment that are caused or exacerbated by the use of the substances of abuse.

KEY CONCEPTS
- hallucinogens
- inhalants
- opioids
- psychological dependence
- sedatives/hypnotics
- self-medication
- stimulants
- tolerance
- withdrawal

INTRODUCTION

Substance use is studied in psychology from personality, social, and biological perspectives. Social and personality studies of individuals with substance use disorders have produced a variety of theories. These theories have focused on issues such as difficulties people might have with tolerating stress, being unable to delay gratification, developing social skills, being socially isolated or marginalized, being attracted to taking risks, and having difficulties regulating their own behavior. Additionally, environmental issues, such as poverty or high levels of stress, have been linked to substance use problems. Biological theories of these disorders suggest that genetic and conditioned sensitivities to substances of abuse and their effects may predispose individuals to acquire these disorders. For instance, people who have increased needs to seek relief from pain or have an increased need to seek pleasure or euphoria might be at greater risk for developing such problems. Pain is broadly defined as any feeling of dysphoria. Because both pain and euphoria can be produced by psychosomatic or somatopsychic events, these two biological categories can subsume most of the stated nonbiological correlates of substance abuse.

There are several forms of substance use disorders including abuse and dependence. These should be contrasted to normal experimentation, normal use without problems, and limited instances of misuse that are more appropriately attributed to situational factors than an underlying psychiatric disorder.

There are several types of substances of abuse, and some of these are not typically viewed as problematic. Major categories include sedatives/hypnotics; alcohol; nicotine; marijuana; opioids, such as heroin; stimulants, including amphetamine, cocaine, crack, and caffeine; inhalants, such as glue, paint, nitrous oxide (laughing gas), and shoe polish; hallucinogens, including phencyclidine (PCP or "angel dust"), lysergic acid diethylamide (LSD, or "acid"), MDMA (an amphetamine-like drug with hallucinogenic effects, also known as X or ecstasy); anabolic steroids; and even some types of prescription drugs, such as diazepam (Valium) or oxycodone (Oxycontin).

When diagnoses are given for substance use disorders, diagnoses should be given in terms of a specific type of substance. A diagnosis of "substance abuse" would be too general, because it does not specify the substance causing the problem. Having problems with one substance does not automatically mean that a person has problems with all substances. Thus, any diagnosis for a substance use disorder should be substance specific; examples might include alcohol abuse, inhalant abuse, marijuana dependence, marijuana abuse, cocaine dependence, or stimulant abuse.

For the substance abuse category, the key features of the disorder are patterns of repeated problems in individual functioning in terms of roles at work, school, or home; legal status; use of the substance in hazardous situations, or the consequences of the use on interpersonal relationships. For the substance dependence category, the key features of the disorder are patterns of repeated problems in several areas that are distinct from those considered for abuse. Diagnosis of dependence relies on factors such as tolerance; withdrawal; new or worsened physical or emotional problems directly resulting from the use of the substance; loss of control over the use of the substance; unsuccessful efforts to cut down or quit coupled with intense desire to quit; excessive periods of time spent obtaining, using, or recovering from using the substance; and the displacement of social or occupational activities to use the substance.

PAIN AND EUPHORIA

The experience of pain or the seeking of euphoria as causes of substance use disorders can be measured physically or can be perceived by the individual without obvious physical indicators. The relative importance of pain and euphoria in determining the development and maintenance of substance use disorders requires consideration of the contributions of at least five potential sources of behavioral and physical status: genetic predisposition, dysregulation during development, and dysregulation from trauma at any time during the life span, the environment, and learning. Any of these can result in or interact to produce the pain or feelings of euphoria that can lead to substance use disorders.

The key commonality in pain-induced substance use disorders is that the organism experiences pain that it does not tolerate. Genetic predisposers of pain include inherited diseases and conditions that interfere with normal pain tolerance. Developmental dysregulations include physical and behavioral arrests and related differences from developmental norms. Trauma from physical injury or from environmental conditions can also result in the experience of pain, as can the learning of a pain-producing response.

Several theories of pain-induced substance use

Substance-Related Disorders in DSM-IV-TR

- Substance Use Disorders:
  Dependence; Abuse
- Substance-Induced Disorders:
  Intoxication; Withdrawal; Anxiety Disorder; Persisting Amnestic Disorder; Intoxication Delirium; Persisting Dementia; Mood Disorder; Psychotic Disorder; Sexual Dysfunction; Sleep Disorder; Withdrawal Delirium
- Alcohol-Related Disorders:
  Abuse; Dependence; Anxiety Disorder; Intoxication; Intoxication Delirium; Mood Disorder; Persisting Amnestic Disorder; Persisting Dementia; Psychotic Disorder; Sexual Dysfunction; Sleep Disorder; Withdrawal; Withdrawal Delirium; Alcohol-Related Disorder Not Otherwise Specified
- Amphetamine- (or Amphetamine-like) Related Disorders:
  Abuse; Anxiety Disorder; Intoxication Delirium; Dependence; Intoxication; Psychotic Disorder; Mood Disorder; Sexual Dysfunction; Sleep Disorder; Withdrawal; Amphetamine-Related Disorder Not Otherwise Specified
- Caffeine-Related Disorders:
  Anxiety Disorder; Intoxication; Sleep Disorder; Caffeine-Related Disorder Not Otherwise Specified
- Cannabis-Related Disorders:
  Abuse; Anxiety Disorder; Intoxication; Dependence; Intoxication Delirium; Psychotic Disorder; Cannabis-Related Disorder Not Otherwise Specified
- Cocaine-Related Disorders:
  Abuse; Anxiety Disorder; Dependence; Intoxication; Intoxication Delirium; Mood Disorder; Psychotic Disorder; Sleep Disorder; Withdrawal; Cocaine-Related Disorder Not Otherwise Specified
- Hallucinogen-Related Disorders:
  Abuse; Anxiety Disorder; Dependence; Intoxication; Intoxication Delirium; Mood Disorder; Persisting Perception Disorder; Psychotic Disorder with Delusions; Hallucinogen-Related Disorder Not Otherwise Specified
- Inhalant-Related Disorders:
  Abuse; Anxiety Disorder; Dependence; Intoxication; Intoxication Delirium; Mood Disorder; Persisting Dementia; Psychotic Disorder; Inhalant-Related Disorder Not Otherwise Specified
- Nicotine-Related Disorders:
  Dependence; Withdrawal; Nicotine-Related Disorder Not Otherwise Specified
- Opioid-Related Disorders:
  Abuse; Intoxication Delirium; Dependence; Intoxication; Mood Disorder; Psychotic Disorder; Sleep Disorder; Sexual Dysfunction; Withdrawal; Opioid-Related Disorder Not Otherwise Specified
- Phencyclidine- (or Phencyclidine-like) Related Disorders:
  Abuse; Anxiety Disorder; Intoxication Delirium; Dependence; Intoxication; Mood Disorder; Psychotic Disorder; Phencyclidine-Related Disorder Not Otherwise Specified
- Sedative-, Hypnotic-, or Anxiolytic-Related Disorders:
  Abuse; Persisting Amnestic Disorder; Anxiety Disorder; Persisting Dementia; Dependence; Intoxication; Intoxication Delirium; Mood Disorder; Psychotic Disorder; Withdrawal; Withdrawal Delirium; Sexual Dysfunction; Sleep Disorder; Sedative-, Hypnotic-, or Anxiolytic-Related Disorder Not Otherwise Specified
- Polysubstance-Related Disorder:
  Dependence
- Other (or unknown) Substance-Related Disorders:
  Other (or unknown) Substance Use Disorders; Other (or unknown) Substance-Induced Disorders

disorders can be summarized as self-medication theories. In essence, these state that individuals misuse substances to correct an underlying disorder that presumably produces some form of physical or emotional distress or discomfort. Self-medication theories are useful because they take into account the homeostatic (tendency toward balance) nature of the organism and because they include the potential for significant individual differences in problems with pain.

Relief from pain by itself does not account entirely for drug use that goes beyond improvement in health or reachievement of normal status and certainly cannot account entirely for drug use that becomes physically self-destructive. Thus, the use of substances to achieve positive effects such as euphoria or pleasure is also important to consider as a cause of these disorders. Associative conditioning and operant conditioning effects play an important role as well. This type of substance misuse can be distinguished from the relief caused by substance use to decrease pain because the substance use does not stop when such relief is achieved, but continues until the person experiences the pleasurable effects.

Euphoria-induced substance use, or pleasure seeking, is characteristic of virtually all species tested. Some theorists have proposed that pleasure seeking is an innate drive not easily kept in check even by socially acceptable substitutes. Other theorists believe that these types of substance use disorders related to the positively reinforcing aspects of the substances may have developed as a function of biological causes such as evolutionary pressure and selection. For example, organisms that could eat rotten, fermented fruit (composed partly of alcohol) may have survived to reproduce when others did not; people who could tolerate or preferred drinking alcohol instead of contaminated water reproduced when those who drank contaminated water did not.

SUBSTANCE USE DISORDER RESEARCH

Laboratory studies of the biological bases of substance abuse and dependence involve clinical (human) and preclinical (animal) approaches. Such research has demonstrated that there are areas of the brain that can provide powerful feelings of euphoria when stimulated, indicating that the brain is primed for the experience of pleasure. Direct electrical stimulation of some areas of the brain, including an area first referred to as the medial forebrain bundle, produced such strong addictive behaviors in animals that they ignored many basic drives including those for food, water, mating, and care of offspring.

Later research showed that the brain also contains highly addictive analgesic and euphoriant chemicals that exist as a normal part of the neural milieu. Thus, the brain is also predisposed to aid in providing relief from pain and has coupled such relief in some cases with feelings of euphoria. It is not surprising, therefore, that substance abuse, dependence, and other behaviors with addictive characteristics can develop so readily in so many organisms.

The effects of typical representatives of the major categories of abused substances can be predicted. Alcohol can dis-

rupt several behavioral functions. It can slow reaction time, movement, and thought processes and can interfere with needed rapid eye movement (REM) sleep. It can also produce unpredictable emotionality, including violence. Those who abuse alcohol may go on to develop the symptoms of physiological dependence (a condition in which tolerance or withdrawal are present) and may go on to develop the full diagnosis of alcohol dependence, and it is important to note that the symptoms of alcohol withdrawal can be life-threatening. Heroin, an opioid, has analgesic (pain-killing) and euphoriant effects. It is also highly addictive, but withdrawal seldom results in death. Marijuana, sometimes classified as a sedative, sometimes as a hallucinogen, has many of the same behavioral effects as alcohol.

Stimulants vary widely in their behavioral effects. Common to all is some form of physiological and behavioral stimulation. Some, such as cocaine and the amphetamines (including methamphetamine), are extremely addictive and seriously life-threatening and can produce violence. Others, such as caffeine, are relatively mild in their euphoriant effects. Withdrawal from stimulants, especially the powerful forms, can result in profound depression.

Hallucinogens are also a diverse group of substances that can produce visual, auditory, tactile, olfactory, or gustatory hallucinations, but most do so in only a small percentage of the population. Some,

Cocaine is a frequently abused substance. (©Delphine Mayeur/Dreamstime.com)

such as PCP, can produce violent behavior, while others, such as LSD, are not known for producing negative emotional outbursts. Inhalants usually produce feelings of euphoria; they are most often used by individuals in their adolescent years who cannot afford to buy other types of drugs such as marijuana, as well as by adult individuals who have easy access to these substances in their work environments or social circles.

BRAIN CHEMISTRY

It is noteworthy that some of the pharmacological effects of very different drugs are quite similar. Marijuana and alcohol affect at least three of the same brain biochemical systems. Alcohol can become a form of opiate in the brain following some specific chemical transformations. These similarities raise an old and continuing question in the substance use field: Is there a fundamental addictive mechanism common to everyone that differs only in the level and nature of expression? Older theories of drug-abuse behavior approached this question by postulating the addictive personality, a type of person who would become indiscriminately addicted as a result of his or her personal and social history. With advances in neuroscience have come theories concerning the possibility of an addictive brain, which refers to a neurological status that requires continued adjustment provided by drugs.

An example of the workings of the addictive brain might be a low-opiate brain that does not produce normal levels of analgesia or normal levels of organismic and behavioral euphoria (joy). The chemical adjustment sought by the brain might be satisfied by use or abuse of any drug that results in stimulation of the opiate function of the brain. As discussed above, several seemingly unrelated drugs can produce a similar chemical effect. Thus, the choice of a particular substance might depend both on brain status and on personal or social experience with the effects and availability of the drug used.

The example of the opiate-seeking brain raises at least two possibilities for prevention and treatment, both of which have been discussed in substance use literature: reregulation of the brain and substitution. So far, socially acceptable substitutes or substitute addictions offer some promise, but reregulation of the dysregulated brain is still primarily a hope of the future. An example of a socially acceptable substitute might be opiate production by excessive running, an activity that can produce some increase in opiate function. The success of such a substitution procedure, however, depends on many variables that may be quite difficult to predict or control. The substitution might not produce the required amount of reregulation, the adjustment might not be permanent, and tolerance to the adjustment might develop. There are a host of other possible problems.

FUTURE POSSIBILITIES

Use of psychoactive substances dates from the earliest recorded history and most likely predates it. Historical records indicate that many substances with the potential for abuse were used in medicinal and ceremonial or religious contexts, as tokens in barter, for their euphoriant properties during recreation, as indicators of guilt or innocence, as penalties, and in other practices.

Substance use disorders are widespread in virtually all countries and cultures, and can be extremely costly, both personally and socially. There is no doubt that most societies would like to eliminate substance use disorders, as many efforts are under way to prevent and treat their occurrence. It is obvious that economic as well as social factors contribute both to substance use disorders and to the laws regulating substance use, and possibly create some roadblocks in eliminating abuse and dependence.

In psychology, the systemic and popular study of substance use became most extensive as the field of pharmacology blossomed and access to substances of abuse increased. The creation of the National Institute of Alcohol Abuse and Alcoholism and the National Institute on Drug Abuse helped to fuel research in this area in the 1970's and later. During the 1980's and 1990's, there was an increase in exploration of the biological mechanisms underlying substance use disorders and the possibility that pharmacological interventions might be useful to prevent and treat substance use disorders. The 1990's also brought an increase in awareness among the research and clinical communities that attention to specific demographic characteristics, such as age, gender, and ethnicity, was also important for understanding the etiology, prevention, and treatment of substance use disorders. As research progresses, these factors and the impact of the environment on behavior are increasingly the focus of study, and attention to the diagnosis of abuse is increasing.

Future research on substance use disorders is

likely to focus on biological determinants of the problem for the purposes of prevention and treatment, environmental circumstances related to problem development, the interaction of culture and gender as they relate to substance use disorders and treatments, and how other mental illnesses can compound problems related to substance use. Many people erroneously consider biological explanations of problematic behaviors to be an excuse for such behaviors. In fact, discoveries regarding the neural contributions to such behaviors are the basis on which rational therapies for such behaviors can be developed. Recognizing that a disorder has a basis in the brain can enable therapists to address the disorder with more useful therapeutic tools. In this way, simple management of such disorders can be replaced by real solutions to the problems created by substance abuse.

SOURCES FOR FURTHER STUDY

Brunton, Laurence L., ed. *Goodman and Gilman's The "Pharmacological Basis of Therapeutics."* 11th ed. New York: McGraw-Hill, 2006. A standard reference for students interested in an overview of the pharmacological aspects of selected addictive drugs. Of greater interest to those interested in pursuing the study of substance abuse from a neurological and physiological perspective.

Gitlow, Stuart. *Substance Use Disorders: A Practical Guide.* 2d ed. Philadelphia: Lippincott, Williams & Wilkins, 2007. Provides basic explanations for different diagnoses of substance use disorders and explains other diagnostic terms.

Inaba, Daryl. *Uppers, Downers, All Arounders: Physical and Mental Effects of Psychoactive Drugs.* 6th ed. Ashland, Oreg.: CNS Productions, 2007. An easy-to-read, practical book on what substance use disorders look like to the everyday person, as well as a description of related problems and concerns.

Julien, Robert M., Claire D. Advokat, and Joseph E. Comaty. *A Primer of Drug Action.* 11th ed. New York: Worth Publishers, 2008. An introductory treatment of types and actions of many abused and therapeutic substances. A useful, quick reference guide for psychoactive effects of drugs used in traditional pharmacological therapy for disorders and abused substances. Contains good reference lists and appendices that explain some of the anatomy and chemistry required to understand biological mechanisms of substance abuse.

Weil, Andrew, and Winifred Rosen. *From Chocolate to Morphine: Everything You Need to Know About Mind Altering Drugs.* Rev. ed. Boston: Houghton Mifflin, 2004. This classic, popular text discusses mind-altering substances, from foods that alter moods to illicit drugs of abuse.

Rebecca M. Chesire; updated by Nancy A. Piotrowski

SEE ALSO: Addictive personality and behaviors; Alcohol dependence and abuse; Caffeine and mental health; Codependency; Endorphins; Motivation; Nicotine dependence; Optimal arousal theory.

Suicide

TYPE OF PSYCHOLOGY: Psychopathology
FIELD OF STUDY: Depression

Suicide is the deliberate ending of one's own life; roughly 12 per 100,000 Americans commit suicide annually and it is the eleventh leading cause of death in the United States. Suicide rates are higher for men than women and increase with age; risk for suicide also increases with clinical depression, so suicide may be considered the most severe consequence of any psychological disorder.

KEY CONCEPTS
- altruistic suicide
- anomic suicide
- egoistic suicide
- epidemiological research
- psychological autopsy
- suicidal gesture

INTRODUCTION

Suicide is the intentional taking of one's own life. Psychologists have devoted much effort to its study, attempting to identify those at greatest risk for suicide and to intervene effectively to prevent suicide.

Sociologist Émile Durkheim introduced what has become a well-known classification of suicide types. Altruistic suicides, according to Durkheim, are those that occur in response to societal demands (for example, the soldier who sacrifices himself to save his comrades). Egoistic suicides occur when the individual is isolated from society and so does not expe-

Émile Durkheim classified suicides as altruistic, egoistic, and anomic. (Library of Congress)

rience sufficient societal demands to live. The third type is the anomic suicide. Anomie is a sense of disorientation or alienation that occurs following a major change in one's societal relationships (such as the loss of a job or the death of a close friend); the anomic suicide occurs following such sudden and dramatic changes.

Research supports Durkheim's ideas that suicide is associated with social isolation and recent loss. Many other variables, both demographic and psychological, have also been found to be related to suicide. Numerous studies have shown that the following demographic variables are related to suicide: sex, age, marital status, employment status, urban/ rural dwelling, and race. Paradoxically, more women than men attempt suicide, but more men than women commit suicide. Nearly four times the number of men commit suicide as women, and statistics from the National Institute of Mental Health and the Centers for Disease Control and Prevention

from 2004 indicate that death by suicide was the eighth leading cause of death for men and the sixteenth leading cause of death for women. The difference between the sexes in terms of attempted and completed suicide is generally explained by the fact that men tend to employ more lethal and less reversible methods than do women (firearms and hanging, for example, are more lethal and less reversible than ingestion of drugs).

Age is also related to suicide. In general, risk for suicide increases with increasing age; however, even though the risk of suicide is higher in older people, much attention has been devoted to suicide among children and adolescents. This attention is attributable to two factors. First, since 1960, there has been an increase in the suicide rate among people under twenty-five years of age. Second, suicide has become one of the leading causes of death among people under the age of twenty-one, whereas suicide is surpassed by many illnesses as a cause of death among older adults. Other demographic variables are related to suicide. Suicide risk is higher for divorced than married people. The unemployed have a higher suicide rate than those who are employed. Urban dwellers have a higher suicide rate than rural dwellers. Whites have a higher suicide rate than African Americans. According to the *Journal of Epidemiology and Community Health*, 2007 research indicates that male veterans have double the suicide rate of civilians because of exposure to both stress-related elements and knowledge of the lethal methods to commit the act.

In addition to these demographic variables, several psychological or behavioral variables are related to suicide. Perhaps the single best predictor of suicide is threatening to commit suicide. Most suicide victims have made some type of suicide threat or indicated an intent to commit suicide in another way (the threat may be veiled or indirect, such as putting one's affairs in order or giving away one's belongings). For this reason, psychologists consider seriously any threat of suicide. A related index of suicide risk is the detail or clarity of the threat, such as the creation of a suicidal note. Individuals who describe a suicide method in detail are at greater risk than those who express an intent to die but who describe the act only vaguely. Similarly, the lethality and availability of the proposed method provide additional measures of risk. Suicide risk is higher if the individual proposes using a more lethal method and if the individual has access to the proposed method, such as if the person has firearms in the home.

Another useful indicator of suicide risk is previous suicide attempts. People who have made prior attempts are at higher risk for suicide than people who have not. The lethality of the method used in the prior attempt is a related indicator. An individual who survives a more lethal method, such as a wound inflicted by a firearm or suffocation, is considered at higher risk than one who survives a less lethal attempt, such as a drug overdose.

Suicide risk is associated with particular behavioral or psychological variables: depression, isolation, stress, pain or illness, recent loss, and drug or alcohol use. These factors may help explain why certain of the demographic variables are related to suicide. For example, people who are unemployed may experience higher levels of stress, depression, and isolation than people who are employed. Similarly, divorced people may experience more stress and isolation than married people. The elderly may experience more isolation, depression, and pain or illness than younger people.

Although the demographic and psychological variables summarized above have been found to be related to suicide, the prediction of suicide remains extremely difficult. Suicide is a statistically rare event; according to basic laws of probability, it is very difficult to predict such rare occurrences. What happens in actual attempts to predict suicide is that, to identify the "true positives" (individuals who actually attempt suicide), one must accept a very large number of "false positives" (individuals who are labeled suicidal but who in fact will not attempt suicide). Many psychological disorders other than depression, particularly schizophrenia or borderline personality disorder, are also risk factors for suicide. Another factor associated with risk and prevention is the likelihood of imminent death, such as in patients with a terminal illness.

Since the 1990's, euthanasia, particularly the practices of physician Jack Kevorkian, has been controversial. Kevorkian aided terminally ill patients with their suicides via a lethal injection and was imprisoned in 1999 for administering the lethal injection himself. The controversy surrounding euthanasia involves a debate between whether the action is criminal or is a medical procedure to end suffering. As of 2009, the only state to allow doctor-assisted euthanasia was Oregon.

RESEARCH AND PREVENTION

Several methods have been used to study the psychology of suicide. Epidemiological research determines the distribution of demographic characteristics among suicide victims. Another method is to study survivors of suicide attempts. Estimates show that for every twenty-five suicide attempts, one death by suicide occurs. This enables psychologists to examine intensively their psychological characteristics. A third method is to analyze suicide notes, which may explain the individual's reasons for suicide. A final method is the psychological autopsy. This involves interviewing the victim's friends and family members and examining the victim's personal materials, such as diaries and letters, in an attempt to identify the psychological cause of the suicide.

Although all these approaches have been widely used, each has its limitations. The epidemiological method focuses on demographic characteristics and so may overlook psychological influences. Studying survivors of suicide attempts has limitations because survivors and victims of suicide attempts may differ significantly. For example, some suicide attempts are regarded as suicidal gestures, or "cries for help," the intent of which is not to die but rather to call attention to the self to gain sympathy or assistance. Thus, what is learned from survivors may not generalize to successful suicide victims. The study of suicide notes is limited by the fact that, contrary to popular belief, most suicide victims do not leave notes. For example, in a study of all suicides in Los Angeles County in a single year, psychologists Edwin Shneidman and Norman Farberow found that only 35 percent of the men and 39 percent of the women left notes. Finally, the psychological autopsy is limited in that the victim's records and acquaintances may not shed light on the victim's thought processes.

In 1988, Harry Hoberman and Barry Garfinkel conducted an epidemiological study to identify variables related to suicide in children and adolescents. They examined death records in two counties in Minnesota over an eleven-year period for individuals who died at age nineteen or younger. Hoberman and Garfinkel examined in detail the death records of 225 suicide victims. They noted that 15 percent of their sample had not been identified as suicides by the medical examiner but had instead been listed as accident victims or as having died of undetermined causes. This finding suggests that official estimates of suicide deaths in the United States are actually low.

Consistent with other studies, Hoberman and Garfinkel found that suicide was related to both age and sex. Men accounted for 80 percent of the suicides, women for only 20 percent. Adolescents aged fifteen to nineteen years composed 91 percent of the sample, with children aged fourteen and under only 9 percent. In addition, Hoberman and Garfinkel found that a full 50 percent of the sample showed evidence of one or more psychiatric disorders. Most common were depression and alcohol and drug abuse. Finally, Hoberman and Garfinkel found that a substantial number of the suicide victims had been described as "loners," "lonely," or "withdrawn." Thus, several of the indicators of suicide in adults also are related to suicide in children and adolescents.

ASSESSING RISK

Psychiatrist Aaron Beck and his colleagues developed the Hopelessness Scale in 1974 to assess an individual's negative thoughts of the self and future. In many theories of suicide, an individual's sense of hopelessness is related to risk for suicide. Beck and others have demonstrated that hopelessness in depressed patients is a useful indicator of suicide risk. For example, in 1985, Beck and his colleagues reported a study of 207 patients who were hospitalized because of suicidal thinking. Over the next five to ten years, fourteen patients committed suicide. Only one demographic variable, race, differed between the suicide and nonsuicide groups: White patients had a higher rate of suicide (10.1 percent) than African American patients (1.3 percent). Of the psychological variables assessed, only the Hopelessness Scale and a measure of pessimism differed between suicides and other patients. Patients who committed suicide were higher in both hopelessness and pessimism than other patients. Beck and his colleagues determined the Hopelessness Scale score, which best discriminated suicides from nonsuicides. Other mental health professionals can use this criterion to identify those clinically depressed patients who are at greatest risk for suicide.

Warning Signs for Suicide

No suicide attempt should be dismissed or treated lightly

The following can be warning signs:
- verbal threats such as "You'd be better off without me" or "Maybe I won't be around anymore . . . "
- Expressions of hopelessness and/or helplessness
- Previous suicide attempts
- Daring and risk-taking behavior
- Personality changes (such as withdrawal, aggression, moodiness)
- Depression
- Giving away prized possessions
- Lack of interest in the future

Source: National Mental Health Association (NMHA) factsheet "Suicide: General Information."

Several approaches have been developed in efforts to prevent suicide. Shneidman and Farberow developed what may be the most well-known suicide-prevention program, the Los Angeles Suicide Prevention Center. This program, begun in 1958, helped popularize telephone suicide hotlines. Staff members are trained to interact with individuals who are experiencing extreme distress. When an individual calls the center, staff members immediately begin to assess the caller's risk for suicide, considering the caller's demographics, stress, lifestyle, and suicidal intent. Staff members attempt to calm the caller, so as to prevent an immediate suicide, and to put the person in contact with local mental health agencies so that the individual can receive more extensive follow-up care.

Psychologists William Fremouw, Maria de Perczel, and Thomas Ellis published a useful guide for those who work with suicidal clients. Among their suggestions are to talk openly and matter-of-factly about suicide, to avoid dismissing the client's feelings or motives in a judgmental or pejorative way, and to adopt a problem-solving approach to dealing with the client's situation.

Suicide-prevention programs are difficult to evaluate. Callers may not identify themselves, so it is difficult to determine whether they later commit suicide. Still, such programs are generally thought to be useful, and suicide-prevention programs similar to that created by Shneidman and Farberow have been developed in many communities. Prevention measures are also available on the Internet; however, some Web sites may promote or encourage suicide.

SOCIAL AND CULTURAL CONTEXTS

Suicide is one of the most extreme and drastic behaviors faced by psychologists. Because of its severity, psychologists have devoted considerable effort to identifying individuals at risk for suicide and to developing programs that are effective in preventing suicide.

Psychological studies of suicide have shown that many popular beliefs about suicide are incorrect. For example, many people erroneously believe that people who threaten suicide never attempt suicide, that all suicide victims truly wish to die, that only the mentally ill commit suicide, that suicide runs in families, and that there are no treatments that can help someone who is suicidal. Because of these and other popular myths about suicide, it is especially important that psychological studies of suicide continue and that the results of these studies be disseminated to the public.

Suicide risk increases in clinically depressed individuals. In depressed patients, suicide risk has been found to be associated with hopelessness: As one's sense of hopelessness increases, one's risk for suicide increases. Since the 1970's, Beck's Hopelessness Scale has been used in efforts to predict risk for suicide among depressed patients. Although the suicide rate has been relatively stable in the United States since the early twentieth century, the suicide rate of young people has increased since the 1960's.

For this reason, depression and suicide among children and adolescents have become major concerns of psychologists. Whereas childhood depression received relatively little attention from psychologists before the 1970's, psychologists have devoted considerable attention to this condition since then. Much of this attention has concerned whether biological, cognitive, and behavioral theories of the causes of depression and approaches to the treatment of depression, which were originally developed and applied to depressed adults, may generalize to children. In the 1980's, psychologists developed several innovative programs that attempt to identify youths who are depressed and experiencing hopelessness, and therefore may be at risk for suicide; evaluations and refinements of these programs will continue.

PHARMACOLOGY AND TREATMENT

Because suicide is not a condition, but the result of a condition or a disorder, there is no set pharmaceutical treatment for those who attempt or threaten suicide; however, since depression is a determining factor in suicide, many of those suffering from depression take antidepressant drugs, such as selective serotonin reuptake inhibitors (SSRIs), which may aid in suicide prevention by stabilizing mood. Drug treatment is often accompanied by therapy, which also can reduce risk. Heavily debated studies as of 2005 have indicated controversy that some SSRIs, such as fluoxetine (Prozac), can actually increase the chance of suicide up to 5 percent, particularly in younger patients. Other conditions, such as schizophrenia, are treated with psychotropic drugs that can aid in suicide prevention, such as clozapine (Clozaril). For those who are at risk because of substance abuse, treatment may first entail eliminating that substance from the patient's environment.

SOURCES FOR FURTHER STUDY

Durkheim, Émile. *Suicide.* Reprint. Glencoe, Ill.: Free Press, 1951. In this work, originally published in 1897, Durkheim introduced his system for classifying suicide types—altruistic, egoistic, and anomic suicides—and examined the relationship of suicide to isolation and recent loss.

Fremouw, William J., Maria de Perczel, and Thomas E. Ellis. *Suicide Risk: Assessment and Response Guidelines.* New York: Pergamon, 1990. This book presents useful guidelines, based on both research and clinical practice, for working with suicidal individuals.

Hawton, Keith. *Suicide and Attempted Suicide Among Children and Adolescents.* Beverly Hills, Calif.: Sage Publications, 1986. Presents an overview of research results concerning the causes of youth suicide and treatment programs for suicidal youngsters.

Jobes, David A., and Edwin S. Shneidman. *Managing Suicidal Risk: A Collaborative Approach.* New York: Guilford Press, 2006. A clinical book intended for psychologists and therapists who are working with suicidal patients. Includes visual aids on how to assess risk and develop treatment plans.

Lann, Irma S., Eve K. Moscicki, and Ronald Maris, eds. *Strategies for Studying Suicide and Suicidal Behavior.* New York: Guilford Press, 1989. This book examines the various research methods used to study suicide. Considers the relative strengths and weaknesses and offers examples of each method.

Lester, David, ed. *Current Concepts of Suicide*. Philadelphia: Charles Press, 1990. A useful overview of research results on the possible causes of suicide and on programs designed both to prevent suicide and to treat suicidal patients.

Peck, Michael L., Norman L. Farberow, and Robert E. Litman, eds. *Youth Suicide*. New York: Springer, 1989. A useful overview of the psychological influences on youth suicide and on the treatment and prevention programs that have been used with suicidal youths.

Shneidman, Edwin S. *The Suicidal Mind*. New York: Oxford University Press, 1996. An overview of patients who commit suicide, examined by asking questions such as, "Why do we kill ourselves?"

Shneidman, Edwin S., and Judy Collins. *Autopsy of a Suicidal Mind*. New York: Oxford University Press, 2004. An intense look at suicide via a psychological analysis of the suicidal mind. Includes interviews with the top suicide experts in the country.

Shneidman, Edwin S., Norman L. Farberow, and Robert E. Litman. *The Psychology of Suicide*. New York: Science House, 1970. This is a collection of articles, some of which are now regarded as classics in the study of suicide.

Michael Wierzbicki; updated by Jean Prokott

SEE ALSO: Antidepressant medications; Antipsychotic medications; Beck, Aaron T.; Bipolar disorder; Crisis intervention; Death and dying; Depression; Drug therapies; Elders' mental health; Teenage suicide.

Sullivan, Harry Stack

BORN: February 21, 1892, in Norwich, New York
DIED: January 14, 1949, in Paris, France
IDENTITY: American psychiatrist and social analyst
TYPE OF PSYCHOLOGY: Personality; psychotherapy
FIELDS OF STUDY: Interpersonal relations; personality theory; psychodynamic and neoanalytic models; schizophrenias

Sullivan created an interpersonal psychiatry using an integration of experience, development, pathology, culture, and system.

Harry Stack Sullivan was an American physician who studied psychopathology and psychiatry. He was born of Irish-Catholic stock in Chenango County, south central New York State. After a troubled early life, he entered the psychiatric world at St. Elizabeths Hospital in Washington, D.C., in 1920. Influenced by Swiss psychiatrist Adolf Meyer and analyzed by American psychiatrist Clara Thompson, he joined Karen Horney and Erich Fromm in promoting a social (interpersonal) form of psychoanalysis. He was an inspiring teacher, which brought him a loyal following. He worked clinically with varied groups, including schizophrenics. He never married.

Sullivan took an eclectic and interpersonal approach to understanding personality that later influenced British psychoanalyst R. D. Laing. Sullivan provided an integration in self theory between the social role orientation and mirroring approach of philosopher George H. Mead and the psychoanalytic view of unconscious processes pioneered by Sigmund Freud. In creating a unique mixture, Sullivan added his own view of development, a view that came out of his own experience in growing up and his diagnostic and therapeutic work with severely disturbed patients. His ideas about developmental eras predate an American focus on cognitive development as articulated by Swiss psychologist Jean Piaget and the American response of Jerome Bruner and others. Consideration of a developmental mode of functioning—prototaxic, parataxic, and syntaxic—added to his description of experience. He viewed the self as a system that included significant others, especially their anxiety, before psychiatrist Murray Bowen introduced the notion of system into family therapy. His contacts with cultural anthropologists such as Edward Sapir and Ruth Benedict led him to views that prefigured social constructionism, the postmodern view that society exclusively shapes the self.

Sullivan's approach has been synthesized with that of Piaget by James Youniss, who has applied this integrated approach to the study of social development, looking at ways of understanding friendship, kindness, and reciprocity in youth.

As cofounder and editor of the journal *Psychiatry*, Sullivan wrote a number of short articles and editorials. His several books were assembled and published after his death. His 1939 lectures are summed up in *Conceptions of Modern Psychiatry* (1953), and his

1948 notes for lectures were edited and published in *The Interpersonal Theory of Psychiatry* (1953).

SOURCES FOR FURTHER STUDY

Evans, F. Barton, III. *Harry Stack Sullivan: Interpersonal Theory and Psychotherapy*. New York: Routledge, 1996. Examines Sullivan's theory of personality development over the life cycle, his view of psychopathology and his detailed exploration of the psychiatric interview as it relates to interpersonal psychotherapy.

Mullahy, Patrick, ed. *The Contributions of Harry Stack Sullivan: A Symposium on Interpersonal Theory in Psychiatry and Social Science*. 1952. Reprint. Northvale, N.J.: Jason Aronson, 1995. Contemporaries of Sullivan view his contributions as clinician and social scientist.

Sollod, Robert N., John P. Wilson, and Christopher F. Monte. *Beneath the Mask: An Introduction to Theories of Personality*. 8th ed. Hoboken, N.J.: John Wiley & Sons, 2009. The chapter on Harry Stack Sullivan and interpersonal theory integrates theory and significant events with his life history.

Everett J. Delahanty, Jr.

SEE ALSO: Bruner, Jerome; Fromm, Erich; Horney, Karen; Piaget, Jean; Social psychological models: Erich Fromm; Social psychological models: Karen Horney.

Support groups

TYPE OF PSYCHOLOGY: Cognition; emotion; language; learning; memory; motivation; personality; psychological methodologies; psychopathology; psychotherapy; social psychology; stress

FIELDS OF STUDY: Adolescence; adulthood; aggression; aging; anxiety disorders; attitudes and behavior; behavioral therapies; childhood and adolescent disorders; cognitive therapies; coping; critical issues in stress; depression; group and family therapies; group processes; interpersonal relations; motivation theory; personality disorders; prejudice and discrimination; problem solving; prosocial behavior; schizophrenias; sexual disorders; sleep; social motives; social perception and cognition; stress and illness; substance abuse

The history of support groups in modern times begins with the formation of the Oxford Group in 1908 and the subsequent development of Alcoholics Anonymous. For the participants, support groups reduce feelings of isolation, offer information, instill hope, provide feedback and social support, and teach new social skills. At the opening of the twenty-first century, support groups exist for persons suffering from all kinds of medical and psychological conditions and for victims of violent crime.

KEY CONCEPTS
- cohesion
- exchange theory
- group dynamics
- networks
- norms
- roles
- social facilitation
- social inhibition
- social learning
- sociobiology

INTRODUCTION

Humans are social animals in that they live in groups. These networks among people are powerful in shaping behavior, feelings, and judgments. Groups can lead to destructive behavior, such as mob violence and aggression, but they can also encourage loyalty, nurturing of others, and achievement, as found in cancer-support groups. Scientific investigation of how groups affect human behavior began as early as 1898, but the main body of research on group functioning began only in the 1940's and 1950's. The study of groups is still a major topic of scientific enquiry.

D. R. Forsyth defined a group as "two or more individuals who influence each other through social interaction." A group may be permanent or temporary, formal or informal, structured or unstructured. Those groups known as support groups may share any of these characteristics.

Why do human beings seek out groups? Social learning theorists believe that humans learn to depend on other people because most are raised within families, where they learn to look to other people for support, validation, amusement, and advice. Exchange theorists, on the other hand, reason that groups provide both rewards (such as love and approval) and costs (such as time and effort). Membership in a group will "profit" the individual if the rewards are greater than the costs. Yet another set of theorists, the sociobiologists, argue that humans form groups because this has a survival benefit for the species. They hypothesize a genetic predisposition toward affiliation with others. It is within groups that the fittest have the greatest chance of survival.

Whatever the reason for forming groups, all groups have important characteristics that must be addressed in seeking to understand why support groups work. First of all, group size is important. Larger groups allow more anonymity, while smaller groups facilitate communication, for example. Group structure includes such elements as status differences, norms of conduct, leaders and followers, and subgroups. Individuals in groups develop social roles—those expected behaviors associated with the individual's position within the group. Roles are powerful in influencing behavior and can even cause individuals to act contrary to their private feelings or their own interests. These roles carry varying degrees of status within the group—who is influential and respected and who is less so. Groups may have subgroups, based on age, residence, roles, interests, or other factors. These subgroups may contribute to the success of the whole or may become cliquish and undermine the main group's effectiveness.

Groups also have varying degrees of cohesion. Cohesion reflects the strength of attachments within the group. Sometimes cohesion is a factor of how well group members like one another, sometimes a factor of the need to achieve an important goal, and sometimes a factor of the rewards that group membership confers. All groups have communication networks, or patterns of openness and restrictions on communication among members.

Group norms are those attitudes and behaviors that are expected of members. These norms are needed for the group's success because they make life more predictable and efficient for the members. Leadership may be formal or informal, may be task oriented or people oriented, and may change over time. Finally, all groups go through fairly predictable stages as they form, do their work, and conclude. The comprehensive term for the way a group functions is "group dynamics."

How Groups Influence Individuals

Researchers have found that for all animals, including human beings, the mere presence of other members of the same species may enhance performance on individual tasks. This phenomenon is known as social facilitation. However, with more complex tasks the presence of others may decrease performance. This is known as social inhibition or impairment. It is not clear whether this occurs because the presence of others arouses the individual, leads individuals to expect rewards or punishments based on past experience, makes people self-conscious, creates challenges to self-image, or affects the individual's ability to process information. Most theorists agree that the nature of the task is important in the success of a group. For example, the group is more likely to succeed if the individual members' welfare is closely tied to the task of the group.

Groups provide modeling of behavior deemed appropriate in a given situation. The more similar the individuals doing the modeling are to the individual who wants to learn a behavior, the more powerful the models are. Groups reward members for behavior that conforms to group norms or standards and punish behaviors that do not conform. Groups provide a means of social comparison—how one's own behavior compares to others' in a similar situation. Groups are valuable sources of support during times of stress. Some specific factors that enhance the ability of groups to help individuals reduce stress are attachment, guidance, tangible assistance, and embeddedness. Attachment has to do with caring and attention among group members. Guidance may be provision of information or it may be advice and feedback provided by the group to its members. Tangible assistance may take the form of money or of other kinds of service. Embeddedness refers to the sense the individual has of belonging to the group. Some researchers have shown that a strong support system actually increases the body's immune functioning.

Alcoholics Anonymous

The most well-known support group is Alcoholics Anonymous (AA), formed in Akron, Ohio, in the late 1930's. AA groups now number in the tens of thousands and are found across the globe. What is less well known is that AA is an outgrowth of the Oxford Group, an evangelical Christian student and athlete group formed at Oxford University in England in 1908. The Oxford Group's ideals of self-examination, acknowledgment of character defects, restitution for harm done, and working with others directly influenced the steps to recovery practiced by members of AA and other so-called twelve-step groups, including Al-Anon, Narcotics Anonymous, and Smokers Anonymous.

For addicts, support groups are important for a number of reasons. They provide peer support for the effort to become "clean and sober." They provide peer pressure against relapsing into substance use. They assure addicts that they are not alone—that others have suffered the destruction brought about by drinking or drug use. Addicts in twelve-step groups learn to interact with others on an emotional level. Importantly, members of AA and other support groups for addicts are able to confront the individual's maladaptive behaviors and provide models for more functional behavior. The norm for AA is sobriety, and sobriety is reinforced by clear directions on how to live as a sober person. Another important aspect of AA is the hope that it is able to inspire in persons who, while using, saw no hope for the future. This hope comes not only from seeing individuals who have successfully learned to live as sober persons but also from the group's emphasis on dependence on a higher power and the importance of a spiritual life.

OTHER SUPPORT GROUPS

Not all support groups are for addicts. Support groups exist for adoptive parents, children who have been adopted, persons with acquired immunodeficiency syndrome (AIDS), caregivers for patients with Alzheimer's disease, amputees—and that is just the beginning. Why are these groups so popular? Some writers believe that Americans have turned away from the "rugged individualism" that has characterized the national psyche in the past and are searching for meaning in groups to replace the extended families found in other societies. However, this does not explain why support groups are also popular in other parts of the world. The answer probably lies in the characteristics of groups.

Support groups are generally composed of small numbers of people who are facing similar challenges in their lives. They meet, with or without a trained facilitator, to explore their reactions, problems, solutions, feelings, frustrations, successes, and needs in relation to those challenges. They build bonds of trust. Members show compassion for one another. Groups may provide material support or simply assure the individual member he or she is not alone.

They help minimize stress and maximize coping. They model strategies for dealing with the given challenge. They provide information. They nurture their members. They encourage application of new learning. Through this sharing, each member grows, and through individual growth, the group matures.

Support groups have traditionally met in person, but the Internet has altered this expectation. Many support groups now meet online. These may take the form of synchronous or asynchronous chat groups, bulletin boards, Web sites with multiple links to information sources, referrals, and collaboration with professionals. These groups, while not well studied, seem to serve the same purposes as in-person groups. In addition, they provide a possible advantage: The anonymity of the Web makes it possible to observe and to learn from observing without actually participating until one is comfortable doing so.

Support groups may not be sufficient in and of themselves to solve individual problems. They are probably most effective as a part of an integrated plan for addressing the challenge in the individual's life that involves other resources as appropriate. For example, the caregiver of a person with Alzheimer's disease may also need social services support, adult daycare or respite care facilities, medical assistance for control of problem behaviors, and home health services to deal successfully with the day-to-day challenges of dealing with the patient. The support group can facilitate access to these other resources in addition to serving as an important stress reducer and support system for the caregiver.

SOURCES FOR FURTHER STUDY

Carlson, Hannah. *The Courage to Lead: Start Your Own Mutual Help Support Group—Mental Illnesses and Addictions.* Madison, Conn.: Bick, 2001. A complete how-to manual for creating small groups for persons striving against addiction or to overcome mental illnesses.

Klein, Linda L. *The Support Group Sourcebook: What They Are, How You Can Find One, and How They Can Help You.* New York: John Wiley & Sons, 2000. The most comprehensive guide to how groups work and develop, and how they assist people. Good advice on how to start or find a group.

Mowat, Joan. *Using Support Groups to Improve Behaviour.* Thousand Oaks, Calif.: PCP/Sage Publications, 2007. Mowat describes how to change undesirable behaviors through support groups.

Nichols, Keith, and John Jenkinson. *Leading a Support Group: A Practical Guide.* New York: Open University Press, 2006. Nichols and Jenkinson explain the benefits of support groups and describe a step-by-step guide to forming and running one.

O'Halloran, Sean. *Talking Oneself Sober: The Discourse of Alcoholics Anonymous.* Amherst, N.Y.: Cambria Press, 2008. Discusses the techniques followed by one of the best-known support groups.

Rebecca Lovell Scott

SEE ALSO: Alcohol dependence and abuse; Computer and Internet use and mental health; Coping: Social support; Group therapy; Groups; Internet psychology; Self-help groups; Social networks.

Survey research
Questionnaires and interviews

TYPE OF PSYCHOLOGY: Psychological methodologies
FIELDS OF STUDY: Descriptive methodologies; experimental methodologies; methodological issues

Psychologists use survey research techniques, including questionnaires and interviews, to evaluate specific attitudes about social or personal issues and to find out about people's behaviors directly from those people. Questionnaires are self-administered and in written form; interviews entail the psychologist asking questions of a respondent. There are strengths along with limitations for both of these data collection methods.

KEY CONCEPTS
- attitudes
- demographics
- interview
- population
- questionnaire
- respondent
- sample

INTRODUCTION
Survey research is common in both science and daily life. Almost everyone has been exposed to survey research in one form or another. Data about the social world can be obtained in many ways, including observation, field studies, and experimentation. Two key methods for obtaining data—questionnaires and interviews—are survey research methods. Most of the social research conducted or published involves these two data collection methods.

In general, when using survey methods, the researcher gets information directly from each person (or respondent) by using self-report measurement techniques to ask people about their attitudes, behaviors, and demographics (statistical features of populations, such as age, income, race, and marital status), in addition to past experiences and future goals. In questionnaires, the questions are in written format and the subjects write down their answers. In interviews, the interviewer engages in one-to-one verbal communication with the respondent, either face-to-face or by means of a telephone. Both techniques are flexible and adaptable to the group of people being studied and the particular situation. Both can range from being highly structured to highly unstructured.

STRENGTHS AND LIMITATIONS
Questionnaires can be completed in groups or self-administered on an individual basis. They can also be mailed to people. They are generally less expensive than conducting interviews. Questionnaires also allow greater anonymity of the respondents. One drawback is that a questionnaire requires that the subjects understand exactly what the questions are asking. Also, people filling out the questionnaire may get bored or find it tedious to write down their answers. The survey researcher must therefore make sure that the questionnaire is not excessively long or complex.

In contrast, with an interview there is a better chance that the interviewer and subject will have good communication and that all questions will be understood. Telephone interviews are less expensive than face-to-face interviews; still, questionnaires tend to be less costly. In an interview, the respondent is presented with questions orally, whereas in the questionnaire, regardless of type or form, the respondent is presented with a written question. Each data collection device has pros and cons. The decision to use questionnaires versus interviews depends on the purpose of the study, the type of information needed, the size of the sample (the number of people who participate in a study and are part of a population), the resources for conducting the study, and the variable(s) to be measured. Overall, the interview is probably the more flexible device of the two.

DESIGNING BIAS-FREE QUESTIONS

When creating a questionnaire, the researcher must give special thought to the wording of the questions. Researchers must avoid questions that would lead people to answer in a biased way, or ones that might be easily misinterpreted. For example, the questions "Do you favor eliminating the wasteful excesses in the federal budget?" and "Do you favor reducing the federal budget?" might well result in different answers from the same respondent.

Questions are either closed- or open-ended, depending on the researcher's choice. In a closed-ended question, a limited number of fixed response choices are provided to subjects. With open-ended questions, subjects are able to respond in any way they like. Thus, a researcher could ask, "Where would you like a swimming pool to be built in this town?" as opposed to "Which of the following locations is your top choice for a swimming pool to be built in this town?" The first question allows the respondent to provide any answer; the second provides a fixed number of alternative answers from which the person must choose. Use of closed-ended questions is a more structured approach, allowing greater ease of analysis because the response alternatives are the same for everyone. Open-ended questions require more time to analyze and are therefore more costly. Open-ended questions, however, can provide valuable insights into what the subjects are actually thinking.

CLINICAL INTERVIEW

A specialized type of interview is the clinical, or therapeutic, interview. The specific goal of a particular clinical interview depends on the needs and the condition of the individual being interviewed. There is a distinction between a therapeutic interview, which attempts both to obtain information and to remedy the client's problem, and a research interview, which attempts solely to obtain information about people at large. Because the clinical interview is a fairly unstructured search for relevant information, it is important to be aware of the factors that might affect its accuracy and comprehensiveness. Research on hypothesis confirmation bias suggests that it is difficult to search for unbiased and comprehensive information in an unstructured

setting such as the clinical interview. In the context of the clinical interview, clinicians are likely to conduct unintentionally biased searches for information that confirm their early impressions of each client. Research on self-fulfilling prophecies suggests a second factor that may limit the applicability of interviews in general: The interviewer's expectations may affect the behavior of the person being interviewed, and respondents may change their behavior to match the interviewer's expectations.

ROLE OF SCIENTIFIC METHOD

Knowing what to believe about research is often related to understanding the scientific method. The two basic approaches to using the scientific method, the descriptive and the experimental research approaches, differ because they seek to attain different types of knowledge. Descriptive research tries to describe particular situations; experimental research tries to determine cause-and-effect relationships. Independent variables are not manipulated in descriptive research. For that reason, it is not possible to decide whether one thing causes another. Instead, survey research uses correlational techniques, which allow the determination of whether behaviors or attitudes are related to one another and whether they predict one another. For example, how liberal a person's political views are might be related to that person's attitudes about sexuality. Such a relationship could be determined using descriptive research.

Survey research, as a widely used descriptive technique, is defined as a method of collecting standardized information by interviewing a representative sample of some population. All research involves sampling of subjects. That is, subjects must be found to participate in the research, whether that research is a survey or an experiment. Sampling is particularly important when conducting survey research, because the goal is to describe what a whole population is like based on the data from a relatively small sample of that population.

KINSEY GROUP RESEARCH

One famous survey study in the mid-1930's was conducted by Alfred Kinsey and his colleagues. Kinsey studied sexual behavior. Until that time, most of what was known about sexual behavior was based on what biologists knew about animal sex; what anthropologists knew about sex among indigenous peoples in non-Western, nonindustrialized societies; or what

Sigmund Freud learned about sexuality from his emotionally disturbed patients. Kinsey and his colleagues were the first psychological researchers to interview volunteers from mainstream American society about their sexual behaviors. The research was hindered by political investigations and threats of legal action. In spite of the harassment encountered by the scientists on the project, the Kinsey group published *Sexual Behavior in the Human Male* in 1948 and *Sexual Behavior in the Human Female* in 1953.

The findings of the Kinsey group have benefitted the public immensely. As a result, it is now known that the majority of people (both men and women) interviewed by the Kinsey group masturbated at various times, but that more men than women said they masturbated. Data collected by the Kinsey group on oral-genital sexual practices have allowed researchers to discover that, since the 1930's, attitudes toward oral-genital sex have become more positive. Their research also shocked the nation with the discovery that the majority of brides at that time were not virgins.

When scientific sampling techniques are used, the survey results can be interpreted as an accurate representation of the entire population. Although Kinsey and his associates helped to pave the way for future researchers to be able to investigate sexual behaviors and attitudes, there were some problems with the research because of its lack of generalizability. The Kinsey group's research is still the largest study of sexual behavior ever completed. They interviewed more than ten thousand people; however, they did not attempt to select a random or representative sample of the population of the United States, which meant that the responses of middle-class, well-educated whites were overrepresented. There is also a problem with the accuracy of the respondents' information, because of memory errors, exaggerations, or embarrassment about telling an interviewer personal, sensitive information. Despite these limitations, the interviewing conducted by Kinsey and associates made great strides for the study of sexuality and great strides for psychology in general.

IMPORTANCE OF SAMPLING PROCEDURES

When research is intended to reveal very precisely what a population is like, careful sampling procedures must be used. This requires defining the population and sampling people from the population in a random fashion so that no biases will be intro-

duced into the sample. To learn what elderly people think about the medical services available to them, for example, a careful sample of the elderly population is needed. Obtaining the sample only from retirement communities in Arizona would bias the results, because these individuals are not representative of all elderly people in the population.

Therefore, when evaluating survey data, a researcher must examine how the responses were obtained and what population was investigated. Major polling organizations such as the Gallup organization typically are careful to obtain representative samples of people in the United States. Gallup polls are frequently conducted to survey the voting public's opinions about the popularity of a presidential candidate or a given policy. Many other surveys, however, such as surveys that are published in popular magazines, have limited generalizability because the results are based on people who read the particular magazine and are sufficiently motivated to complete and mail in the questionnaire. When *Redbook*, for example, asks readers to write in to say whether they have ever had an affair, the results may be interesting but would not give a very accurate estimate of the true extent of extramarital sexual activity in the United States. An example of an inaccurate sampling technique was a survey by *Literary Digest* (a now defunct magazine) sampling almost ten million people in 1936. The results showed that Alfred Landon would beat Franklin D. Roosevelt by a landslide in that year's presidential election. Although the sample was large, the results were completely inaccurate.

EARLY SURVEY METHODS

One of the earliest ways of obtaining psychological information using descriptive techniques was through clinical interviewing. The early interviews conducted by Freud in the late 1800's were based on question-and-answer medical formats, which is not surprising, considering that Freud was originally a physician. Later, Freud relied on the less structured free-association technique. In 1902, Adolf Meyer developed a technique to assess a client's mental functioning, memory, attention, speech, and judgment. Independent of the style used, all the early clinical interviews sought to get a psychological portrait of the person, determine the source of the problem, make a diagnosis, and formulate a treatment. More detailed studies of interviews were conducted in the 1940's and 1950's to compare and contrast interviewing styles and determine how much structure was necessary. During the 1960's, much research came about as a result of ideas held by Carl R. Rogers, who emphasized the interpersonal elements he thought were necessary for the ideal therapeutic relationship; among them are warmth, positive regard, and genuineness on the part of the interviewer.

In the 1800's and early 1900's, interviews were used mainly by psychologists who were therapists helping people with problems such as fear, depression, and hysteria. During that same period, experimental psychologists had not yet begun to use survey research methods. Instead, they used introspection to investigate their own thought processes. For example, experimental psychologist Hermann Ebbinghaus gave himself lists of pronounceable nonsense syllables to remember; he then tested his own memory and attempted to improve it methodically. Many experimental psychologists during this period relied on the use of animals such as dogs and laboratory rats to conduct behavioral research.

EVOLUTION OF QUESTIONNAIRES

As mentioned above, one of the first attempts by experimental psychologists to study attitudes and behaviors by means of the interview was that of the Kinsey group in the 1930's. At about that same time, L. L. Thurstone, an experimental social psychologist, formalized and popularized the first questionnaire methodology for attitude measurement. Thurstone devised a set of questionnaires, or scales, that have been widely used for decades. He is considered by many to be the father of attitude scaling. Soon thereafter, Rensis Likert made breakthroughs in questionnaire usage with the development of what are known as Likert scales. A Likert scale provides a series of statements to which subjects can indicate degrees of agreement or disagreement. Using the Likert technique, the respondent answers by selecting from predetermined categories ranging from "strongly agree" to "strongly disagree." It is fairly standard to use five categories (strongly agree, agree, uncertain, disagree, strongly disagree), but more categories can be used if necessary. An example of a question using this technique might be, "Intelligence test scores of marijuana users are higher on the average than scores of nonusers." The respondent then picks one of the five categories mentioned above in response. Likert scales have been widely used and have resulted in a vast amount of information about human attitudes and behaviors.

SOURCES FOR FURTHER STUDY

Bordens, Kenneth S., and Bruce B. Abbott. *Research Design and Methods: A Process Approach.* 7th ed. Boston: McGraw-Hill, 2008. Places the techniques of surveys, interviews, and questionnaires for collecting data in the context of conducting research as a process from start to finish.

Cozby, Paul C. *Methods in Behavioral Research.* 10th ed. Boston: McGraw-Hill Higher Education, 2009. Examines the importance of survey research in the context of conducting experiments and doing research in psychology in general. Allows the reader to understand the research process from a broader perspective.

Dillman, Don, Jolene D. Smyth, and Leah Melani Christian. *Internet, Mail, and Mixed-Mode Surveys: The Tailored Design Method.* 3d ed. Hoboken, N.J.: Wiley & Sons, 2009. Details how to design and implement surveys, as well as when and how to use a multimedia approach.

Hoyle, Rick H., Monica J. Harris, and Charles M. Judd. *Research Methods in Social Relations.* 7th ed. Fort Worth, Tex.: Wadsworth, 2002. Offers thorough information that introduces the reader to the process of doing research in psychology, including how to get an idea for a research topic, how to collect the information, how to be ethical with subjects, and how to report the results. Detailed information is provided on questionnaires and interviews.

Stewart, Charles J., and William B. Cash, Jr. *Interviewing Principles and Practices.* 12th ed. Boston: McGraw-Hill Higher Education, 2008. A hands-on introduction to interviewing that provides practical suggestions and tips along with background information.

Deborah R. McDonald

SEE ALSO: Behavioral assessment; Case study methodologies; Clinical interviewing, testing, and observation; Complex experimental designs; Data description; Kinsey, Alfred; Personality interviewing strategies; Personality rating scales; Qualitative research; Quasi-experimental designs; Sampling; Statistical significance tests; Within-subject experimental designs.

Synaptic transmission

TYPE OF PSYCHOLOGY: Biological bases of behavior
FIELD OF STUDY: Nervous system

A neuron transmits chemical or electrical signals to other cells and controls their functions through an intercellular space called synaptic cleft. Synaptic transmission is a key to understanding various normal and abnormal behavioral and physiological phenomena as well as the effects of various neuroactive drugs.

KEY CONCEPTS

- agonist
- antagonist
- neuropsychopharmacology
- neurotransmitter
- receptor
- synaptic cleft
- synaptic transmission
- vesicle

INTRODUCTION

Transmission refers to the transferring of signals from a source to a receiving end through or across a medium. Synaptic transmission specifically refers to the transferring of a signal from a neuron (a nerve cell) across a space called the synaptic cleft to a target cell. The nerve impulse is generated in the cell body of the neuron and is related to the movement of sodium ions across the cell membrane of the axon (the axon is an extension of the neuron cell body). This impulse is known as an action potential. When the impulse reaches the axon terminal, this presynaptic signal either remains as an electrical signal or is converted to a chemical signal; either way, it is then transmitted through this space and exerts an influence on the target cell. The synapse contains three areas: the presynaptic terminal, the synaptic cleft, and the postsynaptic membrane.

Physical activity and behavior involve neuronal activities and the resulting contractions and relaxations of many muscles. The winking of an eye, for example, involves the control of contraction and relaxation of eyelid muscles. The axon terminals of the motor neurons must synapse with the eyelid muscles. A synapse between neuron and muscle cells is called a neuromuscular junction. The axon terminal releases a neurochemical that acts on the recep-

tors embedded in the cell membrane of the postsynaptic muscle cells, resulting in muscle contraction. The synaptic area is a key to the control of neural effects; most chemicals that affect the nervous system vary physiological and behavioral responses at this site.

ELECTRICAL AND CHEMICAL MODES

Two distinct modes of synaptic transmission have been delineated, one electrical and the other chemical. At an electrical synapse, the presynaptic current spreads across the intercellular gap to the target cell. For this spreading to occur, a low-resistance pathway is required; this is achieved by a close apposition of cells with a gap of about 2 nanometers (1 nanometer is one-billionth of a meter). This type of coupling is called a gap junction. In electrical transmission, unlike chemical transmission, an impulse in the presynaptic terminal is transmitted to the postsynaptic terminal with little attenuation (lessening) and with no time delay. Electrical synapses are very common in the nervous systems of invertebrates, lower vertebrates, and embryonic animals.

At a chemical synapse, the gap is about 20 to 30 nanometers. The high resistance does not allow the presynaptic current to spread to the postsynaptic current. On arrival of impulses, a presynaptic terminal releases chemicals termed neurotransmitters. These molecules then diffuse through the cleft and interact with receptors, complex protein molecules embedded in the postsynaptic membrane. The neurotransmitter molecules are stored in vesicles. The wall of the vesicle becomes fused to the presynaptic membrane because of the influx of calcium ions on arrival of the impulse; this results in release of the molecules. The interaction between neurotransmitter and receptor results in certain electrical and chemical events in the target cell. In chemical transmission, the signals are attenuated, and the process takes more time than electrical transmission—about 0.3 millisecond, which is termed the synaptic delay. Neurotransmitters secreted by the presynaptic terminals include acetylcholine, dopamine, epinephrine, norepinephrine, serotonin, certain amino acids (gamma-aminobutyric acid, glutamate, glycine, aspartate), and many peptides.

Neurons come in various shapes and possess varying numbers of branches. Basically, however, each consists of the dendrites, the soma (cell body), and the axon. Synapses are classified in terms of the nature of the presynaptic terminal and the postsynaptic end. The presynaptic terminal is usually an axon; however, it has been found that dendrites may communicate with other dendrites directly at a synapse termed a dendrodendritic synapse. Three types of synapses between neurons are axodendritic, axosomatic, and axoaxonic. An axodendritic synapse couples an axon terminal to a dendrite of another neuron and usually produces a depolarization or excitatory postsynaptic potential. An axosomatic synapse couples an axon terminal to the soma of another neuron, and it may produce a hyperpolarization or inhibitory postsynaptic potential as well as an excitatory postsynaptic potential. An axoaxonic synapse couples an axon terminal to another axon terminal, which results in reduction of excitatory postsynaptic potential in the target neuron of the second neuron, so the net effect is inhibitory. When an axon terminal is coupled to a muscle cell or a glandular cell, the synapse is called a neuromuscular junction or a neuroeffector junction. The excitatory postsynaptic potential occurring in the muscle is called end-plate potential. When the sum of those potential changes reaches the threshold of firing, an action potential is generated, resulting in a propagating impulse or muscular contraction.

STUDYING THE NERVOUS SYSTEM

The release of a neurotransmitter substance, the binding of neurotransmitter molecules to receptors, and the termination of neurotransmitter activities are among the key considerations in understanding the regulation of the effects of the nervous system. The synthesis and storage (in vesicles) of these substances are also important. The magnitude and duration of many physiological and behavioral responses are jointly determined by various neuronal effects. Neuroactive drugs are crucial tools, and various ones manipulate different phases of transmission, synthesis, storage, release, binding, and termination of neurotransmitters. These drugs may be used to study the functions of various neurochemicals as well as to control synaptic transmission for therapeutic purposes.

Neuroactive drugs and chemicals are classified in terms of their facilitating or inhibitory effects. Agonists are those that enhance the effects of a neurotransmitter; antagonists inhibit the effects. For example, curare, a compound extracted from a vine by South American Indians for use as an arrow

posion to paralyze animals, is an antagonist of the neurotransmitter acetylcholine at the neuromuscular junction. Curare interferes with synaptic transmission at this junction, resulting in muscle paralysis.

A lock-and-key analogy is often employed to explain how synaptic transmission works. The neurotransmitter molecule represents the key, and the receptor molecule represents the lock. Just as the correct key is needed to open the lock on a door, the appropriate chemical "key" is needed to start the effect. The molecular lock has the recognition site and the active site as well as the support structure, just as the door has the keyhole with specific notch configurations, as well as other parts. A neurotransmitter may be able to open several different locks, termed receptor subtypes, which are named for the chemical compounds specific to each subtype. (In this sense, a neurotransmitter is like a submaster key that will fit several doors, while a subtype-specific compound is the key for only one door.) The neurotransmitter acetylcholine, for example, acts on two receptor subtypes—nicotinic and muscarinic. The nicotinic receptor is so named because it reacts specifically to nicotine, a substance found in tobacco. This receptor subtype is found in the smooth and cardiac muscles; the muscarinic subtype, on the other hand, is abundant in the brain.

Nicotine and muscarine, in other words, each affect only one subtype, but acetylcholine affects both; thus, acetylcholine and nicotine are both nicotinic receptor agonists, and acetylcholine and muscarine are both muscarinic receptor agonists. To return to the example of curare, it is a subtype-specific blocker that acts on the nicotinic receptor to block the effect of acetylcholine, causing paralysis of the skeletal muscles. Chemical variants of curare are used clinically to cause muscle relaxation before surgery.

Atropine is a muscarinic receptor blocker, so the cholinergic effects that are mediated by this subtype are antagonized. This drug is used to reduce motion sickness, to induce pupillary dilation for retinal examination, and to fight the sickening effects of certain gases used in chemical warfare. It is because those gases often involve cholinergic agonists that atropine is an appropriate antidote. There are many other compounds that can affect cholinergic effects through interfering with the release, receptor binding, and termination mechanisms. For example, the venom of the black widow spider facilitates the release of acetylcholine, whereas botulinum food poison inhibits its release. Physostigmine, a compound obtained from the Calabar bean in West Africa, enhances acetylcholine effects. Physostigmine is used to treat glaucoma and to help control the forgetfulness of Alzheimer's disease patients.

SYNTHETIC NEUROTRANSMITTERS
The potency and efficacy of a drug are presumably related to the degree of fit between the drug molecule and the receptor molecule; a potent drug is one with a good fit to a receptor or subtype. The pharmaceutical industry is constantly working to synthesize variants of neurotransmitters and neuroactive compounds to make the effects of the drug both potent and specific, thus reducing undesirable side effects.

Because acetylcholine in the brain is known to be related to learning and memory, and since Alzheimer's disease involves memory loss, it is theorized that the disease may involve cholinergic subfunctioning. Indeed, cholinergic neurons have been found to be lacking in Alzheimer's patients' brains. Thus, drugs that could alleviate the symptoms are cholinergic agonists of various kinds, such as physostigmine, and various cholinomimetics, drugs that mimic acetylcholine. Many cholinomimetics are so-called nootropic drugs, compounds that may be able to improve learning, memory, and cognitive functions. Dopamine, another neurotransmitter in the brain, has been found to be involved with the hallucinations and delusions of schizophrenics, and dopamine antagonists are used as antipsychotic drugs. Amphetamine is known to induce those psychotic symptoms; this type of drug promotes the release of dopamine.

Furthermore, a lack of dopamine activity has been linked to the symptoms of Parkinson's disease, so anti-Parkinson's drugs tend to be dopamine agonists. Depression has been found to be related to reduced activity of norepinephrine in the brain, so some antidepressants are norepinephrine agonists. Morphine is a well-known pain reducer; in the body, there are chemically similar compounds known as endorphins (from "endogenous morphine"). They are released by neurons within the spinal cord, resulting in a reduction of the release of the neurotransmitter (called substance P) related to pain signaling, thus suppressing pain. Arousal is known to be related to acetylcholine and norepinephrine in the brain; dreaming has also been related to nor-

epinephrine. The action of the tranquilizer diazepam (Valium), the most commonly prescribed drug in the United States, is related to the activity of an inhibitory neurotransmitter, gamma-aminobutyric acid. Neuropsychopharmacology is the area of study that explores the relationships among neurophysiology, neuroanatomy, and pharmacology. Neurotransmission is an important key to discovering these relationships. Beyond the importance of such research efforts, however, it must also be remembered that behavior, both normal and abnormal, is inextricably related to the effects of synaptic transmission.

DISCOVERING NEW NEUROTRANSMITTERS
In the earliest years of the twentieth century, neurotransmission was thought to be solely electrical. The discovery of the synaptic cleft, however, made neuroscientists wonder whether an electrical current could jump a gap of this magnitude. The chemical hypothesis of neurotransmission was then proposed, although it was not until 1921 that convincing evidence of chemical transmission was obtained. Otto Loewi, a German physiologist, electrically stimulated the parasympathetic vagus nerve of a frog and recorded the effect on the frog's heart. He then transferred the liquid from the stimulated heart to an unstimulated frog heart and observed that the recipient heart reacted as if it were stimulated. The effect of the vagal stimulation—decreasing the heart rate—was transferred to the unstimulated heart via the liquid from the stimulated heart. This transferral could only occur if the electrical stimulation of the vagus had resulted in the release of a chemical into the heart and this chemical was transferred to the new heart, thus inducing the same effect. Loewi called this substance *Vagusstoff*, since it was released from the vagus nerve. Later chemical analysis revealed the substance to be acetylcholine, the first neurotransmitter to be identified.

No fewer than fifty neurotransmitter substances have been identified, and researchers are still discovering new ones. To classify a substance as a neurotransmitter, a scientist needs to show that it fulfills a number of conditions. The substance (referred to as a putative neurotransmitter) should be found in the presynaptic terminals. Exogenous applications of the substance should mimic the effect of endogenously released substance when the presynaptic neurons are electrically stimulated. The drug effect should be the same as the effect of the exogenously applied substance and the same as the effect of the endogenously released transmitter substance. A mechanism must exist for the synthesis of the substance in the presynaptic neuron. A mechanism must also exist for the termination of the transmitter activity of the substance. As can be seen, it is not easy to identify and define a new neurotransmitter substance.

The United States Public Health Service proclaimed the 1990's to be the decade of the brain. The synthesis of drugs that may be related to brain functions is still an area of intense research activity. Neuropsychopharmacological studies test the effects of various compounds; the new compounds are also used to test for specific neuronal bases of brain functions. New drugs not only increase the possibilities for controlling neuronal function but also reduce the undesirable side effects of drug therapy by making the effects specific to receptor subtypes. Better, more effective drugs will undoubtedly continue to be produced.

SOURCES FOR FURTHER STUDY

Binder, Mark D., Nobutaka Hirokawa, and Uwe Windhorst, eds. *Encyclopedia of Neuroscience.* New York: Springer, 2008. A very comprehensive source of information on neuroscience, including the synapses.

Charney, Dennis S., and Eric J. Nestler, eds. *Neurobiology of Mental Illness.* 3d ed. New York: Oxford University Press, 2009. Neurobiology is explained in terms of how it is affected in patients with mental illnesses.

Iversen, Leslie L., et al. *Introduction to Neuropsychopharmacology.* New York: Oxford University Press, 2009. A basic text that looks at drugs and their interactions with the central nervous system.

Julien, Robert M., Claire D. Advokat, and Joseph E. Comaty. *A Primer of Drug Action.* 11th ed. New York: Worth Publishers, 2008. This book describes how synaptic transmission can be manipulated by drugs to effect physiological and psychological responses. Historical episodes about drugs and coverage of various "street" compounds make this interesting reading.

Nicholls, John G., et al. *From Neuron to Brain.* 4th ed. Sunderland, Mass.: Sinauer Associates, 2001. The authors are well-known researchers. This widely used neuroscience text covers historical and modern approaches to neurophysiology in general and synaptic transmission in particular.

Siegel, George J., et al., eds. *Basic Neurochemistry: Molecular, Cellular, and Medical Aspects.* 7th ed. Boston: Elsevier, 2006. The book covers more than forty topics, each discussed by one or more authoritative researchers in the respective fields. More than ten topics fall under "Synaptic Function," covering the major neurotransmitter systems.

Sigmund Hsiao

SEE ALSO: Inhibitory and excitatory impulses; Nervous system; Neurons; Neurotransmitters; Reflexes.

Synesthesia

TYPE OF PSYCHOLOGY: Biological bases of behavior; sensation and perception
FIELDS OF STUDY: Auditory, chemical, cutaneous, and body senses; vision

Synesthesia, from a Greek word meaning "to perceive together," is the experience of two or more sensations occurring simultaneously. People with synesthesia may hear, smell, taste, or feel in color, while others may taste shapes. The most common form of synesthesia is colored hearing, in which sounds are also experienced as colors.

KEY CONCEPTS
- congruence effect
- induced sensation
- perceived sensation
- semantic-encoding hypothesis
- sensory leakage theory

INTRODUCTION

The first medical reference to synesthesia, the experience of two or more sensations simultaneously, was circa 1710, when an English ophthalmologist described a case of a blind man who described colored vision in response to auditory stimulation. Although there are a number of other isolated accounts of this condition, a sharp rise in publications on synesthesia occurred in the 1880's. At least twenty-seven articles on this topic appeared from 1882 to 1892.

Several key findings emerged from the classical studies of synesthesia: Colored hearing seems to be the most common form. Other forms, such as colored taste and pain are reported but are apparently quite rare. People who experience synesthesia report that they have experienced it for as long as they can remember and often report that family members have the same condition. In cases of colored hearing, merely reading is insufficient to elicit synesthesia; the words must be heard.

At the beginning of the twentieth century, there was a marked drop in research attention. This drop continued until the 1960's. This period in which synesthesia was relatively ignored by researchers coincides with the behavioral era, in which U.S. psychologists limited their studies to observable behaviors rather than to mental processes that can only be measured indirectly and subjectively. The cognitive revolution in psychology in the 1960's allowed internal mental processes, such as synesthesia, to become objects of study. What followed was a slow increase of research on this phenomenon.

STRONG SYNESTHESIA

Many researchers distinguish between strong and weak synesthesia. Strong synesthesia tends to run in families, is more common in women than in men, and is relatively rare. Scientists estimate that it occurs in approximately one person in two thousand. Strong synesthesia is typically noticed in early childhood. The connection between the two sensations seems to be actually experienced and is not just a metaphorical description created by the person.

The most common form of strong synesthesia is colored hearing, in which sounds, music, or voices are perceived as colors. People with strong synesthesia (often referred to as synesthetes) may hear, smell, taste, feel pain, or experience written language in color, while others may taste shapes. In one account, a woman described that, as a little girl, she had problems writing the letter *R*. She remembered that it eventually dawned on her that all she had to do was make the letter *P* and draw a line down from the loop. She then commented to her father that she had just "turned a yellow letter into an orange letter." For as long as she could remember, each letter of the alphabet elicited an experience of color.

Nineteenth century researcher Sir Francis Galton, who is thought to have been a strong synesthete, wrote, "Each word is a distinct whole. I have always associated the same colors with the same letters, and no amount of effort will change the color

of one letter. Occasionally, when uncertain how a word should be spelt, I have considered what color it ought to be and have decided in that way."

In his book *The Man Who Tasted Shapes* (1998), Richard Cytowic, a neurologist who has done extensive study of strong synesthesia, described how Michael, the subject of the book, invited him to dinner. Michael said, as he cooked a roast chicken, that "there aren't enough points on the chicken." When questioned by Cytowic, Michael explained that "flavors have shape" and that he wanted the "chicken to be a pointed shape, but it came out round." On further inquiry, Michael stated,

> Nobody's ever heard of this. They think I'm on drugs or that I'm making it up. That's why I never intentionally tell people about my shapes. Only when it slips out. It's perfectly logical that I thought everybody felt shapes when they ate. If there's no shape, there's no flavor.

In some cases, the induced sensation in a strong synesthete is so vivid that it becomes distracting. Neuropsychologist Aleksandr Luria wrote, in his book *The Mind of a Mnemonist* (1968), that "S" described "crumbly and yellow" images that flowed from a speaker's mouth. His experience of this image was so strong that it diminished his capacity to attend to what the speaker was saying. "S" was often quite distressed about his inability to separate such strong sensory experiences. "S" described to Luria how the induced visual images were so troubling that he tried describing them in writing and then destroying what he had written in an effort to rid himself of the intrusive experiences.

His experience also exemplifies another general principle of strong synesthesia—that the induced sensory experience is often visual, while inducing stimuli are often auditory, tactile, or gustatory (relating to taste). The underlying reason for this pattern is unknown.

POSSIBLE CAUSES OF STRONG SYNESTHESIA

Many researchers currently believe that strong synesthesia is biologically based, automatic, and unlearned. It is also different from hallucinations or metaphoric descriptions of experience. Various theories have been proposed to explain synesthesia. The sensory leakage theory suggests that synesthesia is caused by an overabundance of neural connections in the brain. Ordinarily, the different sensory systems are assigned to separate areas in the brain during development, which results in distinct sensory experiences. In the synesthete's brain, stronger neural connections among these areas may blur the separation of sensory experiences.

Other researchers have speculated that all people are born with the neural connections that may cause synesthesia, but that these connections are weeded out during normal brain development.

Some scientists, however, object to defining synesthesia as an abnormality. In the brains of nonsynesthetes, higher-level neural connections in the brain that mediate the experience of sensory integration may have feedback connections to the single sensory systems, which gives rise to distinct sensory experiences. In the brains of synesthetes, however, such connections may not be inhibited as they are in the brains of nonsynesthetes. Evidence that supports this explanation is the fact that hallucinogenic drugs can lead to synesthetic experiences. Such drugs may temporarily disinhibit the feedback connections between the brain areas that process multisensory integration and those that mediate distinct sensory experiences.

In the late 1980's, a research team asked people with synesthesia to describe the color perceptions triggered by each of one hundred words. When they repeated the test a year later, the synesthetes described the same associations between the words and colors with over 90 percent accuracy.

The availability of brain imaging techniques, such as positron emission tomography (PET), allows researchers to directly observe synesthesia at work in the brain. PET scans of synesthetes with colored hearing show increased activation in the visual areas of the brain in response to sounds.

WEAK SYNESTHESIA

There is considerable evidence that many people can create, identify, and appreciate less vivid cross-sensory experiences. These abilities are often referred to as weak synesthesia. An example of such associations is found in common metaphorical language (for example, a "sweet smell" or a "warm person").

Weak synesthesia is also evident in the experience of music, such as an association between certain pitches and colors. Laboratory experiments have shown that when people are presented with a set of notes of varying pitch and a set of colors varying in lightness, they will systematically pair lighter colors with higher pitches. This common experience is distinguished from that of strong synesthetes in one important way—in weak synesthesia, the associations are highly influenced by context, so that the lightest color always corresponds to the highest pitch.

Thus, in weak synesthesia, sensory associations are contextual, while those in strong synesthesia cut across time and situations. Another distinction is that in weak synesthesia, both sensory stimuli are perceived simultaneously, while in strong synesthetic experiences, one sensation is perceived and then another (typically visual) is induced.

Researchers have studied the experience of weak synesthesia by measuring a person's ability to respond to a stimulus while receiving simultaneous input from a different, unattended sensory modality. If the unattended stimulus impairs the person's ability to respond to the attended one, then the two stimuli are thought to compete in the processing of information.

In one such experiment, participants were asked to classify the pitch of a sound (low versus high) in the presence of a color. The results showed a pattern of high-pitched tones being classified faster in the presence of a light color and low-pitched tones being associated with darker colors. This pattern is known as the congruence effect, which suggests that there is cross-sensory interaction (unattended signals can affect responses to an attended one) and that these cross-sensory associations are often bidirectional (unlike in strong synesthesia, which is commonly unidirectional).

POSSIBLE CAUSES OF WEAK SYNESTHESIA

Two explanations for weak synesthesia predominate. The sensory hypothesis is consistent with the sensory leakage theory in strong synesthesia. Congruence effects may involve absolute neural connections between areas in the brain that process different sensory experiences.

The semantic-encoding hypothesis is another explanation of weak synesthesia. The term "semantic" refers to meaning, while "encoding" refers to the process in which sensory stimulation from the world is transformed into a mental representation, such as a memory. Information is encoded more easily when the stimulus is meaningful to the person.

The semantic-encoding hypothesis includes several claims. First, cross-sensory associations occur at a perceptual rather than at a sensory level. According to cognitive information processing theory, there is a one-to-one correspondence between a physical stimulus and the way it is encoded in the sensory areas of the brain. Perception, however, is a higher-level process that involves the interpretation of sensory information.

Second, perceptions of various sensory stimuli are strongly influenced by language. For example, four-year-old children match pitch and brightness systematically, but not pitch and visual size. However, by age twelve, such matches are performed as well as they are by adults.

Third, corresponding sensory stimuli are recoded from distinct, one-to-one sensory experiences to an abstract, integrated perception. This suggests that the integration of sensory experiences occurs at a higher level in the brain in which meaning is constructed.

Synesthesia is not a single phenomenon but represents a broad range of cross-sensory experiences, from weak to strong. The two extremes of synesthetic experience also seem to have different theoretical explanations.

SOURCES FOR FURTHER STUDY

Cytowic, Richard E. *The Man Who Tasted Shapes.* Cambridge, Mass.: MIT Press, 1998. This book is a highly readable narrative of synesthetic experiences, based on a fascinating case study.

Cytowic, Richard E., and David M. Eagleman. *Wednesday Is Indigo Blue: Discovering the Brain of Synesthesia.* Cambridge, Mass.: MIT Press, 2009. Explains the neuroscience and genetics behind synesthesia's multisensory experience.

Duffy, Patricia L. *Blue Cats and Chartreuse Kittens: How Synesthetes Color Their Worlds.* New York: Henry Holt, 2001. This book describes the personal, inner experiences of different synesthetes.

Harrison, John. *Synesthesia: The Strangest Thing.* New York: Oxford University Press, 2001. This book is a scholarly, yet accessible, account of the history and science of synesthesia.

Ward, Jamie. *The Frog Who Croaked Blue: Synesthesia and the Mixing of the Senses.* New York: Routledge, 2008. One of the world's leading experts on synesthesia describes his research. He argues that a certain level of sensory mixing may be the norm, although most people are not synesthetes.

Cathy J. Bogart

SEE ALSO: Hallucinations; Hearing; Sensation and perception; Senses; Smell and taste; Touch and pressure; Vision: Brightness and contrast; Vision: Color; Visual system.

Systematic desensitization

DATE: 1950's forward
TYPE OF PSYCHOLOGY: Learning; psychological methodologies; psychopathology
FIELDS OF STUDY: Anxiety disorders; behavioral therapies; Pavlovian conditioning

Systematic desensitization is a behavior therapy based on principles of Pavlovian conditioning. It was developed by the South African psychiatrist Joseph Wolpe in the late 1950's. It is used in the treatment of fears, phobias, and anxiety reactions.

KEY CONCEPTS
- anxiety hierarchy
- counterconditioning
- deep muscle relaxation
- exposure technology
- imaginal exposure
- progressive muscle relaxation
- reciprocal inhibition

INTRODUCTION

Systematic desensitization, also called graduated exposure therapy, is a behavior therapy used in the treatment of fears, phobias, and anxiety disorders. The therapist asks the client to imagine successively more fear- or anxiety-arousing situations while engaging in a behavior, generally relaxation, which competes with being afraid or anxious. With treatment, the client's fear or anxiety reactions gradually subside. Therapeutic intervention is warranted when the intensity of the fear or anxiety is disproportionate to the actual situation, interferes with normal functioning, and affects the quality of life.

Systematic desensitization involves three steps. First, the therapist teaches the client the technique of deep muscle relaxation or some other response that is incompatible with fear or anxiety. Deep muscle relaxation training involves first learning to distinguish between relaxed and tense states of different skeletal muscle groups and then learning to achieve deep muscle relaxation on command without tightening the muscles. Second, the therapist helps the client construct an anxiety hierarchy in which situations are ordered from least to most anxiety-evoking. Multiple hierarchies may be needed if a client has several problems, and the hierarchies may be modified if new concerns arise during treatment. Third, the therapist instructs the client to maintain a state of relaxation while imagining a scene from the anxiety hierarchy as it is described by the therapist (imaginal exposure). Therapy begins with the item on the hierarchy that elicits the least discomfort and advances to the next item only after the client can reliably relax to the presentation of the preceding item. Each scene is imagined for a few seconds at a time. If the client experiences an increase in fear while imagining a scene, the therapist instructs the client to discontinue imagining the fear-eliciting item and to concentrate on relaxing. The third step may be done under hypnosis.

The goal of systematic desensitization is to replace the anxiety associated with an item on the anxiety hierarchy with a new and competing response such as relaxation. The premise underlying this treatment is that a person cannot be simultaneously afraid and relaxed. For example, physiological correlates of fear such as rapid heart beat and increased respiration rate are the opposite of those associated with deep muscle relaxation in which the heart beat and breathing rate are slowed. During therapy, a client will also be encouraged to confront in real life (in vivo exposure) the imagined situations that no longer elicit fear in the treatment sessions.

Clinical psychologists Peter Lang and David Lazovik, along with others, conducted a number of laboratory studies of systematic desensitization in the 1960's using snake-phobic college students. One study of twenty-four snake-phobic students reported that students benefited significantly from their treatment both in the short term and at a six-month follow-up, as measured by avoidance of an actual snake and self-ratings. Moreover, there was no evidence of symptom substitution, a concern Freudian psychoanalysts had expressed about treatment of the overt manifestation of anxiety (fear and avoidance of snakes) rather than the underlying unconscious and unresolved conflict (anxiety about sex).

Subsequent research has shown that the essential component in systematic desensitization is repeated

exposure to situations or stimuli that elicit fear or anxiety but with no actual negative consequences for the client. Exposure is generally considered one of the most powerful and dependable methods for reducing or eliminating human fears and anxiety, and is the key element in the behavioral component of cognitive behavior therapy.

HISTORY

Systematic desensitization was developed by the South African psychiatrist Joseph Wolpe during the 1950's on the basis of counterconditioning experiments he did with cats from June, 1947, to July, 1948, at the University of Witwatersrand. After using classical conditioning to make cats afraid of their cages, Wolpe demonstrated that their conditioned fear response could be eliminated by feeding the cats at locations progressively closer to their cages. This finding confirmed a 1924 report of counterconditioning by Mary Cover Jones, a student of the behaviorist John B. Watson, who successfully extinguished a young boy's fear of rabbits by very gradually moving a rabbit toward the boy as he ate.

In developing a method for extinguishing human fears, Wolpe modified and shortened the progressive muscle relaxation (PMR) method perfected by the physician Edmund Jacobsen in the 1930's, which could take more than two hundred hours to master. Wolpe also pioneered the idea that treatment of anxiety elicited by an imagined situation would transfer to its real-life counterpart. In *Psychotherapy by Reciprocal Inhibition* (1958), Wolpe reported that 90 percent of his clients showed significant improvement with systematic desensitization.

UNDERLYING THEORY

Wolpe's observations of his fearful cats learning to eat in the presence of gradually incremented anxiety-evoking cues convinced him that eating inhibited their fear reactions. He formulated the principle of reciprocal inhibition: When an animal eats in the presence of a fear stimulus, an inhibitory connection is strengthened between the fear stimulus and the fear reaction. Thus, if a response (fear) is inhibited by an incompatible response (eating) and followed by reinforcement (for example, a reduction in drive), a significant amount of conditioned inhibition of the fear response will develop to the fear-eliciting stimulus. The theoretical influences of the Russian physiologist Ivan Petrovich Pavlov and of the psychologist Clark L. Hull are evident in Wolpe's concept of reciprocal inhibition.

Reciprocal inhibition is a defining feature of the widely accepted dual process theory of motivation. According to this theory, there are two motivational systems underlying behavior, one that is appetitive, or positive, and the other that is aversive, or negative. Activation of the positive motivational system inhibits the negative motivational system, and activation of the negative motivational system inhibits the positive motivational system. Such reciprocal inhibitory links explain why an anxious person or fearful animal generally has no appetite.

Clinical psychologists Michael D. Spiegler and David C. Guevremont summarize additional explanations for why systematic desensitization works, including simple extinction; changes in the client's thinking, such as being more realistic, having altered expectations, or increased self-confidence; and attention from the therapist.

VARIATIONS

Relaxation is the most frequently used competing response in systematic desensitization but it is not always optimal for some clients. Children, for example, may find it easier to use pleasant thoughts or humor and laughter as responses incompatible with anxiety. Other competing responses that may, under some conditions, be more appropriate than relaxation are sexual arousal, assertive behavior, and eating.

Fear or anxiety is the most common response to be treated with systematic desensitization, but treatment of other negative reactions including anger, jealousy, motion sickness, speech disorders, and racial prejudice has been successful. In *Psychotherapy by Reciprocal Inhibition*, Wolpe describes the case of a twenty-seven-year-old male client, Mr. E., whose unreasonable jealousy was threatening his engagement to Celia, his girlfriend. Whenever Celia said something nice about another man, Mr. E. experienced intense feelings of jealousy that would persist for days, making him irritable and excessively critical of anything Celia did. Following several interviews and training in relaxation, an anxiety hierarchy was constructed. Treatment was conducted under hypnosis and began with the lowest disturbing item: Celia commenting that his friend John (who was not viewed as much of a competitor by Mr. E.) has a nice way about him. After several months of imaginal ex-

posure and various modifications to the anxiety hierarchy, Mr. E., who by then was married to Celia, could tolerate her speaking excitedly to another young man at a party.

Advances in technology have allowed therapists to use virtual reality or computer simulated exposure to replace in vivo exposure, which is not always practical, affordable, or safe. In a review of the research on virtual reality applications to mental health, clinical psychologists Lynsey Gregg and Nicholas Tarrier conclude that the relative effectiveness of exposure technology, in vivo and imaginal exposure, has yet to be fully determined.

COMPARISONS

A study by clinical psychologist Gordon L. Paul compared systematic desensitization and insight-oriented psychotherapy (which focuses on the source of a phobia) for the treatment of students with severe anxieties about public speaking. In a two-year follow-up, 85 percent of those in the systematic desensitization group showed significant improvement relative to pretreatment compared with 50 percent in the psychotherapy group and 22 percent in an untreated control group. Once again, there was no evidence of symptom substitution: No one in the systematic desensitization group reported new fears.

In their 2004 paper, clinical psychologist F. Dudley McGlynn and colleagues discuss reasons for the abrupt decline in academic-research interest in systematic desensitization based on relaxation in the 1970's and its reduced use in clinical practice since the 1980's. The decrease in peer-reviewed papers on systematic desensitization is attributed to a change in editorial policy toward studies using a pretreatment and posttreatment comparison to assess the effectiveness of systematic desensitization. The methodology used in such analogue desensitization studies was sharply criticized by clinical psychologists Douglas A. Bernstein and Gordon L. Paul. Their influential critique raised concerns about uncontrolled experimental demand effects and whether subjects were sufficiently phobic for meaningful conclusions to be drawn about treatment efficacy. Clinicians lost interest in systematic desensitization first because of the emergence of competing therapies, most notably flooding, implosive therapy, and participant modeling, and later because of the emergence of exposure technology and the shift toward cognitive behavior therapy.

APPLICATION TO ANIMALS

Applied animal behavior science is a field that covers research on and the treatment of behavior problems in companion animals or other domestic animals. Counterconditioning has been used to treat a variety of fear-related behavioral problems in dogs, including fear of other dogs, humans, and loud noises (such as thunderstorm, fireworks, and gunshots). A common protocol for treating a noise phobia usually involves exposing the fearful dog to increasingly louder prerecorded presentations of the sound that elicits fear while simultaneously playing with the dog and rewarding with treats for maintaining a calm and relaxed demeanor. As in systematic desensitization, the dog starts exposure training with a low intensity sound that elicits negligible anxiety and is exposed to an increment in the intensity of the fear-eliciting stimulus only when the dog remains completely relaxed at the preceding volume.

SOURCES FOR FURTHER STUDY

Bernstein, Douglas A., and Gordon L. Paul. "Some Comments on Therapy Analogue Research with Small Animal 'Phobias.'" *Journal of Behavior Therapy and Experimental Psychiatry* 2, no. 4 (1973): 225-237. Influential critique of the limited utility of laboratory analogue studies for the evaluation and development of behavior modification techniques. Identifies various methodological problems and suggests ways to correct the errors.

Gregg, Lynsey, and Nicholas Tarrier. "Virtual Reality in Mental Health." *Social Psychiatry & Psychiatric Epidemiology* 42, no. 5 (2007): 343-354. Reviews more than fifty studies using virtual reality applications to treat patients with various common fears such as fear of flying, fear of heights, social phobia/public speaking anxiety, and spider phobia. Discusses advantages in terms of delivery and disadvantages in terms of the side effects of using virtual reality. Concludes that virtual-reality-based therapy may be superior to no treatment but that evaluation of its effectiveness relative to traditional therapeutic approaches requires more controlled trials with clinically identified populations.

Lang, Peter J., and A. David Lazovik. "Experimental Desensitization of a Phobia." *Journal of Abnormal and Social Psychology* 66, no. 6 (1963): 519-525.
This study compared the effects of systematic desensitization in snake-phobic college students to an untreated control group of college students. It used a behavioral measure as well as self-report to assess the effectiveness of treatment. Design, procedure, and findings are clearly communicated.

McGlynn, F. D., Todd A. Smitherman, and Kelly G. Gothard. "Comment on the Status of Systematic Desensitization." *Behavior Modification* 28, no. 2 (2004): 194-205. Graphs the number of articles on systematic desensitization published in three mainstream behavior therapy journals between 1970 and 2002 and surveys clinical use of systematic desensitization by 310 selected providers. Discusses reasons for the decline in research papers on and clinical use of systematic desensitization with relaxation.

Paul, Gordon L. "Insight Versus Desensitization in Psychotherapy Two Years After Termination." *Journal of Consulting Psychology* 31, no. 4 (1967): 333-348. Discusses problems of follow-up research. Some statistics are presented but the results are clearly explained in the text.

Spiegler, Michael D., and David C. Guevremont. *Contemporary Behavior Therapy.* 5th ed. Pacific Grove, Calif.: Brooks/Cole, 2009. Excellent introduction to systematic desensitization and other behavioral methods for treating clinical problems in humans.

Wolpe, Joseph. *Psychotherapy by Reciprocal Inhibition.* Stanford, Calif.: Stanford University Press, 1980. Generally regarded as one of the most influential books in the history of clinical psychology. Wolpe describes his method of systematic desensitization for the treatment of anxiety derived largely from the work of Pavlov and Hull on learning. He presents his experimental studies on the extinction of learned fear in cats and the results of numerous clinical case studies.

Ruth M. Colwill

SEE ALSO: Anxiety disorders; Aversion therapy; Behavior therapy; Cognitive behavior therapy; Conditioning; Fear; Hull, Clark L.; Implosion; Little Albert study; Meditation and relaxation; Pavlov, Ivan Petrovich; Pavlovian conditioning; Watson, John B.

Systems theories

DATE: 1940's forward
TYPE OF PSYCHOLOGY: Psychological methodologies
FIELDS OF STUDY: Descriptive methodologies; general constructs and issues; group and family therapies

Systems scientists in the natural and social sciences study the interaction between the parts of a system rather than the parts in isolation to better understand the complexity of reality. Systemic thinking has influenced psychological theory and practice, as many subfields in psychology such as industrial and organizational psychology, ergonomics, and family systems theory share the systems perspective.

KEY CONCEPTS
- holistic approach
- integration
- interaction
- organization
- structure

INTRODUCTION

Systems theories provide a general framework for the integration of different fields in science. They are, in essence, theories of organization. Until the beginning of the twentieth century, science was dominated by a reductionist viewpoint. Scientists believed that the way to understand something was to take it apart and see what it was made of. After a while though, all they were left with were molecules. Systems thinking provided another way of looking at the world that better accounted for its complexity. Instead of trying to understand something by studying it in isolation, scientists looked at what types of patterns emerged when elements interacted. Thinking in terms of systems greatly increased after World War II and occurred independently in different parts of the world, thus creating systems science. Influential figures in the development of modern systems thinking include William Ross Ashby, Gregory Bateson, and Kenneth Boulding. In 1945, biologist Ludwig von Bertalanffy formalized general systems theory.

According to systems theorists, reality is a hierarchy of interconnected systems of higher and lower orders. For example, the cell, which is a system on its own, is part of the human body system, which is part of a social system, which is a part of the planetary system, which is a part of the solar system. What all these systems have in common is the way they are organized. They possess general system characteristics, regardless of whether the system is physical, biological, psychological, or social. They may look different, but they all obey the same rules. They all share similar structures and functions.

The structure of a system refers to the way its elements are interrelated. It can be seen as the "program" that determines how elements interact together, or its design. The function of a system refers to what the system is "designed" to do. Some systems are characterized by their tendency to maintain steady states or equilibrium. In this sense, systems appear to be goal-oriented. Systems that achieve a certain balance are said to be self-stabilizing, or self-regulating. One way systems can achieve this stability is via the structure of feedback loops, where information from one part of the system is fed to other parts and back again, creating a continuous flow of communication. This allows the system to adjust by comparing its current state to a "desired" state. This particular type of systems theory, cybernetics, was introduced by Norbert Weiner in 1948. The thermostat is an example of this type of system.

Many different systems theories exist, with applications in physics, chemistry, biology, psychology, sociology, and other fields. Regardless of the specific field of study, scientists find that many different types of phenomena can be categorized under the same "system" umbrella. Because many systems work in essentially the same way, knowledge can be transferred from one field of study to another. In a sense, different fields of study provide different examples of the same types of systems.

SYSTEMS THEORIES AND PSYCHOLOGY

Many psychological theories have been inspired by systems thinking. These include ecological systems theory, cognitive systems theory, and field theory. Fields of applied psychology such as ergonomics, industrial and organizational psychology, and family systems therapy also adopt a systemic perspective. What all these psychological theories and approaches have in common is that they all take a step back and observe how dynamic interaction produces observable behavior. For example, a work environment, a family, and an individual can all be considered systems at different levels. In seeking to solve problems, systems psychologists consider the impact of each of these elements on the functioning of the entire system. They consider, as expressed in Gestalt psychology, that the whole is different from the sum of its parts. Indeed, a human being cannot be adequately represented if reduced only to a body plus mental functioning.

By studying what is common in the way elements of physical, biological, social, or other types of systems interact to create a whole, systems scientists are able to get a clearer view of the big picture. This holistic perspective allows scientists to continually uncover general patterns in nature and ultimately arrive at unifying principles of science.

Sources for Further Study

Kauffman, Draper L. *Systems One: An Introduction to Systems Thinking.* Minneapolis: S. A. Carlton, 1980. An introduction to systems thinking that does not require any background in math or science. Many examples and illustrations of systems in everyday life are provided.

Levine, Ralph L., and Hiram E. Fitzgerald, eds. *Analysis of Dynamic Psychological Systems: Basic Approaches to General Systems, Dynamic Systems, and Cybernetics.* New York: Plenum Press, 1992. Presents the basics of dynamic systems theories, including living systems theory and cybernetics with applications to psychology. Gets technical in the later chapters, but graphs help illustrate the main points.

Luenberger, David G. *Introduction to Dynamic Systems: Theory, Models, and Applications.* New York: Wiley, 1979. Provides a look at the mathematics behind systems theories. The concepts of matrix algebra and dynamic equations are clearly and intuitively presented.

Von Bertalanffy, Ludwig. *General System Theory: Foundations, Development, Applications.* New York: George Braziller, 1968. Presents the essence of general system theory in detail while not being overly technical or mathematical. Provides a good overview of the historical development of systems theories.

Weinberg, Gerald M. *An Introduction to General Systems Thinking.* New York: Wiley, 1975. Considered by many to be a classic, this introductory book explores systems thinking in depth, using various examples and thought problems.

Daniel Lalande and Roy F. Baumeister

See also: Ecological psychology; Family systems theory; Field theory: Kurt Lewin; Industrial and organizational psychology; Organizational behavior and consulting.

T

Taste aversion

Type of psychology: Learning
Fields of study: Biological influences on learning; instrumental conditioning; Pavlovian conditioning

Taste aversion occurs when an animal or person eats a food, becomes ill, and subsequently develops a distaste for the food that motivates avoidance. Most often considered a form of Pavlovian conditioning, taste aversion learning has several unusual characteristics that have made it an important topic in the literature of learning theory.

Key concepts
- avoidance conditioning
- equipotentiality
- instrumental conditioning
- interstimulus interval
- Pavlovian conditioning
- preparedness

INTRODUCTION

When an animal eats a food, especially one with which it has had little experience, and then becomes ill, the food acquires a nauseating or aversive quality and will subsequently be avoided. This phenomenon is called bait shyness, food aversion, or, most commonly, taste aversion, although the odor and sometimes even the sight of the food also become aversive.

When confronted with a new food, rats will investigate it thoroughly by sniffing. If the odor is unfamiliar, and familiar food is available elsewhere, the rats may pass by the novel food without eating it. If sufficiently hungry, the rats may sample the new food by nibbling at it and then withdrawing to wait for adverse effects. If none occurs, the new food may be accepted, but if the rats become ill the food will be avoided; even the trails or runways where the new food is located may be abandoned. This cautiousness toward novel foods makes rats notoriously difficult to poison.

STIMULUS AND RESPONSE

Taste-aversion learning has been construed both as instrumental avoidance learning and as Pavlovian conditioning. Clearly, elements of both are involved. Development of the aversion itself, in which the food takes on a negative motivational quality, is seen by most learning theorists as Pavlovian conditioning. Subsequent avoidance of the food is learned by instrumental conditioning.

In development of the aversion, the smell or taste of the food clearly serves as the conditioned stimulus; however, there has been some confusion in the literature as to what constitutes the unconditioned stimulus in taste-aversion conditioning. In a typical experiment, rats are presented with water that contains a distinctive flavor, such as saccharin or almond extract. After drinking the flavored water, the rats are treated in some way that makes them ill. Illness treatments have been as diverse as X-ray irradiation and spinning on a turntable, but the preferred method is injection of a toxic drug such as lithium chloride or apomorphine. As a result of the treatment-produced illness, the rats subsequently avoid the flavored water.

Most frequently, "illness" is cited as the unconditioned stimulus in these experiments, but one also sees references to "poisoning" or to the "illness treatment" in this regard. These latter references actually make more sense and are more consistent with other research in which a drug treatment (the unconditioned stimulus) is seen as producing an innate drug effect (the unconditioned response).

In 1927, Ivan Petrovich Pavlov described experiments with morphine and apomorphine in which the drug injection, the drug itself, or "changes in the internal environment due to alteration in the composition of the blood" were construed as the unconditioned stimulus. The drug effects, including salivation, nausea, vomiting, and sleep, were construed as unconditioned responses. Pavlov even described an experiment in which tying off the portal vein led to development of an aversion to meat in dogs because of buildup in the blood of toxic substances derived from the digestion of the meat. The implication was that the smell and taste of meat were conditioned stimuli and the toxins (or the alterations in blood chemistry) were unconditioned stimuli.

In taste-aversion conditioning, the smell or taste (and sometimes the sight) of food serves as the conditioned stimulus. This stimulus signals the presence of a toxin, which acts as the unconditioned stimulus by altering body chemistry, which in turn produces nausea, illness, or vomiting, the unconditioned response. Through conditioning, nausea or "aversion" develops as the conditioned response to presentation of the taste, smell, or sight of the food. This aversion then motivates an instrumental avoidance response; that is, because of the conditioned aversion, the animal does not eat the food.

LEARNING AVERSIONS

Taste aversion plays an important adaptive role in the everyday life of animals, especially those that eat a diversity of foods. Food preferences are learned early in the lives of such animals—they eat what they see their mothers eating or, even earlier, they come to prefer foods with flavors encountered previously in mothers' milk. To cope with a variable environment, however, animals must often adopt a new food. Animals with no mechanism for learning to accept safe foods while rejecting toxic ones would soon perish.

Nor is taste-aversion learning seen only in laboratory animals. Humans, too, learn food aversions quickly and convincingly. Martin E. P. Seligman, a prominent learning theorist, has supplied his own autobiographical account of taste aversion learning. Six hours after eating filet mignon flavored with béarnaise sauce, Seligman became violently ill with the stomach flu. "The next time I had sauce béarnaise, I couldn't bear the taste of it," he relates. He did not, however, develop an aversion to the steak, to the white plates from which it had been eaten, or to the opera that he attended during the six-hour interstimulus interval.

Seligman's experience exemplifies several pecu-

liarities of taste-aversion learning that have made it an important topic in the literature of learning theory: A strong conditioned response develops in a single learning trial, the conditioned response develops even when the conditioned and unconditioned stimuli are separated by long interstimulus intervals, the aversion develops selectively to some stimuli but not to others, and the conditioned response is irrational in the sense that it is not much affected by conscious knowledge that the food was not tainted or is not likely to be tainted in the future.

NATURAL AVERSIONS

In nature, taste-aversion learning is a common event. Animals that do not specialize on one or a few foods must be able to reject toxic foods. Rats especially have a problem in this regard, since they do not vomit and therefore cannot expel poisons once they have ingested them. When rats have access to many foods, their behavior is marvelously adapted to detecting toxins. They eat only one or two different food types at a time and may eat these exclusively for days. Then they shift to concentration on another food type. If illness develops, the rats know immediately which type of food is probably to blame and subsequently avoid it. If the rats had eaten a variety of foods all the time, such discrimination would not be possible.

Human infants may adopt a similar strategy when allowed to eat without supervision. In the 1920's, Clara Davis gave infants the opportunity to eat any of a variety of nutritious foods, none of which alone supplied a balanced diet. The infants specialized on one or two foods for days at a time before shifting to another food. Although daily diets were certainly not nutritionally balanced, the infants did, over the long run, eat a balanced, healthful diet. The behavior of one infant was particularly interesting. This child voluntarily consumed cod-liver oil, a vile-tasting fluid usually rejected by children. This child, however, had a vitamin D deficiency, and the cod-liver oil supplied the necessary vitamin. After the deficiency was eliminated, the infant stopped eating cod-liver oil and never went back to it.

The idea that the infant's behavior may be related to taste learning was shown by Paul Rozin, who found that rats fed a thiamine-deficient diet subsequently chose a food laced with thiamine supplements even though thiamine itself is tasteless. The rats apparently were able to use the taste of the food as a discriminative stimulus for its nutritive properties. Thus, the phenomenon is the opposite of taste-aversion learning—the development of specific hungers for foods with nutritive qualities, foods that promote health or recovery from illness. Anecdotal reports suggest that humans sometimes also suddenly develop tastes for foods that contain needed nutrients.

Thus, taste aversion is apparently only one side of the story of food selection and rejection in nature. Both appetitive and avoidance behaviors can be predicated on taste cues. In some cases, these behaviors are innate responses to the taste. Bitter tastes usually indicate the presence of toxic alkaloids and are often rejected by young animals that have had no prior experience with them. Human infants do the same. In other cases, the response to taste cues must be learned. Thus, specific hungers and taste aversions both represent examples of appropriate behaviors that are cued by discriminative taste stimuli.

Lincoln Brower has described a classic example of taste-aversion learning in nature. Blue jays, he noted, typically avoid preying on monarch butterflies. If hungry enough, however, jays will take and eat monarchs. The caterpillars of these butterflies eat milkweed, which contains a poison to which the butterflies are immune but birds are not. Enough of the poison remains concentrated in the tissues of adult monarchs to make a bird that eats one quite sick. The jays subsequently reject monarchs after a brief taste, and eventually the distinctive orange and black insects are rejected on sight.

Blue jays learn to reject the monarch butterfly, which contains a poison that makes the birds sick. (Davidcrehner/Dreamstime.com)

INDUCED AVERSIONS

In more applied settings, Carl Gustavson and John Garcia have described the use of taste-aversion conditioning in wildlife management. On the western ranges where large flocks of sheep are left relatively unprotected, ranchers often face the threat of predation by coyotes, wolves, and mountain lions. One response has been wholesale shooting and poisoning of these wild predators, but this is a less-than-ideal solution. Gustavson and Garcia found that predators, such as coyotes, that scavenge a lamb carcass laced with a sublethal dose of lithium chloride will subsequently develop a strong aversion to lamb and may even avoid areas where lamb and sheep are grazing. The authors proposed a scheme for reducing predation on sheep using taste-aversion conditioning that would drastically reduce the need for shooting and the use of indiscriminate lethal poisons.

In humans, many medical conditions are accompanied by loss of appetite and weight loss. Although this is often attributable to chemical changes within the body, it can also be caused by taste-aversion learning. Ilene Bernstein investigated the loss of appetite, or anorexia, that frequently accompanies cancer chemotherapy and found that, in all likelihood, it was attributable to aversive conditioning caused by the cancer medications, which often induce nausea and vomiting. Bernstein and her colleague, Soo Borson, investigated other anorectic syndromes and found the same possibility. In an important review article published in 1986, they proposed that taste-aversion learning may play a significant role in such conditions as cancer anorexia, tumor anorexia, anorexia nervosa, and the anorexias that accompany clinical depression and intestinal surgery.

On the other hand, taste-aversion learning is intentionally induced in some types of aversion therapy for maladaptive behaviors. Alcoholics are sometimes given a drug called disulfiram (Antabuse) that interferes with alcohol metabolism in the liver. Drinking alcohol after taking this drug results in a very unpleasant illness that conditions an aversion to alcohol. Subsequently, the taste, smell, or even the thought of alcohol can induce nausea. Cigarette smoking has been treated similarly.

EXPERIMENTAL AVERSIONS

Before 1966, psychologists believed that learning obeyed the law of equipotentiality. In Pavlovian conditioning, the nature of conditioned and unconditioned stimuli was seen as unimportant—if they were paired appropriately, learning would occur with equal facility for any stimulus pair. In instrumental conditioning, psychologists believed that any reinforcer would reinforce any behavior.

Equipotentiality had been challenged. Ethologists insisted that each species of animal is unique in what it learns, that learning is an evolutionary adaptation, and that species are not interchangeable in learning studies. Nikolaas Tinbergen, in *The Study of Instinct* (1951), wrote of the innate disposition to learn. Keller and Marian Breland, who trained animals for commercial purposes, discovered that animals drifted toward species-specific food-related behaviors when their arbitary instrumental responses were reinforced with food.

In 1966, Garcia, Robert Koelling, and Frank Ervin published their research on taste-aversion learning. In an article called "Relation of Cue to Consequence in Avoidance Learning," they described an experiment in which rats received aversive consequences for licking water from a drinking spout. In the "tasty water" condition of the experiment, the water was flavored with saccharin, while in the "bright-noisy water" condition, licking the spout activated a flashing lamp and a clicking relay. Half the animals from each condition were made sick after drinking. The other half received a mild but disruptive electric shock after licking the spout. In the tasty water condition, animals that were made sick, but not those that were shocked, avoided drinking. In the bright-noisy water condition, animals that were shocked, but not those that were made sick, avoided drinking. Thus, light and noise were easily associated with shock, and taste was easily associated with illness, but the contrary associations were much more difficult to establish.

In a second article, called "Learning with Prolonged Delay of Reinforcement," Garcia, Ervin, and Koelling demonstrated that taste aversion developed even when the taste and illness treatment were separated by seventy-five minutes. Learning with such prolonged delays had been regarded as impossible, and it could not be reproduced in shock-avoidance experiments. These results were quickly replicated in other laboratories. Similar effects were demonstrated in other types of learning experiments, including traditional avoidance paradigms and even in mazes and Skinner boxes. The fact that something was wrong with traditional learning theory and equipotentiality was soon evident.

The doctrine of prepared learning replaced equipotentiality. Preparedness is the idea that evolution equips animals to learn things that are important to their survival. Examples of prepared learning already existed in the literature, but until 1966 their significance was not widely recognized among psychologists. Ethologists, however, pointed to studies of imprinting, food recognition, song learning, and place learning in a variety of animals, all illustrating prepared learning. Psychologists quickly included language learning and the learning of some phobias under the umbrella of preparedness. It was even proposed that human cognition evolved to cope with widely divergent situations that require unprepared learning. Taste-aversion learning, however, which is strongly prepared apparently even in humans, seems relatively immune to such ratiocination.

SOURCES FOR FURTHER STUDY

Bernstein, Ilene L., and Soo Borson. "Learning Food Aversion: A Component of Anorexia Syndromes." *Psychological Review* 93, no. 4 (1986): 462-472. A review of some of the issues relevant to development of clinically significant food aversions in humans. The authors discuss tumor anorexia, cancer anorexia, anorexia nervosa, and anorexia following intestinal surgery. Technical, but interesting and important.

Bolles, Robert C. *Learning Theory.* 2d ed. New York: Holt, Rinehart and Winston, 1979. One of the most concise and readable textbooks on learning theory; it reads almost like a mystery story in places. Details learning theory both before and after the discovery of the Garcia effect and includes a discussion of learning in its evolutionary context. Chapter 9 is almost entirely on taste aversion and its implications.

Braveman, Norman S., and Paul Bronstein, eds. *Experimental Assessments and Clinical Applications of Conditioned Food Aversions*. New York: New York Academy of Sciences, 1985. This is volume 443 in the Annals of the New York Academy of Sciences, and it reprints papers presented at a 1984 conference. Many of the articles, by experts in the field, deal with the medical relevance of food aversions in humans. Many of the articles are quite technical, but some are accessible to the general reader with some background.

Brower, Lincoln Pierson. "Ecological Chemistry." *Scientific American* 220 (February, 1969): 22-29. An excellent and enjoyable description of taste-aversion learning in nature. Brower describes how birds become averted to insects, such as monarch butterflies, that feed on plants containing chemical toxins. Some of the evolutionary implications of this phenomenon are discussed.

Bures, Jan, Federico Bermudez-Rattoni, and Takashi Yamamoto. *Conditioned Taste Aversion: Learning of a Special Kind*. New York: Oxford University Press, 1998. A comprehensive and up-to-date summary of research into the neuroanatomy, pharmacology, electrophysiology, and functional morphology of conditioned taste aversion.

Gustavson, Carl R., and John Garcia. "Pulling a Gag on the Wily Coyote." *Psychology Today* 8 (August, 1974): 68-72. Very entertaining article describing the research on averting wild predators to sheep as a way of limiting predation on ranchers' herds without destroying the predators themselves. The authors convincingly show that shooting and poisoning coyotes are unnecessary and undesirable.

Reilly, Steve, and Todd R. Schachtman, eds. *Conditioned Taste Aversion: Neural and Behavioral Processes*. New York: Oxford University Press, 2009. Leading scholars in the field of learning provide articles on recent research in conditioned taste aversion. Topics include side effects of chemotherapy, treatment of alcoholism, memory, and addiction.

Seligman, Martin E. P., and Joanne L. Hager, eds. *Biological Boundaries of Learning*. New York: Appleton-Century-Crofts, 1973. Almost a history of the revolution in learning theory brought about by taste aversion, this volume contains reprints of and commentaries on many of the original research articles, including those by Garcia cited in the text. Difficult in places but necessary reading for a complete understanding of taste aversion.

William B. King

SEE ALSO: Conditioning; Defense reactions: Species-specific; Learning; Pavlovian conditioning; Seligman, Martin E. P.

Teaching methods

TYPE OF PSYCHOLOGY: Learning; motivation
FIELDS OF STUDY: Biological influences on learning; cognitive learning

Teaching methods are techniques to induce students to learn. There are six classes of complementary methods: information providing, inquiry oriented, active or performance based, cooperative, mastery based, and creativity inducing. Excellent instruction depends not on how well any one method is implemented, but rather on how well all the techniques can be coordinated to complement one another.

KEY CONCEPTS

- active or performance-based methods
- cooperative methods
- creativity-inducing methods
- information-providing methods
- inquiry-oriented methods
- mastery-based methods
- responsibility for learning

INTRODUCTION

Teaching methods are techniques to induce students to do what they need to do to learn a specific content, skill, or thinking strategy. Two underlying features of this definition—responsibility for learning and the quest for one best method—deserve further consideration.

Regarding responsibility, there is little doubt that, if learners did what they needed to do, teachers would be unnecessary. However, few learners are sufficiently self-motivated or capable of diagnosing what they need. Enter teachers: It is they who can—and must—structure a task so that students are willing to do what they do not yet understand, diagnose errors or misconceptions, provide feedback on how to improve, and encourage or motivate as needed.

Current thinking on the responsibilities of teachers can probably be traced to the book by philosopher and educator John Dewey, *How We Think* (1933), in which Dewey specifically equated the teaching-learning process with selling-buying. Teaching activities that do not culminate in student achievement are every bit as unsuccessful as merchant activities that do not result in a sale. The analogy is not perfect, however, because merchants succeed by selling to only a portion of their customers; teachers are held accountable for each student. Virtually all models of instruction since Dewey make learning a shared or reciprocal responsibility between teacher and student.

Regarding the "one best method" mentality, all models recommend that teachers learn and employ a wide variety of techniques so that, first, students can find different ways to engage the material and, second, students cannot overemphasize one learning strategy and allow others to atrophy. An aphorism makes the point more dramatically: If a child has only a hammer, everything looks like a nail. To get past that narrow perception requires that the child begin to use other tools. Tools of teaching are therefore most profitably conceived as ways to expand the teacher's repertoire, which increases the probability of inducing students to do what they need to do to learn.

TYPES OF TEACHING METHODS

Teaching methods can be classified in a number of ways, none of which is entirely satisfactory because of considerable overlap of purposes and procedures. For example, although lectures can be straight presentation of information with little or no active involvement by an audience, since the 1970's teachers have increasingly woven opportunities for active participation into lectures, even in very large classes. As another example, mastery learning, which requires students to demonstrate competence individually, is often successfully combined with cooperative teams.

Recognizing that overlaps exist, one can divide methods into categories according to whether they are primarily information-providing, inquiry-oriented, active or performance-based, cooperative, mastery-based, or creativity-inducing.

INFORMATION-PROVIDING METHODS

Prime exemplars of information-providing methods are lectures and demonstrations in which authoritative information is presented or a skill or a process

modeled. Strengths of the lecture are not only that much information, including data too recent to be published, can be presented in a relatively short period of time but also that an expert's ways of thinking about the topic can be displayed. Also on display is the lecturer's excitement about the topic, as well as implicit or explicit concern for ethical issues. While many facts can be embedded in a lecture, they will be remembered better by other methods; thus, the lecture is better used to convey how an expert reflects on the chain of logic used to draw inferences about the data or events that constitute the topic.

Demonstrations have many of the same features as lectures—indeed, a lecture could be considered a demonstration of reasoning—but they display skills and performances in modalities beyond the verbal. These include physical skills, artistic performances, and scientific experiments in which experts can model effective, efficient, and aesthetic techniques.

Lectures and demonstrations are often combined to great effect, and they have the advantage of being locally recordable for later viewing or transmission to distant or very large audiences. Conversely, professionally developed videos of actual or simulated research or events—such as space exploration or an experiment involving deoxyribonucleic acid (DNA)—can be made available to students anywhere in the world. Using similar technology, teachers can present complex skills or ideas, dissecting a sports or a musical performance, or even a chemical reaction.

The primary weakness of information-providing methods is, ironically, that they are not very efficient for learning specific information. A popular saying conveys the problem: I hear, I forget; I see, I remember; I do, I understand. Research on verbal and visual elaborations in memory confirms the point that demonstrations provide imagery, which improves memory beyond that of simple verbal processing. To understand and use, which implies beginning to become truly competent, learners must construct their own examples, organize their knowledge, and practice their skills. Thus, lectures and demonstrations are most effective if they are accompanied by other methods.

INQUIRY-ORIENTED METHODS

In general, the word "inquiry" implies some systematic examination of a topic in search of information or discovery of the truth. Hence, inquiry and discovery are often used as synonyms for techniques that require students not only to solve problems but also to pose them, not only to conduct investigations but also to plan them, not only to draw inferences from data but also to elucidate the chain of logic they are using. These are higher levels of thinking, requiring such cognitive processes as planning, critical analysis, organization, and synthesis, as well as such metacognitive processes as self-reflection on "what I know and how I know it."

Case studies—real or simulated—in which illnesses are diagnosed, problems are identified, and alternative solutions or treatments are compared and evaluated are excellent illustrations of inquiry methods. So is the search for historical antecedents or consequences of a scientific finding, sociopolitical event, or ethical-moral debate. Inquiry is integral to progress in science and the social sciences and, if education is preparation for such fields, students need to have such discovery experiences to understand these fields.

Weaknesses of inquiry/discovery learning include the extended time required, the fact that breadth of coverage of a field is sacrificed in favor of in-depth study of only a few topics, and that every student must be involved in all stages of the investigation to reap the benefit (and receive teacher feedback). In practice, therefore, teachers often use inquiry methods in combination with other techniques. For example, they save time by demonstrating an experiment or by having teams of students doing different phases of the research. To the extent that students are excluded from responsibility for various phases, however, their experience with inquiry is diluted.

Still, some practice with inquiry may be better than none, and thus it may be possible to place specific inquiry/discovery methods on a continuum from complete to none. A teacher demonstration followed by students searching for alternative explanations would be a legitimate, if partial, inquiry experience. The other end of the continuum might be a concept attainment lesson, in which elementary students are shown objects or pictures of objects and must decide why they are alike or different, and thereby discover symmetry, even before they know the concept label.

ACTIVE OR PERFORMANCE-BASED METHODS

Active methods are those in which students are continually participating in the lesson, sometimes "hands-on," or overtly, when they are performing, always "minds-on," or covertly, because they may be called on to contribute at any moment. Such methods are usually contrasted with passive learning, in which students just listen for extended periods of time or wait until it is their turn to perform. Examples of passive methods—which active methods were invented to supplement—include long lectures or demonstrations; classroom recitations in which, for example, one student translates a sentence from one language to another or performs a song, while other students wait their turn in sequence; and procedures in which only volunteers participate.

Active methods have long been used to supplement lectures and demonstrations, as well as to monitor learning in performance-based fields such as music or sports. In these fields, information may be provided via brief lectures or demonstrations, following which students practice with feedback and coaching. For academic subjects, lectures or demonstrations could likewise be broken into ten- to twenty-minute segments, followed by such techniques as learning by teaching, in which the teacher demonstrates, say, three concepts and each member of a three-person team teaches one of those concepts to the other two persons (perhaps also inventing their own examples); think-pair-share, in which the lecture is interrupted with a question designed to make individuals process or apply the content, which is then discussed with a partner and subsequently shared with the whole class; one-minute papers, in which students must summarize the main points or central inference to be drawn from the presentation, which can then be discussed further in class (or turned in anonymously as feedback to the instructor); or short quizzes, in which the teacher asks a few true-false, multiple-choice, or short-answer questions to be scored and discussed immediately.

To substitute for recitations in which only the performer is active, it is more desirable to ask questions of, or invent an activity for, the whole class before any individual is called on to respond. Thus, for language translation, all students may be asked to translate the sentence, then compare translations or call on two or three students. For a recital, the student audience may be assigned to assess the difficulty of the piece, find one exemplary aspect of the performance, and make one positive suggestion for improving. (Even if these are not shared with the performer, such exercises give students practice with the higher levels of thinking involved in evaluation of performances.)

Discussions can also be active methods, but not if they are dominated by only the few individuals who are willing to volunteer. At the other extreme is an inquisition-like atmosphere in which the teacher dominates by asking question after question. Somewhere between these extremes is an optimal active method, which may use techniques from other methodologies as precursors to the whole class discussion.

The main weakness of active methods is probably that, in trying to keep them brief enough to fit into the limited class time available, they tend to overemphasize lower-level thinking skills or initial performances. Thus, they need to be supplemented by other information-providing techniques and inquiry projects that can provide experiences with problem posing and sustained reasoning.

COOPERATIVE METHODS

Cooperative methods should also be included in the repertoire of active methods, but what makes them a unique category is that they were explicitly designed to teach collaborative skills as well as traditional academic objectives. They do this through what David and Roger Johnson, pioneers in cooperative teaching methods, in 1975 called cooperative goal structures. In contrast to individualistic or competitive approaches, cooperative goals require individuals to coordinate their efforts to achieve an instructional objective, so that individuals succeed only when all succeed. This is accomplished by two features that both define cooperative teams and distinguish them from the kinds of groups most people have experienced: individual accountability and positive interdependence.

Individual accountability means that, despite having a group assignment or product to complete, all students will be assessed, first, on what each was responsible for doing and, second, on his or her comprehension of the whole task. Positive interdependence means, first, that each student will have a unique role that complements the others' roles, and, second, that each student has an incentive for assuring that all students succeed in fulfilling their roles and comprehending the material.

Using different role assignments, a math or science teacher might identify a leader, a researcher, and a presenter as roles for three-person teams (with different assignments on other days). Leaders will help define the task, distribute responsibilities, keep the group on task, and maintain records of the group's work; researchers will bring class notes, organize and calculate data, or consult the teacher; and presenters will organize the report and present findings to the class.

Other ways of assuring positive interdependence in many subject areas were developed in the 1980's by Robert Slavin and his colleagues. For example, in jigsaw, each member of the team becomes responsible for one aspect of a complex topic and meets with corresponding members of other teams. That is, each team member is given a number from one to four; then the ones get together to study one component of the topic, the twos another, and so on. Following acquisition of expertise in this topic, they return to their groups and teach their team members.

To ensure individual accountability in these approaches, the teacher must still provide incentive for each student to care that all learn. This can be done, for example, by giving a bonus to the whole team when each member individually passes a quiz or mastery test on the material. Alternatively, the teacher can assess individual students' fulfillment of their responsibilities, which might also include students' self-ratings or (if done properly) students rating one another.

MASTERY-BASED METHODS

Both a philosophy and a collection of methods, mastery learning seeks to ensure that each student achieves at least the minimum standard of knowledge or performance for each required objective. Such competencies can be defined formally, as when students will eventually be accountable for professional certifications as lawyers, physicians, and psychologists, or, less formally, as in demonstrating mastery of multiplication tables, rules of grammar, or reading comprehension. In any case, the concern of mastery methods is to teach and monitor the progress of each student's competence in a criterion-referenced fashion—that is, in relation to established standards for the instructional objectives.

To implement mastery learning, one must divide the curriculum into critical and enrichment objectives. The former are basic concepts or skills that must be attained by all to prepare for more advanced study in the course or discipline. These critical objectives need to be divided into manageable units, perhaps two to four weeks in length, and learned to a high level (75 percent correct or higher) on conventional tests. Demonstrating mastery, whether by test or performance, is only the initial acquisition of new material and, as such, the material will surely be forgotten. Unlike poorly learned basics, however, material and skills initially mastered can be relearned quickly when needed in subsequent lessons, providing considerable savings in time overall. For students who do not demonstrate mastery, remedial instruction and retesting must be provided.

Because mastery is conceived as initial acquisition and not expert status, even perfect scores on the test must be graded as the beginning levels of skill. People pass a driver's test or learn a new tennis stroke to begin to drive or to play tennis, not because they are finished learning. Thus, people need enrichment objectives, which provide advanced study and application of the mastered material. These are optional assignments that can be done in different ways and that carry the incentive of raising course grades above basic passing. For example, in science or history, enrichment exercises might be inquiry assignments; in English, writing a poem or critiquing an essay or book; in music, arranging a piece for the instruments just studied; in any field, tutoring students who need help with initial mastery.

Weaknesses of mastery methods are that, in emphasizing basic skills, instruction tends to be at the lowest levels of thinking and to go at the rate of the slowest learners. To avoid this, mastery must be used in combination with other methods, and only for material that all students must know to be certified as competent or to assure that prerequisite knowledge has been attained.

CREATIVITY-INDUCING METHODS

While any teaching method has potential for encouraging creativity, it is easy to become dominated by the established logic and ways of thinking in a field. Edward deBono, a longtime advocate of creativity training, calls such approaches vertical thinking to emphasize their sensible, top-to-bottom structure. While logic is necessary to solve problems and organize thinking, it is often insufficient to generate a wide variety of alternative, uncommon, and even bizarre ideas that can later be evaluated logically. He called this approach lateral thinking.

Similar to William Gordon's synectics, lateral thinking has specific techniques for forcing familiar concepts to seem strange so that knowledge—or assumptions—may be reconsidered. For example, one may consider what life would be like if people were born old and became younger every year (deBono's reversibility method) or what it feels like to be the bull in a bullfight (personal analogy in synectics). While these ideas may not lead to new theories, they may help spice up essays on developmental psychology or dysfunctional families, respectively, if used as warm-up exercises. Like brainstorming, the rules include suspending judgment during the idea-generating phase. Finding fault with an idea shuts out further thinking in that direction, while praising an idea reinforces similar thinking. Evaluation comes later, when the goal shifts from generating ideas to deciding which ones to use. As deBono made explicit in his 1985 *Six Hat Thinking* curriculum, people need to learn to put on different thinking caps for different purposes. Each type has weaknesses. Creative thinking is not logical, by definition, and is therefore a method to be used in combination with other methods. Furthermore, while these techniques can stimulate truly novel inventions, when used in classrooms, creativity is defined as behavior or thinking that is novel for this student. Thus, the goal is to encourage each student to avoid habitual or rigidifying thinking through exercises that expand their thinking.

SOURCES FOR FURTHER STUDY

Block, James H., Helen E. Efthim, and Robert B. Burns. *Building Effective Mastery Learning in Schools.* New York: Longman, 1989. Beginning with John Carroll's redefinition of aptitude as "time needed to learn," the authors describe the logical and empirical bases for mastery learning, along with suggestions for implementing mastery in various fields and levels of schooling.

Bonwell, Charles C., and James A. Eisen. *Active Learning: Creating Excitement in the Classroom.* Washington, D.C.: School of Education and Human Development, George Washington University, 1991. Aimed at teachers in higher education, this book clearly describes practical methods for involving students, even in large lecture classes.

Burden, Paul R., and David M. Byrd. *Methods for Effective Teaching: Meeting the Needs of All Students.* 5th ed. Boston: Pearson/Allyn & Bacon, 2009.

Comprehensive textbook provides information on a wide variety of teaching strategies, which are designed to meet the learning needs of different students.

Johnson, David W., Roger T. Johnson, Edythe J. Holubec, and Patricia Roy. *Circles of Learning: Co-operation in the Classroom.* Alexandria, Va.: Association for Supervision and Curriculum Development, 1984. This practical book makes the case for cooperative methods, as well as how to teach the collaborative skills and establish the procedures for maximizing their effectiveness.

Joyce, Bruce R., Marsha Weil, and Beverly Showers. *Models of Teaching.* 8th ed. Boston: Pearson/Allyn & Bacon, 2009. This book presents dozens of instructional methods from various theoretical approaches: from behavioral to cognitive, from individual to cooperative, from didactic to creative.

Rosenshine, Barak, and Robert Stevens. "Teaching Functions." In *Handbook of Research on Teaching*, edited by Merlin C. Wittrock. 3d ed. New York: Macmillan, 1986. This review of the literature analyzes the effectiveness of various things teachers do, particularly regarding review and homework, lecture presentations, feedback, and practice.

J. Ronald Gentile

SEE ALSO: Concept formation; Creativity and intelligence; Dewey, John; Educational psychology; Intelligence; Learning; Learning disorders; Problem-solving stages; Problem-solving strategies; Thought: Inferential; Thought: Study and measurement.

Teenage suicide

TYPE OF PSYCHOLOGY: Developmental psychology
FIELD OF STUDY: Adolescence

Teenage suicide is a profoundly tragic and unsettling event. The rise in adolescent suicide has been so dramatic since the 1960's that it cannot be ignored as a passing problem; attention has been directed toward gaining insight into the myths, causes, warning signs, treatments, and preventive measures of adolescent suicide.

KEY CONCEPTS
- behavioral psychology
- cognitive limitations
- cognitive psychology
- depression
- psychodynamic orientation
- suicide
- suicide attempt

INTRODUCTION

The statistics on teenage suicide are shocking. Suicide is the fifth leading cause of death for those under age fifteen, and it is the second leading cause of death for those ages fifteen to twenty-four.

In 1960, the suicide rate among fifteen- to nineteen-year-olds was 3.6 per 100,000. By 1990, 11.1 out of every 100,000 teenagers fifteen and older committed suicide, according to the U.S. Centers for Disease Control and Prevention (CDC). In 1997, about 9 percent of suicides in the United States were committed by people aged nineteen or younger. Perhaps even more disturbing are the statistics regarding the classification of attempted suicides. Although it is difficult to determine accurately, it is estimated that for every teenager who commits suicide there are approximately fifty teenagers who attempt to take their own lives.

Females attempt suicide at higher rates than males but are less likely to succeed. Males are much more likely to use violent and lethal methods for trying to kill themselves, such as shooting or hanging. Females are more likely to use passive means to commit suicide; the use of drugs and poisons, for example, is more prevalent among females than males.

As alarming as these facts may be, it should be noted that suicide is still rare among the young. Nevertheless, preventing suicide would save thousands of adolescent lives each year. The problem of suicide is complex, and studying it has been especially difficult because suicidal death is often denied by both the medical professional and the victim's family. The whole subject of suicide is carefully avoided by many people. As a result, the actual suicide rate among adolescents may be significantly higher than the official statistics indicate.

CONTRIBUTING FACTORS

There are no simple answers to explain why adolescents attempt suicide, just as there are no simple solutions that will prevent its occurrence; however, researchers have discovered several factors that are clearly related to this drastic measure. These in-

Warning Signs for Teenage Suicide

Four out of five teenagers who attempt suicide have given clear warnings, such as some of the following signs:
- suicide threats, direct and indirect
- obsession with death
- poems, essays, and drawings that refer to death
- dramatic change in personality or appearance
- irrational, bizarre behavior
- overwhelming sense of guilt, shame, or reflection
- changed eating or sleeping patterns
- severe drop in school performance
- giving away belongings

Source: National Mental Health Association (NMHA) factsheet "Suicide: Teen Suicide," 1997.

clude family relations, depression, social interaction, and the adolescent's concept of death.

Family factors have been found to be highly correlated with adolescent suicide. A majority of adolescent suicide attempters come from families in which home harmony is lacking. Often there is a significant amount of conflict between the adolescent and his or her parents and a complete breakdown in communications. Many suicidal youths feel unloved, unwanted, and alienated from the family. Almost every study of suicidal adolescents has found a lack of family cohesion.

Most adolescents who attempt suicide have experienced serious emotional difficulty prior to their attempt. For the majority, this history involves a significant problem with depression. The type of chronic depression that leads some adolescents to commit suicide is vastly different from the occasional "blues" most people experience from time to time. When depression is life-threatening, adolescents typically feel extremely hopeless and helpless and believe there is no way to improve their situation. These feelings of deep despair frequently lead to a negative self-appraisal in which the young person questions his or her ability to cope with life.

Further complicating the picture is the fact that clinically depressed adolescents have severe problems with relating to other people. As a result, they often feel isolated, which is a significant factor in the decision to end one's life. They may become withdrawn from their peer group and develop the idea that there is something wrong with society. At the same time, they lack the ability to recognize how

their inappropriate behavior adversely affects other people.

Another factor that may contribute to suicidal thoughts is the adolescent's conception of death. Because of developmental factors, a young person's cognitive limitations may lead to a distorted, incomplete, or unrealistic understanding of death. Death may not be seen as a permanent end to life and to all contact with the living; suicide may be viewed as a way to punish one's enemies while maintaining the ability to observe their anguish from a different dimension of life. The harsh and unpleasant reality of death may not be realized. Fantasy, drama, and "magical thinking" may give a picture of death that is appealing and positive. Adolescents' limited ability to comprehend death in a realistic manner may be further affected by the depiction of death in the songs they hear, the literature they read, and the films they watch. Frequently death is romanticized. Often it is presented in euphemistic terms, such as "gone to sleep" or "passed away." At other times it is trivialized to such an extent that it is the stimulus for laughter and fun. Death and violence are treated in a remarkably antiseptic fashion.

PREVENTION ATTEMPTS

Suicide is a tragic event for both the victim and the victim's family. It is also one of the most difficult problems confronting persons in the helping professions. In response, experts have focused their attention on trying to understand better how to prevent suicide and how to treat those who have made unsuccessful attempts to take their own lives.

It is believed that many suicides can be prevented if significant adults in the life of the adolescent are aware of various warning signals that often precede a suicide attempt. Most adolescents contemplating suicide will emit some clues or hints about their serious troubles or will call for help in some way. Some of the clues are easy to recognize, but some are very difficult to identify.

The adolescent may display a radical shift in characteristic behaviors related to academics, social habits, and relationships. There may be a change in sleeping habits; adolescents who kill themselves often exhibit difficulty in falling asleep or maintaining sleep. They are likely to be exhausted, irritable, and anxious. Others may sleep excessively. Any deviation from a usual sleep pattern should be noted. The individual may experience a loss of appetite with accompanying weight loss. A change in eating habits is often very obvious.

A pervasive feeling of hopelessness or helplessness may be observed. These feelings are strong indicators of suicide potential. Hopelessness is demonstrated by the adolescent's belief that his or her situation will never get better. It is believed that current feelings will never change. Helplessness is the belief that one is powerless to change anything. The more intense these feelings are, the more likely it is that suicide will be attempted. The adolescent may express suicidal thoughts and impulses. The suicidal adolescent may joke about suicide and even outline plans for death. He or she may talk about another

person's suicidal thoughts or inquire about death and the hereafter. Frequently, prized possessions will be given away. Numerous studies have demonstrated that drug abuse is often associated with suicide attempts. A history of drug or alcohol abuse should be considered in the overall assessment of suicide potential for adolescents.

A variable that is often mentioned in suicide assessment is that of recent loss. If the adolescent has experienced the loss of a parent through death, divorce, or separation, he or she may be at higher risk. This is especially true if the family is significantly destabilized or the loss was particularly traumatic. A radical change in emotions is another warning sign. The suicidal adolescent will often exhibit emotions that are uncharacteristic for the individual. These may include anger, aggression, loneliness, guilt,

Candles, flowers, and notes mark the spot on a cliff at the Point Fermin Park in San Pedro, California, from which two teenagers were believed to have jumped to their deaths. (AP/Wide World Photos)

grief, and disappointment. Typically, the emotion will be evident to an excessive degree.

Any one of these factors may be present in the adolescent's life and not indicate any serious suicidal tendency; however, the combination of several of these signs should serve as a critical warning and result in some preventive action.

TREATMENT

The treatment of suicidal behavior in young people demands that attention be given to both the immediate crisis situation and the underlying problems. Psychologists have sought to discover how this can best be done. Any effort to understand the dynamics of the suicidal person must begin with the assumption that most adolescents who are suicidal do not actually want to die. They want to improve their lives in some manner, they want to overcome the perceived meaninglessness of their existence, and they want to remove the psychological pain they are experiencing.

The first step in direct intervention is to encourage talking. Open and honest communication is essential. Direct questions regarding suicidal thoughts or plans should be asked. It simply is not true that talking about suicide will encourage a young person to attempt it. It is extremely important that the talking process include effective listening. Although it is difficult to listen to an individual who is suicidal, it is very important to do so in a manner that is accepting and calm. Listening is a powerful demonstration of caring and concern.

As the adolescent perceives that someone is trying to understand, it becomes easier to move from a state of hopelessness to hope and from isolation to involvement. Those in deep despair must come to believe that they can expect to improve. They must acknowledge that they are not helpless. Reassurance from another person is very important in this process. The young person considering suicide is so overwhelmed by his or her situation that there may seem to be no other way of escape. Confronting this attitude and pointing out how irrational it is does not help. A better response is to show empathy for the person's pain, then take a positive position that will encourage discussion about hopes and plans for the future.

Adolescents need the assurance that something is being done. They need to feel that things will improve. They must also be advised, however, that the suicidal urges they are experiencing may not disappear immediately and that movement toward a better future is a step-by-step process. The suicidal young person must feel confident that help is available and can be called on as needed. The adolescent contemplating suicide should never be left alone.

If the risk of suicide appears immediate, professional help is indicated. Most desirable would be a mental health expert with a special interest in adolescent problems or in suicide. Phone-in suicide prevention centers are located in virtually every large city and many smaller towns, and they are excellent resources for a suicidal person or for someone who is concerned about that person. To address long-term problems, therapy for the adolescent who attempts suicide should ideally include the parents. Family relationships must be changed to assist the young person in feeling less alienated and worthless.

SUICIDAL PERSONALITIES

Suicide has apparently been practiced to some degree since the beginning of recorded history; however, it was not until the nineteenth century that suicide came to be considered a psychological problem. Since that time, several theories that examine the suicidal personality have been developed.

Émile Durkheim was one of the first to offer a theoretical explanation for suicidal behavior. In the late nineteenth century, he conducted a now-classic study of suicide and published a book, *Le Suicide: Étude de sociologie* (1897; *Suicide: A Study in Sociology*, 1951). He concluded that suicide is often a severe consequence of the lack of group involvement. He divided suicide into three groupings: egoistic, altruistic, and anomic suicides.

The egoistic suicide is representative of those who are poorly integrated into society. These individuals feel set apart from their social unit and experience a severe sense of isolation. He theorized that people with strong links to their communities are less likely to take their lives. Altruistic suicide occurs when individuals become so immersed in their identity group that group goals and ideals become more important than their own lives. A good example of this type of suicide would be the Japanese kamikaze pilots in World War II: They were willing to give up their lives to help their country. The third type, anomic suicide, occurs when an individual's sense of integration in the group has dissolved. When caught in sudden societal or personal change that creates significant alienation or confusion, some may view suicide as the only option available.

Psychologists with a psychodynamic orientation explain suicide in terms of intrapsychic conflict. Emphasis is placed on understanding the individual's internal emotional makeup. Suicide is viewed as a result of turning anger and hostility inward. Sigmund Freud discussed the life instinct versus the drive toward death or destruction. Alfred Adler believed that feelings of inferiority and aggression can interact in such a way as to bring a wish for death to punish loved ones. Harry Stack Sullivan viewed suicide as the struggle between the "good me," "bad me," and "not-me."

Other areas of psychology offer different explanations for suicidal behavior. Cognitive psychologists believe that suicide results from the individual's failure to use appropriate problem-solving skills. Faulty assessment of the present or future is also critical and may result in a perspective marked by hopelessness. Behavioral psychologists propose that past experiences with suicide make the behavior an option that may be considered; other people who have taken their lives may serve as models. Biological psychologists are interested in discovering any physiological factors that are related to suicide. It is suggested that chemicals in the brain may be linked to disorders that predispose an individual to commit suicide.

Research in the area of suicide is very difficult to conduct. Identification of those individuals who are of high or low suicidal risk is complex, and ethical considerations deem many research possibilities questionable or unacceptable. Theory construction and testing will continue, however, and the crisis of adolescent suicide demands that research address the causes of suicide, its prevention, and treatment for those who have been unsuccessful in suicide attempts.

SOURCES FOR FURTHER STUDY

Boesky, Lisa. *When to Worry: How to Tell If Your Teen Needs Help and What to Do About It.* New York: AMACOM, 2007. A practical handbook for parents who are deciding whether their unpredictable and defiant teen is expressing normal adolescent moods or is in need of professional help. Lists serious warning signs such as school difficul-

ties, alcohol and drug use, bipolar disorder, and low self-esteem.

Friedman, Myra. *Buried Alive: The Biography of Janis Joplin.* Updated ed. New York: Harmony Books, 1992. A powerful biography of a famous rock singer who died of a heroin overdose. It poignantly describes how insecurity and acute loneliness played a significant role in her death. An interesting and informative book that is appropriate for adolescents and adults. Contains photographs.

Hyde, Margaret O., and Elizabeth Held Forsyth. *Suicide: The Hidden Epidemic.* Rev. ed. New York: Franklin Watts, 1991. A book written for grades nine through twelve. Discusses the misconceptions of suicide, self-destructive patterns, and motivation theories. Includes a chapter that specifically addresses teenage suicide. Contains a list of suicide prevention centers located across the nation.

Kaplan, Cynthia S., and Blaise Aguirre. *Helping Your Troubled Teen: Learn to Recognize, Understand, and Address the Destructive Behavior of Today's Teens and Preteens.* Beverly, Mass.: Fair Winds Press, 2007. Explains how parents can recognize teens' self-destructive behaviors—substance abuse, eating disorders, self-mutilation, and inappropriate sexual behavior—before they result in serious consequences, such as suicide.

Peck, Michael L., Norman L. Farberow, and Robert E. Litman, eds. *Youth Suicide.* New York: Springer, 1989. Provides a comprehensive overview of adolescent suicide. Written especially for the individual who is interested in working with suicidal youth, but an excellent resource for all who want to increase their understanding of this topic. Contains information on the psychodynamics of suicide, the impact of social change, the role of the family, and intervention strategies.

Petti, T. A., and C. N. Larson. "Depression and Suicide." In *Handbook of Adolescent Psychology,* edited by Vincent B. Van Hassett and Michel Herson. New York: Free Press, 1995. A well-written chapter that makes the complicated factors involved in depression and suicide accessible to the general audience. The authors discuss the causes of both depression and suicide, as well as how the two are related. Addresses how to help the suicidal adolescent. Very readable and informative.

Robbins, Paul R. *Adolescent Suicide.* Jefferson, N.C.:

McFarland, 1998. Covers racial and gender differences, methods used in the study of suicidal behavior, associated behavioral problems such as drugs and alcohol, psychological profiles, precipitating events for suicide attempts, teenage suicide clusters, the effects of suicide on family and friends, the treatment of suicidal adolescents, and strategies for intervention and prevention.

Doyle R. Goff

SEE ALSO: Adolescence: Cognitive skills; Community psychology; Coping: Social support; Death and dying; Depression; Family systems theory; Identity crises; Suicide; Teenagers' mental health.

Teenagers' mental health

TYPE OF PSYCHOLOGY: Developmental psychology; psychopathology
FIELDS OF STUDY: Adolescence; depression

Teenagers' mental health, like their development, is normally well and adaptable. However, some teenagers have difficulty coping with stress and illness, leading to disorders such as major depression, which places them at risk of committing suicide.

KEY CONCEPTS
- clinical criteria
- depression
- development
- resiliency
- risk factors
- suicide

INTRODUCTION

The term "teenager" refers to a person from around the age of thirteen to nineteen. The teenage years are marked by cognitive advancement, increased social interactions, behavioral and emotional independence, abstract thought, idealism, and physical and sexual maturation. The multifaceted context of development can hinder as well as nurture the well-being of teenagers. For some teenagers, mental health (psychological resiliency and well-being) diminishes at a time when the framework of adulthood is to be constructed.

In the early twentieth century, G. Stanley Hall became one of the first scientists to consider an inter-

lude in human development between the immaturity of childhood and the maturity of adulthood; he called this period adolescence. To Hall, adolescence was a recapitulation of the evolutionary transition from proto-humans to modern humans and therefore was characterized by struggle, confusion, and stress (storm and stress). Although Hall's evolutionary explanation of adolescence was later discredited, his theme of adolescent storm and stress persisted for much of the twentieth century. For many teenagers, the transitions to and pathways through middle and high school are the main source of stressors. Some experts consider adolescence to be a time when the key goal is endurance within a developmental context of negativity.

THE "REAL" TEENAGER

The reality, however, does not back up such negative views of adolescence as those of Hall. Most teenagers lead happy, satisfying lives and sustain positive outlooks even when faced with innumerable challenges. The life of a teenager consists of a wide assortment of biological, psychological, and sociocultural factors that combine to form myriad opportunities and adjustments. Teenagers also face pressure as they formulate their academic and career goals and encounter familial expectations regarding performance and social expectations regarding conformity. However, teenagers effectively face these many challenges and adjustments with advancing developmental capacities that they bring to bear in their lives. Teenagers are not embroiled in Hall's storm and stress but rather enjoy lives filled by stimulating adventures and challenges. Adults should focus on making sure teenagers have the psychological and social resources they need to confront their challenges and grow from them.

MENTAL HEALTH

A teenager's mental health status can be defined as the degree to which an individual exhibits resiliency and effective coping across life circumstances. Mental health is a mediating factor in how well teenagers deal with stress, make decisions, and operate interpersonally. Teenagers' mental health is a reservoir from which they draw a number of important resources such as confidence, self-esteem, and hopefulness. These elements make up a general sense of well-being and fuel teenagers' psychological endurance when they confront difficult challenges.

Teenagers have near-adult capacities of reasoning, self-regulation, behavioral autonomy, and intellectual achievement, but only a narrow repertoire of skills to guide those capacities and few experiences to inform them. When teenagers experience mental problems, there is an associated disruption in normative development and an increased likelihood of persistence of the disorder into adulthood. When mental illness accompanies development, it can initiate a vicious cycle in which a disorder compromises development, then the compromised development makes a disorder more intractable, leading to further compromised development and a worsening of the disorder. Teenagers' mental health problems involve real pain and suffering and have severe acute and long-term consequences if left untreated.

According to the National Institute of Mental Health (NIMH), a person may have a mental health problem if the individual exhibits the following behaviors:

- Consistently experiences anger or worry
- Feels grief or sadness longer than typically expected after a loss or death
- Believes his or her mind is too controlled or out of control
- Uses alcohol or drugs
- Exercises or diets excessively, overeats, or thinks obsessively about exercise and diet
- Act in ways that harm others or damage property
- Acts impulsively or in reckless ways that expose the self or others to harm

RESILIENCY

Resiliency is the sum whole of protective factors in teenagers' lives that serve to buffer against risk and harm. Teenagers' ability to endure and even respond positively to adversity is a product of resiliency and predicts the maintenance of mental health. Resiliency is not a prewired competence but is constructed with internal and external protective factors available to teenagers.

The list of potential protective factors is long but generally incorporates factors from the individual (for example, intelligence), family (for example, nurturing parents), and environment (for example, a supportive and invested teacher). For example, a resilient teenager may have a stable and nurturing family, have access to health care and nutrition, live in a safe neighborhood, have good communication and interpersonal skills, and have access to social supports and mentors outside the family. No single factor is necessarily more protective, although some may more consistently have a positive impact.

RISK FACTORS

Risk factors are those internal and external aspects of teenagers' developmental context that weaken their capacity to effectively cope with challenges and stress. Risk factors, like protective ones, exist within individuals, their families, and their environments. For example, dyslexia, a learning disorder involving difficulties in recognizing and comprehending written language, is a common risk factor for school-age children and teenagers. Dyslexia can disrupt learning, academic performance, and participation in extracurricular activities. Such disruptions can erode basic developmental resources such as self-efficacy and self-esteem, creating further disruption across other domains of development. Fortunately, any given risk factor does not represent an inevitable erosive force on development, although some, more consistently than others, exert a negative effect. Risk factors have a compounding effect; as challenges to development accumulate, so does the likelihood of maladjustment.

Although some teenagers are predisposed to certain psychiatric disorders such as major depression (often because of genetic makeup), whether they develop these disorders is largely a function of resiliency. No teenager is destined to suffer mental health problems; adequate resiliency minimizes the risks and maximizes the effectiveness of a teenager's response if he or she develops the disorder. Overall, the degree of teenagers' resiliency is determined by the number of positive protective factors relative to the total negative impact of risk factors.

DEPRESSION

Discussions of teenagers' mental health generally focus on major depression. No other psychiatric disorder identified among teenagers is as widely intermixed with accompanying disorders and psychological and social problems. Some 40 to 70 percent of teenagers with major depression are diagnosed with a co-occurring disorder such as an anxiety disorder, conduct disorder, eating disorder, oppositional defiant disorder, or substance abuse.

The prevalence of major depression increases with age from 1 to 2 percent among school-aged children to 5 percent among teenagers (about 1.5 million people). An additional 10 to 15 percent of teenagers may experience depressive symptoms that do not meet the clinical criteria for major depression but still generate serious distress and are at risk of intensifying and crossing the threshold into clinical severity. Although up to 25 percent of teenagers will experience major depression by their nineteenth birthday, major depression is not a normal part of teenage life and development. In fact, it involves significant psychological and biological distress that results in serious pain and potentially life-threatening risk.

CHALLENGES OF RECOGNITION

Two primary factors—limited parental scrutiny and the wide variability of symptoms according to age—create challenges for recognizing major depression among teenagers. First, the normative social and emotional context of adolescence generally involves teenagers spending less time with their parents. Teenagers have schedules (school, extracurricular, and personal) that create a rather autonomous social context and minimize the extent to which parents can monitor their psychological and medical health. In addition, many of the symptoms of major depression are not obvious but rather are largely internalized.

Second, the symptoms of major depression vary widely across age groups. Depressed younger adolescents (eleven through twelve years old) may exhibit symptoms such as somatic complaints (including aches, pains, or illness) instead of psychological negativity, and irritability instead of a depressed mood. In contrast, depressed teenagers (thirteen years old and older) are more likely to show persistent inability to experience happiness or pleasure (anhedonia), debilitating reduction in movement (psychomotor retardation), delusions, and a pervasive sense of hopelessness. Some symptoms are consistent across all age groups (including adults), such as thoughts of suicide, disruption of sleep, and poor concentration.

ALCOHOL USE

A particularly important aspect of teenage depression—and mental health in general—is the high incidence of alcohol use and abuse among teenagers. A 2004 study funded by the National Institute on Drug Abuse found that almost 40 percent of Ameri-

can eighth graders, 66 percent of tenth graders, and 75 percent of twelfth graders had used alcohol. Some 25 percent of tenth through twelfth graders had engaged in binge drinking (five or more drinks within a short time period) within the previous two weeks. Teenage alcohol use (abuse) complicates the risk for depression because it can both mask and protract the symptoms of depression, acting as an inappropriate coping strategy that sustains an insidious disruption of normative development. Indeed, depressed teenagers are more likely to have co-occurring substance use behaviors that may call for a further diagnosis of substance abuse or dependence.

IMPACT OF DEPRESSION

In teenagers, depression typically starts as a single episode that averages about nine months in duration and has a 40 percent cumulative chance of recurring within two years. This reflects the disruption that major depression has on the lives of young people. Depression, like most other disorders, is not a fast-resolving condition and may well last an entire school year. As school is an exceptionally important context of teenage development, depressed teenagers experience disruption to some degree across a wide range of social, psychological, and emotional domains. For example, depression among teenagers is associated with interpersonal difficulties, poor academic performance, and weak self-esteem. These and other difficulties often create a vicious cycle of developmental disturbance that can progressively increase vulnerability to further bouts with depression or another disorder over time.

Many of these age-related differences in symptom expression are due to developmental changes. For example, younger adolescents are more likely to interpret their distress in concrete ways that are constrained by their experience. That concrete thinking translates to an interpretation of their pain and distress as a physical injury or illness (for example, gastrointestinal pain). Younger adolescents (and children) are essentially prone to experience depression and other psychiatric distress as a function of physical illness and only rarely as connected to psychological states.

Teenagers develop severe physical symptoms of depression, but the disorder expands deep into their thoughts, self-concept, and future orientation. Depressed teenagers, like depressed adults, have more advanced cognitive abilities (for example, abstraction, idealism, and hypothetical thought), but these are often compromised by thoughts and reflections infiltrated and dominated by negativity. Depressed teenagers commonly operate within an external locus of control in which they view positive events as being outside of their control and interpret negative events as being completely their own fault. They convince themselves that they are worthless and acquire a pessimistic orientation toward the future that gives rise to seemingly intractable hopelessness. These exaggerations are amplified by the idealistic adolescent mind-set, which they bring to the context of the disorder.

SIGNS AND SYMPTOMS OF DEPRESSION

According to the American Psychiatric Association's *Diagnostic and Statistical Manual of Mental Disorders: DSM-IV-TR* (rev. 4th ed., 2000), the clinical criteria threshold for a major depressive episode is at least five (of a possible nine) symptoms exhibited by the teenager for at least two weeks and that represent a change from previous functioning. At least one of two primary symptoms—either depressed mood or loss of interest or pleasure—must be present. The remaining seven symptoms are abnormal weight gain or loss (including a failure to make expected weight gains), almost daily insomnia or hypersomnia, almost daily observable psychomotor agitation or retardation, almost daily fatigue or lack of energy, consistent feelings of worthlessness or exaggerated or inappropriate guilt, consistent diminished ability to think or apply focus, and persistent thoughts of death, suicide without a specific plan, suicide attempt, or specific suicidal plan.

These symptoms must produce a disruption in functioning within social or academic domains. However, additional criteria appropriately frame the existence of the depressive disorder. Depressive symptoms cannot be due to a teenager's substance use (alcohol or other drugs), nor can they be due to a general medical condition. Further, it would be inappropriate to seek a diagnosis within eight weeks of the loss of a loved one, with exceptions made for extreme functional impairment, morbid obsession with worthlessness, suicidal ideation, psychotic symptoms, or psychomotor retardation.

Teenage depression at any level of severity is not an inevitable or normative aspect of development. Many people erroneously assume that teenagers are "normally" emotionally irregular, and this can prevent them from recognizing potentially serious mood disorders in teenagers. Although teenagers confront stressors that can precipitate emotional reactivity, healthy (resilient) teenagers remain emotionally stable and adaptable. Deviations from normally happy day-to-day lives lasting upward of two weeks should be cause for concern and action.

SUICIDE RISK

Teenage suicide is a critical danger that accompanies major depression and subclinical depressive symptoms. It is the third leading cause of death among teenagers (thirteen to nineteen years old), after unintentional injury and homicide. Although life stressors and other disorders are associated with teenage suicide, depression is the most prominent risk factor. Other risk factors include a history of physical, emotional, or sexual abuse; alcohol or drug abuse; any mood disorder, especially depression or bipolar disorder; feelings of hopelessness; disruptive behavior; deficits in interpersonal skills; a family history of suicide or a prior suicide; a suicide within the child's peer group; stress; and permissive or neglectful parenting. It may be that teenagers' developmental advancements, which are not yet mature, act synergistically with the persistent negative thoughts and feelings of depression to amplify the risk of extreme behaviors such as suicide.

SEEKING HELP AND INFORMATION

Seeking help for teenagers' mental health problems can be an intimidating prospect. Teenagers themselves, despite their distress, may not understand or acknowledge the extent to which they need help. Parents or family members, despite their good intentions, may not have enough information to feel confident that they have identified a real problem. However, indecision should not prevent parents from taking action on issues relating to teenagers' mental health. Consulting with professionals (whether in person or through hotlines) is always a prudent and safe choice.

Communities may not always have as many options for referral and treatment of mental health as they should, but people and programs are available to assist teenagers and their parents in securing proper information, referrals, or diagnostic evaluations and treatment. Sometimes getting the best information and help requires some effort, but it is crucial that teenagers receive the assistance they need. Teenagers and their parents should seek out those people or programs that are most likely to have experience with mental health questions and should remember that serious problems require specialized professional help. Some sources of help are community medical or mental health clinics; family assistance programs; religious leaders or counselors; family doctors or nurse practitioners; hospital psychiatry departments; outpatient clinics; mental health specialists (psychiatrists, psychologists, social workers, or counselors); school counselors, nurses, or principals; social service agencies; state hospital outpatient clinics; and local college- or university-affiliated programs.

Teenagers and their families must seek out multiple sources of information to ensure that all aspects of a mental health problem are understood. For instance, the Internet can hold a wealth of information about disorders and symptoms but cannot substitute for in-person assessment, diagnosis, and treatment by a trained professional. Knowledge is empowering, and discomfort is no excuse for not asking questions about diagnoses and treatment services. Teenagers and their families should seek out other families in their communities that share similar mental health challenges to tap into an empathetic source of support and information. In addition, family networks provide extensive sources of support, information, and advocacy.

SOURCES FOR FURTHER STUDY

Hall, G. Stanley. *Adolescence: Its Psychology and Its Relations to Physiology, Anthropology, Sociology, Sex, Crime, Religion, and Education.* New York: Appleton, 1904. Classic work in which Hall lays forth his theories about adolescence and mental illness, among other topics.

Johnston, L. D., P. M. O'Malley, J. G. Bachman, and J. E. Schulenberg. *Monitoring the Future, National Results on Adolescent Drug Use: Overview of Key Findings, 2004.* NIH Publication No. 05-5726. Bethesda, Md.: National Institute on Drug Abuse, 2005. A report on a survey of drug use among adolescents.

Luthar, S. S., and D. Cichetti. *Resilience and Vulnerability: Adaptation in the Context of Childhood Adversities.* New York: Cambridge University Press, 2003. An examination of resiliency and what it means in terms of mental health.

Marcovitz, H. *Teens and Family Issues.* Folcroft, Pa.: Mason Crest, 2004. The results of a Gallup survey on major issues and trends among teenagers and their families.

National Institute of Mental Health (NIMH). http://www.nimh.nih.gov. Governmental site on mental health provides valuable information on mental illness among teenagers.

National Mental Health Consumers' Self-Help Clearinghouse. http://www.mhselfhelp.org. Web site offers self-help for those with mental illnesses and suggestions for getting appropriate care.

Restifio, K., and D. Shaffer. "Identifying the Suicidal Adolescent in Primary Care Settings." *Journal of the American Academy of Child & Adolescent Psychiatry* 27 (1997): 675-687. The authors look at ways to determine which adolescents are suicidal in primacy care contexts.

Substance Abuse and Mental Health Services Administration (SAMHSA), National Mental Health Information Center. http://www.mentalhealth.samhsa.gov. Web site of a governmental agency that looks at the relationship between mental illness and the use of prohibited substances and alcohol.

Thayer, R. E. *The Origin of Everyday Moods: Managing Tension, Energy, and Stress.* New York: Oxford University Press, 1996. A closer look at the biological and psychological bases of everyday moods, with suggestions on how to manage them.

George T. Ladd

SEE ALSO: Adolescence: Cognitive skills; Adolescence: Cross-cultural patterns; Adolescence: Sexuality; Alcohol dependence and abuse; Depression; Suicide.

Temperature

TYPE OF PSYCHOLOGY: Sensation and perception
FIELD OF STUDY: Auditory, chemical, cutaneous, and body senses

Thermoreceptors are specialized to detect a particular physical change in the environment—the flow of heat, detected as a change in temperature—and to convert this information into nerve impulses that can be integrated and processed by the central nervous system to allow an appropriate compensating response.

KEY CONCEPTS
- adaptation
- circadian temperature rhythm
- cold thermoreceptor
- hyperthermia
- hypothalamus
- hypothermia
- pyrogen
- thermoreceptor
- warm thermoreceptor

INTRODUCTION

Humans have thermoreceptors that can detect the flow of heat energy. These specialized sensory receptors can detect the flow of heat as a change in temperature, and convert this information into nerve impulses. Conversion into nerve impulses places the information into a form that can be processed by the central nervous system, allowing a compensating response, if required, to be initiated.

Humans and other mammals have two kinds of thermoreceptors. One type, called the warm thermoreceptor, becomes active in sending nerve impulses when the body surroundings or an object touched reaches temperatures above 30 degrees Celsius. Nerve impulses from the warm thermoreceptors increase proportionately in frequency as the temperature rises to about 43 degrees Celsius; past this temperature, impulses from the warm thermoreceptors drop proportionately in frequency until they become inactive at about 50 degrees Celsius.

The second type of thermoreceptor becomes active in generating nerve impulses at temperatures below about 43 degrees Celsius. Nerve impulses from these receptors, called cold thermoreceptors, increase proportionately as temperatures fall to about 25 degrees Celsius. Below this temperature, the frequency of nerve impulses generated by the receptors drops proportionately; as temperatures fall to about 5 to 10 degrees Celsius, activity of the cold thermoreceptors falls to zero. The activity of cold and warm thermoreceptors overlaps between temperatures of about 30 and 40 degrees Celsius. Within this range, the sensation of heat or cold results from an integration in the brain of nerve impulses generated by both cold and warm receptors.

At temperatures below about 15 degrees and above about 45 degrees Celsius, pain receptors become active and increase proportionately in activity as temperatures rise or fall beyond these levels.

There is a narrow range of overlap of the limits of pain receptors and thermoreceptors, so that temperatures between about 5 and 15 degrees Celsius are felt as both cold and pain (or as "freezing cold") and temperatures between about 43 and 50 degrees Celsius are felt as both heat and pain (or "burning hot"). Temperatures beyond the 5-degree and 50-degree limits for the thermoreceptors stimulate only the pain receptors and are felt primarily or exclusively as pain. Curiously, the cold receptors become active as pain receptors as the temperature rises above about 45 degrees Celsius. The dual activity of the cold thermoreceptors may account for the fact that freezing cold and burning heat may produce a similar sensation.

ADAPTATION PROCESS

Both types of thermoreceptors adapt quickly as the temperature stabilizes. Adaptation refers to the fact that as a stimulus is maintained at a constant level, the nerve impulses generated by a receptor drop in frequency. In effect, the receptor undergoes a reduction in sensitivity if the stimulus remains constant. If the stimulus changes, the receptor again generates nerve impulses at a frequency proportional to the intensity of the stimulus. The ability of receptors to adapt makes them sensitive to a change in stimulus, which is often the factor of greatest importance to an appropriate response.

The rapid adaptation of thermoreceptors is part of common experience. In going from the outdoors into a warm room on a cold day, one immediately detects the warmer temperature and has a resultant strong sense of a temperature change. After a few minutes, one no longer notices the temperature difference, as one's thermoreceptors adapt and reduce their generation of nerve impulses. If the temperature of the room changes by only a degree or so, however, the generation of impulses by the thermoreceptors increases again, and one becomes aware of the change.

SPATIAL SUMMATION AND RECEPTOR LOCATION

Thermoreceptors also show strong spatial summation. If only a very small region of the body is stimulated, one has difficulty discerning whether a temperature change has been experienced, or even whether the stimulus is hot or cold. As the surface area stimulated increases, impulses arriving in the brain from thermoreceptors are summed, so that perception of the change increases proportionately. If only a square centimeter of skin is stimulated by a warm or cold probe, for example, one might not be able to detect a temperature change smaller than about 1 degree Celsius. If the entire body surface is stimulated, as in total immersion in water, one becomes exquisitely sensitive to changes in temperature. Summation of information from all surface thermoreceptors may allow detection of temperature changes as small as one hundredth of one degree Celsius.

Thermoreceptors in humans are most numerous at the body surface, where they are located immediately under the skin. Each thermoreceptor can detect temperature changes over an area of about 1 millimeter in diameter. Cold thermoreceptors occur in greater numbers at the body surface than warm receptors: Depending on the body region, there may be as many as three to ten cold thermoreceptors for each warm thermoreceptor. Thermoreceptors of both types are particularly densely distributed in the skin of the tongue and the lips. In these regions, there may be as many as twenty to thirty or more thermoreceptors per square centimeter of surface. About a third as many thermoreceptors occur in the skin of the fingertips. In other parts of the body surface, only a few thermoreceptors occur per square centimeter.

PHYSICAL AND CHEMICAL MECHANISMS

Although the locations of cold and heat receptors can be pinpointed on the body surface by touching the skin with a warm or cold probe, it has proved difficult to detect particular structures responsible for thermoreception. One group of cold thermoreceptors, however, has been identified as branched nerve endings that terminate near the inner surfaces of cells in the skin. Presumably, other cold thermoreceptors and the warm thermoreceptors are little more than naked nerve endings that cannot be distinguished from pain and some touch receptors, which have a similar appearance.

Little is understood about the physical and chemical mechanisms underlying thermoreception; however, it is considered likely that the reception mechanism depends on increases and decreases in chemical reaction rates in the receptor cells as the temperature rises and falls. In general, chemical reaction rates approximately double for each 10-degree increase in temperature or are halved for

each 10-degree fall. Thermoreceptors probably respond to these increases or decreases in chemical reaction rates rather than directly detecting the changes in heat flow responsible for changes in temperature. The thermoreceptors responsible for detecting heat are also sensitive, to some degree, to chemicals. This explains why spices such as red peppers give the sensation of heat when placed on the tongue or rubbed into the skin. Other chemicals, such as menthol, feel cold on the tongue or skin.

BODY TEMPERATURE MAINTENANCE

Thermoreception has two primary functions in warm-blooded animals such as humans. One is detection of extreme temperatures, so that a person can respond to avoid tissue damage by burning or freezing. The second is maintenance of normal body temperature of 37 degrees Celsius.

Maintenance of body temperature involves both conscious and automated responses. At temperatures not too far above and below the range of comfort (about 22 to 24 degrees Celsius), one feels consciously warm or cool and responds by one or more voluntary methods to decrease or increase skin temperature, such as donning or removing clothing. The automated responses maintaining body temperature are complex and involve a variety of systems. Changes in internal temperature are detected by thermoreceptors in the body interior, particularly in the hypothalamus—a brain structure containing the center that detects and regulates internal body temperature. The thermoreceptors of the hypothalamus are extremely sensitive to shifts from the normal body temperature of 37 degrees Celsius. If such changes occur, the hypothalamus triggers involuntary responses that adjust body temperature.

If the internal body temperature rises above 37 degrees, sweat glands in the skin are stimulated to release their secretion, which evaporates and cools the body surface. Heat loss is also promoted by dilation of the peripheral vessels, which increases blood flow to the body surface. Blood cooled at the surface is carried to the body interior by the circulatory system, where it removes heat from internal regions and causes a drop in body temperature. In addition to these cooling mechanisms, release of thyroxin from the thyroid gland is inhibited. The resulting reduction in the concentration of this hormone in the circulation slows the rate at which body cells oxidize fuel substances and diminishes the amount of heat released by these reactions in the body.

If the internal body temperature falls below 37 degrees Celsius, a series of automated responses with opposite effects triggered. Peripheral blood vessels contract, reducing the flow of blood to the body surface. The output of thyroxin from the thyroid gland increases; the increased thyroxin concentration stimulates body cells to increase the rate at which fuel substances are oxidized to release heat within the body. Although the effect of the response in humans is not pronounced, a drop in internal temperature also stimulates contraction of small muscles at hair roots over the body. The contraction, which is felt as "goose bumps," raises body hairs and increases the dead-air space at the surface of the body. If the drop in internal temperature becomes more extreme, shivering caused by rhythmic contractions of voluntary muscles is induced. Shivering increases body temperature through the heat released by the muscular contractions.

ROLE OF THE HYPOTHALAMUS

The hypothalamus has been identified as the region of the brain regulating body temperature through observations of the effects of injuries and electrical stimulation. Damage to the hypothalamus can inhibit such temperature-regulating responses as sweating and dilation or constriction of peripheral blood vessels. Conversely, experimental electrical stimulation of the hypothalamus can induce the regulatory responses. These observations indicate that the primary temperature-regulating center of the hypothalamus is in its anterior or preoptic region. The automated responses triggered by the hypothalamus in addition to conscious responses allow humans to maintain an almost constant body temperature in the face of a wide variety of environmental conditions. These combined automated and conscious responses allow humans to survive and remain active in a wider range of environmental conditions than any other animal.

The body temperature maintained by the thalamus is not actually set perfectly and constantly at 37 degrees. For most persons, the internal body temperature varies over a range of about 0.6 degree, with the lowest temperatures in the early morning and the highest point at about four to six in the afternoon. This daily variation in body temperature is called the circadian temperature rhythm.

Although the body temperature is normally set at 37 degrees, the set point can be adjusted upward to produce fever as a part of the body's response to infection by invading organisms. Raising the body temperature above 37 degrees results from the same automated responses that normally raise internal temperatures—shivering, constriction of peripheral blood vessels, and an increase in the rate of metabolic reactions.

FEVER

Several types of bacteria secrete substances that can directly stimulate the hypothalamus to raise its set point and induce fever. Substances of this type, capable of inducing fever, are termed pyrogens. Other substances derived through the breakdown of infecting bacteria, or from substances released through the breakdown of body tissues in disease, particularly fragments of some body proteins, can indirectly trigger the hypothalamus to raise its set point. These substances are engulfed by certain types of white blood cells, including macrophages. On engulfing the breakdown substances, the white blood cells release a powerful pyrogen called interleukin-1. This substance stimulates the secretion of a type of hormone, the prostaglandins, which in turn induces the hypothalamus to raise its temperature set point above 37 degrees. The advantage that fever provides to the body in fighting infection is unclear. Aspirin and corticosteroids are able to reduce fever by inhibiting the secretion of prostaglandins.

When the body's ability to regulate temperature is exceeded, resulting in extreme hyperthermia or hypothermia, the results can be extremely serious. Fevers above about 41 to 42 degrees Celsius, or about 106 to 108 degrees Fahrenheit, can cause severe or fatal damage if the body temperature is not quickly lowered by treatments such as water or alcohol sponging of the skin. The high temperatures injure or kill body cells, particularly in the brain, liver, and kidneys, and cause internal bleeding. Damage to brain cells from extremely high fever is essentially irreversible and may cause permanent impairment or even death within minutes.

HYPERTHERMIA AND HYPOTHERMIA

Under some conditions, as on hot and humid days or when the body is immersed in hot water, the normal physiological reactions regulating body temperature are ineffective and body temperature may rise uncontrollably. If the air temperature rises above about 38 degrees Celsius on days in which the humidity approaches 100 percent, for example, temperature regulation by sweating and dilation of peripheral blood vessels is ineffective. Under such conditions, internal body temperature may rise to damaging levels, particularly if physical exercise is attempted. The resulting reaction, known as hyperthermia or heat stroke, may include dizziness and abdominal distress or pain in milder cases; more severe heat stroke may produce delirium or even death. Hyperthermia differs fundamentally from fever in that the set point of the hypothalamus remains at 37 degrees. Another difference is that the circadian temperature rhythm is maintained during fever, but not in hyperthermia. In addition to high environmental heat and humidity, hyperthermia may be caused by cocaine and psychedelic drugs.

Low environmental temperatures can also exceed the body's capacity to regulate its internal temperature. Heat loss attributable to accidental or intentional immersion in ice water, for example, induces a steady drop in internal body temperature that cannot be effectively reversed by shivering, constriction of peripheral blood vessels, or increases in chemical reaction rates. The effects of extreme cold in lowering body temperature are magnified by impairment of the regulatory function of the hypothalamus. At body temperatures below about 34 degrees Celsius, the function of the hypothalamus in temperature regulation becomes severely impaired. Shivering usually stops below 32 degrees. At internal temperatures below about 28 degrees Celsius, the temperature regulation centers of the hypothalamus cease to function entirely. Below this temperature, internal body temperature falls rapidly, breathing slows greatly or arrests, and the heart may develop an irregular beat or stop beating entirely. Death follows quickly if breathing or the heartbeat stops. Any fall of body temperature below 35 degrees is known as hypothermia.

SURGICAL APPLICATIONS

For some surgical procedures, body temperature is deliberately reduced by administering a drug that inhibits activity of the hypothalamus. The body is then immersed in ice water or surrounded by cooling blankets until internal temperatures reach levels of 30 degrees or below. At these temperatures, the heart can be stopped temporarily without significant damage to the brain or other body tissues. Induced reduction of body temperatures in this manner is routinely used in heart surgery.

SOURCES FOR FURTHER STUDY

Berne, Robert M., and Matthew N. Levy, eds. *Physiology*. 5th ed. St. Louis: C. V. Mosby, 2004. The chapter on the somatosensory system in this standard college physiology text outlines the anatomy and physiology of the cells and nerve tracts in the spinal column and brain involved in temperature and other body sensations. Although the text is intended for students at the college level, it is clearly written and should be accessible to high school readers.

Coren, Stanley. *Sensation and Perception*. 6th ed. Hoboken, N.J.: John Wiley & Sons, 2004. This simply written text provides an easily understood discussion of the senses, sensory cells, and the routes traveled by sensory information through the spinal cord to the brain. A clear and interesting description is provided of the basics of perception in the cerebral cortex.

Guyton, Arthur C., and John E. Hall. *Textbook of Medical Physiology*. 11th ed. Philadelphia: Elsevier Saunders, 2006. This readable and clearly written text includes an excellent discussion of thermoreceptors, the role of the hypothalamus in regulation of body temperature, and medical implications of fever, hyperthermia, and hypothermia. It also provides a general description of the structure and function of receptors. Although intended for college and medical students, the text can be easily understood by readers at the high school level.

Schmidt-Nielsen, Knut. *Animal Physiology: Adaptation and Environment*. 5th ed. New York: Cambridge University Press, 1998. This standard college text, by one of the greatest animal physiologists, provides a deeply perceptive comparison of sensory systems in humans and other animals. Chapters 6 and 7 describe temperature effects and temperature regulation. The text is remarkable for its lucid and entertaining descriptions of animal physiology.

Stephen L. Wolfe

SEE ALSO: Nervous system; Neurons; Pain; Sensation and perception; Senses; Signal detection theory; Touch and pressure.

Terrorism
Psychological causes and effects

TYPE OF PSYCHOLOGY: Learning; psychopathology; social psychology

FIELDS OF STUDY: Aggression; behavioral and cognitive models; cognitive development; cognitive learning; cognitive processes; social perception and cognition

Terrorism has been the subject of considerable discussion and study since the terrorist attacks of September 11, 2001. Much like hate crimes, terrorism involves the use of violence to frighten and intimidate members of an identifiable race, nationality, or religion.

KEY CONCEPTS
- collective violence
- fear and intimidation
- noncombatants
- suicide bombers
- victims

INTRODUCTION

Terrorism, from a Latin word meaning "to frighten," has been used by various groups throughout history. During the Reign of Terror in the late eighteenth century, Englishman Edmond Burke used the term "terrorism" to describe the violent acts of the new French rulers. Later, the term "terrorist" was used to describe those who used violence to challenge the ruling powers. In the twentieth century, this included anarchists and violent left-wing groups. However, in the latter half of the twentieth century, terrorism took on a more global aspect, as terrorist groups, including those made up of religious fundamentalists, conducted acts of violence outside their countries of origin.

The global reach of terrorism means that these acts have come to affect more people than just the intended victims and members of targeted groups. The worldwide media coverage of terrorist acts has increased the fear and intimidation that these acts generate. For example, footage of the second airplane striking the World Trade Center on September 11, 2001, was shown live on national television and replayed on televisions around the globe. The Internet has also enabled terrorist groups to in-crease exposure of their activities and threats to the world.

DEFINING TERRORISM

There is no universally accepted definition of this terrorism. It has commonly been used to describe violent, intimidating acts on the part of governments, dissidents, and groups following a particular religion or ideology. Since 1983, the U.S. government has defined terrorism as politically motivated violence perpetrated against noncombatant targets by subnational groups or clandestine agents, usually intended to influence an audience. It also defines a terrorist group as any group practicing, or that has significant subgroups that practice, international terrorism. Terrorists do not view themselves as such but rather as true patriots or true believers. Their efforts are focused on initiating changes they believe will not occur under the present regime (which they believe is misguided), or on enlightening or punishing those who do not share their beliefs.

Although definitions of terrorism vary, terrorist acts tend to share certain elements. Terrorism typically involves the use of collective violence, which often takes an unconventional form. This violence is aimed at innocent citizens and is meant to bring about change by instilling fear and intimidation. Often religion or another ideology is used to justify the acts of terror.

The violence is typically premeditated and functions to reduce or destroy the sense of security felt by a group of citizens within a society. It can take the form of kidnapping, torture, assassination, bombing, poisoning, or destruction of property. Whichever form these violent acts take, they are largely unpredictable, making it difficult for people to protect themselves from becoming victims.

Victims of terrorism are usually noncombatants and, therefore, innocent parties by definition, though terrorists might say that no one is innocent. Regardless, the majority of the victims are not usually in a position to bring about the changes the terrorists are seeking. These sought-after changes range from a new regime, to the destruction or removal of a particular group of citizens within a nation, to political recognition of the terrorist group.

Terrorist acts have the immediate goal of producing damage and the far-reaching goal of creating fear and intimidating government officials or a group of citizens. In addition to producing suffering or death among direct victims, terrorist acts make other members of the victims' group or government officials afraid that they may be the next targets of violence. To add credibility or legitimacy, terrorists often describe their actions in terms of religion. They present acts of terror as attempts to purify a society of infidels, making these acts part of a "holy war."

Some types of terrorism, particularly those involving victims who can be identified based on their race, religion, or ethnicity, resemble hate crimes. In a hate crime, it is the identifiable group that is the primary focus of the attacks, and domination or removal of the group (through death or exile) is the reason for the attacks. Examples of this type of terrorism are the Nazi's attempt to eliminate the Jews in Germany and the Ku Klux Klan's treatment of African Americans in the United States. Both terror-

ism and hate crimes attempt to instill fear in and to intimidate the identified group.

TYPES OF TERRORISTS

Research has attempted to determine the characteristics of terrorists; however, the changes in the nature of terrorism and its diversity have made this a difficult task. Terrorists have ranged from middle class to lower class, from better educated to less educated, and from state-supported to privately funded (mercenaries). Although most terrorists have been men, female terrorists are increasingly common. As long as the label of "terrorist" continues to be used, the profiles of terrorists are likely to change.

In his 1976 book on terrorism, Frederick J. Hacker described three types of terrorists: criminals, crazies, and crusaders. He found that the majority of terrorists fell into the crusader category. However, the tendency to view terrorists as patho-

The towers of the World Trade Center shortly after both buildings were struck by jet airliners. (www.bigfoto.com)

logical or criminal may be an impediment to understanding the psychology of terrorists. Early studies from the Western perspective viewed the terrorists and their actions as abnormal or at the least criminal. However, the growing body of knowledge produced by research shows that the majority of terrorists are psychologically normal and their acts are quite rational. This does not preclude the existence of psychopathic terrorists; it just means that this is not the norm.

It is important when studying terrorism and terrorists to consider the similarities and not just focus on the differences. The differences may be mainly among the methods used to accomplish goals rather than the characteristics of the individual terrorists. To gain a more accurate and realistic understanding of terrorists and how they function, researchers must see the world through their eyes by studying their individual psychopathologies and behavior, as well as their group, social, and organizational psychology.

The typical terrorists' mind-set is us against them. This mind-set usually has been developing for generations and therefore acquired through a socialization process. It may begin with an individual's experiencing a perceived wrong at the hands of a government or a member of some identifiable group (the wrong does not have to be real or intended). As the individual associates with others with similar experiences and perceptions, the individual's personal identity is reinforced, and he or she begins to identify with a group.

Terrorists do not see themselves as terrorists nor do they apply any other socially negative label to their identity. They view themselves as soldiers or warriors with a legitimate cause and, therefore, may share the same psychology as government soldiers. They use violence because they believe it is the only appropriate or available method of achieving the changes they seek. Consequently, they rationally perceive their actions as legitimate acts to accomplish justified goals. The violent nature of their attacks, designed to produce fear and intimidation, is a form of psychological warfare.

Cultural ideologies play an important role in terrorism. For example, cultures and religions have different values and beliefs about life and death. Because some religions believe there are or can be rewards received after death, in these religions, death is not perceived as a loss but as a gain in the afterlife. This makes martyrdom more acceptable in some

cultures and provides a rationale for suicidal terrorist acts.

Research has begun to show that suicide bombers, who are typically volunteers, should not be compared to suicidal individuals. British researcher Ellen Townsend has argued that suicides of terrorists and those of nonterrorists have few factors in common. The suicides of terrorists might be considered to be altruistic suicides (if judged to be any type of suicide) or acts of martyrdom, driven largely by religious convictions, social pressure, and group process. To understand the psychology of suicide bombers, many factors—the individual's development, education, mental status, and environmental influences—must be considered.

VICTIMS

Terrorists usually attack people while they are involved in routine activities, such as work and recreation. Therefore, any place where many people are engaged in everyday activities can become the target of a terrorist attack. In many cases, these locations have not been built or designed with protection in mind, which makes them vulnerable to and attractive targets for terrorists. These areas include offices, shopping centers, restaurants, schools, entertainment venues, and major traffic arteries. Ordinarily, there is little cause to suspect danger in these locations.

When a terrorist attack occurs, the effects go beyond the immediate victims and extend well past the time of the attack. Many of those who survived the attack itself are likely to experience psychological trauma, including post-traumatic stress disorder. In addition, the family members and friends of the deceased and the survivors, as well as the first responders, rescue personnel, and support personnel, will also experience trauma. Many of these individuals will develop secondary post-traumatic stress disorder. Physical and mental recovery may take years, if it can be accomplished.

SOURCES FOR FURTHER STUDY

Combs, Cindy C. *Terrorism in the Twenty-first Century.* 4th ed. Upper Saddle River, N.J.: Pearson/Prentice Hall, 2006. Examines the nature of terrorism in the twenty-first century, and gives a profile of a typical terrorist.

Hacker, Frederick J. *Crusaders, Criminals, Crazies: Terror and Terrorism in Our Time.* New York: W. W.

Norton, 1976. This book on terrorism focuses on the terrorists—who they are and what their goals are.

Martin, Gus. *Essentials of Terrorism: Concepts and Controversies.* Los Angeles: Sage Publications, 2008. Covers all aspects of terrorism, including terrorism by the state, dissidents, and religious and international groups.

Silke, Andrew. "Courage in Dark Places: Reflections on Terrorist Psychology." *Social Research* 71 (2004): 177-198. This article looks into the psychology of terrorists and describes the research that notes that these individuals are typically not mentally ill.

Townsend, Ellen. "Suicide Terrorists: Are They Suicidal?" *Suicide and Life-Threatening Behavior* 37 (2007): 35-49. Townsend looks at research on suicide terrorists and concludes that they are not in the same category as suicidal individuals who are not terrorists.

Richard L. McWhorter

SEE ALSO: Cross-cultural psychology; Hate crimes: Psychological causes and effects; Religion and psychology.

Testing
Historical perspectives

TYPE OF PSYCHOLOGY: Intelligence and intelligence testing

FIELDS OF STUDY: Ability tests; intelligence assessment

Current psychological tests have been historically influenced by French researchers, who emphasized clinical observation; by German researchers, who emphasized experimentation; by British researchers, who were interested in individual differences; and by American researchers, who have been more pragmatic in their approach.

KEY CONCEPTS
- genius
- individual differences
- reaction time
- sensory
- test

INTRODUCTION

Tests are an intrinsic part of people's lives. They are tested as children to determine when they will enter school and how much they will learn in school. They are tested as young adults to determine whether they should receive a high school diploma, whether they should enter college, how much they can learn, or whether they can participate in some specialized training. People are tested if they seek admission to law school or medical school, if they want to practice a profession, and if they want to work for a specific company or show proficiency in a particular talent.

Tests have been used for quite some time. In China around 2000 B.C.E., public officials were examined regularly and were promoted or dismissed on the basis of these examinations. The direct historical antecedents of contemporary testing go back slightly more than one hundred years and reflect contributions made by many individuals representing four historical traditions: the French clinical tradition, the German scientific tradition, the British emphasis on individual differences, and the American practical orientation.

EUROPEAN TRENDS

The French clinical tradition emphasized clinical observation. That is, the French were very interested in the mentally ill and mentally retarded, and a number of French physicians wrote excellent descriptions of patients they had studied. They produced very perceptive and detailed descriptions, or case studies, and thereby contributed the notion that the creation of a test must be preceded by careful observations of the real world. To develop a test to measure depression, for example, one must first carefully observe many depressed patients. The French also produced the first practical test of intelligence: Alfred Binet, a well-known French psychologist, in 1905 devised the Binet-Simon test (with Théodore Simon) to be used with French schoolchildren to identify those who were retarded and hence needed specialized instruction.

A second historical trend that affected testing was the scientific approach promulgated by German scientists in the late 1800's. Perhaps the best-known name in the field was Wilhelm Wundt, who is considered to be the founder of experimental psychology. He was particularly interested in reaction time, the rapidity with which a person responds to a stimulus. To study reaction time, Wundt and his students carried out systematic experimentation in a laboratory, focused mostly on sensory functions such as vision, and developed a number of instruments to be used to study reaction time. Although Wundt was not interested in tests, his scientific approach and his focus on sensory functions did influence later test developers, who saw testing as an experiment in which standardized instructions needed to be followed and strict control over the testing procedure needed to be exercised. They even took the measurement of sensory processes such as vision to be an index of how well the brain functioned and therefore of how intelligent the person was.

Whereas the Germans were interested in discovering general laws of behavior and were trying to use reaction time as a way of investigating the intellectual processes that presumably occur in the brain, the British were more interested in looking at individual differences. The British viewed these differences not as errors, as Wundt did, but as a fundamental reflection of evolution and natural selection, the ideas that had been given a strong impetus by the work of Charles Darwin. In fact, it was Darwin's cousin, Sir Francis Galton, who is said to have launched the testing movement on its course. Galton studied eminent British men and became convinced that intellectual genius was fixed by inheritance: One was born a genius rather than trained to be one. Galton developed a number of tests to measure various aspects of intellectual capacity, tested large numbers of individuals who visited his laboratory, and developed various statistical procedures to analyze the test results.

AMERICAN PERSPECTIVES

It was in the United States, however, that psychological testing really became an active endeavor. In 1890, psychologist James McKeen Cattell wrote a scientific paper that for the first time used the phrase "mental test." In this paper, he presented a series of ten tests designed to measure a person's intellectual level. These tests involved procedures such as the subject's estimating a ten-second interval, and measurement of the amount of pressure exerted by the subject's grip. Cattell had been a pupil of Wundt, and these tests reflected Wundt's heavy emphasis on sensory abilities. The tests were administered to Columbia University students, since Cattell was a professor there, to see if the results predicted grade point

average. They did not; nevertheless, the practice of testing students to predict their college performance was born.

Lewis Terman, a professor at Stanford University, took the French test that Binet had developed and created a new version in English, called the Stanford-Binet test; thus, intelligence testing became popular in America. When the United States entered World War I in 1917, there was a great need in the military to screen out recruits whose intellectual capabilities were too limited for military service, as well as a need to identify recruits who might be given specialized training or be admitted to officer training programs. Several tests were developed to meet these needs and, when the war was over, they became widely used in industry and in schools. By World War II, testing had become quite sophisticated and widespread and was again given impetus by the need to make major decisions about military personnel in a rapid and efficient manner. Thus, not only intellectual functioning but also problems of adjustment, morale, and psychopathology all stimulated interest in testing.

As with any other field of endeavor, advances in testing were also accompanied by setbacks, disputes, and criticisms. In the late 1930's and early 1940's, for example, there was a rather acrimonious controversy between researchers at Iowa University and those at Stanford University over whether the intelligence quotients (IQs) of children could be increased through enriched school experiences. In the 1960's, tests were severely criticized, especially the multiple-choice items used in tests to make admission decisions in higher education. Many books were published that attacked testing, often in a distorted and emotional manner. In the 1970's, intelligence tests again came to the forefront, in a bitter controversy about whether whites are more intelligent than blacks. Many school districts eliminated the administration of intelligence tests, both because the tests were seen as tools of potential discrimination and because of legal ramifications.

Tests are still criticized and misused, but they have become much more sophisticated and represent a useful set of tools that, when used appropriately, can help people make more informed decisions.

TESTING SKILLS

In the everyday world, there are a number of decisions that must be made daily. For example, "Susan" owns a large manufacturing company and has openings for ten lathe operators. When she advertises these positions, 118 prospective employees apply. How will Susan decide which ten to hire? Clearly, she wants to hire the best of the applicants, those who will do good work, who will be responsible and come to work on time, who will follow the expected rules but also be flexible when the nature of the job changes, and so on. She would probably want to interview all the applicants, but it might be physically impossible for her to do so since it would require too much time, and perhaps she might realize that she does not have the skills to make such a decision. An alternative, then, would be to test all the applicants and to use the test information with other data, such as letters from prior employers, to make the needed decision. A test, then, can be looked on as an interview, but one that is typically more objective, since the biases of the interviewer will be held in check; more time effective, since a large number of individuals can be tested at one sitting, whereas interviews typically involve one candidate at a time; more economical, since a printed form will typically cost less than the salary of an interviewer; and, usually, more informative, since a person's results can be compared with the results of others, whereas one's performance in an interview is more difficult to evaluate.

In fact, historically, most tests have been developed because of pressing practical needs: the need to identify schoolchildren who might benefit from specialized instruction, the need to identify Army recruits with special talents or problems, or the need to identify high school students with particular interest in a specific field such as physics. As testing has grown, the applications of testing have also expanded. Tests are now used to provide information about achievement, intellectual capacity, potential talents, career interests, motivation, and hundreds of other human psychological concerns. Tests are also developed to serve as tools for the assessment of social or psychological theories; for example, measures of depression are of interest to social scientists investigating suicide, while measures of social support are useful in studies of adolescents and the elderly.

TESTING POTENTIAL

Another way of thinking about tests is that a test represents an experiment. The experimenter, in this

case usually a psychologist or someone trained in testing, administers a set of carefully specified procedures and just as carefully records the subject's responses or performance on these procedures. Thus, a psychologist who administers an intelligence test to a schoolchild is interested not simply in computing the child's IQ but also in observing how the child goes about solving new problems, how extensive the child's vocabulary is, how the child reacts to frustration, the facility with which the child can solve word problems versus numerical problems, and so on. While such information could be derived by carefully observing the child in the classroom over a long period of time, using a specific test procedure not only is less time-consuming but also allows for a more precise comparison between a particular child's performance and that of other children.

There are, then, at least two ways, not mutually exclusive, of thinking about a test. Both of these ways of thinking are the result of the various historical emphases: the French emphasis on the clinical symptoms exhibited by the individual, the German emphasis on the scientific procedure, the British interest in individual differences, and the American emphasis on practicality: "Does it work, and how fast can I get the results?"

To be sure, tests are only one source of information, and their use should be carefully guided by a variety of considerations. In fact, psychologists who use tests with clients are governed by two very detailed sets of rules. One set has to do with the technical aspects of constructing a test, with making sure that indeed a particular test has been developed according to scientific guidelines. A second set has to do with ethical standards, ensuring that the information derived from a test is to be used carefully for the benefit of the client.

Because the use of tests does not occur in a vacuum, but rather in a society that has specific values and expectations, that emphasizes or denies specific freedoms, and in which certain political points of view may be more or less popular, this use is often accompanied by strong feelings. For example, in the 1970's, Americans became very concerned about the deteriorating performance of high school seniors who were taking the Scholastic Aptitude Test (SAT, later the SAT Reasoning Test) for entrance into college. From 1963 to 1977, the average score on the SAT verbal portion declined by about 50 points, and the average score on the SAT mathematics section declined by about 30 points. Rather than seeing the SAT as simply a nationwide "interview" that might yield some possibly useful information about a student's performance at a particular point in time, the SAT had become a goal in itself, a standard by which to judge all sorts of things, including whether high school teachers were doing their jobs.

TESTING PSYCHOLOGY

Tests play a major role in most areas of psychology, and the history of psychological testing is in fact intertwined with the history of psychology as a field. Psychology is defined as the science of behavior, and tests are crucial to the experimentation that is at the basis of that science. Especially with human subjects, studies are typically carried out by identifying some important dimension, such as intelligence, depression, concern about one's health, or suicide ideation, and then trying to alter that dimension by some specific procedure, such as psychotherapy to decrease depression, education to increase health awareness, a medication designed to lessen hallucinations, and so on. Whether the specific procedure is effective is then assessed by the degree of change, typically measured by a test or a questionnaire.

Psychology also has many applied aspects. There are psychologists who work with the mentally ill, with drug abusers, with college students who are having personal difficulties, with spouses who are not getting along, with business executives who wish to increase their leadership abilities, or with high school students who may not be certain of what career to pursue. All these situations can involve the use of tests, to identify the current status of a person (for example, to determine how depressed the person is), to make predictions about future behavior (for example, to determine how likely it is that a person will commit suicide), to identify achievement (for example, to assess how well a person knows elementary math), or to identify strengths (for example, to gauge whether someone is a people-oriented type of person)—in other words, to get a more objective and detailed portrait of the particular client.

The wide and growing use of computers has also affected the role of tests. Tests can be administered and scored by computer, and the client can receive feedback, often with great detail, by computer. Computers also allow tests to be tailored to the individual. Suppose, for example, a test with one hundred items is designed to measure basic arithmetic

knowledge in fifth-grade children. Traditionally, all one hundred items would be administered and each child's performance scored accordingly. By using a computer, however, a test can present only selected items, with subsequent items being present or absent depending on the child's performance on the prior item. If, for example, a child can do division problems quite well, as shown by his or her correct answers to more difficult problems, the computer can be programmed to skip the easier division problems.

Clearly, tests are here to stay. The task is to use them wisely, as useful but limited tools to benefit the individual rather than facilitate political manipulations.

SOURCES FOR FURTHER STUDY

Anastasi, Anne, and Susan Urbina. *Psychological Testing*. 7th ed. Upper Saddle River, N.J.: Prentice Hall, 1997. An excellent though somewhat technical introduction to psychological testing. Often required reading for students of psychology. Chapter 1 gives an overview of the history of psychological testing.

Ballard, Philip Boswood. *Mental Tests*. London: Hodder & Stoughton, 1920. A fascinating little book, written for schoolteachers, that covers the development of mental tests, the measurement of intelligence, and school-related activities such as reading, spelling, and arithmetic. Gives the English translation of the Binet-Simon test of intelligence as well as a number of tests the author developed. Should be read for historical context; most of the book's contents are clearly outdated, but certainly give a flavor of what testing was like in the 1920's.

Garrett, Henry Edward, and Matthew R. Schneck. *Psychological Tests, Methods, and Results*. New York: Harper & Brothers, 1933. A textbook for courses in psychological testing as given in the 1930's. A book to be read in its historical context.

Gregory, Robert. *Psychological Testing: History, Principles, and Applications*. 7th ed. Boston: Pearson/ Allyn & Bacon, 2007. A good summary of the history of psychological testing in the United States.

Office of Strategic Services. Assessment Staff. *Assessment of Men: Selection of Personnel for the Office of Strategic Services*. New York: Rinehart, 1948. A fascinating book that describes the Office of Strategic Services (the OSS, the forerunner of the Central Intelligence Agency) program during World War II to select potential spies and saboteurs.

Sacks, Peter. *Standardized Minds: The High Price of America's Testing Culture and What We Can Do to Change It.* Cambridge, Mass.: Perseus, 2001. Covers current controversies in standardized testing.

Sokal, Michael M., ed. *Psychological Testing and American Society, 1890-1930.* New Brunswick, N.J.: Rutgers University Press, 1987. This book had its genesis in a symposium given in 1984 at the 150th national meeting of the American Association for the Advancement of Science. Consists of eight chapters, written by seven different authors, that place testing in a historical perspective. For example, chapter 2 talks about Cattell and how his tests came to be.

Stanovich, Keith E. *What Intelligence Tests Miss: The Psychology of Rational Thought.* New Haven, Conn.: Yale University Press, 2009. A critic describes the failings of intelligence tests, suggesting that they do not measure a person's ability to think rationally.

Wise, Paula Sachs. *The Use of Assessment Techniques by Applied Psychologists.* Belmont, Calif.: Wadsworth, 1989. Introduces the reader to the ways in which assessments are conducted in real settings by professional psychologists, especially clinical, counseling, organizational, and school psychologists. Well written, with a minimum of technical detail and many examples. Covers assessment in its broad aspects, rather than simply discussing psychological testing.

George Domino

SEE ALSO: Ability tests; Assessment; Binet, Alfred; Career and personnel testing; Career Occupational Preference System (COPS); College entrance examinations; Creativity: Assessment; General Aptitude Test Battery (GATB); Human resource training and development; Intelligence tests; Interest inventories; Kuder Occupational Interest Survey (KOIS); Peabody Individual Achievement Test (PIAT); Race and intelligence; Scientific methods; Stanford-Binet test; Strong Interest Inventory (SII); Survey research: Questionnaires and interviews; Wechsler Intelligence Scale for Children-Third Edition (WISC-III).

Thematic Apperception Test (TAT)

DATE: 1935 forward
TYPE OF PSYCHOLOGY: Personality
FIELD OF STUDY: Personality assessment

The Thematic Apperception Test is one of the most popular personality assessment instruments. It consists of pictures of ambiguous social situations; the subject makes up a story about each picture. These stories are interpreted by a trained clinician to reveal important aspects of the subject's personality.

KEY CONCEPTS
- apperception
- personality assessment instruments
- projective techniques
- psychological testing

INTRODUCTION

The kind of psychological testing concerned with the affective, or nonintellectual, aspects of behavior is called personality assessment. Personality tests refer to measures of such characteristics as emotional states, motivation, attitudes, interests, and interpersonal relations. There are two general types of personality assessment instruments. Objective assessment instruments require a specific response such as "true" or "false," while projective techniques require that the client respond to a relatively unstructured task that permits a variety of possible responses. Methods for eliciting and interpreting stories told about pictured scenes are one type of projective technique. The most widely used set of pictures is the one introduced in 1935 by Henry A. Murray of the Harvard Psychological Clinic. This set is titled the Thematic Apperception Test (TAT).

Apperception is more than just the recognition or perception of an object based on sensory experience. It is also the addition of meaning to what is perceived. Thus, telling stories about pictured scenes is an apperceptive task requiring the interpretation of what is pictured to discern a character's motives, intentions, and expectations. The TAT shows the actual dynamics of interpersonal relationships. It reveals the testing subject's relationship to peers of both sexes, male and female authority figures, and specific family relationships, such as the relationship between a mother and her son.

The TAT set comprises thirty pictures and one blank card. These cards are organized into four parallel sets of twenty pictures according to the age and gender of the test subject. Thus, these cards are numbered from 1 to 20 and are designated suitable for boys (B), girls (G), males over fourteen (M), females over fourteen (F), or combinations of those groups (MF, BG, BM, GF). Cards with no letters following their numbers are suitable for all subjects. The cards are achromatic and lack racial diversity. However, adaptations of these cards for specialized populations do not result in richer, more productive stories than does the traditional TAT. The primary advantage of the TAT set is that the pictures portray situations conveying unfinished business and are ambiguous, thus allowing many possible interpretations.

ADMINISTRATION AND INTERPRETATION

Generally, the clinician selects eight to twelve of the cards to administer to the client. Leopold Bellak, the author of the most widely used book on the TAT, has suggested certain cards for standard use. For example, Card 1 is recommended for all subjects. It depicts a boy seated at table looking down at a violin resting on the table. The stimulus requires an explanation for the boy's facial expression in relation to the violin. Instructions are given to the client to make up a story for each picture shown. They are told to tell what has happened before the event in the picture, to describe what is happening at the moment, what the characters are thinking and feeling, and what the outcome is. Exact wording of the instructions can vary depending on the age and intellectual level of the subject. Approximately five minutes for storytelling per picture is typical. In the standard procedure, the examiner will write the stories down as the test is given individually. After all the stories are given, the examiner may inquire about any specific dates, places, or names of people. It is also feasible to use self-administration with written instructions and group administration in which the pictures are projected onto a screen and each person writes down a story.

As indicated in the name "Thematic Apperception Test," the clinician examines themes that emerge across all the stories generated by the client. These themes may involve cognition (that is, logic or realism), emotion (and how to cope with emotion), and motivation (what motivates individuals to

act and how they pursue goals). A common theme for Card 1 depicting the boy and violin is that of achievement motivation. Various methods of interpreting the TAT have been developed, and some are fairly structured. Generally, clinicians prefer to use the TAT as a flexible tool for eliciting information that they would interpret based on their professional training and experience.

SOURCES FOR FURTHER STUDY

Anastasi, Anne, and Susan Urbina. *Psychological Testing*. 7th ed. Upper Saddle River, N.J.: Prentice Hall, 1997. An excellent overview of psychological testing by one of the pioneers in the field. Chapters include basics in assessment, including the origins of psychological testing and types of tests, including a chapter on projective techniques. The section on the TAT and related instruments is clear and concise.

Bellak, Leopold. *The TAT, CAT, and SAT in Clinical Use*. 6th ed. Boston: Allyn & Bacon, 1997. The most comprehensive text on the TAT by one of the pioneering investigators in the field and developer of the CAT (for young children) and SAT (for older adults). While this book is primarily for students in psychology, the general reader will find the chapter devoted to analyzing themes from literary products such as the short stories of Somerset Maugham particularly interesting.

Cramer, Phebe. *Storytelling, Narrative, and the Thematic Apperception Test*. New York: Guilford Press, 2004. Examines a variety of ways to interpret the Thematic Apperception Test and describes how test results differ for children and adults and for men and women.

Teglasi, Hedwig. *Essentials of TAT and Other Storytelling Techniques Assessment*. New York: John Wiley & Sons, 2008. An exceptionally clear and well-written presentation of the TAT and related assessment instruments. Discusses administration, scoring, interpretation, and reporting results. This book is conveniently formatted for rapid reference and provides numerous examples, advice on common pitfalls, and self-tests at the end of each chapter. An excellent book for students and professionals, as well as nonprofessional readers.

Karen D. Multon

SEE ALSO: Beck Depression Inventory (BDI); California Psychological Inventory (CPI); Children's

Depression Inventory (CDI); Clinical interviewing, testing, and observation; Depression; Diagnosis; *Diagnostic and Statistical Manual of Mental Disorders* (DSM); Minnesota Multiphasic Personality Inventory (MMPI); Personality: Psychophysiological measures; Personality interviewing strategies; Personality rating scales; State-Trait Anxiety Inventory (STAI).

Thirst

Type of psychology: Motivation
Fields of study: Endocrine system; motivation theory; physical motives

Thirst, along with hunger, is one of the basic biological drives; it motivates humans to drink to ensure their survival.

Key concepts
- antidiuretic hormone (ADH)
- cellular dehydration thirst
- drive
- hypothalamus
- hypovolemic thirst
- motivation

Introduction

The range of human motivation is quite broad in controlling behaviors. Motivation can be defined as a condition that energizes and directs behavior in a particular manner. Different aspects of motivation can be attributed to instinctive behavior patterns, the need to reduce drives, or learned experiences.

Thirst is one of many biologically based motivational factors; among other such factors are those that involve food, air, sleep, temperature regulation, and pain avoidance. Biologically based motivational factors help humans and other organisms to maintain a balanced internal environment. This is the process of homeostasis. Deviations from the norm, such as hunger, excessive water loss, and pain, will cause an organism to seek out whatever is lacking.

Biologically based motivational factors, such as thirst, have been explained by the drive-reduction theory proposed by Clark L. Hull in 1943. The lack of some factor, such as water or food, causes the body to feel unpleasant. This is turn motivates one

to reduce this feeling of unpleasantness, thus reducing the drive. Thirst is considered what is called a primary drive. Primary drives, which are related to biologically based needs such as hunger, thirst, and sleepiness, energize and motivate one to fulfill these biological needs, thus helping the body to maintain homeostasis. Secondary drives fulfill no biological need.

One may wonder what it is that makes one thirsty and how one knows when one has had enough to drink. Seventy-five percent of a human's weight is water. The maintenance of water balance is an ongoing process. In an average day, a person will lose approximately 2.5 liters of water; 60 percent of the water loss occurs through urination, 20 percent is lost through perspiration, and the remainder is lost through defecation and exhalation from the lungs. These 2.5 liters of water must be replaced.

What is the stimulus that motivates one to drink when one is thirsty? The simplest hypothesis, which was proposed by Walter Bradford Cannon in 1934, is the dry mouth hypothesis. According to Cannon, it is a dry mouth that causes one to drink, not the need for water. This hypothesis has not held up under scrutiny. Research has shown that neither the removal of the salivary glands nor the presence of excess salivation in dogs disrupts the animals' regulation of water intake. Studies have indicated that the amount of water consumed is somehow measured and related to the organism's water deficit. This occurs even before the water has been replaced in the person's tissues and cells. Thus, dry mouth is a symptom of the need for water.

Water Regulation Process

When a human being's water intake is lower than its level of water loss, two bodily processes are set in motion. First, the person becomes thirsty and drinks water (provided it is available). Second, the kidneys start to retain water by reabsorbing it and concentrating the urine. Thus, the kidneys can conserve the water that is already in the body. These processes are set in motion by the central nervous system (CNS).

The CNS responds to two primary internal bodily mechanisms. One is cellular dehydration thirst, and the other is hypovolemic thirst (a change in the volume of water in the body). To understand these mechanisms, one must realize that the body contains two main supplies of water. One supply, the intracellular fluid, is in the cells; the other supply consists of the extracellular fluid surrounding the cells and tissues and the fluid in the circulatory system. Water moves between these two areas by means of a process called osmosis, which causes it to move from an area of higher concentration to an area of lower concentration.

A person who is deprived of water will experience cellular dehydration thirst as a result of water loss caused by perspiration and excretion through the urine. This increases the salt concentration in the extracellular fluid, thereby lowering the water concentration. Thus, the cells lose their water to the surrounding extracellular fluid. The increasing salt concentration triggers specialized osmoreceptors located in the hypothalamic region of the brain. Two events occur: First, drinking is stimulated; second, antidiuretic hormone (ADH) is secreted from the pituitary gland in the brain. The ADH helps to promote the reabsorption of water into the kidneys.

The second kind of thirst, hypovolemic thirst, occurs when there is a decrease in the volume of the extracellular fluid as a result of bleeding, diarrhea, or vomiting. This produces a decrease in the salt concentration of the extracellular fluid, which lowers the blood pressure, which in turn stimulates the kidney cells to release a chemical. Eventually, the thirst receptors in the hypothalamus are stimulated; these cause the organism to consume water. In addition, ADH is secreted in this process, which promotes the conservation of water.

The regulation of water intake in humans is thus related to a number of factors and is quite complex. Though cellular dehydration thirst and hypovolemic thirst play a role, it appears that in humans, peripheral factors such as dry mouth play an even larger role. Humans can drink rapidly, replacing a twenty-four-hour water deficit in two to three minutes. This occurs even before the cellular fluid has replaced the water, which takes approximately eight to twelve minutes.

MOTIVATIONAL FACTOR

Thirst is a strong motivational factor. The importance of replacing lost water is underscored by the fact that a person can survive for a month without food but for only several days without water. It appears that both thirst processes help to promote drinking. Researchers have estimated that 64 to 85 percent of the drinking following water loss is caused by cellular dehydration thirst. Hypovolemic thirst accounts for 5 to 27 percent of the drinking, and the remainder is caused by peripheral factors.

The two types of thirst are independent of each other. The receptors for both thirsts are located in the hypothalamic region of the brain, but they are at different locations. Research has shown that lesions in one region will have no effect on thirst regulation in the other region.

Although the motivation to drink in humans is under conscious control by peripheral factors, unconscious control does exert a large influence. A study of cellular dehydration thirst using goats showed that the injection of a saline solution that has a salt concentration of more than 0.9 percent salt (body fluids have a salt concentration of 0.9 percent salt) into the area in which the osmoreceptors are located will produce a drinking response within sixty seconds. Similar results have been found regarding hypovolemic thirst; injecting angiotensin II (a converted protein found in the blood) into the hypothalamus causes a drinking response. This occurs even in animals that are fully hydrated. These animals will consume in direct proportion to the amount of angiotensin II injected into the hypothalamus.

Diet can have a profound effect on water balance in humans. Eating salty foods will produce cellular dehydration thirst despite adequate fluid levels, because water will flow out of the cells into the extracellular fluid. In contrast, salt-free diets will produce hypovolemic thirst by causing water to flow into the cells. Other factors also cause thirst. As stated previously, diarrhea, vomiting, and blood loss will cause hypovolemic thirst as a result of the loss of extracellular fluid. Therefore, significant blood loss will cause a person to become thirsty.

IMPACT OF DISEASES

Diseases can also have an impact on thirst. An interesting example of such a disease is diabetes. Diabetes is a condition in which the body cannot process blood glucose (a type of sugar) properly. Improper diet or medication can cause diabetic ketoacidosis, which causes the levels of glucose and ketone bodies (derivatives from fat) in the blood to rise. This creates a major shift in the water balance of the body. Water leaves the cells and enters the blood system, causing the volume of blood to increase. This extra fluid (along with potassium and sodium) is excreted from the body in the urine, which causes the body to suffer dehydration and triggers a tremendous thirst. Since fluid is lost from both cells and extracellular fluid, this causes both types of thirst. Excessive thirst is still a symptom of diabetes, but it has become rare as a result of education and improved treatment.

IMPACT OF EXERCISE

Thirst motivation also operates during exercise. In short-term exercise, thirst motivation does not come into play because the body usually maintains its temperature. During long-term exercise, however, water intake at intervals facilitates athletic performance by helping to maintain body temperature. The motivation to drink occurs as a result of sweating, which causes the salt concentration in the body to rise during exercise, thereby causing cellular dehydration thirst. Interestingly, voluntary thirst and peripheral factors do not motivate one to take in water during prolonged exercise in the heat until it is too late. Thus, coaches should insist that athletes drink water as they perform.

SOURCES FOR FURTHER STUDY

Carlson, Neil R. *Foundations of Physiological Psychology.* 7th ed. Boston: Allyn & Bacon, 2008. An introductory college textbook. Thirst is covered in the chapter on ingestive behavior.

Levinthal, Charles F. "Chemical Senses and the Mechanisms for Eating and Drinking." In *Introduction to Physiological Psychology.* 3d ed. Englewood Cliffs, N.J.: Prentice-Hall, 1990. A very good chapter on the thirst drive. It is quite detailed, but the clarity of the writing makes it easy to read.

Mader, Sylvia S. *Biology.* 9th ed. Boston: McGraw-Hill, 2007. An easy-to-read introductory textbook on biology that provides a good background on hormones, water regulation, and kidney function, with many fine diagrams and figures. A good basis for understanding physiological psychology.

Lonnie J. Guralnick

SEE ALSO: Drives; Endocrine system; Hormones and behavior; Hull, Clark L.; Hunger; Pituitary gland.

Thorndike, Edward L.

BORN: August 31, 1874, in Williamsburg, Massachusetts
DIED: August 9, 1949, in Montrose, New York
IDENTITY: American psychologist
TYPE OF PSYCHOLOGY: Cognition; learning
FIELDS OF STUDY: Behavioral and cognitive models; cognitive development; cognitive processes

Thorndike, an early behaviorist, was an important contributor to the study of the psychology of learning.

The familiy of Edward L. Thorndike traced its roots back to colonial America. Thorndike's father was a Methodist minister who held up high standards for all of his children. Thorndike took his bachelor's degree at Wesleyan University in Connecticut. While he was an undergraduate student, he read William James's two-volume *Principles of Psychology* (1890). Thorndike was so taken with James's work that he decided to pursue graduate study with him at Harvard. While he was at Harvard, Thorndike had to work part time. Columbia University made him an irresistible offer: to come to New York and devote himself full time to studying. Thorndike placed his two brightest chickens (part of an animal experiment) in a basket, got on the train, and went to Columbia.

After Thorndike finished his doctorate, he taught at Columbia for forty years. During his long and distinguished career, Thorndike made a number of significant contributions to educational research. He is credited with having devised two experimental procedures, the maze and the puzzle box. He also laid the groundwork for educational measurement. Thorndike devised intelligence tests, rating scales, reading tests, composition tests, geography tests, arithmetic tests, and college entrance tests. His dictionaries were used by millions of public-school children.

Thorndike was a pioneer in applying experimental procedures to the study of learning. His work with kittens in puzzle boxes convinced him learning was a trial-and-error process. The kittens were not able to escape from the puzzle boxes by using either reason or instinct. As they dashed madly around the boxes, the kittens—quite by accident—tripped devices that allowed them to escape. They were caught and returned to their boxes. Through repeated trial-

Edward L. Thorndike. (Library of Congress)

and-error procedures, stimulus (S) and response (R) bonds were stamped into the kittens' neural pathways.

Thorndike was committed to the scientific study of education. He formulated three laws of learning. The law of readiness holds that when an organism is ready to act, satisfaction will follow action. The law of effect asserts that when an action is followed by satisfaction, that action will be more likely to be repeated in the future. The law of exercise contends that stimulus and response bonds are strengthened by repetition.

Thorndike collected data that refuted two widely accepted doctrines in education, formal discipline and faculty psychology. Formal discipline held that Latin disciplined the mind. Faculty psychology maintained the mind was composed of separate faculties such as memory, reason, and creativity. These faculties, like muscles, could be strengthened through exercise. Latin improved memory, geometry heightened reasoning, and music furthered cre-

ativity. Thorndike's data indicated these doctrines were faulty. Latin did not discipline the mind, and mental faculties could not be strengthened through exercise. Generalized transfer simply did not exist. If teachers wished their students to transfer information from one area to another, they would have to show them the identical elements that the two subjects shared.

SOURCES FOR FURTHER STUDY

Clifford, Geraldine. *Edward L. Thorndike: The Sane Positivist.* Middletown, Conn.: Wesleyan University Press, 1984. A biography of Thorndike and explanation of his work.

Salkind, Neil J., ed. *Encyclopedia of Educational Psychology.* Thousand Oaks, Calif.: Sage Publications, 2008. This encyclopedia contains many entries that shed light on Thorndike's work.

Zimmerman, Barry J., and Dale H. Schunk, eds. *Educational Psychology: A Century of Contributions.* Mahwah, N.J.: Lawrence Erlbaum, 2003. Contains information on Thorndike and the time in which he was active.

Stanley D. Ivie

SEE ALSO: Behaviorism; Cognitive psychology; James, William; Learning; Structuralism and functionalism.

Thought
Inferential

TYPE OF PSYCHOLOGY: Cognition
FIELD OF STUDY: Thought

An argument is a process that takes assertions as inputs and produces conclusions as outputs; to go beyond the information given and get from the inputs to the outputs is to draw inferences. Formal inferences include deduction and induction. Inferential thought of a formal and informal nature is essential to both scientific reasoning and reasoning in daily life.

KEY CONCEPTS
- argument
- assertion
- belief

- categorical syllogism
- deductive inference
- formal logic
- induction
- pragmatic inferences
- premise
- presupposition

INTRODUCTION

Psychologists are only beginning to understand how human thought processes operate, but there is no doubt that thinking is a critical skill. Reasoning is but one of many types of thought. Others include decision making and concept formation. Reasoning is unique in that it involves drawing inferences from current knowledge and beliefs. Reasoning has multiple components, including the production and evaluation of arguments, the drawing of inferences, and the generation and testing of hypotheses.

The process of inference involves the exploration of alternatives, using evidence. Evidence is information that helps determine the degree to which a possibility achieves a goal. Basically, using inference, each possibility for choice is made stronger or weaker, considering that goal. The process can be done well or poorly. Without the ability to make inferences, there would be no science, mathematics, or even laws.

Almost every statement a person says or writes leads the listener or reader to make inferences. A presupposition is knowledge on which one draws to understand a statement or assertion. Once the assertion is understood, an inference can be drawn. Certain types of inferences, known as logical inferences, *must* follow from what was said. Logical inferences are, in a sense, demanded by the assertions. For example, the statement "Jack's heart problems forced his doctor to put him on a strict diet" logically implies that Jack was put on a diet.

INDUCTION AND DEDUCTION

There are two basic forms of formal, logical inference: induction and deduction. An induction is a judgment that something is probably true on the basis of experience. It involves generalization—that is, reasoning from a few to all, or from the particular to the general. People infer that they should avoid all bees, having been stung by only one or two up to that time. The inductive inference allows one to go beyond the data at hand and draw a useful con-

clusion (*all* bees will sting people) that cannot be proved, because it cannot be exhaustively tested. Induction can extend the content of the assertions at the cost of introducing uncertainty.

In contrast, deductive inference achieves absolute certainty, if performed correctly, at the cost of sacrificing innovation. It requires that two or more separate assertions be integrated to deduce a new assertion as a necessary consequence. Deductive inference deals with the validity, or form, of the arguments, providing methods and rules for restating given information so as to make what is implicit explicit. All valid deductive arguments reformulate knowledge already given in the assertions. They typically utilize key terms, such as quantifiers (such as "all," "some," "none"), connectives (such as "and," "or," "if-then"), and comparatives (such as "more," "less").

INFERRING SENTENCE MEANING

An experiment published in 1972 by John D. Bransford, J. Richard Barclay, and Jeffrey J. Franks illustrated that people could not distinguish sentences that were actually presented from inferences they made in the process of comprehending those sentences. Subjects saw sentences such as "Three turtles rested on a floating log and a fish swam beneath it." Subjects were then given memory tests to see if they recognized logically implied sentences such as "Three turtles rested on a floating log and a fish swam beneath them" that were new, so to speak, because they had not actually been seen by the subjects before the recognition test. A large number of the subjects claimed that they had seen the new sentences, which suggests that the logical inferences were formed and stored at the time when the original sentences were initially presented.

Not all inferences are demanded by formal logic, however; the majority of inferences are *invited* by the assertion, and they are known as pragmatic inferences. A pragmatic inference does not need to follow from an assertion, but rather is reasonable, considering world knowledge. For example, to say that "Albert and Rae were looking at wedding rings" in no way demands the inference that Albert and Rae are to be married; however, that inference is certainly reasonable, given what is known about the world. A large number of experiments have been reported that demonstrate that pragmatic inferences also are remembered as part of the original event.

As a further illustration, additional research by Bransford and other colleagues in 1973 presented subjects with sentences such as "John was trying to fix the birdhouse. He was pounding the nail when his father came out to watch him and to help him do the work." The assertions imply, but do not logically demand, that John was using a hammer. Subjects later falsely recognized the sentence "John was using a hammer to fix the birdhouse when his father came out to watch him and help him do the work." Like the logical inference, the pragmatic inference is usually remembered as if it had actually been presented.

Shortcomings of Inference
Experimental investigations of thinking have revealed a wide range of shortcomings in human inference. Both deductive and inductive reasoning can go astray and produce incorrect conclusions, often either because one of the premises from which the conclusion was drawn is false or because the rules of deductive inference were violated. Many inferential judgments are based on imperfect information, and that means mistakes are unavoidable; however, the shortcomings are not simply errors. Instead, the ones that psychologists have identified involve the way in which information is used to draw the inference. For example, relevant information is sometimes ignored and sometimes relied on too heavily. In addition, multiple pieces of information are often not combined as they should be.

To understand human communication, it is necessary to recognize the prevalence and power of inferential processing. Much of what is communicated is actually left unsaid. Speakers instead rely on listeners to draw appropriate inferences. The ability to communicate without explicitly saying everything one is trying to convey enormously increases efficiency; however, as with other thought processes, increased efficiency comes at the cost of increased error. Everyone occasionally says things in such a way that a listener will infer information that may not be quite accurate. To determine whether a speaker is actually being dishonest, the speaker's intentions need to be discovered, which is a difficult thing to do if the actual assertion is accurate. As a result, it is easy to mislead—either when sufficient information to evaluate an assertion is intentionally withheld or when care in drawing inferences is not taken.

Implied Messages of Advertising
Real-world situations such as advertising copy and courtroom testimony provide interesting examples of the use of potentially misleading information. For example, the Federal Trade Commission was established to make decisions about what constitutes deceptive advertising, but deciding exactly what is deceptive is complex. The decision becomes especially difficult if a claim is not blatant but instead is implied. Consider the following commercial: "Aren't you tired of sneezing and having a red nose throughout the winter? Aren't you tired of always feeling under the weather? Get through the entire winter without colds. Take NuPills as directed."

Notice that the commercial does not directly state that NuPills will get one through the entire winter without colds. The commercial only implies it. To test whether people can distinguish between asserted and implied claims, John Harris, in a study published in 1977, presented people with a series of twenty fictitious commercials, half of which asserted claims and half of which implied claims. The subjects in the experiment were told to rate the claims as true, false, or of indeterminate truth value, based on the presented information. Some of the people made their judgments immediately after hearing each commercial, and others made their judgments after hearing all the commercials. Half the people were given instructions that warned them to take care not to interpret implied claims as asserted ones.

The results were that the subjects responded "true" more often to assertions than to implications, and instructions did help to reduce the number of implications accepted as true. Overall error rates, however, were high. Even in the group that gave an immediate judgment after hearing each commercial, people mistakenly accepted about half the implied statements as asserted ones. Finally, when the judgments were delayed until all commercials were presented, people accepted about as many implied statements as true as they did direct statements, even when they had been specifically warned about implied statements.

Courtroom Testimony
In the context of how information can be misleading in courtroom testimony, Elizabeth F. Loftus published an article in 1975 that described how she showed subjects ("witnesses") a film of a multiple-car accident. Immediately afterward, the witnesses

completed a questionnaire that included questions such as "Did you see a broken headlight?" Half the witnesses, however, were given a question that was worded "Did you see *the* broken headlight?" When the word "the" is used, the question encourages the subject/witness to assume that there was a broken headlight and seems to be asking whether he or she happened to see it. The word "a" does not presuppose the existence of a broken headlight. Questions with "the" more often led to reports that the witness had seen the broken headlight than questions with "a." This was the case regardless of whether the object (a broken headlight) had actually appeared in the film. Thus, in a courtroom situation, attorneys can intentionally or inadvertently influence the memories of witnesses by using leading words that entail presuppositions in their questions, leading to inaccurate inferences.

Regardless of the source of the information, the elaborative nature of comprehension can be and is used to imply potentially inaccurate information. Yet through knowledge of influence, one can be in the position to protect oneself by directly questioning assertions and carefully analyzing one's own inferences.

EVOLUTION OF STUDY

In ancient Greece, the philosopher Aristotle was the main creator of a formal inferential system. Historically, however, the scientific study of inference began fairly recently. Psychologists such as Robert S. Woodworth and S. B. Sells first began publishing articles in the 1930's on errors people made in the process of inferring conclusions. Woodworth and Sells were interested in how a reasoner's personal attitudes toward the conclusion of a syllogistic argument could bias the ability to draw inferences. They, along with other psychologists during the next three decades or so, studied formal inference and mainly looked at logical arguments called categorical syllogisms. As time passed, psychologists began to study other forms of deductive arguments and, later, inductive ones.

In 1962, Mary Henle encouraged psychologists to consider the difference between formal and practical reasoning. Henle attempted to clarify the heated controversy between the psychologists who thought formal logic was largely irrelevant to the thinking process, those who believed the mind contained a formal logic, and those who thought the mind contained other systems of logic that were more practical for day-to-day thinking. Henle pointed out that mathematical logic was never intended to be a direct description of how people think. For example, formal reasoning makes two demands not made in everyday reasoning. First of all, the reasoner must restrict the information to that contained in the premises. Second, the reasoner needs to discover the minimum commitments of the assertions as they are worded, which is not typical of ordinary comprehension. In ordinary comprehension, many inferences are invited that are unacceptable in formal deductive logic.

Linguists have also helped to promote research on inference. A long-standing question posed by linguists is how logic relates to actual conversation and argumentation. In conversation, most utterances have multiple functions. For example, the same utterance could be a description, a persuasion, an emotional expression, or even a warning. Numerous functions can arise, because the speaker may have one of a variety of intentions in mind when making the utterance.

It has been argued by Philip Johnson-Laird, in work he began publishing in 1978, that what subjects use to understand text is a mental model of the textual statements. He claims that people construct representations of models when they read a text. Rather than relying on formal logic in the interpretation of the material, Johnson-Laird believes, people manipulate the models they have formed. He thinks that the psychology of reasoning should describe the degree of competence that people display when it comes to inference, but that the mental processes underlying them—inferential performance—also need to be investigated. Given the increasing interest in the relationship of inference to linguistics, especially considering the applications that can be made in the area of artificial intelligence, such as getting computers to understand speech and to translate from one human language to another, the psychology of inferential thought will undoubtedly continue to be important research.

SOURCES FOR FURTHER STUDY

Baron, Jonathan. *Thinking and Deciding.* 4th ed. New York: Cambridge University Press, 2008. An excellent book that emphasizes the factors that keep people from thinking effectively and provides information to help the reader improve thinking and decision-making skills. The book is clearly written, but many of the ideas are complex. The author describes the role that thinking plays in relationship to learning, intelligence, and creativity.

Evans, Jonathan St. B. T. *Bias in Human Reasoning: Causes and Consequences.* London: Lawrence Erlbaum, 1994. Almost everyone interested in inferential thought should find this short book (slightly more than a hundred pages) a pleasure to read. The book is in an extended essay. Classifies the types of bias and puts them in a general theoretical framework, while considering practical applications. Suggestions, based on research, are provided to help the reasoner avoid bias as much as possible. There are also suggestions for educators.

_____. *The Psychology of Deductive Reasoning.* Boston: Routledge & Kegan Paul, 1982. The author reviews the available research in the area. He has published numerous journal articles on reasoning and is one of the top experts in the area of the psychology of reasoning.

Nickerson, Raymond S. *Reflections on Reasoning.* Hillsdale, N.J.: Lawrence Erlbaum, 1986. This brief book is an adaptation of a report that the author prepared under a project sponsored by the National Institute of Education. It clearly describes reasoning and factors that can impede reasoning, and it provides practical chapters on how to improve one's own reasoning ability and how to use reasoning to win disputes of all kinds.

Sanford, David. *If P Then Q: Conditionals and the Foundations of Reasoning.* 2d ed. New York: Routledge, 2004. This text recounts the historical development and recent research in the field of conditionals.

Deborah R. McDonald

SEE ALSO: Artificial intelligence; Cognitive ability: Gender differences; Cognitive development: Jean Piaget; Computer models of cognition; Concept formation; Decision making; Intelligence tests; Logic and reasoning; Philosophy and psychology; Thought: Study and measurement.

Thought
Study and measurement

TYPE OF PSYCHOLOGY: Cognition
FIELDS OF STUDY: Cognitive processes; thought

The study of thought is probably as old as thought itself. Although the measurement of thought did not originate in psychology, cognitive psychology is primarily dedicated to the study and measurement of thought processes.

KEY CONCEPTS
- cognitive psychology
- Ebbinghaus forgetting curve
- higher mental functions
- information processing model
- parallel processing
- percent savings
- personal equation
- serial processing
- subtraction technique

INTRODUCTION

Cognitive psychologists study many processes basic to human nature and everyday life. Mental processes are central to who people are, what they do, and how they survive. In cognitive psychology, the study of thought necessitates its measurement. For example, much effort has been put forth in cognitive psychology to study how people understand and process information in their environment. One popular approach is to use the idea of a human information-processing system, analogous to a computer. Computers are information-processing devices that use very specific instructions to achieve tasks. A computer receives input, performs certain internal operations on the data (including memory operations), and outputs certain results. Cognitive psychologists often use the information-processing metaphor in describing human operations. People must "input" information from the environment; this process includes sensory and perceptual systems, the recognition of certain common patterns of information, and attention processes.

Once this information has entered the "system," a vast number of operations can be performed. Much of the work by cognitive psychologists has centered on the storage of information during this process—that is, on memory. While memory processes have been of interest since ancient times, it was not until the 1880's that scientists, notably Hermann Ebbinghaus, first systematically and scientifically studied memory. Scientists studying memory today talk about concepts such as short-term and long-term memory as well as about the distinction between episodic and semantic memory systems. The function of memory is essential to human thought and ultimately to the measurement of thought.

In terms of measuring what happens to incoming information, more than memory storage occurs; people manipulate these data. They make decisions based on the information available, and they have capabilities (often referred to as higher mental processes) that in many ways differentiate humans from other animals. Some of the functions commonly studied and measured include reasoning, problem solving, logic, decision making, and language development and use. The information-processing analogy is completed with the "output" of information. When a person is asked a question, the response is the output; it is based on the information stored in memory, whether those items be personal experiences, knowledge gained from books, or awareness of social customs. People do these things so effortlessly, day in and day out, that it is difficult to stop, appreciate, and comprehend how thoughts work. Psychologists have pondered these questions for many years and are only beginning to discover the answers.

MEASURING THOUGHTS
Some of the earliest systematic studies of thought and the accompanying desire to measure it came from astronomy, not psychology or philosophy. From this beginning, Dutch physiologist Frans C. Donders set out specifically to measure a sequence of mental process—thought—in the middle of the nineteenth century. His technique was simple yet elegant in its ability to measure how much time mental processes consume; the procedure developed by Donders is typically referred to as the subtraction technique.

The subtraction technique begins with the timing and measurement of a very basic task. For example, a person might be asked to press a button after hearing a tone. Donders realized that it was fairly easy to time accurately how long subjects took to

perform this task. He believed that two cognitive (thought) processes would be operating: perception of the tone and the motor response of pressing the button. Once the time of this simple task was known, Donders would make the task more difficult. If a discrimination task were added, he believed, the time taken to complete the task would increase compared to the basic perception-motor response sequence. In this discrimination task, for example, Donders might tell a person to press the button only after hearing a high-pitched sound. That person is now faced with an added demand—to make a decision about pitch. Donders believed that with this discrimination stage, the processing of the information would require more mental effort and more time; he was right. More important, Donders could now measure the amount of extra thought required for the decision by subtracting the simple-task time from the discrimination-task time. In a general sense, Donders had a method for measuring thought.

Donders also had the ability to measure and manipulate specific components of the thought process. He even added another component to the sequence of tasks, what he called choice time. For example, the task could be changed so that for a high tone the subject should press the right button, and for a low tone, press the left button. By subtracting the discrimination time from this new choice time, he could estimate how long the added choice contributed to the overall thought process. By means of these ingenious methods, Donders inspired generations of cognitive psychologists to study thought in terms of the time it takes to think.

EBBINGHAUS ON LEARNING AND FORGETTING
The first recognized work done in psychology on the measurement of thought processes was Ebbinghaus's work on memory capacity and forgetting. Working independently in the 1880's in Germany, Ebbinghaus set out to study memory processes, particularly the nature of forgetting. Being the first psychologist to study the issue, he had no precedent as to how to proceed, so Ebbinghaus invented his own procedures for measuring memory. To his credit, those procedures were so good that they are still commonly used. Before describing his measurement of memory, Ebbinghaus made two important decisions about methods for studying memory. First, he studied only one person's memory—his own. He be-

lieved he would have better control over situational and contextual variables that way.

Second, Ebbinghaus decided that he could not use everyday words in his memory studies, because they might have associations that would make them easier to study. For example, if one were memorizing a poem, the story and the writing style might help memory, and Ebbinghaus was interested in a pure measure of memory and forgetting. To achieve this, Ebbinghaus pioneered the use of nonsense syllables. He used three-letter combinations of consonant-vowel-consonant so that the items were pronounceable but meaningless. Nonsense syllables such as "geb," "fak," "jit," "zab," and "buh" were used.

Ebbinghaus used a vigorous schedule of testing and presented himself with many lists of nonsense syllables to be remembered at a later time. In fact, he spent five years memorizing various lists until he published his seminal work on the topic, *Über das gedächtnis: Untersuchurgen zur experimentellen Psychologie* (1885; *Memory: A Contribution to Experimental Psychology,* 1913). He systematically measured memory by memorizing a list, letting some time pass, and testing himself on the list. He devised a numerical measurement for memory called percent savings. Percent savings was a measure of the degree of forgetting that occurred over time. For example, it might take him ten minutes to memorize a list perfectly. He would let forty-eight hours pass, then tell himself to recall the list. Forgetting would occur during that time, and only some items would be remembered. Ebbinghaus would then look at the original list and rememorize it until he knew it perfectly; this might take seven minutes or so. He always spent less time rememorizing the list. Said another way, there was some savings from the earlier experience forty-eight hours before. This percent savings was his measure of memory. The higher the percentage of savings, the more items remembered (or the fewer forgotten), and Ebbinghaus could remember the list in less time.

Ebbinghaus then varied the time between original list learning and later list recall. He found that percent savings drops over time; that is, the longer one waits to remember something, the less one saves from the prior experience, so the more time he had to spend rememorizing the list. Ebbinghaus found fairly good percent savings two or nine hours later, but percent savings dropped dramatically after two or three days. Plotted on a graph, this relationship looks like a downward sloping curve, and it is called the Ebbinghaus forgetting curve. Simply stated, it means that as time passes, memories become poorer. Although this effect is not surprising today, Ebbinghaus was the first (in 1885) to demonstrate this phenomenon empirically.

STERNBERG ON SPEED

Another example of the work in the area of cognitive psychology comes from the studies of Saul Sternberg in the 1960's at Bell Laboratories. Sternberg examined how additional information in memory influences the speed of mental operations in retrieving information stored in memory. Sternberg's task was fairly simple. He presented people with a list of numbers; the list might range from one to six numbers. After the people saw this initial list, a single number (called a probe) was presented. People were asked to identify whether the probe number was on the initial list of numbers. The list might be 2, 3, 9, and 5, for example, and the probe might be 3.

Sternberg's primary interest was in studying how the length of the initial list affected the time it took to make the required yes-or-no decision. Two possibilities typically emerge when people consider this problem. The concept called serial processing holds that the comparison of the probe to each number in the initial list takes time, so that the more items in the initial list, the longer the memory search takes. An alternative idea, parallel processing, suggests that people instantaneously scan all the items in the memory set, and the number of items in the initial list does not make a difference. Another way of saying this is that all the items are scanned at once, in parallel fashion. Sternberg found that people search their memories using the technique of serial processing. In fact, he was able to calculate precisely the amount of additional search time needed for each added item in the memory set—38 milliseconds (a millisecond is a thousandth of a second). Although the search may seem fast, even instantaneous, the more there is to think about, the more time it takes to think.

COGNITIVE PSYCHOLOGY

The study of thought, and particularly its measurement, is a relatively recent development. For centuries, the thinking processes of humans were believed to be somewhat mystical and certainly not available for scientific inquiry. Most philosophers were concerned more with the mind and its relationship to the body or the world than with how people think. The study of thought, although it was generally considered by the ancient Greek philosophers, did not merit serious attention until the emergence of the "personal equation" by astronomers and the realization that thought processes are indeed measurable and can be measured accurately and precisely.

The story of the first recorded measurements of thought begins with the royal astronomer to England, Nevil Maskelyne, and his assistant, David Kinnebrook, in 1794. Astronomers of the day were mostly concerned with stellar transits (measuring the movement of stars across the sky). Using telescopes and specialized techniques, the astronomer sought to measure the time it took for a particular star to move across a portion of the telescopic field. Using a complicated procedure that involved listening to a beating clock and viewing the sky, astronomers could measure the transit time of a star fairly accurately, to within one-tenth or two-tenths of a second. These measurements were particularly important because the clocks of that period were based on stellar transits.

Maskelyne and Kinnebrook often worked together in recording the movement of the stars. While Kinnebrook had no problems during 1794, in 1795 Maskelyne began to notice that Kinnebrook's times varied from his own by as much as one-half of a second—considered a large and important difference. By early 1796, the difference between the astronomers' times had grown to eight-tenths of a second. This was an intolerable amount of error to Maskelyne, and he fired his assistant Kinnebrook.

About twenty years later, a German astronomer named Friedrich Bessel came across the records of these incidents and began to study the "error" in the differing astronomers' measurements. He believed that the different measurements were attributable in part to differences between people and that this difference was not necessarily an error. He found that even the most famous and reliable astronomers of the day differed from one another by more than two-tenths of a second.

This incident between Maskelyne and Kinnebrook, and its later study by Bessel, led to some important conclusions. First, measurements in astronomy would have to consider the specific person making the measurement. Astronomers even went

to the lengths of developing what became known as the personal equation. The personal equation was a verified, quantified account of how each astronomer's thought processes worked when measuring stellar transits. In essence, the personal equation was a measurement of the thought process involved and a recognition of differences between people. Second, if astronomers differ in their particular thought processes, then many people differ in other types of thinking processes as well. Finally, and perhaps most important in the long run, this incident laid the groundwork for the idea that thought could be measured accurately and the information could be put to good use. No longer was thinking a mystical or magical process that was unacceptable for study by scientists.

It is from this historical context that the field of cognitive psychology has emerged. Cognitive psychology is chiefly concerned with the thought processes and, indeed, all the general mental processing of organisms (most often humans). The interests of a cognitive psychologist can be quite varied: learning, memory, problem solving, reasoning, logic, decision making, linguistics, cognitive development in children, and other topics. Each area of specialization continues to measure and examine how people think, using tasks and procedures as ingenious as those of Donders, Ebbinghaus, and Sternberg. The study and measurement of thought (or, more generally, the field of cognitive psychology) will continue to play an important and vital role. Not many questions are more basic to the study of human behavior than how people think, what processes are involved, and how researchers can scientifically study and measure these processes.

SOURCES FOR FURTHER STUDY

Anderson, John R. *Cognitive Psychology and Its Implications.* 6th ed. New York: Worth, 2005. This text is a long-standing leader in the field of cognitive psychology. Provides a wonderful overview of the fundamental issues of cognitive psychology, including attention and perception, basic principles of human memory, problem solving, the development of expertise, reasoning, intelligence, and language structure and use.

Ashcraft, Mark H. *Human Memory and Cognition.* 4th ed. Upper Saddle River, N.J.: Pearson Prentice Hall, 2006. A cognitive psychology textbook that heavily emphasizes the human information-processing metaphor. Arranged differently from Anderson's text, it, too, provides good coverage of all the basic areas of cognitive psychology.

Boring, Edwin G. *A History of Experimental Psychology.* 2d ed. Englewood Cliffs, N.J.: Prentice-Hall, 1957. This text, originally published in 1920, is the foremost authority on the development and history of psychology up to the 1950's. Contains detailed accounts of the work of early philosophers and astronomers who contributed to the study of thought and has an entire chapter devoted to the personal equation. This can be a difficult text to read, but it is the authoritative overview of the early history of psychology.

Goodwin, C. James. *A History of Modern Psychology.* 3d ed. Hoboken, N.J.: John Wiley & Sons, 2008. A readable and understandable treatment of the history of psychology from René Descartes in the Renaissance to the present.

Lachman, Roy, Janet L. Lachman, and Earl C. Butterfield. *Cognitive Psychology and Information Processing: An Introduction.* Hillsdale, N.J.: Lawrence Erlbaum, 1979. One of the earliest texts that adequately captures the coming importance and influence of cognitive psychology. There are outstanding chapters that trace the influences of other disciplines and traditions on what is now known as cognitive psychology. Topic areas within the field are discussed as well.

Mayer, R. E. *Thinking, Problem Solving, and Cognition.* 3d ed. New York: Worth, 2007. A book primarily dedicated to the topic of problem solving, which is unusual. The format is interesting and creative, covering the historical perspective of problem solving, basic thinking tasks, information-processing analysis, and implications and applications. The focus on thought and its measurement is seen throughout, especially in sections discussing mental chronometry.

R. Eric Landrum

See also: Artificial intelligence; Cognitive maps; Cognitive psychology; Computer models of cognition; Ebbinghaus, Hermann; Language; Learning; Logic and reasoning; Memory: Empirical studies; Thought: Inferential.

Thyroid gland

Type of psychology: Biological bases of behavior
Field of study: Endocrine system

The thyroid gland is responsible for the production of three hormones important for proper growth and development: thyroxine and triiodothyronine, which regulate the basal metabolic rate of the body, and calcitonin, which lowers blood calcium levels. Disorders associated with the thyroid may result from either underactivity (hypothyroidism) or overactivity (hyperthyroidism) of the gland.

Key concepts
- calcitonin
- endocrine glands
- hyperthyroidism
- hypothyroidism
- metabolism
- pituitary gland
- thyroid-stimulating hormone (TSH)
- thyroxine
- triiodothyronine

INTRODUCTION

The thyroid gland is the largest endocrine gland in the human body. It is on the upper portion of the trachea (windpipe) near the junction between the larynx (voice box) and the trachea. The thyroid gland is made up of a right lobe and a left lobe, which are joined by a narrow band of tissue called the isthmus, which lies across the trachea.

The thyroid gland is classified as an endocrine gland because it is made up of epithelial cells that are specialized for the production and secretion of specific hormones. Hormones produced by endocrine glands are specialized organic molecules that regulate biological activity by affecting certain cells of the body called target cells. Once the hormones have been produced by the gland, they are released into the bloodstream and carried by the blood throughout the body. The target cells have receptors on their surfaces to which the hormones attach; attachment of the hormone initiates cellular activities that lead to the observed effects of the hormone on body processes.

Internally, the thyroid gland is composed of hollow groups of cells called follicles. The cells are bound together by connective tissue and surround an inner region that contains a protein substance called colloid. The hormones produced by the thyroid gland are stored in the colloid until their release into the bloodstream. The thyroid gland is different from all other endocrine glands in this respect, since the other endocrine glands of the human body store their hormones within the cells of the gland.

The thyroid gland produces the hormones triiodothyronine (T^3), thyroxine (tetraiodothyronine, or T^4), and calcitonin. Triiodothyronine and thyroxine contain iodine, which is obtained from the diet and actively taken up from the bloodstream by the follicle cells. Within the follicle cells, iodine is attached to an amino acid called tyrosine to form a molecule called monoiodotyrosine (MIT). A second iodine may then be attached to form diiodotyrosine (DIT). Thyroxine is produced by coupling two DIT molecules; triiodothyronine is produced by coupling an MIT with a DIT. The thyroid hormones thyroxine and triiodothyronine are then stored extracellularly in the colloid, surrounded by the ball of follicle cells. Normally the thyroid produces 10 percent triiodothyronine and 90 percent thyroxine.

The release of thyroid hormones is controlled by the anterior lobe of the pituitary gland, a small pea-shaped gland located at the base of the brain. The pituitary gland produces a hormone known as thyrotropin, or thyroid-stimulating hormone (TSH), which controls the production and secretion of the thyroid hormones. The release of TSH from the anterior pituitary is in turn regulated by thyrotropin-releasing hormone (TRH), a hormone produced by the hypothalamus. TRH is transported by way of a capillary system to the anterior pituitary, where it stimulates the release of TSH. TSH then travels via the bloodstream to the thyroid, where it stimulates the production and release of the thyroid hormones. When the thyroid is stimulated by TSH to secrete its hormones, triiodothyronine and thyroxine are taken into the follicle cells from the colloid by a process called endocytosis. Triiodothyronine and thyroxine then enter the bloodstream from the follicle cells. While traveling in the bloodstream, the thyroid hormones are bound to thyroid-binding globulin (TBG), a plasma protein. Once the hormones reach the target cells, most of the thyroxine is converted to triiodothyronine, indicating that triiodothyronine is the major active form of the thyroid hormones at the cellular level.

The thyroid hormones influence the metabolic rate of the body primarily by controlling the rate of cell respiration. Most tissues of the body are responsive to the influence of these hormones; exceptions include the testes, uterus, spleen, and brain. Triiodothyronine and thyroxine cause a calorigenic effect on the body by promoting oxygen usage and heat production by the tissues. They promote the synthesis of proteins from amino acids and stimulate the synthesis, mobilization, and degradation of lipids. Thyroid hormones increase the utilization of carbohydrates, promoting their breakdown and the subsequent release of energy, and they increase the rate by which glucose is absorbed from the intestine. Triiodothyronine and thyroxine promote the uptake of glucose from the blood by adipose tissue and muscle, and stimulate a process known as gluconeogenesis, whereby carbohydrates are produced from noncarbohydrate molecules. The effects of thyroid hormones on carbohydrate metabolism are modified by other hormones, especially insulin, epinephrine, and norepinephrine.

Although normal quantities of thyroid hormone

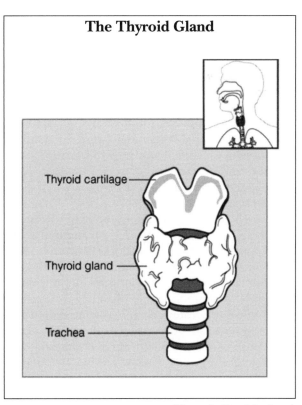

The Thyroid Gland

Thyroid cartilage

Thyroid gland

Trachea

(Hans & Cassidy, Inc.)

stimulate the production of proteins, excessive amounts cause muscle wasting and weakness, especially in the heart and eye muscles. High levels of triiodothyronine and thyroxine also cause an increase in the breakdown of lipids and a decreased amount of cholesterol and phospholipids in the blood plasma.

In addition to triiodothyronine and thyroxine, the thyroid produces and secretes calcitonin. This hormone is produced by parafollicular cells, which are located adjacent to the thyroid follicle cell. Structurally, calcitonin is a polypeptide made up of a chain of thirty-two amino acids. When calcitonin is released into the bloodstream, it primarily affects bone cells, causing them to increase bone formation and suppress bone resorption. As a result, the amount of calcium and phosphate in the blood is lowered. Release of calcitonin is regulated by the amount of calcium ions in the blood plasma; when the concentration of calcium increases, calcitonin production and secretion by the thyroid is stimulated. Some hormones released by the digestive tract during the digestion and absorption of food also promote the secretion of calcitonin from the thyroid. This aids the body's conservation of calcium from the diet by preventing a rapid surge in the amount of calcium in the blood, which could lead to increased excretion of calcium in the urine by the kidneys.

Thyroid dysfunction is a common endocrine condition that demonstrates neuropsychiatric symptoms. Both hyperthyroidism and hypothyroidism occur more often in women than in men and can manifest with psychiatric symptoms including anxiety, depression, and psychosis.

HYPOTHYROIDISM

The psychiatric manifestations of hypothyroidism have been observed for nearly two hundred years. In 1873, British physician William Gull first described the neuropsychiatric manifestations of hypothyroidism and its characteristic clinical picture of mental and physical slowing. It was his fellow Briton William Ord who introduced the term "myxedema" in 1878 and postulated that the overall apathy, fatigue, and weariness of the patients was due to a "jelly-like" swelling of connective tissues. In the later part of nineteen century, the Clinical Society of London released a classic report that revealed that insanity, manifested by delusions and hallucinations, was seen

in more than one-third of the 109 cases of myxedema. Dementia was also found in a significant number of patients, and mental slowing was noticed in all but 3 of 109 patients.

Hypothyroidism has recently received more attention in the medical community, with clinics that specialize in "thyroid optimization" springing up. Overt hypothyroidism occurs in 2 percent of women compared with 0.1 percent of men. Many patients suffering from hypothyroidism frequently exhibit neuropsychiatric symptoms such as apathy, anxiety, suicidal ideation, depression, diminished libido, delusions, memory impairment, and overall slowing. These neuropsychiatric symptoms commonly appear before the onset of other recognizable symptoms and signs of hypothyroidism: cold intolerance, husky voice, constipation, excessive menstrual bleeding, muscle cramps, dry, coarse skin, goiter, mild edema, and slow heart rate. A rapid onset of severe hypothyroidism is sometimes accompanied by delirium with psychotic features (myxedema madness). In most cases of hypothyroidism, the neuropsychiatric symptoms remit with appropriate replacement hormone, resulting in euthyroidism. There is evidence that in some patients with long-standing hypothyroidism, neuronal death may occur and result in persistence of neuropsychiatric manifestations even after adequate hormonal replacement.

More controversial, less understood, and far more easily missed is the diagnosis of subclinical hypothyroidism, which is more common in women. Subclinical forms of hypothyroidism may show few if any nonpsychiatric signs or symptoms. In one study, the researchers found that the prevalence of depression is three times higher among those with subclinical hypothyroidism compared with those with normal thyroid function. In the psychiatric populations, one should not forget that lithium, used in the treatment of mania, could well cause hypothyroidism.

Diagnoses of thyroid dysfunction have increased dramatically, and thyroid disease is one of the most common diseases, affecting more than 200 million people worldwide. In women, thyroid dysfunction has been described during pregnancy, after childbirth or abortion, before menstruation, and at menopause. Patients describe such symptoms as brain fog, Brillo hair, and prune skin. Hypothyroidism is more common in women after delivery of a child and may cause a constellation of symptoms resembling major depressive disorder. Researchers have found a positive correlation between postpartum depression and postpartum thyroiditis. Postpartum thyroiditis (as defined by the presence of thyroid autoantibodies) is caused by heightened immune activity, postpartum, in at-risk individuals. One study found that 38 percent of the women with postpartum thyroiditis experienced either major or minor depression as compared with 9.5 percent of women in a matched control group. Hence it is important to recognize postpartum depression and exclude any organic disease.

In the absence of universal screening, numerous cases of thyroid disorders, including thyroiditis, will remain undiagnosed. Because the symptoms of hypothyroidism mimic so many other conditions—such as chronic fatigue, premenstrual syndrome, and clinical depression—physicians agree that the disorder can be difficult to diagnose. Studies regarding hypothyroidism have come to include children. One study looked at subgroups with different levels of thyroxine and thyrotropin and compared their abilities to perform psychological tasks and their levels of focus and attention. The results demonstrated that although children with high levels of both thyroxine and thyrotropin had significantly lower attention spans, they were reportedly less hyperactive.

HYPERTHYROIDISM

Caleb Parry, a physician at the health resort of Bath, England, first described the hyperthyroid state in 1835, attributing the condition to traumatic fear. In 1835, Irish physician Robert Graves also suggested that a patient's psychological state could play a role in the development of hyperthyroidism, linking it in particular to globus hystericus in women. Since then the relationship between psychological state and hyperthyroidism has gained much attention in the scientific community. Graves' disease, an autoimmune disorder, is more common in women than in men. In Graves' disease, an autoantibody to the thyroid-stimulating hormone receptor on the thyroid follicular cell causes stimulation of the receptor and eventually thyrotoxicosis.

Many common symptoms of hyperthyroidism are behavioral, such as nervousness, irritability, restlessness, insomnia, mood lability, and poor attention, and these symptoms could mislead a clinician into making a diagnosis of anxiety or mood disorder, or even stimulant intoxication. In general, the symptoms are similar to those seen in agitated depression, panic disorder, and anxiety states. Interestingly, the hyperthyroid patient may show several symptoms of anxiety or depression but may not report feeling dysphoric or anxious. Frequently, the behavioral and psychiatric manifestations of hyperthyroidism lead patients to seek medical attention. In the rare form of thyrotoxicosis, the "thyroid storm," the psychiatric features may be more marked and include psychosis and profound agitation. Many of the neuropsychiatric complaints of hyperthyroidism are probably due to the central effects of thyroid hormones. Several of the neuropsychiatric features appear to be consistent with prefrontal lobe dysfunction.

In elderly individuals who suffer from the apathetic form of thyrotoxicosis, features of depression and severe slowing of mental and bodily activities predominate, and such a clinical picture may be mistaken for a major depression. When hyperthyroidism is suspected, clinical clues, including heat intolerance, diaphoresis, warm skin, weight loss (despite increased appetite), palpitations, and faster heart rates, are helpful to establish the clinical diagnosis. However, the biochemical thyroid function tests help to confirm the diagnosis.

Hyperthyroidism can exacerbate chronic psychotic disorders or precipitate manic episodes in susceptible individuals. Psychotic patients may poorly communicate common hallmark signs and symptoms of hyperthyroidism, thereby further obscuring the diagnosis. Transient elevations of thyroid hormone levels have been reported, especially at the height of psychiatric illness or at the time of hospitalization. This possibility of false-positive results from laboratory testing makes the diagnosis of hyperthyroidism especially difficult in psychiatric populations.

In most patients, successful treatment of the hyperthyroidism itself is effective in reducing the neuropsychiatric symptoms. Sometimes beta blockers in conjunction with antithyroid medications ameliorate many of the symptoms of anxiety. Adjunctive antipsychotic therapy may pose risks. Tricyclic antidepressant medications may increase the risk of central toxicity. Lithium is generally avoided in Graves' disease because of the possibility of exacerbating the exophthalmos. Haloperidol has been found to result in neurotoxicity and possibly the initiation of thyroid storm. However, some of the neurocognitive deficits may be irreversible in patients with long-standing hyperthyroidism.

In summary, thyroid disorders are important endocrine abnormalities that are common in women and frequently exhibit neuropsychiatric symptoms. It is important to realize that many of the neuropsychiatric manifestations of both hypothyroid and hyperthyroid states are reversible if the underlying thyroid disturbance is diagnosed and treated in a timely manner.

SOURCES FOR FURTHER STUDY

Braverman, Lewis E., and Robert D. Utiger. *Werner and Ingram's The Thyroid: A Fundamental and Clinical Text.* 9th ed. Philadelphia: Lippincott, Williams & Wilkins, 2005. Compiles information regarding the thyroid from many diverse sources. The book is designed for clinical as well as laboratory use. The text is thorough and detailed, suitable for college students. Extensive reference sections are provided at the end of each chapter.

Corbett, Nancy Sickles. "The Endocrine System." In *Hole's Human Anatomy and Physiology.* 11th ed. Boston: McGraw-Hill, 2007. Presents a well-organized discussion of the endocrine glands, including pertinent information on clinical aspects (such as pathological disorders) and laboratory techniques associated with each gland. The text is suitable for high school and college students.

Friedman, Theodore C., and Winnie Yu. *The Everything Health Guide to Thyroid Disease: Professional Advice on Getting the Right Diagnosis, Managing Your Symptoms, and Feeling Great.* Cincinnati: Adams Media, 2006. Co-authored by the chief of the Division of Endocrinology, Molecular Medicine, and Metabolism at the UCLA School of Medicine, this book provides information on who is at risk for thyroid disease, types of thyroid disorders, the disease's far-reaching effects, and treatments.

Graves' Disease: A Medical Dictionary, Bibliography, and Annotated Research Guide to Internet References. San Diego, Calif.: Icon Health, 2004. This is a three-in-one reference book containing a complete medical dictionary, lists of bibliographic citations, and helpful information on how to use various Internet resources concerning Graves' disease. Although the book is designed for medical researchers, physicians, and medical students preparing for board examinations, it is also useful to patients who want to become familiar with Graves' disease.

Shomon, Mary J. *Living Well with Hypothyroidism: What Your Doctor Doesn't Tell You . . . That You Need to Know.* New York: Collins Living, 2005. Shomon outlines how too few thyroid hormones in the body results in weight gain, depression, fatigue, and what has commonly become referred to brain fog. Includes sections on postpartum thyroid problems, taking antithyroid drugs, and lifelong thyroid hormone replacement.

Debra Zehner; updated by Krishna Bhaskarabhatla and Kausalya Chennapragada; updated by M. Casey Diana

SEE ALSO: Adrenal gland; Endocrine system; Hormones and behavior; Pituitary gland; Stress: Physiological responses.

Tic disorders

TYPE OF PSYCHOLOGY: Emotion; language; personality; psychopathology

FIELDS OF STUDY: Adolescence; anxiety disorders; attitudes and behavior; childhood and adolescent disorders; critical issues in stress; interpersonal relations; personality disorders

A tic is defined as a sudden involuntary movement or twitch, usually in the face but sometimes in the neck or in other parts of the body, that occurs without any obvious external cause and that may also manifest itself in the victim's speech or breathing.

KEY CONCEPTS
- attention-deficit hyperactivity disorder (ADHD)
- chronic tic disorder
- coprolalia
- dopamine
- obsessive-compulsive disorder (OCD)
- phonic tics
- Tourette's syndrome
- transient tic disorder
- vocal tics

INTRODUCTION

The tics that occur with some frequency in young children and in adolescents are often confined to the face, particularly the eyes and lips, although these muscle contractions can also affect other parts of the body, notably the shoulders, the neck, the arms, the hands, and the trunk. They can also affect breathing and may be vocal.

Most people have had some experience with tics, but as people mature, the frequency of such tics usually diminishes. In cases of this sort, the condition is identified as transient tic disorder and does little to interfere with people's normal activities.

Some victims of the disorder, however, experience tics so frequently that it significantly affects their normal functioning. These people have chronic tic disorder, which, especially in its vocal manifestations, called coprolalia, makes it difficult for them to interact with people and to be involved in social and learning situations. Such people may erupt unexpectedly and quite frequently into loud streams of profanity directed to those around them. There usually is not any identifiable trigger for these eruptions, which often leave those who hear and see them bewildered and frightened.

Although coprolalia may be a transient condition, its manifestations require immediate attention, because those who have the condition are usually disruptive in social situations and in school settings. In some situations, this disruptiveness may cause victims of coprolalia to be isolated, because their presence in classroom settings can make it impossible for teachers to deal with them in average-sized classes.

Causes

The presence of tics in young people may be hereditary, although a genetic link has not been firmly established. Environmental causes appear to be present in some cases in which tics develop. It is also thought that stress may contribute to the occurrence of tics, and it has been observed that sometimes people who develop tics experience a reduction in their symptoms if their stress level is reduced.

Among adults, the overuse of caffeine, defined as more than the equivalent of five cups of coffee a day, can result in tics, twitches, or tremors that can be virtually eliminated if caffeine consumption is drastically reduced. The regular use of alcoholic beverages may also result in the tics, twitches, and tremors associated with the overuse of caffeine and can be controlled by eliminating alcoholic beverages from the patient's diet.

In some people, tics coexist with mental disorders and emotional instability, in which case they may be treated by psychologists or psychiatrists. Where a psychological basis exists for the condition, the reduction of stress is imperative.

Types and Frequency

Tics may be motor or verbal. Although they may disappear almost as quickly as they appeared, they are irresistible. Will power and distractions may mitigate them temporarily, but once the distraction disappears, the tic reappears. Researchers have found that tics do a great deal to relieve stress in those experiencing them, so they question the advisability of doing anything to prevent or discourage them.

Although tics are often associated with Tourette's syndrome, they may also occur in people with Asperger syndrome, bipolar disorders, learning disabilities, and attention-deficit hyperactivity disorder (ADHD). Some neurologists have associated them with such conditions as chronic nail biting, nose picking, and air swallowing.

Tics often are closely associated with obsessive-compulsive disorders (OCDs). Those who experience transient tic disorders, defined as those that last for at least four weeks but for no longer than a year, generally exhibit behaviors associated with both motor and verbal (also called phonic) tics, sometimes simultaneously.

The American Psychiatric Associations' *Diagnostic and Statistical Manual of Mental Disorders: DSM-IV-TR* (rev. 4th ed., 2000) classifies tics as sudden, rapid, nonrhythmic, stereotyped, involuntary movements, classifications that were also adopted by the World Health Organization. A chronic tic disorder is defined as one that lasts more than a year.

Transient tic disorders disappear as their victims mature. They are rarely found in people over eighteen years old. In some cases, however, the disorder follows its victims into adulthood, which usually complicates their lives considerably. However, as neurologist Oliver Sacks has shown in seven case studies involving those with Tourette's syndrome, the most difficult type of tic disorder, some of those with the disorder have learned to live with it and lead productive lives in spite of it. Sacks cites case studies he has made of seven physicians who suffer from Tourette's syndrome and practice actively in such fields as surgery, ophthalmology, and internal medicine.

Epidemiological studies contend that between 5 and 15 percent of all children of school age in the

DSM-IV-TR Criteria for Tic Disorders

CHRONIC MOTOR OR VOCAL TIC DISORDER (DSM CODE 307.22)

Single or multiple motor or vocal tics (sudden, rapid, recurrent, nonrhythmic, stereotyped motor movements or vocalizations), but not both, at some time during the disorder

Tics occur many times a day nearly every day or intermittently throughout a period of more than one year; during this period, no tic-free periods of more than three consecutive months

Disturbance causes marked distress or significant impairment in social, occupational, or other important areas of functioning

Onset before age eighteen

Disturbance not due to direct physiological effects of a substance (such as stimulants) or a general medical condition (such as Huntington's disease or postviral encephalitis)

Criteria for Tourette's Disorder never met

TOURETTE'S DISORDER (DSM CODE 307.23)

Both multiple motor and one or more vocal tics (sudden, rapid, recurrent, nonrhythmic, stereotyped motor movements or vocalizations) at some time during the disorder, although not necessarily concurrently

Tics occur many times a day (usually in bouts) nearly every day or intermittently throughout a period of more than one year; during this period, no tic-free periods of more than three consecutive months

Onset before age eighteen

Disturbance not due to direct physiological effects of a substance (such as stimulants) or a general medical condition (such as Huntington's disease or postviral encephalitis)

TRANSIENT TIC DISORDER (DSM CODE 307.21)

Single or multiple motor and/or vocal tics (sudden, rapid, recurrent, nonrhythmic, stereotyped motor movements or vocalizations)

Tics occur many times a day, nearly every day for at least four weeks, but for no longer than twelve consecutive months

Disturbance causes marked distress or significant impairment in social, occupational, or other important areas of functioning

Onset before age eighteen

Disturbance not due to direct physiological effects of a substance (such as stimulants) or a general medical condition (such as Huntington's disease or postviral encephalitis)

Criteria for Tourette's Disorder or Chronic Motor or Vocal Tic Disorder never met

TIC DISORDER NOT OTHERWISE SPECIFIED (DSM CODE 307.20)

United States develop identifiable tics, usually transient ones, during childhood. School-age boys develop tics at a rate of five to one over their female counterparts.

The condition has been reported throughout recorded medical history. At one time, tics were considered to be evidence that those who had them, at least in their more extreme manifestations, were possessed. A degree of shame was associated with them. Tics were considered to stem from psychological causes well into the twentieth century, even though Tourette's syndrome was identified in the last half of the nineteenth century.

In the United States, Tourette's syndrome affects more whites than African Americans or Latinos. Young children suffer more frequently from Tourette's than older children do. The occurrence of the condition in those between kindergarten and eighth grade is about twelve cases in every ten thousand students, whereas the occurrence in those aged sixteen or seventeen is about four cases in every ten thousand students.

Many tic disorders go unobserved and unreported. Therefore, some researchers have speculated that the actual occurrence of some kind of tic disorder may be as high as one in every hundred people between five and eighteen years old.

Young people who suffer from Tourette's syndrome, even if they attend school, are often shunned by their classmates and may be dreaded by their teachers who view them as disruptive. Most school districts have some special education programs for those who need them, but a person with Tourette's can seriously obstruct the learning processes of other students. Teachers on an intellectual level can understand the problems that face the person with Tourette's, but this understanding does little to remedy the disruptions that such a student may create.

Students coping with Tourette's syndrome have legal protection under Section 504 of the American with Disabilities Act (ADA). This law protects the rights of all Americans with disabilities and is particularly relevant in educational and vocational training programs. Protection is granted under ADA to anyone whose physical or mental impairment places a limitation on them in one of several areas, including walking, seeing, hearing, speaking, breathing, and several other areas that are commonly found in those with Tourette's. People with Tourette's often have badly damaged self-images caused by their inability to fit into the social and educational settings in which most young people participate. Discussions of what Tourette's syndrome is and of how it affects people often increase the understanding of the teenage tormentors of those with the syndrome. Researchers have found drastic changes in the attitudes of people who have viewed a single ten-minute videotape that deals with the problem.

TREATMENT

Most tic disorders are sufficiently mild and transient that they do not require treatment. Given time, the symptoms will probably diminish and finally disappear entirely. Those dealing with young people who have tic disorders are usually advised not to encourage them to suppress their tics because they often are essential in helping them release their stress and deal with their emotions.

For cases in which patients experience such severe tics that treatment is indicated, benzodiazepines and antipsychotic medications are sometimes employed. Such treatment is considered extreme and usually is resorted to only in cases in which there are such severe involuntary contractions of the muscles between the chest and the abdomen that the patient makes loud grunting noises and exhibits distinct symptoms of Tourette's syndrome. In such cases, some instances of relief have been reported following accupuncture, accupressure, yoga, and massage.

Tourette's usually involves two or more kinds of motor tics simultaneously as well as a phonic tic, generally coprolalia. Such extreme manifestations of this obsessive-compulsive disorder are infrequent and are usually dealt with both psychologically and medicinally. When it is considered necessary, however, limited doses of dopamine agonists, notably bromocriptine and pramipexole, may be administered.

Mild tics often respond to small quantities of a blood pressure medication, clonidine, or to an anti-seizure medication, clonazepam. Multiple tics can be controlled by small doses of such antipsychotic drugs as haloperidol, pimozide, and fluphenazine, but each of these medications has significant side effects that cause most physicians to limit their use to the most extreme cases.

SOURCES FOR FURTHER STUDY

Bruun, Ruth Dowling, and Bertel Bruun. *A Mind of Its Own: Tourette's Syndrome—A Story and a Guide.* New York: Oxford University Press, 1994. Especially valuable for its chapter "Obsessive-Compulsive Symptoms," and for its discussion of the role heredity plays in the onset of the disease.

Cohen, Donald J., Ruth Dowling Bruun, and James F. Leckman, eds. *Tic and Tic Disorders: Clinical Understanding and Treatment.* New York: John Wiley, 1999. A thorough presentation, clear and direct, of how to deal with tic disorders. The contributors cover every significant aspect of tic disorders and are generally lucid in their presentations.

Kushner, Howard I. *A Cursing Brain? The Histories of Tourette Syndrome.* Cambridge, Mass.: Harvard University Press, 1999. A classic in its field, this book offers a good history of Tourette's syndrome, with special emphasis on the early recognition of the condition in the last half of the nineteenth century by French neurologist Georges Gilles de la Tourette, for whom the condition was named.

Kutscher, Martin L. *Kids in the Syndrome Mix of ADHD, LD, Asperger's, Tourette's, Bipolar, and More! The One Stop Guide for Parents, Teachers, and Other Professionals.* Philadelphia: Jessica Kingsley, 2005. A comprehensive overview of tic disorders in young children and adolescents written by a medical doctor and contributed to by two other professionals who specialize in such disorders. Easily accessible.

Robertson, Mary M., and Simon Baron-Cohen. *Tourette Syndrome: The Facts.* 2d ed. New York: Oxford University Press, 1998. This thin volume directed to those dealing with people—usually children—suffering from Tourette's syndrome is the most usable brief account of how to deal with the condition.

Sacks, Oliver. *An Anthropologist on Mars: Seven Paradoxical Tales.* New York: Alfred A. Knopf, 1995. A collection of seven case studies of patients with whom neurologist Oliver Sacks has come into contact in his career as a therapist. Intriguing accounts of Tourette's patients who have had successful careers as surgeons, ophthalmologists, and internists despite their neuropathology.

Shimberg, Elaine. *Living with Tourette Syndrome.* New York: Simon & Schuster, 1995. The sections on how Tourette's syndrome affects a family and the problems the disease presents for teachers in school settings are practical and detailed.

Woods, Douglas W., John C. Piacentini, and John T. Walkup, eds. *Treating Tourette Syndrome and Tic Disorders: A Guide for Practitioners.* New York: Guilford Press, 2007. The thirteen essays in this book, each written by recognized specialists, provide one of the best overviews available for recognizing, diagnosing, and dealing with tic disorders of every kind.

R. Baird Shuman

SEE ALSO: Abnormality: Biomedical models; Asperger syndrome; Attention-deficit hyperactivity disorder; Caffeine and mental health; Childhood disorders; Speech disorders; Stress: Behavioral and psychological responses; Stress: Physiological responses; Tourette's syndrome.

Time-out

DATE: 1950's forward
TYPE OF PSYCHOLOGY: Learning; psychological methodologies
FIELDS OF STUDY: Aggression; behavioral and cognitive models; childhood and adolescent disorders; instrumental conditioning

Time-out refers to the temporary withdrawal of access to positive reinforcement immediately following performance of an undesirable or maladaptive behavior. It is based on operant conditioning principles and has been widely used to reduce a variety of disruptive behaviors in children.

KEY CONCEPTS
- duration of time-out
- isolation time-out
- positive reinforcement

- punishment
- release from time-out
- suppression of disruptive behaviors

INTRODUCTION

Time-out, also called time-out from positive reinforcement, refers to the temporary suspension of access to reward or positive reinforcement immediately following performance of inappropriate or maladaptive behavior. Child time-out is administered either by removing positive reinforcement from the situation or by removing the misbehaving child from the situation and placing him or her in a time-out room or specially designated area.

Time-out has been used to suppress a wide range of behaviors in children, including tantrums, physical aggression, noncompliance, and self-injurious behavior. For example, psychologists Montrose Wolf, Todd Risley, and Hayden Mees instituted a time-out for Dicky, their three-and-a-half-year-old autistic client. Whenever Dicky threw his glasses, he was sent to his room for ten minutes. When this time-out procedure was in effect, the frequency of throwing glasses declined to zero in five days. The frequency of throwing glasses increased over the course of three weeks when the time-out procedure was suspended and then declined to zero in six days when time-out was reinstated.

Evidence of the selectivity of the suppressive effect of time-out was provided by psychologists Ronald Drabman and Robert Spitalnik, who implemented a time-out procedure for male adolescents in a psychiatric hospital. Boys were placed in a time-out room for ten minutes for being physically aggressive or vacating their seat without permission. Time-out significantly reduced the frequency of both of these target behaviors but did not decrease a nontarget behavior, disallowed vocalizations.

Time-out from positive reinforcement does not have to be administered in a separate room to be effective. In a 1976 study, very young children were required to sit and watch other children for one minute if they exhibited disruptive behavior such as aggression or destruction of toys. In a 1978 study conducted in a special education classroom, a ribbon that signified that a child was eligible to earn social reinforcement in the form of verbal praise and smiles was removed for three minutes if the child was disruptive. Both techniques were effective in reducing disruptive behavior and had the advantage that the children in time-out could observe other children's appropriate behavior and positive reinforcement.

The use of time-out to manage behavioral problems in children has not been without controversy. There is concern that if time-out is used by an adult or perceived by a child as punishment, it may have negative consequences similar to those associated with physical punishment. Potential undesirable effects include generalized suppression of behavior, reduced motivation, and impairment of the adult-child relationship. Isolation time-out also removes the opportunity for learning appropriate behaviors, and its extreme use in schools may violate students' individual rights. Praise and reward for appropriate "time-in" behaviors has been advocated as a substitute for or supplement to the use of time-out for unwanted behavior.

EFFECTIVENESS

Three conditions are considered crucial to the effectiveness of time-out for eliminating disruptive behavior in children. First, the time-out period should be devoid of any positive reinforcement. The location for isolation time-out should be boring and should not permit activities that are more interesting than those available in the "time-in" environment. Ignoring a child in isolation time-out is also important to ensure the absence of social attention, which is a powerful reinforcer for children. Second, release from time-out should occur only after the specified duration has elapsed and appropriate behavior is exhibited. This contingency prevents the reinforcement of an unwanted behavior coincident with release from time-out. Third, time-out should not enable escape from or avoidance of activities that a child finds unpleasant. In such cases, not only will time-out fail, it may actually be countertherapeutic and increase disruptive behavior.

Studies have demonstrated that short duration time-outs may be superior or equal to long duration time-outs unless the child has been exposed to time-outs of longer duration. The general recommendation for children is one minute for each year of the child's age. Research has also suggested that consistent application of the time-out contingency may be more important than the duration of time-out. Finally, time-out from an enriched environment is more effective than time-out from an impoverished one.

ORIGIN OF TIME-OUT

Time-out was introduced by the behavioral psychologists Charles B. Ferster and B. F. Skinner in *Schedules of Reinforcement* (1957). Originally, time-out denoted the removal of all conditioning stimuli and the insertion of a brief period of darkness, a blackout, following an incorrect or nonreinforced response in a discrimination procedure or an error on a matching-to-sample procedure in nonhuman animals. The use of time-out as a procedure for controlling disruptive behavior in children first appeared in the early 1960's. Four decades later, it was recommended by the American Academy of Pediatrics as an alternative to physical reprimands. Its widespread use by parents and teachers to manage children with emotional and behavioral disorders at home and at school, respectively, reflects one of psychology's most successful social inventions.

SOURCES FOR FURTHER STUDY

Harris, Sandra L., and Robin Ersner-Hershfield. "Behavioral Suppression of Seriously Disruptive Behavior in Psychotic and Retarded Patients: A Review of Punishment and Its Alternatives." *Psychological Bulletin* 85, no. 6 (1978): 1352-1375. Discusses the use of differential reinforcement of other behaviors (DRO) and aversive procedures such as time-out, extinction, overcorrection, and electric shock to suppress self-injurious behavior, aggression, and other disruptive behaviors. Also examines studies on generalization, maintenance, and side effects of these procedures and associated ethical issues.

Miltenberger, Raymond G. *Behavior Modification: Principles and Procedures.* 4th ed. Belmont, Calif.: Thomson Wadsworth, 2008. Engaging and readable introduction to behavior modification methods, including time-out. Explanations of concepts and procedures are accompanied by interesting exercises and examples.

Ryan, Joseph B., Sharon Sanders, Antonis Katsiyannis, and Mitchell L. Yell. "Using Time-Out Effectively in the Classroom." *Teaching Exceptional Children* 39, no. 4 (2007): 60-67. Describes various implementations of time-out in the educational setting and their efficacy in reducing maladaptive behaviors in students with disabilities. Covers problems that make time-out ineffective and offers recommendations for its use in the classroom.

Taylor, Jill, and Michelle Miller. "When Timeout Works Some of the Time: The Importance of Treatment Integrity and Functional Assessment." *School Psychology Quarterly* 12, no. 1 (1997): 4-22. Provides empirical evidence that properly implemented time-out is effective in reducing student behavior problems reinforced by attention but not those that allow escape from or avoidance of an unpleasant situation. Mentions ignoring and "working through" as alternative interventions for escape-motivated problem behaviors.

The Behavior Home Page. http://www.state.ky.us/agencies/behave/homepage.html. Offers resources related to interventions for management of problem behavior in special-needs children. Includes advice on using time-out prepared by special education expert C. Michael Nelson and provides links to organizations such as the Council for Children with Behavioral Disorders (CCBD) and the Council for Exceptional Children (CEC).

Ruth M. Colwill

SEE ALSO: Aversion therapy; Behavior therapy; Children's mental health; Punishment; Reinforcement.

Tolman, Edward C.

BORN: April 14, 1886, in West Newton, Massachusetts
DIED: November 19, 1959, in Berkeley, California
IDENTITY: American psychologist
TYPE OF PSYCHOLOGY: Cognition; learning
FIELDS OF STUDY: Behavioral and cognitive models; cognitive learning; instrumental conditioning

Tolman was a pioneer in the study of learning and cognitive processes governing behavior.

Edward C. Tolman was educated in the West Newton, Massachusetts, public school system and earned a bachelor of science degree in electrochemistry from the Massachusetts Institute of Technology in 1911. He entered Harvard's graduate program in philosophy and psychology in fall, 1911, and spent the following summer in Germany studying with the Gestalt psychologist Kurt Koffka. He returned to Harvard to work with psychologists Hugo Münsterberg and Herbert S. Langfeld. Tolman earned

his doctoral degree in 1915, with a dissertation on retroactive inhibition. He married Kathleen Drew on August 30, 1915. They moved to Evanston, Illinois, where Tolman taught at Northwestern University while continuing his work on human memory. In 1918, he accepted a teaching appointment at the University of California, Berkeley, where he remained for the rest of his academic career.

At Berkeley, Tolman established an animal laboratory dedicated to the study of learning. He rejected the introspectionist approach to scientific inquiry but disputed the central tenets of John B. Watson's behaviorism. Based on a series of studies of rats in a maze, Tolman proposed that animals and humans form cognitive maps that represent their learning about what (sign) leads to what (significate). His place learning studies suggested that rats learn where food is rather than a series of stimulus-response (S-R) connections. His latent learning studies challenged the law of effect by showing that reinforcement was not necessary for learning. Tolman introduced the distinction between learning (knowing) and performance (doing), and originated the concept of an intervening variable to explain behavior. His work on the inheritance of maze-learning ability in rats contributed to the nascent field of behavior genetics.

Tolman presented his main ideas in *Purposive Behavior in Animals and Men* (1932). His theory of learning as the acquisition of expectancies set him apart from mainstream behaviorism and drew criticism from the S-R contiguity theorist Edwin R. Guthrie for leaving the rat "buried in thought." Tolman's empirical work is reprinted in *Collected Papers in Psychology* (1951).

Tolman's *Drives Toward War* (1942) explored the motivation for war through studies of animal behavior. In defense of academic freedom, he successfully fought the ultimatum issued to faculty on June 14, 1949, by the Regents of the University of California to sign California's loyalty oath or face dismissal.

Tolman died in 1959, leaving a legacy of scholarship that revealed how subjective processes might be the focus of objective scientific investigation.

SOURCES FOR FURTHER STUDY

Bolles, Robert C. *Learning Theory.* 2d ed. New York: Holt, Rinehart and Winston, 1979. Introduction to work by Tolman and his contemporaries, including Edward L. Thorndike and Clark L. Hull.

Gleitman, Henry. "Edward Chace Tolman: A Life of Scientific and Social Purpose." In *Portraits of Pioneers in Psychology*, edited by Gregory Kimble and Michael Wertheimer. Washington, D.C.: American Psychological Association, 1998. Presents the perspective of a former student.

Innis, Nancy K. "Tolman and Tryon: Early Research on the Inheritance of the Ability to Learn." *American Psychologist* 47 (1992): 190-197. Summary of Tolman's work with his student Tryon on breeding maze-bright and maze-dull rats.

Ruth M. Colwill

SEE ALSO: Cognitive psychology; Genetics and mental health; Learning; Memory; Memory: Animal research; Watson, John B.

Touch and pressure

TYPE OF PSYCHOLOGY: Sensation and perception
FIELD OF STUDY: Auditory, chemical, cutaneous, and body senses

Receptors of touch and pressure are mechanoreceptors that convert mechanical energy into the electrical energy of nerve impulses. Touch receptors detect objects coming into light contact with the body surface and allow a person to reconstruct the size, shape, and texture of objects even if they are unseen; pressure receptors detect heavier contacts, weights, or forces and provide a sense of the position of body parts.

KEY CONCEPTS
- adaptation
- expanded-tip tactile receptor
- free nerve ending
- hair end organ
- mechanoreceptor
- Meissner's corpuscle
- Pacinian corpuscle
- proprioception
- Ruffini's end organ
- somatic sensory cortex

INTRODUCTION

The human body is supplied with an abundance of sensory receptors that detect touch and pressure. These receptors are members of a larger group called mechanoreceptors; they are able to detect energy in mechanical form and convert it to the energy of nerve impulses. Mechanoreceptors occur both on body surfaces and in the interior, and they detect mechanical stimuli throughout the body. Touch receptors are located over the entire body surface; pressure receptors are located only under the skin and in the body interior. The two sensations are closely related. A very light pressure on the body surface is sensed by receptors in the skin and is felt as touch. As the pressure increases, mechanoreceptors in and immediately below the skin and at deeper levels are stimulated, and the sensation is felt as pressure.

TYPES OF MECHANORECEPTORS

Several different types of mechanoreceptors are located in the skin and primarily detect touch. One type, known as free nerve endings, consists simply of branched nerve endings without associated structures. Although located primarily in the skin, some mechanoreceptors of this type are also found to a limited extent in deeper tissues, where they detect pressure.

A second mechanoreceptor type, termed Meissner's corpuscles, consists of a ball of nerve endings enclosed within a capsulelike layer of cells. These mechanoreceptors, which are exquisitely sensitive to the lightest pressure, occur in nonhairy regions of the skin, such as the lips and fingertips.

A third mechanoreceptor type, the expanded-tip tactile receptor, occurs in the same nonhairy regions as Meissner's corpuscles and, in smaller numbers, in parts of the skin that are covered with hair. These mechanoreceptors often occur in clusters that are served by branches of the same sensory nerve cell. Meissner's corpuscles and the expanded-tip tactile receptors, working together in regions such as the fingertips, are primarily responsible for a person's ability to determine the size, surface texture, and other tactile features of objects touched.

A fourth type of mechanoreceptor consists of a network of nerve endings surrounding the root of a hair. The combined nerve-hair root structure, called a hair end organ, is stimulated when body hairs are displaced. These mechanoreceptors, because hairs extend from the body surface, give an early warning that the skin of a haired region of the body is about to make contact with an object. The remaining mechanoreceptors of this group are located in

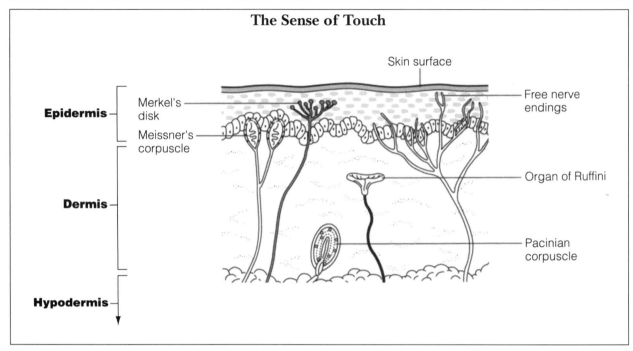

The sensation of touch is produced by special receptors in the skin that respond to temperature and pressure. (Hans & Cassidy, Inc.)

deeper regions of the body; because of their location, they detect pressure rather than touch.

Pacinian corpuscles, which occur just under the skin and in deeper regions of the body, consist of a single sensory nerve ending buried inside a fluid-filled capsule. The capsule is formed by many layers of connective tissue cells, which surround the nerve ending in concentric layers, much like the successive layers of an onion. Pressure displaces the capsule and deforms its shape; the deforming pressure is transmitted through the capsule fluid to the surface of the sensory nerve ending. In response, the sensory nerve generates nerve impulses.

The remaining type of pressure receptor, Ruffini's end organ, consists of a highly branched group of nerve endings enclosed in a capsule. These mechanoreceptors occur below the skin, in deeper tissues, and in the connective tissue capsules surrounding the joints. They detect heavy pressures on the body that are transmitted to deeper layers, and, through their locations in the joints, contribute to proprioception—the sense of the position of the body's limbs.

The various types of mechanoreceptors are believed to convert mechanical energy into the electri-

cal energy of nerve impulses by essentially the same mechanism. In some manner, as yet incompletely understood, the mechanical forces deforming the cell membranes of sensory nerve endings open channels in the membranes to the flow of ions. The ions, which are electrically charged particles, produce the electrical effects responsible for generating nerve impulses.

MECHANORECEPTOR ADAPTATION

The different mechanoreceptor types exhibit the phenomenon of adaptation to varying degrees. In adaptation, the number of nerve impulses generated by a sensory receptor drops off with time if the stimulus remains constant. In the Pacinian corpuscle, for example, which is highly adaptive, adaptation results from flow of the capsule fluid. If pressure against the corpuscle is held at steady levels, deforming the capsule in one direction, the fluids inside the capsule flow in response to relieve the pressure. The new fluid distribution compensates for the applied pressure, and the nerve impulses generated by the Pacinian corpuscle drop in frequency. Any change in the pressure, however, is transmitted through the fluid to the sensory nerve ending before the fluid has a chance to shift in response. As a result, a new volley of nerve impulses is fired by the sensory neuron on a change of pressure until the fluid in the corpuscle shifts again to compensate for the new pressure. In Pacinian corpuscles, compensating movements of the fluid take place within hundredths or even thousandths of a second. Meissner's corpuscles and the hair end organs also adapt quickly.

The expanded-tip tactile receptors and Ruffini's end organs adapt significantly more slowly than the other mechanoreceptors. Expanded-tip tactile receptors adapt initially to a steady touch or pressure but reach a base level at which they continue to generate nerve impulses under steady pressure. The Ruffini's end organs adapt only to a limited extent. The continuing nerve impulses arriving from these mechanoreceptors provide continuous monitoring of a constant stimulus. Thus, some of the mechanoreceptors are specialized to detect changes in touch or pressure and some to keep track of constant stimuli.

MECHANOSENSORY ABILITIES

The combined effects of touch and pressure receptors, along with the varying degrees of adaptation of different receptor types, allow the detection of a range of stimuli, varying from the lightest, most delicate, glancing touch, through moderate pressures, to heavy pressures that stimulate both the body surfaces and interior. People can explore the surface, texture, and shape of objects and can interpret the various levels of touch and pressure so well that they can reconstruct a mental image of objects touched by the fingers with their eyes closed.

Much of this mechanosensory ability depends on the degree to which the different receptor types adapt. The rapid adaptation of Meissner's corpuscles and the hair end organs explains why, if a steady, light to moderate pressure (not heavy enough to cause pain) is maintained on the body surface, the sensation of pressure quickly diminishes. If the pressure is heavy enough to cause pain, a person continues to be aware of the painful sensation, because pain receptors are very slow to adapt. If the degree or location of the pressure is altered, a person again becomes acutely aware of the pressure.

Awareness of continued touch depends primarily on the expanded-tip tactile receptors, which initially adapt but then continue to send nerve impulses when a light surface pressure is held constant. This allows a person to continue to be aware, for example, that some part of the body surface is touching an object. The limited adaptation of Ruffini's corpuscles keeps a person aware of stronger pressures that are felt deeply in the body. Through their locations in joints, these slow-adapting mechanoreceptors also help keep a person continually aware of the positions of the limbs.

The sensory effects of the fast- and slow-adapting mechanoreceptors can be demonstrated by a simple exercise such as pinching the skin on the back of the hand with a steady pressure strong enough to cause only slight pain. The feeling of pressure dissipates rapidly; however, one remains aware of the touch and pain. The rapid dissipation of the sensation of pressure is caused by the fast adaptation of Meissner's corpuscles and any Pacinian corpuscles that may have been stimulated. Some degree of touch sensation is maintained, however, by residual levels of nerve impulses sent by the expanded-tip tactile receptors. The sensation of pain continues at almost steady levels because, in contrast to most of the mechanoreceptors, pain receptors adapt very little. If the pressure is released, the pain stops, and another intense sensation of pressure is felt as all the receptor types fire off a burst of nerve impulses in response to the change.

Mechanoreceptors located at deeper levels keep a person constantly aware of the positions of body parts and the degree of extension of the limbs with respect to the trunk. Ruffini's and Pacinian corpuscles located within the connective tissue layers covering the bones, and within the capsules surrounding the joints, keep track of the angles made by the bones as they are pulled to different positions by the muscles. Ruffini's and Pacinian corpuscles are among the most important mechanoreceptors keeping track of these movements.

MUSCLE SPINDLES AND GOLGI TENDON ORGANS

Touch and pressure receptors represent only a part of the body's array of mechanoreceptors. Other mechanoreceptors located more deeply in the body help monitor the position of body parts and detect the degree of stretch of body cavities.

In addition to the Ruffini's and Pacinian corpuscles detecting the positions of the bones and joints, two further types of mechanoreceptors constantly track the tension developed by the muscles moving the limbs. One is buried within the muscle itself, and one is in the tendons connecting the muscles to the bones. The mechanoreceptors buried within muscles, called muscle spindles, consist of a specialized bundle of five to twelve small muscle cells enclosed within a capsule of connective tissue. Sensory nerve endings surround the muscle cells in a spiral at the midpoint of the capsule and also form branched endings among the muscle cells of the capsule. Because of their position within the muscle spindle, the nerve endings are stretched, and generate nerve impulses, when the surrounding muscle tissue contracts.

The mechanoreceptors of tendons, called Golgi tendon organs, are formed by nerve endings that branch within the fibrous connective tissue cells forming a tendon. The nerve endings of Golgi tendon organs detect both stretch and compression of the tendon as the muscles connected to them move and place tension on the limbs. The combined activities of the deeply located mechanoreceptors keep a person aware of posture, stance, and positions of the limbs. They also allow a person to perform feats such as bringing the thumbs or fingers together behind the back or touching the tip of the nose with the forefinger with the eyes closed.

SOMATIC SENSES

Mechanoreceptors are one of five different types of sensory receptors that also include thermoreceptors, which detect changes in the flow of heat to or from the body; nociceptors, which detect tissue damage and whose nerve impulses are integrated and perceived in the brain as pain; chemoreceptors, which detect chemicals in locations such as the tongue, where they are responsible for the sense of taste, and in the nasal cavity, where they contribute to the sense of smell; and photoreceptors, which detect light. The mechanoreceptors, thermoreceptors, and nociceptors together form what are known as the somatic or body senses.

Sensory nerve tracts originating from mechanoreceptors, particularly those arising from the body surfaces, and their connecting neurons within the spinal cord and the brain are held in highly organized register with one another. Sensory fibers and their connecting nerves originating from the hand, for example, are located in a position near those originating from the wrist. In the cerebral cortex, the organization is retained, so that there is a pro-

jection of the body parts over a part of the cerebrum called the somatic sensory cortex. In this region, which occupies a band running from the top to the lower sides of the brain along anterior segments of the parietal lobes, segments corresponding to major body parts trace out a distorted image of the body from the top of the brain to the sides, with the genitalia, feet, and legs at the top, the arms and hands at the middle region, and the head, lips, tongue, and teeth at the bottom. Sensory information from the right side of the body is received and integrated in the somatic sensory cortex on the left side of the brain, and information from the left side of the body is received and integrated on the right side of the brain. The area of the somatic sensory cortex integrating signals from various body regions depends on the numbers of touch and other sensory receptors in the body regions. The lips and fingers, for example, which are generously supplied with sensory receptors, are represented by much larger areas in the somatic sensory cortex than the arms and legs. Reception and integration of signals in the somatic sensory cortex are partly under conscious control; a person can direct attention to one body part or another and concentrate on the signals arriving from the selected region. The activities of touch, pressure, and other sensory receptors, integrated and interpreted in the somatic sensory cortex, supply people's link to the world around them and supply the information people require to survive and interact with the environment.

SOURCES FOR FURTHER STUDY

Berne, Robert M., and Matthew N. Levy, eds. *Physiology*. 5th ed. St. Louis: C. V. Mosby, 2004. The section on the somatosensory system in this standard college physiology text outlines the anatomy and physiology of the cells and nerve tracts in the spinal column and brain involved in the sensation of temperature and other body sensations. Although the text is intended for students at the college level, it is clearly written and should be accessible to high school readers.

Coren, Stanley. *Sensation and Perception*. 6th ed. Hoboken, N.J.: John Wiley & Sons, 2004. This simply written text provides an easily understood discussion of the senses, sensory cells, and the routes traveled by sensory information through the spinal cord to the brain. A clear and interesting description is provided of the basics of perception in the cerebral cortex.

Guyton, Arthur C., and John E. Hall. *Textbook of Medical Physiology.* 11th ed. Philadelphia: Elsevier Saunders, 2006. This readable and clearly written text includes an excellent discussion of thermoreceptors, the role of the hypothalamus in regulation of body temperature, and medical implications of fever, hyperthermia, and hypothermia. There is also a general description of the structure and function of receptors. Although intended for college and medical students, the text can be easily understood by readers at the high school level.

Schmidt-Nielsen, Knut. *Animal Physiology: Adaptation and Environment.* 5th ed. New York: Cambridge University Press, 1998. This standard college text, by one of the greatest animal physiologists, provides a deeply perceptive comparison of sensory systems in humans and other animals. Chapters 6 and 7 describe temperature effects and temperature regulation. The text is remarkable for its lucid and entertaining descriptions of animal physiology.

Stephen L. Wolfe

SEE ALSO: Hearing; Neurons; Sensation and perception; Senses; Signal detection theory; Smell and taste; Temperature; Visual system.

Tourette's syndrome

TYPE OF PSYCHOLOGY: Psychopathology
FIELD OF STUDY: Nervous system

Tourette's syndrome is classified as a neuropsychiatric disorder because of its roots in neurological functioning, but its prominent features relate to a person's behavior and psychological/psychiatric functioning. The disorder is characterized by motor tics of the face, head, and other extremities that persist for more than one year. There are typically behavioral and cognitive symptoms linked to attention-deficit hyperactivity disorder and obsessive-compulsive disorder.

KEY CONCEPTS
- attention-deficit hyperactivity disorder (ADHD)
- coprolalia
- copropraxia
- echolalia
- incomplete penetrance
- multiple tics
- obsessive-compulsive disorder (OCD)
- variable expressivity

INTRODUCTION

Tourette's syndrome is named for Georges Gilles de la Tourette, the French physician who described the syndrome extensively in 1885. Tourette was the first to describe and publish a case study of a noblewoman who had the disorder. He later identified many of the symptoms that remain associated with the syndrome, including multiple tics, echolalia (the repetition of what is said by other people as if the patient was producing an echo of the other person's speech), and coprolalia (the use of obscene and vulgar language, often in a sexual context). The syndrome is considered to be rare, although estimates suggest it may occur in as many as one in two hundred individuals. Accurate estimates are difficult because of the variability of expression of the condition and the occurrence of multiple tics due to other causes. The incidence of Tourette's syndrome is much higher in children than in adults, and in many cases, motor and vocal tics disappear in adulthood. The incidence of Tourette's syndrome is greater in men than in women, as the generally accepted ratio of male to female patients is 4:1.

The onset of Tourette's syndrome usually occurs in childhood, with the average age of onset being seven years, although cases can occur earlier or later. Typically, the symptoms initially are simple motor tics and progress to more complex motor and vocal tics, although there is considerable variability among patients. The tics often go through periods of waxing and waning, and reach their peak around age ten, after which point they decrease and often disappear in later adolescence.

When Tourette first characterized the syndrome in 1885, he described symptoms in multiple members of a single family. The genetic basis of Tourette's syndrome is still not completely understood, but family studies have indicated that biological relatives of patients appear to have significantly greater risk of developing the syndrome than do relatives of unaffected persons.

Although there is no cure for Tourette's syndrome, medications have been found to be useful in reducing tics and some of the associated abnormal

DSM-IV-TR Criteria for Tourette's Syndrome

TOURETTE'S DISORDER (DSM CODE 307.23)

Both multiple motor and one or more vocal tics (sudden, rapid, recurrent, nonrhythmic, stereotyped motor movements or vocalizations) at some time during the disorder, although not necessarily concurrently

Tics occur many times a day (usually in bouts) nearly every day or intermittently throughout a period of more than one year; during this period, no tic-free periods of more than three consecutive months

Onset before age eighteen

Disturbance not due to direct physiological effects of a substance (such as stimulants) or a general medical condition (such as Huntington's disease or postviral encephalitis)

behaviors. However, many medical practitioners hesitate to prescribe these medications unless symptoms significantly interfere with an individual's day-to-day functioning. Haloperidol is the most well-known medication used to treat Tourette's syndrome.

A surgical procedure called deep brain stimulation (DBS) has yielded promising results by substantially reducing or eliminating tics in affecting individuals. However, this procedure is still experimental and not yet an available or recommended form of treatment.

CLINICAL FEATURES

The presence of motor and vocal tics in young children is not uncommon, occurring in up to 19 percent of children. The type, frequency, and duration of tics are important in classifying the type of disorder that may be affecting a child. The American Psychiatric Association's *Diagnostic and Statistic Manual of Mental Disorders: DSM-IV-TR* (rev. 4th ed., 2000) lists four disorders that involve the presence of motor or vocal tics. Tourette's syndrome is considered as a diagnosis when both motor and vocal tics persist for more than one year. The diagnostic criteria for Tourette's syndrome include multiple motor and one or more vocal tics that have been present at some time during the illness, although not necessarily concurrently. The tics occur many times during a day (usually in bouts), nearly every day or intermittently throughout a period of more than a year. The anatomic location, number, frequency, complexity, and severity of the tics may change over time. There is usually a rostral to caudal movement (from the head to the trunk of the body) of tics that will repeat itself. Onset occurs before the age of eighteen. Occurrence is not exclusively during psychoactive substance intoxication or due to known central nervous system disease, such as Huntington chorea and postviral encephalitis.

The tics that are associated with Tourette's syndrome may be motor tics if movements are involved, or they may be vocal tics if sound is produced. The syndrome commonly begins with facial tics such as blinking, grimacing, and nose twitching. Other involuntary movements may involve head shaking, arm flapping, shoulder shrugging, and foot movements. Head banging and other forms of self-abuse may occur, although these are quite rare. Tics may be simple, as is the case with eye blinking. They may be complex and involve a number of muscle groups, such as jumping up and down or imitating movements of another person. Simple tics tend to be replaced by complex tics, and the severity and frequency of tics tends to wax and wane over time. This can be the most puzzling aspect of the disorder, and research has suggested it is very difficult to predict the course of the tics over time. In some situations, tics are initially mild but become more severe, and in other situations, they may remit for undetermined periods of time. Tics tend to worsen under conditions of stress and tend to subside when the patient is concentrating on some task or activity. Rarely are they present during sleep. As individuals age, it becomes possible to suppress the tics with voluntary effort. A burst of tics generally follows the period of conscious suppression to relieve the mounting inner urge. Some people with Tourette's syndrome have been able to have successful careers as actors, professional athletes, and surgeons.

The most severe aspects of Tourette's syndrome, from a social point of view, are coprolalia and copropraxia (an involuntary use of obscene gestures). Although it is a common belief, it is not correct to think that coprolalia and copropraxia are found in nearly all people with Tourette's syndrome. In fact, coprolalia is found in less than one-third of the cases, and copropraxia is far less common.

Most individuals with Tourette's syndrome have

other mental health concerns, although the severity of these issues varies considerably. The two most common comorbid conditions include attention-deficit hyperactivity disorder (ADHD) and obsessive-compulsive disorder (OCD). Studies have suggested that ADHD occurs in 50 to 60 percent of individuals with Tourette's syndrome and typically develops before the onset of tics. The incidence of OCD and Tourette's syndrome occurs in 30 to 70 percent of cases. OCD symptoms become more evident as the child matures and in many cases become the primary clinical issue in late adolescence and adulthood. The OCD symptoms in individuals with Tourette's syndrome are more often described as sensorimotor compared with individuals with just OCD. That is, individuals with Tourette's syndrome report physical sensations before tics or repetitive behaviors, whereas individuals with OCD describe specific thoughts and anxiety before compulsive behaviors. Although Tourette's syndrome is a chronic disorder, symptoms are usually much more severe in childhood, with the severity of tics peaking by about ten years of age. The tics tend to improve or disappear entirely in more than half of affected adults.

ETIOLOGY

The cause of Tourette's syndrome is not known. It represents a unique diagnosis that involves both neurology and psychiatry. For much of its history, Tourette's syndrome was considered primarily a psychiatric disorder because of the presence of motor and vocal tics and other atpyical behaviors often associated with the syndrome. Psychiatric comorbidity does appear to be a primary feature of Tourette's syndrome, but it is often a secondary consequence of the emotionally disabling physical features. As effective treatment with medications came into use, it became apparent that there was an underlying biochemical basis for the syndrome. The drug haloperidol, which is a dopamine receptor blocker, gave good results in controlling tics, indicating that somehow there was an increased sensitivity of the dopamine system in patients with Tourette's syndrome. Some research suggests that serotonin also plays a role in Tourette's syndrome, but the

primary neurotransmitter of interest is dopamine. Other studies have found some evidence of subtle structural abnormalities in the basal ganglia of the brain. Recent experimental procedures have successfully used deep brain stimulation (DBS) on medial regions of the thalamus, a region with connections to the basal ganglia and brain cortex. The preliminary success of this procedure underscores the basal ganglia as an important brain structure involved in Tourette's syndrome. There have been surprisingly few autopsies to study Tourette's syndrome patients. Both gross and fine anatomical studies have not yielded conclusive findings, but results indicate that multiple structures of the brain may be involved in the syndrome.

Robert Maciunas, a doctor at University Hospital of Cleveland, explains a new surgical technique involving electrode implants for the treatment of Tourette's syndrome. (AP/Wide World Photos)

Although a familiar association of Tourette's syndrome has long been known, two problems have contributed to the difficulty of genetic studies: the problem of variable expressivity and the problem of incomplete penetrance. With variable expressivity, there is a range of phenotypes resulting from a given genotype, and this is very characteristic of Tourette's syndrome, where clinical features range from very mild to very severe. In incomplete penetrance, a genotype that should give rise to a certain expression or phenotype is not expressed at all, and this also seems to be true of Tourette's syndrome. In addition, there is no universal agreement as to what the Tourette syndrome phenotype is. In spite of the limitations, considerable progress has been made in the understanding of the inheritance of Tourette's syndrome.

The agreement between Tourette's syndrome exhibited by both members of monozygotic twins is about 50 percent, compared to 10 percent for dizygotic twins. Since the value for monozygotic twins is less than 100 percent, this indicates that nongenetic and environmental factors play a role in etiology.

Most family studies indicate that Tourette's syndrome is probably due to an autosomal dominant gene with incomplete penetrance. Although simple tics do not seem to have a familial relationship, severe tics do show such a relationship, with relatives of a patient being at an increased risk for tics, if not necessarily severe tics. Relatives of patients also are at increased risks for ADHD and OCD, indicating a possible genetic relationship of the disorders. Although the human genome has been scanned, no single gene has been found that is associated with Tourette's syndrome.

TREATMENT

No medication has been found to eliminate the symptoms of Tourette's syndrome completely. Good progress has been made in using medications in controlling and improving motor and vocal tics and some of the behavioral symptoms. Haloperidol acts as a depressant of the central nervous system and is successful in helping suppress symptoms in many patients. Side effects of haloperidol include drowsiness and alterations in mood, and may be severe enough to limit its use. Also, the effectiveness of haloperidol tends to diminish over time in many patients. Other drugs in use may have fewer side effects than haloperidol, but all drugs may have side effects. If behavioral disorders such as OCD and ADHD present problems, other medications such as risperidone (Risperdal) may need to be prescribed. In general, physicians are reluctant to prescribe medications unless the tics are severe and significantly affecting an individual's daily functioning. The combination of cognitive behavior therapy and medication yields the most significant improvements in children. Other nondrug treatments, such as adaptations to diet, have been recommended.

Since the symptoms of Tourette's syndrome may change over time, it is critical to monitor the levels of medications employed. Since Tourette's syndrome can be a chronic and potentially a socially debilitating disorder, supportive psychotherapy should be available for not only patients but also their families. Until the inheritance of Tourette's syndrome is understood more fully, genetic counseling will continue to be difficult. General information about recurrence risks and gender differences in the incidence of Tourette's syndrome may be transmitted. It also is essential to inform family members and patients of the variability of expression of the disorder in patients and how symptoms may change over time in the same individual.

SOURCES FOR FURTHER STUDY

Brill, Marlene Targ. *Tourette Syndrome.* Brookfield, Conn.: Twenty-first Century Books, 2002. An excellent overview of Tourette's syndrome through the eyes of someone with the disorder. It is well researched and written for a broad audience.

Hayden, Michael R., and Berry Kremer. "Basal Ganglia Disorders." In *Emery and Rimoin's Principles and Practice of Medical Genetics,* edited by David L. Rimoin, J. Michael Connor, and Reed E. Pyeritz. 3d ed. New York: Churchill Livingstone Press, 1996. Reviews basal ganglia disorders that involve involuntary movement syndromes, including Tourette's syndrome.

Hyde, Thomas M., and Daniel R. Weinberger. "Tourette's Syndrome: A Model Neuropsychiatric Disorder." *The Journal of the American Medical Association* 273, no. 6 (1995): 498-501. An overview of Tourette's syndrome with useful information on a case report, genetics, environmental-genetic interactions, and treatment.

Kurlan, Roger, ed. *Handbook of Tourette's Syndrome and Related Tic and Behavioral Disorders.* 2d ed. New York: Marcel Dekker, 2005. An extensive examination of the syndrome that covers its history, associated diagnoses, neurobiology, diagnosis, genetics, and clinical cases.

Kushner, Howard I. *A Cursing Brain? The Histories of Tourette Syndrome.* Cambridge, Mass.: Harvard University Press, 1999. The book examines the history of Tourette's syndrome with exceptionally interesting historical details. There is information concerning the etiology, progression, and treatment of the disorder from the nineteenth century up to the 1980's.

Leckman, James F., and Donald J. Cohen, eds. *Tourette's Syndrome: Tics, Compulsions—Developmental Psychopathology and Clinical Care.* New York: John Wiley & Sons, 1999. A useful book for doctors, students, and families of people with Tourette's syndrome. The book combines basic information and clinical care from neurobiological, developmental, and psychodynamic perspectives.

Shimberg, Elaine. *Living with Tourette's Syndrome.* New York: Simon & Schuster, 1995. A personal account of living with Tourette's syndrome that serves as a good resource for family and individuals with the syndrome.

Donald J. Nash; updated by Martin Mrazik

SEE ALSO: Attention-deficit hyperactivity disorder; Brain structure; Nervous system; Obsessive-compulsive disorder; Parkinson's disease.

Transactional analysis

TYPE OF PSYCHOLOGY: Psychotherapy
FIELDS OF STUDY: Cognitive therapies; humanistic therapies; interpersonal relations

Transactional analysis is a school of psychotherapy and personality theory. Many of TA's key concepts, such as therapeutic contracts, games, and life scripts, have been accepted in the general psychotherapy community.

KEY CONCEPTS
- adult
- child
- decision
- ego state
- games
- life script
- parent
- racket
- stroke

INTRODUCTION

Transactional analysis (TA) is a theory of personality and social interaction originated by Eric Berne in the mid-1950's. TA's popularity has been primarily as a form of psychotherapy and a method for improving social interactions between people in almost any setting—from the group therapy room to business and industry. Berne rejected psychoanalytic therapy, which he considered a type of game called "archaeology," in favor of his own short-term, action-oriented, commonsense approach to psychotherapy. Before entering a group psychotherapy session, Berne would ask himself, "How can I cure everyone in this room today?" In 1964, Berne's book *Games People Play* created a popular interest in a theory of personality and psychotherapy unequaled in the history of psychology; the book sold more than a million copies.

The basic concepts of transactional analysis describe an individual personality and the individual's repetitive patterns of interacting with others. Three distinct ego states compose the individual personality: "parent," "adult," and "child." Berne observed these as distinct phases in his patients' self-presentations. The child ego state within each individual is defined by the feeling, creative, and intuitive part within the person. The child ego state may be approval-seeking or defiant. The fun-loving or "free" side of the child state is curious, spontaneous, and impulsive. Parental discipline, when too harsh or inconsistent, often damages this spontaneous and free child; the adapted child is what then results. The adapted child can have a broken or rebellious spirit and may develop depression or addictions. In either case, the individual, authentic self becomes distorted because of an excessively compliant or defiant adaptation.

The adult ego state is objective and, in a sense, resembles a computer. The adult retrieves, stores, and processes data about physical and social reality. Task-oriented behavior and problem solving are the domain of the adult. If one were trying to build a bridge or do homework, the adult ego state would serve best; however, many problems require the assistance of the intuitive and creative child to be solved most effectively.

The parent ego state is an internalization of one's biological parents or other substitute authority figures in early childhood. The parent state judges, criticizes, and blames. This harsh side of the parent state is the critical parent. In contrast, Berne also recognized the nurturing parent that soothes, encourages, and gently supports the individual. The nurturing parent calls forth the free child, while the critical parent conditions the adapted child. The parent ego state is like a tape recording of the "dos and don'ts" of one's family of origin and culture; it may contain obsolete information. When in the parent state, one may point or shame with an extended index finger or disapproving scowl.

ROLE OF TRANSACTIONS

Transactions are basic units of analysis for the TA therapist. A transaction occurs when one individual responds to the behavior of another. Transactions are called complementary when both persons interact from compatible ego states. For example, a feverish child asks her parent for a glass of water, and the parent complies. A crossed transaction occurs when individuals in incompatible ego states interact. For example, a whining and hungry child asks a parent for an ice cream cone, and the parent (speaking from her adult ego state) reminds the child that it would not be nutritious. The child cannot incorporate the adult data. Another important type of transaction is the ulterior one. An ulterior transaction occurs when the spoken message is undercut by a hidden agenda. To exemplify this, Berne cited a cowboy who asks a woman to leave the dance and go look at the barn with him. The face value of his adult-to-adult question is subtly undercut by a child-to-child sexual innuendo.

Ulterior transactions, when not clearly understood by both parties, lead to "games." A game by definition is a social transaction in which either one or both members of the duo end up feeling "bad." This bad feeling is experienced as a payoff by the game perpetrator; the game pays off by confirming the player's existential life position. For example, the game that Berne called "blemish" involves an existential life position of "I am not OK, you are not OK." In this game, the player exhaustively searches his or her partner for some defect, such as a personality quirk or physical imperfection. Once this de-

fect or blemish is found, the player can hold it up as proof that others are not OK. One thus avoids examining one's own blemish while providing that "others are no good." An example of this can be seen in the chronic bachelor who cannot find a woman who measures up to his perfectionistic standards for marriage.

RACKET FEELINGS AND LIFE SCRIPTS

"Rackets" are the negative feelings that one experiences after a game. Racket feelings are chronic and originate in the early stroking patterns within one's family of origin. In the game of blemish, the player will ultimately feel lonely and sad, while the victim may feel hurt and rejected. Berne compared rackets to stamp collecting: When one collects ten books of brown stamps from playing blemish, they can be cashed in for a divorce or suicide.

Life scripts emerge through repetitive interactions with one's early environment. Messages about what to expect from others, the world, and self become ingrained. A script resembles an actor's role in a drama. An important outcome of one's early scripting is the basic decision one makes about one's existential position. Specifically, the basic identity becomes constellated around feelings of being either OK (free child) or not OK (adapted child). Coping strategies are learned that reinforce the basic decision. Life scripts can often be discovered by asking individuals about their favorite games, heroes, or stories from their childhood. Once individuals become aware of their life scripts, they can be presented with the option of changing them. If a script does not support a person's capacity to be an authentic winner in life, the TA therapist will confront it. TA holds that people are all born to win.

USE IN PSYCHOTHERAPY

Transactional analysis has been applied to the areas of individual and group psychotherapy, couples and family relationship problems, and communication problems within business organizations. This widespread application of TA should not be surprising, since TA's domain is wherever two human beings meet. Berne believed that the playing of games occurs everywhere, from the sandbox to the international negotiation table. Consequently, wherever destructive patterns of behavior occur, TA can be employed to reduce dysfunctional transactions.

TA's most common application is in psychotherapy. The TA therapist begins by establishing a contract for change with his client. This denotes mutual responsibilities for both therapist and client and avoids allowing the client to assume a passive spectator role. The therapist also avoids playing the rescuer role. For example, Ms. Murgatroyd (Berne's favorite hypothetical patient name), an attractive thirty-two-year-old female, enters therapy because her boyfriend refuses to make the commitment to marry her. Her contract with the therapist and group might be that she either will receive a marriage commitment from her boyfriend or will end the relationship. As her specific games and life script are analyzed, this contract might undergo a revision in which greater autonomy or capacity for intimacy becomes her goal.

During the first session, the therapist observes the client's style of interacting. The therapist will be especially watchful of voice tone, gestures, and mannerisms and will listen to her talk about her current difficulties. Since games are chronic and stereotypical ways of responding, they will appear in the initial interview. For example, her dominant ego state might be that of a helpless, whining child looking for a strong parent to protect her. Ms. Murgatroyd may describe her boyfriend in such bitter and negative terms that it is entirely unclear why a healthy adult would want to marry such a man. Discrepancies of this sort will suggest that a tragic script may be operating.

During the first few interviews, the transactional analysis includes game and script analyses. This might require some information about Ms. Murgatroyd's early childhood fantasies and relationships with her parents but would eventually return to her present behavior and relationship. The early history would be used primarily to help the therapist and client gain insight into how these childhood patterns of interacting are currently manifesting. Once the games and script have been clearly identified, the client is in a much better position to change.

After several interviews, in which Ms. Murgatroyd's past and recent history of relationships is reviewed, a pattern of her being rejected is evident. She acknowledges that her existential position is "I am not OK, you are not OK." Her repeated selection of men who are emotionally unavailable maintains her racket feelings of loneliness and frustration. She begins to see how she puts herself in the role of victim. Armed with this new awareness, she is

now in a position to change her script. Through the support of the therapist and the group, Ms. Murgatroyd can learn to catch herself and stop playing the victim.

THERAPIST TECHNIQUES

Berne believed that the original script could best be changed in an atmosphere of openness and trust between the client and therapist. Hence the TA therapist will at all times display respect and concern for his or her client. At the appropriate time in therapy, the therapist delivers a powerful message to the client that serves to counteract the early childhood messages that originally instated the script. Ms. Murgatroyd's therapist, at the proper time, would decisively and powerfully counterscript her by telling her, "You have the right to intimacy!" or "You have the right to take care of yourself, even if it means leaving a relationship." Since the existential life position is supported by lifelong games and scripts, which resist change, TA therapists often employ emotionally charged ways of assisting a client's script redecision.

To catalyze script redecision, a client is guided back in time to the original scene where the destructive message that started the losing life script was received. Simply being told differently by a therapist is not always strong enough to create an emotionally corrective experience that will reverse a life script. Once in the early childhood scene, the client will spontaneously enter the child ego state, which is where the real power to change lies. This time, during the therapeutic regression, the choice will be different and will be for the authentic self.

Ms. Murgatroyd, who is struggling to change an early message, "Don't be intimate," needs to re-experience the feeling she had at the time she first received this message and accepted it from her adapted child ego state. In the presence of the therapist and group, she would role-play this early scene and would tell herself and the significant parent that she *does* have the right to be intimate. These words would probably be spoken amid tears and considerable emotional expression. The parent(s) would be symbolically addressed by her speaking to an empty chair in which she imagines her significant parent sitting: "Whether you like it or not, I'll be intimate!" She would tell herself that it is OK to be intimate. This time she will make a new decision about her script based on her authentic wants and needs, rather than on faulty messages from early childhood. Ms. Murgatroyd's further TA work might involve new contracts with the therapist and group as she integrates her new script into her daily life.

INFLUENCES OF OTHER APPROACHES

The general thesis of TA that current behavior is premised on responses to emotional trauma of early childhood is generally agreed on by most psychologists. Early life experience teaches people a script, a behavioral pattern, which they then repetitively act out in adulthood. Behavioral and humanistic schools alike recognize the formative role that early experiences play in adult behavior patterns; these ideas are not original to TA. TA's contribution is to have created a vocabulary that demystifies many of these ideas and provides a readily learned method of psychotherapy.

Transactional analysis evolved as a form of short-term psychotherapy beginning in the mid-1950's. Berne's early work in groups as a major in the Army during World War II helped him identify the need for both group and short-term therapy. The human growth and potential movement of the 1960's added momentum to the transactional analysis approach. TA's recognition of the innate goodness of the free child prior to the damage of early parental injunctions and self-defeating scripts was consistent with the then-emerging humanistic schools of psychology. Berne began using TA as an adjunct to psychoanalysis, but he eventually rejected the psychoanalytic idea of the dynamic unconscious. Berne's move away from the unconscious and Freudian system paralleled developments in other schools of psychology. Both behavioral psychologists and the cognitive school wished to move away from what they saw as "depth psychology" fictions.

Most of the TA jargon and concepts can be readily seen to correspond to equivalent ones used by other psychologists. Sigmund Freud's constructs of the superego, ego, and id bear a noteworthy similarity to Berne's parent, adult, and child. The superego as the internalized voice of parental and societal values to regulate behavior nearly coincides with Berne's parent ego state. Freud's ego and the adult ego state similarly share the responsibility of solving the individual's problems with a minimum of emotional bias. Freud's id as the instinctual, spontaneous part of the personality shares many characteristics with Berne's child ego state.

Berne's concept of a game's "payoff" is clearly what the behaviorists call a reinforcer. The idea of scripts corresponds to the notion of family role or personality types in other personality theories. For example, an individual with a dominant child ego state would be labeled an orally fixated dependent type in Freudian circles.

INTEREST IN DYSFUNCTIONAL FAMILIES

The psychological role of dysfunctional families has become a topic of conversation for many nonspecialists. The explosion of twelve-step self-help groups has evidenced growing concern about America's mental health; the prominent role of shame and abandonment experiences in early childhood is receiving widespread interest. This surge of interest in making mental health services available to all society is a continuation of what TA practitioners pioneered. It is likely that future developments in the mental health field will draw on the rich legacy of TA.

RESCRIPTING METHODS

Finally, pure transactional analysis as practiced by Berne in the 1960's right before his death has been modified by TA therapists who combine it with emotive and experiential techniques. Many TA therapists found that life scripts failed to change when their clients merely executed new adult decisions. Powerful therapeutic experiences in which the individual regresses and relives painful experiences were necessary. These enable the client to make script redecisions from the child ego state, which proved to be an effective source of change. Future TA therapists are likely to continue enhancing their methods of rescripting by eclectically drawing on new methods of behavior change that go beyond traditional TA techniques. The intuitive child ego state, on which TA therapists freely draw, promises creative developments in this school of psychotherapy.

SOURCES FOR FURTHER STUDY

Berne, Eric. *Games People Play.* 1964. Reprint. New York: Ballantine, 2004. A national best seller that provides a highly readable introduction to the basic ideas of TA and games. Provides an interesting catalog of the most common games played in groups of many kinds. The reader will find that he or she can immediately apply the ideas contained here.

_____. *What Do You Say After You Say Hello?* New York: Grove Press, 1985. This is another excellent primary source for the reader who wants to apply TA to everyday life. Focuses on games and on Berne's final development of his script theory shortly before his death.

Corey, Gerald. *Theory and Practice of Counseling and Psychotherapy.* 8th ed. Belmont, Calif.: Thomson Brooks/Cole, 2009. TA is covered in a brief twenty-five pages but is treated with excellent scholarship. Ideal for the reader who would like a sound overview of TA before moving on to the particular works of Berne. A two-page bibliography is included.

Dusay, J., and K. Dusay. "Transactional Analysis." In *Current Psychotherapies*, edited by Raymond J. Corsini and Danny Wedding. 8th ed. Belmont, Calif.: Thomson Brooks/Cole, 2008. This forty-two-page article contains five pages of bibliography and is cowritten by a leading TA therapist and writer. Thorough and scholarly. The Dusays go into considerable depth in explaining Berne's ideas. Egograms, the drama triangle, and many more key TA concepts are excellently covered. Recommended for the reader who wants a serious introduction to TA.

Goulding, Mary McClure, and Robert L. Goulding. *Changing Lives Through Redecision Therapy.* Rev. ed. New York: Grove, 1997. This three-hundred-page book is written by the two therapists who pioneered the integration of TA with Gestalt therapy. Both Gouldings studied directly with Berne and Fritz Perls. An overview of TA, contracts, and stroking is covered. The clinical use of TA with depression, grieving, and establishing "no suicide contracts" is handled with many case examples and some transcripts of actual sessions. Recommended for the advanced student of TA.

James, Muriel, and Dorothy Jongeward. *Born to Win.* 1971. Reprint. Cambridge, Mass.: Perseus, 1996. Another TA work that became a best seller. An optimistic and humanistic version of TA mixed with Gestalt experiments gives the reader a rich firsthand experience of TA. Contains many experiential and written exercises that enable readers to diagnose their own scripts and rackets. A practical program in how to apply the ideas of TA immediately to improve one's life is provided.

Paul August Rentz

SEE ALSO: Affiliation and friendship; Cognitive therapy; Ego, superego, and id; Existential psychology; Family systems theory; Group therapy; Rational emotive therapy; Self.

Transtheoretical model

DATE: 1980's forward
TYPE OF PSYCHOLOGY: Psychotherapy
FIELDS OF STUDY: Behavioral and cognitive models; behavioral therapies

The transtheoretical model was developed by James O. Prochaska and his colleagues in the 1980's as a way to change behavior, including helping individuals make healthful lifestyle changes. The model has been applied to many risky behaviors including, but not limited to, smoking, obesity, alcohol addiction, and lack of exercise.

KEY CONCEPTS
- action
- contemplation
- maintenance
- precontemplation
- preparation
- stages of change

INTRODUCTION

Changing negative behaviors has been an important interest of psychologists for many years. Psychotherapists have used many strategies with patients to rehabilitate juvenile delinquency, depression, and addictions. In the 1980's, the transtheoretical model was developed by James O. Prochaska in collaboration with Carlo DiClemente and James Norcross. This model was developed not only to guide psychotherapists to positively change behaviors in their patients but also to explain how individuals can change behaviors themselves.

The main premise of the transtheoretical model is that people go through several stages before change occurs. For this reason, the model is also known as the stages of change. An important feature of the model is that regression is as real as progression. Just because individuals move toward a positive behavioral change does not mean that they will not at some point move back in a negative direc-

Original Transtheoretical Model for Behavioral Change

Stages	Characteristics
Precontemplation	No awareness that a problem exists or that a behavioral change is necessary
Contemplation	Realization that behavioral problem exists and a change is necessary
Preparation	Plan for change has been devised; indicates a progression from thinking about a change to enacting one
Action	Behavioral change has been undertaken, but the process is less than six months old
Maintenance	Process of behavioral change passes the six-month mark, indicating consistency and persistence; regression remains a possibility
Termination	Change has taken effect with little or no chance of regression

havior as a problem, they do not have a plan for change. In the preparation stage, people have identified a problem behavior and have developed a plan to make a positive change. The plan may or may not be a good plan. These people have progressed from thinking about starting a change to planning for it.

In the action stage, individuals have implemented the plan and have begun to make the behavioral change. However, the behavior has been changed for less than six months. Once the change has been sustained for more than six months, individuals progress to the maintenance stage. Although people in the maintenance stage have been successful for six months, they are always at risk of reverting back to the negative behavior.

tion. Another characteristic of the model is that strategies used to help people move toward positive behaviors are different at the various stages. Therefore, the objective is to methodically move the person in the positive direction, not jump straight to the positive behavior that the person may not be prepared to sustain.

STAGES OF CHANGE

In the original model, Prochaska and his colleagues identified six stages through which a person must move to fully implement the positive behavioral change: precontemplation, contemplation, preparation, action, maintenance, and termination. After many years of research, the termination stage was dropped because it was determined that changing forever is not guaranteed for those who reach a desired behavioral change. There is always the risk of returning to a negative behavior.

The first stage is precontemplation. Individuals in this stage are not considering a change in a specific behavior. In many cases, these individuals are not aware that their behavior is problematic, nor do they believe there is anything they can do about it. Individuals in the contemplation stage have realized that they have a problem behavior, and they are thinking that they need to make a change in that behavior. While they have identified a specific be-

APPLICATIONS OF THE MODEL

When using the stages of change model, different strategies are used for individuals at different stages. Precontemplators need assistance to make changes. They should not be pushed into action. The focus must be on getting these individuals to realize that a behavioral change is needed and is possible to achieve. When this is accomplished, these individuals become contemplators. The strategy used with contemplators is to prepare them to plan the change by getting them excited about it and getting them to reevaluate themselves. This will help them move into the preparation stage. The key to this stage is commitment. Commitment can be developed by developing a plan of action, setting a date for the change, and letting others know about the planned change. Then these individuals are ready for action. The behavioral change is attempted but not guaranteed. Attention is still needed to substitute good behaviors for those being changed, by controlling the environment that affects the changed behavior and rewarding the individuals for the new behavior. After the behavioral change has been maintained for six months, individuals move to the maintenance stage. The threat of going back to the negative behavior is still real, and interventions are required. Maintaining a positive environment, positive thinking, and using the help of others make maintaining the change more permanent.

SOURCES FOR FURTHER STUDY

Cottrell, Randall R., James T. Girvan, and James F. McKenzie. *Principles and Foundations of Health Promotion and Education.* San Francisco: Pearson Benjamin Cummings, 2009. Discusses the application of the transtheoretical model to the field of health promotion, with a smoking cessation example. Contains a diagram of how the model works.

Edberg, Mark. *Essentials of Health Behavior: Social and Behavioral Theory in Public Health.* Sudbury, Mass.: Jones and Bartlett, 2007. In Chapter 4, the transtheoretical model is discussed and compared to the precaution adoption process model, another model that involves change in stages.

Hayden, Joanna Aboyoun. *Introduction to Health Behavior Theory.* Sudbury, Mass.: Jones and Bartlett, 2009. Discusses many health behavior theories and presents an overview of the transtheoretical model in Chapter 6. It concludes with a research article that uses the model.

Prochaska, James O., John C. Norcross, and Carlo C. DiClemente. *Changing for Good.* New York: Avon Books, 1994. This work, written by the authors of the model for the general public, clearly explains how the model works and presents many of its applications. This publication is designed as a self-help book.

Prochaska, James O., Colleen A. Redding, and Kerry E. Evers. "The Transtheoretical Model and Stages of Change." In *Health Behavior and Health Education,* edited by Karen Glanz, Barbara K. Rimer, and Frances Marcus Lewis. San Francisco: Jossey-Bass, 2002. A detailed description of the transtheoretical model is presented by one of its developers. Provides a long reference list.

Bradley R. A. Wilson

SEE ALSO: Alcohol dependence and abuse; Behavior therapy; Cognitive behavior therapy; Exercise and mental health; Obesity; Positive psychology.

Transvestism

DATE: 1910 forward
TYPE OF PSYCHOLOGY: Psychopathology
FIELD OF STUDY: Sexual disorders

Transvestism is often used to refer to acts of cross-dressing in which men or women wear clothing designed for the other gender. However, in psychology, transvestism is specifically associated with transvestic fetishism, which is properly identified only in heterosexual men who cross-dress in stereotypical female clothing such as dresses and hosiery. The degree of cross-dressing varies from a single undergarment to an entire ensemble, including makeup. Sexual arousal while cross-dressed is a standard feature.

KEY CONCEPTS
- covert sensitization
- cross-dressing
- homosexuality
- paraphilia
- sexual arousal
- transsexualism

INTRODUCTION

As defined in psychology, transvestism (transvestic fetishism) is poorly understood by the public, who often confuse it with homosexuality and transsexualism. Transvestites are heterosexual men, while homosexuals are either men or women sexually attracted to individuals of their own gender. Transsexualism, or gender identity disorder, is when either men or women express discomfort with their biological gender and persistently identify themselves as being, or wishing to be, the other gender.

DSM-IV-TR Criteria for Transvestic Fetishism (DSM code 302.3)

Occurring over a period of at least six months, recurrent, intense sexually arousing fantasies, sexual urges, or behaviors involving cross-dressing in a heterosexual male

The fantasies, sexual urges, or behaviors cause clinically significant distress or impairment in social, occupational, or other important areas of functioning

In psychology, transvestism is marked by sexual arousal. Cross-dressing men, or drag queens such as this man, are not necessarily transvestites by this definition. (©Karen Struthers/Dreamstime.com)

Male cross-dressing is actually common in some societies and is frequently portrayed in entertainment. Some films (such as *Tootsie*, 1982; and *Mrs. Doubtfire*, 1993) and television shows *(Bosom Buddies* and *M*A*S*H)* have featured cross-dressing. Many comedians have used cross-dressing in their acts, including Milton Berle and Dana Carvey. Some men, such as RuPaul, have made a career out of appearing in "drag." These individuals, called "drag queens," cross-dress as performance art. Historically, the Roman emperors Caligula and Nero cross-dressed, and cross-dressing was common on the stage in Shakespearean theater. Men play all the female roles in Kabuki, a traditional type of Japanese theater. Although Caligula and Nero's reasons for cross-dressing are unclear, most examples discussed here would not indicate transvestic fetishism. Actors playing roles or comedians seeking laughs are not transvestites because their motives for cross-dressing are external and not normally associated with sexual arousal. Similarly, drag queens or male homosexuals dressing as females at a costume party are not cross-dressing for sexual arousal.

DETAILS AND POSSIBLE CAUSES

Transvestic fetishism is a paraphilia, a disorder in which intense sexual urges and fantasies center on behaviors or objects other than those seen in typical male-female intercourse. Other paraphilias are exhibitionism and voyeurism. When not cross-dressed, individuals exhibiting transvestic fetishism appear typically male. Many are married and have children, and they cross-dress only in private. However, they typically have few sexual relationships and may have engaged in occasional homosexual behavior. Sexual masochism, the enjoyment of personal suffering, as in bondage, is an associated feature in some people.

The urge to cross-dress typically appears in late childhood or early adolescence. Some researchers suggest a biological predisposition for this disorder, but most explanations involve learned experiences. Many transvestites report experiencing difficult family issues, such as an uncomfortable father-son relationship. Some transvestites report being praised as children for looking "cute" in female clothing, while others were "forced" to wear such clothing as punishment. Certainly, many transvestites masturbated during adolescence while either wearing female garments or with such garments nearby. Because orgasm is a strong reinforcer, associating masturba-

Transvestic fetishism is typically not diagnosed if there are gender identity issues. In rare cases, individuals with transvestic fetishism may develop gender dysphoria, a sense of discomfort with their biological sex. Such individuals sometimes develop a desire to live permanently as women.

The garments that constitute cross-dressing are culturally determined. A Scottish man wearing a kilt is not cross-dressing, even though kilts resemble feminine skirts in other cultures. Also, the mere act of cross-dressing in a man does not necessarily indicate transvestic fetishism or any sexual dysfunction.

tion with female clothing can produce classical conditioned arousal to such clothing.

Cross-dressing increases in frequency for transvestites when they are stressed, and it seems to calm them. The sexual arousal aspect also decreases as many transvestites age, without lessening the cross-dressing urge. Cross-dressing apparently helps some individuals escape the strictures of the traditional male role. Therefore, more than just sexual arousal may be involved. Other than a tendency toward introversion and inhibition in relationships, the personality profiles for transvestites and nontransvestites are typically indistinguishable.

TREATMENT ISSUES

Unlike many paraphilias, transvestic fetishism has little potential to cause physical harm to the individual or others. However, transvestites often feel guilty about their behavior, and it can damage their sexual relationships, especially if wives or girlfriends do not approve. In addition, men cross-dressing as women is illegal in some jurisdictions, and cross-dressers appearing in public may face legal risks.

Most therapies used with transvestites are based on learning model explanations for the disorder. Some therapists have claimed success by strengthening the individual's confidence and adequacy in male sex roles. Attempts to pair cross-dressing with electrical shock in aversive conditioning procedures have been relatively unsuccessful. Covert sensitization, in which the individual first imagines engaging in the desired behavior of cross-dressing, then vividly visualizes humiliating outcomes for doing so, has been more successful. The negative visualization counters the reinforcing arousal of cross-dressing with a punishing emotional state, thus decreasing sexual excitement. However, most individuals with transvestic fetishism do not want to change, and the general prognosis is poor.

SOURCES FOR FURTHER STUDY

Bloom, Amy. *Normal.* New York: Random House, 2002. Contains a lengthy chapter on transvestism. Bloom interviewed numerous cross-dressers and their wives. Includes a bibliography.

Bullough, Vern L., and Bonnie Bullough. *Cross Dressing, Sex, and Gender.* Philadelphia: University of Pennsylvania Press, 1993. Includes historical information and discusses different types of cross-dressing and the relevance for various gender disorders. Reports the results of numerous research studies.

Rudd, Peggy J. *My Husband Wears My Clothes: Cross-dressing from the Perspective of a Wife.* 2d ed. Katy, Tex.: PM, 1999. A personal account of living with a transvestite. Answers questions that family members and friends might have. In part, takes a counseling approach for family members.

Stryker, Susan, and Stephen Whittle, eds. *The Transgender Studies Reader.* New York: Routledge, 2006. Collects many essays on gender issues, including transvestism. Also includes articles on other gender disorders and gender issues, which provides a context for understanding transvestism.

Suthrell, Charlotte A. *Unzipping Gender: Sex, Cross-Dressing, and Culture.* New York: Berg, 2004. A cross-cultural look at transvestism, including cultures where it is more accepted.

Charles A. Gramlich

SEE ALSO: Aversion therapy; Behavior therapy; Body dysmorphic disorder; Fetishes; Gay, lesbian, bisexual, and transgender mental health; Gender identity disorder; Homosexuality; Sexual variants and paraphilias.

Type A behavior pattern

TYPE OF PSYCHOLOGY: Stress
FIELD OF STUDY: Stress and illness

The Type A behavior pattern has been related to coronary artery disease; individuals who exhibit the Type A behavior pattern have been shown to be at a greater risk of coronary artery disease in some studies.

KEY CONCEPTS
- hard-driving behavior
- hurry sickness
- job involvement
- speed and impatience
- stress

INTRODUCTION

The Type A behavior pattern, often simply called the Type A personality, identifies behaviors which have been associated with coronary artery disease.

Although these behaviors appear to be stress related, they are not necessarily involved with stressful situations or with the traditional stress response. Instead, the behaviors are based on an individual's thoughts, values, and approaches to interpersonal relationships. In general, Type A individuals are characterized as ambitious, impatient, aggressive, and competitive. Individuals who are not Type A are considered Type B. Type B individuals are characterized as relaxed, easygoing, satisfied, and non-competitive.

Cardiologists Meyer Friedman and Ray H. Rosenman began work on the Type A behavior pattern in the mid-1950's. It was not until the completion of some retrospective studies in the 1970's, however, that the concept gained credibility. During the 1950's, it was noticed that younger and middle-aged people with coronary artery disease had several characteristics in common. These included a hard-driving attitude toward poorly defined goals; a continuous need for recognition and advancement; aggressive and at times hostile feelings; a desire for competition; an ongoing tendency to try to accomplish more in less time; a tendency to think and act faster and faster; and a high level of physical and mental alertness. These people were classified as "Pattern A" or "Type A."

CORRELATION TO HEART DISEASE

Following their work on identifying the characteristics of the Type A personality or behavior pattern, Friedman and Rosenman began conducting studies to determine if it might actually cause coronary artery disease. First they conducted several correlational studies to determine if there was a relationship between the Type A behavior pattern and metabolic function in humans. They found that healthy persons with the Type A behavior pattern had elevated levels of fat in the blood (serum cholesterol and triglycerides), decreased blood-clotting time, increased catecholamine secretion (which increases heart contractility) during normal work hours, and decreased blood flow to some tissues. These studies indicated that the Type A behavior pattern may precede coronary artery disease.

Following these studies, Friedman, Rosenman, and their research team initiated the Western Collaborative Group Study in 1960. This large study, which went on for more than eight years, attempted to determine if the presence of the Type A behavior

pattern increased the risk of coronary artery disease. The results of Rosenman and Friedman's study in 1974 indicated that the subjects with the Type A pattern had more than twice the incidence of the disease than subjects with the Type B pattern. More specifically, Type A individuals (when compared to Type B individuals) were twice as likely to have a fatal heart attack, five times more likely to have a second heart attack, and likely to have more severe coronary artery disease (of those who died). These results were found when other known risk factors, such as high blood pressure, smoking, and diet, were held constant. This study was followed by numerous other studies that linked coronary artery disease to the Type A behavior pattern. In 1978, the National Heart, Lung, and Blood Institute sponsored a conference on the Type A behavior pattern. As a result of the Review Panel on Coronary-Prone Behavior and Coronary Heart Disease, a document was released in 1981 that stated that the Type A behavior pattern is related to increased risk of coronary artery disease.

IDENTIFYING TYPE A BEHAVIOR

Another product of the Western Collaborative Group Study was a method for assessing the Type A behavior pattern, developed by Rosenman in 1978. This method was based on a structured interview. A predetermined set of questions was asked of all participants. The scoring was based on the content of the participants' verbal responses as well as their nonverbal mannerisms, speech style, and behaviors during the interview process. The interview can be administered in fifteen minutes. Because the interview was not a traditional type of assessment, however, many interviewers had a difficult time using it.

In an effort to simplify the process for determining Type A behavior, many self-report questionnaires were developed. The first developed and probably the most-used questionnaire is the Jenkins Activity Survey, which was developed by C. David Jenkins, Stephen Zyzanski, and Rosenman in 1979. This survey is based on the structured interview. It gives a Type A score and three related subscores. The subscores include speed and impatience, hard driving, and job involvement. The Jenkins Activity Survey is a preferred method, because the questionnaire responses can be tallied to provide a quantitative score. Although this instrument is easy to use and provides consistent results, it is not considered as good as the structured interview because many believe the Type A characteristics can best be identified by observation.

The Type A behavior pattern continues to be studied, but research appears to have reached a peak in the late 1970's and early 1980's. Researchers are challenging the whole concept of coronary-prone behavior, because many clinical studies have not shown high correlations between the Type A behavior pattern and the progression of coronary artery disease. Other risk factors for coronary artery disease, such as smoking, high blood pressure, and high blood cholesterol, have received increasing attention.

BIOCHEMICAL AND PHYSIOLOGICAL MECHANISMS

The Type A behavior pattern, or personality, has been used to explain in part the risk of coronary artery disease; however, many risk factors for the disease have been identified. Since the various risk factors interact with one another, it is difficult to understand any one risk factor clearly.

Efforts have been made to explain the mechanism by which the Type A behavior pattern affects coronary artery disease. It has been theorized that specific biochemical and physiological events take place as a result of the emotions associated with Type A behavior. The neocortex and limbic system of the brain delivers emotional information to the hypothalamus. In a situation that arouses the Type A characteristics, the hypothalamus will cause the pituitary gland to stimulate the release of the catecholamines epinephrine and norepinephrine (also known as adrenaline and noradrenaline) from the adrenal glands, as well as other hormones from the pituitary itself. These chemicals will enter the blood and travel throughout the body, causing blood cholesterol and fat to increase, the ability to get rid of cholesterol to decrease, the ability to regulate blood sugar levels to decrease (as with diabetics), and the time for the blood to clot to increase. This response by the body to emotions is normal. The problem with Type A individuals arises because they tend to maintain this heightened emotional level almost continually, and the constant release of pituitary hormones results in these negative effects on the body being continuous as well.

The connection between Type A behavior and coronary artery disease actually results from the continuous release of hormones controlled by the pituitary gland. Through complex mechanisms, the constant exposure to these hormones causes several problems. First, cholesterol is deposited on the coronary artery walls as a result of the increase in blood cholesterol and the reduced ability to rid the blood of the cholesterol. Second, the increased ability of the blood to clot results in more clotting elements being deposited on the arterial walls. Third, clotting elements can decrease blood flow through the small capillaries that feed the coronary arteries, resulting in further complications with the cholesterol deposits. Fourth, increased insulin in the blood further damages the coronary arteries. Therefore, the reaction of the pituitary gland to the Type A behavior pattern is believed to be responsible for the connection with coronary artery disease.

MODIFICATION TECHNIQUES

Fortunately, it is believed that people with the Type A behavior pattern can modify their behavior to reduce risk of coronary artery disease. As with many health problems, however, denial is prevalent. Therefore, it is important that Type A individuals become aware of their problem. In general, Type A individuals need to focus on several areas. These include hurry sickness, speed and impatience, and hostility.

Type A individuals try to accomplish more and more in less and less time (hurry sickness). Unfortunately, more is too often at the expense of quality, efficiency, and, most important, health. Type A individuals need to make fewer appointments related to work, and they need to schedule more relaxation time. This includes not starting the day in a rush by getting out of bed barely in time to get hurriedly to work. Finally, Type A individuals need to avoid telephone and other interruptions when they are working, because this aggravates hurry sickness. Therefore, it is recommended that individuals who suffer from hurry sickness avoid scheduling too much work; take more breaks from work (relaxation), including a lunch hour during which work is not done; and have calls screened to get blocks of working time.

Type A individuals typically do things rapidly and are impatient. For example, they tend to talk rapidly, repetitiously, and narrowly. They also have a hard time with individuals who talk slowly, and Type A individuals often hurry these people along by finishing their sentences. Additionally, Type A individuals try to dominate conversations, frequently focusing the discussion on themselves or on their interests. In an effort to moderate speed and impatience, Type A individuals need to slow down, focus their speech in discussions to the specific problem, and cut short visits with individuals who waste their time. They should spend more time with individuals who enhance their opportunities.

The other area is hostility, or harboring destructive emotions. This is highly related to aggressiveness. Aggressive Type A individuals must learn to use their sense of humor and not look at situations only as challenges set up to bother or to upset them. One way to accomplish this is for them consciously to attempt to socialize with Type B individuals. Obviously, this is not always possible, since Type A individuals have certain other individuals with whom they must associate, such as colleagues at work and certain family members. Nevertheless, Type A individuals must understand their hostilities and learn to regulate them. In general, Type A individuals must learn to control their feelings and relationships. They must focus more attention on being well-rounded individuals rather than spending most of their time on work-related successes. Type A individuals can learn the Type B behavior pattern, resulting in a lower risk for coronary artery disease.

BEHAVIOR PATTERN VERSUS PERSONALITY

Since Friedman and Rosenman defined the Type A behavior pattern in the 1950's, many researchers have studied the Type A behavior pattern. Initially, most of the researchers were cardiologists. Gradually, more and more psychologists have become involved with Type A research.

Since the concept of relating coronary heart disease with human behavior was developed by cardiologists instead of psychologists, it was initially called the Type A behavior pattern rather than the Type A personality. "Personality" relates to an individual's inner traits, attitudes, or habits and is very complex and generally studied by psychologists. As Type A was defined, however, it only related specific behaviors with disease and was observed openly. Therefore, it seemed appropriate to label Type A a behavior pattern. Over the years, Type A has been assumed to be a personality; technically, this is not accurate, although many people now refer to it as the Type A personality.

Another reason Type A is most accurately considered a behavior pattern rather than a personality relates to the way it is assessed. Whether the structured interview or the written questionnaire is utilized, a predetermined set of questions and sequence is used. While this approach can assess a behavior pattern adequately, different skills, which allow the interviewer to respond appropriately to an individual's answers and probe specific responses further, are needed to assess personality.

CONTRIBUTIONS AND FUTURE RESEARCH

The Type A behavior pattern was originally identified as a risk factor for coronary artery disease. The original need for this idea was not psychologically based. Instead, it was based on a need to understand further the factors that are involved with the development of coronary artery disease, a major cause of death. Therefore, the role of the Type A behavior pattern in psychology has been limited. Nevertheless, Type A studies have benefitted humankind's understanding of an important disease and, to a certain extent, the understanding of psychology.

The future study of the Type A behavior pattern is in question. Research continually shows conflicting results about its role in coronary artery disease. As more research is conducted by both medical clinicians and psychologists, the true value of the Type A behavior pattern will become evident. Until then, health care professionals will continually have to evaluate the appropriateness of using the Type A behavior pattern as an identifier of the risk of artery or heart disease.

SOURCES FOR FURTHER STUDY

Chesney, Margaret A., and Ray H. Rosenman, eds. *Anger and Hostility in Cardiovascular and Behavior Disorders.* Washington, D.C.: Hemisphere, 1985. Integrating psychology and the Type A behavior pattern, this book provides in-depth information on the technical aspects of behavior. Although some portions of the book are technical, the introductions to each chapter provide historical and nontechnical information related to the broader topic of behavior.

Friedman, Meyer. *Type A Behavior: Its Diagnosis and Treatment.* New York: Springer, 2008. The physician who first identified Type A behavior and its relation to cardiovascular illnesses provides an overview of the treatments he has used in his Recurrent Coronary Prevention Program.

Houston, B. Kent, and C. R. Snyder, eds. *Type A Behavior Pattern: Research, Theory, and Intervention.* New York: John Wiley & Sons, 1988. Contains thirteen chapters by various authors. The first three chapters nicely introduce the topic in relatively simple terms. Subsequent chapters tend to be more technical and require a better background for understanding. A wealth of references is listed throughout.

Price, Virginia Ann. *Type A Behavior Pattern.* New York: Academic Press, 1982. A good technical resource for Type A behavior. Very comprehensive.

The introductory chapters provide the nontechnical reader with valuable, understandable information. More than three hundred references are listed at the end of the book.

Bradley R. A. Wilson

SEE ALSO: Aggression; Aggression: Reduction and control; Biofeedback and relaxation; Coping: Social support; Environmental psychology; Fight-or-flight response; General adaptation syndrome; Health psychology; Stress: Physiological responses; Stress-related diseases.

V

Violence and sexuality in the media

TYPE OF PSYCHOLOGY: Social psychology
FIELD OF STUDY: Aggression

The American mass media, especially films and television, contain high levels of violence. In some pornography, violence is presented in a sexual context. The consensus among social scientists, based on both laboratory experiments and field studies, is that nonsexual and sexual violence causes aggressive behavior in the audience but that nonviolent pornography does not.

KEY CONCEPTS
- aggression machine
- aggressive cues
- arousal
- catharsis hypothesis
- desensitization
- disinhibition
- excitation transfer
- imitation
- mean world syndrome
- priming
- rape myths
- script

INTRODUCTION

The world of the American mass media is much more violent than the real world. Communication researcher George Gerbner has found that approximately 80 percent of television programs contain some violence, for an average of almost ten violent acts per hour. Some prime-time television programs and R-rated action films contain as many as 50 to 150 violent acts per hour. Cartoons average 25 violent acts per hour. It has been estimated that by the age of eighteen, the average American has witnessed 100,000 acts of violence, including 25,000 killings, on television alone. There are many cases of direct copying of media violence. For example, at least twenty-eight people have killed themselves in apparent imitation of the Russian roulette scene in the film *The Deer Hunter* (1978). Reactions to such anecdotal evidence, however, must be tempered by the knowledge that many millions of people have seen these programs and films.

In the early 1960's, psychologist Leonard Berkowitz devised a laboratory procedure to study the effects of filmed violence on aggressive behavior. In a typical experiment, subjects are made angry by a confederate or accomplice of the experimenter. They then watch a ten-minute film clip containing a high level of violence (a boxing match) or an equally exciting control film (a foot race). Finally, subjects are permitted to evaluate the confederate's work using an "aggression machine," an apparatus that they think delivers electric shocks to the confederate. Results of these studies consistently show that subjects who have seen a violent film deliver longer and more intense shocks than control subjects do. This experiment has been repeated at least 150 times with the same results, making its findings among the most reliable in social psychology. Similar effects have been found with other measures of verbal and physical aggression.

Four variables have been shown to influence the amount of imitation of media violence. First, the more realistic the portrayal of violence, the greater the imitation. The same violence is more effective when presented as a real event than as fiction. "Aggression cues," or points of similarity between the filmed violence and the subject's real-life experience, such as a weapon or a character's name, can increase aggression. Second, more imitation occurs when violence is presented as justified. Violence committed by the hero in revenge for previous harm produces greater imitation than violence that is unfair to the victim. Third, imitation increases when violence is effective—that is, when aggressors are rewarded with wealth, happiness, and social approval. Fourth, imitation is more likely when the viewer is in a psychological state of readiness to aggress—for example, when he or she is emotionally aroused or angry. Anger, however, is not a necessary condition for imitation of violence.

Critics have argued that laboratory studies of aggression are so different from everyday experience that the results are not generalizable to the real world. This skepticism produced a second generation of studies using field-research methodologies. These included correlational studies in which subjects' exposure to violent programs was related to ratings of their aggressiveness by parents, teachers, or peers; field studies in which the exposure of institutionalized boys to media violence was controlled and physical and verbal aggression was observed; "natural experiments" in which communities or nations that were slow to receive television were compared with others that received it sooner; and archival studies of the effects of highly publicized suicides or homicides on the suicide or homicide rate. Although the results of these studies are not as clear as those of laboratory experiments, they have generally supported the hypothesis.

In summary, there is substantial evidence from studies using a variety of research methods converging on the conclusion that filmed and televised violence increases aggression. Although any single study can be criticized on methodological grounds, there are no convincing alternative explanations for all of them.

Media violence can affect attitudes as well as behavior. The prevalence of crime and violence on television appears to cultivate a "mean world syndrome." For example, heavy viewers are more likely than infrequent viewers to overestimate the frequency of crime. It is not clear, however, whether television causes these attitudes or pessimistic and fearful people are more attracted to television.

PORNOGRAPHY EFFECTS

Laboratory research on the effects of pornography has used procedures similar to those of aggression research. In several studies, male subjects were angered by a female confederate. They watched either violent pornography (a sexually explicit rape scene) or a control film. The men who saw the rape film showed more violence against women than did control subjects. Violent pornography, however, contains two distinct variables that might plausibly be related to aggression: violence and sexual explicitness. To determine whether either or both contribute to aggression, it is necessary to compare four conditions: sex plus violence (a sexually explicit rape scene), violence only (a nonexplicit rape scene), sex only (sexually explicit but with willing participants), and a control film. Researchers who have made this comparison find that the sex-plus-violence and violence-only conditions increase aggression toward women (to about the same degree), but nonviolent pornography does not usually produce any more aggression than a control film. This suggests that the effect of violent pornography is a special case of the well-established effect of filmed violence. Nonviolent pornography does not increase aggression. This is important, because only a small percentage of pornography—for example, about 15 percent of pornography videotapes—contains violence.

Studies show that men exposed to violent (and, in some cases, nonviolent) pornography in laboratory experiments show undesirable changes in attitude. They are more likely to endorse rape myths, such as the belief that women secretly enjoy being raped. They recommend less severe punishment for the defendant in a hypothetical rape trial, suggesting that they regard rape as a less serious crime. There is no evidence, however, that these attitudes are directly related to the likelihood of raping someone. It should be noted that these attitude changes are small and temporary and that similar effects have been obtained with nonpornographic violence, such as R-rated "mad slasher" films.

Field research on the effects of pornography falls into two categories. Some researchers have examined the relationship between the availability of pornography and the incidence of reported rape in various locales. Others have interviewed convicted sex offenders to see whether they differ from nonoffenders in their history of exposure to pornography. Both approaches have produced mixed results, suggesting that, at most, pornography plays a minor role in sexual assault once alternative explanations have been removed.

AN ONGOING DEBATE

The effects of media violence have been vigorously debated for several decades. Televised violence is of special concern because of its vivid and realistic nature and its easy accessibility to children. The most extensive government investigation of the effects of television on children was the 1972 Surgeon General's Scientific Advisory Committee on Television and Social Behavior, which conducted forty scientific studies. It concluded that television can cause aggression, but the committee's report contained so many qualifications that it was widely perceived as indicating that television is not really an important cause of aggressive behavior. This ambiguity may have resulted from the fact that the television networks were allowed to appoint five of the twelve commissioners and to blackball several proposed members. A 1982 update by the National Institute of Mental Health stated more directly that television violence is indeed a cause of aggression. In spite of these investigations and the lobbying of pressure groups such as Action for Children's Television, the amount of violence on television has changed little since the late 1960's. The television networks believe (with some justification) that violent programs are more popular, and they have considerable power to resist governmental regulation.

Pornography in all media, from print to film to the Internet, has also been an issue of great concern to the American public. The country's ambivalence about media sexuality is illustrated by the contrasting recommendations of two government commissions. The 1970 Commission on Obscenity and Pornography consisted primarily of social scientists. It funded nineteen original studies (all of nonviolent pornography) and concluded that pornography had no proven harmful effects. Political reaction to the report was primarily negative. In 1986, President Ronald Reagan appointed the Attorney General's Commission on Pornography (the Meese Commission), consisting primarily of antipornography activists with little social scientific background. The Meese Commission came to the following conclusions: Violent pornography causes aggression toward women and harmful attitude change; nonviolent pornography that is degrading to women (although the report was not very clear about what "degrading" means) does not cause aggressive behavior but produces harmful attitude change; and nonviolent and nondegrading pornography has no specific negative effects, although certain moral and aesthetic harms were claimed. In spite of the different effects attributed to each type, the commission concluded that all pornography should be banned and proposed ninety-two recommendations for doing so.

Social scientists criticized the Meese Commission for failing to define categories of pornography clearly, for biased selection and presentation of research, for not distinguishing between low- and high-quality evidence, and for obscuring differences between the effects of violent and nonviolent pornography.

Attempts to regulate media violence and pornography would appear to be in conflict with the First Amendment to the United States Constitution, which states that "Congress shall make no law . . . abridging the freedom of speech, or of the press." The courts have historically permitted many exceptions to the First Amendment, however, and there is a long history of legal censorship of news and entertainment media. Social scientists disagree on whether there is enough evidence of antisocial effects of violence or pornography to justify censorship. Many social scientists would insist, however, that the Constitution places a strong burden of proof on the censor, that a much stronger case could be made for censorship of violence (including violent pornography) than of nonviolent pornography, and that attempts to censor media content because it is alleged to produce "bad attitudes" are in conflict with the free marketplace of ideas model assumed by the Constitution.

While social scientists see media violence as more harmful than pornography, the American public favors censorship of nonviolent pornography more than of violence. This suggests that people underestimate the effects of media violence, overestimate the effects of nonviolent pornography, or object to pornography for reasons other than its alleged harmful effects.

PSYCHOLOGICAL MODELS

Two early psychological approaches to the study of aggression made different predictions about the effects of media violence. Instinct and drive theories of aggression suggested that watching media violence would provide a catharsis, or release of aggressive energy, which would reduce the likelihood of subsequent aggression. Social learning theory proposed that much of one's knowledge of how to behave comes from observing and sometimes imitating the behavior of others. Exposure to media violence would be expected to increase aggression. The majority of research has supported the social learning theory position.

There are several contemporary explanations for

the effects of media violence. The imitation approach emphasizes the direct transmission of information about when, why, and how to commit aggressive behaviors. This theory accounts for copycat aggression but has difficulty explaining more general effects. The disinhibition approach points out that adults already know how to aggress, and that media violence reduces restraints that would normally cause people to inhibit their aggressive impulses by suggesting that aggression is socially acceptable. The arousal and desensitization approaches suggest that watching violence will have different short- and long-term effects. In the short run, violence is exciting and increases physiological arousal, which can spill over and energize real aggressive behavior. This effect would appear to be temporary. In the long run, each exposure produces progressively less arousal, called desensitization. This implies that a steady diet of media violence can make people indifferent to the pain and suffering of victims and increase their tolerance of real violence.

In the 1970's and 1980's, cognitive theories became more popular in psychology. The cognitive priming approach proposes that media violence increases the availability of aggressive thoughts in the viewer for as long as several days, and these thoughts increase the probability of aggressive behavior. A related approach suggests that media portrayals contribute to the formation and maintenance of aggressive behavioral scripts, which are later activated by real situations similar to those observed in the media.

The effects of violent pornography can be explained by the same theories that explain the effects of general film violence. Those who claim that nonviolent pornography causes aggression are faced with the problem of explaining how nonaggressive content (sexuality) can activate aggressive behavior. A variation on arousal theory, the excitation transfer theory, suggests that the physiological arousal caused by pornography can subsequently be confused with anger and can energize aggression. Any source of arousal, such as music or exercise, can have this effect if the timing is right. This theory predicts very subtle, temporary effects of exposure to pornography, and, as noted, research does not consistently support it.

Effects of aggression and pornography on attitudes can be explained on the basis of theories of attitude change, which show that, not surprisingly, almost any media presentation produces small, temporary changes of attitude in the direction advocated by its author. Resistance to attitude change occurs when the audience has the information and the motivation to argue with the media effectively.

SOURCES FOR FURTHER STUDY

Donnerstein, Edward I., Daniel Linz, and Steven Penrod. *The Question of Pornography*. New York: Free Press, 1987. Review of laboratory research on effects of pornography. Distinguishes between the proven antisocial effects of violent pornography and the more speculative claims against nonviolent pornography. Accessible to the general reader.

Huesmann, L. Rowell, and Neil M. Malamuth. "Media Violence and Antisocial Behavior." *Journal of Social Issues* 42, no. 3 (1986): 125-139. This article is in a special issue of a psychological journal containing eleven articles that summarize the effects of media violence and pornography.

Joy, Leslie A., Meredith M. Kimball, and Merle L. Zabrack. "Television and Children's Aggressive Behavior." In *The Impact of Television*, edited by Tannis MacBeth Williams. Orlando, Fla.: Academic Press, 1986. Presents a study of the effects of the introduction of cable television in an isolated community in western Canada on the aggressive behavior of its children.

Kirsh, Steven J. *Children, Adolescents, and Media Violence: A Critical Look at the Research*. Thousand Oaks, Calif.: Sage, 2006. A review of the research literature on effects of media violence on young people. The author identifies some critical age gaps in the research.

Liebert, Robert M., and Joyce Sprafkin. *The Early Window: Effects of Television on Children and Youth*. 3d ed. Elmsford, N.Y.: Pergamon, 1988. Excellent overview of the socializing effects of television. Discusses the effects of televised violence and the politics of governmental regulation of television content.

Signorelli, Nancy, and George Gerbner, comps. *Violence and Terror in the Mass Media: An Annotated Bibliography*. New York: Greenwood Press, 1988. Citations and paragraph-length summaries of 784 studies of violent media content and its effects. Very helpful when doing a literature survey.

Trend, David. *The Myth of Media Violence: A Critical Introduction.* Malden, Mass.: Wiley-Blackwell, 2007. Reviews the decades-long debates over whether media violence is harmful. Despite an army of critics arrayed against media violence—on television, in films, and in video games—media violence has proliferated.

Zillmann, Dolf, and Jennings Bryant, eds. *Pornography: Research Advances and Policy Considerations.* Hillsdale, N.J.: Lawrence Erlbaum, 1989. Fifteen papers dealing with the content and effects of pornography and the legal debate over pornography regulation. Papers are sometimes difficult but are generally rewarding.

Lloyd K. Stires

SEE ALSO: Aggression; Aggression: Reduction and control; Attitude-behavior consistency; Attitude formation and change; Children's mental health; Sexism; Social learning: Albert Bandura; Social schemata; Violence: Psychological causes and effects.

Violence by children and teenagers

TYPE OF PSYCHOLOGY: Developmental psychology; emotion; personality; psychopathology; social psychology

FIELDS OF STUDY: Adolescence; aggression; attitudes and behavior; childhood and adolescent disorders; infancy and childhood; interpersonal relations; personality disorders; social perception and cognition; substance-related issues

Some children and teenagers commit acts of violence on their families, peers, authority figures, or strangers. Such antisocial behavior may result from psychiatric disorders or social catalysts.

KEY CONCEPTS
- aggression
- antisocial behavior
- predatory violence
- psychopathological violence
- relational violence
- situational violence

INTRODUCTION

Some children and teenagers prey on vulnerable people, exhibiting antisocial behavior, neurological dysfunctions, and mental illnesses. These youths may assault other children or adults for a variety of reasons, ranging from invoking fear as a form of entertainment to causing bodily harm as retribution for perceived wrongs such as social ostracism.

Youth crimes doubled during the late 1980's and early 1990's and included shocking crimes that exceeded those committed by previous generations. Although homicide rates for teenage perpetrators began to decline in the United States by 1997, youth violence remained an urgent issue. By the beginning of the twenty-first century, violent youths were committing callous acts at increasingly younger ages. They also behaved more extremely with regard to weapons used or number of victims attacked during violent sprees. Crimes such as school shootings targeted individuals both known and unfamiliar to perpetrators.

WHO IS VIOLENT?

Violent youths represent varying social classes and ethnicities, living in both rural and urban areas. Young males are twice as likely to act violently outside the home than are young females, but both genders are equally likely to be violent toward their families. Violent tendencies sometimes emerge when children are toddlers. Aggressive children may fight with other youngsters, act up in class, challenge authority figures, or steal. Some sadistically abuse animals. Such aberrant behaviors can intensify during adolescence.

Researchers offer contrasting theories about why some youths become violent. Violent youths may suffer from severe mental illnesses, display disruptive behavior disorders or antisocial personalities, or have experienced brain damage. Some researchers suggest that brain circuits containing the neurotransmitter serotonin have malfunctioned in violent youths. A few researchers speculate that some infants have innate repressed violent characteristics that develop when the child encounters biological or psychological triggers, such as sexual or physical abuse, illegal substances, or peer pressure.

Authorities agree that many violent children and teenagers have been exposed to violence in their homes or communities. Inadequate or abusive parenting can prevent children from learning appropriate values of right and wrong. Neglected or

In 1999, police stand outside the east entrance of Columbine High School, where two students killed fellow students. This incident prompted many studies of why teenagers become violent. (Getty Images)

abused children can feel emotionally abandoned and become self-centered. Egocentric youths are more likely to lack consciences and to be incapable of feeling empathy or compassion for others. Emotions such as depression, frustration, rage, and shame can intensify a child's perceived inadequacies. Many violent youths are alienated from emotional support systems and feel isolated and discriminated against. They may become desensitized to violence or emotionally numb and seek excitement through violence. Some are suicidal and resigned to accepting and participating in violence.

How Violence Is Committed

Youth violence can be categorized into four major types. Situational violence, one of the most common types of violence committed by children and teenagers, is sparked by an event that upsets or enrages the victimizer. For example, a student might assault a teacher who gave a failing grade. Rela-

tional violence occurs when a child or teenager is violent toward a relative or friend with whom he or she has a personal dispute. Dating violence is one of the most prevalent forms of this type of violence, as when a teenage boy attacks a girl who terminates their relationship. Predatory violence describes thefts and muggings involving violence or violent activities carried out to prove loyalty and ensure acceptance by a group. Violence connected to competition, drug dealing, riots, and gang fights and the use of concealed weapons with intent to maim or murder is considered predatory. Less than 1 percent of juvenile cases involve psychopathological violence, which involves perpetrators who probably are neurologically damaged or mentally ill and who commit extremely violent acts. These individuals require pharmaceutical and management therapy. Other violent acts that may be committed by youths include hate crimes, vandalism, bombings, or activism such as ecoterrorism. Some violent youths are attention seekers who believe that they will become celebrities through their acts.

While engaged in violent acts, youths may be dis-associated from what they are doing and may feel as if they are experiencing a dreamlike or fantastical state instead of reality. Violent youths may verbally antagonize and ridicule their victims, who are often people whom the perpetrators view as weak, such as young children, the elderly, and handicapped individuals. Sometimes, groups of youths plan assaults to surround and attack one person. Preteens have raped or murdered children their own age or younger. A notorious case of youth violence occurred in England in 1993, when two ten-year-olds kidnapped and beat to death a two-year-old. Some children who commit violent acts are not sufficiently mature, intellectually and morally, to realize that their actions can hurt other people. In 2000, a six-year-old who shot a classmate at a Michigan school expressed confusion when she died.

INTERVENTION

Mental health professionals stress that children who display violent behaviors should be identified as young as possible so that intervention measures can be implemented to prevent them from harming other youths. Facilities that treat violent juvenile offenders include boot camps, detention centers, wilderness programs, and group or private psychotherapy sessions. Both public and private schools attempt to identify emotionally disturbed students who might interfere with the learning process of other students by disrupting classes and challenging faculty members.

Violent youths who are mentally ill should receive counseling and medication. Other options are available to those whose behavior has social and emotional roots. These youths may be enrolled in programs that promote self-esteem, emotional resilience, and self-control. Parents can teach their children appropriate coping techniques to prevent violence. Communities and churches can provide children with supervised recreational activities during afternoons, which are the hours when youths are most likely to act violently. Mentoring programs can demonstrate alternatives to destructive behavior. Peer counseling has been shown to be an effective deterrent to violence. Violence-prevention curricula can teach children to resolve conflicts creatively and help them develop skills to control emotional outbursts.

SOURCES FOR FURTHER STUDY

Eron, Leonard D., Jacquelyn H. Gentry, and Peggy Schlegel. *Reason to Hope: A Psychosocial Perspective on Violence and Youth.* Washington, D.C.: American Psychological Association, 1996. Discusses youth violence as a form of juvenile delinquency and social handicap that can be rehabilitated.

Garbarino, James. *Lost Boys: Why Our Sons Turn Violent and How We Can Save Them.* New York: Anchor Books, 2000. Focuses on why young males are more likely to commit extremely antisocial acts such as school shootings.

Gentile, Douglas A., ed. *Media Violence and Children: A Complete Guide for Parents and Professionals.* Westport, Conn.: Praeger, 2008. An expert on media violence collects essays from researchers who report on such topics as television violence, video games, and violent music.

Holden, Constance. "The Violence of the Lambs." *Science* 289 (July 28, 2000): 580-581. Commentary on the various risk factors that investigators suggest cause children to become violent. This issue of the American Association for the Advancement of Science's magazine is devoted to scientific research concerning violence in humans and animals.

Katch, Jane. *Under Deadman's Skin: Discovering the Meaning of Children's Violent Play.* Boston: Beacon Press, 2001. Explores how violence is learned and displayed by children through games and in social groups.

Kellerman, Jonathan. *Savage Spawn: Reflections on Violent Children.* New York: Ballantine, 1999. Analyzes the psychopathology exhibited by children with conduct disorders.

Richman, Jack M., and Mark W. Fraser, eds. *The Context of Youth Violence: Resilience, Risk, and Protection.* Westport, Conn.: Praeger, 2001. Examines personality traits associated with violence in children and teenagers and addresses why children and teenagers target their peers for victimization.

Elizabeth D. Schafer

SEE ALSO: Aggression; Aggression: Reduction and control; Anger; Children's mental health; Conduct disorder; Juvenile delinquency; Law and psychology; Misbehavior; Psychotic disorders; Suicide; Teenage suicide; Teenagers' mental health; Violence and sexuality in the media; Violence: Psychological causes and effects.

Violence
Psychological causes and effects

Type of psychology: Developmental psychology; social psychology; stress

Fields of study: Adolescence; aggression; anxiety disorders; childhood and adolescent disorders; cognitive development; depression; social perception and cognition; stress and illness

Violent behavior erupts in response to the presence or absence of particular psychological and environmental factors. Children growing up in violent households or communities who lack important social and psychological resources have a higher tendency to behave violently and to become adults who are either perpetrators or victims of violence. In poorer households with an unemployed male head of household, women and children are more prone to domestic abuse. The psychological effects of violence include depression and hopelessness in perpetrating adolescents and post-traumatic stress, depression, insecurity, and fear in the victims.

Key concepts
- cycle of violence
- environmental factors
- intimate partner violence
- post-traumatic stress disorder (PTSD)
- resilience to violence

Introduction

Many factors, including both external and psychological, can provoke violence. External factors include violent childhood and adolescent home and community environments and intimate partner violence. Experiencing violence can cause victims to behave violently themselves and continue the cycle of violence as adults by becoming perpetrators or victims of violent behavior. Socioeconomic factors play a role in the development of violent behavior, with households in which the head of household is of lower socioeconomic status or unemployed more likely to be affected by violence. However, some children are resilient to the negative effects of violence. Key social and psychological resources appear to be important in the development of this resilience. The psychological effects of violence include feelings of depression and hopelessness and a de-

creased belief in a positive future in perpetrators, as well as post-traumatic stress, depression, fear, insecurity, and poor self-esteem in victims. These effects can occur in the short term or may develop years after the violence has ended. To break the cycle of violence and reduce the negative psychological effects of violence, it is important to initiate therapy when predisposing factors are identified.

Childhood and Adolescence

Children and adolescents are particularly vulnerable to the effects of violence. The experience of violence as a child can have deep and lasting effects on a person's development and psychology and behavior as an adult. To understand the causes of violence, it is important to examine both the psychological and environmental factors that can provoke violence. External causes of violence that may occur during childhood include having a violent or neglectful childhood environment, experiencing violence during childhood and adolescence, and viewing violence in the media (including television, films, music, and video games). A longitudinal study of boys found significant correlation between viewing of television violence as eight-year-olds and exhibition of violent behavior as thirty-year-old adults. These experiences may result in desensitization to violence and in the perception that violence is a suitable means of obtaining one's desires. Impulsivity, learning difficulties, low intelligence quotient (IQ), and fearlessness have also been linked to violent behavior.

Violence breeds violence. Violent individuals often learn violent behavior from family members and friends, including fellow gang members. Children who witness violence are more aggressive and are more likely to become involved in violence as adults, either as victims or perpetrators. Children who are rejected by their parents are more likely to experience symptoms of post-traumatic stress disorder (PTSD) and problems with social information processing (for example, interpreting innocuous speech or gestures as hostile), which can then manifest as violence toward their intimate partners. A violent upbringing, combined with a lack of early positive experiences, predisposes a child to becoming involved in violence as an adult. For example, among African American adolescents living in a high-crime, urban environment, those who self-reported use of violence were more likely to be male; to have been exposed to violence, victimization, and family conflict; and to report hopelessness and depression. These adolescents were also more likely to score lower on ratings of purpose in life and the expectancy of being alive at age twenty-five. The adolescents' scores on these two measures and on hopelessness were correlated with the employment status of the head of the household in which the adolescents lived. African American adolescents from homes with employed heads of households showed higher purpose in life and expectancy of being alive at age twenty-five, as well as fewer feelings of hopelessness. The increased rate of depression among the adolescents who self-reported violent behavior may either be a cause or an effect of violence.

Interestingly, not all children and adolescents growing up in violent homes or communities display violent behavior or become susceptible to violence. It is probable that some children are born resilient. For other children, several factors may influence whether they develop resilience against violence. These factors include the presence of positive role models, exposure to positive behaviors, having supportive relationships, being able to develop self-esteem and self-efficacy (belief in one's ability to cope with a particular situation), and possessing the ability to develop self-esteem in work, hobbies, and creative pursuits. A child growing up in the midst of violence who possesses one or more of these factors, either from birth or through early positive experiences, has a higher likelihood of becoming resilient to violence. The study of urban African American adolescents found less violence among adolescents who participated more frequently in religious activities or who belonged to households with higher socioeconomic status.

INTIMATE PARTNER VIOLENCE ON WOMEN

Socioeconomic factors may also play a significant role in the occurrence of intimate partner violence. Across cultures and ethnicities, violence is most prevalent among the poor. Male unemployment and the resulting inability of men to provide for their families often induce considerable psychological stress. Some unemployed men vent their frustration by exerting violence on their domestic partners. When women start working and become partial or major breadwinners, "male exclusion" may occur, in which the man suffers a crisis in his traditional, masculine identity as the family provider. The results of this gender crisis include confusion, frustration, aggressive behavior, and intimate partner violence. Some men use violence against women in an attempt to reassert their control and regain a dominant male role. In one study of women with unemployed husbands in Papua New Guinea, a higher rate of domestic violence was reported among working wives than among wives who did not work outside of the home. Violence was especially high at the beginning of the year, when couples argued over how to pay school fees. The frustration of men over their inability to provide for their families and their feelings of being threatened by their wives' perceived independence precipitated violence.

Children and adolescents who experience violence in their homes or communities may learn that violence is an acceptable way to solve conflicts or to obtain desired objects. Some children, especially girls, may learn to expect violent treatment from others. If these children and adolescents lack resources and characteristics that aid in resilience, they may perpetrate the cycle of violence by behaving violently toward others. Adolescents who practice violence are in turn more likely to experience depression and feelings of hopelessness. They are also more likely to become adults who either practice violence or are victims of violence. In a study of southern female adolescents, sexually abused girls were more likely to have feelings of depression and to experience suicidal ideation. They also had a higher probability of being physically abused and of initiating sexual intercourse at a younger age. A high proportion of children and adolescents (approximately 80 percent) who were physically or sexually abused before age eighteen met the American Psychiatric Association's *Diagnostic and Statistical Manual of Mental Disorders* (rev. 3d ed., 1987, DSM-III-R) criteria for at least one psychiatric disorder at age twenty-one. These young adults had higher rates of psychiatric disorders, depressive and anxiety symptoms, emotional and behavioral problems, suicidal ideation, and suicide attempts at ages fifteen and twenty-one. Overall, their psychosocial functioning was poorer than that of their nonabused peers.

POST-TRAUMATIC STRESS DISORDER IN CHILDREN

Post-traumatic stress disorder (PTSD) can occur in children in response to witnessing or experiencing violence, whether in the midst of war or as a result of domestic or community violence. According to the American Psychiatric Association's diagnostic manual, PTSD is diagnosed if the following criteria are met: the presence of a stressor that would produce significant distress symptoms in most people; the re-living of the trauma, manifested as recurrent and intrusive memories of the event, recurrent dreams of the event, and the sudden feeling of the traumatic event happening again in response to experiencing a certain environmental or thought stimulus; numbing of responses or withdrawal from the external world, evidenced by diminished interest in activities, detachment or withdrawal from others, or reduced affect; and emergence of at least two of the following new symptoms: being hyperalert or demonstrating an exaggerated startle response, disturbed sleep, guilt at surviving when others perished or guilt over actions performed for survival, difficulty concentrating or impaired memory, avoiding activities that provoke memories of the traumatic event, and intensification of symptoms by experiencing events that resemble the traumatic event.

The impact of trauma on a child depends on several factors. These include the acute or chronic nature of the trauma and the presence of a maternal figure. If the trauma is acute and lasts for a finite period of time, children may need only situational adjustment, in which children assimilate the event into their understanding of the situation and continue living a normal life. This can be performed through reassuring children that they are safe and everything is back to normal. However, if the trauma is chronic or more severe, children may be psychologically affected. Children who have lost parents or whose relationships have been affected because of the traumatic event are especially vulnerable to psychological damage. Psychological symptoms include extreme sensitivity to stimuli reminiscent of the traumatic event and decreased expectations for the future. These children are also more likely to have impaired development and emotional trauma. They may require developmental adjustment, which involves using the children's key relationships (for example, with their parents and immediate families) to create a new positive reality to replace the worldview that traumatized children are likely to have constructed concerning their self-worth, their attitude toward the world, and the reliability of adults and institutions. Helping children reestablish confidence in the key adults in their lives and in their ability to survive in the world can enable them to better cope with the effects of trauma and danger.

IMPACT OF INTIMATE PARTNER VIOLENCE

The effects of intimate partner violence on women's health include both physical and psychological damages, and can take the form of PTSD, depression, fear, and insecurity. A study of married and single mothers in Ontario, Canada, revealed that women who reported past physical abuse were significantly more likely to have experienced clinical depression and lower self-esteem, as well as a feeling that they lacked control. They were also more likely to have chronic physical health problems and to report a lack of social and economic resources. Some of these health effects were experienced years after the occurrence of abuse.

SOURCES FOR FURTHER STUDY

Bandari, S., et al. "Comparative Analyses of Stressors Experienced by Rural Low-Income Pregnant Women Experiencing Intimate Partner Violence and Those Who Are Not." *Journal of Obstetric, Gynecologic, & Neonatal Nursing* 37 (2008): 492-501. A study of factors associated with intimate partner violence among rural, low-income, pregnant women.

DuRant, R. H., et al. "Factors Associated with the Use of Violence Among Urban Black Adolescents." *American Journal of Public Health* 84, no. 4 (1994): 612-617. This study assesses factors that influence whether adolescents raised in violent environments engage in violent behavior.

Leavitt, L. A., and N. A. Fox, eds. *The Psychological Effects of War and Violence on Children.* Hillsdale, N.J.: Lawrence Erlbaum, 1993. Presents a comprehensive view of the physical and psychological effects of war and violence on children, including a chapter on post-traumatic stress disorder.

McAlpine, D., and L. Davies. "The Long Term Health Effects of Violence Against Women." *Abstracts of Academy Health Meetings* 20 (2003). Abstract no. 257. This paper describes a University of Minnesota study of Canadian women that reported a correlation between past physical abuse and clinical depression and chronic physical health problems, some of which appeared years after incidents of abuse.

Nagy, S., R. DiClemente, and A. G. Adcock. "Adverse Factors Associated with Forced Sex Among Southern Adolescent Girls." *Pediatrics* 96, no. 5, part 1 (1995): 944-946. A large-scale survey of southern adolescent girls that examines the effects of sexual abuse on the psychology and sexual behavior of adolescent girls.

Pickup, F., S. Williams, and C. Sweetman. *Ending Violence Against Women: A Challenge for Development and Humanitarian Work.* Oxford, England: Oxfam, 2001. A comprehensive treatise on sociological, economical, and cultural issues surrounding violence against women in the developing world. Created and published by the United Kingdom-based, nonprofit humanitarian group, Oxfam.

Silverman, A. B., H. Z. Reinherz, and R. M. Giaconia. "The Long-Term Sequelae of Child and Adolescent Abuse: A Longitudinal Community Study." *Child Abuse & Neglect* 20, no. 8 (1996): 709-723. Effects of childhood abuse on psychosocial functioning in mid-adolescence and early adulthood.

Taft, C. T., et al. "Family-of-Origin Maltreatment, Posttraumatic Stress Disorder Symptoms, Social Information Processing Deficits, and Relationship Abuse Perpetration." *Journal of Abnormal Psychology* 117 (2008): 637-646. A study examining the correlation of childhood parental rejection with adult violent behavior, demonstrating that use of violence may be at least partially caused by abnormal social information processing in some individuals.

Ing-Wei Khor

SEE ALSO: Air rage; Anger; Attitude formation and change; Battered woman syndrome; Child abuse; Depression; Domestic violence; Elder abuse; Hope and mental health; Post-traumatic stress disorder; Road rage; Self-efficacy; Violence and sexuality in the media; Violence by children and teenagers.

Virtual reality

DATE: Early 1990's forward

TYPE OF PSYCHOLOGY: Cognition; learning; memory; psychological methodologies; psychopathology; psychotherapy; sensation and perception; social psychology; stress

FIELDS OF STUDY: Anxiety disorders; attitudes and behavior; behavioral therapies; cognitive therapies; experimental methodologies; problem solving

Virtual reality is a form of computer-generated technology that offers innovative alternative therapies through human-machine interactions to treat psychological disorders by creating environments in which people can address and confront situations that cause stress, fear, or other unwanted behaviors. It also presents potential dangers for the development of pathological behavior.

KEY CONCEPTS
- augmented virtual reality
- cave virtual reality
- desktop virtual reality
- immersive virtual reality
- phobias
- post-traumatic stress disorder
- projected virtual reality
- Second Life
- ELIZA
- telepresence

INTRODUCTION

After World War II, computer scientists and engineers developed technology, such as flight simulators, that provided an early foundation for virtual reality through digitization, real-time graphics, and interactive and pointing devices. By the early 1980's, medical and computer science professionals collaborated to integrate their specialties. Some medical professionals incorporated virtual reality as a tool to learn and practice medical procedures, especially surgery, by manipulating virtual organs. Virtual reality underwent a transition from laboratories to hospitals. Physicians reported that virtual reality eased the pain that burn patients felt by distracting them and making them unaware of the real world through immersion in alternative environments such as snowy landscapes, which convinced patients that they felt coolness.

Another foundation for modern virtual reality was the computer program ELIZA. Created in 1966 by Joseph Weizenbaun, ELIZA was not strictly a virtual reality environment but an early form of computer-simulated psychotherapy. Although ELIZA was a grammar program that used only text, it seemed to engage the user in Rogerian therapy. By the early 1990's, virtual reality had expanded to creating both visual and auditory environments.

Virtual reality techniques were appropriated for psychological applications by the early 1990's to influence people's perceptions and psychological processes. Computer hardware and software were developed to simulate specific situations for therapeutic sessions. This technology enabled phobic patients to interact safely with situations that arouse fear. Phobic patients often prefer virtual reality therapy because they can encounter their fears in private instead of in public situations. In 1998, *CyberPsychology and Behavior: The Leading Psychology Journal for Internet, Multimedia, and Virtual Reality Research* began providing a centralized forum to advance virtual reality as a therapeutic tool. Software improvements enabled the creation of more virtual environments to meet therapeutic demands. Although there was significant interest in virtual reality therapy early in the twenty-first century, by 2005 much of that enthusiasm had cooled, although there has been renewed interest in using virtual reality platforms such as Second Life, Multiverse, and Active Worlds to address psychological issues.

THERAPIES

Six types of virtual reality therapies have been tested. All rely on convincing people that they are experiencing an environment by making it realistic to their senses of sight, hearing, and touch. The desktop method involves interacting with images on a computer screen by using pointing devices. Projected virtual reality casts the patient's image into an artificial setting. Cave virtual reality displays images on the walls of a small room, allowing several people to participate in therapy simultaneously. Telepresence delivers a setting from another place on a video screen that the patient observes. Augmented virtual reality uses objects that enhance the setting for specific therapies. Immersive virtual reality is used most frequently and includes aspects of other virtual reality types. In contrast to two-dimensional computer images, virtual reality creates a three-dimensional environment composed of computer graphics. People believe they are immersed in and participating in the simulation. This illusion is enabled by devices that participants wear that aid them to interact with and manipulate the virtual setting. A head-mounted visor has a stereoscopic optical display. The scenery is adjusted by motion-tracking sensors attached to people's heads and limbs, and the experience seems more realistic because graphics respond convincingly to movement. Additional sensors in datagloves improve the illusion by suggesting that the participant is interacting with items located in the virtual world and navigating through the setting.

TREATMENT

Many psychologists have been skeptical as to whether virtual reality can be advantageous for therapeutic use. Many professionals consider the expense associated with equipment and operation of some types of virtual reality therapy to be prohibitive. In addition, they consider virtual reality at worst to be an irrelevant technology more suitable for entertainment than therapy and at best to be an experimental therapy requiring additional research. Gradually, the benefits of virtual reality have secured the approval of some mental health practitioners, many of whom admit to being surprised at patients' successful improvement due to virtual reality exposure (VRE) therapy. Virtual reality therapy has been used to address a variety of potential psychological problems and other difficulties, including phobias, posttraumatic stress disorder, autistic spectrum disorders, and addictive behaviors. It has been used in the area of cognitive assessment and for self-improvement in the area of weight management.

PHOBIAS

Virtual reality's most frequent psychological application is treatment for phobias. VRE therapy parallels traditional therapy in which patients's exposure to a situation or object stimulus that arouses acute fear and anxiety is gradually increased. Such exposure is either in vivo (actually experienced by the patient) or in vitro (imagined by the patient). The degree of exposure is deliberately increased over time. Individuals become conditioned and desensitized, learn not to panic, and develop more receptive attitudes.

Virtual reality creates a safe, private environment in which patients can confront their fears without being publicly embarrassed or risking physical harm. Compared with most real settings and props, such as airplanes and animals, that are necessary for conventional phobia therapy, virtual reality is inexpensive and more controllable. Multiple stimuli can be presented. Specific stimuli can be isolated, and distractions can be eliminated. Virtual reality also allows therapists to develop settings not easily located in their communities.

Patients can face frightening situations and objects virtually that they could not initially handle in person. These virtual depictions of dangerous settings are more realistic than most patients would imagine. Virtual reality enables people to overcome the limitations of their imagination and memory. Active interaction with anxiety-arousing stimuli causes patients to feel more in control, confident, and capable than undergoing more passive observational and listening therapies. Virtual reality allows people in remote places to experience settings and fears that are not available to them in their immediate surroundings.

Virtual reality has proven effective in countering acrophobia (fear of heights), claustrophobia (fear of enclosed spaces), agoraphobia (fear of open spaces), arachnophobia (fear of spiders), and aerophobia (fear of flying). Patients with social phobias such as fear of public speaking can practice skills with virtual reality to interact more comfortably with people. Research teams are also considering the possibilities of patients and therapists being immersed in virtual reality settings together.

POST-TRAUMATIC STRESS DISORDER

Chronic post-traumatic stress disorder (PTSD) has been addressed through the use of virtual reality. At the Georgia Institute of Technology's College of Computing, a group of Vietnam veterans with PTSD were treated using virtual reality therapy. During virtual reality sessions, therapists encouraged veterans to narrate their military experiences. The veterans were asked to repeat their stories many times to bolster their memories. Although many veterans were reticent to share their stories in traditional therapy, virtual reality freed them to become more talkative and physical as they interacted with virtual comrades and enemies in a setting that included combat sounds.

Such experiences helped the veterans deal with guilt about such things as being the sole survivor of an attack. Although their PTSD was not eliminated, many veterans experienced a lessening of problems after they revisited their memories via virtual reality. Veterans' hospitals have incorporated virtual reality equipment into therapy treating chronic anxiety disorders.

The Weill Cornell Medical Center in New York City has used virtual reality to address a variety of PTSD situations, including among veterans of the Persian Gulf and Iraq wars. Virtual reality therapy has also helped survivors of the terrorist attacks on the World Trade Towers on September 11, 2001. The treatment includes virtual exposure to the towers before, during, and after their collapse for indi-

viduals who experienced the attacks from within the towers and from afar. All treatment is under the guidance of a therapist who makes sure the patient does not become overwhelmed by the experience.

AUTISTIC SPECTRUM DISORDERS

Through virtual reality worlds such as Second Life, individuals can seek out others for social interaction. In Second Life, users create an avatar that is a representative of themselves and use that avatar to interact with the virtual environment and other avatars in that virtual environment. Self-help groups are not uncommon in Second Life. Through virtual reality, individuals with autistic spectrum disorders can reach out to others with similar concerns and problems. Geographically diverse individuals can interact and help each other. For example, a young man with Asperger syndrome established Naughty Auties, a resource center for individuals with autistic spectrum disorders, in Second Life. However, seeking help in the unregulated environment of virtual reality carries significant risk in that the avatars' real identities are unknown, as is the veracity of their statements. Despite this drawback, virtual reality, which does not have the same pressures as real-life social interactions, seems to provide an optimum place for individuals to practice social interactions in a variety of virtual settings without the risk of failing in the real world. Research is just beginning in this area, but some results have been promising.

ADDICTIVE BEHAVIORS AND SELF-IMPROVEMENT

Virtual reality has been used to deal with addictive behaviors such as smoking. In virtual reality environments, patients can practice coping skills when confronted with virtual simulations of situations and stimuli that trigger their addictive behaviors. The virtual environment seems to provide the right balance of believability of stimuli without the risk of real-life failure. Virtual reality also has been used therapeutically for patients' self-improvement.

Eating disorders have been successfully treated with virtual reality methods that often supplement traditional forms of therapy. The virtual-reality-based experiential cognitive treatment of obesity and binge-eating disorders assists people to modify their flawed body perceptions. Improved body awareness obtained through an integration of virtual environments and traditional cognitive behavioral and visual-motor therapies results in awareness of latent feelings, decreased problematic eating, and displays of more normal social behavior.

Research has also confirmed that virtual reality can be used to make exercising more enjoyable. Similar to watching television or listening to music while exercising, virtual reality can provide a distraction. Instead of biking in the gym, virtual reality can allow the individual to bike through the English countryside or on the course for the Tour de France.

MEASUREMENT, NEUROSCIENCE, AND EDUCATION

Virtual reality environments allow patients who are unable to function in normal settings to respond to stimuli presented in real time. Neuroscientists can then gauge individuals' cognitive abilities. Virtual reality has proven effective in rehabilitating some individuals who are cognitively impaired because of brain injuries or diseases such as Alzheimer's. Patients are tested with virtual reality scenarios that researchers can control and adjust as needed to assess how well individuals function.

Virtual settings offer people with neurological impairments the opportunity to interact with an environment to which they would otherwise lack physical access to enrich their sensory and motor skills. Virtual reality classrooms have been designed to evaluate and measure the cognitive abilities of children who possibly have attention-deficit hyperactivity disorder (ADHD). Most cognitive researchers consider virtual reality tests less biased than traditional tools and do not consider its lack of realism, comparable to that of a photograph, problematic. Virtual reality has proven beneficial in working with children with a variety of reading disabilities and delays. School districts have used virtual reality games that engage students with a story line to increase reading scores. Virtual reality has also been used to successfully teach other subjects.

SIDE EFFECTS AND RISKS

Virtual reality is limited by its costs, complexity, technology, and reliability, as well as the technical proficiency of users. Time delays, noise, and distortions (particularly in body image sessions) can impede therapy, although technological advances will continue to address these issues. To improve techniques, virtual reality researchers have begun investigating human-computer interaction with clinical tests. They are interested in how people perceive and accept or reject computer-generated worlds as a mental health treatment method. Researchers evaluate whether virtual reality therapy is more time- and cost-effective than traditional techniques.

Some patients may experience simulation sickness, which is a form of motion sickness, and nausea. Careful design of virtual scenarios and screening of patients can minimize such adverse reactions. Some people's neck muscles are too weak to support heavy virtual reality helmets, and many claustrophobic patients are reluctant to wear the bulky helmets. Some users experience depth perception problems. Sometimes virtual reality confuses patients, and virtual experiences replace real experiences in memories. Migraines and seizures are also a possibility. Despite these risks, many patients, however, seem receptive to virtual reality techniques.

Although virtual reality does present many opportunities for treatment and growth, the unregulated environment of many virtual reality worlds, such as Second Life, Multiverse, and Active Worlds, presents many opportunities for the development and expression of pathologies. This particular negative aspect of virtual reality has received little research attention, although warnings abound. In virtual reality, just as in the online environment in general, where the usual social constraints on behavior are often lacking, individuals can behave in very pathological ways, and far from practicing positive social interactions, individuals may find themselves engaging in relationships that mirror the negative patterns they follow in real life or that exhibit an even higher degree of pathology. Behaviors such as stalking, emotional abuse, and manipulation are all possible. Vulnerable and needy individuals may lose sight of where reality ends and virtual reality begins. Their online relationships and interactions can become more real to them than their real-life relationships and interactions.

In the virtual environment, people engage in all sorts of behavior that they would not otherwise engage in. They have virtual sex with strangers and sell their virtual bodies. In a recent divorce case in England, the husband was engaging in virtual sex with prostitutes in Second Life. His wife cited his online behavior as a cause for divorce. The virtual world also offers a multitude of opportunities to find others who share a person's pathologies and thereby can confirm these negative beliefs and reinforce them.

SOURCES FOR FURTHER STUDY

Baumann, Stephen, and Michael A. Sayette. "Smoking Cues in a Virtual World Provoke Craving in Cigarette Smokers." *Psychology of Addictive Behaviors* 20, no. 4 (December, 2006): 484-489. Discusses how virtual reality was used to immerse subjects in a realistic environment to induce cravings, enabling researchers to study the use of cognitive behavioral therapy and desensitization therapy.

Mühlberger, Andreas, Heinrich H. Bülthoff, Georg Wiedemann, and Paul Pauli. "Virtual Reality for the Psychophysiological Assessment of Phobic Fear: Responses During Virtual Tunnel Driving." *Psychological Assessment* 19, no. 3 (September, 2007): 340-346. Address the use of virtual reality to treat the phobia of driving in tunnels.

North, Max M., Sarah M. North, and Joseph R. Coble. *Virtual Reality Therapy: An Innovative Paradigm.* Colorado Springs, Colo.: IPI Press, 1996. One of the first texts describing the potential of virtual reality to provide alternative treatments for a variety of psychological disorders.

Riva, Giuseppe, Brenda K. Wiederhold, and Enrico Molinari, eds. *Virtual Environments in Clinical Psychology and Neuroscience: Methods and Techniques in Advanced Patient-Therapist Interaction.* Amsterdam: ISO Press, 1998. Pioneer researchers in the field of virtual reality therapy compare virtual reality versus traditional methods and discuss the roles of humans and technology in mental health.

Rothbaum, Barbara O., and Larry F. Hodges. *Virtually Better: Therapist Manual for Fear of Flying.* Atlanta: Virtually Better, 1997. Guide based on the authors' research, which promotes computer-generated techniques to prepare patients for experiences aboard airplanes.

Villani, D., F. Riva, and G. Riva. "New Technologies for Relaxation: The Role of Presence." *International Journal of Stress Management* 14, no. 3 (August, 2007): 260-274. Virtual reality is another tool that can be used to help individuals learn to relax and alleviate stress.

Elizabeth D. Schafer;
updated by Ayn Embar-Seddon O'Reilly
and Allan D. Pass

SEE ALSO: Agoraphobia and panic disorders; Alcohol dependence and abuse; Anxiety disorders; Asperger syndrome; Autism; Aversion therapy; Body dysmorphic disorder; Cognitive behavior therapy; Eating disorders; Implosion; Post-traumatic stress disorder; Systematic desensitization.

Vision
Brightness and contrast

TYPE OF PSYCHOLOGY: Sensation and perception
FIELDS OF STUDY: Cognitive processes; vision

Brightness refers to one's perception of the intensity of light reflected from a surface; contrast refers to one's perception of differences in light reflected from two surfaces. Contrast enhances perception of intensity differences, thereby accentuating lines, colors, and borders; it makes a dark area appear darker and a bright area appear brighter when they are juxtaposed.

KEY CONCEPTS
- assimilation
- complementary color
- contrast sensitivity function
- hue
- retina
- simultaneous contrast
- successive contrast

INTRODUCTION

Brightness is the perception of intensity of light. Roughly, the more intense a light is, the brighter it seems to be. Intensity refers to the physical energy of light, as measured by a photometer. Brightness, however, is a perceptual phenomenon: It cannot be measured by physical instruments. It is a basic perception, difficult if not impossible to describe; it must be experienced. Measurements of brightness are generally observers' reports of their experience viewing lights of different intensities. Only in living systems—that is, only in the eye of the perceiver—is the term "brightness" relevant.

The brightness of a spot of light, although related to the intensity of light reflected from that spot, is also influenced by other factors. It varies with the intensity of light reflected from the immediately surrounding area at any given time and at immediately preceding times. In general, a spot appears brighter if the surrounding areas are dark or are stimulated with light perceived as complementary in color; it also appears brighter if the eye has become accustomed to the dark ("dark-adapted"). These factors contribute contrast, the perception of differences in light intensity, which enhances brightness. Brightness and contrast are perceptually linked.

INFLUENCES ON PERCEPTION

A light of a given physical intensity may appear quite bright when viewed with an eye that has been dark-adapted, perhaps by being covered for ten to fifteen minutes. That same light may seem dim in comparison to an eye exposed to bright light for the same time period. This is largely attributable to the fact that a dark-adapted eye has more photopigment available to respond to incoming light; when this pigment has been exposed, it becomes bleached and needs time to regenerate. The enhancement of differences in brightness by an adapting light or other stimulus preceding the test light is called successive contrast and is primarily attributable to the state of adaptation of the retina.

Simultaneous contrast can also affect brightness perception. In this case, a spot of light at one place on the retina can be made to appear brighter or dimmer depending only on changes in the lighting of adjacent retinal locations. A small gray paper square placed on a sheet of black paper appears brighter than an identical square on a sheet of white paper. This is mostly a result of lateral inhibition, or photoreceptors stimulated by the white background inhibiting the receptors stimulated by the square so it appears less dazzling on white than on black. In general, differences are enhanced when the stimuli are side by side.

Sensitivity to contrast also varies with the detail of the object being viewed. Reading a book involves attending to high spatial frequencies, closely spaced lines, and minute detail. Recognizing a friend across the room or finding one's car in a parking lot involves attention to much broader spatial frequencies; that is, the lines important for recognition are much farther apart. The visual system handles low, moderate, and high spatial frequencies, although not equally well. A contrast sensitivity function may be plotted to show which spatial frequencies are most easily detected—that is, to which frequencies the eye-brain system is most sensitive.

The peak of this function, the highest sensitivity to spatial frequency, is within the midrange of detectable frequencies. At this peak, it takes less physical contrast (a smaller intensity difference) for an observer to report seeing the border between areas of different frequency. At higher and lower spatial frequencies, sensitivity drops off, so greater intensity differences must be made for perception in those ranges.

While perceptual systems exaggerate physical contrast, they fail to notice lack of contrast, change, or movement. Changes in brightness, for example, can be made so gradually that no notice of them is taken at all. In fact, the visual system, while signaling changes well, does not respond to seemingly constant stimulation. When an image, a bright pattern of light projected on the retina, is stabilized so it does not move at all, the observer reports first seeing the image and then, in a few seconds, its fading from view. The field does not turn gray or black or become empty; it simply ceases to exist. A border circumscribing a pattern within another pattern, perhaps a red-filled circle within a green-filled one, may be stabilized on the retina. In this case, the inner border disappears completely: The observer continues to see an unstabilized green-filled circle with no pattern in it. The area that formerly appeared red—and which indeed does reflect long-wavelength light—is perceived only as a part of the homogeneous green circle. Thus, while borders and movement creating physical contrast are exaggerated in perception, a stimulus signaling no change at all is simply not perceived.

COLOR PERCEPTION

Brightness and contrast are especially well illustrated in color perception. In the retina, three different cone pigments mediate color perception. Each pigment maximally absorbs light of certain wavelengths: One maximally absorbs the short lengths that are perceived as blue, one the medium wavelengths perceived as green, and one the red or long-wavelength region of the spectrum. The outputs of the cones interact with one another in the visual system in such a way that reds and greens stand in opposite or complementary roles, as do blues and yellows, and black and white. A gray square reflects light of all wavelengths equally. It has no hue, or color. Yet when it is placed on a red background, it appears greenish; if placed on a blue background, that same gray square appears yellowish. In each case, the neutral square moves toward the complement of its background color. The background has induced the perception of hue, tinting the gray with the color of its complement. Brightness of the background can also affect hue. A royal-blue square against a moderately white background can appear deep navy when the background intensity is increased or seem to be a powder blue when it is decreased. The same color in two different settings or under two different brightness conditions is not the same color.

The appearance of color is not a simple property of the color pigment itself but is defined in its relationship to others. Simultaneous color contrast can be quite startling, depending on the color relationships chosen. For example, if two squares of different hues but the same brightness are juxtaposed, colors appear very strong and exaggerated. One's attention goes immediately to the contrast. If they are complementary colors such as red and green, the contrast is heightened. If they are close to the complements of each other, they are perceived in the direction of complementarity.

Yet not all colors are contrasting. A color configuration that does not move toward contrast moves toward assimilation—toward being united with the major color present. For example, a painting's central blue feature may bring out subtly blue features elsewhere in the painting. Whenever colors show enough similarity to one another, they approach one another, emphasizing similarity rather than contrast. Both color contrast and assimilation are beautifully illustrated in Josef Albers's book *Interaction of Color* (1987).

THE PULFRICH PHENOMENON

Another visual demonstration of brightness effects is the Pulfrich pendulum effect, or the Pulfrich phenomenon. To observe this, tie a pendulum bob to a two-foot length of string. Swing this in a plane normal to the line of sight, moving it back and forth as a pendulum. Then observe this continuing motion while wearing glasses, one lens of which is darkened or covered with a sunglass cover. Suddenly the pendulum appears to move in an ellipse instead of an arc. This illusion is a brightness effect. The shaded or sunglass-covered eye does not receive as much light as the other eye at any given time. It takes this eye longer to integrate the light information it does receive and so, by the time it sends location information to the brain, the other eye is sending its in-

formation of another location. The brain interprets disparity, this difference in the locations, as depth. Therefore the pendulum appears to move closer and farther away from the observer in elliptical depth and not constantly in a single plane. Intriguingly, switching the covered eye changes the elliptical path from clockwise rotation to counterclockwise or vice versa.

The Pulfrich phenomenon is a demonstration of changes in perception with changes in brightness; such changes have very practical effects. Driving at dusk, for example, can be dangerous, because light levels are suddenly lower than expected. Although the eye gathers the available light for form, distance, and depth perception, it takes a longer period of time to do so. Unaware of this, a driver may find reaction time to be longer than in the middle of the day and not allow enough braking distance. Similarly, an umpire may halt an evening soccer game earlier than the spectators think is necessary because of low light levels. The spectators can see well enough, as they gather the light needed to perceive what is happening. The players, on the other hand, notice that their reaction times are extended and that they are having trouble localizing the ball.

For a third application, the fact that contrast sensitivity shows peaks in particular spatial frequencies bears explanatory if not practical value. Robert Sekule, Lucinda Hutman, and Cynthia Owsley showed, in a 1980 study, that as one grows older, sensitivity to low spatial frequencies decreases. This may partly explain why older people may show greater difficulty recognizing faces or locating an automobile than the young, even though the two groups may be equally able to discriminate fine structural details. Making an older person aware of this change in sensitivity may be of assistance in defining the difficulty and in providing assurance that this is not a memory problem or a sign of decreasing cognitive ability.

SENSATION AND PERCEPTION

In the late nineteenth century, much of the early development of psychology as a science came about through work in sensation and perception. As empirical evidence grew, theories of contrast perception took shape. Two of the most notable are those of Hermann von Helmholtz and Ewald Hering.

Helmholtz had a psychological theory—a cognitive theory that explained color and brightness changes with contrast as errors in judgment. Errors were attributed to lack of practice in making brightness judgments, not in any physiological change in the neural input. Something suddenly looked brighter simply because it was misinterpreted, probably because one was focusing on some other aspect.

At the same time, Hering insisted and provided convincing demonstrations that contrast involves no error in judgment but has a physiological base. The neural response of any region of the retina, he argued, is a function not only of that region but also of neighboring regions. These neighboring sensations were postulated as having an effect opposite in brightness, or in the complementary color, of the region being viewed. Hering showed with successive contrast and simultaneous contrast studies that the outputs of different places on the retina could be modified by one another.

In 1890, William James described this controversy and gave, in *The Principles of Psychology*, his support to Hering's physiological position. With some modifications, it may be supported today. Yet the Helmholtz theory has some supportive evidence as well. For example, John Delk and Samuel Fillenbaum showed in 1956 that an object's characteristic color influences an observer's perception of that object's color. In this way, for example, an apple cut out of red paper is identified as redder than it actually is. This line of evidence would support Helmholtz in his theory of errors in judgment.

Almost any modern consideration of contrast includes a discussion of brightness changes at borders, commonly called Mach bands. This dates to 1865, when Ernst Mach, an Austrian physicist, described borders as places where differences in brightness are shown side by side. One way to observe these is to create a shadow by holding a book or other object with a sharp edge between a light source and the surface it illuminates. The border of the shadow is not crisp; in fact, it seems to be made of several lines. On the inside there is a dark stripe, darker than the central shaded object that separates it from the unshaded region. Adjacent to this, on the bright side of the shadow, is another stripe that appears brighter than the rest of the illuminated surface. These additional bands are an example of brightness contrast at a border where the physical contrast between shadow and light is exaggerated in perception. As true brightness phenomena, Mach bands do not exist in the physics of the situation (that is, in the distribution of light intensity). They are purely a perceptual phenomenon, their brightness depending not only on the intensity of an area but also on the intensity of surrounding areas.

SOURCES FOR FURTHER STUDY

Albers, Josef. *Interaction of Color.* Rev. ed. New Haven, Conn.: Yale University Press, 2007. Albers, an artist and teacher, presents commentary on form and color in addition to his paintings. Many of his works illustrate simultaneous contrast, successive contrast, assimilation, and other brightness effects. They are especially intriguing in that they were not designed to support psychological theories but to be viewed as art.

Bloomer, Carolyn M. *Principles of Visual Perception.* 2d. ed. New York: Design Press, 1990. Bloomer interweaves visual perception and art theory in an easily comprehensible explanation of perceptual principles complete with illustrations from the fine arts. She includes a full chapter on color, including illustrations of contrast and suggestions for making one's own demonstrations. Annotated bibliography.

Gregory, R. L. *Eye and Brain: The Psychology of Seeing.* 5th ed. Princeton, N.J.: Princeton University Press, 1998. An introduction to the basic phenomena of visual perception that was clearly written to be read and enjoyed by general readers as well as serious students. Gregory gives a full chapter on seeing brightness, including an excellent discussion of the eye's sensitivity to light. Well illustrated.

Lee, Hsien-Che. *Introduction to Color Imaging Science.* New York: Cambridge University Press, 2005. Fascinating look at how the eye perceives color, with a focus on scientific and engineering principles. Of interest are the sections on computer monitors, liquid crystal screens, and digital cameras.

Palmer, Stephen. *Vision Science.* Cambridge, Mass.: MIT Press, 2002. A groundbreaking textbook covering all areas of visual perception, reflecting an integrated computational approach to the subject. Presents theoretical approaches and then places empirical data within that framework.

Bonnie S. Sherman

SEE ALSO: Depth and motion perception; James, William; Pattern recognition; Pattern vision; Sensation and perception; Vision: Color; Visual system.

Vision
Color

TYPE OF PSYCHOLOGY: Sensation and perception
FIELD OF STUDY: Vision

Color vision depends on three types of photoreceptors in the retina of the eye. Each photoreceptor type absorbs light maximally at a wavelength corresponding to one of the three primary colors. The colors perceived in the brain result from integration of the degree to which each photoreceptor type is stimulated by light at given wavelengths.

KEY CONCEPTS
- chlorolabe
- cone
- cyanolabe
- dark adaptation
- deuteranope
- erythrolabe
- photoreceptor
- protanope
- rod
- tritanope

INTRODUCTION
Light is a form of radiant energy that is absorbed by sensory cells in the retina of the eye. The absorbing cells, the photoreceptors, convert light into the electrical energy of nerve impulses. The impulses generated by photoreceptors travel along the optic nerves to the optic lobes of the brain, where they are integrated into perception of a visual image.

The energy of light follows a wave path through space. The distance from crest to crest in a wave path is called the wavelength; the wavelengths of light that are visible to humans fall between about 400 nanometers (seen as blue light) and 750 nanometers (seen as red light). Wavelengths outside this range are invisible to humans because human photoreceptors are not "tuned" to receive and convert them to electrical energy.

The cornea and lens of the eye, acting together, focus light rays reflected from objects in the environment into a picturelike image that falls on the retina of the eye. The retina contains the photoreceptors of the eye, called rods and cones because of their elongated shapes. The cones, which are shorter in length than rods and conically shaped at their outer tips, are the photoreceptor type responsible for color vision. The retina contains about 110 to 120 million rods and 6 million cones. More than half the cones are concentrated in the fovea, where rods are completely absent.

CONES
There are three types of cones in the retina. Each type absorbs light maximally at a different wavelength. One absorbs maximally at 445 nanometers (blue light), one at 535 nanometers (green light), and one at 570 nanometers (yellow light near the border of the spectrum with orange). The absorption maxima at these wavelengths depend on three types of pigment molecules that absorb light in the cones. One pigment, cyanolabe, absorbs maximally at blue wavelengths; the second, chlorolabe, absorbs maximally at green wavelengths; and the third, erythrolabe, absorbs maximally at yellow wavelengths.

Each type of cone cell contains only one of the three pigments. As a result, there is one population of cones in the retina that absorbs blue light maximally, one population absorbing green, and one absorbing yellow. The three types of cones are mixed intimately in the fovea, the region of clearest vision in the retina.

The 445-, 535-, and 570-nanometer wavelengths are the colors absorbed most efficiently by each type of cone; however, each photoreceptor type also absorbs other wavelengths near their absorption maxima, although less efficiently. For example, the cone type absorbing maximally at yellow wavelengths actually absorbs wavelengths beginning at about 460 nanometers and extending to nearly 700. As wavelengths are encountered farther from the absorption maximum, light absorption becomes progressively less efficient. The pattern produces a smooth absorption curve that starts near zero on each side and peaks at the 570-nanometer wavelength.

The total ranges absorbed by the three cone types overlap, so that light at any wavelength in the visible range is likely to be absorbed by and stimulate at least two of the three photoreceptor types. For example, orange light at 580 nanometers is absorbed by and stimulates both the green and yellow cone types but not the blue photoreceptors. The green and yellow photoreceptor types, however, are stimulated to a different extent: At 580 nanometers, the yellow photoreceptors would be stimulated almost maximally, but the green photoreceptors would be stimulated to only about 40 percent of their maximum.

COLOR PERCEPTION

This difference in the absorption and stimulation of cones by light of a given wavelength is considered to underlie human perception of color. For example, when light stimulates the yellow photoreceptors at 99 percent, the green photoreceptors at 40 percent, and the blue photoreceptors at 0 percent, the color is perceived as orange. A wavelength stimulating the blue and green photoreceptors at 50 percent of their maxima, and yellow photoreceptors at 5 percent, is perceived as a blue-green color.

Light at wavelengths above about 620 nanometers stimulates only the yellow photoreceptors at or below 70 percent of their maximum; these wavelengths are perceived as red colors. For this reason, the photoreceptors absorbing maximally in the yellow wavelengths are often identified as red rather than yellow cones. Similarly, light at about 420 nanometers stimulates only the blue photoreceptors and is perceived as a deep blue. Light stimulating all three cone types equally is perceived as white. White is strictly a perceived color; there is no wavelength of light corresponding to white.

In response to absorbing light at various levels nearer or farther from their maxima, the photoreceptors generate nerve impulses. When absorbing at its maximum, a photoreceptor generates impulses at the highest frequency; at levels farther from the maximum, the frequency of impulses is proportionately reduced. The impulses sent by the three types of cones at various frequencies are partially integrated into color perception in the complex nerve circuitry of the retina, which may be considered as an extension of the brain into the eye, and partly in the optic lobes at the rear of the cerebral cortex. When objects are viewed in bright light, the total integration reconstructs the image focused in the fovea of the retina as a full-color perception of the scene viewed.

Each cone in the fovea has essentially a straight-line connection through neurons to the optic lobes. As a result, each detail of light, shade, and color in the image is likely to register as differences in stimulation between neighboring cones in the fovea and to be registered and transmitted separately to the visual area of the brain. This arrangement specializes the cones in the fovea for the detection of minute details in full color.

DARK ADAPTATION

Color reception by the cones is most efficient in bright light. As light intensity falls during and after sunset, stimulation of the cones drops off rapidly. (The cones have relatively little ability to adapt to dark as compared to the rods of the retina.) The yellow photoreceptors drop out first, so that colors in the yellow, orange, and red wavelengths fade and, in deep twilight, appear gray or black. The blue and green photoreceptors still retain some sensitivity at twilight, so that blues and greens can still be perceived. In deepest twilight, only the blue photoreceptors are stimulated, so that if any color can be perceived at all, the scene appears blue-black. The shift in color sensitivity toward the greens and blues in reduced light also explains why green fields and trees look so rich in color, and reds and yellows seem dull, on overcast or rainy days.

Adaptation to darkness occurs through an increase in the amount of pigment molecules in both the cone and rod photoreceptors. The ability of the cone cells to increase their quantities of pigment molecules is limited as compared to the rods, which can greatly increase their pigment quantities and their sensitivity to light. As a result, as light intensity decreases, visual perception shifts from the cones to the rods, which detect light but are not stimulated differentially by different wavelengths. This produces the perception of images of grays and blacks rather than color in light that is too dim to stimulate the cones. Because the rods are outside the region of sharp vision in the fovea, objects are perceived only as relatively unfocused, fuzzy images in light of very low intensity.

The rods are completely insensitive to red light. Therefore, it is possible to become completely dark-adapted even if relatively bright red light is used as a source of illumination. For this reason, persons who must work under conditions of reduced light, such as pilots flying at night, commonly use red light for required illumination.

COLOR BLINDNESS

Individuals who are color-blind carry gene mutations that reduce or inhibit the synthesis of one or more of the three color-absorbing pigments of the cones in the retina. A protanope, an individual who carries a mutation inhibiting synthesis of the erythrolabe, or yellow-absorbing pigment, is insensitive to red, orange, and yellow wavelengths and perceives all these colors as the same gray or greenish hue. Typically, such individuals cannot distinguish between green and red. A deuteranope, a person lacking the chlorolabe, or green-absorbing pigment, is also unable to distinguish between red, orange, yellow, and green. Since their inability to distinguish among red, orange, yellow, and green is similar, both protanopes and deuteranopes are classified as red-green color-blind. A tritanope, an individual deficient in the cyanolabe, or blue-absorbing pigment, cannot distinguish between blue and green. Persons deficient in all three pigments cannot perceive color and see the world only in shades of gray. Mutations affecting synthesis of the chlorolabe and erythrolabe pigments, producing green and red color blindness, are most common. About 2 percent of men are deficient in the erythrolabe pigment, and about 6 percent of men are deficient in the chlorolabe pigment, giving a total of about 8 percent of men who are red-green color-blind. The total red-green color blindness among women is about 2 percent. Blue color blindness is relatively rare in the human population; only about one in as many as sixty-five thousand people is deficient in the blue-absorbing pigment.

Color blindness affects males more often than females—about twenty times more frequently—because it is a sex-linked, recessive trait. A color-blind father cannot pass the trait to any of his sons. A color-blind mother married to a man with normal vision will pass the trait to all of her sons. Her daughters will have normal vision but will be carriers of the trait. The sons of a female carrier of the trait married to a man with normal vision have a 50 percent chance of being color-blind; all the daughters are expected to have normal vision. Half of the daughters, however, will be carriers of the trait. Deficiencies in color vision are presently uncorrectable.

Color Commentary

The beginnings of an understanding of color vision go back to 1801, when the English physicist Thomas Young proposed that the human eye has only three different kinds of receptors for color. According to Young, an ability to sense the hundreds of different colors that humans can recognize depends on an interaction among the three receptor types. Young based his idea on the fact that painters can mix any color by starting from only three: the red, the blue, and the yellow primary colors. Orange, for example, can be mixed from equal quantities of red and yellow. Young's highly perceptive explanation for this was that wavelengths in the orange range are not actually produced when light is reflected from mixed red and yellow pigments. Instead, he proposed that the mixture of red and yellow stimulates red and yellow receptors in the eye equally. This equal stimulation is summed and interpreted in the brain as the color orange. Young proposed that the sensation of white, which can be mixed from pigments by adding equal quantities of red, yellow, and blue, is produced through equal stimulation of all three receptors. Young's proposals, which turned out to be essentially correct, were later expanded by the German physicist and physiologist Hermann von Helmholtz into what is now known as the Young-Helmholtz trichromatic theory of color vision.

Two lines of later research revealed that there are only three types of color photoreceptors in the eye, as Young and Helmholtz proposed. One series of experiments, carried out in the 1960's by Paul K. Brown and George Wald at Harvard University, and Edward F. MacNichol, William H. Dobelle, and William B. Marks at The Johns Hopkins University, measured the wavelengths of light stimulating individual cones to generate nerve impulses. This work revealed that there are actually only three different types of cones, each absorbing light maximally at the blue (445-nanometer), green (535-nanometer), or yellow-orange (570-nanometer) wavelength. These colors differ to some extent from the red, blue, and yellow photoreceptors proposed by Young and Helmholtz, whose ideas were derived primarily from the results obtained by mixing painter's pigments; however, they are exactly the colors used if colored lights rather than painter's pigments are used to mix additional colors from three primary colors.

The second line of major supporting evidence came from experiments carried out by George Wald, William A. H. Rushton, and others, identifying and isolating the pigments responsible for light absorption in the eye. Some of these experiments were done by the simple but elegant technique of shining a white or colored light into the eye and then analyzing the light reflected from the retina. The reflected light was missing the colors absorbed by the pigments in the eye; the colors absorbed in the eye were those absorbed by the pigments in rod cells. Only three different pigments were detected in the cones—the cyanolabe, chlorolabe, and erythrolabe pigments—by these experiments, as predicted by Young and Helmholtz so many years ago.

SOURCES FOR FURTHER STUDY

Albers, Josef. *Interaction of Color.* Rev. ed. New Haven, Conn.: Yale University Press, 2007. Albers, an artist and teacher, presents commentary on form and color in addition to his paintings. Many of his works illustrate simultaneous contrast, successive contrast, assimilation, and other brightness effects. They are especially intriguing in that they were not designed to support psychological theories but to be viewed as art.

Ball, Philip. *Bright Earth: Art and the Invention of Color.* London: Vintage, 2008. Primarily a history of art, but covers subjects such as the physiology of color perception and the cultural factors, such as the range of color vocabulary, that influence color perception.

Berne, Robert M., and Matthew N. Levy, eds. *Physiology.* 5th ed. St. Louis: C. V. Mosby, 2004. The chapter on the visual system in this standard college physiology text outlines the anatomy and physiology of the human organ systems integrated in the detection and perception of vision, including the eye and the optic lobes of the brain, and the nerve tracts connecting them. Intended for students at the college level but written clearly enough so that it should be accessible to high school readers.

Gegenfurtner, Karl R., and Lindsey T. Sharpe, eds. *Color Vision: From Genes to Perception.* New York: Cambridge University Press, 2001. A multidisciplinary textbook on color vision, ranging from the physiology of perception to the cognitive psychology of color. Contains twenty review essays written by thirty-five internationally renowned experts in the field.

Palmer, Stephen. *Vision Science.* Cambridge, Mass.: MIT Press, 2002. A groundbreaking textbook covering all areas of visual perception, reflecting an integrated computational approach to the subject. Presents theoretical approaches and then places empirical data within that framework.

Stephen L. Wolfe

SEE ALSO: Brain structure; Depth and motion perception; Pattern recognition; Pattern vision; Sensation and perception; Vision: Brightness and contrast; Visual system.

Visual system

TYPE OF PSYCHOLOGY: Sensation and perception
FIELDS OF STUDY: Biological influences on learning; vision

The visual system allows perception of an object's form, color, size, movement, and distance. In seeing, light passes through a transparent lens in each eye, is focused, enters the inner eye, and falls on the retina. The resultant nerve impulses move to the brain through the optic nerve to create sight.

KEY CONCEPTS
- blindness
- cornea
- fovea centralis
- night blindness
- peripheral vision
- photopic and scotopic vision
- retina
- rods and cones
- sclera
- vision defects

INTRODUCTION

The visual system is one of the primary means by which humans are aware of and monitor their environment. The visual system provides information on the form, color, size, movement, and distance of any object in sight range. Its importance is seen in the fact that sight loss (blindness) is much more debilitating than any other sensory deprivation.

The anatomy of the eye is quite complex. Each eye sits in a protective, bony skull cavity, an eye socket. The human eye is roughly spherical and about one inch in diameter. Six muscles, attached at one end to the eyeball and at the other end to the eye socket, control the directional movements of each eye.

The semiliquid eyeball interior is surrounded by three tissue layers. Outermost is the tough and protective sclera, made up of fibrous tissue. The sclera, or "white of the eye," has at its front a circular cornea. This sclera segment is modified to allow light rays to enter the eye and to aid in the focusing of light reflected from objects seen. At the front of each eye, paired eyelids protect the sclera's outer surface, removing dirt and lubricating with tears by blinking. The eyelids also close reflexively for protection when an object comes close to an eye.

The middle and inner tissue layers of the eye are the choroid and the retina. The choroid holds all the blood vessels that feed the eye and a muscular ciliary body that alters the shape of the eye lens to help to focus light. The retina lines most of the eyeball interior, except at its front. Retinal tissue converts light energy to nerve impulses carried to the brain. Choriod blood vessels extend throughout the retina, except at its front. There, a hole, the pupil, allows light entry into the eye. A circular iris around the pupil gives each eye its color.

The retina translates light energy into nerve impulses, using rod cells, cone cells, bipolar cells, and ganglion cells. Rods and cones are light-sensitive,

yielding nerve impulses when they are struck by light. Bipolar cells transfer the acquired information to the brain via ganglion cell fibers in the optic nerve at the rear of the eye. The rods, sensitive to tiny amounts of light, enable dim light vision. Cones enable the perception of color and detail. Rods and cones hold the pigment rhodopsin (RO, or visual purple). When it interacts with light, RO decomposes to a protein (opsin) and a form of vitamin A called retinol1. More RO must be made before a rod's next operation. Unless the diet provides vitamin A (as retinol1) in amounts enabling this, an afflicted person has night blindness (nyctalopia). Nyctalopics cannot see well in dim light.

A small region in the retina's center, the fovea centralis, contains cones but no rods, and cone number per unit of retinal area decreases as the front edge of the retina—near the pupil—is approached from the fovea. In contrast, the relative number of rods increases as the number of cones diminishes. Humans see most clearly in daylight, using the fovea almost exclusively. At night, vision is ac-

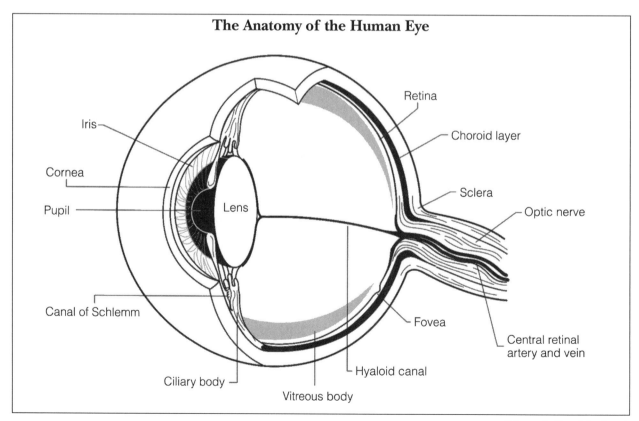

The Anatomy of the Human Eye

Iris — Cornea — Pupil — Canal of Schlemm — Ciliary body — Vitreous body — Hyaloid canal — Fovea — Lens — Retina — Choroid layer — Sclera — Optic nerve — Central retinal artery and vein

(Hans & Cassidy, Inc.)

complished mostly by using a retina region at the side of each eye.

A blind spot in the visual field occurs when objects cast images on the retina's optic disk. This disk, the point where the optic nerve leaves the eye, lacks both rods and cones. The optic nerves from the two eyes pass through the optic chiasma. Fibers from the inner half of each retina cross to the opposite side of the brain. Those from the outer half remain on the same side of the brain. This causes the right visual field, which stimulates the left half of each retina to activate the left half of the thalamus and visual cortex. The left visual field affects the right half of the brain, a situation similar to that of the other human sensory systems.

The visual cortex includes the occipital lobe of each cortical hemisphere, and there is a point-for-point correspondence between the retinas and the cortex. This yields a "map," whose every point represents a point on the retina and visual space seen by each eye. Vision simultaneously depicts object color, shape, location, movement, and orientation in space. Seeking a model to explain the overall brain action in vision, neurophysiologists have identified various cortical cell types, each involved selectively in these features. Retinal maps from each eye merge in a cortical projection area, which allows images from the two eyes to yield stereoscopic vision. Other brain regions also participate in vision; for instance, the cortex appears to be involved in perceiving form and movement.

LENSES AND VISION TYPES

Just behind the cornea, a transparent, elastic lens is attached to a ligament that controls its shape. Lens shape focuses light reflected from an object and forms on the retina the sharpest possible visual image. The eyes regulate the amount of light reaching retinal rods and cones by contracting or expanding the pupil by means of the iris. These involuntary responses are controlled by brain reflex pathways. The lens also divides the eye into two compartments. The small compartment in front of the lens holds watery aqueous humor. The much larger rear compartment between lens and retina is full of jellylike vitreous humor. This humor maintains the eye's shape.

Usable visible (380- to 730-nanometer) light enters the eye through the pupil and excites color sensations by interacting with retinal cones. Light re-

flected from an object passes through the lens to form a focused retinal image, similar to what a camera forms on film. Focusing a visual image also requires regulation of the amount of light passing through the pupil by making the iris larger or smaller. The eye lens produces an inverted retinal image, interpreted in the brain right-side-up. Binocular vision enables accurate depth perception. Each eye gets a slightly different view of any object, and the two retina images are interpreted by the brain as a three-dimensional view.

Nocturnal animals see in low-light environments with black-and-white (scotopic) vision. Diurnal (day-living) animals have photopic vision, which needs much more light to perceive colors and textures. Humans have both photopic and scotopic vision. Scotopic vision uses the rods as well as photosensitive RO. RO is bleached by bright light, so scotopic animals are almost blind by day. Humans suffer brief blindness on walking indoors on bright days. Then, by dark adaptation, scotopic vision quickly begins to function. Faulty dark adaptation (night blindness) occurs in humans who lack rods or are vitamin A deficient. Afflicted individuals cannot find their way around at night without artificial light. Photopic vision mostly uses the fovea, so it is due to cones, the only foveal visual cells. In the central fovea there are approximately 100,000 cones per square millimeter of retinal surface. Each cone associates with nerve cells that process the incoming visual data, convey them to the brain cortex, and provide detailed information on objects whose images fall in the fovea.

Peripheral vision occurs outside of the fovea, as may be seen by looking directly at one letter on a page. That letter and a few others nearby look very sharp and black because they are seen by foveal vision. The rest of the page, seen by peripheral vision, blurs. The clarity of foveal vision versus peripheral vision is due to the increasing scarcity of cones in retinal areas farther and farther from the fovea. Also, the nerve connections in the retinal periphery result in each optic nerve fiber being activated by hundreds of rods. This shared action is useful in detecting large or dim objects at night. However, it prevents color vision, which requires the brain to differentiate among many signals.

VISUAL DEFECTS AND THEIR SYMPTOMS

Human eyes can have numerous vision defects. The most common of these defects are small, opaque bodies (floaters) in the eye humors. Usually, floaters are only an inconvenience. Much more serious are lens opacities called cataracts. They develop for several reasons, including advancing age and diabetes. Opacity of the cornea can also cause obscured vision. It can be repaired through the transplantation of a section of clear cornea from another person. Three very dangerous eye diseases that can cause blindness are detached retinas (retina rips), glaucoma (eye pressure buildup due to blocked tear ducts), and macular degeneration (destruction of the retinal areas responsible for sight).

Six serious, but relatively easily treated, vision problems are myopia, hyperopia, presbyopia, astigmatism, diplopia, and strabismus. They are due to incorrect eyeball length, to lens defects, or to external eye muscle weakness. In myopia (nearsightedness) the eyeball is too long. Light from nearby objects will focus well on the retina. Distant rays focus before it, yielding blurry images. Conversely, farsightedness (hyperopia) occurs because the eyeball is too short. As a result, the light from distant objects focuses on the retina, but that from nearby objects focuses behind it and makes them blurry. An eye can also lose the ability to adapt quickly from far vision to near vision. This problem, presbyopia, usually happens after age forty. In an astigmatism, uneven curvature of an eye lens causes retinal images to be made up of short lines, not sharp points. Weakness or paralysis of external eyeball muscles may cause diplopia (double vision) and strabismus (squint).

Blindness, the most serious vision problem, is much more debilitating than any other sensory deprivation. It occurs in many forms. Some are temporary, mild, and readily treated. Others are severe and untreatable. Color blindness is an incurable lack of some or all color vision. This congenital form of blindness is attributed to genetic defects in the retina or some part of the optic tract. It is mild, causing, at worst, no color perception and a life spent in a black-and-white world. Amblyopia, weak vision without apparent structural eye damage, is another type of acquired blindness, due to toxic drugs, alcoholism, or hysteria. Blindness may also be caused by diseases such as iritis and trachoma.

Blindness varies in extent, from inability to distinguish light from darkness (total blindness) to inability to see well enough to do any job requiring use of the eyes (economic blindness) to vocational and educational blindness: inability to work in a job done before becoming blind, and inability to become educated by methods commonly used in school, respectively. Most severe blindness is permanent and incurable. There are about two blind people per thousand in industrialized nations and two per hundred in underdeveloped countries. The causes of blindness include genetic abnormalities of components of the eye or brain, pressure on the optic nerve from a brain tumor, detachment of the retina from the choriod, damage to the eyes or brain by excess light, or severe head trauma.

TREATMENT OPTIONS FOR VISION PROBLEMS

Visual defects are most often identified by ophthalmologists who prescribe eye treatments such as the use of eyeglasses, contact lenses, or surgery. Detached retinas and glaucoma can both be repaired by surgery, and most night blindness is cured by adding sufficient vitamin A to the diet to allow optimal cone and rod operation. Amblyopia is treated by psychologists or psychiatrists who identify its basis and work with afflicted individuals to reassure them or apply pharmacological treatment of the problem. Some kinds of structurally based blindness may be cured by surgery (such as removing brain tumors). However, in a great many cases the blindness is incurable. When blindness is acquired by sighted people (adventitious blindness), it can be important to receive the help of a mental health professional to gain the ability to live with it successfully. This is most crucial early in the adventitious blindness, when afflicted individuals are least likely to be able to cope with being cut off from a major source of their contact with the world.

The adjustments that must be made on occurrence of adventitious blindness are so extensive that the blind person eventually becomes a different individual from the sighted person he or she once was. Usually, the initial response to adventitious blindness is apathy and severe depression. These symptoms are followed by the return of interest in living and coping with the practical problems caused by blindness. The function of a psychologist or a psychiatrist is the careful combination of psychotherapy and pharmacological treatment—varied, individually, in its length and scope—to ready each afflicted individual to function well in a sighted world. After an adventitiously blind individual is capable of coping well with being blind, there are several federal and private agencies aimed at teaching such individuals to operate well and to engage in training so as to allow them to reachieve gainful employment.

SOURCES FOR FURTHER STUDY

Chalkley, Thomas. *Your Eyes.* 4th ed. Springfield, Ill.: Charles C Thomas, 2000. Thoroughly covers the human eye; light and vision; diseases such as cataracts, glaucoma, and strabismus; how eyes and brain relate; and eye changes due to general disease and injury.

De Valois, Karen K., ed. *Seeing.* 2d ed. San Diego, Calif.: Academic Press, 2000. This work has chapters on vision, physiological aspects of vision, color perception, binocular vision processes, and motion perception. It includes a bibliography.

Hollins, Mark. *Understanding Blindness: An Integrative Approach.* Hillsdale, N.J.: Lawrence Erlbaum, 1989. A well-done book, covering blindness, its causes, and its psychological aspects. It also has a complete bibliography.

Hubel, David H. *Eye, Brain, and Vision.* New York: W. H. Freeman, 1995. Thoroughly covers the eye, the brain's function in vision, and vision. Includes a bibliography.

Rodieck, Robert W. *The First Steps in Seeing.* Sunderland, Mass.: Sinauer Associates, 1998. Covers vision, the physiology of vision and the eye, and the anatomy and histology of the eye. Good bibliography.

Schwartz, Steven H. *Visual Perception.* 3d ed. New York: McGraw-Hill, 2004. Covers many aspects of vision, including the retina, functional retinal physiology, the cortex, color vision and its anomalies, depth perception, and the anatomy of the eye. Has a good bibliography.

Tovée, Martin J. *An Introduction to the Visual System.* New York: Cambridge University Press, 2008. Covers many vision topics, including the eye and image formation, color vision, organization of the visual system, the visual cortex, object perception and recognition, and motion perception.

Sanford S. Singer

SEE ALSO: Brain structure; Depth and motion perception; Hearing; Pattern recognition; Pattern vision; Sensation and perception; Smell and taste; Touch and pressure; Vision: Brightness and contrast; Vision: Color.

W

Watson, John B.

BORN: January 9, 1878, near Greenville, South
Carolina
DIED: September 25, 1958, in New York City
IDENTITY: American psychologist
TYPE OF PSYCHOLOGY: Learning; origin and
definition of psychology; psychological
methodologies
FIELDS OF STUDY: Anxiety disorders; infancy and
childhood

*Watson founded a school of psychology known as
behaviorism.*

John B. Watson was born into a strict religious
family. At the age of sixteen, he entered Fur-
man University in Greenville, South Carolina,
and eventually received a master's degree. He
then enrolled at the University of Chicago,
where he became the youngest student ever at
the university to earn a Ph.D.

Watson was an instructor at the University
of Chicago for four years before becoming a
professor at The Johns Hopkins University.
When the department chairman resigned, Watson replaced him and also assumed editorship
of *Psychological Review,* a respected journal. In
1913, he published "Psychology as the Behaviorist Views It" in the journal; this launched a
new school of psychology. In the paper, Watson rejected the introspective techniques of
the school of structuralism and declared that
psychology must become the science of behavior by examining overt behavior in an objective fashion. Mentalistic concepts must be
replaced by empirical study of observable behavior only. In 1915, Watson was elected president of the American Psychological Association,
and he used this position to promote behaviorism.

Watson's behaviorism incorporated a strong
form of environmentalism; he argued that there
were no genetic influences on behavior and that humans were simply a product of their environment.
In one famous demonstration, he and his graduate
assistant Rosalie Rayner used Pavlovian conditioning to instill a phobia in a young boy. "Little Albert,"
an eleven-month-old infant, was conditioned to fear
a rat after the animal's appearance was paired with a
loud noise. The boy also cried when shown other
furry objects, such as a rabbit and fur coat, even

John B. Watson. (Hulton Archives/Getty Images)

though these objects had not been paired with the noise. The boy's fear had generalized to objects similar to the rat. Watson argued, therefore, that phobias are simply learned behavior and not the result of unconscious sexual conflict, as Sigmund Freud had claimed.

Unfortunately, Watson's academic career ended unexpectedly in 1920. He was having an affair with Rayner and was forced to resign after his wife began divorce proceedings. Watson moved to New York and began a successful career in advertising. Throughout the 1920's, he continued to promulgate his ideas through several books, most notably *Behaviorism* (1924), and numerous articles. Many of these writings were read by general audiences and solidified behavioristic views in the United States.

By emphasizing the study of overt behavior, Watson's behaviorism moved psychology away from its philosophic roots and helped fashion it into a science. In many areas, such as learning, behaviorism dominated American psychology throughout much of the twentieth century. B. F. Skinner, one of the most famous twentieth century American psychologists, was a strong advocate of behaviorism.

SOURCES FOR FURTHER STUDY

Buckley, Kerry W. *Mechanical Man: John Broadus Watson and the Beginnings of Behaviorism.* New York: Guilford Press, 1989. Provides a comprehensive examination of how Watson's personal and scientific lives affected each other.

Cohen, David. *J. B. Watson, the Founder of Behaviourism: A Biography.* London: Routledge & Kegan Paul, 1979. Persuasively demonstrates the breadth of Watson's psychological contributions and vision.

Fancher, Raymond E. *Pioneers of Psychology.* 3d ed. New York: W. W. Norton, 1996. Includes a chapter on Watson's and Pavlov's contributions in making psychology the science of behavior.

Charles H. Evans

SEE ALSO: Behaviorism; Learning; Radical behaviorism: B. F. Skinner; Skinner, B. F.

Wechsler Intelligence Scale for Children-Third Edition (WISC-III)

DATE: 1949 forward

TYPE OF PSYCHOLOGY: Intelligence and intelligence testing

FIELD OF STUDY: Intelligence assessment

The Wechsler Intelligence Scale for Children-Third Edition is an individually administered test battery developed to measure the intellectual ability of children aged six years through sixteen years, eleven months. The WISC-III is commonly used for the psychoeducational, neurological, and clinical assessment of school-aged children and for the diagnosis of mental retardation, learning disabilities, brain injury, and giftedness.

KEY CONCEPTS

- culture bias
- intelligence test
- performance subtests
- psychoeducational assessment
- verbal subtests

INTRODUCTION

The Wechsler Intelligence Scale for Children-Third Edition (WISC-III) retains the essential content and structure of the original Wechsler Intelligence Scale for Children (WISC), published in 1949, and its 1974 revision (WISC-R). The third edition, however, provides current representative normative data, updated test items that attempt to minimize culture bias and gender bias, more contemporary and visually appealing testing materials, and clearer administrative procedures, factor structure rules, and scoring rules. These improvements make the test more interesting and fairer for the child and more user-friendly for the examiner.

HISTORY OF DEVELOPMENT

David Wechsler defined intelligence as the overall capacity of an individual to act purposefully, think rationally, and deal effectively with the environment. He believed intelligence to be a general concept that is multidetermined and multifaceted, rather than a specific trait or type of intellectual ability. An intelligence test is a device that assesses an individual's potential for purposeful and useful behavior. To measure intelligence at the adult level, he selected eleven subtests from a wide range of existing standardized tests and published the Wechsler-Bellevue Intelligence Scale in 1939. This assessment became the Wechsler Adult Intelligence Scale in 1955 and is currently the Wechsler Adult Intelligence Scale-Third Edition (WAIS-III), published in 1998.

In 1949, to provide an instrument to measure the intelligence of children as young as five years old, he developed the Wechsler Intelligence Scale for Children by designing easier items appropriate for children and adding them to the original scales. Due to suspected ethnic and socioeconomic bias in the standardization sample, the test was revised in 1974 to establish normative data that were more representative of ethnic minorities and children from lower socioeconomic levels. The present form, the Wechsler Intelligence Scale for Children-Third Edition, was published in 1991.

DESCRIPTION OF THE TEST

The WISC-III consists of thirteen subtests organized into two groups: the verbal subtests and the performance subtests. The verbal subtests require language to administer the items and the child must provide a verbal response. These subtests and the behaviors assessed include information (knowledge of general information), similarities (abstract and conceptual thinking), arithmetic (arithmetic knowledge and short-term memory), vocabulary (general vocabulary knowledge and long-term memory), comprehension (social judgment), and digit span (short-term auditory memory). The performance subtests consist of perceptual-motor items that also must be administered verbally but require minimal or no verbal response. The performance subtests and behaviors measured are picture completion (perceptual discrimination), coding (visual-motor coordination), picture arrangement (visual perception), block design (abstract visual-spatial reasoning), object assembly (visual-motor coordination and integration), mazes (visual planning ability), and a new item labeled symbol search (perceptual discrimination). Subtests are reported as scaled (standard) scores with a mean of 10 and a standard deviation of 3.

The performance on each of these subtests yields three composite intelligence quotient (IQ) scores, which are also reported as scaled scores. The sum of the scaled scores on the verbal subtests yields the verbal IQ score, and the sum of the scaled scores on the performance subtests results in the performance IQ scores. The verbal and performance subtests are then added to compute the full-scale IQ. The mean of each IQ is 100, and the standard deviation is 15. The WISC-III also provides four new index scores that are composites of subtests identified by a previous factor analytic study that reported the existence of four factors. The verbal comprehension index, perceptual organization index, freedom from distractibility index, and processing speed index also have a mean of 100 and a standard deviation of 15.

STANDARDIZATION, RELIABILITY, AND VALIDITY

The WISC-III was standardized on groups considered representative of the United States population of children according to 1988 census data. A stratified sampling plan was used to select children in representative proportions according to age, gender, race/ethnicity, geographic region, and parent education. A total of 2,200 children in eleven age groups ranging from six years to sixteen years, eleven months of age were selected, with 200 children (100 males and 100 females) in each group. Both public and private schools were sampled, and students receiving special services in school settings were included if they could speak and understand English. Thus, 7 percent of the sample consisted of students identified as having a learning disability, speech/language impairment, emotional disorder, physical disability, or reading challenge that qualified them for Chapter 1 programs. Also, 5 percent of the sample consisted of students identified as gifted and/or talented.

Split-half reliability coefficients reported in the manual for the verbal, performance, and full-scale IQ scores range from an average of 0.91 to 0.96. Due to the considerable overlap of test items, as well as the acceptable IQ score correlations and subtest correlations between the WISC-R and the WISC-III (0.42 to 0.90), the validity research on the WISC-R was generalized to the WISC-III. The findings from these studies supported the construct, concurrent, and predictive validity of the WISC-R.

APPLICATIONS OF THE WISC-III

The WISC-III is commonly used for the psychoeducational assessment, neurological assessment, and clinical assessment of school-aged children. As a psychoeducational tool, the WISC-III is often part of the assessment battery used for the diagnosis of mental retardation and giftedness and for the appropriate placement in special school-based programs. Moreover, the separation of verbal and performance subtests allows the examiner to select portions of the test that can be successfully completed by children with hearing impairments, visual impairments, and orthopedic handicaps. Studies have shown that responses to WISC-III subtests have provided information useful for the diagnosis and remediation of learning disabilities, brain injury, and other cognitive deficits.

Sources for Further Study

Cooper, Shawn. *The Clinical Use and Interpretation of the Wechsler Intelligence Scale for Children.* 3d ed. Springfield, Mass.: Charles C Thomas, 1995. The author describes the history and development of the WISC-III and provides detailed information and advice on the administration, analysis, and interpretation of the test. He offers a number of alternative approaches to the intellectual assessment of children and adolescents.

Groth-Marnat, Gary. *Handbook of Psychological Assessment.* Rev. ed. New York: John Wiley & Sons, 2009. The author dedicates a chapter to a thorough overview of the measurement of intelligence as a construct as well as to the development of the Wechsler Intelligence Scales. The sections describing assessment of brain damage and special populations of school-age children are particularly interesting and useful to clinicians and educators.

Newmark, Charles S. *Major Psychological Assessment Instruments.* 2d ed. Boston: Allyn & Bacon, 1996. The author describes the psychometric properties of the WISC-III, the specific abilities measured by each of the subtests, and the sources of IQ scores and index scores. The book provides very clear descriptions of the clinical uses of the test, approaches to interpret test results, and the assets and liabilities of the test.

Sattler, Jerome M. *Assessment of Children.* 5th ed. San Diego, Calif.: Author, 2008. Presents a highly detailed description of the development, characteristics, subtests, and interpretation of the WISC-R. The writing style is directed toward students and professionals who might not have a strong background in tests and measurements.

_____. *WISC-III and WPPSI-R Supplement to As-sessment of Children.* 5th ed. San Diego, Calif.: Author, 2008. This supplement to *Assessment of Children* compares the WISC-R and the WISC-III and describes the WISC-III in detail. The supplement was designed to be more readable and comprehensive than the main text. However, according to the author, the supplement should be used in conjunction with the main text to have all the tables and guidelines needed to interpret the WISC-III.

Wechsler, David. *Manual for the Wechsler Intelligence Scale for Children.* 3d ed. New York: Psychological Corporation, 1991. The technical manual that was published with the WISC-III provides information on the development and application of the test, standardization procedures, administration and scoring procedures, and statistical information on reliability and validity. Chapter 2 provides a detailed description of the changes made to update and improve the WISC-R.

"The Wechsler Intelligence Scale for Children-Third Edition." In *The Twelfth Mental Measurement Yearbook*, edited by Jane C. Conoley and James C. Impara. Lincoln: University of Nebraska Press, 1995. Technical information about the WISC-III is provided, and 409 references are listed that relate to the development, psychometric quality, and use of the test. Two independent reviews of the test by measurement specialists describe the characteristics, updates, changes, strengths, and weaknesses of the test.

Woodrich, David L. *Children's Psychological Testing: A Guide for Nonpsychologists.* 3d ed. Baltimore: Brookes, 1997. This resource describes the reasons for psychological testing, explains the principles of assessment, and provides a nontechnical overview of the WISC-III. The writing style is very appropriate for nonprofessional readers.

Lyn T. Boulter

See also: Ability tests; Assessment; Career and personnel testing; Career Occupational Preference System (COPS); College entrance examinations; Creativity: Assessment; General Aptitude Test Battery (GATB); Human resource training and development; Intelligence tests; Interest inventories; Kuder Occupational Interest Survey (KOIS); Peabody Individual Achievement Test (PIAT); Race and intelligence; Scientific methods; Stanford-Binet test; Strong Interest Inventory (SII); Survey research: Questionnaires and interviews; Testing: Historical perspectives.

Within-subject experimental designs

TYPE OF PSYCHOLOGY: Psychological methodologies
FIELD OF STUDY: Experimental methodologies

Within-subject designs are experimental plans in which each participant in the experiment receives every level of the independent variable. Such designs are powerful, because individual differences cannot confound the effects of the independent variable.

KEY CONCEPTS
- balanced Latin square
- between-subject designs
- carryover effects
- confounding
- counterbalancing
- dependent variable
- independent variable
- reversal design
- small-n designs

INTRODUCTION

In an experiment, a particular comparison is produced while other factors are held constant. For example, to investigate the effects of music on reading comprehension, an experimenter might compare the effects of music versus no music on the comprehension of a chapter from a history textbook. The comparison that is produced—music versus no music—is called the independent variable. An independent variable must have at least two levels or values so that a comparison can be made. The behavior that is observed or measured is called the dependent variable, which would be some measure of reading comprehension in the example.

Presumably, any changes in reading comprehension during the experiment depend on changes in the levels of the independent variable. The intent of an experiment is to hold everything constant except the changes in the levels of the independent variable. If this is done, the experimenter can assume that changes in the dependent variable were caused by changes in the levels of the independent variable.

ROLE OF INDEPENDENT VARIABLE

Experimental design concerns the way in which the levels of the independent variable are assigned to experimental subjects. This is a crucial concern, because the experimenter wants to make sure that it is the independent variable and not something else that causes changes in behavior. Between-subject designs are plans in which different participants receive the levels of the independent variable. Therefore, in terms of the example already mentioned, some people would read with music playing and other people would read without music. Within-subject designs are plans in which each participant receives each level of the manipulated variable. In a within-subject design, each person would read a history chapter both while music is playing and in silence. Each of these designs has unwanted features that make it difficult to decide whether the independent variable caused changes in the dependent variable.

Because different subjects receive each level of the independent variable in a between-subject design, the levels of the independent variable vary with the subjects in each condition. Any effect observed in the experiment could result from either the independent variable or the characteristics of the subjects in a particular condition. For example, the people who read while music is playing might simply be better readers than those who read in silence. This difference between the people in the two groups would make it difficult to determine whether music or reading ability caused changes in comprehension. When something other than the independent variable could cause the results of an experiment, the results are confounded. In between-subject designs, the potential effects of the independent variable are confounded with the different subjects in each condition. Instead of the independent variable, individual differences, such as intelligence or reading ability, could account for differences between groups. This confounding (the variation of other variables with the independent variable of interest, as a result of which any effects cannot be attributed with certainty to the independent variable) may be minimized by assigning participants to conditions randomly or by matching the different subjects in some way, but these tactics do not eliminate the potential confounding. For this and other reasons, many experimenters prefer to use within-subject designs.

Because each subject receives each level of the independent variable in within-subject designs, subjects are not confounded with the independent variable. In the example experiment, this means that both good and bad readers would read with and without music. Yet the order in which a subject receives the levels of the independent variable is confounded with the levels of the independent variable. Therefore, determining whether a change in the dependent variable occurred because of the independent variable or as a result of the timing of the administration of the treatment might be difficult. This kind of confounding is called a carryover effect. The effects of one value of the independent variable might carry over to the period when the next level is being tested. Just as likely, an unwanted carryover effect could result because the subject's behavior changes as the experiment progresses. The subject might become better at the task because of practicing it or worse because of boredom or fatigue. Whatever the source of the carryover effects, they represent serious potential confounding.

COUNTERBALANCING

Carryover effects can be minimized by counterbalancing. Counterbalancing means that the order of administering the conditions of an experiment is systematically varied. Consider the reading experiment: One condition is reading with music (M), and the comparison level is reading in silence (S). If all subjects received S before M, order would be confounded with condition. If half the subjects had M before S and the remaining subjects had S before M, the order of treatments would not be confounded with the nature of the treatments. This is so because both treatment conditions occur first and second equally often.

Complete counterbalancing is done when all possible orders of the independent variable are administered. Complete counterbalancing is easy when there are two or three levels of the independent variable. With four or more levels, however, complete counterbalancing becomes cumbersome because of the number of different orders of conditions that can be generated. With more than three levels, experimenters usually use a balanced Latin square to decide the order of administering conditions. In a balanced Latin square, each condition occurs at the same time period on average, and each treatment precedes and follows each other treatment equally often. Imagine an experiment with four levels of the independent variable, called A, B, C, and D. One might think of these as four different

types of music that are being tested in the reading-comprehension example. Suppose there are four subjects, numbered 1, 2, 3, and 4. In a balanced Latin square, the following would be the orders for the four subjects: subject 1, A, B, D, C; subject 2, B, C, A, D; subject 3, C, D, B, A; subject 4, D, A, C, B. Notice that across subjects each treatment occurs first, second, third, and fourth. Notice also that each treatment precedes and follows each other treatment. Although these four orders do not exhaust the possibilities for four treatments (there are a total of twenty-four), they do minimize the confounding from carryover effects.

INFERENTIAL STATISTICS AND TESTING SUBJECTS

Another feature favoring within-subject designs concerns inferential statistics. Because each participant serves in all conditions in within-subject designs, variability associated with individual differences among subjects has little influence on the statistical significance of the results. This means that within-subject designs are more likely than between-subject designs to yield a statistically significant result. Experimenters are more likely to find an effect attributable to the independent variable when its levels vary within subjects rather than between them.

A final reason within-subject designs are preferred to between-subject ones is that they require fewer subjects for testing. To try to minimize the confounding effects of individual differences in between-subject designs, experimenters typically assign many subjects randomly to each condition of the experiment. Since individual differences are not a hindrance in within-subject designs, fewer subjects can be tested, and there is a corresponding savings in time and effort.

REVERSAL DESIGN

Experimenters in all areas of psychology use within-subject designs. These designs are used whenever the independent variable is unlikely to have permanent carryover effects. Thus, if the characteristics of the subjects themselves are the variable of interest (such as place of birth or reading ability), those variables must be varied between subjects. If permanent carryover effects are of interest (such as learning to type as a function of practice), however, experimenters use within-subject plans.

Many experiments undertaken to solve practical problems use within-subject designs. These experiments are often small-n designs, which means that the number of subjects (n) is small—sometimes only one. Consider an experiment conducted by Betty M. Hart and her associates. They wanted to decrease the amount of crying exhibited by a four-year-old boy in nursery school. They observed his behavior for several days to find the baseline rate of crying episodes. During a ten-day period, the boy had between five and ten crying episodes each day that lasted at least five seconds. Hart and her associates noted that the teacher often tried to soothe the boy when he began crying. The researchers believed that this attention rewarded the crying behavior. Therefore, in the second phase of the experiment, the teacher ignored the boy's crying unless it resulted from an injury. Within five days, the crying episodes had decreased and remained at no more than one per day for a week. To gain better evidence that it was the teacher's attention that influenced the rate of crying, a third phase of the experiment reinstated the conditions of the baseline phase. The teacher paid attention to the boy when he whined and cried, and in a few days the level of crying was back to six or seven episodes per day.

The small-n design used by Hart and her associates is an example of a reversal design. In a reversal design, there is first a baseline phase, then a treatment phase, and finally a return to the baseline phase to make sure that it was the treatment that changed the behavior. Hart's experiment had a fourth phase in which the teacher again ignored the boy's crying, because the purpose of the treatment was to reduce the crying. In the fourth phase, the level of crying dropped to a negligible level.

When there is only one subject in an experiment, counterbalancing cannot be used to minimize carryover effects. Thus, the experience in the treatment phase of a reversal design might carry over into the second baseline phase. Experimenters seek an approximate return to the original behavior during the second baseline phase, but the behavior is seldom exactly as it was before the treatment period. Therefore, deciding about the effectiveness of the treatment introduced in the second phase may be difficult. This means that the reversal design is not a perfect experimental design. It has important applications in psychology, however, especially in clinical psychology, where practical results rather than strict experimental control are often very important.

TRAPPERS CASE STUDY

Lise Saari conducted an experiment that used a more conventional within-subject design. Saari wanted to assess the effect of payment schedule on the performance and attitudes of beaver trappers. The trappers received an hourly wage from a forest-products company while they participated in the following experiment.

Initially, trapping performance was measured under the ordinary hourly payment plan. Later, the trappers worked under two incentive plans manipulated in a within-subject design. In the continuous-reward condition, trappers received an additional dollar for each animal that was trapped. In the second condition, trappers received a reward of four dollars when they brought in a beaver. They obtained the four dollars only if they correctly predicted twice whether the roll of a die would yield an even or an odd number. In this variable-ratio condition, the trapper could guess the correct roll one out of four times by chance alone. In summary, the trappers always received a one-dollar reward in the continuous-reward condition. In the variable-ratio condition, however, the payment of four dollars occurred once every four times on average. Therefore, the trappers averaged an extra dollar for each beaver in each condition.

To minimize carryover effects, counterbalancing the order of treatments occurred as follows. The trappers were split into two groups, which alternated between the two schedules, spending a week at a time on each. This weekly alternation of experimental payment continued for the entire trapping season.

Compared to the amount of trapping that occurred under the hourly wage, the results showed that beaver trapping increased under both the continuous and the variable-payment scheme. The increase was, however, much larger under the variable payment plan than under the continuous one. In addition, Saari found that the trappers preferred to work under the variable-ratio scheme. Since both plans yielded the same amount of extra money on average, the mode of giving the payment (continuous or variable) seems crucial.

The experiment by Saari has obvious important practical implications concerning methods of payment. Still, it is equally important that the design of the experiment was free of confounding. The counterbalancing scheme minimized the possibility of confounding the payment scheme with order. Thus, Saari could conclude that the change in attitudes and the increased trapping performance resulted from the variable payment plan, not from some confounding carryover effect.

USE IN PSYCHOLOGY

Within-subject designs have a long history of use in psychology. The psychophysics experiments conducted by Ernst Weber and Gustav Fechner in the nineteenth century were among the first within-subject experiments in psychology. The tradition of obtaining many observations on a few subjects started by Weber and Fechner continues in modern psychophysical scaling and signal-detection experiments.

One of the most famous small-n experiments in psychology is that reported by Hermann Ebbinghaus in his book *Über das gedächtnis: Untersuchurgen zur experimentellen Psychologie* (1885; *Memory: A Contribution to Experimental Psychology*, 1913). Ebbinghaus tested himself in a series of memory experiments. In his work on remembering nonsense syllables and poetry, he discovered many laws of retaining and forgetting. These laws are now firmly established. Numerous modern experiments with larger numbers of experimental participants and various verbal materials have yielded results confirming Ebbinghaus's work. Among the most important findings are the shape of the curve of forgetting over time, the important role of practice in improving retention, and the benefits of distributing practice as opposed to cramming it.

B. F. Skinner pioneered the use of small-n designs for laboratory experiments on rats and pigeons in the 1930's. Skinner's work on schedules of reinforcement is among the most frequently cited in psychology. In his work, Skinner insisted on making numerous observations of few subjects under tightly controlled conditions. His ability to control the behavior of experimental subjects and obtain reliable results in within-subject plans such as the reversal design has led to the wide acceptance of within-subject plans in laboratory and applied experimental work.

Developmental psychologists regularly use a variant of the within-subject design. This is the longitudinal design, in which repeated observations are made as the subject develops and grows older. In a typical longitudinal experiment, a child first might receive a test of problem solving when he or she is three years old. Then the test would be repeated at ages five and seven.

CROSS-SECTIONAL PLAN

The longitudinal design inherently confounds age or development with period of testing, since age cannot be counterbalanced for an individual. An alternative developmental design is the cross-sectional plan. In this design, subjects of different ages are tested at the same time. Since participants of different ages have grown up in different time periods with different people, age is confounded with generation of birth in the cross-sectional design. Thus, the cross-sectional plan is between subjects and cannot control for individual differences. Although the longitudinal design confounds age with time of testing, individual differences do not confound the results. Therefore, the longitudinal design is a valuable research tool for the developmental psychologist.

Because of their control, efficiency, and statistical power, within-subject designs are popular and important in psychology. All areas of applied and basic scientific psychology rely heavily on within-subject designs, and such designs are likely to remain important in the field.

SOURCES FOR FURTHER STUDY

Gescheider, George A. *Psychophysics: Method and Theory.* 2d ed. Hillsdale, N.J.: Lawrence Erlbaum, 1984. This is a standard work on psychophysical methods. Gescheider describes the many experimental plans used to examine the sensory judgments that people make. The student will find the discussion of method more valuable than the sections that deal with the theories of psychophysics.

Gravetter, Frederick J., and Larry B. Wallnau. *Essentials of Statistics for the Behavioral Sciences.* 6th ed. Belmont, Calif.: Thomson/Wadsworth, 2008. This accessible statistics text shows the strength of within-subject designs. The authors do not assume that the reader has a sophisticated mathematical background, but understanding the statistical analysis of within-subject designs may require some effort.

Kantowitz, Barry H., David G. Elmes, and Henry L. Roediger III. *Experimental Psychology: Understanding Psychological Research.* 9th ed. Belmont, Calif.: Wadsworth, 2009. A standard textbook on all aspects of research in psychology. Chapters focus on experimental design, detailed methods of counterbalancing, and small-*n* designs besides the reversal design. Can be understood by college students and sophisticated high school students.

Martin, David W. *Doing Psychology Experiments* 7th ed. Belmont, Calif.: Wadsworth, 2008. Martin presents humorous examples that may help the reader comprehend the important principles of experimental design.

Reis, Harry T., and Charles M. Judd, eds. *Handbook of Research Methods in Social and Personality Psychology.* New York: Cambridge University Press, 2000. A very thorough overview of psychological research methods. Within-subject experimental design is discussed at several points throughout.

David G. Elmes

SEE ALSO: Complex experimental designs; Developmental methodologies; Ebbinghaus, Hermann; Experimentation: Independent, dependent, and control variables; Sampling; Scientific methods; Signal detection theory; Statistical significance tests.

Women's mental health

TYPE OF PSYCHOLOGY: Psychopathology; psychotherapy; stress

FIELDS OF STUDY: Behavioral and cognitive models; depression; schizophrenias; stress and illness

Women experience a higher rate of depression than men do, and they are more likely to experience depression related to life changes, including trauma and stress, hormonal changes, and role changes. Other serious mental illnesses such as bipolar disorder and schizophrenia are as likely to occur in men as in women, but they may manifest differently in women.

KEY CONCEPTS
- bipolar disorder
- depression
- major depressive disorder
- schizophrenia

INTRODUCTION
During their lifetimes, women undergo multiple biological and psychological changes involving hormonal fluctuations, childhood trauma, physical and emotional stress, and role changes. Combined with genetic dispositions and environmental factors, these events can result in mental diseases such as depression, schizophrenia, and bipolar disorder.

Depression, in particular, is highly prevalent in women, with women having twice the incidence of depression as men do. The menstrual cycle, pregnancy, infertility, childbirth, and menopause are associated with depression in women. Although there are many studies examining possible links between abnormalities in sex hormone levels and depression, no conclusive relationships have been established. In the absence of identifiable markers and biochemical diagnostic tests, practitioners have to rely on careful evaluation of symptoms and the taking of medical and mood histories. A variety of diagnostic tools are available to aid in the collection of this information. For women suspected of having depression related to the menstrual cycle, childbirth, or menopause, records of how their moods and symptoms fluctuate over time are important for diagnosis.

Unlike depression, schizophrenia and bipolar disorder are equally prevalent in men and women. However, these diseases may manifest differently in women and men. There are a variety of pharmacological and cognitive and behavioral treatment options for women with mental disorders. In some cases, treatment with a single therapy works well, and in other cases, a combination of different therapies results in optimal outcomes.

PREVALENCE AND CAUSES OF DEPRESSION
Major depressive disorder, which affects twice as many women as men, is characterized by decreased energy, reduced concentration, loss of interest or pleasure in activities that an individual used to enjoy, feelings of hopelessness, and disordered sleep (sleeping too much or too little). Some depressed patients may also have suicidal thoughts. Depression in women may be triggered by hormonal changes, stressful events, and seasonal fluctuations. Apart from the psychological effects, depression also causes problems in work and social functioning and is associated with comorbid diseases and a 10 to 15 percent suicide rate. Although depression has many causes, with both biological and environmental influences, there are specific conditions in women that are associated with especially high rates of depression. These conditions include the experience of

---

Women and Depression

STATISTICS AND FACTS
- about twelve million American women report experiencing clinical depression each year
- women experience depression at approximately double the rate of men
- approximately 3 to 5 percent of women who experience premenstrual syndrome have symptoms severe enough to be classified as Premenstrual Dysphoric Disorder (PMDD)
- approximately 10 to 15 percent of new mothers experience postpartum depression
- research indicates that a strong relationship exists between eating disorders and depression in women

WOMEN'S ATTITUDES TOWARD DEPRESSION
More than 50 percent of women believe:
- depression during menopause is normal and that treatment is not necessary
- depression is a normal aspect of the aging process
- feeling depressed for at least two weeks after giving birth is normal
- they are more informed about depression than men are

Source: National Mental Health Association (NMHA) factsheet "Depression in Women."

childhood trauma, the presence of certain personality traits, hormonal changes associated with the menstrual cycle, infertility, the aftermath of giving birth (postpartum), and the experiences of entering into and undergoing menopause.

Women are more likely than men to experience childhood trauma such as childhood sexual abuse, which predisposes for adult depression. Certain personality traits such as strong interpersonal sensitivity and a more passive, ruminative type of coping are more prevalent in women and are also associated with depression. Some women experience depressive symptoms, mood fluctuations, and social and work impairment in the ten days before the onset of menses. This condition, termed premenstrual dysphoric disorder, is gaining recognition as a bona fide mood disorder separate from major depression. Infertility is an increasingly prevalent condition in women, with a 1995 study reporting 6.1 million infertile women aged fifteen to forty-four and 9.3 million women using infertility services in the United States. This condition is frequently associated with symptoms of depression and anxiety. Women experi-

encing infertility report twice the depression rates of fertile women. For women undergoing in vitro fertilization (IVF), depression appears to fluctuate with the phases of the IVF cycle. Depression rates are particularly high after a failed IVF attempt, with a high percentage (13 percent) of women having thoughts of suicide. Postpartum depression occurs in 8 to 22 percent of women, depending on the diagnostic method used. Women with a history of depression and other psychiatric illnesses, teenage mothers, and mothers living in poverty are more prone to developing postpartum depression, with the latter two groups having incidence rates of approximately 26 percent and 27 percent, respectively. The causes of postpartum depression are unclear; although there are many hypotheses and some circumstantial evidence about the role of abnormal sex hormone levels (cortisol is elevated and serum thyroid hormone suppressed in women with postpartum depression), there is a lack of reproducible and conclusive studies.

Menopause is a process that stretches out over a number of years. Perimenopause starts one year before a woman's last period and ends one year after her last period. When the woman has gone one year without a period, she can be referred to as postmenopausal. Perimenopausal and postmenopausal women experience hormonal changes, resulting in a wide range of physical and emotional symptoms. One of these symptoms is depression, which is especially common in women with a history of depression. This may be due to the reduced levels of estrogen and other sex hormones in menopausal women.

DIAGNOSIS OF DEPRESSION
To treat women with depression, accurate diagnosis is essential. An important consideration in diagnosis is that depression manifests differently in men and women, with depressed women having more abnormal eating problems (either loss of appetite or overeating), anxiety, and atypical symptoms, while depressed men have higher rates of substance and alcohol abuse as well as higher rates of completed suicide. Women also tend to have longer depressive

episodes and are more likely to have chronic or recurrent depression. Physicians make use of information such as a patient's symptoms and history of depression and other psychiatric disorders, as well as the patient's past responses to medications to make a diagnosis of depression. Diagnostic tools may help in the process of obtaining important information and making an accurate diagnosis.

One tool that is especially conducive to the primary care setting, where there is limited time for patient evaluations, is the two-question depression screen. This consists of the following two questions:

- In the last month, have you lost pleasure in the activities you normally enjoy?
- In the last month, have you felt sad, down, depressed, or hopeless?

If the answer is yes to both questions, the patient is considered positive by this depression screen and is likely to be depressed. Additional information should be obtained to make a definitive diagnosis of major depression.

Other, more complex diagnostics tools include the BATHE technique, the SIG-E-CAPS system, and the PHQ-9 questionnaire. The BATHE technique includes questions about life events, emotions, what is troubling the patient most, and the patient's methods for dealing with these emotions. The last component of the BATHE technique is empathizing with the patient. The SIG-E-CAPS system determines the degree to which a patient is experiencing each of the diagnostic symptoms of depression, according to the American Psychiatric Association's *Diagnostic and Statistic Manual of Mental Disorders: DSM-IV-TR* (rev. 4th ed., 2000). The PHQ-9 contains nine questions and allows the severity of depression to be determined.

For depression occurring in specific conditions, additional symptoms and characteristics may be helpful in establishing an accurate diagnosis. Postpartum depression usually occurs in the first month postpartum and remains through the first six months postpartum, after which symptoms tend to lessen and resolve. Symptoms of postpartum depression include fatigue, sleep problems, decrease in libido, and disruptions in appetite, features that are commonly mistaken as part of the normal course of childbirth and the postpartum period. Rating scales such as the Edinburgh Postnatal Depression Rating Scale and the Postpartum Depression checklist may be helpful in diagnosing postpartum depression.

TREATMENT OPTIONS FOR DEPRESSION

Once a diagnosis of depression is made, appropriate treatment can be initiated. Depression may be treated with various medications, including those that block the reuptake of specific neurotransmitters. This class of agents includes selective serotonin reuptake inhibitors (SSRIs) and serotonin-norepinephrine reuptake inhibitors (SNRIs). Older antidepressants such as monoamine oxidase inhibitors (MAOIs) and tricyclic antidepressants (TCAs) may also be used, although these therapies are accompanied by more adverse effects than are SSRIs and SNRIs. There is some evidence that women respond more slowly to antidepressants than men do, and that women respond better to treatment with SSRIs, SNRIs, and MAOIs than to treatment with TCAs. Whenever antidepressants are used to treat depression, three factors are important in ensuring successful treatment outcomes: sufficient length of treatment, adequate antidepressant dose, and frequent monitoring for symptomatic or functional improvement. In addition, antidepressant treatment may be combined with psychotherapy, cognitive behavior therapy, or both if patients do not respond completely to antidepressants alone. Cognitive behavior therapy has also been shown to maintain remission and prolong the time to relapse in patients who have responded well to antidepressants.

There are additional considerations that need to be considered when treating depression in specific groups of women. Treatment with estrogen appears to improve depressive and physical symptoms in perimenopausal and postmenopausal women, but more research is required to confirm this benefit. The addition of estrogen therapy also appears to boost the response of perimenopausal women to SSRIs but not to SNRIs. In postmenopausal women, on the other hand, evidence suggests that SNRIs may promote remission more effectively than SSRIs. However, because of the potential risks of estrogen treatment, risk-benefit assessments need to be determined for each patient before initiating estrogen therapy. Prophylactic antidepressant treatment has been used in women who have given birth and who have a history of postpartum depression or recurrent depression.

PREVALENCE AND CAUSES OF SCHIZOPHRENIA

Schizophrenia is a disease in which internal realities are separated from external realities, and thought is separated from perception. The behavior of schizophrenics appears to be motivated by inner demons that confuse senses, disrupt logical thinking, and interfere with social functioning. There is an equal incidence of schizophrenia in women and men, but the peak age of onset differs between the genders. Schizophrenia is most likely to develop in men between the ages of seventeen and twenty-seven. In women, the peak onset of schizophrenia occurs three to four years later than in men, followed by another peak around menopause. Schizophrenia afflicts all ethnic groups and social classes, although it appears to be more prevalent among people of lower socioeconomic status. Although there appears to be a genetic component, with children of schizophrenic parents having a 35 percent probability of developing the disease, cases have been reported in people who lack a family history of schizophrenia. External factors that have been suggested to play a role in schizophrenia onset include complications in birth and pregnancy, in utero exposure to a viral agent, and influenza infection. Another factor that has been recently linked to schizophrenia in women is reduced estrogen levels. Reduced estrogen and androgen levels in men have also been associated with more severe schizophrenia symptoms.

DIAGNOSIS OF SCHIZOPHRENIA

Symptoms of schizophrenia can generally be classified as either positive symptoms, which are the result of an excess or abnormality of normal functions, or negative symptoms, which are the result of attenuation or loss of normal functions. Positive symptoms include hallucinations (visual, auditory, or olfactory), delusions, disjointed speech, and loss of logical association. Negative symptoms include apathy, poverty of speech (reduced speech and decreased vocabulary), social withdrawal, blunted or inappropriate emotional responses, and dysphoric mood (depressed, anxious, or irritable). The DSM-IV diagnostic criteria for schizophrenia include having two or more positive symptoms for at least one month, unless hallucinations or delusions are particularly bizarre, in which case only one positive symptom is required. Negative symptoms are harder to diagnose, because they are an absence or reduction in normal functioning. This is especially true in treated schizophrenic patients, in whom an adverse effect of antipsychotics may be a blunted affect.

TREATMENT OPTIONS FOR SCHIZOPHRENIA

The most frequently prescribed treatments for schizophrenia are antipsychotics, both the first-generation antipsychotics, such as haloperidol (Haldol), and the newer atypical antipsychotics, including aripiprazole (Abilify), clozapine (Clorazil), olanzapine (Zyprexa), quetiapine (Seroquel), risperidone (Risperdal), ziprasidone (Geodon, Zeldox), and paliperidone (Invega). The newer atypical antipsychotics generally cause fewer extrapyramidal side effects (EPS), which include repetitive, involuntary movements, and prolactin elevation, which are major adverse effects that plague the first generation antipsychotics. Atypical antipsychotics, however, are associated with weight gain, hyperglycemia, and insulin resistance, with varying effects depending on the particular drug. When treated with the appropriate psychopharmacological regimens, schizophrenia can be effectively controlled, with only 10 to 15 percent of patients suffering a relapse. Without treatment, 65 to 70 percent of schizophrenic patients suffer relapses. Cognitive behavioral therapy has not been used to much success in treating schizophrenia. Women with schizophrenia may also benefit from estrogen therapy administered together with their regular medications for schizophrenia. In a study conducted in Melbourne, Australia, schizophrenic women were treated with either a combination of estradiol (a type of estrogen) administered through the skin and oral antipsychotics, or with antipsychotics alone. The women who received estradiol and antipsychotics showed improvement in positive symptoms of schizophrenia compared with women treated with antipsychotics alone.

PREVALENCE AND CAUSES OF BIPOLAR DISORDER

Bipolar disorder affects women and men equally. The first manifestation of bipolar disorder usually occurs as a manic episode in men and as a depressive episode in women. Bipolar I disorder is present in 0.4 percent to 1.6 percent of the population and appears to have a genetic component, with offspring of people with bipolar disorder or depression being more likely to have bipolar disorder. A small proportion of bipolar patients experience symptoms of psychosis, such as hallucinations, delusions, and paranoia; this is often accompanied by violent behavior. In rare cases, women may experience psychosis in the first four to six weeks postpartum. This is a psychiatric emergency in which mothers exhibit obsessive thoughts about the baby, hallucinations, paranoia, and disturbed sleep.

DIAGNOSIS OF BIPOLAR DISORDER

Bipolar disorder is underdiagnosed in both primary care and psychiatry. There are several reasons for this, including the fact that patients frequently seek medical help while in a depressive rather than a manic episode. Another reason is that approximately 50 percent of bipolar patients do not realize that they have manic symptoms, and either fail to seek treatment or do not report their manic symptoms to their practitioner. Bipolar disorder is thus often misdiagnosed as depression. The DSM-IV details diagnostic criteria for bipolar disorder, including bipolar I disorder, bipolar II disorder, and bipolar disorder with rapid cycling.

Bipolar I disorder is characterized by one or more manic episodes or mixed episodes (featuring rapidly alternating symptoms of mania and depression) for at least one week. Bipolar II disorder is characterized by one or more hypomanic episodes (a less severe form of mania) and major depression for at least one week. A manic episode or mania is defined by the DSM-IV as the presence of abnormally and persistently elevated, expansive, or irritable mood, lasting at least one week, plus three or more of the following symptoms (or four if the mood is only irritable): inflated self-esteem or grandiosity, decreased need for sleep, unusually talkative or expansive mood, flight of ideas (many ideas appearing at once or in rapid succession), distractibility, increase in goal-directed activity, and excessive involvement in pleasurable activities that have a high potential for painful consequences (for example, risky investments and sexual indiscretions). In addition, the episode must be severe enough to cause marked impairment in work or social functioning or to necessitate hospitalization to prevent harm to the self or others, or if psychotic features are present. The diagnostic criteria for a hypomanic episode is similar to that for a manic episode, with the exception that work and social functioning are not severely affected, hospitalization is not warranted, and there are no psychotic features.

Some individuals suffer from bipolar disorder with rapid cycling; in these patients, four or more manic or depressive episodes occur in one year. Some experts, however, believe that the DSM-IV criteria are overly strict and may exclude individuals who have some symptoms of bipolar disorder but do not precisely fulfill the criteria. An alternative view of bipolar disorder has been proposed that presents a spectrum of mood conditions, with depression at one end and mania at the other. All individuals fall somewhere along this spectrum. Those with some symptoms of both depression and mania are considered to be in the bipolar spectrum and may benefit from therapy.

Bipolar disorder with psychosis is typically characterized by hallucinations, delusions, or paranoia. Some people with this condition also exhibit violent behavior and are in danger of hurting themselves and others. The rare cases of women with postpartum psychosis appear to be linked to bipolar disorder. Women with a personal and family history of bipolar disorder have a higher risk of developing postpartum psychosis.

TREATMENT OPTIONS FOR BIPOLAR DISORDER

Bipolar disorder can be most effectively treated with a combination of medications and psychotherapy, including cognitive behavioral therapy. Expert guidelines recommend that bipolar patients should typically be treated first with a mood stabilizer such as lithium, lamotrigine (Lamictal), or valproic acid (Valproate, Depakene), or with a mood stabilizer and an antipsychotic. Patients with depressive symptoms that do not respond to mood stabilizers may be treated with a combination of mood stabilizers and antidepressants. A bipolar patient should never be treated with antidepressants alone, because this can trigger rapid cycling or the emergence of a manic episode. Many bipolar patients mistakenly diagnosed as having major depression are discovered to have bipolar disorder when mania occurs in response to antidepressant treatment. A major problem for patients with mental diseases is poor adherence to medications. Bipolar patients often stop taking their medications because of a lack of insight into their condition or because of their inability to tolerate adverse effects, such as the weight gain that is often experienced with lithium, antidepressants, and some antipsychotics.

SOURCES FOR FURTHER STUDY

Abma, Joyce C., et al. "Fertility, Family Planning, and Women's Health: New Data from the 1995 National Survey of Family Growth." *National Center for Health Statistics: Vital Health Statistics* 23, no.

19 (1997). Presents statistical data about the prevalence of infertility in women and the number of women seeking in vitro fertilization treatment.

American Psychiatric Association. *American Psychiatric Association Practice Guideline for the Treatment of Patients with Bipolar Disorder.* 2d ed. Arlington, Va.: Author, 2002. This is a set of recommendations by experts for treatment of bipolar disorder in clinical practice.

Daniel, Jessica H., and Amy E. Banks. *The Complete Guide to Mental Health for Women.* Boston: Beacon Press, 2003. A comprehensive resource of the gamut of mental disorders afflicting women. It is written in an informative but conversational style.

Kulkarni, Jayashri, et al. "Estrogen in Severe Mental Illness: A Potential New Treatment Approach." *Archives of General Psychiatry* 65, no. 8 (2008): 955-960. This peer-reviewed article discusses the effects of administering transdermal estrogen and oral antipsychotics to women with chronic schizophrenia.

MGH Center for Women's Mental Health. Harvard Medical School. http://www.womensmentalhealth.org. This Web site is a perinatal and reproductive psychiatry information resource maintained by the Massachusetts General Hospital Center for Women's Mental Health.

Office on Women's Health of the U.S. Department of Health and Human Services. "Achieving Remission in Depression: Managing Women and Men in the Primary Care Setting." *Clinical Courier* 21, no. 28 (2003). This government report specifically addresses the issues surrounding treating depression in primary care, as well as strategies that can be used toward the ultimate goal of achieving remission.

Parikh, Rakesh M. "Depression and Anxiety in Couples Presenting for In Vitro Fertilization." In *Women's Health and Psychiatry.* Philadelphia: Lippincott, Williams & Wilkins, 2002. This study from the Jaslok Hospital and Research Center in Mumbai, India, describes symptoms of depression and anxiety in couples undergoing in vitro fertilization treatments.

Ing-Wei Khor

SEE ALSO: Antidepressant medications; Antipsychotic medications; Bipolar disorder; Depression; Femininity; Gender differences; Gender roles and gender role conflicts; Hormones and behavior; Postpartum depression; Schizophrenia: Background, types, and symptoms; Schizophrenia: Theoretical explanations; Stress: Behavioral and psychological responses; Stress-related diseases.

Women's psychology
Carol Gilligan

TYPE OF PSYCHOLOGY: Social psychology
FIELDS OF STUDY: Adolescence; classic analytic themes and issues; general constructs and issues; social motives

Gilligan's theories of girls' and women's different moral voice and development led many researchers to examine the ways boys and girls, men and women develop morality and have been instrumental in drawing attention to the importance of the study of the lives of girls and women.

KEY CONCEPTS
- ethic of care
- ethic of justice
- moral orientation
- relational self
- voice

INTRODUCTION
Within the fields of the moral psychology and the psychology of women, Carol Gilligan, a developmental psychologist, has raised a number of important questions about moral psychology and has generated a great deal of research on girls and their development. Her theory about the "different voice" of girls and women, described in her 1982 book, *In a Different Voice: Psychological Theory and Women's Development,* has been used to explain gender differences in such diverse fields as children's play, the speech of children, adult conversation, women in academia, leadership style, career choice, war and peace studies, the professions of law, nursing, and teaching, and theories about women's epistemologies (or ways of knowing).

Originally Gilligan's work was conducted in the field of moral psychology. She followed a tradition of social scientists and moral philosophers who associated moral development with cognitive development. Gilligan argued that boys and men apply rational, abstract, or objective thought to moral questions; as a result they are likely to appeal to the principle of justice when describing their thinking about moral issues. In contrast, Gilligan asserted, girls and women are more likely than boys and men to focus on the relationships between people and the potential for human suffering and harm. When this thinking is applied to moral issues, girls and women appeal to the ethic of care. The ethic of care, she claims, reflects women's "different voice."

In the preface written to the 1993 edition of her book, Gilligan describes "voice" as the core of the self. She calls it "a powerful psychological instrument and channel, connecting inner and outer worlds . . . a litmus test of relationships and a measure of psychological health." Gilligan and colleagues in the Harvard Project on Women's Psychology and the Development of Girls designed an interview and qualitative scoring method to study moral orientation and voice. They interviewed, held focus groups, and used sentence-completion measures to examine female adolescent and adult development. They argued that girls "lose voice" in adolescence; they dissociate from their real selves, a loss that puts them at risk for depression and anxiety.

DEVELOPMENT OF THE ETHIC OF CARE AND VOICE

Gilligan offers two explanations regarding how the ethic of care and women's different voice develop. The first draws from the psychoanalytic theory of Nancy Chodorow. According to Chodorow, from infancy both boys and girls develop a strong attachment to their mothers, which is the basis for their relational selves. However, during the Oedipal period (about age five), boys must separate from their mothers and must form an autonomous and separate identity as a male. This leads them to repress their relational selves and identify with their fathers. For girls, it is not necessary to detach themselves psychologically from their mothers to develop a gender role identity as a female; their attachment to their mothers is not repressed, and girls maintain a strong relational self.

Gilligan claimed to find a developmental pattern in her study of women facing a decision to have an abortion, described in her 1982 book. The first level, called "orientation to individual survival," focused on caring for oneself. The second level, called "goodness as sacrifice," focused on care of self. The third level, "the morality of nonviolence," is a morality of care for both self and others. Gilligan's levels have not been validated in any subsequent studies, raising questions about whether the ethic of care is a developmental construct.

Socialization also affects women's sense of self and is connected with the development of voice. According to Gilligan, society reinforces the male/female gender roles, rewarding boys and men for being autonomous, independent, and rational while their relational voices are silenced. In contrast, girls' independent autonomous voices are silenced during adolescence when they experience a conflict. If they become "good women" by conforming to societal stereotypes, they risk losing their authentic (independent) self, or voice. However, if girls resist social pressures to conform to an ideal of femininity, they risk damaging their connections to others. Most girls do not resist and, as a consequence, learn to doubt their true selves.

HISTORICAL CONTEXT FOR GILLIGAN'S THEORY

Gilligan's theory of moral development was an attempt to correct psychological theories that overlooked the experiences of women or discredited women's moral psychology. For example, Sigmund Freud, the "father" of psychoanalysis, had claimed that women and men differ in their moral capacity because girls' superegos are less developed than those of boys. While Freud found women's morality inferior to men's, Gilligan claimed that women's moral thinking was different from men's but of great, if not greater, moral value.

Gilligan's theory drew from the developmental work of Lawrence Kohlberg but corrected what she claimed was a gender bias in Kohlberg's theory. Kohlberg's theory of moral development was based on six stages of moral thinking that develop universally in an invariant sequence as a result of maturation and experience. In 1969, Kohlberg published results comparing men's and women's moral reasoning and reported that women typically scored at stage three, "mutual interpersonal expectations, relationships, and conformity," while men typically scored at stage four, "social system and conscience maintenance." Since developmental theories such as Kohlberg's assume that higher stages are more adequate, this was tantamount to saying that the moral reasoning of women was less developed than that of men. However, Kohlberg made no claim regarding gender differences in moral reasoning. It is likely that in the 1960's, when his study was conducted, his sample of working men and their wives had very different life experiences and that these differences account for his findings.

Gilligan's influential book *In a Different Voice* entered the field of the psychology of women at an important time. In the 1960's and 1970's, researchers who were studying the psychology of women had argued that empirical evidence shows that psychological differences between men and women are small, and, if they exist at all, gender differences are due to socialization and experience. If no relevant differences exist, there is no basis for assigning men and women to different spheres; gender cannot be used to exclude women from education, political life, or work.

Androgyny theorists in the 1960's and 1970's sought to discredit claims of gender differences that denigrate women or bar them from educational or career opportunities. They argued that with proper gender role socialization, boys and girls, men and women would be equal in psychological attributes. However, by the late 1970's, feminist psychologists began pointing out that androgyny theory contained its own problems: the qualities of competitiveness, aggression, independence, and autonomy, which characterized the masculine norm, might not be the best ideal for either men or women. Some feminist psychologists, such as Jean Baker Miller, sought a new norm for human development, an ideal that celebrated the alternative, feminine virtues of care, concern for others, and the ability to maintain strong relationships with others.

In this postandrogyny period, Gilligan's theory was hailed as a corrective to psychological studies based on male samples that posited masculinity as normative. Gilligan called attention to the study of adolescent girls and claimed to map a new psychological theory that begins with the experience of girls and women and reveals women's different voice.

RESEARCH ON MORAL REASONING, MORAL ORIENTATION, AND VOICE

Research on moral psychology shows that children are concerned with moral issues at a very early age. They care about "what's fair" and they are disturbed when someone has been hurt, suggesting that both justice and care orientations can be identified early in life. Research also shows that in Western culture, girls and women are expected to be more concerned

with relationships and more in tune with their feelings than boys. However, a great deal of research since the 1970's has shown that girls and boys are not as different in moral reasoning and voice as Gilligan claims.

Studies using the Kohlbergian Moral Judgment Interview (MJI) reveal that males and females at the same age and educational levels are equally able to resolve moral dilemmas by appealing to justice principles. Similar results have been obtained with the Defining Issues Test (DIT), the most frequently used objective test of comprehension of and preference for moral issues. Meta-analysis on DIT scores reveals that education is 250 times more powerful than gender in predicting principled moral reasoning. Narrative and longitudinal studies also have shown that women are as likely as men at the same educational level to advance in the sequential order of development predicted from Kohlberg's theory. In sum, evidence does not support the assertions that, compared with females, males are more principled in their moral reasoning, more concerned with conflicts resulting from conflicting claims about rights, or more capable of using abstract principles of justice in their moral reasoning. Evidence does not support the claim that Kohlberg's theory or measure of moral reasoning is biased against girls or women.

Are women more caring or more relational than men? Are they more likely to be silenced, silence themselves, or lose their voice than men? The evidence to support or refute Gilligan's assertion that the ethic of care characterizes female morality or voice is inconclusive. In part, this is because there are so many different ways that care and voice as psychological constructs are measured; it is difficult to compare across studies that operationalize the constructs differently. Different researchers view the ethic of care as a moral theory, an interpersonal orientation, a perceptual focus, or an epistemological theory. Voice is understood variously as a theory of self, a moral perspective, or a defensive posture. Furthermore, most of Gilligan's qualitative studies of girls' development only present girls' voices, and gender differences cannot be tested.

Research on the ethic of care suggests that the majority of people, both males and females, can and do use both care and justice orientations. Some studies, particularly those conducted using Gilligan's qualitative interview, report that females tend to focus on the care orientation and males on the justice orientation, particularly in self-identified moral dilemmas. While qualitative research is very important in developing a theory and understanding a construct, testing specific hypotheses (such as that there are gender differences in voice) requires quantitative studies. Most such studies fail to support Gilligan's theory of gender differences in moral orientation.

Some researchers have found that whether someone uses an ethic of care or an ethic of justice depends on the type of moral dilemma they discuss. Lawrence J. Walker and his colleagues found that when participants talk about their own moral dilemmas, females were more likely to identify interpersonal dilemmas, whereas males were more likely to choose impersonal dilemmas. If respondents focus on people and their relationships (a friend who betrays another friend), they are more likely to see that the ethic of care has been violated. If respondents focus on issues in which the rights of others are violated or societal rules are transgressed (breaking a law), they are more likely to be concerned about justice. Interpersonal conflicts elicit a care orientation, while issues of conflicting rights elicit a justice orientation for both men and women. However, when asked to think about an issue differently, both boys and girls are able to change and use either justice or care reasoning.

Gilligan's studies of adolescent girls' voices, using her methods of interview, focus groups, and open-ended sentence-completion measures, depict a conflicted adolescence, loss of voice, and growing dissociation from what girls know. While some girls resist, most strive to retain their relationships and thus seek to please others even if it means developing an inauthentic self.

Research conducted by Susan Harter using more standardized measures and large samples of both boys and girls indicates that adolescence is a challenging time for girls, and that they are concerned about their relationships. Girls feel silenced by others and they silence themselves, but not more so than adolescent boys. Harter's studies of loss of voice indicate there are not gender differences in voice, that girls do not have lower levels of voice than boys, and voice does not decline with age.

GENDER DIFFERENCE RESEARCH

Given the empirical results that gender differences, when they exist, are small and usually attributable to

different socialization, why do such claims persist? In part the answer lies in the methodology that is used in research on gender. Gilligan and her colleagues' work, particularly their research using qualitatively analyzed interviews, leads to the conclusion that there are large differences in the ways boys and girls view moral issues, think, react emotionally, and commit to relationships. However, studies that use standardized measures to compare men and women reveal more similarities than differences. Either conclusion has important implications.

Rachel Hare-Mustin and Jeanne Marecek claim that since knowledge in the social sciences is always incomplete, interpretation of events, including research findings, is always subject to bias. They suggest that two forms of bias influence beliefs about gender differences. Alpha bias is the tendency to emphasize gender difference; beta bias is the tendency to emphasize similarity. In beta bias, underemphasizing gender differences can lead to ignoring the different resources men and women need. In contrast, alpha bias, overestimating differences, can lead one to advocate different roles for men and women. If women are more caring, ought they be the caregivers? If men are more justice oriented, ought they be judges? If there is no difference in moral orientation between boys and girls, ought all children be taught to use both principles? Ought care and justice be expected from all adults?

GILLIGAN'S CONTRIBUTION

Gilligan raised important questions in the field of the psychology of morality and in so doing drew attention to the ethic of care. While the gender differences that she originally asserted have not been found, her work draws on the experience of girls and women in ways that value that experience. Her insistence that studying the lives of girls is as important as studying the lives of boys brought a good deal of research attention that can lead to new knowledge and new ways to promote the well-being of all boys and girls, men and women.

SOURCES FOR FURTHER STUDY

Brown, Lyn Mikel, and Carol Gilligan. *Meeting at the Crossroads: Women's Psychology and Girls' Development.* New York: Ballantine Books, 1993. This book describes interviews conducted at the Laurel School, a private day school for girls. The authors describe the listener's guide, a method of listening to girls' thoughts and feelings. The interviews demonstrate that relationships are central concerns for middle and high school girls.

Chodorow, Nancy. *The Reproduction of Mothering: Psychoanalysis and the Sociology of Gender.* 1978. Reprint. Berkeley: University of California Press, 1999. Chodorow draws on psychoanalytic theory to describe how women's mothering is reproduced across culture and across time. The book requires a fairly good background in psychoanalytic theory.

Freud, Sigmund. "Some Psychical Consequences of the Anatomical Distinction Between the Sexes." In *The Standard Edition of the Complete Psychological Works of Sigmund Freud.* Vol. 19. Translated and edited by James Strachey. London: The Hogarth Press, 1961. Freud claimed that because of anatomical differences, girls do not have an Oedipal conflict as emotionally strong as that of boys. As a consequence, boys develop a stronger superego, the structure of the psyche responsible for morality.

Gilligan, Carol. *In a Different Voice.* 1982. Reprint. Cambridge, Mass.: Harvard University Press, 2000. The theory of ethic of care and girls' and women's different moral voice is described. This often-cited book launched a great deal of discussion and prompted many studies of adolescent girls. Gilligan describes her theory of gender differences in moral orientation and of women's voice as different from men's voice.

Gilligan, Carol, Nona Lyons, and Trudy Hanmer, eds. *Making Connections: The Relational Worlds of Adolescent Girls at Emma Willard School.* Cambridge, Mass.: Harvard University Press, 1990. The voices of girls and their resistance to imposed silencing of their voices are described through interviews conducted at the Emma Willard School, a private day and boarding school for girls.

Gilligan, Carol, Annie G. Rogers, and Deborah L. Tolman, eds. *Women, Girls, and Psychotherapy: Reframing Resistance.* New York: Harrington Park Press, 1991. This collection of essays describes the social pressures that silence girls' voices and demonstrates girls' resistance to being silenced.

Gilligan, Carol, Janie Victoria Ward, and Jill McLean Taylor, eds. *Mapping the Moral Domain: A Contribution of Women's Thinking to Psychological Theory and Education.* Cambridge, Mass.: Harvard Graduate School of Education, 1988. These essays describe research on gender and morality and the book includes a chapter on the origins of gender differences in moral orientation. Many of the chapters were previously published as journal articles or book chapters.

Hare-Mustin, Rachel, and Jeanne Marecek, eds. *Making a Difference: Psychology and the Construction of Gender.* New Haven, Conn.: Yale University Press, 1990. The essays describe how gender differences are socially constructed and includes Hare-Mustin and Marecek's discussion of alpha and beta bias, a distinction that is useful in interpreting findings of gender differences.

Harter, Susan. *The Construction of the Self: A Developmental Perspective.* New York: Guilford Press, 1999. Harter describes her theory and the measurement of the self from a developmental perspective. This book includes an important summary and discussion of her research on gender differences in voice.

Hyde, Janet Shibley. *Half the Human Experience.* 7th ed. Boston: Houghton Mifflin, 2007. Presents the latest research in the relationship between gender and emotion and in feminist psychology.

Matlin, Margaret W. *The Psychology of Women.* Belmont, Calif.: Wadsworth/Thomson, 2008. Introductory text is valuable for students, and it is especially helpful in references to women of color and in providing demonstrations and exercises.

Miller, Jean Baker. *Toward a New Psychology of Women.* 2d ed. New York: Penguin, 1991. Miller draws on her clinical experience with women to describe and value a relational self, as defined through connections and relationships with others. This is an essential text for understanding relational theories about women's psychology.

Walker, Lawrence J. "Sex Differences in the Development of Moral Reasoning: A Critical Review." *Child Development* 55 (1984): 677-691. Walker's first meta-analysis revealed no gender differences in moral reasoning among men and women. Subsequent studies conducted by Walker and associates have confirmed these initial findings.

Mary Brabeck

SEE ALSO: Feminist psychotherapy; Kohlberg, Lawrence; Moral development; Women's mental health; Women's psychology: Karen Horney; Women's psychology: Sigmund Freud.

Women's psychology
Karen Horney

TYPE OF PSYCHOLOGY: Personality
FIELDS OF STUDY: Classic analytic themes and
    issues; personality theory

Horney's theories emphasize the effects of cultural influences on women's personality development. Her theories modified classical psychoanalytic views and provided new insights into women's interpersonal relationships.

KEY CONCEPTS
- biological influences
- classical psychoanalysis
- cultural influences
- instinct
- neo-Freudians
- sexual instinct
- unconscious

INTRODUCTION

Karen Horney considered people to be products of their environment as well as of biology. She stressed the ways in which cultural influences affect women's personality development. These cultural influences include interpersonal relationships and society's attitudes about women.

Cultural influences are overlooked by classical psychoanalysis—a system of psychology based on Freudian doctrine and procedure that seeks the root of human behavior in the unconscious, a region of the mind that is the seat of repressed impulses and experiences of which the conscious mind is unaware. Unconscious motivation and conflict, particularly sexual conflict, according to Horney, play an important role in women's development. She viewed women as living in a male-oriented world in which they are judged by men according to male standards. Women have come to believe that these male-based standards represent their true nature. As a result, according to Horney, women live with the dilemma of having to choose between fulfilling their ambitions and meeting their needs for love by adhering to the passive role that society assigns to them. These circumstances contribute to depression and low self-esteem.

Horney described three basic patterns of behavior by which people relate to others: moving toward (or self-effacing), moving away from (or distancing), and moving against (or expanding). The moving-toward behavior involves dependency and taking care of others as well as self-effacement. Women have been conditioned since birth to relate to others in this manner, according to Horney.

RELATIONSHIP TO FREUDIAN THEORY

Horney's theories were modifications of classical psychoanalytic beliefs. Her theories are best understood when viewed in relation to the Freudian concepts that were prevalent during her lifetime. According to Sigmund Freud, who founded classical psychoanalysis during the late nineteenth century, biological influences determine human behavior. Of these biological factors, sexual instincts are the strongest motivators of human behavior. Neurosis, or mental disorder, was considered by Freud to be the result of unconscious sexual conflicts that began in early childhood.

Horney was grounded in psychoanalytic thinking and agreed with many of Freud's concepts. She disagreed radically, however, with the heavy sexual content of Freudian theory. A major point of departure was the Freudian concept of penis envy. Freud essentially viewed all psychological problems in women to be the result of the woman's inherent wish to be a man. Freud maintained that girls are not born with a natural sense of their femininity and regard themselves as inferior, castrated boys. As a result of penis envy, the female rebels against her biological inferiority. The consequences, according to Freud, are resentment, devaluation of her "negative sexual endowments," envy of the opposite sex, and a constant search for compensation.

Horney considered penis envy to be contrary to biological thinking. She maintained that little girls are instinctively feminine and aware of their femaleness in early childhood. Thus, girls are not programmed to feel inferior. Women may envy men the power and freedom they have in their private and professional lives, but women do not envy men's genitals. The behaviors that Freud associated with penis envy—including greed, envy, and ambition—Horney attributed to the restrictions society places on females.

Horney also disagreed with the Freudian theory that viewed frigidity and masochism as biologically determined aspects of woman's nature. Frigidity, or the inability of a woman to experience sexual desire, is neither a normal condition for a woman nor an illness, according to Horney. She considered frigidity to be a symptom of an underlying psychological disturbance, such as chronic anxiety. Frequently, it is caused by tensions between marital partners. Powerful forces in society restrict a woman in the free expression of her sexuality. Custom and education promote female inhibitions. Men's tendency to view their wives as spiritual partners and to look for sexual excitement with prostitutes or others whom they do not respect may also cause frigidity in wives.

Masochistic tendencies, wherein a woman seeks and enjoys pain and suffering, particularly in her sexual life, result from special social circumstances, Horney maintained. Freudian theory, holding that women are biologically programmed for masochism, is associated with the Freudian concept of the female as having been rendered less powerful than the male through castration. Horney, on the other hand, believed that society encourages women to be masochistic. Women are stereotyped as weak and emotional, as enjoying dependence, and these qualities are rewarded by men. Masochistic tendencies, according to Horney, are a way of relating by which a woman tries to obtain security and satisfaction through self-effacement and submission.

Horney's theories stressed the positive aspects of femininity. As her ideas developed, she became more influenced by social scientists of her period. Her theories placed increasing emphasis on interpersonal and social attitudes in determining women's feelings, relations, and roles. Her ideas about the development of women's sexuality were focused on adolescent girls, rather than on young children, as in Freudian theory. According to Horney, adolescents develop attitudes to cope with sexual conflict, and these attitudes carry over into adulthood.

NEW APPROACH TO WOMEN AND RELATIONSHIPS

Horney's theories opened the door for new ways of understanding women's personalities and relationships. In a 1984 study of women's reaction to separation and loss, psychotherapist Alexandra Symonds found Horney's theories to be relevant to what she encountered in her female patients. Writing in the *American Journal of Psychoanalysis*, Symonds reported female reaction to separation and loss to be a frequent motivation for women to enter therapy. In contrast, she found that men come into therapy in these circumstances mainly because of pressure from a wife or girlfriend. According to Symonds, women are more eager than men to create relationships, and women express more feeling when the relationships end.

Symonds considered these behaviors from the viewpoint of the three basic patterns of behavior described by Horney: moving toward, moving away from, and moving against. Symonds viewed the moving-toward, self-effacing type of behavior as love oriented, or dependent; the moving-away-from, detached type as freedom oriented; and the moving-against, expansive type as power oriented. According to Symonds's views, society assigns the love-oriented, dependent pattern to women, while men are encouraged to develop power- and freedom-oriented patterns. She described a frequent combination in a couple to be a detached, expansive, power-oriented man married to a dependent, self-effacing, love-oriented woman. Relationships often develop between the silent, strong, withdrawn, noncommunicative man and the loving, dependent woman who always wants to talk about feelings.

As people develop character patterns, such as love-oriented and dependent, they suppress feelings that cause inner conflicts, such as aggressiveness, according to Symonds. By contrast, power-oriented people suppress dependent feelings. People idealize their self-values and feel contempt for what is suppressed; thus, the power-oriented person views dependency and need as contemptible weaknesses. This contempt is conveyed to those who are aware of their dependency needs. Women then add self-hate for needing others to the anxiety they feel when a relationship ends.

Extremely dependent, self-effacing women often stay in poor and even abusive relationships rather than separate, according to Symonds. They are victims of a culture that considers a woman nothing unless attached to a man. Symonds found these women to be coming from two different backgrounds: either having been held close by mother or father during childhood and adolescence, thus having no opportunity for healthy growth, or having separated prematurely from parents in childhood in an effort to become self-sufficient at an early age, often having developed a facade of self-sufficiency with deep, unresolved dependency needs.

UNDERSTANDING FEAR OF SUCCESS

Horney's theories predicted the anxiety women feel about their own ambition and the ways in which women sabotage their competence and success. In the book *Women in Therapy* (1988), psychotherapist Harriet Goldhor Lerner discusses female work inhibition in the light of Horney's theories. Lerner views work inhibition as an unconscious attempt to preserve harmony within a relationship as well as to allay fears of being unfeminine. Women often fear success because they fear they will pay dearly for their accomplishments. Women frequently equate success, or the wish for it, with the loss of femininity and attractiveness, loss of significant relationships, loss of health, or even loss of life. Feelings of depression and anxiety are ways women either apologize for their competence and success on one hand or ensure the lack of success on the other hand, according to Lerner. She views self-sacrifice or self-sabotage to be other common ways women react to their feelings of guilt and anxiety about becoming successful.

When faced with the choice (real or imagined) of sacrificing the self to preserve a relationship or strengthening the self at the risk of threatening a relationship, women often choose the former, according to Lerner. She applies Horney's views to the situation of a thirty-year-old married woman who entered therapy because of personal distress and marital tension over her desire to enroll in graduate school and embark on a career. Lerner found that multigenerational guilt on the part of the woman was involved, as well as fears of destroying her marriage. The woman's husband was opposed to his wife's enrolling in graduate school. In addition, the woman was the first female in her family to aspire to graduate school. In the face of these circumstances, she put aside her ambitions to preserve harmony in her relationships. The woman's work inhibition involved profound anxiety and guilt over striving for things previous generations of women in her family could not have. Work inhibition also may result when a woman perceives her strivings as "too masculine," a perception Lerner sees as reinforced by society. Being labeled "masculine" triggers deep guilt and anxiety in women.

BACKGROUND AND ACCOMPLISHMENTS

Horney's theories on female psychology developed from a series of papers she wrote over a thirteen-year period in response to Freud's views on female sexuality. The last paper was published after Horney emigrated to the United States from Germany at a highly productive point in her career.

One of the first women admitted to medical school in Berlin, she had completed her psychiatric and psychoanalytic training there by 1913. By that time, Freud had passed the peak of his greatest creative years. Horney was thirty years younger than Freud and a product of the twentieth century. Her views were more in tune with the relatively open structure of twentieth century science than with the more closed science of Freud's period. Horney was influenced greatly by sociologists of her time. She and other neo-Freudians, such as Harry Stack Sullivan, Alfred Adler, and Erich Fromm, were the first psychoanalysts to emphasize cultural influences on personality development.

Horney's theories grew out of a need for a feminine psychology different from male psychology. She believed that women were being analyzed and treated according to a male-oriented psychology that considered women to be biologically inferior to males. She did not find these male theories supported by what she observed in her female patients or in her own life experience.

Horney was the first female doctor to challenge male theory and went on to take a position in the foreground of the psychoanalytic movement. In so doing, she became a role model for women in general and professional women in particular. She was a controversial figure, and her career involved many disputes with the established psychoanalytic world. She and her followers eventually were ostracized by the establishment, and for a time her name disappeared from the psychoanalytic literature. Her biographers attribute this to a fear on the part of some Freudians of being contaminated by association with her ideas.

MODERN-DAY IMPACT

A growing interest in Horney's work occurred during the women's liberation movement in the 1970's. The women's movement brought her name back into the literature as a pioneer in upgrading women's status. Her name began appearing more frequently in literature associated with women's therapy. The series of important books that she had written throughout her career remain popular and continue to be used as textbooks.

An independent thinker, Horney is considered an individual who was always ahead of her time. Her work anticipated a revival of interest in the narcissistic personality. Her theories predicted popular trends in psychology, although she often is not credited for her ideas. One of these trends is the increasing emphasis on social and cultural factors as causes of emotional illness. Systems theory is another popular trend related to Horney's concepts. Systems theory, which includes a type of psychology called family therapy, emphasizes the continuous interaction between cultural conditions, interpersonal relations, and inner emotional experience.

SOURCES FOR FURTHER STUDY

Hitchcock, Susan Tyler. *Karen Horney: Pioneer of Feminine Psychology*. Philadelphia: Chelsea House, 2005. Written for readers of high school age and above, this biography describes the life and works of Horney in an accessible style.

Horney, Karen. *Feminine Psychology*. 1967. Reprint. New York: W. W. Norton, 1993. A collection of all of Horney's writings on feminine psychology. Gives a flavor of Horney's personality and force as a psychoanalyst and educator. Includes an informative introduction by Harold Kelman, one of Horney's colleagues.

Lerner, Harriet Goldhor. *Women in Therapy*. 1988. Reprint. New York: Harper & Row, 1992. Discusses women and their psychotherapists from a psychoanalytic perspective, with references to Horney's theories. Illustrates how Horney's theories apply to many themes and issues in women's psychology.

Paris, Bernard J. *Karen Horney: A Psychoanalyst's Search for Self-Understanding*. New Haven, Conn.: Yale University Press, 1996. A biography of Horney that places her theories squarely within the context of her life history. Written by the editor of the papers unpublished during Horney's lifetime (*The Unknown Karen Horney*, 2000).

Quinn, Susan. *A Mind of Her Own: The Life of Karen Horney*. New York: Other Press, 2003. This biography is an excellent source of information about Horney's personal and professional life. Much of it is devoted to her female psychology. Easy to read; contains photographs, biographical essays, extensive source notes, and a complete list of Horney's work.

Rubins, Jack L. *Karen Horney: Gentle Rebel of Psycho-*

analysis. New York: Dial Press, 1978. The first biography of Karen Horney. Thorough and well documented, it includes detailed discussions of Horney's theories on women. Lengthy but well organized. Can be read by the college or high school student.

Solomon, Irving. *Karen Horney and Character Disorder: A Guide for the Modern Practitioner*. New York: Springer, 2006. Written by a psychologist-psychoanalyst, this guide is helpful for practitioners who want to offer Horney's theories in treatment.

Symonds, Alexandra. "Separation and Loss: Significance for Women." *American Journal of Psychoanalysis* 45, no. 1 (1985): 53-58. Discusses women's feelings about separation and loss. Important illustration of how Horney's theories help explain women's role in interpersonal relationships. Available in college libraries.

Margaret M. Frailey

SEE ALSO: Abnormality: Psychological models; Consciousness; Dreams; Feminist psychotherapy; Gender differences; Gender roles and gender role conflicts; Instinct theory; Penis envy; Psychoanalysis; Psychoanalytic psychology; Psychoanalytic psychology and personality: Sigmund Freud; Psychosexual development; Sadism and masochism; Social psychological models: Karen Horney; Women's mental health; Women's psychology: Carol Gilligan; Women's psychology: Sigmund Freud.

Women's psychology
Sigmund Freud

TYPE OF PSYCHOLOGY: Personality
FIELDS OF STUDY: Classic analytic themes and issues; personality theory

Freud, the first person to develop a comprehensive theory of personality, thought that women undergo distinct experiences in the development of their personalities. He believed that traumatic events during the phallic stage (from approximately three to five years of age) were likely to hinder normal female development, the results being a failure of same-sex identification and a diminished superego or moral capacity.

KEY CONCEPTS

- free association
- id
- identification
- instincts
- Oedipus complex
- penis envy
- psychosexual stages of development
- superego

INTRODUCTION

Two central concepts underlie Sigmund Freud's theory of personality development. The first is the notion of the unconscious; the second concept has to do with the role of infantile sexuality. Freud believed that consciousness could be viewed as a continuum of experience, with one pole being the familiar one of acute awareness of one's thoughts, feelings, and behaviors and the other pole being a state of profound unconsciousness in which one's feelings, thoughts, and wishes are completely beyond one's awareness. Midway between these poles is the preconscious, which Freud believed contained material or mental life from both the conscious and the unconscious and could, with effort, be made totally conscious. Freud believed that the bulk of mental life is represented in the unconscious, with only a small portion, "the tip of the iceberg," being conscious awareness.

Operating from the depths of the unconscious, a structure of personality known as the id operates to seek pleasure, to avoid pain at all costs, and to accomplish solely selfish aims. The id is the source of all psychic energy, including both sexual and aggressive instincts.

PSYCHOSEXUAL STAGES OF DEVELOPMENT THEORY

Freud proposed that the sexual instincts are critical and that personality develops over time as the individual responds to these instincts. He believed that a number of component instincts arise from various regions of the body. These instincts strive for satisfaction in what he calls organ pleasure. Each of these organs is the focus of a phase or stage of development, the first of which is the oral stage. The oral stage begins at birth and continues through the first year, as the infant seeks pleasure through the mouth and the mouth becomes the source of all gratification. Milk from the mother's breast or a bottle is devoured, just as, later, any object that the child can

reach will be manipulated and explored orally. The child takes in physical nourishment in the same way that he or she takes in, in a very rudimentary way, the behaviors, values, and beliefs of others, beginning the basis for later identification with others.

The second psychosexual stage of development is the anal stage, which Freud believed revolved around the pleasure associated with elimination. During the second year of life, the child begins taking control of urination and defecation, trying to do so within parental and societal limits.

Freud believed that both boys and girls proceed through the oral stage in essentially the same manner. For both, the mother is the primary love object. Sometime after the third year, however, Freud believed that the sexes diverge. In the third, or phallic, stage of development, both boys and girls discover the pleasurable nature of the genitals. For boys, the stage is centered on the Oedipus complex, in which they develop strong sexual feelings toward their mothers. These feelings are accompanied by others, such as anger and jealousy, as fathers are perceived as competitors for mothers' affection and attention. As sexual desires heighten, the boy begins to perceive competition and hostility from the father. The sense of peril becomes located in the physical source of the boy's feelings for his mother, the penis, and the result is a phenomenon that Freud called castration anxiety—the fear that the father will retaliate. Over time, fear of castration motivates the boy to give up the mother as a love object and turn toward the father in same-sex identification. According to Freud, this strengthening identification with the father is essential for the development of a solid superego, which, in turn, empowers the male, making possible major contributions to culture and society.

Unlike the male's experience, the onset of the phallic stage for females entails a major trauma: the realization that she does not have a penis. Often, the realization is accompanied by the notion that the mother is responsible for her own and her daughter's castrated state. Here the little girl turns away from her mother as the primary love object and turns toward her father, limiting her future chances for same-sex identification. Feelings of inferiority pervade, and she falls victim to penis envy, a chronic wish for the superior male organ. Freud believed that, as a result of this trauma, the remaining course of female development would be difficult at best and that the accomplishment of same-sex identification was questionable. The girl's life is thus spent in search of a substitute penis, which Freud thought might be a husband or a child, particularly a male child. Indeed, Freud believed that the single most rewarding relationship in a woman's life would be her relationship with her son, regarding which her feelings would be totally unambivalent.

Freud believed that the foundations of personality were in place by the end of the phallic stage. He described the post-Oedipal period, beginning with the latency stage, as a period when children repress, or make unconscious, the sexual conflicts of the Oedipal period. Females during this time are said to be more passive and less aggressive than boys, but, like boys, they tend to seek out same-sex play groups.

The final psychosexual stage of development is the genital stage. Unlike the previous, more self-centered periods of stimulation and gratification, the genital stage marks a period of sexual attraction to others and a time during which social activities and career goals become important before marriage.

The child is thus transformed into an adult. Freud believed that, in some cases, failure to resolve the female Oedipus complex results in neurosis, which he often observed in his practice with female patients. He believed that in other cases the lack of resolution caused a masculinity complex in which women attempt to succeed in traditionally male endeavors (he offered this explanation to his contemporary female analysts for their behavior). Freud believed that the female's failure to unite with her mother in post-Oedipal identification, and her subsequent diminished superego capacity, caused her to have a tendency toward negative personality traits and an inability to apply objective standards of justice.

CRITICISMS

Several of Freud's contemporaries, including some female analysts, were critical of Freud's views on the psychology of women. Among his critics was Karen Horney, who rejected the idea that penis envy is central to normal female development. She acknowledged, however, that from a cultural point of view,

Sigmund Freud in London in 1938, a year before his death at age eighty-three. (Library of Congress)

envy of the male role might explain some of Freud's clinical observations better than the biological notion of penis envy. In addition, after many years of analyzing female patients, Horney began analyzing males; from her observations, she concluded that males often exhibit an intense envy of pregnancy, childbirth, and motherhood, as well as of the breasts and of the act of suckling.

FREE INTERPRETATION AND DREAM ANALYSIS

Historically, psychoanalysis has represented a method of psychological observation, a set of theoretical constructs or ideas, and an approach to psychotherapy. When Freud began psychoanalysis, it was a method of observation intended to broaden the knowledge of human behavior. Believing that the unconscious is the major clue to solving problems of human behavior, Freud used two processes to understand it: free association and dream interpretation. Free association, the reporting of what comes to mind in an unedited fashion, was an important tool used to discover the contents of the unconscious. Freud believed that all thoughts are connected in some fashion and that therefore the spontaneous utterances of the patient are always meaningful clues to what has been repressed or buried in the unconscious. Freud also believed that the unconscious can be clarified by means of dream interpretation. Those thoughts and impulses that are unacceptable to the conscious mind are given symbols in dreams.

An interesting study conducted by Calvin Hall in 1964 illustrates how the interpretation of dreams has been used in research—in this case, to test Freud's observation that the female superego is not as strong as it appears to be in males. Hall reasoned that a person with a strong internalized superego would be independent of external agents, whereas a person who has a less internalized superego would tend to disown his or her own guilt and blame external authority figures. Hall further made the assumption that dreams in which the dreamer was the victim of aggression were expressions of an externalized superego, whereas dreams in which the dreamer was the victim of misfortune (accident, circumstance) were expressions of an internalized superego. It was hypothesized that females would be more likely to dream of themselves as victims of aggression and males would be more likely to dream of themselves as victims of misfortune. Careful content analysis of

more than three thousand dreams of young adults was performed. Results supported the hypotheses, although Hall cautioned that additional hypotheses should be tested and more diverse data collected to support thoroughly Freud's theory of the differences between the male and the female superego.

TRANSFERENCE AND THE UNCONSCIOUS

Freud was also the first to understand and describe the concept of transference, the patient's positive or negative feelings that develop toward the therapist during the long, intimate process of analysis. These feelings often relate to earlier ones that the patient has had for significant others: namely, mother, father, or sibling. The analysis of transference has become extremely important to neo-Freudian analysts, particularly as it relates to the treatment of borderline and other personality disturbances.

Another aspect of Freud's legacy involves the many theoretical constructs that psychoanalysis has generated. Among these is the concept of the unconscious. Freud provided many everyday examples of the operation of the unconscious as he described slips of the tongue and other phenomena. He was convinced that such slips, now known as "Freudian slips," were not accidental at all, but somehow expressed unconscious wishes, thoughts, or desires. For example, the woman who loses her wedding ring wishes she had never had it.

MENTAL ILLNESS THERAPY

Finally, psychoanalysis also represents a method of therapy that Freud and later analysts used to treat the symptoms of mental illness. Practicing for many years, Freud refined his technique, using free association and dream interpretation to help patients gain insight into themselves by recognizing their unconscious patterns and to help them work through the unconscious conflicts that affect everyday life. Many of Freud's patients were women, and it was from these women's recollections in analysis that Freud built his theory of female development. Some of Freud's critics argue that building a theory of normal development from the observation of pathology or abnormality represents an inappropriate conceptual leap.

SEXUAL BASIS OF NEUROSIS

During years of analysis, Freud became convinced of the sexual basis of neurosis. He believed that sexual experiences occurring prior to puberty and stored in the unconscious as memories produced conflict that later caused certain neurotic conditions. These ideas, often referred to as Freud's seduction theory, were used to explain hysterical symptoms such as paralysis, blindness, inability to understand the spoken word (receptive aphasia), and sexual dysfunction as the result of sexual abuse probably occurring before ages six to eight. It is important to note, however, that Freud later revised his thinking on infantile sexuality and concluded that it is the thought or psychic reality of the individual that counts more than the physical reality of events. In other words, a person might fantasize a seduction, store the fantasy in unconscious memory (repress it), and have that conflictual memory cause neurosis just as readily as the memory of an actual seduction. Some recent critics have suggested that Freud's reformulation represented a form of denial of his inability to recognize the prevalence of sexual abuse at that time.

FREUD'S BACKGROUND AND IMPACT

Born in 1856 to Jewish parents, Freud lived and practiced most of his life in Vienna. He graduated from medical school in 1881 and practiced as a clinical neurologist for several years before becoming interested in the "talking cure" that his colleague Josef Breuer had developed as a means of dealing with his patients' emotional symptoms. Freud's writings and lectures on the subject of hysteria and its sexual roots led him to be ostracized by most of his medical colleagues. His medical training and the influence of the work of Charles Darwin were largely responsible for his emphasis on sexual and aggressive instincts as the basis for behavior.

Freud's theory was important because it was the first of its kind and because it was controversial, generating further research into and theorizing about the female personality.

CHALLENGES TO FREUDIAN THEORY

Over the years, many aspects of Freudian theory have been challenged. Freud's notion that penis envy is a primary motivator in the female personality was challenged by Horney, who believed that, if it existed, a woman's envy was related to the man's privileged role in society. Freud's idea that the clitoral orgasm is immature and must be surrendered for the vaginal orgasm at puberty spurred

work by William H. Masters and Virginia E. Johnson, who concluded, after much rigorous research, that orgasm is a reaction of the entire pelvic area.

Freud's theory has forced critics to determine what is uniquely female about personality. In *Toward a New Psychology of Women* (1976), Jean Baker Miller attempted to show how traditional theories of female behavior have failed to acknowledge the essence of the female personality. Miller suggested that affiliation is the cornerstone of the female experience and that it is in response to her relationships with others that a woman's personality grows and develops.

In her book *In a Different Voice* (1982), Carol Gilligan disputes Freud's notion that females show less of a sense of justice than males and have weak superegos. She argues that morality involves respect for the needs of self balanced with respect for the needs of others; thus, it is not that females lack the justice principle, but rather that they have different expressions of justice and different internal and external demands.

Heavily influenced by Freud, many object-relations theorists continue to make contributions in the area of psychotherapy with clients whose early relationships have been disturbed or disrupted. This work will continue to constitute the basis for decisions made by courts, adoption agencies, and social-service agencies regarding the placement of children.

Freud's views on the origins of neurosis may continue to play a role in the understanding of multiple personality disorder and its roots in early sexual abuse. The concept of body memory, the physical memory that abuse has occurred, may well bridge the gap between Freud's concepts of repressed psychic memory and repressed actual memory of early sexual abuse; it may streamline the treatment of this condition. Finally, Freud's theory will no doubt continue to generate controversy, motivating both theory and research in the area of women's personality development.

SOURCES FOR FURTHER STUDY

Baraitser, Lisa. *Maternal Encounters: The Ethics of Interruption.* London: Routledge, 2009. Compilation of research on motherhood and the changes it causes in the lives of women. Includes many references to Freud and his theories on motherhood and identity.

Freud, Sigmund. *New Introductory Lectures on Psycho-analysis.* 1933. Reprint. New York: W. W. Norton, 1989. This volume contains seven lectures or papers that Freud wrote toward the end of his career. Among them is "The Psychology of Women," in which Freud attempts to explain some fundamental differences between the sexes. Freud describes female behavior and the Oedipus complex for males and females, and he elaborates on the role of penis envy in female development. The volume also contains lectures on dreams, on the structure of personality, and on anxiety and the instincts.

_____. *The Standard Edition of the Complete Psychological Works of Sigmund Freud.* Edited by James Strachey. London: Hogarth Press, 1953-1974. Volume 7 in this collection of Freud's works contains a detailed case history of a woman named Dora, whom Freud treated over a period of years. This case history illustrates Freud's ideas about the causes of neurosis and hysterical symptoms. The work also contains three essays on sexuality, including sexual aberrations, infantile sexuality, and puberty.

Gilligan, Carol. *In a Different Voice.* 1982. Reprint. Cambridge, Mass.: Harvard University Press, 2000. Traditional theories of development have tried to impose male thinking and values on female psychology. Gilligan discusses the importance of relationship as well as female conceptions of morality, challenging Freud's views on female superego development.

Horney, Karen. *Feminine Psychology.* 1967. Reprint. New York: W. W. Norton, 1993. A collection of some of Horney's early works in which she describes Freudian ideas on the psychology of women and offers her own observations and conclusions. Horney disputes Freud's notion of penis envy and in later essays explores such topics as distrust between the sexes, premenstrual tension, and female masochism.

Miller, Jean Baker. *Toward a New Psychology of Women.* 2d ed. New York: Penguin, 1991. Miller proposes that traditional theories of female development have overlooked a critical ingredient in female behavior—affiliation—which she believes is a cornerstone of female psychology.

Miller, Jonathan, ed. *Freud: The Man, His World, His Influence.* Boston: Little, Brown, 1972. Miller has edited a series of essays that put Freud's work in historical, social, and cultural perspectives. One essay, by Friedrich Heer, describes the impact of Freud's Jewish background on his life and work in Vienna. Another, by Martin Esslin, describes Vienna, the exciting and culturally rich background for Freud's work.

Rychlak, Joseph F. *Introduction to Personality and Psychotherapy.* 2d ed. Boston: Houghton Mifflin, 1981. This introductory personality text carefully reviews the work of several leading psychologists and psychotherapists, including Freud. Rychlak describes the gradual development of Freud's structural hypothesis, and he reviews Freud's ideas about the instincts, dynamic concepts such as defense mechanisms, and the development of the Oedipus complex for males and females, noting the concerns of modern feminists who have found Freud's work offensive.

Ruth T. Hannon

SEE ALSO: Abnormality: Psychological models; Consciousness; Dreams; Feminist psychotherapy; Instinct theory; Penis envy; Psychoanalysis; Psychoanalytic psychology; Psychoanalytic psychology and personality: Sigmund Freud; Psychosexual development; Women's mental health; Women's psychology: Carol Gilligan; Women's psychology: Karen Horney.

Work motivation

TYPE OF PSYCHOLOGY: Motivation
FIELDS OF STUDY: Motivation theory; social motives

Work motivation theories describe the psychological processes that affect people's choices regarding their work-related behaviors; the theories provide managerial guidelines for increasing worker productivity.

KEY CONCEPTS
- expectancy theory
- extrinsic motivation
- goal setting
- hierarchy of needs theory
- intrinsic motivation
- job enrichment
- scientific management

INTRODUCTION

Motivation is the psychological process that directs people's choices regarding the type and intensity of their behavior. A common misconception among managers is that motivation is merely the desire to work hard. Consequently, managers often think that only productive workers possess motivation. In contrast, psychologists define motivation as a general process that influences virtually all behavior. Thus, psychologists believe that all workers are motivated. Some workers are motivated to work hard; other workers are motivated to stay home.

A basic principle that underlies most modern theories of motivation is that motivated behavior is performed to obtain pleasurable outcomes. Based on this principle, motivational theorists have defined two types of motivation: intrinsic motivation and extrinsic motivation. A behavior is intrinsically motivated if the valued or pleasurable outcome associated with the behavior is in the behavior itself. The intrinsically motivated employee works because the work itself is enjoyable. A behavior is extrinsically motivated if the valued outcome associated with the behavior is performed only as a means to obtain the outcome. The extrinsically motivated worker works not because the work is pleasurable but because working leads to a pleasurable outcome external to the job, such as money, status, security, or friendship.

EXPECTANCY THEORY

The most popular and widely accepted theory of work motivation is the expectancy theory. Originally proposed by Victor Vroom, this model has been elaborated on by a large number of researchers. The expectancy theory describes the decision-making process that people experience when they choose which behavior to perform. It suggests that a person's motivation to perform some behavior is a function of three components: expectancy, instrumentality, and valence.

"Expectancy" refers to a person's beliefs about his or her ability to perform a behavior. "Instrumentality" refers to a person's beliefs about the likelihood that a number of outcomes will occur if the behavior is performed. "Valence" refers to how positively or negatively a person values these outcomes. The expectancy theory suggests that when people are deciding which of a number of behaviors they will perform, they consider the three components associated with each behavior and choose the behavior that is most likely to lead to positive outcomes.

For example, a worker is given an opportunity to receive a bonus for completing a project early. The employee's motivation to work on the project is a function of the worker's beliefs about her ability to get the project done early (expectancy), her beliefs about the likelihood that she will actually receive a bonus for completing the project early (instrumentality), and the degree to which she values the bonus (valence). To the extent that the worker values the bonus, is certain that the bonus will be awarded if the project is completed early, and is certain that she is capable of completing the project, the worker will be motivated to complete the project early. Whether the worker attempts to complete the project, however, is influenced by her competing motivation to perform other behaviors. While the worker may be motivated to complete the project, she may also feel that other activities, such as going on vacation or calling in sick, are more likely to lead to equally or more pleasurable outcomes than the bonus.

MASLOW'S HIERARCHY OF NEEDS

The expectancy theory is considered a cognitive model. The theory proposes that behavior is guided by choices based on beliefs and values. The theory describes the process of decision making. "Needs models" are another type of motivation model. Needs models complement the process-oriented cognitive models by suggesting the categories of outcomes that people typically value. Needs models also provide insight into how the values of outcomes change.

The most widely known needs model is the hierarchy of needs theory, proposed by Abraham Maslow. Maslow suggested that all people have five categories of needs, which are arranged in a hierarchy. From lowest level to highest level, these needs include physiological needs, safety needs, social needs, esteem needs, and self-actualization needs. Maslow argued that a person's first concern is to fulfill the lowest level of unsatisfied need. When a need is not satisfied, opportunities to fill the need gain value. As the need is met, opportunities to fill the satisfied need lose value, and opportunities to satisfy the next higher level of need gain value. For example, once a worker has enough air, water, and food, thus satisfying his or her physiological needs, the worker will become less concerned about these needs and will value opportunities to fill safety needs. The process of unsatisfied needs gaining value and satisfied needs losing value continues up the hierarchy through safety, social, and esteem needs. When all the lower-level needs are reasonably well satisfied, people will most highly value opportunities for self-actualization. Self-actualization can be thought of as the process of developing one's physical and mental skills to the limit of one's potential.

Maslow's theory helps define the distinction between extrinsic and intrinsic motivation. Extrinsic motivation usually involves performing a job as a way to meet physiological, safety, and social needs. Intrinsic motivation typically occurs when a job offers opportunities to meet higher-level needs. That is, the work itself becomes enjoyable when performance of the job leads to greater self-esteem and self-actualization.

ROLE OF A SUPERVISOR

The supervisor's job is to increase a subordinate's motivation to be productive. The supervisor does this by defining productivity and establishing a contingency between productive behavior and the attainment of an outcome the worker values. That valued outcome can be either in the job itself, involving intrinsic motivation, or external to the job, involving extrinsic motivation. The expectancy theory offers a number of guidelines for helping supervisors establish productivity-outcome contingencies.

First, a supervisor must make certain that the employee believes she or he can be productive. That is, the supervisor must heighten the employee's expectancy beliefs. For example, the supervisor must clearly explain to the employee what behaviors or levels of performance constitute productivity. The supervisor may then need to provide training, giving the employee the skills necessary to meet the performance criteria. Additionally, the supervisor may need to coach the employee, convincing the employee that he or she has the potential to be productive.

Next, a supervisor must make certain that the employee believes that productive performance will lead to positive outcomes. (The supervisor must strengthen the employee's instrumentality beliefs.) In doing this, the supervisor must clearly explain the potential benefits of productive behavior, including any organizational policies regarding compensation and promotion. Finally, a supervisor must make certain that the employee values the outcome associated with productive behavior—that is, the supervisor must heighten the valence of productive performance. If the supervisor wants to increase intrinsic motivation, the supervisor must make certain that the employee can find the job itself enjoyable. If the supervisor wants to increase extrinsic motivation, he or she must offer a performance reward that the employee enjoys.

ENHANCING EMPLOYEE MOTIVATION

The expectancy theory provides useful theoretical guidelines for shaping employee motivation. Over the years, researchers have developed a number of specific techniques for increasing employee motivation to be productive. Two of the most useful techniques involve goal setting and job enrichment.

Goal setting involves assigning specific objectives for employee performance. For example, goal setting might be applied to the job of a computer disk-drive assembler in the following way. The assembler would meet with his or her supervisor. Using information about the worker's past performance, the supervisor and assembler would set a challenging goal regarding the number of disk drives to be assembled per week. The supervisor and assembler would then negotiate rewards for completing the goal on time. Each day, the supervisor would give the worker feedback by posting a running total of the number of disk drives assembled. At the end of the week, the worker's production would be reviewed and appropriate rewards would be given.

Edwin Locke and Gary Latham have studied goal setting extensively. They found that goals will lead to greater productivity if the goals are specific, difficult, and set with time deadlines. Further, goal setting programs will be more effective if the employee receives frequent feedback, allowing the employee to monitor his or her progress toward goal attainment. Additionally, goal setting will increase productivity if the employee is highly committed to the goal; giving employees the opportunity to participate in setting goals is one way to increase goal commitment. Finally, the effects of goal setting may be improved by establishing rewards for meeting goals on time. Other popular motivational techniques that involve goal setting include management by objectives (MBO) and organizational behavior modification (often called OBMod).

Job enrichment, a technique designed specifically to increase intrinsic motivation, was introduced by Frederick Herzberg. Herzberg argued that people will find a job enjoyable if the job provides opportunities to learn, to be responsible, and to experience a sense of achievement. For example, job enrichment might also be applied to the assembler's job. To enrich the job of the disk-drive assembler, the supervisor might change the job so that the assembler assembles a whole computer rather than only the disk drives. This would require greater knowledge and skills. The assembler could be given greater responsibility and be made accountable for the quality of each of the computers he or she assembles. Additional responsibility could be given to the assembler by providing the assembler a budget and requiring the assembler to order all the parts needed for assembly. Finally, the assembler might be given the opportunity to schedule his or her own hours.

Herzberg, like Maslow, argued that people have an innate need to grow psychologically and to develop their skills. Herzberg enriched the jobs of mechanics, secretaries, janitors, managers, and assembly-line workers. He found that giving workers challenging and interesting work, personal accountability for success and failures, control over organizational resources, and opportunities to self-schedule increased production quantity, improved production quality, and heightened job satisfaction.

THEORETICAL EVOLUTION

Modern work motivation theories span three eras. The first period was the scientific management era, which began around the beginning of the twentieth century, when Frederick Winslow Taylor applied scientific methodology to the study of worker efficiency. Taylor assumed that workers were basically lazy and incapable of self-direction. He proposed that the best way to motivate workers was to simplify the worker's job as much as possible, to determine empirically the most efficient movements the worker needed to perform the job, and to make pay contingent on job performance. Taylor applied the principles of scientific management to steelworkers and was able to increase productivity dramatically. The result of scientific management was that managers treated employees as if they were simply part of the production machinery. By making jobs specialized and repetitive, the manager could structure and fine-tune a worker's performance. Job routinization,

coupled with the assumption that employees were naturally uninterested in work, led managers to use extrinsic motivation techniques.

The next period of work motivation theory was the human relations era. This period began in the 1930's, with a classic study by Elton Mayo, Fritz Roethlisberger, and William Dickson at the Hawthorne Western Electric Plant, near Chicago, Illinois. These researchers conducted numerous experiments and interviews that led them to question the fundamental assumptions of scientific management. The researchers found that workers were strongly influenced by social norms and that peers could have as much influence on productivity as rules and incentives. They also found that workers expressed a strong desire to have their opinions heard and to make decisions regarding their jobs. The outcome of the human relations era was that managers began to show greater concern for employees' opinions and social needs. Managers assumed that the best way to motivate employees was to alleviate employee morale problems and to improve social relations on the job.

It was not until the human potential movement that managers and psychologists began to emphasize intrinsic motivation. This period began in the 1960's, with a growing concern over job satisfaction. Attracted to the work of Maslow and Herzberg, managers began to recognize employees' needs for psychological growth. Managers thus assumed that the best way to motivate workers was to give workers more opportunities to learn and to experience responsibility.

Beginning in the 1970's, motivational theorists and researchers became less concerned about finding the one best way to motivate employees. Instead, they took a more eclectic approach, elaborating on and integrating established motivation theories. For example, researchers have become interested in the degree to which extrinsic motivational strategies, such as performance bonuses, interfere with or supplement intrinsic motivation.

As work roles become more central to people's identity, as world economic competition increases, and as telecommunications and the Internet change the dynamics of work and the workplace, work motivation should remain a popular area of research. Managers will continue to find motivation theories useful in improving job satisfaction and increasing worker productivity.

SOURCES FOR FURTHER STUDY

Doyle, Christine E. *Work and Organizational Psychology: An Introduction with Attitude.* New York: Psychology Press, 2003. A cutting-edge introduction to work psychology. Covers work motivation as well as other topics relevant to organizational and work psychology. Suitable for undergraduate and graduate students.

Hodson, Christine. *Psychology and Work.* New York: Routledge, 2001. Chapter 3 covers a number of topics related to work motivation, including overviews of Maslow's hierarchy of needs and David McClelland's research on the need for achievement.

Maslow, Abraham H. *Toward a Psychology of Being.* 3d ed. New York: John Wiley & Sons, 1999. Maslow describes his needs hierarchy model of motivation and presents an interesting discussion of self-actualization.

Pinder, Craig C. *Work Motivation in Organizational Behavior.* 2d ed. New York: Psychology Press, 2008. This textbook gives a thorough overview of all the research related to work motivation, and it emphasizes that workplace behavior is the product of several factors, including emotions such as love and attitudes such as those related to power.

Smither, Robert D., ed. *The Psychology of Work and Human Performance.* Reading, Mass.: Addison Wesley, 1998. Chapter 7 covers work motivation, with emphasis on understanding individual differences among employees in motivation and performance.

Taylor, Frederick Winslow. *The Principles of Scientific Management.* New York: Cosimo, 2006. This management classic, originally published in 1911, describes Taylor's studies at the Midvale Steel Mill. Taylor was one of the first authors to discuss such concepts as wage incentives, time and motion studies, employee selection, and planning.

Daniel Sachau

SEE ALSO: Achievement motivation; Affiliation motive; Hierarchy of needs; Human resource training and development; Incentive motivation; Industrial and organizational psychology; Motivation; Motivation: Intrinsic and extrinsic; Self-actualization; Social support and mental health; Workplace issues and mental health.

Workforce reentry

TYPE OF PSYCHOLOGY: Social psychology
FIELDS OF STUDY: Interpersonal relations; motivation theory; prejudice and discrimination; social perception and cognition; stress and illness; substance-related issues

Appropriately timed workforce reentry is a priority for individuals suffering from mental disorders, including drug and alcohol addiction. Approximately one in five employees may have a mental condition, and many employers say the condition with the highest indirect cost to the company is mental illness. The World Health Organization states that mental health problems may be the factor most responsible for employee disability. Providing a safe and accepting work environment is essential to workforce reentry.

KEY CONCEPTS
• Americans with Disabilities Act
• reasonable accommodations
• reintegration
• self-reliance
• unemployment

INTRODUCTION

The unemployment rate for individuals with persistent mental illness is estimated to be as high as 90 percent, even when these individuals want to work or are able to work. With treatment, many people have manageable symptoms or recover from their disease, and can lead productive lives. Reintegration into society, including a return to the workforce, is a priority of mental health management. Work is an important step in becoming self-reliant and provides a focus away from the mental illness.

Research has demonstrated that there is no significant difference in the productivity of employees with and without mental illness. In 1990, President George H. W. Bush signed into law the Americans with Disabilities Act (ADA), which prohibits discrimination against people with a variety of disabilities, including psychiatric disabilities, in employment and other services. Under the ADA, reasonable accommodations are required when workforce reentry occurs. In 1999, President Bill Clinton signed legislation to eliminate work disincentives called the Ticket to Work and Work Incentives Improvement

Act. The act provided people with disabilities the opportunity to pursue a job without losing health care coverage.

The ADA defines a disability as a physical or mental impairment that substantially limits major life activities, including work. Mental impairment may be any mental or psychological disorder, including emotional or mental illness such as depression, anxiety disorders, schizophrenia and other personality disorders. Addictions to drugs or alcohol are also impediments to workforce reentry. Employers should define a program to enable potential and existing employees with mental health issues to reenter the workforce.

IMPLICATIONS FOR EMPLOYERS

The cost of care for mental-health-related conditions is often the highest percentage of health care insurance dollars spent by a company, according to the Partnership for Workplace Mental Health: A Program of the American Psychiatric Foundation. Managing the employee's return to work after mental health care ensures that the dollars spent were worthwhile. The goals for employers are to improve and maintain the employee's outcomes of treatment, decrease future absenteeism, and minimize the cost and impact of behavioral health conditions on the workplace and the employee's colleagues.

Regardless of the underlying cause of mental illness, an employee's return to work poses a challenge to coworkers and supervisors. Behavioral health problems, poor self-esteem and work habits, and fear of the work environment may cause the employee to stay away from work longer than necessary, increasing the workload for coworkers. Colleagues may grow to resent the employee because of frequent absences. The same stigma attached to mental illness that prevents individuals from seeking care may also negatively affect coworkers' support for the returning employee if they know why the coworkers was absent. If the workplace and colleagues are unprepared to provide necessary support, the stress of returning to work may prevent the affected individual from moving into an environment that will enhance recovery.

To enhance assimilation of the employee into the workforce, a program designed to support reentry while minimizing disruption is critical. The company's leadership must communicate a clear message of a nondiscriminatory workplace, whether illness is physical or mental. Supervisors are essential to a successful employee reentry and must receive education and training to understand their role. All employees must be educated to issues surrounding mental health and the need to seek care for mental health issues promptly. A greater understanding of mental health issues by employees in the workplace encourages a climate of acceptance and support should the returning employee choose to share personal information.

Employers are also required by the ADA to hold all information about the employee reentering the workforce in strict confidence. Supervisors and select others may receive information necessary to manage the work and needs of the returning employee. The employer is also not allowed to disclose any medical information about the returning employee to coworkers. If employees question why the returning worker is receiving different or special treatment, the employer can only state that it is acting in compliance with a federal law for legitimate business reasons.

REASONABLE ACCOMMODATIONS

The ADA requires reasonable accommodations for individuals with disabilities. Changes to workplace policies, procedures or practices that are not excessive in cost or disruption are expected. Changing a schedule to allow the returning employee to gradually increase to full-time work or to carpool if unable to drive; providing a quiet workspace to minimize sensory stimulation, such as for the employee with severe attention deficit disorder; and providing time off for recurrent physician visits are examples of reasonable accommodations. Employers are not expected to make changes that are an undue hardship or to allow a disruptive or threatening employee to return to the workforce, but a health care professional must participate in the decision to refuse workforce reentry.

Successful reentry into the workplace requires trust and a partnership between the employer and employee. Open, honest communication and dialogue will facilitate the reentry process.

SOURCES FOR FURTHER STUDY

Kessler, R. C., et al. "Prevalence and Effects of Mood Disorders on Work Performance in a Nationally Representative Sample of U.S. Workers." *American Journal of Psychiatry* 163 (2006): 1561-1568.

Essay examines work issues surrounding those with mood disorders and how common this disorder is.

Lengnick-Hall, Mark L., ed. *Hidden Talent: How Leading Companies Hire, Retain, and Benefit from People with Disabilities*. Westport, Conn.: Praeger, 2007. Takes a positive approach to workforce re-entry, looking at the practices of major companies such as IBM, Dow Chemical, and Microsoft, and how they successfully employ people with disabilities.

National Council on Disability. *Implementation of the Americans with Disabilities Act: Challenges, Best Practices, and New Opportunities for Success*. Washington, D.C.: Author, 2007. Looks at the key issues involving implementation, focusing on what has worked well and problematic areas.

Rubin, Stanford E., and Richard T. Roessler. *Foundations of the Vocational Rehabilitation Process*. 6th ed. Austin, Tex.: PRO-ED, 2008. Examines a variety issues surrounding vocational rehabilitation, including the role of the counselor and sociological aspects.

Warren, Frank, and Richard G. Luecking. *Jobs for People: A Handbook—Finding Employment Opportunities for Citizens Who Have Disabilities*. Rockville, Md.: TransCen, 1989. A brief manual that is designed to help those assisting people with disabilities who are seeking to join the workforce.

Patricia Stanfill Edens

SEE ALSO: Alcohol dependence and abuse; Career selection, development, and change; Law and psychology; Personality disorders; Prejudice; Quality of life; Work motivation; Workplace issues and mental health.

Workplace issues and mental health

TYPE OF PSYCHOLOGY: Social psychology

FIELDS OF STUDY: Adulthood; anxiety disorders; attitudes and behavior; behavioral therapies; cognitive therapies; coping; critical issues in stress; depression; group and family therapies; group processes; motivation theory; personality disorders; prejudice and discrimination; problem solving; schizophrenias; social perception and cognition; stress and illness; substance-related issues

Life and job stresses are increasingly affecting the mental health of employees, thereby reducing their productivity and creating problems for their employers. More and more employers are striving to create healthful workplaces through programs designed to enhance employees' mental health and to enable managers to recognize signs and symptoms of developing mental health disorders.

KEY CONCEPTS

- alcohol and drug abuse
- anxiety disorders
- bipolar disorders
- disability
- disease management
- major and nonmajor depression
- productivity

INTRODUCTION

Approximately 20 percent of employees may exhibit some type of mental illness, and 50 percent of disability worldwide is mental health-related, according to the World Health Organization and the International Labor Organization. According to many employers, mental illness is the condition with the highest indirect cost to their companies. Alcohol and drug abuse, bipolar disorder, major depression, obsessive-compulsive disorder, and schizophrenia, coupled with anxiety, stress, and nonmajor depression, present a growing problem in the workforce. These disorders may lead to productivity loss, employee turnover, and long-term disability in employees. Depression is often reported as the mental health disorder that has the greatest effect in the workplace, leading to approximately 200 million days of lost work annually in the United States.

Globalization has resulted in workers in the United States and other developed nations losing their jobs due to downsizing, outsourcing, and factory closings; those who remain employed experience increased workloads, pressure to perform, and uncertainty about their futures. In economic downturns, falling purchasing power and the decreased demand for goods can lead to a rise in drug and alcohol abuse as well as in stress and domestic violence, according to the International Labor Organization.

Historically, employers have viewed mental health disorders in applicants and workers in a negative manner. The stigma attached to mental illness has affected both hiring and retention of individuals perceived to have mental health issues. By the twenty-first century, however, efforts at educating employers regarding mental health issues have ameliorated some of the stigma associated with mental illness and allowed workers with mental illnesses to receive appropriate treatment. In addition, companies have altered their hiring practices to comply with the Americans with Disabilities Act (ADA) of 1990, which prohibits discrimination against people with disabilities, including psychiatric disabilities, in employment and other activities. Studies have shown that employees either entering or returning to the workplace after successful treatment for mental health issues are as productive as their coworkers.

To provide a healthful workplace and decrease employee turnover, many companies have begun educating employees and managers to recognize the signs and symptoms of mental health disorders, enabling them to identity early indications of problems and to refer individuals to the appropriate course of treatment. Many companies have also found that providing an environment conducive to good mental health in employees enhances productivity and product quality.

RECOGNIZING SIGNS OF MENTAL HEALTH DISORDERS

Employers are encouraged to consider hiring individuals with managed mental health disorders. Research has shown that employees with select psychiatric disorders can be stable, functional, and productive employees. Understanding the pathology of mental illness can assist managers in providing an environment that encourages success for employ-

ees. When employers are aware of mental health disorders affecting employees, accommodations can be made to better meet their needs.

Both managers and employees should be educated to recognize the early signs of mental health disorders. Early recognition of signs indicating a problem in an employee will lead to early intervention, prompt referral for treatment, and better outcomes of therapy. Employees may also be able to recognize their developing problems if mental health education has been provided in the workplace. Education also creates the opportunity to remove the stigma surrounding mental health issues and encourages both managers and employees to feel comfortable acknowledging a need for assistance.

The most visible sign of a potential mental health issue with an employee is absenteeism. If an employee calls in sick several times a month for a few days at a time, this should alert the individual's supervisor to a potential problem. Employees who exhibit sadness, irritability, or make inappropriate comments should also be observed carefully. Employees may also complain of burnout or their frustration with assigned tasks and, in extreme cases, may even make comments about violence or suicide. General poor health—including high blood pressure, skin rashes, sleeping disorders, and frequent infections—is often associated with mental health disorders. Lethargy, abnormally slow movements, or periods of hyperactivity may indicate substance abuse, and slurred speech, confusion, clumsiness, and the smell of alcohol on the breath may indicate alcohol abuse.

Changes in work performance are often noted in mental health disorders. Decreased productivity and work output, and increased errors and accidents are indicators that should be carefully evaluated. An inability to prioritize work, poor decision making, and a loss of commitment and motivation are also signs that an employee may have a problem. If staff in an area demonstrate a poor attitude or there is a high rate of turnover, it may indicate a problem with the supervisor or the workplace environment.

Poor relationships at work with colleagues or clients may also be an indication that an employee is experiencing difficulties. Visible tension or conflicts, an increase in actions requiring discipline, or avoidance of an employee by colleagues are also warning signs for employers. Social support from colleagues is important to mental health and work productivity.

Although absenteeism, changes in work performance, and deteriorating relationships may indicate a problem with an individual, the diagnosis of a mental health disorder must be made by a mental health professional. Educating individuals about warning signs of a potential issue is the first step in determining if an employee or manager needs professional intervention.

Facts About Depression in the Workplace

- depression ranks third in workplace problems for employee assistance professionals
- the employee was female in more than 75 percent of short-term disability days taken because of depressive disorders
- approximately 15 percent of workers suffering from severe depression will commit suicide
- many times a depressed employee does not seek treatment for depression because he or she thinks it will affect how he or she will be perceived on the job

Source: National Mental Health Association (NMHA) factsheet "Depression in the Workplace."

COMMON PSYCHIATRIC CONDITIONS

Many employees with diagnosed psychiatric conditions are capable of working and being productive members of society when given the opportunity. Understanding the definition of common mental health disorders is important for managers of employees with a diagnosed condition, and managers are encouraged to research known diagnoses in more depth to increase understanding of a specific disease.

Bipolar disorders, also known as manic-depressive disorders, cause changes in mood, function, and energy levels. Manic phases with hyperactivity, lack of impulse control, and irritability, alternating with depressive phases of sad, anxious, or hopeless moods are the hallmarks of bipolar disorders. Often the disease is not recognized in a timely manner, but when diagnosed, the disease is treatable, and patients can lead full and productive lives.

Major depression is a disorder that interferes with the ability to carry on a normal life and should not be confused with mild episodes of sadness or a blue mood. Depressive disorders are evidenced by persistent sadness, feelings of hopelessness, decreased energy levels, thoughts of death or suicide, loss of interest in pleasurable activities or work, difficulty concentrating or trouble making decisions. Depression may be treated with psychotherapy and medication, and individuals are capable of leading a productive life after intervention.

Substance abuse remains a growing problem in the workplace. A compulsion to drink; being unable to limit drinking; the development of withdrawal symptoms such as nausea, sweating, and anxiety; and an increasing need for greater amounts of alcohol all indicate a problem. Drug abuse is defined as repeated use of harmful agents but does not include tolerance or compulsive use. Drug dependence is also known as addiction and implies an inability to do without an agent. Substance abuse and mental health conditions often occur together. Behavioral therapies and medication may be used to treat addictions, and positive responses may occur with continued support and the individual's commitment to staying sober.

An individual with obsessive-compulsive disorder, an anxiety disorder, has unwanted thoughts or demonstrates repetitive behaviors such as hand washing or counting in attempt to control unwanted thoughts. Medication, psychotherapy, and self-help groups may be effective in managing this disorder.

Schizophrenia is a severe and disabling disorder that may cause individuals to hear voices, experience paranoia, or withdraw. Antipsychotic medications and long-term psychosocial interventions may allow the individual to manage the chronic disorder, but recovery does not occur. Entry into the workforce for more complex mental disorders is possible in a carefully selected and managed setting.

Anxiety, stress, and nonmajor depression may be evident in individuals who are in the workplace. Stressors such as life events (divorce, death, or other loss) may lead to nonmajor depressions and anxiety disorders such as post-traumatic stress disorder (PTSD). Cognitive behavioral therapy and medications may be used to treat anxiety disorders.

Hiring an individual with a diagnosed mental health disorder requires a commitment to providing accommodations based on the needs of the individual. There may be funding available to assist companies in providing a job opportunity for individuals entering or returning to the workforce after therapy for mental illness.

INTERVENTION PROGRAMS

The most commonly implemented intervention program related to mental health in the workplace is the Employee Assistance Program (EAP), available in more than 75 percent of companies in the United States, according to the Society for Human Resource Management. The EAP provides a confidential resource for employees to seek help with mental health issues and is a nonthreatening option for managers to suggest to employees. Although the EAP was originally designed to assist with drug and alcohol disorders, its programs have expanded to cover a variety of issues, including depression, stress management, marital problems, or legal and financial problems. Many plans also allow limited care for employees'

family members. The program is conducted by an outside third party, and confidentiality is assured.

Many employers have implemented disease management programs for mental illness. Disease management programs generally assign a case manager to monitor the care of an employee undergoing therapy to be sure that timely and appropriate care is provided. An additional focus of disease management programs is to facilitate the employee's reentry into the workplace.

SUPPORTING EMPLOYEES WITH MENTAL HEALTH PROBLEMS

Individuals with mental health disorders benefit from work during their treatment and recovery. Having a purposeful and supportive place to go on a daily basis provides structure and financial security to individuals experiencing mental illness. Often

This call center in Greensboro, N.C., allows employees to bring their dogs to work to promote workers' mental well-being. (AP/Wide World Photos)

job-related health benefits are needed to pay for therapy and medications that lead to recovery. Colleagues and friends are an important part of recovery. Individuals receiving care may share their issues and concerns with coworkers.

If the workplace provides education about good mental health, employees have a foundation from which to support the colleague with a mental health issue. Some more formal work reentry programs allow a therapist to come to the workplace and provide an orientation to coworkers to ease the employee's return. This program must be conducted without violating patient confidentiality and with the individual's written, legal permission. Recovery is more likely in a supportive environment, and a workplace that is accepting and supportive is important.

PROMOTING GOOD MENTAL HEALTH

Employers have a responsibility to create a work environment that promotes good mental health. An assessment of physical conditions, such as lighting, temperature, cleanliness, and noise level, may indicate that the physical environment needs attention. A safe and secure work environment is the first step in promoting good mental health in the workplace.

Managers are also critical to a positive work experience, leading to a less stressful and healthy workplace. Providing management training for newly promoted supervisors and ongoing education for all managers is important. Understanding how to manage and motivate employees to achieve their potential in a positive and supportive manner may contribute to good employee mental health. Measuring employee morale and satisfaction in the workplace is also important to track measures that affect good mental health and to determine if managers are meeting the needs of their employees.

Some companies provide screening programs to detect mental health risk factors in employees. Mental health screenings must be confidential and should be interpreted by a mental health professional. Employees may feel threatened by the findings of a mental health screening and its relationship to continued employment or advancement within the company. Some mental health screening questionnaires allow individuals to self-evaluate using a set of indicators, and if the individual crosses a certain threshold of response, the person is advised to seek additional assistance from a mental health pro-

fessional. These are similar to cancer or heart disease screening questionnaires, which are used to refer individuals who possibly have problems to their doctors. Most general health screening questionnaires include some mental-health-related questions. Many employers also have preemployment drug testing or, depending on the industry, may have a policy of ongoing, random drug testing. In some instances, this may be a deterrent to substance abuse in the workplace.

Companies should provide education that assists individuals in learning how to deal with stress, anxiety, and substance abuse both in and out of the workplace. Learning stress relief measures, such as meditation, guided imagery, and relaxation, helps employees deal with day-to-day issues. Learned coping mechanisms may also improve employees' personal lives, leading to less stress at home and improved performance at work. It may also lead to less reliance on drugs and alcohol as coping mechanisms. Educating employees may also be effective in preventing the development of drug or substance abuse.

Proactive measures designed to enhance employee health contribute to positive mental health and may decrease behaviorally related mental health disorders. Wellness programs such as smoking cessation, weight loss, and grief recovery programs are used to enhance employee health and self-esteem. Allowing community agencies or twelve-step programs such as Alcoholics Anonymous to use meeting space at a company is a way to provide cost-effective intervention programs. Educational programs such as on-site literacy programs, high school completion programs, and special training or college courses all contribute to a positive self-image and may inhibit development of some mental health disorders.

Companies should provide their employees with health insurance with equivalent coverage of physical and mental health problems. If employees have access to inpatient or outpatient care, those with recognized signs of mental health issues may be referred for care more easily.

SOURCES FOR FURTHER STUDY

Dunnagan, T., M. Peterson, and G. Haynes. "Mental Health Issues in the Workplace: A Case for a New Managerial Approach." *Journal of Occupational & Environmental Medicine* 43, no. 12 (December, 2001): 1073-1080. Examines the impact of a traditional worksite health promotion program on mental health, finding that this type of program played a limited role and that managers should pay greater attention to addressing workplace stress, anger, and depression.

Kawada, T., and S. Suzuki. "Physical Symptoms and Psychological Health Status by the Type of Job." *Work* 31, no. 4 (2008): 397-403. Compares and contrasts the stresses on workers at a dairy product company depending on whether they were in production process, technical or clerical, or transportation or sales work. The transportation or sales work employees were observed to have the most health problems.

Kessler, R. C., et al. "Prevalence and Effects of Mood Disorders on Work Performance in a Nationally Representative Sample of U.S. Workers." *American Journal of Psychiatry* 163 (2006): 1561-1568. Addresses issues of productivity, absenteeism, and other effects on performance of workers with mood disorders, contrasting bipolar disorder with major depression.

Langlieb, A. M., and J. P. Kahn. "How Much Does Quality Mental Healthcare Care Profit Employers?" *Journal of Occupational and Environmental Medicine*, November, 2005, pp. 1099-1109. This study found that anxiety disorders and depression were very costly to employers, yet most companies did not realize the importance of providing high-quality mental health care for their workers.

Partnership for Workplace Mental Health: A Program of the American Psychiatric Foundation. http://www.workplacementalhealth.org/ This program is designed to advance effective employer approaches to mental health. Contains resources for both employers and employees.

Thomas, Jay C., and Michel Hersen, eds. *Handbook of Mental Health in the Workplace*. Thousand Oaks, Calif.: Sage Publications, 2002. Explores how psychological disorders affect individuals' ability to work and recommends treatments. Looks at legal rights and responsibilities of the employer and employee and at areas such as anger, grieving, and the effects of abuse.

Patricia Stanfill Edens

SEE ALSO: Alcohol dependence and abuse; Anxiety disorders; Career and personnel testing; Depression; Health insurance; Intervention; Law and psychology; Mental health parity; Mood disorders; Posttraumatic stress disorder; Stress: Behavioral and psychological responses; Substance use disorders; Workforce reentry.

Y

Yalom, Irvin D.

BORN: June 13, 1931, in Washington, D.C.
IDENTITY: American psychiatrist
TYPE OF PSYCHOLOGY: Psychotherapy
FIELDS OF STUDY: Adulthood; aging; group and
family therapies; humanistic therapies

*Yalom advanced the theory and practice of psycho-
therapy techniques for groups and existential therapy
methods for individuals.*

Irvin D. Yalom was born to Russian immigrants Benjamin Yalom and Ruth Yalom, who owned a Washington, D.C., grocery. Yalom enrolled in George
Washington University, receiving a bachelor's of art
degree in 1952. He attended his alma mater's medical school for one year, then transferred to Boston
University's medical program. Yalom married Marilyn Koenick in 1954 and earned an M.D. two years
later.

Yalom completed a Mount Sinai Hospital intern-
ship in New York City in 1957 and began his residency at The Johns Hopkins University's Henry
Phipps Psychiatric Clinic in Baltimore, Maryland.
His mentor, Jerome Frank, invited Yalom to watch
group therapy, assisting him to establish a group.
Rollo May's *Existence: A New Dimension in Psychiatry
and Psychology* (1958; edited with Ernest Angel and
Henri F. Ellenberger) influenced Yalom, who took
philosophy classes to enhance his psychotherapy approaches.

In 1962, Yalom accepted a position at Stanford
University's medical school in Palo Alto, California.
He wrote *The Theory and Practice of Group Psychotherapy* (1970), emphasizing what he called curative factors, including group cohesiveness and universality.
That book has been translated into several languages
and revised numerous times.

By 1973, Yalom had become a full professor and
assistant director of Stanford's Adult Psychiatric

Clinic. The Institute of Pennsylvania Hospital honored him with its 1974 Edward Strecker Award. He
received the American Psychiatric Association
(APA) Foundation's Fund Award in 1976. Yalom was
a Center for Advanced Study in Behavioral Sciences
fellow in 1977 and 1978. He wrote *Existential Psychotherapy* (1980), addressing four basic concepts related to human existence: death, freedom, isolation,
and meaning.

In 1981, Yalom began directing medical services
for Stanford University Hospital's Psychiatry Inpatient Unit. His book *Inpatient Group Psychotherapy*
(1983) discussed treating patients in psychiatric
wards. Reviewers praised Yalom's *Love's Executioner
and Other Tales of Psychotherapy* (1989) for honestly
depicting therapist-patient interactions, revealing
failures associated with therapy, and acknowledging
therapists' uncertainties.

Yalom's novels *When Nietzsche Wept* (1992), *Lying
on the Couch* (1996), and *The Schopenhauer Cure* (2005)
featured historical existential figures and situations.
He retired from Stanford in 1994. Yalom was general editor of the Jossey-Bass Library of Current
Clinical Technique. In 2001, he received the APA's
Oscar Pfister Award.

In *The Gift of Therapy: An Open Letter to a New Generation of Therapists and Their Patients* (2002), Yalom
offered insights and criticisms regarding the psychotherapy profession. His *Staring at the Sun: Overcoming
the Terror of Death* (2008) focused on existentialism
and mortality.

SOURCES FOR FURTHER STUDY

Josselson, Ruthellen. *Irvin D. Yalom: On Psychotherapy
and the Human Condition*. New York: Jorge Pinto
Books, 2008. Includes two interviews, chapters
exploring Yalom's psychotherapy education and
practices, and a bibliography.
Shaughnessy, Michael F., Douglas Main, and Judy
Madewell. "An Interview with Irvin Yalom." *North*

American Journal of Psychology 9, no. 3 (December, 2007): 511-518. Yalom discusses his mentors, responsibilities as a therapist, professional concerns, existential factors, and writing.

Yalom, Irvin D., ed. *The Yalom Reader: Selections from the Work of a Master Therapist and Storyteller.* New York: Basic Books, 1998. Excerpts represent Yalom's innovative group and existential therapies and fiction. Supplemented with annotations and introduction by Yalom.

Elizabeth D. Schafer

SEE ALSO: Existential psychology; Group therapy; Groups; Psychotherapy: Goals and techniques.

Z

Zimbardo, Philip

BORN: March 23, 1933, in New York, New York
IDENTITY: American social psychologist
TYPE OF PSYCHOLOGY: Personality; social
   psychology
FIELDS OF STUDY: Personality assessment; social
   motives; social perception and cognition

*Zimbardo is a leading authority on the dynamics of
shyness and the psychology of time perspective.*

Philip Zimbardo, the son of poor, uneducated Sicilian American parents, was reared in the South Bronx ghetto of New York City. In that environment, he learned the importance of people versus material possessions and of education in rising from poverty. He earned a bachelor's degree in psychology, sociology, and anthropology from Brooklyn College in 1954. After earning his doctorate in psychology from Yale University in 1959, Zimbardo taught psychology courses at Yale (1959-1960), at New York University (1960-1967), and at Columbia University

Philip Zimbardo. (AP/Wide World Photos)

(1967-1968). In 1968, he accepted a position in the department of psychology at Stanford University.

Zimbardo's most notable study was the infamous Stanford prison experiment in 1971. He assigned twenty-four mentally normal students to act as either guards or prisoners in a mock prison constructed in the psychology building at Stanford. It was a classic demonstration illustrating the power of social situations to distort personalities, personal values, and moral standards, as the students took on the identities of the persons they were portraying. The guards exhibited sadistic characteristics, while the prisoners demonstrated passivity and depression.

To help people through the application of psychology, Zimbardo founded the Shyness Clinic at Stanford in 1975 to treat shyness in adolescents and adults. The clinic became the Palo Alto Shyness Center in 1982. Zimbardo's best-known books are *Shyness: What It Is, What to Do About It* (1977) and *The Shy Child: A Parent's Guide to Preventing and Overcoming Shyness from Infancy to Adulthood* (with Shirley L. Radl, 1981). Zimbardo and Floyd L. Ruch published *Psychology and Life* (1971), a textbook used in numerous undergraduate psychology courses (an eighteenth edition was published in 2008, with Richard J. Gerrig as Zimbardo's co-author).

In 1990, Zimbardo designed, wrote, and hosted the twenty-six-part award-winning Public Broadcasting Service television series *Discovering Psychology*. It has been used widely in high schools and colleges. It was translated into ten different languages and updated in 2001. Zimbardo has also appeared on the British reality television show, *The Human Zoo*, in which the behavior of participants in a controlled setting is analyzed.

In 2002, Zimbardo was elected president of the American Psychological Association (APA). His later research efforts concentrated on the psychology of time perspective, the ways that individuals develop temporal orientations associated with personal experiences that are related to past, present, or future events, or with beliefs about life after death. He retired from Stanford in 2003 but continued to teach part time at the Pacific Graduate School of Psychology.

SOURCES OF FURTHER STUDY

Crozier, W. Ray. *Understanding Shyness: Psychological Perspectives.* New York: Palgrave, 2001. Zimbardo's contributions to understanding and dealing with shyness are examined.

Lane, Christopher. *Shyness: How Normal Behavior Became a Sickness.* New Haven, Conn.: Yale University Press, 2007. Lane explores the history of mental illness and discusses some of Zimbardo's research and insights into the treatment of bashfulness.

Simonton, Dean Keith. *Great Psychologists and Their Times: Scientific Insights into Psychology's History.* Washington, D.C.: American Psychological Association, 2002. Zimbardo's contributions to the advancement of psychological science are discussed along with the work of other prominent psychologists.

Alvin K. Benson

SEE ALSO: Aggression: Reduction and control; Depersonalization; Experimental psychology; Experimentation: Ethics and subject rights; Shyness; Stanford prison experiment.

Appendixes

GLOSSARY

Absolute threshold: The smallest amount of stimulus that elicits a sensation 50 percent of the time.

Accommodation: In Jean Piaget's theory of development, adjusting the interpretation (schema) of an object or event to include a new instance; in vision, the ability of the lens to focus light on the retina by changing its shape.

Acetylcholine (ACh): A cholinergic neurotransmitter important in producing muscular contraction and in some autonomic nerve transmissions.

Achievement motivation: The tendency for people to strive for moderately difficult goals because of the relative attractiveness of success and repulsiveness of failure.

Acquisition: In learning, the process by which an association is formed in classical or operant conditioning; in memory, the stage at which information is stored in memory.

Action potential: A rapid change in electrical charges across a neuron's cell membrane, with depolarization followed by repolarization, leading to a nerve impulse moving down an axon; associated with nerve and muscle activity.

Actor-observer bias: The tendency to infer that other people's behavior is caused by dispositional factors but that one's own behavior is the product of situational causes.

Actualizing tendency: The force toward maintaining and enhancing the organism, achieving congruence between experience and awareness, and realizing potentials.

Adaptation: Any heritable characteristic that presumably has developed as a result of natural selection and thus increases an animal's ability to survive and reproduce.

Addiction: Physical dependence on a substance; components include tolerance, psychological dependence, and physical withdrawal symptoms.

Adolescence: The period extending from the onset of puberty to early adulthood.

Adrenal glands: The suprarenal glands. Small, caplike structures sitting each on top of one kidney; in general, they function in response to stress, but they are also important in regulating metabolic and sexual functions.

Affect: A class name given to feelings, emotions, or dispositions as a mode of mental functioning.

Affective disorders: Functional mental disorders associated with emotions or feelings (also called mood disorders); examples include depression and bipolar disorders.

Afferent: A sensory neuron or a dendrite carrying information toward a structure; for example, carrying sensory stimuli coming into the reticular formation.

Affiliation motive: The motive to seek the company of others and to be with one's own kind, based on such things as cooperation, similarity, friendship, sex, and protection.

Aggression: Behavior intended to harm or injure another person or thing.

Agoraphobia: An intense fear of being in places or situations in which help may not be available or escape could be difficult.

Allele: One of the many forms of a gene; it may be dominant (needing only one copy for the trait to appear) or recessive (needing two copies).

Altruism: A phenomenon in human and animal behaviors in which individuals unselfishly sacrifice their own genetic fitness in order to help other individuals in a group.

Alzheimer's disease: A form of presenile dementia, characterized by disorientation, loss of memory, speech disturbances, and personality disorders.

Amplitude: The peak deviation from the rest state of the movement of a vibrating object, or the ambient state of the medium through which vibration is conducted.

Anal stage: According to Sigmund Freud, the second psychosexual stage of personality development, approximately from ages two to four; sexual energy is focused on the anus and on pleasures and conflicts associated with retaining and eliminating feces.

Analgesia: The reduction or elimination of pain.

Analytical psychology: A school of psychology founded

by Carl Jung that views the human mind as the result of prior experiences and the preparation of future goals; it deemphasizes the role of sexuality in psychological disorders.

Androgens: Male sex hormones secreted by the testes; testosterone, the primary mammalian male androgen, is responsible for the development and maturation of male sexual structures and sexual behaviors.

Androgyny: The expression of both traditionally feminine and traditionally masculine attributes.

Anorexia nervosa: An eating disorder characterized by an obsessive-compulsive concern for thinness achieved by dieting; often combined with extreme exercising and sometimes part of a binge-purge cycle.

Anterograde amnesia: An inability to form new memories after the onset of amnesia.

Antidepressants: Drugs that are used in the treatment of depression, many of which affect or mimic neurotransmitters; classes of antidepressants include the tricyclics and monoamine oxidase inhibitors (MAOIs).

Antisocial personality disorder: A personality disorder characterized by a history of impulsive, risk-taking, and perhaps chronic criminal behavior and by opportunistic interpersonal relations.

Anxiety: A chronic fearlike state that is accompanied by feelings of impending doom and that cannot be explained by an actual threatening object or event.

Aphasia: Partial or total loss of the use of language as a result of brain damage, characterized by an inability to use and/or comprehend language.

Applied research: Research intended to solve existing problems, as opposed to "basic research," which seeks knowledge for its own sake.

Aptitude: The potential to develop an ability with training and/or experience.

Archetypes: In Carl Jung's theory, universal, inherited themes—such as the motifs of the self, hero, and shadow—that exercise an influence on virtually all human beings.

Archival data: Information collected at an earlier time by someone other than the present researcher, often for purposes very different from those of the present research.

Artificial intelligence: The use of computers to simulate aspects of human thinking and, in some cases, behavior.

Assimilation: The interpretation of a new instance of an object or event in terms of one's preexisting schema or understanding.

Attachment: An emotional bond between infant and caregiver based on reciprocal interaction patterns.

Attention: The ability to focus mentally.

Attitude: A relatively stable evaluation of a person or thing; it can be either positive or negative, can vary in level of intensity, and has an affective, cognitive, and behavioral component.

Attribution: The process by which one gathers information about the self and others and interprets it to determine the cause of an event or behavior.

Attributional biases: Typical motivational and cognitive errors in the attribution process; tendencies that are shared among people in using information in illogical or unwarranted ways.

Autonomic nervous system: The division of the peripheral nervous system that regulates basic, automatically controlled life processes such as cardiovascular function, digestive function, and genital function.

Availability heuristic: A decision-making heuristic whereby a person estimates the probability of some occurrence or event depending on how easily examples of that event can be remembered.

Aversion therapy: A therapy that involves pairing something negative (such as electric shock) with an undesired behavior (such as drinking alcohol or smoking cigarettes).

Axon: The single fiberlike extension of a neuron that carries information away from the cell body toward the next cell in a pathway.

Beck Depression Inventory (BDI): A brief questionnaire used to measure the severity of depression; developed by Aaron Beck.

Behavior therapy: A branch of psychotherapy narrowly conceived as the application of classical and operant conditioning to the alteration of clinical problems, but more broadly conceived as applied experimental psychology in a clinical context.

Behaviorism: A theoretical approach which states that the environment is the primary cause of behavior and that only external, observable stimuli and responses are available to objective study.

Between-subject designs: Experimental plans in which

different participants receive each level of the independent variable.

Bilingual: A person who has enough control of two languages to function well with both languages in a number of different contexts.

Binocular cues: Visual cues that require the use of both eyes working together.

Biofeedback: A psychophysiological technique in which an individual monitors a specific, supposedly involuntary, bodily function such as blood pressure or heart rate and consciously attempts to control this function through the use of learning principles.

Bipolar disorder: A disorder characterized by the occurrence of one or more manic episodes, usually interspersed with one or more major depressive episodes.

Bottom-up processing: Information processing guided by simple stimulus features of units rather than by a person's general knowledge, beliefs, or expectations.

Brain stem: The lower part of the brain, between the brain and spinal cord, which activates the cortex and makes perception and consciousness possible; it includes the midbrain, pons, medulla, and cerebellum.

Bystander effect: The tendency for an individual to be less likely to help as the number of other people present increases.

Cardinal trait: According to Gordon W. Allport's theory of personality, a single outstanding characteristic that dominates a person's life; few individuals are characterized by a cardinal disposition.

Case study: An in-depth method of data collection in which all available background data on an individual or group are reviewed; typically used in psychotherapy.

Catecholamines: A neurotransmitter group derived from the amino acid tyrosine that includes dopamine, epinephrine, and norepinephrine; they are activated in stressful situations.

Catharsis: A reduction of psychological tension and/or physiological arousal by expressing (either directly or vicariously) repressed aggressive or sexual anxieties.

Central nervous system: The nerve cells, fibers, and other tissues associated with the brain and spinal cord.

Central traits: According to Gordon W. Allport's the-

ory, the relatively few (five to ten) distinctive and descriptive characteristics that provide direction and focus to a person's life.

Cephalocaudal development: A pattern of early physical growth consisting of motor development that proceeds from head to foot.

Cerebellum: The portion of the brain that controls voluntary muscle activity, including posture and body movement; located behind the brain stem.

Cerebral commissures: Fiber tracts, such as the corpus callosum and anterior commissure, that connect and allow neural communication between the cerebral hemispheres.

Cerebral cortex: The outer layer of the cerebrum; controls higher-level brain functions such as thinking, reasoning, motor coordination, memory, and language.

Cerebral hemispheres: Two anatomically similar hemispheres that make up the outer surface of the brain (the cerebral cortex); separated by the cerebral longitudinal fissure.

Cerebrospinal fluid: A fluid, derived from blood, that circulates in and around the ventricles of the brain and the spinal cord.

Cerebrum: The largest and uppermost portion of the brain; the cerebrum performs sensory and motor functions and affects memory, speech, and emotional functions.

Chaining: The process by which several neutral stimuli are presented in a series; they eventually assume reinforcing qualities by being paired with an innate reinforcer.

Children's Depression Inventory (CDI): A modified version of the Beck Depression Inventory (BDI) that was developed to measure the severity of depression in children; developed by Maria Kovacs.

Chromosomes: Microscopic threadlike bodies in the nuclei of cells; they carry the genes, which convey hereditary characteristics.

Circadian rhythm: A cyclical variation in a biological process or behavior that has a duration of about a day; in humans under constant environmental conditions, the rhythm usually reveals its true length as being slightly more than twenty-four hours.

Classical conditioning: A form of associative learning in which a neutral stimulus, called the conditioned stimulus (CS), is repeatedly paired with a biologically significant unconditioned stimulus (US) so that the CS acquires the same power to elicit response as the US; also called Pavlovian conditioning.

Clinical psychologist: A person with a Ph.D. in psychology, specially trained to assess and treat mental disorders and behavior problems.

Cochlea: The snail-shell-shaped portion of the inner ear, which contains the nerve connections to the auditory nerve.

Code-switching: A speech style used by many bilinguals that is characterized by rapid shifts back and forth between two languages within a single conversation or sentence.

Cognition: Mental processes involved in the acquisition and use of knowledge, such as attention, thinking, problem solving, and perception; cognitive learning emphasizes these processes in the acquisition of new behaviors.

Cognitive appraisal: An assessment of the meaningfulness of an event to an individual; events that are appraised as harmful or potentially harmful elicit stress.

Cognitive behavior therapy: Therapy that integrates principles of learning theory with cognitive strategies to treat disorders such as depression, anxiety, and other behavioral problems (such as smoking or obesity).

Cognitive dissonance theory: Leon Festinger's theory that inconsistencies among one's beliefs cause tension and that individuals are motivated to reduce this tension by changing discrepant attitudes.

Cognitive map: A mental representation of an external area that is used to guide one's behavior.

Cognitive processes: The processes of thought, which include attending to an event, storing information in memory, recalling information, and making sense of information; cognitive processes enable people to perceive events.

Cognitive psychology: An area of study that investigates mental processes; areas within cognitive psychology include attention, perception, language, learning, memory, problem solving, and logic.

Cognitive science: A multidisciplinary approach to the study of cognition from the perspectives of psychology, computer science, neuroscience, philosophy, and linguistics.

Cohort: An identifiable group of people; in developmental research, group members are commonly associated by their birth dates and shared historical experiences.

Collective unconscious: In Carl Jung's theory, memory traces of repeated experiences that have been passed down to all humankind as a function of evolutionary development; includes inherited tendencies to behave in certain ways and contains the archetypes.

Color: The brain's interpretation of electromagnetic radiation of different wavelengths within the range of visible light.

Color blindness: An inability to perceive certain colors; the most common type is green-minus color blindness, involving a defect in the eyes' green cones.

Compensation: In Alfred Adler's theory, a defense mechanism for overcoming feelings of inferiority by trying harder to excel; in Sigmund Freud's theory, the process of learning alternative ways to accomplish a task while making up for an inferiority—a process that could involve dreams that adjust psychologically for waking imbalances.

Complementary color: Light that complements another light in that their addition produces white light and their juxtaposition produces high contrast.

Compulsions: Ritualistic patterns of behavior that commonly follow obsessive thinking and that reduce the intensity of the anxiety-evoking thoughts.

Concrete operations stage: The third stage of Jean Piaget's theory, during which children acquire basic logical rules and concrete concepts; occurs between the ages of seven and eleven.

Conditioned response (CR): In Pavlovian conditioning, the behavior and emotional quality that occurs when a conditioned stimulus is presented; related to but not the same as the unconditioned response.

Conditioned stimulus (CS): A previously neutral stimulus (a sight, sound, touch, or smell) that, after Pavlovian conditioning, will elicit the conditioned response (CR).

Conditioned taste aversion: An avoidance of a food or drink that has been followed by illness when consumed in the past.

Conditioning: A type of learning in which an animal learns a concept by associating it with some object or by the administration of rewards and/or punishments.

Conditions of worth: In Carl Rogers's theory, externally based conditions for love and praise; the expectation that the child must behave in accordance with parental standards in order to receive love.

Cone: One type of visual receptor found in the retina of the eye; primarily for color vision and acute daytime vision.

Confounding of variables: The variation of other variables along with the independent variable of interest, as a result of which any effects cannot be attributed with certainty to the independent variable.

Consciousness: A level of awareness that includes those things of which an individual is aware at any given moment, such as current ideas, thoughts, accessed memories, and feelings.

Consensual validation: The verification of subjective beliefs by obtaining a consensus among other people.

Consensus information: Information concerning other people's responses to an object; in attribution theory, high consensus generally leads people to attribute situational rather than personal causes to a behavior.

Conservation: In Jean Piaget's theory, understanding that the physical properties (number, length, mass, volume) remain constant even though appearances may change; a concrete-operational skill.

Consistency information: Information concerning a person's response to an object over time. In attribution theory, high consistency implies that behavior is dispositional or typical of a person.

Consolidation: A neural process by which short-term memories become stored in long-term memory.

Construct: A formal concept representing the relationships between variables or processes such as motivation and behavior; may be empirical (observable) or hypothetical (inferred).

Construct validity: A type of validity that assesses the extent to which a test score (variable) correlates with other tests (variables) already established as valid measures of the item.

Consumer psychology: The subfield of psychology that studies selling, advertising, and buying; the goals of its practitioners are generally to communicate clearly and to persuade consumers to buy products.

Context dependence: The phenomenon in which memory functions more effectively when material is recalled in the same environment in which it was originally learned, compared with recall in a different environment.

Contingency: A relationship between a response and its consequence or between two stimuli; sometimes considered a dependency.

Contingency management: A method of behavior modification that involves providing or removing positive rewards in accordance with whether the individual being treated engages in the expected behavior.

Continuous reinforcement: A schedule in which each response is followed by a reinforcer.

Control group: A group of subjects that are like the experimental groups in all ways except that they do not experience the independent variable; used as a comparison measure.

Control variable: An extraneous factor that might influence the dependent variable, making it difficult to evaluate the effect of the independent variable; in an experiment, attempts are made to isolate or control such effects systematically.

Convergence: In perception, the turning of the eyes inward from parallel lines of sight to look at a nearby object; a depth cue.

Convergent thinking: Creative thinking in which possible solutions to a problem are systematically eliminated in search for the best solution; the type of ordinary thinking in which most people generally engage.

Conversion disorder: A psychological disorder in which a person experiences physical symptoms, such as the loss or impairment of some motor or sensory function (paralysis or blindness, for example), in the absence of an organic cause.

Coping: Responses directed at dealing with demands (in particular, threatening or stressful ones) upon an organism; these responses may either improve or reduce long-term functioning.

Correlation: The degree of relatedness or correspondence between two variables, expressed by a coefficient that can range from +1.00 to −1.00; 0.00 signifies no correspondence.

Cortex: The surface (or outer layer) of the brain, which receives sensory input, interprets it, and relates behavior to external stimuli; responsible for perception and conscious thought.

Cortical brain centers: The portions of the brain making up the cerebral cortex and controlling voluntary behavior, higher reasoning, and language skills; they develop rapidly during the first two years of life.

Countertransference: The phenomenon in which an

analyst either shifts feelings from his or her past onto a patient or is affected by the client's emotional problems; caused by a patient's perceived similarity to individuals or experiences in the analyst's life.

Creativity: Cognitive abilities in areas such as fluency, flexibility, originality, elaboration, visualization, metaphorical thinking, and problem definition; the ability to originate something that is both new and appropriate.

Criterion group: A group used to validate a measurement instrument; in the case of interest inventories, it refers to persons in a particular occupational group.

Critical period: A time during which the developing organism is particularly sensitive to the influence of certain inputs or experiences necessary to foster normal development; in nonhuman animals, a specific time period during which a certain type of learning such as imprinting must occur.

Cross-sectional design: A design in which subgroups of a population are randomly sampled; the members of the sample are then tested or observed.

Cue-producing response: A response that serves as a cue for other responses; words (speech) can cue behaviors, and thoughts can cue other thoughts.

Cutaneous sense: Relating to the skin sense, as in responses to touch or temperature.

Cyclothymia: A milder version of a cyclical mood disorder in which mood swings can occur but are not as intense as in bipolar disorder.

Daily hassles: Seemingly minor everyday events that are a constant source of stress.

Dark adaptation: An increase in the sensitivity of rods and cones to light through an increase in the concentration of light-absorbing pigments.

Data: A collection of observations from an experiment or survey.

Death instinct: The unconscious desire for death and destruction in order to escape the tensions of living.

Debriefing: Discussing an experiment and its purpose with subjects after its completion; required if the experiment involved deception.

Decay: The disappearance of a memory trace.

Deduction: A type of logic by which one draws a specific conclusion from one or more known truths or premises; often formed as an "if/then" statement.

Defense mechanism: According to Sigmund Freud, a psychological strategy by which an unacceptable sexual or aggressive impulse may be kept from conscious thought or expressed in a disguised fashion.

Deindividuation: The loss of self-awareness and evaluation apprehension that accompanies situations that foster personal and physical anonymity.

Delusion: A symptom of psychosis that consists of a strong irrational belief held despite considerable evidence against it; types include delusions of grandeur, reference, and persecution.

Dementia: Globally impaired intellectual functioning (memory reasoning) in adults as a result of brain impairment; it does not mean "craziness," but a loss or impairment of mental power.

Dendrite: A branching extension of a neuron through which information enters the cell; there may be one or many dendrites on a neuron.

Dependent variable: The outcome measure in a study; the effect of the independent variable is measured by changes in the dependent variable.

Depolarization: A shift in ions and electrical charges across a cell membrane, causing loss of resting membrane potential and bringing the cell closer to the action potential.

Depression: A psychological disorder characterized by extreme feelings of sadness, hopelessness, or personal unworthiness, as well as loss of energy, withdrawal, and either lack of sleep or excessive sleep.

Depth perception: The ability to see three-dimensional features, such as the distance of an object from oneself and the shape of an object.

Descriptive statistics: Procedures that summarize and organize data sets; they include mean, median, range, correlation, and variability.

Desensitization: A behavioral technique of gradually removing anxiety associated with certain situations by associating a relaxed state with these situations.

Determinism: The theory or doctrine that acts of the will, occurrences in nature, or social or psychological phenomena are causally determined by preceding events or natural laws.

Development: The continuous and cumulative process of age-related changes in physical growth, thought, perception, and behavior of people and animals; a result of both biological and environmental influences.

Developmental psychology: The subfield of psychology that studies biological, social, and intellectual changes as they occur throughout the human life cycle.

Deviancy: The quality of having a condition or engaging in behavior that is atypical in a social group and is considered undesirable.

Diagnosis: The classification or labeling of a patient's problem within one of a set of recognized categories of abnormal behavior, determined with the aid of interviews and psychological tests.

Diagnostic and Statistical Manual of Mental Disorders (DSM): A handbook created by the American Psychiatric Association for diagnosing and classifying mental disorders; used by mental health professionals and insurance companies.

Dichotic listening: A technique in which two different messages are simultaneously played through earphones, with a different message to each ear.

Diffusion of responsibility: The reduction of personal responsibility that is commonly experienced in group situations; diffusion of responsibility increases as the size of the crowd increases.

Discounting: Reducing the role of a particular cause in producing a behavior because of the presence of other plausible causes.

Discrimination: In perception, the ability to see that two patterns differ in some way; in intergroup relations, behavior (usually unfavorable) toward persons that is based on their group membership rather than on their individual personalities.

Discriminative stimulus: A stimulus that signals the availability of a consequence, given that a response occurs.

Dispersion: A statistical measure of variability; a measure (range, semi-interquartile range, standard deviation, or variance) that provides information about the difference among the scores.

Displacement: According to Sigmund Freud, a defense mechanism by which a person redirects his or her aggressive impulse onto a target that may substitute for the target that originally aroused the person's aggression.

Display: A visual dance or series of movements or gestures by an individual or animal to communicate such things as dominance, aggression, and courtship to other individuals.

Display rules: Culturally determined rules regarding the appropriate expression of emotions.

Dispositional: Relating to disposition or personality rather than to situation.

Dissociative disorder: A disorder that occurs when some psychological function, such as memory, is split off from the rest of the conscious mind; not caused by brain dysfunction.

Dissonance: An unpleasant psychological and physiological state caused by an inconsistency between two thoughts or beliefs.

Distal stimulus: An object or other sensory element in the environment.

Distinctiveness information: Information concerning a person's response to an object under given conditions; in attribution theory, high distinctiveness suggests that individuals are behaving uniquely toward a given target/object.

Diurnal enuresis: The presence of enuretic episodes when the individual is awake.

Divergent thinking: Thinking that results in new and different responses that most people cannot, or do not, offer; the type of thinking most clearly involved in creativity.

Domestic violence: Physical, emotional, psychological, or sexual abuse perpetrated by a family member toward another family member; typically the abuse follows a repetitive, predictable pattern.

Dominance hierarchy: An ordered arrangement of dominant to subordinate individuals in an animal population that serves numerous social functions, including protection; a pecking order.

Dopamine: One type of neurotransmitter, a chemical that is released from one nerve cell and stimulates receptors on another, thus transferring a message between them; associated with movement and with treatment of depression.

Double bind: A form of communication that often occurs when a family member sends two messages, requests, or commands that are logically inconsistent, contradictory, or impossible, resulting in a "damned if one does, damned if one doesn't" situation; a hypothesis about the development of schizophrenia.

Double-blind method: A procedure in which neither the experimenter nor the subjects know who is receiving treatment and who is not; this controls for subject and experimenter biases and expectations.

Down syndrome: A chromosomal abnormality that causes mental retardation as well as certain physical defects, such as extra eyelid folds and a thick tongue; caused by an extra (third) chromosome on chromosome pair 21.

Drive: The tendency of a person or animal to engage in behaviors brought about by some change or condition inside that organism; often generated by deprivation (hunger or thirst) or exposure to painful or other noxious stimuli.

Drive reduction hypothesis: The idea that a physiological need state triggers a series of behaviors aimed at reducing the unpleasant state; drive reduction is reinforcing.

Dysfunctional family: A family grouping that is characterized by the presence of disturbed interactions and communications; particularly an abusive, incestuous, or alcoholic family.

Dyslexia: Difficulties in reading, usually after damage to the left cerebral hemisphere.

Dysphoria: A symptom of clinical depression; extreme sadness.

Dysthymic disorder: A form of depression in which mild to moderate levels of depressive symptoms persist chronically.

Early recollections: A projective technique in which the patient attempts to remember things that happened in the distant past; these provide clues to the patient's current use of private logic.

Eating disorders: Afflictions resulting from dysfunctional relationships to hunger, food, and eating.

Echoic memory: Sensory memory for sound.

Echolalia: An involuntary and parrotlike repetition of words or phrases spoken by others.

Eclectic therapy: Therapy in which a combination of models and techniques is employed, rather than a single approach.

Educational psychology: The subfield of psychology that studies the effectiveness of education, usually formal education; educational psychologists seek to develop new educational techniques and to improve the learning process.

Efferent nerve: A motor neuron or an axon carrying information away from a structure; for example, in the transmission of stimuli from the reticular formation to the cerebral cortex.

Ego: In psychoanalytic theory, the part of the personality responsible for perceiving reality and thinking; mediates between the demands of the pleasure-seeking id, the rule-following superego, and reality.

Egocentric thought: A cognitive tendency in childhood in which the child assumes that everyone shares his or her own perspective; the cognitive inability to understand the different perspective of another.

Elaborative rehearsal: Giving meaning to information to enable encoding it in memory.

Electroconvulsive therapy (ECT): A treatment for severe depression in which an electric current is passed through the brain of the patient.

Electroencephalogram (EEG): The graphic recording of the electrical activity of the brain (brain waves).

Electroencephalography: Measurement of the electrical output of the brain, which may then sometimes be brought under voluntary control by biofeedback and relaxation.

Embryonic phase: The period of rapid prenatal change that follows the zygote period; extends from the second to the eighth week after conception.

Emotion: A psychological response that includes a set of physiological changes, expressive behaviors, and a subjective experience.

Empathy: In therapy, the therapist's ability to focus attention on the needs and experience of the client; also refers to the therapist's ability to communicate an understanding of the client's emotional state.

Empirical evidence: Data or information derived objectively from the physical senses, without reliance on personal faith, intuition, or introspection.

Empiricism: A philosophy holding that knowledge is learned through experience and that infants begin life like blank slates, learning about their environment through experience.

Encoding: The transformation of incoming sensory information into a form of code that the memory system can accept and use.

Endocrine gland: A gland that produces one or more hormones and secretes them into the blood so that they can serve as intercellular messengers.

Endocrine system: A system of ductless glands in the bodies of vertebrate animals that secretes hormones which travel through the bloodstream to target tissues, whose functioning is altered by the hormones.

Endogenous behavior: An innate, or inborn, behavior that is established by the animal's inherited genetic code (DNA) and that is not influenced by the animal's experiences or environment.

Endorphins: A group of endogenous, opiate-like neuropeptides of the central nervous system that simulate analgesia and interfere with transmission of pain impulses; the brain's own morphine.

Enkephalins: Peptides containing five amino acids, within the endorphin group, that may act as neurotransmitters; the first of the endorphins to be discovered.

Enmeshment: An excessively close relationship between parent and child in which adult concerns and needs are communicated and in which overdependence on the child is apparent.

Entitlement: The expectation of special or unusually favorable treatment by others; commonly seen among narcissistic personalities.

Entropy: In Carl Jung's analytical theory, a concept maintaining that aspects of a person's psychic energy which are not in balance will tend to seek a state of equilibrium.

Enuresis: The inability to control the release of urine; nocturnal enuresis is also called bed-wetting.

Environmental psychology: The subfield of psychology that studies the relationship between the environment and behavior, particularly the effects of the physical and social environments (such as noise or crowding) on behavior.

Environmental stressor: A condition in the environment, such as crowding, noise, toxic chemicals, or extreme temperatures, that produces stress (bodily or mental tension).

Epilepsy: A disorder of the nervous system in which the cortex produces electrical firing that causes convulsions and other forms of seizures; thought by some to be linked to the reticular formation.

Epinephrine: The neurotransmitter released from the adrenal gland as a result of innervation of the autonomic nervous system; formerly called adrenaline.

Episodic memory: A form of long-term memory involving temporal and spatial information, including personal experiences.

Equipotentiality: In Pavlovian conditioning, the idea that any stimulus paired with an effective unconditioned stimulus will come to elicit a conditioned response with equal facility.

Equity theory: A theory in attraction and work motivation that contends that individuals are motivated to remain in relationships they perceive to be fair, just, and equitable—that is, where one's outcomes are proportional to one's inputs, particularly when contrasted with others in the relationship.

Equivalence: A principle stating that an increase in energy or value in one aspect of the psyche is accompanied by a decrease in another area.

Estradiol: The primary sex hormone of mammalian females, which is responsible for the menstrual cycle and for development of secondary sex characteristics; a primary estrogen, secreted by the corpus luteum.

Ethnocentrism: An attitude of uncritically assuming the superiority of the in-group culture.

Ethology: A branch of zoology that studies animals in their natural environments; often concerned with investigating the adaptive significance and innate basis of behaviors.

Etiology: The factors that are thought to cause or contribute to the development of a particular disorder.

Eustress: Positive arousal or stress, appraised as a challenge rather than as a threat.

Evoked potential: A brain response that is triggered by electroencephalography using discrete sensory stimuli.

Excitation transfer: The theory that arousal from one source can intensify an emotional reaction to a different source (for example, that sexual arousal can increase the response to an aggressive cue).

Existentialism: A philosophical viewpoint emphasizing human existence and the human situation in the world that gives meaning to life through the free choice of mature values and commitment to responsible goals; the critical goal involves finding one's true self and living according to this potential.

Exogenous substances: Substances not normally occurring in the body, present only when administered; exogenous substances include substances such as drugs or synthetic test compounds mimicking endogenous substances.

Expectancy confirmation bias: Interpreting ambiguous information as being supportive of expectations; mistakenly "seeing" what is expected.

Expectancy theory: A cognitive motivation model which proposes that people choose to perform behaviors they believe to be the most likely to lead to positive outcomes; in work theory, workers are more motivated when they perceive congruence between their efforts, products, and rewards.

Experiment: One of several data collection methods;

requires systematically manipulating the levels of an independent variable under controlled conditions in order to measure its impact on a dependent variable.

Experimenter bias: Biases introduced into a research study as a result of the expectations of the experimenter.

Expressive aphasia: Difficulties in expressing language, usually after damage to Broca's area in the left frontal lobe of the cerebral cortex.

External validity: The extent to which the results of a research study can be generalized to different populations, settings, or conditions.

Externalization: A defense mechanism in which one experiences unresolved, repressed inner turmoil as occurring outside oneself; holding external factors responsible for one's problems.

Extinction: A process by which the probability of a response is decreased; in classical or Pavlovian conditioning, a process in which the temporal contiguity of the conditioned stimulus and the unconditioned stimulus is disrupted and the learned association is lost; in operant or instrumental conditioning, a process in which undesirable behavior is not followed by reinforcement.

Extraneous variable: A variable that has a detrimental effect on a research study, making it difficult to determine if the result is attributable to the variable under study or to some unknown uncontrolled variable; for example, in jury decision making, the effect of defendant attractiveness.

Extrinsic motivation: Motivation to perform an activity only because the activity leads to a valued outcome external to the activity itself.

Extrinsic religion: An immature religious orientation that uses religion for self-serving purposes such as security or a sense of social or economic well-being.

Factor analysis: A statistical technique wherein a set of correlated variables can be regrouped in terms of the degree of commonality they share.

Family therapy: A type of psychotherapy that focuses on correcting the faulty interactions among family members that maintain children's psychological problems.

Farsightedness: An inability to focus clearly on nearby objects that is caused by the point of focus of the lens falling behind the retina.

Feminist analysis: The examination of the ways in which inequality, injustice, or oppression devalues women and/or limits their potential, both individually and collectively.

Fetal phase: The third period of prenatal development, extending from the ninth week of pregnancy until birth.

Fetishism: A sexual behavior in which a person becomes aroused by focusing on an inanimate object or a part of the human body.

Field research: An approach in which evidence is gathered in a "natural" setting, such as the workplace; by contrast, laboratory research involves an artificial, contrived setting.

Fight-or-flight response: A sequence of physiological changes, described by Walter B. Cannon, that occurs in response to a threat and prepares the organism to flee from or fight the threat; includes increases in heart rate, blood pressure, and respiration rate.

Fixation: In psychoanalytic theory, an inability to progress to the next level of psychosexual development because of overgratification or undergratification of desires at a particular stage.

Flashback: A type of traumatic reexperiencing in which a person becomes detached from reality and thinks, feels, and acts as if a previous traumatic experience were happening again.

Flocking: A defensive maneuver in many mammalian and bird species in which a scattered group of individuals implodes into a compact cluster at the approach of a predator.

Flooding: A type of therapy in which a phobic person imagines his or her most-feared situation until fear decreases.

Fluid intelligence: The form of intelligence that reflects speed of information processing, reasoning, and memory capacity rather than factual knowledge (crystallized intelligence); associated with Raymond Cattell.

Forebrain: A developmentally defined division of the brain that contains structures such as the cerebral hemispheres, the thalamus, and the hypothalamus.

Forensic psychology: The application of psychological skills in the legal profession—for example, in jury selection, sanity determination, and assessing competency to stand trial.

Forgetting: The loss of information from memory.

Formal operations: According to Jean Piaget, the fourth stage of cognitive development, reached at adolescence; characterized by the ability to engage in abstract thinking, hypothetical constructs, and unobserved logical possibilities.

Fovea: The central part of the retina, which is densest in cone cells and is therefore the area of sharpest visual acuity.

Free association: The psychoanalytic method in which a patient talks spontaneously without restriction; thought to reveal repressed conflicts of the unconscious.

Frequency: The number of complete back-and-forth movements or pressure changes (cycles) from the rest or ambient state that occur each second; measured in units called hertz.

Frequency distribution: The pairing of a measurement or score with the number of people or subjects obtaining that measurement.

Frontal lobe: The anterior portion of each cerebral hemisphere, containing control of motor areas and most of the higher intellectual functions of the brain, including speech.

Frustration: A psychological state of arousal that results when a person is prevented from attaining a goal.

Frustration-aggression hypothesis: A concept, pioneered by John Dollard, stating that aggressive behavior is born of frustration in attempting to reach a goal.

Fugue state: A flight from reality in which the individual develops amnesia, leaves his or her present situation, travels to a new location, and establishes a new identity.

Function word: A word that has little meaning in itself yet signals grammatical relationships between other words in a sentence, such as an article ("the" or "a") or a preposition (for example, "in," "on," "of").

Functional autonomy: A concept, pioneered by Gordon W. Allport, that many adult motives are independent in purpose from their childhood origins.

Functional disorders: Signs and symptoms for which no organic or physiological basis can be found.

Functional fixedness: An inability to think of novel uses for objects because of a fixation on their usual functions.

Functionalism: An early school of American psychology that argued for the study of the human mind from the standpoint of understanding consciousness in terms of its purpose rather than its elements.

Fundamental attribution error: Underestimating the influence of situations and overestimating the influence of personality traits in causing behavior.

Fundamental frequency: The lowest frequency in a harmonic series of complex overtones; the overtones are integer multiples of the fundamental.

Gamete: A reproductive sex cell; the female cell is known as the ovum, and the male cell is known as the sperm.

Gamma-aminobutyric acid (GABA): The most common neurotransmitter in the brain, derived from the amino acid glutamic acid; an inhibitor that seems to affect mood and emotion.

Gender: Social maleness or femaleness, reflected in the behaviors and characteristics that society expects from people of one biological sex.

Gender identity: A child's accurate labeling of himself or herself by gender; also, a person's inner sense of femaleness or maleness.

Gender schema: A general knowledge framework that organizes information and guides perceptions related to males and females.

Gene: The basic unit of heredity; a segment of a DNA molecule that contains hereditary instructions for an individual's physical traits and abilities and for the cell's production of proteins.

General adaptation syndrome: The three-stage physiological response pattern of the body to stress that was proposed by Hans Selye; the three stages are the alarm reaction, resistance stage, and exhaustion stage.

Generalization: The process by which behavior learned in one situation transfers to new situations.

Generativity: In Erik Erikson's theory of personality, the seventh stage, associated with the desire to leave a legacy; the need to take care of future generations through the experiences of caring, nurturing, and educating.

Genetics: The biochemical basis of inherited characteristics.

Genital stage: In Sigmund Freud's theory, the fifth psychosexual stage, beginning at adolescence and extending throughout adulthood; the individual learns to experience sexual gratification with a partner.

Genotype: The genetic makeup of an individual.

Gestalt: A German word, for which there is no precise translation, that is generally used to refer to a form, a whole, or a configuration.

Gestalt school of psychology: A school of psychology which maintains that the overall configuration of a stimulus array, rather than its individual elements, forms the basis of perception.

Gestalt therapy: A form of psychotherapy, initiated by Fritz Perls, that emphasizes awareness of the present and employs an active therapist-client relationship.

Giftedness: A marked ability to learn more rapidly, perform more intricate problems, and solve problems more rapidly than is normally expected for a given age; operationally defined as an IQ score above 130 on an individually administered test.

Goal setting: A motivational technique used to increase productivity in which employees are given specific performance objectives and time deadlines.

Gray matter: Unmyelinated neurons that make up the cerebral cortex, so called because they lack the fatty covering (myelin) found on neurons of the white matter.

Group dynamics: The study of how groups influence individual functioning.

Gustation: The sense of taste.

Gyrus: A convolution on the surface of the brain that results from the infolding of the cortex (surface).

Habit: An association or connection between a cue and a response, such as stopping (the response) at a red light (the cue).

Habituation: A decrease in response to repeated presentations of a stimulus that is not simply caused by fatigued sensory receptors.

Hallucinogen: A drug that can alter perception (vision and audition, in particular); examples include LSD, PCP, peyote, psilocybin, and possibly marijuana.

Hardiness: A constellation of behaviors and perceptions, characterized by perceptions of control, commitment, and challenge, that are thought to buffer the effects of stress; introduced by Suzanne Kobasa.

Hawthorne effect: A phenomenon that occurs when a subject's behavior changes after the subject discovers that he or she is being studied.

Hedonic: Associated with the seeking of pleasure and the avoidance of pain.

Helplessness: The belief that one has little or no con-

trol over the events in one's life; viewed by Martin Seligman as an important cause of depression.

Heredity: The transmission of characteristics from parent to offspring through genes in the chromosomes.

Heuristic: A shortcut or rule of thumb used for decision making or problem solving that often leads to, but does not guarantee, a correct response.

Higher-order conditioning: The linking of successive conditioned stimuli, the last of which elicits the conditioned response; higher-order associations are easily broken.

Hindbrain: A developmentally defined division of the brain that contains the pons, medulla, and cerebellum.

Hippocampus: A structure located in the temporal lobe (lateral cortical area) of the brain that has important memory functions.

Homeostasis: A term referring to the idea that the body tries to maintain steady states—that is, to maintain physiological characteristics within relatively narrow and optimum levels.

Homophobia: A fear, prejudice, or hatred toward homosexuals, usually based upon irrational stereotyping.

Hormone: A chemical "messenger," usually composed of protein or steroids, that is produced and secreted by an endocrine gland and released into the bloodstream; it targets specific genes in certain body-tissue cells.

Hostile aggression: Aggressive behavior that is associated with anger and is intended to harm another.

Hue: The chromatic or color sensation produced by a certain wavelength of light.

Humanistic psychology: A branch of psychology that emphasizes the human tendencies toward growth and fulfillment, autonomy, choice, responsibility, and ultimate values such as truth, love, and justice; exemplified by the theories of Carl Rogers and Abraham Maslow.

Hypermetropia: Hereditary farsightedness caused by the length of the eyeball in the anterior-posterior direction being too short.

Hypnagogic hallucination: A vivid auditory or visual hallucination that occurs at the transition from wakefulness to sleep or from sleep to wakefulness; associated with narcolepsy.

Hypnosis: An altered state of consciousness brought on by special induction techniques (usually progressive relaxation instructions) and characterized by varying degrees of responsiveness to suggestions.

Hypnotic susceptibility: A subject's measured level of responsiveness to hypnotic suggestions on standardized scales.

Hypochondriasis: A psychological disorder in which the person is unrealistically preoccupied with the fear of disease and worries excessively about his or her health.

Hypothalamus: A small region near the base of the brain that controls the pituitary gland, autonomic nervous system, and behaviors important for survival, including eating, drinking, and temperature regulation.

Hypothesis: An educated guess about the relationship between two or more variables, derived from inductive reasoning; often tested by an experiment.

Iconic memory: Brief sensory memory for vision.

Id: The part of the psyche that contains the instincts and is directed solely by pleasure seeking; it is the most primitive part of the psyche and was thought by Sigmund Freud to fuel the ego and superego.

Idealized self: Alienation from the real self that is characterized by grandiose, unrealistic conceptions of the self and unattainable standards; part of Karen Horney's psychology.

Identification: The internalization of parental or societal values, behaviors, and attitudes; in Freudian theory, a defense and resolution of incestuous feelings toward the opposite-sex parent that is important in the development of the superego.

Identity: A personal configuration of occupational, sexual, and ideological commitments; according to Erik Erikson, the positive pole of the fifth stage of psychosocial development.

Identity crisis: According to Erik Erikson, the central developmental issue in adolescence; encompasses a struggle between an integrated core identity and role confusion.

Idiographic study: The study of the unique patterns of the individual through methods such as case studies, autobiographies, and tests that examine patterns of behavior within a single person.

Illusions: Beliefs that are unsupported by evidence or that require facts to be perceived in a particular manner.

Imagery: The use of visualization to imagine the physical movements involved in executing a skill.

Imitation: The performance of behaviors that were learned by observing the actions of others.

Immune response: The body's response to invasion by disease-producing organisms; proteins (antibodies) are produced that mark the unwanted cells for destruction.

Immutable characteristics: Physical attributes (such as gender) that are present at birth and that other people assume gives them information as to the kind of person they are seeing.

Implosion therapy: A therapy in which the patient imagines his or her feared situation, plus elements from psychodynamic theory that are related to the fear until fear decreases.

Impression management: The attempt to control the impressions of oneself that others form; synonymous with "self-presentation."

Imprinting: The innate behavioral attachment that a young animal forms with another individual (for example, its mother), with food, or with an object during a brief critical period shortly after birth; especially seen in ducks and chicks.

In-group: A social group to which a person belongs or with which a person is identified, thereby forming part of the self-concept.

In-group bias: The tendency to discriminate in favor of one's own group.

Incentive: A motivating force or system of rewards that is presented to an individual if he or she behaves or successfully performs specified tasks according to the norms of society; a goal object.

Incompetency: The legally established lack of sufficient knowledge and judgment to maintain a given right or responsibility.

Incongruence: In Carl Rogers's theory, inconsistency or distortion between one's real and ideal self; a lack of genuineness.

Independent variable: The factor that is manipulated by the experimenter in order to assess its causal impact on the dependent variable.

Individual psychology: Alfred Adler's school of personality theory and therapy; stresses the unity of the individual and his or her striving for superiority to compensate for feelings of inferiority.

Induction: A type of logic by which one arrives at a general premise or conclusion based on generalization from a large number of known specific cases.

Industrial and organizational psychology: The subfield of psychology that studies behavior in business and industry; practitioners analyze placement, training, and supervision of personnel, study organizational and communication structures, and explore ways to maximize efficiency.

Inflection: An addition to the stem of a word that indicates subtle modulations in meaning, such as plurality (more than one) or tense (present time or past time); in English, inflections are all suffixes.

Information processing model: The approach of most modern cognitive psychologists; it interprets cognition as the flow of information through interrelated stages (input, processing, storage, and retrieval) in much the same way that information is processed by a computer.

Innate: A term describing any inborn characteristic or behavior that is determined and controlled largely by the genes.

Insanity: A legal term for having a mental disease or defect so great that criminal intent or responsibility and punishability are not possible; it renders one incompetent.

Insight: A sudden mental inspiration or comprehension of a problem that was previously unsolved.

Insomnia: Difficulty in falling asleep or in remaining asleep for sufficient periods.

Instinct: An innate or inherited tendency that motivates a person or animal to act in often complex sequences without reasoning, instruction, or experience; in Freudian theory, a biological source of excitation that directs the development of personality into adulthood, such as the life instinct (Eros) and death instinct (Thanatos).

Institutional racism: The behavior patterns followed in organizations and in society at large that produce discrimination against members of racial minorities regardless of the prejudice or lack thereof of individuals.

Instrumental aggression: Aggressive behavior that is a by-product of another activity; instrumental aggression occurs only incidentally, as a means to another end.

Instrumental conditioning: The learning of the relationship between a voluntary action and the reinforcements or punishments that follow that action; also known as operant conditioning.

Integration: The function of most of the neurons of the cerebral cortex; summarizing incoming sensory information and producing a consensus as to what the nervous system will do next.

Intelligence: The ability to perform various mental tasks, including reasoning, knowledge, comprehension, memory, applying concepts, and manipulating figures; thought to reflect one's learning potential.

Intelligence quotient (IQ): A measure of a person's mental ability (as reflected by intelligence test scores) in comparison with the rest of the population at a comparable age.

Intensity: A measure of a physical aspect of a stimulus, such as the frequency of a sound or the brightness of a color.

Interest inventory: A type of test designed to determine areas of interest and enjoyment, often for the purpose of matching a person with a career.

Interference: The loss or displacement of a memory trace because of competing information that is presented.

Intermittent reinforcement: Any reinforcement schedule in which some but not all responses are rewarded; particularly difficult to extinguish.

Internal validity: The extent to which the dependent variable is caused by the independent variable; if rival alternative hypotheses, which are both relevant and plausible, can be ruled out, the study has strong internal validity.

Interneuron: A neuron that receives information from a sensory neuron and transmits a message to a motor neuron; very common in the brain and important in integration.

Interrater reliability: The obtained level of agreement between two observers when scoring the same observations with the same behavioral taxonomy.

Interval schedule: A schedule in which reinforcer delivery is contingent upon performance of a response after a specified amount of time has elapsed.

Intrinsic motivation: Motivation based on the desire to achieve or perform a task for its own sake, because it produces satisfaction or enjoyment, rather than for external rewards.

Introspection: The self-report of one's own sensations, perceptions, experiences, and thoughts; analyses of and reports on the content of one's own conscious experiences.

Irradiation: Nervous excitement generated in a specific brain center by an unconditioned stimulus that spreads to surrounding areas of the cerebral cortex.

Kinesthetic: Related to the sensation of body position, presence, or movement, resulting mostly from the stimulation of sensory nerves in muscles, tendons, and joints.

Korsakoff's syndrome: Alcohol-induced brain damage that causes disorientation, impaired long-term memory, and production of false memories to fill memory gaps.

Latency: In Sigmund Freud's theory, the period between approximately age six and adolescence, when sexual instincts are not strongly manifested; strictly speaking, not a psychosexual stage.

Latent content: According to psychoanalytic theory, the hidden content of a dream, camouflaged by the manifest content.

Lateral geniculate nucleus: A subdivision of the thalamus in the brain, which receives the nerve impulse from the retina; it assembles visual information.

Laterality: Specialization by sides of almost symmetrical structures; speech is lateralized in human brains, because it is mainly controlled by the left hemispheres of almost all right-handed people.

Law of Effect: Thorndike's basic law of instrumental conditioning, which holds that responses followed by certain events will be either more or less likely to recur.

Leakage: Nonverbal behavior that reveals information that a person wishes to conceal; especially useful in deception detection.

Learned helplessness: The hypothesized result of experiences in which behavior performed seems to bear no relationship to the appearance or control of a stressor.

Learning: A modification in behavior as the result of experience that involves changes in the nervous system which are not caused by fatigue, maturation, or injury.

Lesion: Damage or injury to brain tissue that is caused by disease or trauma or produced experimentally using mechanical, electrical, or chemical methods.

Levels-of-processing model: The perspective that holds that how well something is remembered is based on how elaborately incoming information is mentally processed.

Libido: The energy used to direct behavior that is pleasurable either for the self or others; when it is directed toward the self, it results in self-gratifi-

cation, follows the pleasure principle, and is immature.

Limbic system: An integrated set of cerebral structures (including the amygdala, hypothalamus, hippocampus, and septal area) that play a vital role in the regulation of emotion and motivation.

Linguistic relativity hypothesis: The idea that the structure of particular languages that people speak affects the way they perceive the world.

Linguistics: A field of inquiry that focuses on the underlying structure of language; linguists study phonology (sound system), syntax (sentence structure), and semantics (meaning), among other topics.

Lipids: Fats and oils.

Lithium carbonate: An alkaline compound that modulates the intensity of mood swings and is particularly effective in the dampening of symptoms of manic excitability.

Loci method: A serial-recall mnemonic consisting of visualizing items to be remembered along a known path of distinct locations.

Locus of control: Beliefs concerning the sources of power over one's life; persons who believe they can generally control the direction of their lives have an internal locus of control, whereas those who believe that their lives are influenced more by fate have an external locus of control.

Long-term memory: A memory system of unlimited capacity that consists of more or less permanent knowledge.

Longitudinal study: A research methodology that requires the testing of the same subjects repeatedly over a specified period of time.

Loudness: The strength of sound as heard; related to sound pressure level but also affected by frequency.

Magnitude estimation: A technique for measuring perceptual experience by having persons assign numbers to indicate the "magnitude" of an experience.

Main effect: A statistically significant difference in behavior related to different levels of a variable and not affected by any other variable.

Major depressive episode: A disorder of mood and functioning, meeting clearly specified criteria and present for at least two weeks, which is characterized by dysphoric mood or apathy.

Mania: A phase of bipolar disorder in which the

mood is one of elation, euphoria, or irritability; a disorder in which manic symptoms occur—including hyperactivity, agitation, restlessness, and grandiosity—and then are followed by a return to a normal mood state.

Manifest content: In Freudian theory, the content of a dream just as it is experienced or recalled; masks the dream's latent content.

Masculine protest: The denying of inferiority feelings through rebelliousness, violence, or maintaining a tough exterior.

Maturation: Development attributable to one's genetic timetable rather than to experience.

Mean: The arithmetic average of all the data measuring one characteristic; it can be used as a descriptive or inferential statistic.

Mechanoreceptor: A sensory receptor that is sensitive to mechanical stimulation, such as touch, movement of a joint, or stretching of a muscle.

Medical model: A view in which abnormality consists of a number of diseases that originate in bodily functions, especially in the brain, and have defined symptoms, treatments, and outcomes.

Medulla oblongata: The bulbous portion of the brain stem, which directly connects with the spinal cord; controls cardiac and respiratory activity.

Melatonin: A hormone produced by the pineal gland within the forebrain that is usually released into the blood during the night phase of the light-dark cycle.

Memory: The mental processes that are involved in storing and recalling previously experienced images, information, and events.

Mere exposure: A psychological phenomenon in which liking tends to increase as a person sees more of something or someone.

Meta-analysis: A set of quantitative (statistical) procedures used to evaluate a body of empirical literature.

Metastasis: The transfer of disease from one part of the body to an unrelated part, often through the bloodstream or lymphatic system.

Midbrain: The section of the brain just above the hindbrain; influences auditory and visual processes and arousal.

Midlife crisis: A sense of reevaluation, and sometimes panic, that strikes some individuals during middle age; impulsive behavior, reassessment of goals, and career changes can result.

Mind-body problem: A psychological question originat-ing from philosophy and religion that concerns how to understand the relationship between a physical body or brain and a nonphysical mind or subjective experience.

Mineralocorticoids: The proinflammatory hormones aldosterone and deoxycorticosterone, secreted by the adrenal cortex and having a role in salt metabolism.

Misattribution: Attributing an event to any factor other than the true cause.

Mnemonics: Strategies for improving memory through placing information in an organized context.

Monoamine oxidase inhibitors (MAOIs): A class of antidepressant drugs.

Monoamines: A group of neurotransmitters derived from a single amino acid; they include serotonin and the catecholamines.

Monocular cue: A visual cue available to each eye separately; often used by artists to portray depth.

Monosynaptic reflex: A reflex system that consists of only one synapse, the one between the sensory input and motor output.

Monotic: Referring to the stimulation of only one ear.

Morpheme: The smallest part of a word that has a discernible meaning.

Morphology: The rules in a given language that govern how morphemes can be combined to form words.

Motivation: A hypothetical construct used to explain behavior and its direction, intensity, and persistence.

Motor neurons: The cells of the central nervous system responsible for causing muscular activity.

Multiple personality disorder: A rare mental disorder characterized by the development and existence or two or more relatively unique and independent personalities in the same individual.

Myopia: Hereditary nearsightedness caused by the length of the eyeball in the anterior-posterior direction being too long.

Nanometer: A billionth of a meter.

Narcolepsy: A condition in which an individual is prone to fall suddenly into a deep sleep.

Nativism: A philosophy which holds that knowledge is innate and that the neonate enters the world prepared for certain kinds of environmental inputs.

Natural selection: The process by which those characteristics of a species that help it to survive or adapt to its environment tend to be passed along by members that live long enough to have offspring.

Need: A state of an organism attributable to deprivation of a biological or psychological requirement; it is related to a disturbance in the homeostatic state.

Negative reinforcement: The procedure whereby the probability of a response is increased by the contingent removal of an aversive stimulus.

Neo-Freudian: A term for psychoanalysts who place more emphasis on security and interpersonal relations as determining behavior than on the biological theories of Sigmund Freud; Neo-Freudians include Alfred Adler, Carl Jung, Karen Horney, Harry Stack Sullivan, and Erik Erikson.

Nerve impulse: Electrical activity transmitted through a nerve fiber.

Nervous system: An array of billions of neurons (conducting nerve cells) that transmits electrical information throughout the body and thereby controls practically all bodily processes.

Neurologist: A physician who specializes in the diagnosis and treatment of disorders of the nervous system.

Neuron: An individual nerve cell, the basic unit of the nervous system; receives and transmits electrical information and consists of a cell body, dendrites, and an axon.

Neuropsychology: The study of brain-behavior relationships, usually by using behavioral tests and correlating results with brain areas.

Neuropsychopharmacology: The field of study of the relationship among behavior, neuronal functioning, and drugs.

Neurosis: Any functional disorder of the mind or the emotions, occurring without obvious brain damage and involving anxiety, phobic responses, or other abnormal behavior symptoms.

Neurotransmitter: A chemical substance released from one nerve cell that communicates activity by binding to and changing the activity of another nerve cell, muscle, or gland; some stimulate, others inhibit.

Nomothetic study: A research approach that compares groups of people in order to identify general principles; the dominant method of personality research.

Nonparticipant observation: A field technique in which the researcher passively observes the behavior of the subjects, trying not to get involved in the setting.

Nonverbal communication: Communication through any means other than words, such as facial expression, tone of voice, and posture.

Normal distribution: A bell-shaped curve that often provides an accurate description of the distribution of scores obtained in research; it forms the basis of many statistical tests.

Observational learning: Learning that results from observing other people's behavior and its consequences.

Observational study: A research technique in which a scientist systematically watches for and records occurrences of the phenomena under study without actively influencing them.

Obsessions: Intrusive, recurrent, anxiety-provoking thoughts, ideas, images, or impulses that interfere with an individual's daily functioning.

Obsessive-compulsive disorder: A chronic, debilitating anxiety disorder characterized by continuous obsessive thinking and frequent compulsive behaviors.

Occipital lobe: The posterior portion of each cerebral hemisphere, where visual stimuli are received and integrated.

Oedipal complex: In Freudian theory, sexual attraction to the parent of the opposite sex and jealousy of and fear of retribution from the parent of the same sex; first manifested in the phallic stage (in girls, sometimes called the "Electra complex").

Olfaction: The sense of smell.

Operant: The basic response unit in instrumental conditioning; a response which, when emitted, operates upon its environment and is instrumental in providing some consequences.

Operant conditioning: Learning in which a behavior increases or decreases depending on whether the behavior is followed by reward or punishment; also known as instrumental conditioning.

Operational definition: A description of a measurement or manipulation in terms that are unambiguous, observable, and easily identified.

Opiates: A class of drugs that relieve pain; opiates include morphine, heroin, and several naturally occurring peptides.

Oral stage: In Freudian theory, the first stage of psychosexual development, from birth to approximately age two; sexual energy focuses on the mouth, and conflicts may arise over nursing, biting, or chewing.

Organic disorder: A symptomatology with a known physiological or neurological basis.

Organizational effects: The early and permanent effects of a hormone; for example, the sex hormones, which produce differentiation in the developing embryo of primordial gonads, internal reproductive structures, and external genitalia.

Ossicle: Any of the three bones of the middle ear (the hammer, anvil, and stirrup) that are involved in conduction of sound into the inner ear.

Out-group: Any social group to which an individual does not belong and which, as a consequence, may be viewed in a negative way.

Overextension: The application of a word to more objects than ordinary adult usage allows; for example, when children refer to all small four-legged animals as "dog."

Overjustification effect: The tendency of external factors that are perceived to be controlling an individual's behavior to undermine the individual's intrinsic motivation to engage in that behavior.

Overtone: One of several sine waves simultaneously generated by most sound sources; these pure tones are all integer multiples of the fundamental.

Papilla: A small bundle of taste receptor cells surrounded by supportive cells and communicating with the exterior through a small pore.

Paradoxical intervention: A therapeutic technique in which a therapist gives a patient or family a task that appears to contradict the goals of treatment.

Parallel distributed processing (PDP): A neurally inspired model in which information is processed in a massively parallel and interactive network; the course of processing is determined by the connection strengths between units of the network.

Paranoia: A psychosis characterized by delusions, particularly delusions of persecution, and pervasive suspiciousness; paranoia rarely involves hallucinations.

Parasympathetic nervous system: A branch of the autonomic nervous system; responsible for maintaining or reestablishing homeostasis.

Parietal lobe: The side and upper-middle part of each cerebral hemisphere and the site of sensory reception from the skin, muscles, and other areas; also contains part of the general interpretive area.

Pavlovian conditioning: Learning in which two stimuli are presented one after the other, and the response to the first changes because of the response automatically elicited by the second; also called classical conditioning.

Penis envy: In Freudian theory, the strong envy that females develop of the male organ because they subconsciously believe they have been castrated; Sigmund Freud proposed that penis envy dominates the female personality.

Perception: The psychological process by which information that comes in through the sense organs is meaningfully interpreted by the brain.

Perceptual constancy: The tendency to perceive figures as constant and stable in terms of shape, color, size, or brightness.

Peripheral nervous system: All the nerves located outside the bones of the skull and spinal cord.

Persona: A major Jungian archetype representing one's public personality; the mask that one wears in order to be acceptable to society at large.

Personality: An individual's unique collection of behavioral responses (physical, emotional, and intellectual) that are consistent across time and situations.

Personality disorder: A disorder involving deep-rooted behavior patterns that are inflexible and maladaptive and that cause distress in an individual's relationships with others.

Personality trait: A stable disposition to behave in a given way over time and across situations.

Phallic stage: In Freudian theory, the third stage of psychosexual development, from approximately age four to age six; sexual energy focuses on the genitals.

Phenomenology: An approach that stresses openness to direct experience in introspective or unsophisticated ways, without using analysis, theory, expectations, or interpretation.

Pheromone: A hormone or other chemical that is produced and released from the tissues of one individual and targets tissues in another individual, usually with a consciously or unconsciously detectable scent.

Phobia: An anxiety disorder involving an intense irrational fear of a particular class of things (such as horses) or a situation (such as heights).

Phoneme: A minimal unit of sound that can signal a difference in meaning.

Phonology: The specification, for a given language, of which speech sounds may occur and how they may be combined, as well as the pitch and stress patterns that accompany words and sentences.

Photoreceptor: A specialized nerve cell that can transform light into a neural message; rods are specialized for black-and-white vision, cones for color vision.

Pineal gland: A light-sensitive endocrine gland that is located toward the back of the brain and that controls reproductive cycles in many mammalian species.

Pitch: The highness or lowness of a sound as heard; related to frequency but also affected by loudness.

Pituitary: An endocrine gland located in the brain that controls several other endocrine glands and that cooperates with the hypothalamus of the nervous system in controlling physiology.

Placebo: A substance or treatment (such as a pill or an injection) that has no intrinsic effect but is presented as having some effect.

Placebo effect: The relief of pain or the causing of a desired behavioral effect as a result of a patient's belief that a substance or treatment which has no known psychological or biological effect will in fact be effective; for example, a sugar pill may relieve a backache if given by a trusted doctor.

Plasticity: The ability of neurons and neural networks to grow into specific patterns based partially upon the organism's genetics and partially upon the organism's learned experience; in the brain, neurons can modify the structural organization in order to compensate for neural damage.

Play therapy: A system of individual psychotherapy in which children's play is utilized to explain and reduce symptoms of their psychological disorders.

Pons: A part of the brain stem that serves as the nerve connection between the cerebellum and the brain stem.

Population: All members of a specified group that a researcher is interested in studying.

Positive reinforcement: A procedure used to increase the frequency of a response by presenting a favorable consequence following the response.

Positron emission tomography (PET): An imaging technique that allows blood flow, energy metabolism, and chemical activity to be visualized in the living human brain.

Post-traumatic stress disorder (PTSD): A pathological condition caused by severe stress such as an earthquake or a divorce; it has an acute stage and a chronic stage, and symptoms involve reexperiencing the traumatic event.

Postsynaptic potential: A chemical stimulus that is produced in a postsynaptic cell; may excite the cell to come nearer to electrical firing, or may inhibit firing.

Power law: A statement of the lawful relationship between two variables that expresses one of them as the other raised to some exponent.

Pragmatism: A philosophical position that provides the framework of functionalism by proposing that the value of something lies in its usefulness.

Prejudice: Liking or disliking of persons based on their category or group membership rather than on their individual personalities; predominantly refers to unfavorable reactions.

Preoperational stage: In Jean Piaget's theory, a transitional stage of the preschool child (ages two to seven, approximately), after mental representations (symbols) are acquired but before they can be logically manipulated.

Preparedness: The idea that, through evolution, animals have been genetically prepared to learn certain things important to their survival.

Presbyopia: Farsightedness resulting from decreased flexibility of the lens of the eye and other age-related factors.

Primacy effect: The tendency for things that are seen or received first to be better recalled and more influential than things that come later.

Primary motive: A motive that arises from innate, biological needs and that must be met for survival.

Primary reinforcer: A stimulus that acts as a natural, unlearned reinforcer.

Primary sex characteristics: The physiological features of the sex organs.

Priming: An increase in the availability of certain types of information in memory in response to a stimulus.

Prisoner's dilemma: A laboratory game used by psychologists to study the comparative strategies of cooperation and competition.

Probability: The proportion of times a particular event will occur; also, the study of uncertainty that is the foundation of inferential statistics.

Progesterone: A female sex hormone secreted by the corpus luteum of the ovary; maintains the lining of the uterus during pregnancy and the second half of the menstrual cycle.

Programmed instruction: A self-paced training program characterized by many small, increasingly difficult lessons separated by frequent tests.

Progressive muscle relaxation: A relaxation technique that systematically works through all the major muscle groups of the body by first tensing, then relaxing each group and paying attention to the changes.

Projective task: Any task that provides an open-ended response that may reveal aspects of one's personality; tasks or tests commonly include standard stimuli that are ambiguous in nature.

Proposition: A mental representation based on the underlying structure of language; a proposition is the smallest unit of knowledge that can be stated.

Prosocial behavior: Behavior intended to benefit another; can be motivated by either egoistic or altruistic concern.

Prototype: A "best example" of a concept—one that contains the most typical features of that concept.

Proxemics: The use of space as a special elaboration of culture; it is usually divided into the subfields of territory and personal space.

Proximo-distal development: Motor development that proceeds from the center of the body to its periphery.

Psychoactive drugs: Chemical substances that act on the brain to create psychological effects; usually classified as depressants, stimulants, narcotics (opiates), hallucinogens, or antipsychotics.

Psychoanalytic theory: A set of theories conceived by Sigmund Freud that see the roots of human behavior and mental disorders in unconscious motivation and in childhood and early adulthood conflict.

Psychobiology: The study of the interactions between biological and psychological processes.

Psychogenic disorder: An illness that is attributable primarily to a psychological conflict or to emotional stress.

Psychometrics: The theory or technique of psychological measurement; the measurement of psychological differences among people and the statistical analysis of those differences.

Psychophysics: The study of the relationship between physical units of a stimulus, such as amplitude, and its sensory, experienced qualities, such as loudness.

Psychophysiology: The study of the interaction between the psyche (mind and emotions) and the physiology (physical processes such as blood pressure and heart rate) of the organism.

Psychosis: A general term referring to a severe mental disorder, with or without organic damage, characterized by deterioration of normal intellectual and social function and by partial or complete withdrawal from reality; includes schizophrenia and mood disorders such as bipolar disorder.

Psychosocial crisis: In Erik Erikson's theory, a turning point in the process of development precipitated by the individual having to face a new set of social demands and new social relationships.

Psychosomatic disorder: A physical disorder that results from, or is worsened by, psychological factors; synonymous with psychophysiological disorder and includes stress-related disorders.

Psychosurgery: Brain surgery conducted to alter an inappropriate or maladaptive behavior.

Psychotherapy: A general category of treatment techniques for mental disorders; most psychotherapy uses talking as a tool and centers on the client-psychotherapist relationship to develop awareness and provide support.

Punishment: The procedure of decreasing the probability of a behavior by the response-contingent delivery of an aversive stimulus.

Pure tone: A sound produced by a vibration of a single frequency, the amplitude of which changes over time as a sinusoidal function; a sine wave.

Quasi-experimental designs: Experimental plans that do not allow subjects to be assigned randomly to treatment conditions.

Random assignment: The most common technique for establishing equivalent groups by balancing subject characteristics through the assigning of subjects to groups through some random process.

Rapid eye movement (REM) sleep: A special stage of sleep that involves desynchronized electrical brain activity, muscle paralysis, rapid eye movements, and narrative dream recall.

Ratio schedule: A reinforcement schedule in which reinforcer delivery is contingent upon the performance of a specified number of responses.

Rational-emotive therapy: A cognitive-based psychotherapy, pioneered by Albert Ellis, that attempts to replace or modify a client's irrational, inappropriate, or problematic thought processes, outlooks, and self-concept.

Realistic conflict theory: A theory from social psychology that suggests that direct competition for scarce or valued resources can lead to prejudice.

Receptive aphasia: Difficulties in comprehending spoken and written material, usually after damage to Wernicke's area in the left temporal lobe of the cerebral cortex.

Receptive field: The region and pattern in space to which a single neuron responds.

Receptor: A specific protein structure on a target cell to which a neurotransmitter binds, producing a stimulatory or inhibitory response.

Recessive gene: A gene whose corresponding trait will not be expressed unless the gene is paired with another recessive gene for that trait.

Reciprocal determinism: An interactional model proposing that environment, personal factors, and behavior all operate as interacting determinants of one another.

Reductionism: An aspect of the scientific method which seeks to understand complex and often interactive processes by reducing them to more basic components and principles.

Reflex: An unlearned and automatic biologically programmed response to a particular stimulus.

Reflex arc: The simplest behavioral response, in which an impulse is carried by a sensory neuron to the spinal cord, crosses a synapse to a motor neuron, and stimulates a response.

Regression: An ego defense mechanism that a person uses to return to an earlier stage of development when experiencing stress or conflict.

Regulators: Facial gestures and expressions by listeners that are informative for speakers; they convey comprehension or acceptance, or indicate when the other person may speak.

Reinforcement: An operation or process that increases the probability that a learned behavior will be repeated.

Reinforcer: A stimulus or event that, when delivered contingently upon a response, will increase the probability of the recurrence of that response.

Relative deprivation: The proposition that people's attitudes, aspirations, and grievances largely depend on the frame of reference within which they are conceived.

Reliability: The consistency of a psychological measure, which can be assessed by means of stability over repeated administrations or agreement among different observers.

Representativeness: A heuristic in which an estimate of the probability of an event or sample is determined by the degree to which it resembles the originating process or population.

Repression: In psychoanalytic theory, a defense mechanism that keeps unacceptable thoughts and impulses from becoming conscious.

Response cost: Negative consequences that follow the commission of an undesired behavior, decreasing the rate at which the misbehavior will recur.

Response hierarchy: An arrangement of alternative responses to a cue, from that most likely to occur to that least likely to occur.

Resting membrane potential: The maintenance of difference in electrical charges between the inside and outside of a neuron's cell membrane, keeping it polarized with closed ion channels.

Retardation: A condition wherein a person has mental abilities that are far below average; other skills and abilities, such as adaptive behavior, may also be marginal; measured by an IQ score of less than 70.

Reticular formation: A core of neurons extending through the medulla, pons, and midbrain that controls arousal and sleeping/waking as well as motor functions such as muscle tone and posture.

Retina: The light-sensitive area at the back of the eye, containing the photoreceptors (rods and cones) that detect light.

Retrieval: The process of locating information stored in memory and bringing it into awareness.

Retrograde amnesia: The type of amnesia that involves an inability to remember things that occurred before the onset of the amnesia.

Rhodopsin: The visual pigment in the cells of the rods that responds to light.

Rod: A photoreceptor of the retina specialized for the detection of light without discrimination of color.

Role: A social position that is associated with a set of behavioral expectations.

Rule-governed behavior: Behavior that is under the discriminative control of formalized contingencies.

Sample: A subset of a population; a group of elements selected from a larger, well-defined pool of elements.

Sampling error: The extent to which population parameters deviate from a sample statistic.

Satiety: A feeling of fullness and satisfaction.

Schema: An active organization of prior knowledge, beliefs, and experience which is used in perceiving the environment, retrieving information from memory, and directing behavior (plural, schemata).

Schizophrenia: Any of a group of psychotic reactions characterized by withdrawal from reality with accompanying affective, behavioral, and intellectual disturbances, including illusions and hallucinations.

Schwann cell: A type of insulating nerve cell that wraps around neurons located peripherally throughout the organism.

Script: An event schema in which a customary sequence of actions, actors, and props is specified; for example, behavior at a restaurant.

Seasonal affective disorder (SAD): Bipolar disorder that undergoes a seasonal fluctuation resulting from various factors, including seasonal changes in the intensity and duration of sunlight.

Secondary reinforcement: A learned reinforcer that has acquired reinforcing qualities by being paired with other reinforcers.

Secondary sex characteristics: Physical features other than genitals that differentiate women and men; for example, facial hair.

Self: The unified and integrated center of one's experience and awareness, which one experiences both subjectively, as an actor, and objectively, as a recipient of actions.

Self-actualization: A biologically and culturally determined process involving a tendency toward growth and full realization of one's potential, characterized by acceptance, autonomy, accuracy, creativity, and community; pioneered by Abraham Maslow.

Self-concept: The sum total of the attributes, abilities, attitudes, and values that an individual believes defines who he or she is.

Self-efficacy: The perception or judgment of one's ability to perform a certain action successfully or to control one's circumstances.

Self-esteem: The evaluative part of the self-concept; one's feeling of self-worth.

Self-image: The self as the individual pictures or imagines it.

Self-perception: A psychological process whereby individuals infer the nature of their attitudes and beliefs by observing their own behavior.

Semantic memory: The long-term representation of a person's factual knowledge of the world.

Semicircular canals: The three structures in the inner ear that together signal acceleration of the head in any direction.

Sensation: The process by which the nervous system and sensory receptors receive and represent stimuli received from the environment.

Sensorimotor stage: The first of Jean Piaget's developmental stages, lasting from birth to about two years of age, during which objects become familiar and are interpreted by appropriate habitual, motor, and sensory processes.

Sensory memory: The persistence of a sensory impression for less than a second; it allows the information to be processed further.

Serial processing: A theory concerning how people scan information in memory that suggests that as the number of items in memory increases, so does the amount of time taken to determine whether an item is present in memory.

Set point: An organism's personal homeostatic level for a particular body weight, which results from factors such as early feeding experiences and heredity.

Sex: Biological maleness or femaleness, determined by genetic endowment and hormones.

Sex typing: The process of acquiring traits, attitudes, and behaviors seen as appropriate for members of one's gender; gender-role acquisition.

Sexual instinct: In Sigmund Freud's theory, the innate tendency toward pleasure seeking, particularly through achieving sexual aims and objects.

Shaping: The acquiring of instrumental behavior in small steps or increments through the reinforcement of successively closer approximations to the desired final behavior.

Short-term memory: A memory system of limited capacity that uses rehearsal processes either to retain current memories or to pass them on to long-term memory.

Significance level: The degree of likelihood that research results are attributable to chance.

Skinner box: The most commonly used apparatus for studying instrumental conditioning; manipulation of a lever (for rats, monkeys, or humans) or an illuminated disk (for pigeons) produces consequences.

Social categorization: The classification of people and groups according to attributes that are personally meaningful.

Social cognition: The area of social psychology concerned with how people make sense of social events, including the actions of others.

Social comparison: Comparing attitudes, skills, and feelings with those of similar people in order to determine relative standing in a group or the acceptability of one's own positions.

Social facilitation: The enhancement of a person's most dominant response as a result of the presence of others; for some tasks, such as simple ones, performance is enhanced, while for others, such as novel tasks, performance is impaired.

Social identity theory: A theory maintaining that people are motivated to create and maintain a positive identity in terms of personal qualities and, especially, group memberships.

Social learning theory: The approach to personality that emphasizes the learning of behavior via observations and direct reward; exemplified by the theories of Albert Bandura, Walter Mischel, and Julian Rotter.

Social loafing: The tendency to expend less effort while in the presence of others; most likely to occur on additive tasks in which one's individual effort is obscured as a result of the collective efforts of the group.

Social phobia: A condition characterized by fear of the possible scrutiny or criticism of others.

Social psychology: A subfield of psychology that studies how individuals are affected by environmental factors and particularly by other people.

Social support: The relationships with other people that provide emotional, informational, or tangible resources that affect one's health and psychological comfort.

Socialization: The process of learning and internalizing social rules and standards.

Sociobiology: The application of the principles of evolutionary biology to the understanding of social behavior.

Somatization disorder: A mental syndrome in which a person chronically has a number of vague but dramatic medical complaints that apparently have no physical cause.

Somatoform disorders: A group of mental disorders in which a person has physical complaints or symptoms that appear to be caused by psychological rather than physical factors; for example, hypochondriasis.

Somnambulism: The scientific term for sleepwalking; formerly a term for hypnosis.

Spectrum analysis: The ability of a system, such as hearing, to decompose a complex wave into its sine-wave components and their respective amplitudes.

Spinal cord: The part of the central nervous system that is enclosed within the backbone; conducts nerve impulses to and from the brain.

Spontaneous recovery: The recovery of extinguished behaviors over time in the absence of any specific treatment or training.

Sports psychology: The subfield of psychology that applies psychological principles to physical activities such as competitive sports; frequently concerned with maximizing athletic performance.

Sprouting: A process that occurs when remaining nerve fibers branch and form new connections to replace those that have been lost.

Stage theory of development: The belief that development moves through a set sequence of stages; the quality of behavior at each stage is unique but is dependent upon movement through earlier stages.

Standard deviation: A measure of how variable or spread out a group of scores is from the mean.

Standardization: The administration, scoring, and interpretation of a test in a prescribed manner so that differences in test results can be attributed to the testee.

Statistical significance: Differences in behavior large enough that they are probably related to the subject variables or manipulated variables; differences too large to be caused by chance alone.

Stereogram: A two-dimensional image that appears three-dimensional when viewed binocularly, typically consisting of two images of the same scene as viewed from slightly disparate viewpoints. When special glasses are worn, the images are fused into one image with the full three-dimensional effect.

Stereotype: A set of beliefs, often rigidly held, about the characteristics of an entire group.

Stimulants: Drugs that cause behavioral and/or physiological stimulation. Examples of stimulants: amphetamines, cocaine, and their respective derivatives; caffeine; nicotine; and some antidepressants.

Stimulus: An environmental circumstance to which an organism may respond; it may be as specific as a single physical event or as global as a social situation.

Stimulus generalization: The ability of stimuli that are similar to other stimuli to elicit a response that was previously elicited only by the first stimuli.

Storage: The stage of memory between encoding and retrieval; the period for which memories are held.

Strange situation: A particular experimental technique designed to measure the quality of the mother-infant attachment relationship.

Stress: The judgment that a problem exceeds one's available resources, resulting from a primary appraisal of the problem and a secondary appraisal of the coping resources.

Stressor: Anything that produces a demand on an organism.

Striate cortex: The region of the occipital lobe that reconstitutes visual images for recognition.

Stroke: A vascular accident resulting from either the rupture of a vessel or the blocking of blood flow in an artery.

Structuralism: An early school of psychology that sought to define the basic elements of mind and the laws governing their combination.

Sublimation: According to Sigmund Freud, a defense mechanism by which a person may redirect aggressive impulses by engaging in a socially sanctioned activity.

Suffix: A morpheme that attaches to the end of a word.

Superego: In Freudian theory, the part of the psyche that contains parental and societal standards of morality and that acts to prohibit expression of instinctual drives; includes the conscience and the ego-ideal.

Syllogism: A logical argument constructed of a major premise, a minor premise, and a conclusion, the validity of which is determined by rules of inference.

Symbiotic relationship: An overprotective, often enmeshed relationship between a parent and child.

Sympathetic nervous system: A division of the autonomic nervous system that prepares the organism for energy expenditure.

Synapse: The junction between two neurons over which a nerve impulse is chemically transduced.

Synchronized electroencephalogram: A regular, repetitive brain-wave pattern that is caused by multitudes of neurons firing at the same time and the same rate in a given brain region.

Systematic desensitization: An exposure therapy in which the phobic person is gradually presented with a feared object or situation.

Systems theory: A concept in which the family grouping is viewed as a biosocial subsystem existing within the larger system of society; intrafamilial communications are the mechanisms of subsystem interchange.

Tachistoscope: An experimental apparatus for presenting visual information very briefly to the right or left visual field; sometimes called a T-scope.

Tardive dyskinesia: Slow, involuntary motor movements, especially of the mouth and tongue, which can become permanent and untreatable; can result from psychoactive drug treatment.

Temporal lobe: The lower portion on the side of each cerebral hemisphere, containing the sites of sensory interpretation, memory of visual and auditory patterns, and part of the general interpretive area.

Test-retest reliability: A common way of determining consistency, by administering the same test twice to the same person.

Testosterone: The principal male sex hormone produced by the testes.

Thalamus: A portion of the diencephalon, located at the base of the forebrain, which receives sensory information from the body and relays these signals to the appropriate regions of the cerebrum.

Thematic Apperception Test (TAT): A personality test in which individuals demonstrate their needs by describing what is happening in a series of ambiguous pictures.

Theory: A model explaining the relationship between several phenomena; derived from several related hypotheses which have survived many tests.

Therapy: The systematic habilitation of a disorder.

Thermoreceptor: A sensory receptor specialized for the detection of changes in the flow of heat.

Threshold: The minimum stimulus intensity necessary for an individual to detect a stimulus; usually defined as that intensity detected 50 percent of the time it is presented.

Thyroxine: The major hormone produced and secreted by the thyroid gland; stimulates protein synthesis and the basal metabolic rate.

Timbre: The sound quality produced by the respective amplitude and frequency of the overtones.

Top-down processing: A situation in which a person's perception of a stimulus is influenced by nonstimulus factors such as the person's general knowledge, beliefs, or expectations.

Trait theory: A way of conceptualizing personality in terms of relatively persistent and consistent behavior patterns that are manifested in a wide range of circumstances.

Transduction: The process of changing physical energy, such as light, into neural messages.

Transference: The phenomenon in which a person in psychoanalysis shifts thoughts or emotions concerning people in his or her past (most often parents) onto the analyst.

Transvestite: A person who, for fun or sexual arousal, often dresses and acts like a member of the opposite sex (going "in drag"); most are heterosexual males.

Tricyclics: A class of antidepressant drugs.

Two-factor theory: A behavioral theory of anxiety stating that fear is caused by Pavlovian conditioning and that avoidance of the feared object is maintained by operant conditioning.

Type A personality: A behavior pattern that describes individuals who are driven, competitive, highstrung, impatient, time-urgent, intense, and easily angered; some researchers have associated this pattern with increased risk of heart disease.

Unconditional positive regard: The attempt by a therapist to convey to a client that he or she genuinely cares for the client.

Unconditioned response (UR): An innate or unlearned behavior that occurs automatically following some stimulus; a reflex.

Unconditioned stimulus (US): A stimulus that elicits an unconditioned response; the relation between unconditioned stimuli and unconditioned responses is unlearned.

Unconscious: The deep-rooted aspects of the mind; Sigmund Freud claimed that the unconscious includes negative instincts and urges that are too disturbing for people to be aware of consciously.

Unipolar depression: A disorder characterized by the occurrence of one or more major depressive episodes but no manic episodes.

Validity: A statistical value that tells the degree to which a test measures what it is intended to measure; the test is usually compared to external criteria.

Vicarious learning: Learning (for example, learning to fear something) without direct experience, either by observing or by receiving verbal information.

Visual cortex: The top six cell layers in the back of the brain, which are specialized for organizing and interpreting visual information.

Visual dyslexia: The lack of ability to translate observed written or printed language into meaningful terms.

Voyeurism: The derivation of sexual pleasure from looking at the naked bodies or sexual activities of others without their consent.

Wavelength: The distance traveled by a wave front in the time given by one cycle (the period of the wave); has an inverse relation to frequency.

White matter: The tissue within the central nervous system, consisting primarily of nerve fibers.

Within-subject design: An experimental plan in which each subject receives each level of the independent variable.

Working through: A psychoanalytical term that describes the process by which clients develop more adaptive behavior once they have gained insight into the causes of their psychological disorders.

Yerkes-Dodson law: The principle that moderate levels of arousal tend to yield optimal performance.

Zeitgeber: A German word meaning "time giver"; a factor that serves as a synchronizer or entraining agent, such as sunlight in the morning.

BIBLIOGRAPHY

This bibliography is divided into the following categories:

Aggression 2116
Aging 2117
Anxiety Disorders 2117
Attitudes 2117
Behavior 2118
Brain 2118
Childhood and Adolescence 2119
Cognition 2119
Consciousness 2120
Depression 2120
Development 2120
Emotion 2121
Freudian Psychology 2121
Gender Studies 2122
Hormones 2122
Intelligence 2123
Language 2123

Learning 2123
Memory 2124
Mental Illness 2125
Motivation 2125
Nervous System 2126
Pavlovian Conditioning 2126
Personality 2127
Psychotherapy 2127
Schizophrenia 2128
Sensation and Perception 2129
Sexuality 2129
Sleep 2130
Social Psychology 2130
Stress 2131
Substance Abuse 2132
Testing 2132

AGGRESSION

Archer, John. *Behavioural Biology of Aggression.* New York: Cambridge University Press, 1988. Archer considers possible chemical and biological determinants of aggressive behavior, particularly in young males.

Bandura, Albert. *Aggression: A Social Learning Analysis.* Englewood Cliffs, N.J.: Prentice-Hall, 1973. This volume in Prentice-Hall's Social Learning Analysis Series considers the roots of violence and the psychological and biological causes of such behavior.

Baron, Robert Alex, and Deborah R. Richardson, eds. *Human Aggression.* 2d ed. New York: Plenum, 2004. The nine essays in this book consider the development of aggressive behavior, aggression in natural settings, the biological sources of aggression, and the prevention and control of human aggression.

Berkowitz, Leonard. *Aggression: Its Causes, Consequences, and Control.* Philadelphia: Temple University Press, 1993. A thorough consideration of aggression in humans and other animals. Berkowitz identifies psychological and biological roots of aggression, the outcomes of aggressive behavior, and its control.

Cavell, Timothy A., and Kenya T. Malcolm, eds. *Anger, Aggression and Interventions for Interpersonal Violence.* Mahwah, N.J.: Lawrence Erlbaum Associates, 2007. An examination of interventions for interpersonal violence, particularly in schools and homes. Looks at venting and children's aggression.

Geen, Russell G., and Edward Donnerstein, eds. *Human Aggression: Theories, Research, and Implications for Social Policy.* San Diego, Calif.: Academic Press, 1998. Among the contributions to this volume are valuable essays on the effects of the mass media on aggressive behavior in young people.

Lesko, Wayne A., comp. *Readings in Social Psychology: General, Classic, and Contemporary Selections.* 6th ed. Boston: Pearson/Allyn & Bacon, 2006. The discussion of aggression is clear and forthright. This resource is a desirable starting point for those who are not experienced in the field.

Nelson, Randy J. Biology of Aggression. New York: Oxford University Press, 2006. Examines the biological basis of aggression, paying attention to androgens, serotonin, dopamine, vasopressin, and other factors, such as nitric oxide. Genetics of aggression in numerous species is also covered.

AGING

Abeles, Ronald P., Helen C. Gift, and Marcia G. Ory, eds. *Aging and the Quality of Life*. New York: Springer, 1994. This book's nineteen chapters touch on matters of socioeconomics, helping the aged to remain independent, dealing with health problems that afflict the aging, and sources of social, economic, and medical support for the aged.

Bergeman, Cindy S. *Aging: Genetic and Environmental Influences*. Thousand Oaks, Calif.: Sage Publications, 1997. Considers how different people age differently, the biology and psychology of aging, genetics and aging, and the social implications of aging.

Davey, Basiro, ed. *Birth to Old Age: Health in Transition*. Philadelphia: Open University, 2001. Deals with the development of children, the progression through the aging process, and the problems of old age. Strong discussion of the developmental biology of aging, cradle to grave.

Ebersole, Priscilla. *Geriatric Nursing and Healthy Aging*. 2d ed. St. Louis: Elsevier Mosby, 2005. Ebersole deals with a broad spectrum of questions relating to aging, including mobility, families and aging, coping with loss and grief, dealing with bone, joint, and cardiac health problems, and with the need for rest.

Hummert, Mary Lee, and Jon F. Nussbaum, eds. *Aging, Communication, and Health: Linking Research and Practice for Successful Aging*. Mahwah, N.J.: Lawrence Erlbaum, 2001. This volume's eleven essays deal with physician-patient relationships among the aging, the roles of family caregivers, and the responsibility for decision-making as people age.

Lear, Martha Weinman. *Where Did I Leave My Glasses? The What, When, and Why of "Normal" Memory Loss*. New York: Wellness Central, 2008. Interweaving medical findings with real-life anecdotes, this well-researched book is written with humor and clarity.

McFadden, Susan, and Robert C. Atchley, eds. *Aging and the Meaning of Time: An Interdisciplinary Exploration*. New York: Springer, 2006. This book's thirteen essays focus on perspectives of time among

the aging, dealing with how personal narratives can be useful in keeping older people alert and interested. Considers the role of religious beliefs among the aging.

Nuland, Sherwin B. *The Art of Aging: A Doctor's Prescription for Well-Being*. New York: Random House, 2007. Explores the impact of aging on people's minds and bodies, emphasizing the variability of the aging experience.

ANXIETY DISORDERS

Buss, Arnold H. *Self-Consciousness and Social Anxiety*. San Francisco: W. H. Freeman, 1980. Valuable observations about the relationship of guilt and shame to anxiety disorders. Readable, well researched, and clearly presented.

Crozier, W. Ray, ed. *Understanding Shyness: Psychological Perspectives*. New York: Palgrave, 2001. The chapter on overcoming social anxiety is of special interest. Investigates the nature of shyness. Analyzes its causes genetically and environmentally.

Goodwin, Donald W. *Anxiety*. New York: Oxford University Press, 1986. Offers a lucid and accurate overview of the causes and consequences of anxiety. Considers means of coping with this disabling psychological condition.

Kase, Larina, and Deborah Roth Ledley. *Anxiety Disorders*. Hoboken, N.J.: John Wiley & Sons, 2007. Comprehensive discussion of the theory and practice of identifying and treating anxiety disorders in patients of all ages.

Leitenberg, Harold, ed. *Handbook of Social and Evaluation Anxiety*. New York: Plenum Press, 1990. Valuable perspectives on the social aspects of anxiety. Focuses on self-consciousness and bashfulness. Solid overview of the psychological connections of anxiety disorders.

Rugh, Jayne L., and William C. Sanderson. *Treating Generalized Anxiety Disorder: Evidence-Based Strategies, Tools, and Techniques*. New York: Guilford Press, 2004. Examines the disorder and its treatments, with emphasis on how they are applied and how they work.

ATTITUDES

Allport, Gordon W. *The Nature of Prejudice*. 1954. Reprint. Cambridge, Mass.: Addison-Wesley, 1990. A quintessential source outlining the roots and causes of prejudice, linking such attitudes to feelings of personal inadequacy, the lust for power, and aggression born of feelings of inferiority. Considers both the environmental and psychological sources of prejudice.

Baumeister, Roy F., ed. *Self-Esteem: The Puzzle of Low Self-Regard.* New York: Plenum, 1993. The thirteen essays in this volume consider salient aspects of low self-esteem, considering its relationship to clinical depression, its presence in young children and adolescents, and self-esteem resulting from negative and positive life experiences.

Bowser, Benjamin P., and Raymond G. Hunt, eds. *Impacts of Racism on White Americans.* 2d ed. Thousand Oaks, Calif.: Sage Publications, 1996. This collection of twelve essays is strong in assessing the political and economic implications of racism, particularly in corporate America.

Branch, Taylor. *Parting the Waters: America in the King Years, 1954-1963.* New York: Simon & Schuster, 2005. Branch evaluates the psychological factors present in the racial tensions of the 1950's and 1960's that preceded Martin Luther King's assassination.

BEHAVIOR

Bugliosi, Vincent T., and Curt Gentry. *Helter Skelter.* New York: Bantam Books, 1995. Details the murder of Sharon Tate and others by the followers of Charles Manson, whose psychological control over his followers provides a chilling study of how one magnetic personality influences the behavior of innumerable people.

Burger, Jerry M. *Desire for Control: Personality, Social, and Clinical Perspectives.* New York: Plenum, 1992. Deals effectively with personality assessment and behaviorism. Presented from the practitioner's standpoint.

Carlson, Neil R. *Physiology of Behavior.* Boston: Allyn & Bacon, 1998. Comprehensive overview of the physiological roots of some behaviors with psychological manifestations.

Chagnon, Napoleon A., and W. Irons, eds. *Evolutionary Biology and Social Behavior.* North Scituate, Mass.: Duxbury Press, 1979. Focuses on the biological bases for behaviors common to humans.

O'Donohue, William, and Jane E. Fisher, eds. *Cognitive Behavior Therapy: Applying Empirically Supported Techniques in Your Practice.* 2d ed. Hoboken, N.J.: John Wiley & Sons, 2009. Describes the major techniques used in cognitive behavior therapy and how practitioners can effectively apply them.

Richard, David C. S., and Steven K. Huprich, eds. *Clinical Psychology: Assessment, Treatment, and Research.* London: Academic Press, 2008. This is a comprehensive look at the assessment, treatment, and research aspects of clinical psychology. With case studies and comparisons of therapeutic styles, this research examines the clinical and ethical challenges facing psychological practice.

Schlenker, Barry R. *The Self and Social Life.* New York: McGraw-Hill, 1985. Deals with the roles of interpersonal interactions in human relationships. Concerned with the self versus the members of the group.

Schroeder, David A., ed. *Social Dilemmas: Perspectives on Individuals and Groups.* Westport, Conn.: Praeger, 1995. The eleven essays in this book deal with various social dilemmas, including the famed Prisoner's Dilemma, and work through them, demonstrating the dynamics of groups solving them.

Skinner, B. F. *The Behavior of Organisms: An Experimental Analysis.* Englewood Cliffs, N.J.: Prentice-Hall, 1938. Well worth reading as an introductory text to the field by the father of behaviorism.

Smith, John L. *The Psychology of Action.* New York: St. Martin's Press, 2000. A strong chapter on enigmas, masochism and suicide, and the weakness of will. Quite specialized.

BRAIN

Berthoz, Alain. *The Brain's Sense of Movement.* Translated by Giselle Weiss. Cambridge, Mass.: Harvard University Press, 2000. Excellent review of the motor theory of perception. Solid material on the predictive uses of memory and of how coherence evolves.

Davidoff, Jules. *The Brain and Behavior: Critical Concepts in Psychology.* New York: Routledge, 2000. Strong in discussing cognition in relation to mental activity. Somewhat specialized.

Drubach, Daniel. *The Brain Explained.* Upper Saddle River, N.J.: Prentice-Hall, 2000. Lucid presentation of the structure and function of the brain as related to intelligence and language. Quite readable.

Edelman, Gerald M., and Jean-Pierre Changeux, eds. *The Brain.* New Brunswick, N.J.: Transaction Publishers, 2001. Sixteen photographic plates enhance this solid volume that presents an overview of the brain's activities.

Feinberg, Todd E. *Altered Egos: How the Brain Creates*

the Self. New York: Oxford University Press, 2002. Imaginative and readable account of the brain's capabilities. Chapter on deconstructing the self is exciting, as are chapters entitled "Missing Pieces, Familiar Places," and "Mything Persons."

Glynn, Ian. *An Anatomy of Thought: The Origin and Machinery of the Mind*. New York: Oxford University Press, 2003. Comprehensive view of neuropsychological aspects of cognition. Compelling philosophy of the mind and the brain's activities.

Hendleman, Walter J. *Atlas of Functional Neuroanatomy*. 2d ed. Boca Raton, Fla.: CRC Press, 2006. Hendleman presents a visual tour of the brain through drawings, photographs, and computer-generated illustrations. Three-dimensional images of the brain can be observed by using the accompanying CD-ROM.

Ornstein, Robert, Richard F. Thompson, and David Macaulay. *The Amazing Brain*. Boston: Houghton Mifflin, 1991. This is one of the best introductory books about the brain, written with a light and humorous touch. The lay reader will enjoy the accessibility of the text, the excellent (and unique) sketches, and the fanciful flair the authors use in examining a complicated subject.

Samples, Bob. *The Metaphoric Mind: A Celebration of Creative Consciousness*. 2d ed. Rolling Hills Estates, Calif.: Jalmar Press, 1993. Written with the layperson in mind, this consideration of the bicameral mind is exciting, informative, and accessible.

CHILDHOOD AND ADOLESCENCE

Bowlby, John. *A Secure Base: Parent-Child Attachment and Healthy Human Development*. London: Routledge, 2007. Explores in depth the long-term effects of parent-child relationships.

Byrne, Donn E., and William Fisher. *Adolescents, Sex, and Contraception*. Hillsdale, N.J.: Lawrence Erlbaum, 1983. Well-documented assessment of the sexual habits of adolescents, including those of college age. Their attitudes toward contraception is largely determined by cultural factors.

Clutton-Brock, T. H. *The Evolution of Parental Care*. Princeton, N.J.: Princeton University Press, 1991. The author considers parental care among various animal species and as compared to humans, focusing on how modes of parental care have evolved.

Gentile, Douglas A., ed. *Media Violence and Children: A Complete Guide for Parents and Professionals*. West-port, Conn.: Praeger, 2008. An expert on media violence collects essays from researchers who report on such topics as television violence, video games, and violent music.

Horne, Arthur M., and Mark S. Kiselica, eds. *Handbook of Counseling Boys and Adolescent Males: A Practitioner's Guide*. Thousand Oaks, Calif.: Sage Publications, 1999. Focuses largely on growing up as a male in America, giving special attention to the question of bullying and its victims.

Kirsh, Steven J. *Children, Adolescents, and Media Violence: A Critical Look at the Research*. Thousand Oaks, Calif.: Sage, 2006. A review of the research literature on effects of media violence on young people.

Luthar, S. S., and D. Cichetti. *Resilience and Vulnerability: Adaptation in the Context of Childhood Adversities*. New York: Cambridge University Press, 2003. An examination of resiliency and what it means in terms of mental health.

COGNITION

Bandura, Albert. *Social Foundations of Thought and Action: A Social-Cognitive Theory*. Englewood Cliffs, N.J.: Prentice-Hall, 1986. Emphasizes the social aspects and social perspectives of cognition. Somewhat specialized.

Flavell, John, Patricia H. Miller, and Scott Miller. *Cognitive Development*. 4th ed. Englewood Cliffs, N.J.: Prentice-Hall, 2002. Presents theory and research on cognitive development from an information-processing approach. Discusses relationship between information-processing and Piagetian theory. An excellent effort to compare and contrast these two perspectives.

Honeycutt, James M. *Cognition, Communication, and Romantic Relationships*. Mahwah, N.J.: Lawrence Erlbaum, 2001. Investigates the role of memory structures in romantic relationships. The chapter on emotion and cognition in relationships is particularly cogent, as is that on memory structures and decaying relationships.

Rowlands, Mark. *The Body in Mind: Understanding Cognitive Processes*. New York: Cambridge University Press, 1999. Chapters on language, perception, thought, and memory are relevant in the context of cognitive learning.

Solowij, Nadia. *Cannabis and Cognitive Functioning*. New York: Cambridge University Press, 2006. Solowij considers the effects of long-term use of cannabis on cognitive processes. Considers the reversibility of such effects when drug use ceases.

Turner, Mark. *Cognitive Dimensions of Social Science.* New York: Oxford University Press, 2001. Explores the development and use of cognitive processes in relation to all of the social studies, emphasizing their psychological dimensions.

CONSCIOUSNESS

Baars, Bernard J. *A Cognitive Theory of Consciousness.* New York: Cambridge University Press, 1995. Carefully reasoned psychological consideration of how consciousness is intertwined with cognition and with the learning process.

Carter, Rita. *Exploring Consciousness.* Berkeley: University of California Press, 2004. Using information derived from recent discoveries about the brain, Carter considers whether consciousness is an illusion—a byproduct of our brain—or a property of the material universe.

Dodwell, Peter. *Brave New Mind: A Thoughtful Inquiry into the Nature and Meaning of Mental Life.* New York: Oxford University Press, 2000. Deals well with psychological underpinnings of cognitive science. Unique perspectives on representation versus reality.

Hutto, Daniel D. *Beyond Physicalism.* Philadelphia: John Benjamins, 2000. Provocative discussion of the pluralism of naturalism compared to absolute idealism. Sharp insights on nonconceptual expression.

Ornstein, Robert E., ed. *The Nature of Human Consciousness: A Book of Readings.* New York: Viking, 1974. Comprehensive overview of the psychophysiological aspects of consciousness. Clear presentation of hemisphericity.

Ramachandran, V. S. *A Brief Tour of Human Consciousness: From Impostor Poodles to Purple Numbers.* New York: Pi Press, 2005. Neuroscientist Ramachandran explains the physical structures of the brain and how they relate to psychological disorders and how they illuminate the connection between the brain and the mind.

Underwood, Jeffrey, and Robin Stevens. *Aspects of Consciousness.* New York: Academic Press, 1979. Offers valuable information about states of consciousness and their relationship to cognitive development.

DEPRESSION

Bauer, Mark, and Linda McBride. *Structured Group Psychotherapy for Bipolar Disorder: The Life Goals Program.* 2d ed. New York: Springer, 2003. Considers what bipolar disorder is pathologically, biologically, and psychosocially. Outlines the success of the Life Goals Program in treating depression.

Baumeister, Roy F., ed. *Self-Esteem: The Puzzle of Low Self-Regard.* New York: Plenum, 1993. Brett W. Pelham's essay, "On the Highly Positive Thoughts of the Highly Depressed," which deals with how low self-esteem affects clinical depression, is relevant.

Becker, Howard S. *Outsiders.* New York: Free Press, 1997. Considers the effects of social exclusion upon individuals and links such exclusion to psychological depression.

Court, Bryan L., and Gerald E. Nelson. *Bipolar Puzzle Solution: A Mental Health Client's Perspective.* Washington, D.C.: Accelerated Development, 1996. A part of the Psychological Disorders Series, this book provides answers to 187 questions asked by members of a support group for manic-depressive people.

Kendall, Philip C., and David Watson, eds. *Anxiety and Depression: Distinctive and Overlapping Features.* San Diego, Calif.: Academic Press, 1989. Comprehensive view of how anxiety leads to psychological depression. Identifies causes and suggests psychotherapeutic remedies.

Solomon, Andrew. *The Noonday Demon: An Atlas of Depression.* New York: Charles Scribner's Sons, 2003. Solomon, who suffered serious depression himself, provides an insightful investigation of the subject from multiple perspectives of history, psychology, literature, psychopharmacology, law, and philosophy.

DEVELOPMENT

Axelrod, Robert M. *The Evolution of Cooperation.* Rev. ed. New York: Basic Books, 2006. Discusses human development from the standpoints of cooperativeness and consensus. Considers egoism. Suggests means of managing conflict.

Baumeister, Roy F., Todd F. Heatherton, and Dianne M. Tice. *Losing Control: How and Why People Fail at Self-Regulation.* San Diego, Calif.: Academic Press, 2002. Considers why people fail to take control of their lives through self-management. Suggests protocols for coping with the problem. Considers addictions and why people feel helpless to control them.

Briggs, Jean L. *Never in Anger: Portrait of an Eskimo Family*. Cambridge, Mass.: Harvard University Press, 1981. Socioethnographic study of an Eskimo family. Reveals developmental processes of children within that family.

Parker, Sue Taylor, Jonas Langer, and Michael L. McKinney. *Biology, Brains, and Behavior: The Evolution of Human Development*. Santa Fe, N.M.: School of American Research Press, 2000. Particularly relevant among the ten contributions to this collection are those on the development of primate behavior, the focus of two engrossing chapters.

Schlinger, Henry D., Jr. *A Behavior Analytic View of Child Development*. New York: Plenum, 1995. Provides information about the motor, perceptual, cognitive, language, social, and emotional development of children as they mature.

Unell, Barbara C., and Jerry L. Wyckoff. *The Eight Seasons of Parenthood: How the Stages of Parenting Constantly Reshape Our Adult Identities*. New York: Times Books, 2000. Interesting contrasts between parent-child and parent-adult child relationships and their effect upon people as they mature.

EMOTION

Bar-on, Reuven, and James D. A. Parker, eds. *The Handbook of Emotional Intelligence*. San Francisco: Jossey-Bass, 2000. Assesses emotional intelligence neurologically, psychologically, and socially. Material on purposive behavior and emotional competence is excellent.

Charrochi, Joseph, Joseph P. Forgas, and John D. Mayer. *Emotional Intelligence in Everyday Life: A Scientific Inquiry*. Philadelphia: Psychology Press, 2001. Focuses on emotional intelligence in intimate relationships and in the workplace. Views emotional intelligence in terms of self-actualization and empathetic accuracy.

Cherniss, Cary, and Daniel Goleman, eds. *The Emotionally Intelligent Workplace: How to Select for, Measure, and Improve Emotional Intelligence in Individuals, Groups, and Organizations*. San Francisco: Jossey-Bass, 2001. Among this volume's dozen essays are those dealing with the development of emotional intelligence and how to bring such intelligence into the workplace. Stresses the economic value of achieving emotional intelligence within corporations.

Saarni, Carolyn. *The Development of Emotional Competence*. New York: Guilford Press, 1999. Considers how to cope with adverse emotions. Links emotional development to overall social development and recommends that people be sensitive to the emotions of others.

Saul, Leon Joseph. *Emotional Maturity: The Development and Dynamics of Personality and Its Disorders*. Philadelphia: J. B. Lippincott, 1971. Deals with the psychopathology that accompanies emotional immaturity and leads to emotional disorders. Suggests ways to overcome this psychopathology and become an emotionally healthy person.

Zeidner, Moshe, Gerald Matthews, and Richard D. Roberts. *What We Know About Emotional Intelligence: How It Affects Learning, Work, Relationships, and Our Mental Health*. Cambridge, Mass.: MIT Press, 2009. Examines all facets of emotional intelligence, including how it is developed and measured. Discusses how it relates to work and school.

FREUDIAN PSYCHOLOGY

Fordham, Michael. *Freud, Jung, Klein—The Fenceless Field: Essays on Psychoanalysis and Analytical Psychology*. Edited by Roger Hobdell. New York: Routledge, 1998. Sections reviewing major works in psychoanalysis are useful, as is the hundred-page section on analytical psychology.

Gossy, Mary S. *Freudian Slips: Woman, Writing, the Foreign Tongue*. Ann Arbor: University of Michigan Press, 1995. Overview of Freudian psychoanalysis and its relation to feminism is fresh and challenging. Fine study of Freud's views on gender.

Hall, Kirsty. *The Stuff of Dreams: Fantasy, Anxiety, and Psychoanalysis*. London: Karnac, 2007. Reading of the place of anxiety alongside fantasy in the construction and interpretation of dreams.

Kase, Larina, and Deborah Roth Ledley. *Anxiety Disorders*. Hoboken, N.J.: John Wiley & Sons, 2007. Comprehensive discussion of the theory and practice of identifying and treating anxiety disorders in patients of all ages.

Ornstein, Robert E. *The Evolution of Consciousness: Of Darwin, Freud, and Cranial Fire—The Origins of the Way We Think*. New York: Simon & Schuster, 1992. Considers thought processes genetically, biologically, and neuropsychologically. Analysis of Freud's mental processes is revealing.

Sander, Joseph, Ethel Spector Person, and Peter Fonagy, eds. *Freud's "On Narcissism—An Introduc-*

tion." New Haven, Conn.: Yale University Press, 1991. English-language version of Sigmund Freud's *Zur Einführung des Narzissmus* (1924). Presents Freud's feelings about self-love and egoism.

Young-Bruehl, Elisabeth, ed. *Freud on Women: A Reader.* New York: W. W. Norton, 1990. Provides a representative selection of Freud's writing about women. Dated but interesting historically.

GENDER STUDIES

Archer, John. *Sex and Gender.* New York: Cambridge University Press, 2002. Comprehensive assessment of sexual differences, sex roles, and gender considerations in sexual relationships.

Ashmore, Richard D., and Frances K. Del Boca, eds. *The Social Psychology of Female-Male Relations: A Critical Analysis of Central Concepts.* New York: Academic Press, 1986. Presents material on interpersonal relations involving sex roles, identity, and the psychology of both genders.

Beall, Anne E., and Robert J. Sternberg, eds. *The Psychology of Gender.* 2d ed. New York: Guilford Press, 2005. The ten essays in this collection deal with the relationship of gender to biology and environment, a cognitive approach to considering gender, and a social constructionist view of gender.

Blakemore, Judith E., Sheri A. Berenbaum, and Lynn S. Liben. *Gender Development.* New York: Psychology Press, 2008. A well-written textbook on all aspects of gender development that gives fair coverage of biological and social influences across family, peers, and school and media contexts.

Bonvillain, Nancy. *Women and Men: Cultural Constructs of Gender.* 4th ed. Upper Saddle River, N.J.: Pearson Prentice Hall, 2007. Examines the gender roles in different economies, including the industrial economy of the United States. Also examines the influence of reproduction and religion.

Brehm, Sharon S. *Seeing Female: Social Roles and Personal Lives.* Westport, Conn.: Greenwood, 1988. This volume in Greenwood's Women's Studies Series assesses the social roles and social conditions of women in the United States during the 1980's.

Burn, Shawn M. *The Social Psychology of Gender.* New York: McGraw-Hill, 1996. Balanced discussion of the motivating forces that shape views of gender and sexual differentiation from a psychological standpoint.

Kalbfleish, Pamela J., and Michael J. Cody, eds. *Gender, Power, and Communication in Human Relation-*

ships. Hillsdale, N.J.: Lawrence Erlbaum, 1995. Among the fourteen essays in this volume, those on the role of power in matters of gender, as well as the politics of gender and the presence of nonverbal communication in dealings between men and women are especially relevant.

Keough, Kelli A., and Julio Garcia. *Social Psychology of Gender, Race, and Ethnicity: Readings and Projects.* New York: McGraw-Hill, 2000. Interactive text on sexual differences and on attitudes toward gender. Engaging and informative.

Narrow, William D., et al., eds. *Age and Gender Considerations in Psychiatric Diagnosis.* Arlington, Va.: American Psychiatric Association, 2007. These essays discussing gender and mental health examine issues such as diagnostic criteria, childhood trauma, sociobiology, neurobiology, and children.

HORMONES

Carlson, Neil R. *Foundations of Physiological Psychology.* 7th ed. Boston: Allyn & Bacon, 2007. One of the standard texts on the physiological basis of human and animal behavior. The importance of sex hormones in development and motivation is emphasized throughout the chapter on reproductive behavior.

Conn, P. Michael, and Shlomo Melmed, eds. *Endocrinology: Basic and Clinical Principles.* 2d ed. Totowa, N.J.: Humana, 2004. Among the twenty-seven contributions to this collection are psychologically relevant essays by George P. Chrousos on the effect of hormones on the hypothalamus and by Gregory Brent on thyroid hormones.

Ellison, Peter T., and Peter B. Gray, eds. *Endocrinology of Social Relationships.* Cambridge, Mass.: Harvard University Press, 2009. Collection of essays on how the endocrine system and hormones influence aspects of human and animal relationships. Includes information on oxytocin, vasopressin, androgens, human mating, and fatherhood.

Neave, Nick. *Hormones and Behaviour: A Psychological Approach.* New York: Cambridge University Press, 2008. Neave explains the endocrine system and how hormones can influence brain structure and function. He also presents a series of examples to show the influence of hormones on specific behaviors, including sexual determination, neurological differentiation, parental and aggressive behaviors, and cognition.

Pinel, John P. J. *Biopsychology.* 7th ed. Boston: Allyn

& Bacon, 2007. Another good introductory text on the physiology of human and animal behavior. The chapter "Hormones and Sex" is detailed and clearly presented; several good case studies are offered to illustrate how hormonal problems can affect human sexual development.

Svare, Bruce B. *Hormones and Aggressive Behavior.* New York: Plenum, 1983. Assesses chemical effects hormones have on certain forms of aggressive behavior, particularly in young males.

Swearingen, Brooke, and Beverly M. K. Biller, eds. *Diagnosis and Management of Pituitary Disorders.* Totowa, N.J.: Humana Press, 2008. With contributions for radiologists, ophthalmologists, pathologists, radiation oncologists, and neurologists, this comprehensive resource focuses on all the clinical aspects of hormones and the pituitary gland.

INTELLIGENCE

Deary, Ian J. *Intelligence: A Very Short Introduction.* New York: Oxford University Press, 2001. Considers the relationship between genetics and environment in determining intelligence. Speculates that IQs increase overall from generation to generation.

Howe, Michael J. A. *IQ in Question: The Truth About Intelligence.* London: Sage, 2000. Deals in ten well-written chapters with such questions as whether IQ can be increased, relationships between race and intelligence as it is usually measured, and how reliable IQ measurements are. Explodes twelve commonly held beliefs about IQ.

Lynn, Richard. *The Global Bell Curve: Race, IQ, and Inequality Worldwide.* Augusta, Ga.: Washington Summit Publishers, 2008. An examination of the bell curve theory and IQ worldwide.

Martinez, Michael E. *Education as the Cultivation of Intelligence.* Mahwah, N.J.: Lawrence Erlbaum, 2000. Sound definition of intelligence considered genetically and experientially. Considers psychometric models of intelligence.

Naglieri, Jack A., and Sam Goldstein, eds. *Practitioner's Guide to Assessing Intelligence and Achievement.* Hoboken, N.J.: Wiley, 2009. Looks at questions of assessment in general and by specific tests, including the assessment of intellectual strengths and weaknesses with the Stanford-Binet test.

Scheibel, Arnold B., and J. William Schopf, eds. *The Origin and Evolution of Intelligence.* Boston: Jones

and Bartlett, 1997. Studies origins of intelligence from prerational intelligence, through intelligence among primates—essentially apes—to that of humans. Steven Pinker's essay on the biology of intelligence is especially challenging.

Sternberg, Robert J. *Handbook of Intelligence.* New York: Cambridge University Press, 2000. Considers biological factors associated with intellect. Presents common theories and frequently used means of measuring intelligence.

LANGUAGE

Brown, Penelope, and Stephen C. Levinson. *Politeness: Some Universals in Language Usage.* New York: Cambridge University Press, 2008. Intriguing assessment of nonverbal aspects of communication and their psychological components. Imaginative approach.

Chomsky, Carol. *The Acquisition of Syntax in Children from Five to Ten.* Cambridge, Mass.: MIT Press, 1979. Brief, compelling study of how children acquire language and of what environmental and psychological forces affect the process.

Chomsky, Noam. *Language and Mind.* 3d ed. Cambridge University Press. 2006. Builds on Chomsky's earlier psycholinguistic approach to language, demonstrating how the mind operates in relation to words, meanings, and syntactic structures.

_____. *Syntactic Structures.* 2d ed. New York: Mouton de Gruyter, 2002. Brief, landmark volume in which Chomsky establishes the field of transformational-generative grammar that affected directly subsequent theories of language learning.

Pinker, Steven. *The Language Instinct.* New York: HarperPerennial, 2007. Hypothesizes that all humans are born with a language instinct, so that certain language protocols are inherent rather than learned. Controversial book that stimulates productive thought. Well written. Can be appreciated by nonspecialists.

LEARNING

Amsel, Abram. *Behaviorism, Neobehaviorism, and Cognition in Learning Theory: History and Contemporary Perspectives.* Hillsdale, N.J.: Lawrence Erlbaum, 1989. Presents and evaluates various theories of learning, assessing them historically and contrasting them to earlier theories.

Bandura, Albert. *Social Learning Theory*. Englewood Cliffs, N.J.: Prentice-Hall, 1977. Considers learning as a preparation of people for productive functioning in society. Considers substantive learning in relation to more general forms of learning with social outcomes.

Mazur, James E. *Learning and Behavior*. 6th ed. Upper Saddle River, N.J.: Prentice Hall, 2006. Excellent introduction to the topic of learning and behavior assumes no prior knowledge of psychology. The reading is straightforward though sometimes challenging as it covers the basics of classical and operant conditioning, biological bases of learning and behavior, and applications to complex human learning situations.

Mowrer, Robert R., and Stephen B. Klein, eds. *Handbook of Contemporary Learning Theories*. Mahwah, N.J.: Lawrence Erlbaum, 2001. Deals with the psychology of learning and the general field of cognition. Accessible to nonspecialists.

Smith, Frank. *The Book of Learning and Forgetting*. New York: Teachers' College Press, 1998. Undermines much traditional learning theory, investigating the immensity of learning in early childhood and assessing decreases in learning surges as people age.

Tileston, Donna Walker. *Ten Best Teaching Practices: How Brain Research, Learning Styles, and Standards Define Teaching Competencies*. 2d ed. Thousand Oaks, Calif.: Corwin Press, 2005. Practical book aimed at in-service teachers and those preparing to become teachers. Tileston has a broad knowledge of brain research and applies it effectively to learning styles currently in widespread use.

MEMORY

Baddeley, Alan D. *Human Memory: Theory and Practice*. Rev. ed. Boston: Psychology Press, 1998. Updated edition of a classic text. The original emphasis on history of memory research continues, along with experimental views of consciousness and implicit memory.

Berkowitz, Leonard. *Consequences and Causes of Feelings*. New York: Cambridge University Press, 2000. Particularly relevant are Berkowitz's chapters on the influence of feelings on memory and the ways feelings affect memory.

Engel, Susan. *Context Is Everything: The Nature of Memory*. New York: W. H. Freeman, 2000. Explores where memory begins and suggests ways of evoking memory, largely through recalling contexts. Differentiates between remembering things in print and things heard or seen.

Hunt, R. Reed, and Henry Ellis. *Fundamentals of Cognitive Psychology*. Los Angeles: Sage, 2007. The authors approach the role of cognitive psychology in memory using an experimental problem-solving approach. Updated theories explaining both long-term and short-term memory, as well as retrieval, are included.

Martinez, Joe L., and Raymond P. Kesner. *Neurobiology of Learning and Memory*. 2d ed. Boston: Academic Press, 2007. An overview of information on the neurobiology of learning and memory from developmental, pharmacological, and psychobiological perspectives. A good introductory-level source.

Pribram, Karl H., and Donald E. Broadbent, eds. *Biology of Memory*. New York: Academic Press, 1970. Sound presentation of memory psychophysically and biologically, including molecular biological influences on short-term memory.

Richter, Derek. *Aspects of Learning and Memory*. New York: Basic Books, 1966. Explores the relationships between memory and learning, developing a psychologically and biologically based learning theory.

Rose, Steven, ed. *From Brains to Consciousness?* Princeton, N.J.: Princeton University Press, 1998. Striking essays on neurocomputational models of memory, on the physiological basis of memory, and aging from a neurobiological standpoint among the fourteen essays in the collection.

Shank, David R., ed. *Human Memory: A Reader*. New York: St. Martin's Press, 1997. Among the fourteen essays, those on short-term memory, on the reliability of memory, and the neuropsychology of memory are particularly useful.

Squire, Larry R., and Eric Kandel. *Memory: From Mind to Molecules*. 2d ed. Greenwood Village, Colo.: Roberts, 2009. An approachable volume summarizing the major developments in understanding the anatomy and physiology of vertebrate and invertebrate learning. This text contains an extensive discussion of Kandel's work with the molecular biology of memory in Aplysia and Squire's work on the neuroanatomy of memory with monkeys. An excellent source for people with a limited background in biology and chemistry.

Tulving, Endel, and Fergus I. M. Craik. *The Oxford Handbook of Memory.* New York: Oxford University Press, 2005. A comprehensive volume dealing with a wide variety of topics related to both animal and human memory. An excellent general reference source.

MENTAL ILLNESS

Andreasen, Nancy C. *Brave New Brain: Conquering Mental Illness in the Era of the Genome.* New York: Oxford University Press, 2004. Valuable for its consideration of how mapping the genome and mapping the mind through neuroimaging may offer hope to those suffering from degenerative forms of mental illness.

Barlow, David H., and Mark Durand. *Abnormal Psychology: An Integrative Approach.* 5th ed. Belmont, Calif.: Wadsworth Cengage Learning, 2009. Considers among its sixteen clearly presented chapters disorders related to substance abuse, eating and sleeping disorders, problems with anxiety, and a considerable panoply of ills leading to mental illness.

Millon, Theodore, Paul H. Blaney, and Roger D. Davis, eds. *Oxford Textbook of Psychopathology.* 2d ed. New York: Oxford University Press, 2009. An advanced textbook for readers who have at least a college background in psychology and basic knowledge of the field of psychopathology. Twenty-seven chapters span almost seven hundred pages, and experts in the field author each chapter. Theory and assessment of disorders are emphasized.

Morrison, Michelle. *Foundations of Mental Health Nursing.* St. Louis: Mosby, 1997. Comprehensive consideration of the history of caring for the mentally ill. Considers the ethical and legal issues associated with mental health care and the sociocultural issues affecting such care.

Tessler, Richard, and Gail Gamache. *Family Experiences with Mental Illness.* Westport, Conn.: Auburn House, 2000. This book's thirteen chapters deal with the desirable extent of family involvement, economic and emotional costs to family caregivers, and relationships between professional and family caregivers. Focuses on two Ohio families caring for family members, one from 1989 to 1992, the other from 1995 to 1997.

MOTIVATION

Boekaerts, Monique, Paul R. Pintrich, and Moshe Zeidner, eds. *Handbook of Self-Regulation.* San Diego, Calif.: Academic Press, 2007. Offers essays that deal specifically with motivation, presenting unique perspectives that are both physiological and social. The approach of this volume is essentially humanistic.

Deckers, Lambert. *Motivation: Biological, Psychological, and Environmental.* 3d ed. Boston: Allyn & Bacon, 2009. Provides a history of the research in the field of motivation and suggests that motivation is produced by a combination of physiological, psychological, and environmental elements.

Elliot, Andrew J., and Carol S. Dweck, eds. *Handbook of Competence and Motivation.* New York: Guilford, 2007. Essays on diverse topics relating to motivation, with an emphasis on the importance of competence.

French, Jeffrey A., Alan C. Kamil, and Daniel W. Leger, eds. *Evolutionary Psychology and Motivation.* Lincoln: University of Nebraska Press, 2001. These seven contributions were papers delivered at the Nebraska Symposium on Motivation in 2001. They deal with some of the biological aspects of motivation, notably sexual motivation related to pheromones.

Higgins, E. Tory, and Arie Kruglanski, eds. *Motivational Science: Social and Personality Perspectives.* Philadelphia: Psychology Press, 2000. The twenty-three readings in this volume include excellent material on the dynamics of stressful encounters as they relate to motivation and the cognitive-affective theory of personality.

Kenrick, Douglas T., Steven L. Neuberg, and Robert B. Cialdini. *Social Psychology: Unraveling the Mystery.* 3d ed. Boston: Allyn & Bacon, 2005. This is one of the best-written, most accessible books in introductory psychology. It is replete with examples to illustrate what is being said. The prose style is enticing and the intellectual content is exceptional. The chapter entitled "The Motivational Systems: Motives and Goals" is particularly relevant to those studying motivation. Strongly recommended for those unfamiliar with the field.

Lennon, Kathleen. *Explaining Human Action.* La Salle, Ill.: Open Court Press, 1990. Deals with motivation in relation to intention, reductionism, and functionalism. Specialized approach.

Pinder, Craig C. *Work Motivation in Organizational Be-

havior. 2d ed. New York: Psychology Press, 2008. This textbook gives a thorough overview of all the research related to work motivation, and it emphasizes that workplace behavior is the product of several factors, including emotions such as love and attitudes such as those related to power.

Reeve, Johnmarshall. *Understanding Motivation and Emotions.* 5th ed. Hoboken, N.J.: John Wiley & Sons, 2009. Relates motivation to emotional reactions, positive and negative. Suggests a positive approach results in greater motivation than a negative approach.

Nervous System

Deutsch, Sid, and Evangelia Micheli-Tzanakou. *Neuroelectric Systems.* New York: New York University Press, 1987. Detailed consideration of the electrophysiology and the neurophysiology of the nervous system.

Kraemer, W. J., and Alan D. Rogol, eds. *The Endocrine System in Sports and Exercise.* Malden, Mass.: Blackwell, 2005. Collection of essays that looks at the principles and mechanism of endocrinology as related to sports and exercise. Contains several essays on growth hormone factors involved in exercise and examines how the endocrine system affects the nervous system and competition.

Leonard, Charles T. *The Neuroscience of Human Movement.* St. Louis: Mosby, 1998. Considers principles of motor control, the neural control of human locomotion, and the role the cerebral cortex plays in movement.

Marshall, Bruce. *The Nervous System: Circuits of Communication.* New York: Torstar Books, 1985. Focuses on neurophysiology and diseases of the nervous system that affect locomotion and communication. Relevant for those concerned with Alzheimer's disease.

Nathan, Peter. *The Nervous System.* London: Whurr Press, 1997. One of the best overviews of the nervous system, its functioning, and diseases affecting it. Eight useful pages of illustrations.

Sherwood, Lauralee. *Human Physiology: From Cells to Systems.* Pacific Grove, Calif.: Brooks/Cole, 2009. Drawing on recent experimentation, the author provides extensive background material for those chapters that explain the function of the nervous system. The text includes comprehensive details, but tables and diagrams clarify the material and provide numerous examples.

Willott, James F. *Neurogerontology: Aging and the Nervous System.* New York: Springer, 1999. Excellent presentation of how aging affects the nervous system. Valuable for those interested in Alzheimer's disease.

Pavlovian Conditioning

Baldwin, John D., and Janice I. Baldwin. *Behavior Principles in Everyday Life.* 4th ed. Upper Saddle River, N.J.: Prentice-Hall, 2001. Written by two sociologists, this book provides an overview of psychological principles of behavior, including many details about Pavlovian conditioning. The authors provide hundreds of plausible and interesting examples of how behavior principles show up in everyday life. An excellent book for those interested in an interpretation of how Pavlovian and instrumental conditioning work together in daily life.

Gray, Jeffrey A. *Ivan Pavlov.* New York: Penguin Books, 1981. Intriguing biography of Pavlov. Directed at nonspecialists. Solid overview of Pavlov's experiments in classical conditioning.

Klein, Stephen B., and Robert R. Mowrer, eds. *Contemporary Learning Theories—Pavlovian Conditioning and the Status of Traditional Learning Theory.* Hillsdale, N.J.: Lawrence Erlbaum, 1989. Presents thorough information about conditioning in laboratory animals and lucid accounts of Pavlov's experiments with dogs.

Lavond, David G., and Joseph E. Steinmetz. *Handbook of Classical Conditioning.* New York: Springer, 2003. This reference by two experts in conducting classical conditioning experiments shows how to perform a conditioning experiment, describing useful techniques and equipment.

Martin, Irene, and A. B. Levey. *The Genesis of Classical Conditioned Response.* New York: Pergamon Press, 1969. Pavlovian conditioning and its relationship to similar theories is emphasized.

Reilly, Steve, and Todd R. Schachtman, eds. *Conditioned Taste Aversion: Neural and Behavioral Processes.* New York: Oxford University Press, 2009. Leading scholars in the field of learning provide articles on recent research in conditioned taste aversion, based on Pavlovian conditioning. Topics include side effects of chemotherapy, treatment of alcoholism, memory, and addiction.

Schmajuk, Nestor A., and Peter C. Holland, eds. *Occasion Setting: Associative Learning and Cognition in Animals.* Washington, D.C.: American Psychological Association, 1998. Several of the thirteen contributions to this collection deal with Pavlov's experiments, including a chapter on the real-time theory of Pavlovian conditioning and one on Pavlov's notion of feature-ambiguous discrimination.

PERSONALITY

Allport, Gordon W. *Becoming: Basic Considerations for a Psychology of Personality.* 1955. Reprint. New Haven, Conn.: Yale University Press, 1983. In this brief (106-page) book, the father of the five-factor model of personality clearly and directly sets forth his basic theory.

Craik, Kenneth H., Robert Hogan, and Raymond Wolfe, eds. *Fifty Years of Personality Psychology.* New York: Plenum, 1993. Considerable focus on the psychology of personality set forth by Gordon Allport. Presents current status and contemporary perspectives.

De Raad, Boele. *The Big Five Personality Factors: The Psycholexical Approach to Personality.* Seattle: Hogrefe and Huber, 2000. The major focus of this well-researched book is personality assessment.

Dobbert, Duane L. *Understanding Personality Disorders: An Introduction.* Westport, Conn.: Praeger, 2007. This resource introduces the problems of personality-disordered people and suggests ways to work with those who may be obsessive-compulsive, paranoid, antisocial, or overly dependent.

Drapela, Victor J. *A Review of Personality Theories.* 2d ed. Springfield, Ill.: Charles C Thomas, 1995. Overview of work in the field of personality theory. Comprehensive, essentially philosophical.

Eysenck, Hans J. *The Biological Basis of Personality.* New Brunswick, N.J.: Transaction, 2006. This book, originally published in 1967, provides a thorough, in-depth discussion of Eysenck's theories of how neuroticism, introversion, and extroversion are related to physiology.

Mischel, Walter. *Introduction to Personality.* 8th ed. Belmont, Calif.: Wadsworth, 2008. A college-level personality textbook with an emphasis on contemporary issues and research. Each major orientation to personality—psychodynamic, trait, phenomenological (humanistic), and behavioral—is presented with thorough discussions of measurement and research.

Mowen, John C. *The 3M Model of Motivation and Personality: Theory and Empirical Applications to Consumer.* Boston: Kluwer Academic, 2000. Comprehensive consideration of personality and human motivation applied to consumer habits. Discusses impulsive and compulsive behavior.

Pervin, Lawrence A., and Oliver John, eds. *Handbook of Personality: Theory and Research.* 10th ed. New York: Guilford Press, 2008. A compilation of personality theory and research for the sophisticated reader. Chapters by Mischel ("Personality Dispositions Revisited and Revised: A View After Three Decades"), David Magnusson ("Personality Development from an Interactional Perspective"), and Bernard Weiner ("Attribution in Personality Psychology") may be of particular interest.

Staats, Arthur W. *Behavior and Personality: Psychological Behaviorism.* New York: Springer, 1997. This book's nine chapters emphasize abnormal personality development and both cognitive and behavioral aspects of personality. Outlines psychological behavioral therapy.

PSYCHOTHERAPY

Bauer, Mark, and Linda McBride. *Structured Group Psychotherapy for Bipolar Disorder: The Life Goals Program.* 2d ed. New York: Springer, 2003. Deals with treating bipolar disorder through psychotherapy. Explains elements of the Life Goals Program, which has yielded fruitful results in treating bipolar disorders.

Brems, C. *A Comprehensive Guide to Child Psychotherapy.* 3d ed. Long Grove, Ill.: Waveland Press, 2008. Discusses the basic principles of child therapy. Topics covered include intake and assessment, treatment planning, therapeutic process, cross-cultural issues, and termination.

Burns, George W. *101 Healing Stories: Using Metaphors in Therapy.* New York: John Wiley & Sons, 2001. Emphasizes the role of storytelling in psychotherapy, emphasizing the uses of metaphor, which permits patients to focus on their own situations without revealing details that they prefer to suppress.

Corsini, Raymond J., comp. *Current Psychotherapies.* 8th ed. Belmont, Calif.: Thomson-Brooks/Cole, 2008. An excellent survey of more than a dozen approaches to psychotherapy, with a brief historical description of the origin of each.

Eells, Tracy D., ed. *Handbook of Psychotherapy Case Formulation.* 2d ed. New York: Guilford Press,

2007. Guidelines for case formulation, including references to a wide range of therapeutic approaches. Several examples of completed case formulations are helpful.

Freedheim, Donald, Jane Kessler, and Donald Peterson, eds. *History of Psychotherapy: A Century of Change.* 5th ed. Washington, D.C.: American Psychological Association, 2003. A collection of more than sixty papers on the history of psychotherapy in the United States. Covers theoretical approaches, the biographies of leading figures, and the projects of current major research centers.

Hartman, Loren M., and Kirk T. Blankenstein, eds. *Perception of Self in Emotional Disorder and Psychotherapy.* New York: Plenum, 1986. Consideration of the etiology of mental illness and of its treatments through psychotherapy. Emphasizes the role of self-perception in psychotherapy.

Norcross, John C., ed. *Psychotherapy Relationships That Work: Therapist Contributions and Responsiveness to Patients.* New York: Oxford University Press, 2002. Provides insight into the importance of the therapeutic relationship and guidelines on creating effective relationships. Covers such topics as empathy, cohesion in group therapy, and customizing treatment to each patient.

Teyber, Edward. *Interpersonal Process in Psychotherapy: A Guide to Clinical Training.* 5th ed. Belmont, Calif.: Thomson-Brooks/Cole, 2006. An extremely clear and readable guide to modern eclectic therapy. Full of practical examples and written as a training manual for beginning psychotherapy students.

Wen-sheng, Tseng, and Jon Stretzer, eds. *Culture and Psychotherapy: A Guide to Clinical Practice.* Washington, D.C.: American Psychological Association, 2001. Tseng Wen-sheng's title article, "Culture and Psychotherapy," provides a splendid overview. The book's seventeen essays are practical guides for psychotherapists.

SCHIZOPHRENIA

Aleman, André, and Frank Larøi. *Hallucinations: The Science of Idiosyncratic Perception.* Washington, D.C.: American Psychological Association, 2008. Using brain imaging and neurotransmission studies, the authors present a multicomponent model of hallucinations, which can accompany schizophrenia. Includes questionnaires and scales to assist in clinical assessment.

Gelman, Sheldon. *Medicating Schizophrenia: A History.* New Brunswick, N.J.: Rutgers University Press, 1999. Traces the history of chemical treatment of schizophrenia and presents valuable material on current chemical treatment of the disorder.

Green, Michael Foster. *Schizophrenia Revealed: From Neurons to Social Interactions.* New York: W. W. Norton, 2003. Discusses the early symptoms of schizophrenia and genetic predispositions for it. The final chapter, following one dealing with interventions, reviews ways of overcoming the condition.

Harrison, Paul J., and Gareth W. Roberts, eds. *The Neuropathology of Schizophrenia: Progress and Interpretation.* New York: Oxford University Press, 2000. A specialized book—not for the beginner. Its thirteen chapters by experts in the field deal accurately and in detail with biological and psychological aspects of the disorder.

Hirsch, Steven R., and Daniel R. Weinberger. *Schizophrenia.* Oxford: Blackwell Science, 2002. A comprehensive review by two masters in the field.

Kingdon, David G., and Douglas Turkington. *Cognitive Therapy of Schizophrenia.* New York: Guilford Press, 2008. Written for clinicians, this resource provides guidelines for treating schizophrenics suffering from delusions. visions, voices, and disordered thinking.

Maj, Mario, and Norman Sartorius. *Schizophrenia.* Hoboken, N.J.: John Wiley & Sons, 2003. This book, part of a World Psychiatric Association series bringing evidence from empirical studies to clinical practitioners, is an integration of the worldwide research literature on schizophrenia.

Torrey, Edwin Fuller. *Surviving Schizophrenia: A Family Manual.* 5th ed. New York: Collins, 2006. One of the best books available for the general reader on schizophrenia. Intended primarily for members of families that have a schizophrenic family member, this book should be read by everyone who is interested in the disorder, including mental health workers. Torrey writes wonderfully and pulls no punches when dealing with outmoded theories and poorly done experiments.

Zahavi, Dan, ed. *Exploring the Self: Philosophical and Psychopathological Perspectives on Self-Experience.* Philadelphia: John Benjamins, 2000. Six of the thirteen papers, presented originally at a conference at the University of Copenhagen in May 1999, deal with matters relating to schizophrenia.

SENSATION AND PERCEPTION

Berkowitz, Leonard. *Consequences and Causes of Feelings.* New York: Cambridge University Press, 2000. In seven chapters arranged under four major headings, Berkowitz deals with the psychological effects feelings have on human behavior and the consequences of such feelings.

Classen, Constance. *Worlds of Senses: Exploring the Senses in History and Across Cultures.* New York: Routledge, 1993. An anthropological approach. Considers literacy as anticulture in the Andes. Discusses the words and worlds of the senses.

Gifford, Don. *The Farther Shore: A Natural History of Perception.* New York: Vintage Books, 1991. Considers the history of the senses and sensation as well as the history of perception.

Goldstein, E. Bruce. *Sensation and Perception.* Belmont, Calif.: Wadsworth, 2009. Excellent overview of the field of sensation and perception. Chapters focus on subjects dealing with vision, hearing, and touch, but Goldstein also adds chapters on perceived speech and the chemical senses.

Howes, David, ed. *The Varieties of Sensory Experience: A Sourcebook in the Anthropology of the Senses.* Toronto, Ont.: University of Toronto Press, 1991. Focuses on anthropological considerations of the senses and perception.

Humphrey, Nicholas. *A History of the Mind.* New York: Copernicus, 1992. Presents a history of the senses and sensation, and a history of consciousness, the mind, and body.

Laming, Donald R. J. *The Measurement of Sensation.* New York: Oxford University Press, 1997. Questions whether sensation can be measured effectively. Considers the physiological basis of sensation. Suggests ways of scaling sensation. Shows how to judge relations between sensations.

Matlin, M. W. *Sensation and Perception.* Boston: Allyn & Bacon, 2009. Matlin's book is an introductory text covering all general areas of sensation and perception. Themes carried throughout the text are intended to provide additional structure for the material; these themes reflect the author's eclectic, theoretical orientation.

Sekuler, Robert, and Robert R. Blake. *Perception.* 5th ed. New York: McGraw-Hill, 2006. Sekuler and Blake attempt to explain seeing, hearing, smelling, and tasting to students of perception. Extensive use of illustrations allows the reader to understand materials more fully. A series of short illustrations is also utilized by the authors to depict additional concepts.

SEXUALITY

Aron, Arthur, and Elaine N. Aron. *Perspectives on Close Relationships.* Boston: Allyn & Bacon, 1994. Links the success of close relationships to self-understanding and fulfillment in other walks of life.

Bieschke, Kathleen J., Ruperto M. Perez, and Kurt A. DeBord, eds. *Handbook of Counseling and Psychotherapy with Lesbian, Gay, Bisexual, and Transgender Clients.* 2d ed. Washington, D.C.: American Psychological Association, 2007. This work explores the scientific study of the psychology of gay, lesbian, bisexual, and transgender individuals. Studies include GLBT identity, mental health issues facing these populations, and effective psychotherapeutic strategies with GLBT individuals and couples.

Blakemore, Judith E., Sheri A. Berenbaum, and Lynn S. Liben. *Gender Development.* New York: Psychology Press, 2008. A well-written textbook on all aspects of gender development and sexuality that gives fair coverage of biological and social influences across family, peers, and school and media contexts.

Brookey, Robert Alan. *Reinventing the Male Homosexual: The Rhetoric and Power of the Gay Gene.* Bloomington: Indiana University Press, 2002. Discusses recent attempts to identify a genetic component to sexual orientation and the cultural effect of such research on gay identity.

Buss, David M., and Neil M. Malamuth, eds. *Sex, Power, Conflict.* New York: Oxford University Press, 1996. These twelve essays deal with such questions as sexual aggression, male aggression, and the relationship between power and aggression.

Dean, Tim, and Christopher Lane, eds. *Homosexuality and Psychoanalysis.* Chicago: University of Chicago Press, 2001. Reviews the often-conflicted relationship between psychoanalytic theory and homosexuality. Covers the attitudes toward homosexuality found in the writings of Sigmund Freud, Melanie Klein, Wilhelm Reich, Jacques Lacan, and Michel Foucault, among others.

Kinsey, Alfred C., and Paul H. Gebhard. *Sexual Behavior in the Human Female.* New York: Pocket Books, 1973. Originally published in 1953, this sequel to *Sexual Behavior in the Human Male* presents the other half of human sexuality.

Kinsey, Alfred C., Wardell B. Pomeroy, and Charles E. Martin. *Sexual Behavior in the Human Male.* Bloomington: Indiana University Press, 1998. Originally published in 1948, this landmark study of sexual behavior, based on extensive interviews, changed forever the ways in which Americans viewed human sexuality.

Libby, Roger W. *The Naked Truth About Sex: A Guide to Intelligent Sexual Choices for Teenagers and Twentysomethings.* Topanga, Calif.: Freedom Press, 2006. A guide for adolescents and young men and women about sex, containing contraceptive and other information. Also deals with gay and lesbian teenagers.

SLEEP

Cooper, Rosemary, ed. *Sleep.* New York: Chapman and Hall, 1994. Considerations of the function of sleep, the classification of sleep disorders, sleep apnea, and such matters as sleeping at high altitudes.

Dement, William C. *The Promise of Sleep.* New York: Dell, 2000. Dement, founder of the sleep disorders clinic at Stanford University, provides a nontechnical, personal report of current findings in sleep research, drawing a connection between sleep and general health. Offers a guide to remedying sleep deficits and alleviating insomnia.

Empson, Jacob, and Michael B. Wang. *Sleep and Dreaming.* 3d ed. New York: St. Martin's Press, 2002. An overview of scientific sleep research and popular beliefs about sleep.

Fosgate, Blanchard. *Sleep Psychologically Considered with Reference to Sensation and Memory.* New York: Da Capo Press, 1982. Considers sleep and dreaming in relation to the unconscious mind. Links sleep with memory. Suggests that dreaming is a form of remembering. Shows how sleep promotes memory by fixing ideas in the mind.

Hobson, J. Allan. *Dreaming: An Introduction to the Science of Sleep.* New York: Oxford University Press, 2005. Traces theories and physiological research into sleep and dreaming since the 1950's. Addresses dreaming disorders such as nightmares, night terrors, and sleepwalking.

Houvel, Michael. *The Paradox of Sleep: The Story of Dreaming.* Translated by Lawrence Garey. Cambridge, Mass.: MIT Press, 2001. Explores the func-

tions and natural history of dreaming and dream memories. Regards sleep as the guardian of psychological individuality.

Kryger, Meir H., Thomas Roth, and William C. Dement, eds. *Principles and Practice of Sleep Medicine.* 4th ed. Philadelphia: Elsevier/Saunders, 2005. An examination of sleep and its disorders. Includes bibliography references and an index.

Monk, Timothy H., ed. *Sleep, Sleepiness, and Performance.* New York: John Wiley & Sons, 1991. Extremely interesting contribution on circadian rhythms. Material on sleep-wake cycles, effects of sleep deprivation, and several sleep disorders.

Rosen, Marvin. *Sleep and Dreaming.* Philadelphia: Chelsea House, 2006. Addresses topics such as the biology of sleep, sleep disorders, dreams, and the application of dreams in psychotherapy.

Schenck, Carlos H. *Sleep: A Groundbreaking Guide to the Mysteries, the Problems, and the Solutions.* New York: Avery, 2008. A sleep researcher looks at all aspects of sleep and discusses some unusual conditions that can develop related to sleep, such as sleepwalking, sleep terrors, and sleep-related eating disorders.

SOCIAL PSYCHOLOGY

Berkowitz, Leonard, ed. *Advances in Experimental Social Psychology.* Orlando, Fla.: Academic Press, 1964-present. This series appears annually and deals with all aspects of experimental social psychology.

Dovidio, John F., Jane Allyn Piliavin, David A. Schroeder, and Louis A. Penner. *The Social Psychology of Prosocial Behavior.* Mahwah, N.J.: Lawrence Erlbaum Associates, 2006. Evaluates new concepts explored in twenty-first century research, such as behavioral genetics and neuroscience and interdisciplinary approaches involving neuroscientists, biologists, sociologists, social and evolutionary psychologists, and experts in other fields. Other topics addressed are how groups influence planned prosocial behavior and how givers and recipients are affected by altruism.

Eichelberger, Julia. *Prophets of Recognition: Ideology and the Individual in Novels by Ralph Ellison, Toni Morrison, Saul Bellow, and Eudora Welty.* Baton Rouge: Louisiana State University Press, 1999. Considers four contemporary American authors from the standpoint of social psychology and documentation.

Farr, Robert M. *The Roots of Modern Social Psychology, 1872-1954.* New York: Basil Blackwell, 1996. Considers social psychology an American phenomenon. Traces its history. Places special emphasis on George Herbert Mead, a leading philosopher and pioneer in modern social psychology.

Gilbert, David T., Susan T. Fiske, and Gardner Lindzey, eds. *Handbook of Social Psychology.* New York: McGraw-Hill, 1998. A serviceable quick reference book in the field of social psychology.

Henrich, Natalie S., and Joseph Henrich. *Why Humans Cooperate: A Cultural and Evolutionary Explanation.* Oxford, England: Oxford University Press, 2007. Analyzes how ethnic, heritage, and familial factors influenced members of an Iraqi Chaldean community residing in Detroit, Michigan, to pursue and accept cooperation.

Kotre, John. *Outliving the Self: How to Live on in Future Generations.* New York: W. W. Norton, 1996. Interesting and useful case studies in social psychology, including both children and adults. Considerable emphasis on social psychologist Erik Erikson.

Rickels, Laurence A., ed. *Acting Out in Groups.* Minneapolis: University of Minnesota Press, 1999. Several of this volume's fourteen essays deal with the group dynamics of forms of popular culture such as the talk show. An interesting essay on the trial of host Jenny Jones following a murder resulting from the outing of a gay man on her television show.

Willis-Esqueda, Cynthia. *Motivational Aspects of Prejudice and Racism.* New York: Springer, 2008. The motivation behind prejudice was an area of study in social psychology that fell out of interest. However, recent research is demonstrating that motivational aspects in prejudice, especially racism, are compelling.

STRESS

Bloch, Sidney, and Bruce S. Singh. *Understanding Troubled Minds: A Guide to Mental Illness and Its Treatment.* New York: New York University Press, 1999. Chapter 6 in this twenty-two chapter book is entitled "Coping with Stress." Details ways to handle stress and psychological tensions.

Brannon, Linda, and Jess Feist. *Health Psychology: An Introduction to Behavior and Health.* 7th ed. Belmont, Calif.: Wadsworth Cengage Learning, 2009. Written for undergraduate students. A very readable overview of the field of health psychology.

Provides the reader with chapters on stress and health, and various stress-related diseases.

Fink, George, et al., eds. *Encyclopedia of Stress.* 2d ed. 4 vols. Boston: Academic Press, 2007. This multivolume set looks at stress from all aspects, including its physiological effects.

Greenberg, Jerrold S. *Comprehensive Stress Management.* 11th ed. New York: McGraw-Hill, 2009. Looks at what stress is and how it affects people, and contains numerous chapters on stress-reduction methods.

Kahn, Ada P., ed. *The Encyclopedia of Stress and Stress-Related Diseases.* 2d ed. New York: Facts on File, 2005. This encyclopedia of stress, while covering all aspects, focuses on diseases caused or made worse by stress.

Karren, Keith J., et al. *Mind/Body Health: The Effects of Attitudes, Emotions, and Relationships.* 4th ed. San Francisco: Pearson/Benjamin Cummings, 2009. Argues that there is a disease-prone personality and looks at the general connection between stress and disease.

Kendall-Tackett, Kathleen, ed. *The Psychoneuroimmunology of Chronic Disease: Exploring the Links Between Inflammation, Stress, and Illness.* Washington, D.C.: American Psychological Association, 2009. Examines the relationship between stress, inflammation, and disease, particularly chronic disease.

Lovallo, William R. *Stress and Health: Biological and Psychological Interactions.* 2d ed. Thousand Oaks, Calif.: Sage Publications, 2005. This book examines the biological links between thoughts and feelings and the potential health changes that can result from stress. Also discusses how individual differences in physiology and in perceptions and evaluations of events can have physical and long-term health consequences.

Miley, William M. *The Psychology of Well-Being.* Westport, Conn.: Praeger, 1999. Chapter entitled "Dealing with Stress" examines causes of stress. Other chapters deal with the stress related to obesity, a sedentary lifestyle, or such illnesses as AIDS, cancer, heart disease, or diabetes.

Monat, Alan, Richard S. Lazarus, and Gretchen Reevy, eds. *The Praeger Handbook on Stress and Coping.* Westport, Conn.: Praeger, 2007. In this manual on stress and coping strategies, Lazarus describes the link between emotion and stress in a section on the concept of stress. Other sections cover stress and illness (heart disease, gastrointestinal disorders, and depression) and post-traumatic stress (terrorism and violence).

Ritchie, Sheila, and Peter Martin. *Motivational Management.* Brookfield, Vt.: Gower, 1999. One fourteen-page chapter deals specifically with stress and its implications in the workplace.

Schroeder, David A., ed. *Social Dilemmas: Perspectives on Individuals and Groups.* Westport, Conn.: Praeger, 1995. Most of the eleven essays in this book deal with the stress accompanying social dilemmas. Suggests ways of dealing with it.

Sher, Leo, ed. *Psychological Factors and Cardiovascular Disorders: The Role of Stress and Psychosocial Influences.* New York: Nova Science, 2009. Examines the link between stress and other psychological factors and heart disease.

SUBSTANCE ABUSE

Doweiko, Harold E. *Concepts of Chemical Dependency.* 7th ed. Belmont, Calif.: Thomson Brooks/Cole, 2009. Consideration of the causes and manifestations of major addictions, including alcohol, tobacco, and both prescription and illegal drugs. Considers means of coping with substance abuse problems.

Horne, Arthur M., and Mark S. Kiselica, eds. *Handbook of Counseling Boys and Adolescent Males: A Practitioner's Guide.* Thousand Oaks, Calif.: Sage Publications, 1999. Of particular interest is Richard C. Page's "Counseling Substance-Abusing Young Males," the book's last chapter.

Schaler, Jeffrey A. *Addiction Is a Choice.* Chicago: Open Court, 2002. Solid presentation of compulsive behavior as related to substance abuse and addiction. Considers the psychological aspects of choice among substance abusers.

Solowij, Nadia. *Cannabis and Cognitive Functioning.* New York: Cambridge University Press, 2006. Considers how long-term use of cannabis affects people's ability to think. Concerned with how the effects of drugs can be reversed when use is discontinued.

Walters, Glenn O. *The Addiction Concept: Working Hypothesis or Self-Fulfilling Prophesy?* Boston: Allyn & Bacon, 1999. Walters deals with addiction in the light of its biological, psychological, sociological, and pragmatic constructs.

TESTING

Bormuth, John R. *On the Theory of Achievement Test Items.* Chicago: University of Chicago Press, 1970. Presents solid information fruitfully supplemented by Peter Menzel's excellent essay on the linguistic bases of the theory of writing test items.

Kaagan, Stephen S. *Leadership Lessons: From a Life of Character and Purpose in Public Affairs.* Lanham, Md.: University Press of America, 1997. The twenty-two page chapter entitled "Reestablishing the Educational Testing Service" is relevant to those interested in tests and measurements.

Kapes, Jerome T., Marjorie Moran Mastie, and Edwin A. Whitfeld. *A Counselor's Guide to Career Assessment Instruments.* Broken Arrow, Okla.: National Career Development Association in cooperation with the Association for Assessment in Counseling and Education, 2008. This resource contains descriptions of more than fifty tests. In addition to test descriptions, it also provides publisher information, test reviews, and critiques.

Lemann, Nicholas. *The Big Test: The Secret History of the American Meritocracy.* New York: Farrar, Straus and Giroux, 2000. Presents an accurate history of intelligence testing, discussing elitism as it pertains to such testing. Emphasis on Henry Chauncey's contributions to standardized testing.

Lidz, Carol, and Julian G. Elliott, eds. *Dynamic Assessment: Prevailing Models and Applications.* New York: JAI, 2000. Useful suggestions for the psychological testing of handicapped children. Sensitive presentation of material on cognition in children.

Murdoch, Stephen. *IQ: A Smart History of a Failed Idea.* Hoboken, N.J.: J. Wiley & Sons, 2007. A critical assessment of IQ testing and the uses to which it is put.

Naglieri, Jack A., and Sam Goldstein, eds. *Practitioner's Guide to Assessing Intelligence and Achievement.* Hoboken, N.J.: Wiley, 2009. Describes the theory and practice related to a number of popular intelligence and achievement assessment tests.

Reynolds, Cecil R., and Randy W. Kamphaus, eds. *Handbook of Psychological and Educational Assessment of Children.* 2d ed. New York: Guilford Press, 2003. The contributions to this resource deal with psychological tests for children and with achievement tests in general.

R. Baird Shuman

WEB SITE DIRECTORY

AAASP Online: Association for the Advancement of Applied Sport Psychology

http://www.aaasponline.org/index2.html

Offers valuable background information that explains the nature of sport psychology, the growing variety and number of people who use it, the services provided by sport psychologists, and how to find a qualified sport psychology professional. The site also has a member services page which includes AAASP's code of ethics and explains how to become an AAASP-certified consultant. Other features include a consultant finder, a list of AAASP publications, and links to other sport psychology sites.

American Academy of Child and Adolescent Psychiatry (AACAP)

http://www.aacap.org

This organization hopes its site will aid the treatment and understanding of children and youth who have behavioral, mental, or developmental disorders. Particularly useful are the factsheets for family members and other caregivers. The Facts for Families series of more than fifty downloadable texts includes discussions of alcohol, bed-wetting, divorce, guns, lying, pregnancy, talking about sex, and violent behavior. The site also provides a downloadable glossary of symptoms and mental illnesses that might affect teenagers; AACAP policy statements on topics such as juvenile death sentences and psychoactive medications for children and youth; press releases about children online and the influence of music and music videos; and information for professionals.

American Association of Suicidology (AAS)

http://www.suicidology.org/web/guest/home

This site's sections include a detailed background document featuring a focused outline for understanding and helping someone who is suicidal; book recommendations and reviews; recent suicide news; search forms for locating crisis centers or support groups by state and city; guidance on obtaining organizational or individual AAS certification; and a resource page, listing suicide statistics, school guidelines, specifics on suicide among youth and the elderly, and resources for the clinician who has lost a patient to suicide.

American Psychological Association (APA)

http://www.apa.org

This extensive site, from the world's largest professional association for psychologists, offers a wide range of information for a variety of audiences. Though content-rich and detailed, the site is clearly organized and easy to navigate. The main page has sections providing recent news; a featured article; classified ads; portals for psychologists, students, and the public; membership information; APA books, videos, and databases; and quick links. Resources for the public include full text reports from APA's PsycPORT news site; links to information pages on numerous topics (including addiction, anxiety, depression, eating disorders, ethics, and teens); and links to help pages (including finding a psychologist, a psychology glossary, and educational resources). Resources for psychologists include job search information, conferences, ethics statements, practice-related information (such as record-keeping guidelines), and patient brochures.

Association for the Study of Dreams

http://www.asdreams.org/index.htm

This international, nonprofit organization's site features information about the international conference; information about the association's magazine, *Dream Time*, and its journal, *Dreaming*, educational pages, with answers to common questions about dreams and nightmares, and a science project file; the association's ethics statement; a classified list of dream-related and dream-sharing Web sites and e-mail lists; and a calendar of scheduled events.

Attention Deficit Disorder Association

http://www.add.org/

This is the official Web site of the Attention Deficit Disorder Association (ADDA), an organization dedicated to the needs of those who suffer from the disorder and the professionals who treat them. The home page provides updates on the most recent developments in research and links to support groups and general information pertaining to the disorder. Also posted are the ADDA's newsletter, a weekly blog, and relevant articles. Furthermore, there is a list of appropriate questions about attention deficit disorder that patients may ask a doctor.

Autism Collaboration
http://www.autism.org

This Web site contains the Collaboration's statement of purpose and discusses its Parents as Partners program, which outlines the group's general philosophy: that parents of children with autism can spark change in research and that autism is not an incurable disease but a mental disorder that can be remedied. The site also acts a portal to other autism-focused Web sites, such as Autism Research Institute, Autism Society of America, and Talk About Curing Autism (TACA).

Birth Psychology
http://www.birthpsychology.com

This site is provided by the Association for Pre- and Perinatal Psychology and Health (APPAH). Its sections include life before birth (fetal senses, sound, prebirth communication, and prenatal memory and learning); birth and the origins of violence; the birth scene (circumcision, obstetrics, and more); healing of prenatal and perinatal trauma; abstracts and index for APPAH's *Journal of Prenatal and Perinatal Psychology and Health*; a classified bibliography of one hundred books, videos, and journals; and a current list of practitioners and programs.

C. G. Jung Page
http://www.cgjungpage.org

This full-featured site aids novice readers with an introduction to Jungian psychology in the form of a Jung Lexicon. The site's Jungian Resources Page includes links to the Web sites of institutes and societies offering Jungian training. There are also links to the numerous full-text analytical psychology articles from the *Journal of Analytical Psychology*, covering 2003 to 2008; and film commentaries, book reviews, and literary articles employing Jungian criticism.

Classics in the History of Psychology
http://psychclassics.yorku.ca

This site collects important public-domain scholarly texts from psychology and related fields. There are more than two hundred articles and twenty-five books, with links to more than two hundred related works on other sites. To aid undergraduates, some texts are accompanied by introductory essays written for the site. The texts can be accessed by author or by topic (including behaviorism, intelligence testing, psychoanalysis and psychotherapy, cognition, and women and psychology). Within topics, texts are arranged chronologically. Users can also search the entire site by keyword.

Criminal Profiling Research
http://www.criminalprofiling.ch

This Swiss site focuses on presenting the results of scientific research. Besides a detailed, referenced introduction to the topic, it offers brief accounts of how profiling is used in the United States and Europe, a case analysis page, bibliographies of books and journal articles, links to sites explaining how profiling is done, information on profiling as a career, and a discussion board.

depressedteens.com
http://www.depressedteens.com/indexnf.html

This educational site strives to help teenagers and their parents and teachers recognize and understand the symptoms of adolescent depression and ensure that depressed teenagers get help. An essential part of the site is a podcast series called Flipswitch, which covers topics ranging from adjusting to college to isolation and loneliness. Other areas of the site are a factsheet on adolescent depression and an online store that sells books and videos.

Dr. Ruth Westheimer
http://drruth.com/

Dr. Ruth is a highly visible, longtime sex therapist who has written several books (including *Dr. Ruth's Encyclopedia of Sex*) and worked as a professor at New York University, a lecturer, and a television and radio commentator. This content-rich site features a biographical sketch of Dr. Ruth and a wide-ranging archive of nearly five hundred question-and-answer topics. The latter include affairs, childhood trauma, fantasy, homosexuality and bisexuality, infidelity, sex aids, sexually transmitted diseases, and sexual dysfunctions. In addition, the site provides a monthly archive of more than four hundred varied, practical, and fun-loving sex tips dating to November, 2006.

Eating Disorder Referral and Information Center (EDRIC)

http://www.edreferral.com

EDRIC provides information for friends and family members as well as treatment referrals for individuals with all forms of eating disorders. The sections of the site include a referral form for searching for a therapist or treatment center, job openings at treatment centers, treatment scholarships, and recommended books and Web sites. Addresses such topics as how family members can deal with a loved one who has an eating disorder. Also examines binge eating, causes, assessment, treatment, consequences, body image, introductory information on specific disorders, and eating disorders among males, athletes, and celebrities.

ECT.org: Information About Electroconvulsive Therapy

http://ECT.org

This attractive site aims to be the Web's most comprehensive source of Electroconvulsive Therapy (ECT), or "shock therapy," information. Juli Lawrence, the site's creator, had ECT in 1994 and hopes her site, which discusses all sides of the topic, will help others considering ECT make an informed decision. The site provides attractive, clearly arranged links (with annotations) to information on these topics: effects (particularly memory loss and, possibly, brain damage); resources (studies, statistics, and official statements from organizations); news (breaking stories, personal stories, lawsuits, legislative battles); self-help (alternatives to ECT); community (message boards and event calendars); and the Hall of Shame ("the very worst ECT practitioners and researchers").

Encyclopedia of Psychology

http://www.psychology.org

This site, "intended to facilitate browsing in any area of psychology," provides access to nearly two thousand Web sites. The main method of access is by category—including careers, environment behavior relationships (with fifty-three subcategories and nearly one thousand links), organizations, para-

digms and theories, people and history, publications, and resources. All categories are further divided into subtopics. The Web page for each subtopic will include two types of links: those which go to texts and those which go to Web sites. An annotation for each site is generally provided.

Explorations in Learning and Instruction: The Theory into Practice Database

http://tip.psychology.org

This site provides brief but detailed summaries of fifty major theories of human learning and instruction. All the theories have extensive scientific support, and the summaries are drawn from published primary and secondary writings. The summaries include the name of the theory's originator, an overview of the theory, its principles and application, an example, references for further study, and sometimes a video clip or Web site link. The theories include adult learning, andragogy, cognitive dissonance, Criterion Referenced Instruction, experiential learning, lateral thinking, multiple intelligences, operant conditioning, and more.

Freud Net

http://www.psychoanalysis.org/

The site of the New York Psychoanalytic Society and Institute. The site features information on training, education, and treatment, and a schedule of events, including lectures, held at the institute's auditorium. The site also offers information pertaining to the Abraham A. Brill Library, which houses more than forty thousand books, periodicals, and reprints focused on the field of psychoanalysis.

Great Ideas in Personality

http://www.personalityresearch.org

This site deals with scientific research in personality psychology. It provides detailed information on personality theories that are empirically testable, grouping them into thirteen sections. The sections include behaviorism, evolutionary psychology, attachment theory, basic emotions, personality disorders, interpersonal theory, and more. The page describing each theory includes a brief description, the theory's beginning date, names of the theorists involved, references to published works, and links to additional Web sources. The site also features sections on personality in general, practical information for psychology students, links to personality journal sites, and to personality course sites for professors.

Health Emotions Research Institute
http://www.healthemotions.org

This clear, attractive site of the University of Wisconsin's Health Emotions Research Institute provides information on studies of positive emotions, their influence on the body, and the implications of this research for preventing disease, affecting definitions of health, and fostering resilience. The site explains the institute's mission and its current projects (both human and private)—including biological consequences of meditation, biological substrates of resilience, and biological bases of positive affective styles.

Holistic-online.com
http://holistic-online.com

This comprehensive site serves to provide accurate information on both conventional and alternative treatment options for a variety of conditions. It emphasizes treatment of the whole person, prevention of illness, and self care. Separate pages are devoted to conditions such as anxiety, back pain, depression, insomnia, migraine, panic attack, seasonal affective disorder, and stress. The alternative therapies featured include biofeedback, guided imagery, humor therapy, hydrotherapy, imagery, light therapy, massage, meditation, prayer healing, and yoga.

The Humor Project, Inc.
http://www.humorproject.com

The Humor Project, founded in 1977 by Joel Goodman, focuses on the positive power of humor by training individuals and organizations (through its lectures, workshops, conferences, and publications) to use humor and creativity. The site's playful spirit is immediately apparent in the visitor counter, with its constantly whirling numbers. The impressive list of clients who have used the project's services includes American Express, Kodak, Xerox, Mobil Oil, Harvard University, and the American Hospital Association. The site provides descriptions of the speaker's bureau program offerings, the annual workshop, and the annual international humor conference; an on-line bookstore; a daily article, interview, and reader's "di-jest"; a spotlight column; and "today's laffirmation."

Internet Mental Health
http://www.mentalhealth.com

This award-winning site, established in 1995, is intended for both professionals and the general public. It functions as an encyclopedia for the fifty-eight most common mental disorders. For each disorder, the site gives both the American and European description, treatment information (meant for therapists and written by the site's author), research information, booklets prepared by professional organizations and support groups, and magazine articles. The site has links to online diagnostic programs for personality, anxiety, mood, eating, and substance-abuse disorders, as well as for schizophrenia and attention-deficit/hyperactivity disorder (ADHD). It also provides encyclopedic information on common psychiatric medications, a mental-health magazine, and links to popular mental-health sites.

Internet Psychology Lab
http://www.ipsych.com

This award-winning site provides a multimedia, interactive system for psychology lab instruction at the University of Illinois, enabling the university's students—and visitors to the site—to work remotely on lessons, experiments, and demonstrations. The instruction modules include cognition, memory and learning, visual perception, and auditory perception. Experiments include the Stroop Effect, choice reaction time, visual cognition, basic reaction time, and chimeric faces.

MedlinePlus: Phobias
http://www.nlm.nih.gov/medlineplus/phobias.html

MedlinePlus is a service of the U.S. National Library of Medicine and the National Institutes of Health and provides a variety of health information. The phobias page offers a general definition as well as links to Web pages of official medical organizations, such as the Mayo Clinic. The MedlinePlus site is divided into six major categories—Basics, Learn More, Multimedia and Cool Tools, Research, Reference Shelf, and For You—each of which is subdivided into additional sections. The Basics page provides access to the American Psychiatric Association's facts page about phobias, while the Reference Shelf has a glossary of terms related to phobias and a list of organizations that deal with the disorder.

Memory and Reality: Website of the False Memory Syndrome Foundation

http://fmsonline.org

This foundation works to prevent False Memory Syndrome, investigate reasons for its spread, and help families affected by it. Includes a detailed FAQ; the current newsletter; a searchable archive of newsletter issues back to 2003 in both text and PDF formats and to 1992 in text format only; a document explaining hypnosis and hypnotic susceptibility and their role in creating false memories; information about *USA v. Peterson, Seward, Mueck, Keraga, and Davis*, the first criminal trial to bring charges against therapists regarding false memories; a detailed page dealing with retractors; and discussions of scientific studies on whether people can actually repress memories and how false memories can be engendered.

Mental Health America

http://www.nmha.org/

Formerly the National Mental Health Association, Mental Health America is a group composed of people who have suffered through mental illness, their friends and family members, advocates for mental-health awareness, and doctors and others in the mental-healthcare field. The Web site includes a section entitled "Fact Sheets" that provides information grouped by audience (African American, troops and military families), issue (depression, eating disorders), and disorders and treatments (Alzheimer's disease, obsessive-compulsive disorder). Also listed on the site are FAQs, a crisis hotline, and ways to get involved with the organization.

MHN: Mental Help Net

http://mentalhelp.net

Developed in 1994, this award-winning site strives "to promote mental health and wellness education and advocacy." The site includes a drop-down menu with a list of featured topics, including addictions, anxiety disorders, bipolar disorder, and schizophrenia. Each topic is accompanied by a list of resources with links to relevant Web sites. Furthermore, the site features articles on a variety of topics related to mental health posted by professionals.

NAMI: The Nation's Voice on Mental Illness

http://www.nami.org

This site represents the National Alliance on Mental Illness (NAMI), a support and advocacy organization for friends and family of people with severe mental illnesses—and for the individuals themselves. The site contains a search form for locating NAMI affiliate organizations; information about the NAMI helpline; factsheets on specific illnesses, treatments, and medications; purchase information for NAMI's books, videos, brochures, and magazines; public policy information and statements; and a research page with links to NAMI research reports.

National Association for Self-Esteem (NASE)

http://www.self-esteem-nase.org

This association works to integrate self-esteem into American society and thus enhance the personal worth and happiness of every individual. The site provides a review of research on self-esteem, relating it to problems such as substance abuse, violence, crime, teenage pregnancy, and suicide. There are also articles from NASE's newsletter, a categorized reading list, a list of published self-esteem educational programs, and a description of NASE's Parent Link Network for raising socially responsible children.

Positive Psychology

http://psych.upenn.edu/seligman/pospsy.htm

This content-rich site is maintained by Martin Seligman, past president of the American Psychological Association and a researcher on positive psychology, optimism, and learned helplessness. The site offers several readable and well-documented articles, columns, and book chapters by Seligman that define and explore the parameters of positive psychology. There are also links for past positive psychology conferences, additional readings, and video.

Postpartum Support International

http://postpartum.net/

This Web site is dedicated to offering support to parents and families suffering through postpartum depression. Postpartum Support International's site provides numerous resources, including links to and phone numbers of support groups. Articles pertaining to different aspects of the postpartum experience share space with testimonials, research findings, and other news. An online bookstore is also available.

Procrastination Research Group (PRG)

http://www.carleton.ca/~tpychyl

This clear, attractive site is provided by a university learning group at Carleton University's psychology department (Ottawa, Canada), but it collects research and information on procrastination worldwide. The Research Resources section includes a featured journal article, summaries of student papers (undergraduate through doctoral levels) written by the PRG, and a comprehensive procrastination bibliography. The site also has a useful self-help page. The latter includes a brief outline of signs of procrastination, suggested strategies for reducing procrastination, a list of recommended readings, and a concise grouping of links to other sites.

Psybersquare: Strength and Healing Through Community and Self-Help

http://www.psybersquare.com/index.html

This award-winning site aims to provide compassionate advice and guidance to enable visitors to function well in their lives. Consists mainly of brief, warm, and helpful articles (many written by the site's author and most accompanied by recommended readings). Categories include "Me," "Us," "Family," "Work," "Women," "Men," "Anxiety," "Depression," and "Recovery." Each category covers a handful of topics. "Me" includes essays on "getting unstuck," resentment, expectations, learning new tools for strength and health, gratitude, motivation, self-esteem, holidays, self-assertion, and self-improvement. The site also included the "Winner's Circle," subscription service featuring interactive self-help tools.

Psych Central: Dr. Grohol's Mental Health Page

http://psychcentral.com/grohol.htm

This award-winning site, in existence since 1992, provides links to more than 4,432 Web sites that have been personally reviewed by the author. Its main access point is the Resources section, which consists of twenty-one categories (some as specific as "Bipolar" and "Attack on America," others as broad as "Professional Psychology Resources"). Each category ("Sexuality and Gender," for example) is further subdivided into topics (such as men's issues, symptoms, and women's issues) and/or formats (such as books or support groups). The page for each of the 4,432 Web sites gives a brief but usually detailed description of the site, the date last updated, the number of hits it has received from *Psych Central*, the number of votes from *Psych Central* users, and its rating by those users. Besides the Web site links, *Psych Central* provides links to numerous blogs highlighting mental health and psychology.

Psychology

http://psychology.about.com/mbody.htm

This content-rich, attractively formatted site is part of About.com's Homework Help series. About.com focuses on using people (its guides) to carefully select and organize links, texts, forums, and how-to's to answer questions. The site's main organization is its nine Psychology Basics, including brain and behavior, states of consciousness, memory, social psychology, and more. The site also allows the user to browse numerous topics on psychology, which provide definitions, basic information, and links to related articles, and career resources. The site has numerous ads, many of which are related to psychology.

The Psychology of Cyberspace

http://www-usr.rider.edu/~suler/psycyber/psycyber.html

This Web site, dubbed a hypertext by its author, John Suler of Rider University, outlines the psychological effects of Internet usage on modern society. Suler's text is divided into five topics, which examine how an individual or group functions in cyberspace. Suler discusses issues such as online gender switching, identity creation, and relationship building. An article index is part of a drop-down menu that also includes a blog and a search engine.

Psychology Information Online

http://www.psychologyinfo.com

This site provides a wide range of information (aimed at consumers, college students, and psychologists) on the practice of psychology. The information falls into these categories: psychotherapy and counseling, diagnosis and disorders, psychological testing and evaluation, other forms of treatment, behavior therapy, forensic psychiatry, and psychological consultations for legal situations. There are separate access points for the three categories of users. In addition, users can consult the navigation guide, the list of links, or the alphabetical subject index for each category.

Psychology Matters

http://psychologymatters.apa.org/

This is a Web site that highlights the everyday usefulness of psychology and is divided into nineteen research subheads, including sexuality, memory, parenting, safety, and sports. Each category provides at least one, but sometimes more than ten, articles on a variety of topics related to psychology. The homepage also includes a brief definition of psychology, a history of the science and a glossary of its terms, and resources for better understanding of psychology's practical application.

Psychology Today

http://www.psychologytoday.com/

Psychology Today is a comprehensive Web site designed in a bright and easy-to-navigate manner. Its central feature is a compilation of blogs from therapists and other professionals. Also included are a series of quizzes, with topics such as relationships and arguing style, that allow visitors to become better acquainted with the inner workings of their own minds. The site also provides a detailed list of disorders and other topics and a built-in search engine in which a therapist can easily be located by city or ZIP code.

Psychology Virtual Library

http://www.dialogical.net/psychology/index.html

This clear, attractive site is part of the World Wide Web Virtual Library, which evaluates each site it includes. The seventeen categories include academic psychology, books, journals, university psychology departments, clinical social work, directories of psychology sites, mental health, history of psychology, and more. Each category has its own subsections. The Stress Virtual Library includes, for example, links for books and publishers, e-mail lists and newsgroups, mental health resources, professional organizations, stress management, and commercial products. The links on each page are annotated.

RxList: The Internet Drug Index

http://www.rxlist.com

This site, founded in 1995, is maintained by Neil Sandow, a licensed, experienced California pharmacist. The site's primary content includes FAQs on thousands of popular drugs, hundreds of professional monographs, and hundreds of patient-oriented monographs. Visitors can search for drugs by brand name, generic name, ID imprint code, or NDC code. Each FAQ explains the purpose of the drug, who should not use it, how to take it, potential problems, and what to do if you miss a dose or overdose yourself. Other features include a search page for alternatives (such as homeopathies or herbal remedies) and a list of the top prescriptions medications.

schizophrenia.com

http://www.schizophrenia.com

This site was established in 1996 by Brian Chiko in memory of his brother, a schizophrenia patient who committed suicide. Its purpose is to provide, free of charge, accurate information for those who have the disorder or whose lives have been affected by it. The site's introduction to schizophrenia is clear and well organized. Other topics covered are symptoms, treatment, managing depression, preventing suicide, and a history of schizophrenia. Also included is a list of blogs dedicated to the subject.

School Psychology Resources Online

http://www.schoolpsychology.net/

This Web site, run by school psychologist Sandra K. Steingart, is aimed at parents, teachers, and psychologists. It is separated into three easy-to-navigate columns: Features; Specific Conditions, Disorders, Disabilities (which details issues especially encountered by school psychologists, such as suicide, learning disabilities, and drugs and alcohol); and Other Information. The latter section provides links to school psychology journals, laws, and organizations. Also part of the site is a job board, a bookstore, and a daily cartoon.

Self Psychology Page

http://www.selfpsychology.com/

This clear, attractive site is devoted to the study of psychoanalytic self psychology, a theoretical school founded by Heinz Kohut. Its "About" page provides a brief introduction to and definitions of self psychology. There are lengthy bibliographies on self psychology and on its approaches to topics such as children, the elderly, parenting, marital and family therapy, and addictions. The site also provides a news page, a page listing original self psychology papers, and a directory of self psychology training programs.

The Shyness Home Page

http://www.shyness.com

This small site is sponsored by the Shyness Institute in Palo Alto, California. It is grouped into three subsections: Announcements, Shyness Surveys, and Resources. The latter section provides links to, or contact information for, a wide range of other shyness resources, including support groups, treatment centers, and university programs. Also listed are names and affiliations of specific therapists trained to assist those who suffer from social phobia.

Sleepnet.com

http://www.sleepnet.com

Provides information (not medical advice) to improve sleep and aims to link to all noncommercial sleep-information sites. Sections include information on a wide range of sleep disorders and sleep-related conditions (sleep apnea, insomnia, narcolepsy, restless legs, shift work, and circadian rhythms); a detailed glossary; a categorized list of links to news articles; public sleep forums, grouped by topic; and an e-mail newsletter.

Social Phobia/Social Anxiety Association Home Page

http://www.socialphobia.org

The site explains that this frequently misdiagnosed condition is the world's third largest mental-health problem. It provides definitions and background information; a weekly mailing list for individuals with social phobia; a link to the Social Anxiety Institute's page, which offers a variety of therapy programs; and other social-phobia links, including personal testimonies and reading lists.

Social Science Information Gateway: Psychology

http://www.intute.ac.uk/socialsciences/psychology/

This well-organized, attractive site lists and describes high-quality Web sites and texts useful for all audiences. The sites are arranged into seventeen subcategories. Users can search by keyword or browse within the subcategories—including mental health, general psychology, consumer psychology, animal psychology, psychological disorders, developmental psychology, sport psychology, and more. Each subcategory contains further groupings by subject and by type of site. The latter might include books, bibliographies, journals, educational materials, e-mail lists and discussion groups, organizations, research projects, and resource guides. The page describing each Web site gives a descriptive summary, keywords, the site administrator's name and e-mail address, and the site's language.

Society for Light Treatment and Biological Rhythms

http://www.sltbr.org

This society supports those with research or clinical interests in biological rhythm disorders—including seasonal affective disorder, sleep disorders, jet lag, shift work, and premenstrual syndrome—and therapies for those conditions. The information for the general public includes a detailed "Questions and Answers About Seasonal Affective Disorder and Light Therapy" page as well as links to other Web articles and sites about seasonal affective disorder, sleep disorders, melatonin, and circadian rhythm.

Traffic Psychology at the University of Hawaii

http://www.soc.hawaii.edu/leonj/leonj/leonpsy/traffic/tpintro.html

This site, maintained by Dr. Leon James, a psychology professor at the University of Hawaii, has extensive texts and references on the origins and theories of traffic psychology. In addition, James provides an inventory of driving behavior and the psychological aspects of traffic flow, a comprehensive bibliography on driving psychology, a self-test for individuals to determine how they would operate within the nine zones of the driving personality, an outline for presentations on aggressive driving and road rage, and an overview of what James has learned from teaching his traffic psychology course.

The Whole Brain Atlas

http://www.med.harvard.edu/AANLIB

This site is managed by Keith A. Johnson, of the Harvard Medical School and J. Alex Becker of the Massachusetts Institute of Technology. The images it provides were created using magnetic resonance, X-ray computed tomography, and nuclear medicine images. Sections of this award-winning site cover the normal brain (with images of normal aging), cerebrovascular disease, brain tumors, degenerative disorders (such as Alzheimer's and Huntington's diseases), and inflammatory or infectious diseases (such as multiple sclerosis, AIDS dementia, Lyme disease, and herpes).

WholeFamily

http://www.wholefamily.com/index.html

This site, enhanced by its comforting, inviting appearance, offers problem-solving texts (written by credentialed professionals) about situations encountered within family relationships. The site's main portals are its centers for marriage, parents, seniors, and teens. The Marriage Center, for instance, has segments on ten issues (including work, money, in-laws, communication, and parenting). There is a drop-down menu that features twenty commonly asked questions, answered in brief page-long essays, regarding family issues. The site also provides real letters and library links.

Glenn Ellen Starr Stilling;
updated by Christopher Rager

MEDIAGRAPHY

Psychology is a common theme in films, television programs, and literature. Therapists and patients represent many archetypes such as heroes, villains, and victims. Glen O. Gabbard and Krin Gabbard identified 450 films with mental health themes and characters, which they discussed in *Psychiatry and the Cinema* (2d ed. Washington, D.C.: American Psychiatric Press, 1999). Many of those films are adapted from books, plays, and short stories which portray psychology in such genres as drama, comedy, mystery, or horror.

Media depictions of mental health professionals and people with mental illnesses vary in accuracy. Psychiatrists and patients are often stereotyped, misrepresented, and either vilified or celebrated to extremes. Media sometimes distort realities of psychotherapy, cheer pathological behaviors, and show mental health professionals acting unethically, erratically, or irresponsibly. The following list describes selected representatives of psychological media.

FILMS

After Dark, My Sweet
DATE: 1990
DIRECTOR: James Foley

Based on Jim Thompson's 1990 novel of the same title. Mentally ill Collie (Jason Patric) tells Doc Goldman (George Dickerson) about being institutionalized and is advised to seek additional treatment. Instead, he joins a kidnapping plot and is killed. This film is presented from Collie's point of view, which causes audiences to wonder if his perceptions are accurate or blurred by his mental instability.

American Psycho
DATE: 2000
DIRECTOR: Mary Harron

Based on a 1991 novel of the same name by Bret Easton Ellis. A satirical look at the duplicitous life of a 1980's investment banker, Patrick Bateman (Christian Bale), who engages in the superficial rituals of the yuppie culture while alternately committing heinous acts of murder, rape, and torture. The film is meant to lambaste the excesses of the 1980's; however, the reality of the acts that Bateman commits remains ambiguous.

Analyze This
DATE: 1999
DIRECTOR: Harold Ramis

Dr. Ben Sobel (Billy Crystal) treats a gangster (Robert De Niro), who expects his therapist to focus only on him. The sequel, *Analyze That*, in which De Niro's character feigns insanity while in prison and is released to Sobel's care, was released in 2002.

Antonia and Jane
DATE: 1991
DIRECTOR: Beeban Kidron

British. Lifelong friends Antonia McGill (Saskia Reeves) and Jane Hartman (Imelda Staunton) see the same therapist (Brenda Bruce). The women express their emotional feelings, including love, jealousy, and anger concerning their friendship.

Antz
DATE: 1998
DIRECTOR: Erich Darnell and Tim Johnson

Neurotic worker ant Z-4195 (Woody Allen) talks to a psychologist (Paul Mazursky) about his frustrations with work and romantic aspirations with Princess Bala (Sharon Stone).

As Good as It Gets
DATE: 1997
DIRECTOR: James L. Brooks

Melvin (Jack Nicholson) has obsessive-compulsive disorder. He begins taking his psychotropic medication when he falls in love with waitress Carol (Helen Hunt). Psychiatrists state that the character probably should have been described as having a personality disorder.

The Assault (Misshandlingen; Mistreatment, Assault and Battery)
DATE: 1969
DIRECTOR: Lasse Forsberg

Black-and-white Swedish film, based on a 1968 official Swedish sociopathy report. This fictional film resembles a documentary in its critical depiction of how the Swedish Social Democracy controlled radicals by manipulating the meaning of insanity in courts. Socialist Knut Nielsen (Knut Pettersen) is institutionalized in a psychiatric ward because of his protests. Characters denounce how mental institutions are used as weapons against dissenters. Psychologists assisted in film production.

A Beautiful Mind
DATE: 2001
DIRECTOR: Ron Howard

Based on Sylvia Nasar's 1998 book. Mathematician John Nash (Russell Crowe), a paranoid schizophrenic, is depicted as a genius who developed game theory and won a Nobel Prize despite his illness. His psychiatrist, Dr. Rosen (Christopher Plummer), treats Nash with insulin shock therapy and antipsychotic drugs. Psychiatrists served as film consultants. Film won the Academy Award for Best Picture. Nash was also the subject of *A Brilliant Madness*, a 2002 PBS *American Experience* documentary.

Beauty and the Beast
DATE: 1991
DIRECTOR: Gary Trousdale and Kirk Wise

Animated film in which an evil psychiatrist in control of an asylum accepts a bribe from the villain, Gaston, to commit the heroine's father so that Gaston can marry her.

The Bell Jar
DATE: 1979
DIRECTOR: Larry Peerce

Adapted from Sylvia Plath's 1963 autobiographical novel. Esther Greenwood (Marilyn Hassett) succumbs to depression.

Benny and Joon
DATE: 1993
DIRECTOR: Jeremiah Chechik

Benny (Aidan Quinn) protects his schizophrenic sister Joon (Mary Stuart Masterson) and is unwilling to institutionalize her as advised by Dr. Garvey (C. C. H. Pounder). Joon disrupts Benny's life and acts hostilely toward caretakers. She falls in love with eccentric Sam (Johnny Depp) but is briefly institutionalized after she has a public outburst. Sam and Benny cooperate to secure Joon's release.

Best in Show
DATE: 2000
DIRECTOR: Christopher Guest

A neurotic couple, Meg and Hamilton Swan (Parker Posey and Michael Hitchcock), take their dog to a therapist.

Betrayal
DATE: 1978
DIRECTOR: Paul Wendkos

Based on the case *Julie Roy v. Renatus Hartogs, M.D.*, Lesley Ann Warren stars in this drama about a woman who sues her psychiatrist after he seduces her.

Beyond Therapy
DATE: 1987
DIRECTOR: Robert Altman

Based on a 1982 Broadway play written by Christopher Durang. Couple Bruce (Jeff Goldblum) and Prudence (Julie Hagerty) consult their psychotherapists, Charlotte (Glenda Jackson) and Stuart (Tom Conti). Both therapists are portrayed as acting unethically and having personality disorders themselves.

Birdy
DATE: 1984
DIRECTOR: Alan Parker

An adaptation of William Wharton's 1979 novel of the same title. Vietnam veteran Birdy (Matthew Modine) is institutionalized in a Veterans Administration Hospital mental ward. Ineffectively treated by Dr. Weiss (John Harkins), Birdy lives in silence, obsessing about flying like the pigeons he raised as a teenager. Birdy's best friend, Al Columbato (Nicolas Cage), helps him regain his voice and retain mental stability despite the insanity of his surroundings.

Blue Sky
DATE: 1994
DIRECTOR: Tony Richardson

Manic-depressive Carly Marshall (Jessica Lange) disrupts her children's lives and the military career of her husband, Major Hank Marshall (Tommy Lee

Jones), during the 1960's. Hank's credibility as a military scientist, recommending that nuclear testing should be conducted underground to avoid radiation contamination, is undermined by his wife's bizarre and adulterous behavior. Carly has a brief affair with base commander Vince Johnson (Powers Boothe), who forces her to have Hank hospitalized. There he is drugged to prevent him from revealing atomic hazards. Carly ultimately rescues her husband and attracts media attention to the dangers of atomic testing. Lange won an Academy Award for Best Actress for this role.

The Cabinet of Dr. Caligari (*Das Cabinet des Dr. Caligari*)
DATE: 1920
DIRECTOR: Robert Wiene
German expressionistic silent film. Francis (Friedrich Feher) is a delusional mental hospital patient. He conveys information about an evil hypnotist named Caligari and the somnambulist Cesare (Conrad Veidt) whom Caligari hypnotizes to kill people. When Caligari is accused of murder, he hides in the mental institution where Francis is committed. Viewers soon realize that Francis and many of the characters in his story, including Cesare, are mental patients and that Caligari is sane. Many film scholars consider this film the catalyst for quality German cinema. The film was remade in 1962.

Camille Claudel
DATE: 1988
DIRECTOR: Bruno Nuytten
French film based on Reine-Marie Paris's biography and the Claudel family archives. This film features the life of sculptor Camille Claudel (Isabelle Adjani) who became insane and was committed to a mental institution. Claudel was the lover of sculptor Auguste Rodin (Gérard Depardieu), who refused to marry her after using her artistic ideas. Her brother Paul Claudel's (Laurent Grevill) abandonment further agitated her precarious mental condition.

Captain Newman, M.D.
DATE: 1963
DIRECTOR: David Miller
Based on Leo Rosten's 1961 novel. Captain Josiah Newman (Gregory Peck) treats patients at a World War II neuropsychiatric ward. Neurotic Corporal Jackson Leibowitz (Tony Curtis) is an orderly.

Carefree
DATE: 1938
DIRECTOR: Mark Sandrich
Psychiatrist Dr. Tony Flagg (Fred Astaire) hypnotizes his best friend's fiancé Amanda Cooper (Ginger Rogers), to overcome her fear of commitment and reluctance to marry. The first hypnosis goes awry when she falls in love with Flagg instead; a second hypnosis to reverse the first causes her to hate him intensely. When Flagg realizes that he is in love with her himself, he must attempt a third hypnosis to erase the effects of his previous attempts.

Cat People
DATE: 1942
DIRECTOR: Jacques Tourneur
Psychiatrist Dr. Judd (Tom Conway) attempts to treat Irena Dubrovna (Simone Simon), who is obsessed by a family curse that she will become a panther and kill her husband if she is sexually aroused.

Catch-22
DATE: 1970
DIRECTOR: Mike Nichols
Based on Joseph Heller's 1961 novel. In this dark comedy, a World War II bombardier (Alan Arkin) pleads insanity in an attempt to avoid more missions. The "catch-22," however, is that knowing he is crazy is proof of mental competence.

Charly
DATE: 1968
DIRECTOR: Ralph Nelson
Adapted from Daniel Keyes's 1966 novel *Flowers for Algernon*. Surgery gives the mentally disabled adult Charly (Cliff Robertson) a genius intelligence quotient without emotional maturity. The effects are impermanent, causing tragedy when Charly begins to slip back into his preoperative state.

The Couch Trip
DATE: 1988
DIRECTOR: Michael Ritchie
Based on Ken Kolb's 1970 novel. John Burns (Dan Aykroyd) is a prisoner who switches places with his psychiatrist Dr. Baird (David Clennon). He travels to Los Angeles to substitute for radio psychiatrist, Dr. Maitlin (Charles Grodin), who is mentally disintegrating.

David and Lisa
DATE: 1962
DIRECTOR: Frank Perry

Adapted from a 1961 book based on a case study by psychiatrist Dr. Theodore Isaac Rubin. This film features interactions between two teenagers at a school for mentally disturbed students. David Clemens (Keir Dullea), who is highly intelligent and obsessive, cringes at the suggestion of being touched. Lisa (Janet Margolin) is schizophrenic and also displays a personality named Muriel. Dr. Alan Swinford (Howard da Silva) observes the pair's friendship, which aids the beginning of their recovery.

Diary of a Mad Housewife
DATE: 1970
DIRECTOR: Frank Perry

An unhappy housewife, Tina Balser (Carrie Snodgress), participates in group therapy to learn how to resolve issues she has with her chauvinistic husband Jonathan (Richard Benjamin), demanding daughters, and narcissistic lover George Prager (Frank Langella). Tina realizes she must become responsible for her life to achieve happiness.

Dr. Dippy's Sanitarium
DATE: 1906
DIRECTOR: American Mutoscope and Biograph

Silent; the first film to depict a psychiatrist. Lunatics seize control of an asylum until the superintendent restores order.

Eternal Sunshine of the Spotless Mind
DATE: 2004
DIRECTOR: Michel Gondry

Joel Barish (Jim Carrey) learns that his former girlfriend (Kate Winslet) has undergone a radical psychiatric procedure to erase all of her memories. Barish decides to take part in the same procedure, in order to forget the pain of their breakup, but he begins to have regrets as he pieces together the rapidly evaporating images of a psychological puzzle.

Eyes Wide Shut
DATE: 1999
DIRECTOR: Stanley Kubrick

Psychiatrist Dr. William Harford (Tom Cruise) and his wife Alice Harford (Nicole Kidman) explore their sexuality with patients, individually, and in groups.

Face to Face (*Ansikte mot Ansikte*)
DATE: 1976
DIRECTOR: Ingmar Bergman

Swedish. While in a coma after attempting suicide, psychiatrist Dr. Jenny Isaksson (Liv Ullmann) recognizes the childhood sources of her repressed anger. Her colleague, psychiatrist Dr. Helmuth Wankel (Ulf Johansson), dismisses psychoanalysis as a treatment. Isaksson heals by forgiving her grandparents who raised her. This film reveals the director's personal interest in Jungian therapy and the subconscious.

Family Life
DATE: 1971
DIRECTOR: Ken Loach

British. Adapted from the play *Two Minds*. Schizophrenic teenager Janice Baildon (Sandy Ratcliffe) suffers a nervous breakdown aggravated by the domineering behavior of her parents (Grace Cave and Bill Dean). Her condition is exacerbated by uncaring medical and psychiatric treatment that appears aimed at alleviating her parents' problems rather than hers.

Frances
DATE: 1982
DIRECTOR: Graeme Clifford

Based on the life of 1930's actress Frances Farmer (Jessica Lange), who has a nervous breakdown. She is wrongly declared criminally insane and institutionalized by those who are threatened by her female independence and autonomy. Contains scenes of Frances receiving a prefrontal lobotomy.

Freud: The Secret Passion
DATE: 1962
DIRECTOR: John Huston

Montgomery Clift portrays Sigmund Freud at the beginning of his career. Public and professional rejection of his theories of the unconscious and infantile sexuality are depicted. The film portrays Freud's interactions with patients, and the conscious and unconscious perceptions that molded his psychoanalytic theories.

Garden State
DATE: 2004
DIRECTOR: Zach Braff

Andrew Largeman (Zach Braff) returns to his

hometown after years of separation from his family. After a near lifetime of taking antidepressant medication prescribed by his psychiatrist father, Largeman decides to face life without the assistance of prescription drugs. At the same time, he meets Sam (Natalie Portman), a psychologically troubled but ebullient young woman who helps Largeman cast away the memories of a troubled adolescence.

Gaslight
DATE: 1944
DIRECTOR: George Cukor

The sadistic Gregory Anton (Charles Boyer) tries to make his wife, Paula Alquist (Ingrid Bergman), insane. Alquist, pondering her aunt's decade-old unsolved murder, suffers memory loss, delusions, and hysteria after she marries Anton. Anton constantly threatens to have her declared insane and institutionalized before he is exposed as her aunt's strangler.

Girl, Interrupted
DATE: 1999
DIRECTOR: James Mangold

Based the 1993 autobiography by Susanna Kaysen. A psychiatrist admits a teenager (Winona Ryder) to a psychiatric ward after she attempts suicide. Diagnosed as having borderline personality disorder, she is held forcibly and medicated. She interacts with other patients before being deemed fit for release.

Good Will Hunting
DATE: 1997
DIRECTOR: Gus Van Sant

Psychiatrist Sean McGuire (Robin Williams) counsels Will Hunting (Matt Damon) concerning his abusive childhood. In the process, McGuire unprofessionally reveals details of his life and is physically aggressive toward Hunting.

Grosse Pointe Blank
DATE: 1997
DIRECTOR: George Armitage

Professional hit man Martin Blank (John Cusack) forces his therapist Dr. Oatman (Alan Arkin) into continuing to treat him by threatening to kill his family. Nonetheless, he is hurt by Oatman's reluctance to listen to his problems.

Hannibal
DATE: 2001
DIRECTOR: Ridley Scott

Based on Thomas Harris's 1999 novel, the third one featuring former psychiatrist and cannibal Dr. Hannibal Lecter, now living free in Italy and still killing and eating victims.

Harvey
DATE: 1950
DIRECTOR: Henry Koster

Adapted from Mary C. Chase's Pulitzer Prize-winning play about fantasy versus reality. Veta (Josephine Hull) and her daughter, Myrtle Mae (Victoria Horne), attempt to have Veta's alcoholic brother, Elwood P. Dowd (James Stewart), committed to an asylum because he has an invisible human-size rabbit friend he calls Harvey. Veta admits to Dr. Sanderson (Charles Drake) that she, too, has seen Harvey and is admitted to the Chumley Rest Home. Psychiatrist Dr. Chumley (Cecil Kellaway) intends to help Elwood but instead sees Harvey. Veta decides to prevent Elwood from receiving an injection which would make him stop seeing Harvey because she realizes that Elwood would lose his amiable personality and that Harvey represents sanity.

Heavenly Creatures
DATE: 1994
DIRECTOR: Peter Jackson

New Zealand. Based on a true crime. Two teenage girls, Juliet (Kate Winslet) and Pauline (Melanie Lynskey), form an obsessive friendship based on their mutual creation of a fantasy kingdom. When Juliet's parents decide to move back to England, the two kill Pauline's mother, who they believe is standing in the way of Pauline accompanying her friend.

High Anxiety
DATE: 1977
DIRECTOR: Mel Brooks

Parody of psychiatrist films in general and *Vertigo* in particular, in which Brooks plays a psychiatrist who is the director of the Psycho-Neurotic Institute for the Very, Very Nervous.

I Live in Fear (Ikimono No Kiroku)
DATE: 1955
DIRECTOR: Akira Kurosawa

Japanese film created for the tenth anniversary

of the Hiroshima and Nagasaki atomic bombings. Dentist Dr. Harada (Takashi Shimura) and businessman Kiichi Nakajima (Toshiro Mifune) represent the emotional impact of the atomic bombs on the Japanese. Dr. Harada responds with fear yet is optimistic. Nakajima becomes paranoid, then psychotic, and plans to move to Brazil, where he thinks he will be safe. His family tries to have him declared mentally incompetent. When Nakajima burns his foundry, he is placed in a psychiatric hospital. He believes his padded room is actually a fallout shelter and that Earth is burning from another atomic bomb. His psychiatrist (Nobuo Nakamura) questions whether it is more insane to be afraid of atomic weapons or to accept them.

I Never Promised You a Rose Garden
DATE: 1977
DIRECTOR: Anthony Page
　　Adapted from Hannah Green's 1964 book about schizophrenia. Psychiatrist Dr. Fried (Bibi Andersson) treats teenaged Deborah (Kathleen Quinlan) in an asylum. Deborah has constructed an elaborate fantasy world, which provided her comfort in her childhood years but which now threatens to overwhelm her and prevent her from facing adulthood.

Is This Goodbye, Charlie Brown?
DATE: 1983
DIRECTOR: Phil Roman
　　Short animated film in which Snoopy becomes responsible for Lucy's psychiatric booth when she moves out of town with her family.

Jacob's Ladder
DATE: 1990
DIRECTOR: Adrian Lyne
　　Jacob Singer (Tim Robbins) suffers from posttraumatic stress disorder as he has graphic nightmares and flashbacks about service in the Vietnam War and the death of his son (Macaulay Culkin). He becomes increasingly paranoid when his psychiatrist's car explodes. Aspects of the film suggest that Singer is actually the restless spirit of someone who is dead.

Kings Row
DATE: 1942
DIRECTOR: Sam Wood
　　Dr. Alexander Tower (Claude Rains) is a psychia-

trist in a Midwestern town, where some characters are insane or suffer other mental disorders, including his own daughter Cassandra (Betty Field).

Klute
DATE: 1971
DIRECTOR: Alan J. Pakula
　　Prostitute Bree (Jane Fonda) sees a therapist, who learns about her weaknesses and strengths.

K-PAX
DATE: 2001
DIRECTOR: Iain Softley
　　Based on Charles Brewer's 1995 novel. Prot (Kevin Spacey) is a mugging victim who insists he is an alien from the planet K-PAX. Committed to a public mental hospital, Prot becomes the patient of Dr. Mark Powell (Jeff Bridges), who medicates Prot for delusions but then begins to question whether his claims might be true.

Lady in the Dark
DATE: 1944
DIRECTOR: Mitchell Leisen
　　Adapted from a play written by Moss Hart, influenced by his personal psychoanalysis experience. Magazine editor Liza Elliott (Ginger Rogers) undergoes psychiatric treatment to address her indecisiveness and fears. Psychiatrist Dr. Brooks (Barry Sullivan) helps Elliott understand childhood traumas and her need to dominate men. Dream sequences represent her unconscious.

Life Upside Down (*La Vie à l'envers*)
DATE: 1964
DIRECTOR: Alain Jessua
　　French. Depicts the alienated estate agent Jacques (Charles Denner), who prefers to live in a mental clinic rather than with his wife, model Viviane (Anna Gaylor). She attempts suicide as a result of his odd behavior.

Lilith
DATE: 1964
DIRECTOR: Robert Rosen
　　Based on J. R. Salamanca's 1961 novel. Warren Beatty plays an occupational therapist at a mental hospital for wealthy schizophrenics.

Little Miss Sunshine
DATE: 2006
DIRECTORS: Jonathan Dayton and Valerie Faris
A young girl (Abigail Breslin) enters a beauty pageant and leads her dysfunctional family on a cross-country trip of self-discovery and reconciliation. Though the girl may be described as optimistically delusional, she acts as a de facto therapist for a family that exhibits multiple psychological conditions, including feelings of failure (her father), depression (her brother), suicidal tendencies (her uncle), drug addiction (her grandfather), and neurosis (her mother).

Love Crazy
DATE: 1941
DIRECTOR: Jack Conway
William Powell plays a husband who pretends to be insane to prevent his wife (Myrna Loy) from divorcing him after she finds him with a former girlfriend.

The Madness of King George
DATE: 1994
DIRECTOR: Nicholas Hytner
British; adapted from Alan Bennett's play. This film portrays the period when King George III (Nigel Hawthorne) of England was temporarily insane in 1788. The film suggests that he had an organic psychosis such as intermittent porphyria. The king's supporters ask Dr. Willis (Ian Holm) to apply his expertise in psychological disorders to cure the king.

Man Facing Southeast (*Hombre Mirando al Sudeste*)
DATE: 1986
DIRECTOR: Eliseo Subiela
Argentina. A man confined to a mental hospital claims to be an extraterrestrial, causing his psychiatrist to question his treatment.

The Man Who Loved Women
DATE: 1983
DIRECTOR: Blake Edwards
Psychiatrist Marianna (Julie Andrews) relates incidents in the Lothario-esque life of former patient David Fowler (Burt Reynolds) at his funeral.

The Man with Two Brains
DATE: 1983
DIRECTOR: Carl Reiner
Neurosurgeon Dr. Michael Hfuhruhurr (Steve Martin), the inventor of Screw Top, Zip Lock Brain Surgery, marries a gold digger (Kathleen Turner) for her looks but falls in love with the brain—preserved in a jar by mad scientist Dr. Necessiter (David Warner)—of a chubby musician whose thoughts he can hear telepathically.

The Manchurian Candidate
DATE: 1962
DIRECTOR: John Frankenheimer
Based on Richard Condon's 1959 novel. American soldier Raymond Shaw (Laurence Harvey), son of a politically ruthless woman (Angela Lansbury) married to a McCarthyesque senator (John Gregory), is brainwashed by the Chinese during the Korean War to become a sleeper agent/assassin as part of a Communist plot. An updated, thematically similar version starring Denzel Washington was released in 2004.

Manhunter
DATE: 1986
DIRECTOR: Michael Mann
Adapted from Thomas Harris's 1981 novel *Red Dragon*. This film introduces the character Dr. Hannibal Lecter (Brian Cox), a psychiatrist gone insane who has become a cannibal.

M*A*S*H
DATE: 1970
DIRECTOR: Robert Altman
Based on Richard Hooker's 1968 novel. Korean War surgeons Hawkeye Pierce (Donald Sutherland) and Trapper John MacIntyre (Elliott Gould) cope with what they consider wartime insanity by tormenting unbearable colleagues. They provoke Major Frank Burns (Robert Duvall) to go berserk.

Me, Myself, and Irene
DATE: 2000
DIRECTOR: Bobby Farrelly and Peter Farrelly
An inaccurate portrayal of a mentally ill policeman (Jim Carrey) with two personalities (not schizophrenia, as the film states). Heavily criticized by psychiatric and mental health organizations for its negative images of psychology.

The Mirror Crack'd
DATE: 1981
DIRECTOR: Guy Hamilton
Based on a 1962 Agatha Christie mystery. Marina Rudd (Elizabeth Taylor) is an actress struggling to recover from a nervous breakdown.

Mr. Jones
DATE: 1993
DIRECTOR: Mike Figgis
Psychiatrist Dr. Libbie Bowen (Lena Olin), under the supervision of Dr. Catherine Holland (Anne Bancroft), treats Mr. Jones (Richard Gere), who suffers from bipolar affective disorder. Bowen falls in love with him. This film explores the psychiatrist-patient relationship, the use of the psychotropic drug Haldol, forced hospitalization, and Jones's resistance to accepting that he has a mental illness.

Mumford
DATE: 1999
DIRECTOR: Lawrence Kasdan
Dr. Mickey Mumford (Loren Dean) is a popular psychologist in the community where he has recently moved. His patients are unaware that he is recovering from drug addiction and has assumed a deceased friend's identity. Mumford's psychological methods to treat patients are unusual, and he gradually realizes why most psychologists are professionally educated and trained to practice competently.

Nell
DATE: 1994
DIRECTOR: Michael Apted
Adapted from Mark Handley's 1989 play *Idioglossia*. Nell (Jodie Foster) grew up in complete isolation because her mother was a recluse. When Nell's mother dies, physician Jerome Lovell (Liam Neeson) discovers Nell and is puzzled by her private language. He contacts psychologist Paula Olsen (Natasha Richardson), who assumes Nell is mentally disturbed. Psychiatrist Alexander Paley (Richard Libertini) decides to institutionalize Nell to protect her. Lovell removes Nell from the institution, and she speaks in court to demonstrate that she is mentally competent.

Now, Voyager
DATE: 1942
DIRECTOR: Irving Rapper
Based on Olive Higgins Prouty's 1941 novel. Psy-chiatrist Dr. Jaquith (Claude Rains) treats repressed Charlotte Vale (Bette Davis). Dr. Jaquith helps Charlotte function normally in the world and find love.

Nuts
DATE: 1987
DIRECTOR: Martin Ritt
Adapted from a play by Tom Topor. After prostitute Claudia Draper (Barbra Streisand) murders her client (Leslie Nielsen) in self-defense, her parents hire attorney Clarence Middleton (William Prince) to convince the judge that Draper is mentally unfit to stand trial and should remain institutionalized. Middleton resigns when an angry Draper assaults him. Public defender (Richard Dreyfuss) is assigned her case and sides with Draper, arguing that she is competent. Psychiatrist Dr. Herbert A. Morrison (Eli Wallach) also evaluates Draper.

One Flew over the Cuckoo's Nest
DATE: 1975
DIRECTOR: Milos Forman
Adapted from Ken Kesey's 1962 novel. McMurphy (Jack Nicholson) and the inmates of a mental asylum rebel against the institutionalized system. Film graphically portrays shock therapy.

Ordinary People
DATE: 1980
DIRECTOR: Robert Redford
Based on Judith Guest's 1976 novel. Focuses on parents (Donald Sutherland and Mary Tyler Moore) coping with their suicidal son (Timothy Hutton), who feels guilty after he was unable to prevent his brother's drowning. The appealing Dr. Berger (Judd Hirsch) helps the family recover emotionally. Many psychiatrists identified his character as the type of therapist they aspire to be. Won the Academy Award for Best Picture.

Pi
DATE: 1998
DIRECTOR: Darren Aronofsky. A gifted but manic mathematician seeks to decode the secret structures of the universe by mathematically mapping the patterns he sees in nature. His quest eventually drives him mad.

Possessed
DATE: 1947
DIRECTOR: Curtis Bernhardt
Through narcohypnosis, a schizophrenic (Joan Crawford) remembers events that led to her admission to a hospital psychiatric ward.

The Prince of Tides
DATE: 1991
DIRECTOR: Barbra Streisand
Adapted from Pat Conroy's 1986 novel. Dr. Susan Lowenstein (Barbra Streisand) helps Tom Wingo (Nick Nolte) deal with his sister's mental illness.

Prozac Nation
DATE: 2002
DIRECTOR: Erik Skjoldburg
Based on the 1994 memoir by Elizabeth Wurtzel. Dr. Sterling (Anne Heche) treats Wurtzel (Christina Ricci) for depression.

Psycho
DATE: 1960
DIRECTOR: Alfred Hitchcock
Based on a 1959 novel by Robert Bloch. Psychiatrist Dr. Richmond (Simon Oakland) declares Norman Bates (Anthony Perkins) insane after he kills guest Marion Crane (Janet Leigh) and a detective at the Bates Motel and his mother's mummified corpse is found. This film initiated a genre of films about psychotic killers. A shot-for-shot remake directed by Gus Van Zant and starring Vince Vaughn as Bates was released in 1998.

Psycho II
DATE: 1983
DIRECTOR: Richard Franklin
In this sequel, psychiatrist Dr. Raymond (Robert Loggia) releases Norman Bates (Anthony Perkins) from the mental institution where he was committed after murdering motel guests. More murders soon occur, and Bates's sanity is uncertain.

Psycho III
DATE: 1983
DIRECTOR: Anthony Perkins
Another sequel which features murderous mayhem at the Bates Motel, where Norman Bates (Anthony Perkins) continues to be mentally unstable.

Psycho IV: The Beginning
DATE: 1990
DIRECTOR: Mick Garris
A made-for-cable film which attempts to explain why Norman Bates (Anthony Perkins) was mentally flawed.

Rain Man
DATE: 1988
DIRECTOR: Barry Levinson
Adapted from Barry Morrow's story. Autistic savant Raymond Babbitt (Dustin Hoffman), who is gifted mathematically, inherits $3 million from his deceased father. Younger brother Charlie Babbitt (Tom Cruise) abducts Raymond from his institution and challenges his guardian, Dr. Bruner (Jerry Molen), for Raymond's custody. Film won an Academy Award for Best Picture.

Random Harvest
DATE: 1942
DIRECTOR: Mervyn LeRoy
Based on a 1941 novel by James Hilton. World War I army officer Charles Rainier (Ronald Colman) has amnesia due to shell shock and is institutionalized. He escapes and marries Paula (Greer Garson). When Charles is in a car accident, he regains his memory but forgets his wife. She works as his secretary, and he eventually remembers that they are married.

Repulsion
DATE: 1965
DIRECTOR: Roman Polanski
Carol Ledoux (Catherine Deneuve) is a paranoid schizophrenic who kills men who try to befriend her.

Requiem for a Dream
DATE: 2000
DIRECTOR: Darren Aronofsky
Based on a 1978 novel of the same name by Hubert Selby, Jr. Examines the psychological unraveling of four drug addicts in Brooklyn. Dreams and goals are destroyed by harrowing hallucinations, and the nature of reality is questioned.

Return to Oz
DATE: 1985
DIRECTOR: Walter Murch
Dorothy Gale (Fairuza Balk) is admitted to a men-

tal hospital, where her Aunt Em (Piper Laurie) believes electric shock therapy administered by Dr. J. B. Worley (Nicol Williamson) will stop the girl's claims to have visited a fantasy land.

sex, lies, and videotape
DATE: 1989
DIRECTOR: Steven Soderbergh
Ann Millaney (Andie MacDowell) confides her feelings about sex and her unhappy marriage to her therapist (Ron Vawter).

The Shining
DATE: 1980
DIRECTOR: Stanley Kubrick
Based on Stephen King's 1977 novel. Jack Torrance (Jack Nicholson) becomes insane when his family is snowed in at the Overlook, a huge, isolated hotel where he works as the winter custodian. He had been told that a former caretaker had a nervous breakdown and murdered his family.

The Silence of the Lambs
DATE: 1991
DIRECTOR: Jonathan Demme
Based on Thomas Harris's 1988 novel. Held in a maximum security mental institution, cannibal and former psychiatrist Dr. Hannibal Lecter (Anthony Hopkins) antagonizes FBI agent Clarice Starling (Jodie Foster) as she pursues a serial killer.

The Sixth Sense
DATE: 1999
DIRECTOR: M. Night Shyamalan
Child psychologist Malcolm Crowe (Bruce Willis) helps Cole Sear (Haley Joel Osment) comprehend his visions of ghosts seeking his help.

Slingblade
DATE: 1996
DIRECTOR: Billy Bob Thornton
Karl Childers (Billy Bob Thornton) is released from a mental hospital for criminals and has difficulty adjusting when he returns home.

The Snake Pit
DATE: 1948
DIRECTOR: Anatole Litvak
Adapted from Mary Jane Ward's 1946 novel. Virginia Cunningham (Olivia de Havilland) plays a

woman committed for insanity. Her psychiatrist Dr. Mark Kick (Leo Gunn) is resolved to cure her despite her recurrent breakdowns.

Spellbound
DATE: 1945
DIRECTOR: Alfred Hitchcock
Adapted from Hilary Aidan St. George Saunders's 1927 psychological mystery *The House of Dr. Edwardes*. When amnesiac J. B. (Gregory Peck) thinks he has committed a murder that he cannot remember, psychiatrist Dr. Constance (Ingrid Bergman) tries to exonerate him.

The Story of Adèle H. (L'Histoire d'Adèle H.)
DATE: 1975
DIRECTOR: François Truffaut
French. Based on the life of the second daughter of French writer Victor Hugo. In 1843, Adèle (Isabelle Adjani) follows a man she believes to be her lover, the English Lieutenant Pinson (Bruce Robinson), to Halifax, Nova Scotia. Spurned by Pinson, she slowly descends into an obsessive madness.

Sybil
DATE: 1976
DIRECTOR: Daniel Petrie
Made-for-television film in which a psychiatrist (Joanne Woodward) treats Sybil (Sally Field), who has seventeen personalities as a result of a childhood trauma.

The Testament of Dr. Mabuse (Das Testament des Dr. Mabuse)
DATE: 1933
DIRECTOR: Fritz Lang
German film in which Dr. Mabuse (Rudolf Klein-Rogge), an insane criminal and mental patient introduced in a 1922 film, seizes control of the lunatic asylum from its administrator Dr. Baum (Oskar Beregi), who cooperates with his criminal activities. Chief Inspector Lohmann (Otto Wernicke) finds the deceased Mabuse, whose spirit has possessed Baum. Lang made *Die Tausend Augen des Dr. Mabuse* (*The Thousand Eyes of Dr. Mabuse*) in 1950.

Three Faces of Eve
DATE: 1957
DIRECTOR: Nunnally Johnson
Adapted from psychiatrists Corbett H. Thigpen

and Hervey M. Cleckley's 1957 book based on a case study. Joanne Woodward won an Oscar for portraying a woman with three distinct personalities. The film depicts hypnosis during therapy sessions.

Through a Glass Darkly (*Sasom i en Spegel*)
DATE: 1961
DIRECTOR: Ingmar Bergman
Swedish film that begins a trilogy. Schizophrenic Karin (Harriet Andersson) breaks down mentally while on vacation. She realizes that she must be hospitalized but pleads not to be medicated with anything that might worsen her hallucinations.

Tie Me Up! Tie Me Down! (*¡Átame!*)
DATE: 1990
DIRECTOR: Pedro Almodovar
Spanish. On his release from a mental hospital, Ricky (Antonio Banderas) tracks down a porn star, Marina (Victoria Abril), with whom he once had sex and holds her hostage in an attempt to make her love him. Oddly enough, it works.

Vanilla Sky
DATE: 2001
DIRECTOR: Cameron Crowe
Based on a 1997 Spanish film entitled *Abre los Ojos* (*Open Your Eyes*). David Aames (Tom Cruise) plays a publishing scion whose reality is fractured by illogical dreamscapes. He comes to find that his brain functions are implanted with images, and he is in a cryogenically frozen state in which his past life is colluded with unreal memories.

The Vanishing
DATE: 1988
DIRECTOR: George Sluizer
Dutch. A sociopath (Bernard Pierre Donnadieu) taunts, then ensnares Rex (Gene Bervoets), who is obsessed by learning what happened to his girlfriend who disappeared.

Vertigo
DATE: 1958
DIRECTOR: Alfred Hitchcock
An acrophobic San Francisco detective (James Stewart) must cope with his phobia as he trails a woman (Kim Novak) in a very complicated plot.

The Village
DATE: 2004
DIRECTOR: M. Night Shyamalan
A remote village engenders a fear of the unknown, convincing its citizens to remain within its boundaries by indoctrinating the children with a mythology based on an unseen beast that terrorizes the populace.

The Virgin Suicides
DATE: 1999
DIRECTOR: Sofia Coppola
The five Lisbon sisters commit suicide, and psychiatrist Dr. Horniker (Danny DeVito) attempts to comprehend why. Their parents (James Woods and Kathleen Turner) are rigidly religious and did not allow the girls to interact in normal social situations as they matured.

What About Bob?
DATE: 1991
DIRECTOR: Frank Oz
Bob Wiley (Bill Murray) follows his narcissistic psychiatrist Dr. Leo Marvin (Richard Dreyfuss) on vacation, annoying him and befriending his family.

What's New, Pussycat?
DATE: 1965
DIRECTOR: Clive Donner
Written by Woody Allen. Incorrigible womanizer Michael James (Peter O'Toole) sees Viennese psychiatrist Dr. Fritz Fassbender (Peter Sellers) to help him commit to one girlfriend.

When the Clouds Roll By
DATE: 1919
DIRECTOR: Victor Fleming
Silent. Dr. Ulrich Metz (Herbert Grimwood) is a psychiatrist—actually an escaped mental patient—who tries to cause Daniel Boone Brown (Douglas Fairbanks) to commit suicide.

Zelig
DATE: 1983
DIRECTOR: Woody Allen
In a film that is presented to resemble a 1920's documentary, psychiatrist Dr. Eudora Fletcher (Mia Farrow) helps hospital patient Leonard Zelig (Woody Allen) realize that he suffered identity crises throughout his childhood, which resulted in him

lacking a personality and mirroring the people whom he meets. Dr. Fletcher hypnotizes him in what are called the White Room Sessions, and his own personality emerges.

TELEVISION

Ally McBeal
DATE: 1997-2002

In this comedic drama, neurotic lawyer Ally McBeal (Calista Flockhart) sees a therapist (Tracey Ullman) who is humorous but unprofessional, controlling, and mentally imbalanced.

The Bob Newhart Show
DATE: 1972-1978

In this situation comedy, Bob Hartley (Bob Newhart) is a Chicago psychologist who counsels patients individually and in group therapy. Patients seek help for phobias, depression, and neuroses. Elliot Carlin is a recurring character with a persecution complex. Hartley is more competent at handling his patients' problems than his own relationships.

Buffy the Vampire Slayer
DATE: 1997-2003

In one plotline of this tongue-in-cheek drama, Professor Maggie Walsh (Lindsey Crouse), Buffy's (Sarah Michelle Gellar's) psychology teacher and an expert in operant conditioning, is revealed as the evil mastermind of a secret military force, the Initiative. The Initiative captures vampire Spike (James Marsters) and implants a chip in his brain, preventing him from harming any living creature. Subsequent seasons show Spike's behavior continually being modified by the implant. In the episode "Normal Again," Buffy is infected with a demon poison causing her to believe that her town is a hallucination and that she is a schizophrenic in a mental hospital.

Celebrity Rehab
DATE: 2008-

Dr. Drew Pinsky presides over the treatment and rehabilitation of celebrities with substance addictions and related problems. The celebrities include television and film actors, musicians and singers, models, and those with other tenuous claims to fame.

Cheers
DATE: 1982-1993

This situation comedy includes characters Dr. Frasier Crane (Kelsey Grammer) and his wife Dr. Lilith Sternin Crane (Bebe Neuwirth). The uptight psychiatrists provide comic relief through their elitist and pretentious reactions to the problems of their acquaintances at a Boston bar.

Cracker
DATE: 1993-1996

In this British drama, Eddie "Fitz" Fitzgerald (Robbie Coltrane) is a criminal psychologist who works as a profiler. He is also a compulsive gambler and drinker. Psychologist Ian Stephen was a show consultant.

Days of Our Lives
DATE: 1965-

In this soap opera, leading character Dr. Marlena Evans (Deidre Hall) is pivotal to plots. Her office is often the scene of therapy sessions with other characters. Psychiatrist Dr. Laura Horton also is a recurring character.

Dexter
DATE: 2006-

Dexter (Michael C. Hall), a psychopathic antihero, straddles two realities, working in a crime lab by day and committing darkly benevolent acts of murder at night. He takes justice into his own hands by hunting down the perpetrators of the murders whose victims he has examined.

Dr. Katz, Professional Therapist
DATE: 1995-1999

This animated comedy explores the world from the perspective of a psychiatrist.

ER
DATE: 1994-2009

This hospital drama often features psychiatric consultations by such characters as Dr. Kim Legaspi (Elizabeth Mitchell). Sally Field guest starred as Maggie Wycenski, the bipolar mother of nurse Abby Lockhart (Maura Tierney).

Felicity
DATE: 1998-2002

In this drama, college student Felicity (Keri Russell) undergoes counseling with Dr. Toni Pavone

(Amy Aquino), who helps her cope with her parents' divorce. Other characters are in therapy and take antidepressants. Felicity's roommate, Meghan (Amanda Foreman), aspires to become a psychiatrist.

Frasier
DATE: 1993-2004
A spinoff of *Cheers.* Dr. Frasier Crane (Kelsey Grammer) is the host of a Seattle radio talk show which promotes "good mental health." His brother, Dr. Niles Crane (David Hyde Pierce), has a private psychiatric practice. The brothers' psychiatric interests, insecurities, and misunderstandings are the basis of most plots.

Friends
DATE: 1993-2004
In one episode of this ensemble comedy, actor Joey Tribbiani (Matt LeBlanc) plays Sigmund Freud in a musical titled *Freud!*

Futurama
DATE: 1999-2002
In one episode of this animated comedy, Bender and Fry are committed to a robot asylum after being falsely accused of robbing a bank and declared insane.

Good Advice
DATE: 1993
In this situation comedy, Susan DeRuzza (Shelley Long) good-naturedly attempts to help patients while experiencing chaos in her own life.

I'll Fly Away
DATE: 1991-1993
Set in a small Georgia town between 1958 and 1960, this drama features local district attorney Forrest Bedford (Sam Waterston), whose wife Gwen Bedford (Deborah Hedwall) is mentally ill and a resident of a private hospital outside of town.

Intervention
DATE: 2005-
In this documentary-style reality series, friends and family confront alcohol and drug abusers about their addictions in an attempt to force the users into rehabilitation. The addicts are tricked into believing they are part of a documentary of alcohol and drug use and are invariably surprised to discover the true purpose of the show. Each episode also features follow-up footage that traces the addicts' progress, or lack thereof, after the intervention.

In Treatment
DATE: 2008-
An inside look at a psychotherapist, played by Gabriel Byrne, and his patients. Each episode in the series is composed of one therapy session in which myriad topics are discussed and analyzed. Every fifth episode features Byrne's character in session with his own therapist.

King of the Hill
DATE: 1997-
In an episode of this animated comedy called "Naked Ambition," Boomhauer is mistakenly admitted to a Dallas state mental hospital. Friends Dale and Bill also are admitted when they attempt to have Boomhauer released. Hank Hill rescues everyone except Bill, a mentally troubled man who finds group therapy comforting.

Law and Order
DATE: 1990-
This dramatic series chronicles the efforts of the police and legal systems to bring criminals to justice. The characters often seek out the advice of police psychiatrists Dr. Elizabeth Olivet (Carolyn McCormick) or Dr. Emil Skoda (J. K. Simmons).

Mad About You
DATE: 1992-1999
The main characters in this situation comedy, Paul Buchman (Paul Reiser) and his wife Jamie (Helen Hunt), undergo therapy with Sheila (Mo Gaffney), who first appears in the episode "Therapy." Other episodes depict the Buchmans confronting Sheila about her steep therapy fees and searching for more affordable therapists.

Malcolm in the Middle
DATE: 2000-2006
In this situation comedy, Andy Richter plays a psychiatrist who is asked to determine why the three brothers are so destructive. The brothers also see a school therapist in an attempt to avoid unappealing school activities.

M*A*S*H
DATE: 1972-1983

This wartime comedy based on the 1970 film features the supporting character of Corporal Klinger (Jamie Farr), who dresses in women's clothing in hopes of receiving a Section 8 discharge for insanity. The "Dear Sigmund" episode focuses on a visiting psychologist who comforts the characters and is amused by Klinger's efforts.

Monk
DATE: 2002-2009

Tony Shalhoub plays Monk, a brilliant detective formerly of the San Francisco Police Department but forced to work for a private firm, whose idiosyncrasies brought on by obsessive-compulsive disorder (OCD) both aid and inhibit his investigative ability.

My Living Doll
DATE: 1964-1965

In this situation comedy, Bob Cummings plays Dr. Robert McDonald, a psychiatrist who finds himself in control of an attractive female robot.

Once and Again
DATE: 2000-2002

Edward Zwick plays a psychiatrist who helps teenaged Jessie (Evan Rachel Wood) with an eating disorder in this family drama.

Party of Five
DATE: 1994-2000

In this dramatic series, an education student, Kirsten Bennett (Paula Devicq) suffers depression and a nervous breakdown after her fiancé cancels their wedding and she is accused of plagiarizing her doctoral dissertation. She stabilizes with medication and later works as a children's counselor.

Profiler
DATE: 1996-2000

Dr. Sam Walters (Ally Walker) is a forensic psychologist for the Violent Crimes Task Force in this drama.

Seinfeld
DATE: 1990-1998

One plotline in this situation comedy has the psychiatrist of Elaine Benes (Julia-Louis Dreyfus), Dr. Reston (Stephen McHattie), fall in love with her.

Seventh Heaven
DATE: 1996-2007

Reverend Eric Camden (Stephen Collins) is a minister who counsels congregation and community members in this family drama. Episode themes often address mental health issues such as depression, suicide, abuse, and alcoholism.

The Simpsons
DATE: 1989-

In an episode of this animated comedy called "There's No Disgrace Like Home," the Simpson family participates in shock therapy with Dr. Marvin Monroe. In another episode, "Stark Raving Dad," Homer Simpson is placed in a mental institution with a man who claims he is singer Michael Jackson.

Sisters
DATE: 1991-1996

One of the sisters in this dramatic series, Georgie Reed (Patricia Kalember), is seduced by her therapist, Dr. Caspian (Daniel Gerroll), who takes her to a psychiatric conference and suggests that she was molested. She files ethics charges against him with the medical licensing board.

The Sopranos
DATE: 1999-2007

In this dramatic series, Mafia hit man Tony Soprano (James Gandolfini) is in therapy with Dr. Jennifer Melfi (Lorraine Bracco), who urges him to keep a journal.

thirtysomething
DATE: 1987-1991

Most of the characters undergo therapy at some point in this dramatic series. The episode "Therapy" features Elliott (Timothy Busfield) and his wife Nancy (Patricia Wettig) in marriage counseling.

United States of Tara
DATE: 2009-

Toni Collette plays a housewife who suffers from dissociative identity disorder, more commonly referred to as multiple personality. The series was criticized by some for taking a lighthearted view of the disorder.

Elizabeth D. Schafer;
updated by Christopher Rager

ORGANIZATIONS AND SUPPORT GROUPS

Organizations

- **NORTH AMERICAN ORGANIZATIONS**

American Psychiatric Association
1000 Wilson Boulevard
Suite 1825
Arlington, VA 22209-3901
Phone: (888) 35-PSYCH (357-7924)
E-mail: apa@psych.org
http://www.psych.org

American Psychoanalytic Association
309 East 49th Street
New York, NY 10017-1601
Phone: (212) 752-0450
Fax: (212) 593-0571
E-mail: info@apsa.org
http://www.apsa.org

American Psychological Association
750 First Street, NE
Washington, DC 20002-4242
Phone: (800) 374-2721 *or* (202) 336-5500
TDD/TTY: (202) 336-6123
http://www.apa.org

American Psychological Society
1133 15th Street, NW
Suite 1000
Washington, DC 20005
Phone: (202) 293-9300
Fax: (202) 293-9350
http://www.psychologicalscience.org

Canadian Mental Health Association
595 Montreal Road
Suite 303
Ottawa, Ontario K1K 4L2 Canada
Phone: (613) 745-7750

Fax: (613) 745-5522
E-mail: info@cmha.ca
http://www.cmha.ca

Canadian Psychiatric Association
141 Laurier Avenue West
Suite 701
Ottawa, Ontario K1P 5J3 Canada
Phone: (613) 234-2815
Fax: (613) 234-9857
E-mail: cpa@cpa-apc.org
http://www.cpa-apc.org

Canadian Psychological Association
141 Laurier Avenue West
Suite 702
Ottawa, Ontario K1P 5J3 Canada
Phone: (888) 472-0657 *or* (613) 237-2144
Fax: (613) 237-1674
E-mail: cpa@cpa.ca
http://www.cpa.ca

Mental Health America (formerly the National Mental Health Association)
2000 North Beauregard Street, 6th Floor
Alexandria, VA 22311
Phone: (703) 684-7722
TTY: (800) 433-5959
Fax: (703) 684-5968
http://www.mentalhealthamerica.net *or*
    http://www.nmha.org

- **SPECIALTIES**

Academy for the Study of the Psychoanalytic Arts
E-mail: email@AcademyAnalyticArts.org
http://www.AcademyAnalyticArts.org

Academy of Organizational and Occupational Psychiatry
402 East Yakima Avenue
Suite 330
Yakima, WA 98901
Phone: (509) 457-4611
Fax: (509) 454-3295
http://www.aoop.org

Academy of Psychosomatic Medicine
5272 River Road
Suite 630
Bethesda, MD 20816-1453
Phone: (301) 718-6520
Fax: (301) 656-0989
E-mail: apm@apm.org
http://www.apm.org

American Academy of Addiction Psychiatry
345 Blackstone Boulevard, 1st Floor
Weld Building
Providence, RI 02906
Phone: (401) 524-3076
Fax: (401) 272-0922
E-mail: information@aaap.org
http://www.aaap.org

American Academy of Child and Adolescent Psychiatry
3615 Wisconsin Avenue, NW
Washington, DC 20016-3007
Phone: (202) 966-7300
Fax: (202) 966-2891
http://www.aacap.org

American Academy of Clinical Psychiatrists
P.O. Box 458
Glastonbury, CT 06033
Phone: (860) 635-5533
Fax: (860) 613-1650
E-mail: aacp@cox.net
http://www.aacp.com

American Academy of Neurology
1080 Montreal Avenue
St. Paul, MN 55116
Phone: (800) 879-1960 *or* (651) 695-2717
Fax: (651) 695-2791
E-mail: memberservices@aan.com
http://www.aan.com

American Academy of Psychiatry and the Law
One Regency Drive
P.O. Box 30
Bloomfield, CT 06002
Phone: (860) 242-5450 *or* (800) 331-1389
Fax: (860) 286-0787
http://www.aapl.org

American Academy of Psychoanalysis and Dynamic Psychiatry
One Regency Drive
P.O. Box 30
Bloomfield, CT 06002
Phone: (888) 691-8281
Fax: (860) 286-0787
E-mail: Info@AAPDP.org
http://www.aapdp.org

American Academy of Psychotherapists
605 Poole Drive
Garner, NC 27529
Phone: (919) 779-5051
Fax: (919) 779-5642
http://www.aapweb.com

American Art Therapy Association
11160-C1 South Lakes Drive
Suite 813
Reston, VA 20191
Phone: (888) 290-0878
Fax: (571) 333-5685
E-mail: info@arttherapy.org
http://www.arttherapy.org

American Association for Emergency Psychiatry
One Regency Drive
P.O. Box 30
Bloomfield, CT 06002
Phone: (888) 945-5430
Fax: (860) 286-0787
E-mail: AAEP@EmergencyPsychiatry.org
http://www.emergencypsychiatry.org

American Association for Geriatric Psychiatry
7910 Woodmont Avenue
Suite 1350
Bethesda, MD 20814-3004
Phone: (301) 654-7850
Fax: (301) 654-4137

E-mail: main@aagponline.org
http://www.aagpgpa.org

American Association for Marriage and Family Therapy
112 South Alfred Street
Alexandria, VA 22314-3061
Phone: (703) 838-9808
Fax: (703) 838-9805
E-mail: central@aamft.org
http://www.aamft.org

American Association for Technology in Psychiatry
P.O. Box 11
Bronx, NY 10464-0011
Phone: (718) 502-9469
E-mail: aatp@techpsych.org
http://www.techpsych.org

American Association of Children's Residential Centers
11700 West Lake Park Drive
Milwaukee, WI 53224
Phone: (877) 332-2272
E-mail: info@aacrc-dc.org
http://www.aacrc-dc.org

American Association of Community Psychiatrists
c/o Francis Roton Bell
P.O. Box 570218
Dallas, TX 75228-0218
Phone: (972) 613-0985 *or* (972) 613-3997
Fax: (972) 613-5532
E-mail: frda1@airmail.net
http://www.comm.psych.pitt.edu

American Association of Directors of Psychiatric Residency Training
c/o Lucille Meinsler
Suite 319
1594 Cumberland Street
Lebanon, PA 17042
Phone: (717) 270-1673
E-mail: aadprt@verizon.net
http://www.aadprt.org

American Association of Pastoral Counselors
9504A Lee Highway
Fairfax, VA 22031-2303
Phone: (703) 385-6967
Fax: (703) 352-7725
E-mail: info@aapc.org
http://www.aapc.org

American Association of Psychiatric Administrators
P.O. Box 570218
Dallas, TX 75357-0218
Phone: (800) 650-5888
Fax: (972) 613-5532
E-mail: frda1@airmail.net
http://www.psychiatricadministrators.org

American Association of Suicidology
5221 Wisconsin Avenue, NW
Washington, DC 20015
Phone: (202) 237-2280
1-800-SUICIDE (784-2433)
Fax: (202) 237-2282
E-mail: info@suicidology.org
http://www.suicidology.org

American Board of Psychiatry and Neurology
500 Lake Cook Road
Suite 900
Deerfield, IL 60015
Phone: (847) 229-6500
Fax: (847) 229-6600
http://www.abpn.com

American College of Forensic Psychiatry
P.O. Box 130458
Carlsbad, California 92013-0458
Phone: (760) 929-9777
Fax: (760) 929-9803
E-mail: psychlaw@sover.net
http://www.forensicpsychonline.com

American College of Neuropsychopharmacology
545 Mainstream Drive
Suite 110
Nashville, TN 37228
Phone: (615) 324-2360
Fax: (615) 324-2361
E-mail: acnp@acnp.org
http://www.acnp.org

American College of Psychiatrists
122 South Michigan Avenue
Suite 1360
Chicago, IL 60603
Phone: (312) 662-1020
Fax: (312) 662-1025
E-mail: angel@ACPsych.org
http://www.acpsych.org

American Counseling Association
5999 Stevenson Avenue
Alexandria, VA 22304
Phone: (800) 347-6647
Fax: (800) 473-2329 *or* (703) 823-0252
http://www.counseling.org

American Group Psychotherapy Association
25 East 21st Street, 6th Floor
New York, NY 10010
Phone: (212) 477-2677 *or* (877) 668-2472
Fax: (212) 979-6627
E-mail: info@agpa.org
http://www.agpa.org

American Horticultural Therapy Association
201 East Main Street
Suite 1405
Lexington, KY 40507-2004
Phone: (800) 634-1603 *or* (859) 514-AHTA (9177)
Fax: (859) 514-9166
E-mail: ghorton@amrms.com
http://www.ahta.org

American Mental Health Counselors Association
801 North Fairfax Street
Suite 304
Alexandria, VA 22314
Phone: (703) 548-6002 *or* (800) 326-2642
Fax: (703) 548-4775
http://www.amhca.org

American Neurological Association
5841 Cedar Lake Road
Suite 204
Minneapolis, MN 55416
Phone: (952) 545-6284
Fax: (952) 545-6073
E-mail: ana@llmsi.com
http://www.aneuroa.org

American Orthopsychiatric Association
P.O. Box 1564
Clemson, SC 29633
Phone: (864) 656-4230
Fax: (864) 656-6281
E-mail: americanortho@gmail.com
http://www.amerortho.org

American Psychiatric Nurses Association
2107 Wilson Boulevard
Suite 530
Arlington, VA 22209
Phone: (703) 243-2443 *or* (866) 243-2443
Fax: (703) 243-3390
http://www.apna.org

American Psychopathological Association
722 West 168th Street
Box 14
New York, NY 10032
Phone: (212) 543-5880
http://www.appassn.org

American Psychosomatic Society
6728 Old McLean Village Drive
McLean, VA 22101-3906
Phone: (703) 556-9222
Fax: (703) 556-8729
E-mail: info@psychosomatic.org
http://www.psychosomatic.org

American Psychotherapy Association
2750 East Sunshine Street
Springfield, MO 65804
Phone: (800) 205-9165
Fax: (417) 823-9959
E-mail: info@americanpsychotherapy.com
http://www.americanpsychotherapy.com

American Society for Adolescent Psychiatry
P.O. Box 570218
Dallas, TX 75357-0218
Phone: (972) 613-0985
Fax: (972) 613-5532
E-mail: info@adolpsych.org
http://www.adolpsych.org

American Society of Addiction Medicine
4601 North Park Avenue
Upper Arcade Suite 101

Chevy Chase, MD 20815
Phone: (301) 656-3920
Fax: (301) 656-3815
E-mail: email@asam.org
http://www.asam.org

American Society of Clinical Psychopharmacology
P.O. Box 40395
Glen Oaks, NY 11004
Phone: (718) 470-4007
Fax: (718) 343-7739
http://www.ascpp.org

American Society of Consultant Pharmacists
1321 Duke Street
Alexandria, VA 22314
Phone: (703) 739-1300 *or* (800) 355-2727
Fax: (703) 739-1321 *or* (800) 220-1321
E-mail: info@ascp.com
http://www.ascp.com

American Society of Group Psychotherapy and Psychodrama
301 North Harrison Street
Suite 508
Princeton, NJ 08540
Phone: (609) 737-8500
Fax: (609) 737-8510
E-mail: asgpp@asgpp.org
http://www.asgpp.org

American Society of Psychoanalytic Physicians
13528 Wisteria Drive
Germantown, MD 20874
Phone: (301) 540-3197
E-mail: cfcotter@aspp.net
http://www.aspp.net

American Society on Aging
833 Market Street
Suite 511
San Francisco, CA 94103
Phone: (800) 537-9728 *or* (415) 974-9600
Fax: (415) 974-0300
E-mail: info@asaging.org
http://www.asaging.org

Animal Behavior Society
Indiana University
402 North Park Avenue

Bloomington, IN 47408
Phone: 812-856-5541
Fax: 812-856-5542
E-mail: aboffice@indiana.edu
http://www.animalbehavior.org

Assisted Living Federation of America
1650 King Street
Suite 602
Fairfax, VA 22314-2747
Phone: (703) 894-1805
Fax: (703) 894-1831
E-mail: info@alfa.org
http://www.alfa.org

Association for Academic Psychiatry
c/o Dawn M. Levreau
1127 Gate Post Court
Powder Springs, GA 30127
Phone: (770) 222-2265
E-mail: dlevreauaap@gmail.com
http://www.academicpsychiatry.org *or* http://www.hsc.wvu.edu/aap

Association for Ambulatory Behavioral Healthcare
247 Douglas Avenue
Portsmouth, VA 23707
Phone: (757) 673-3741
Fax: (757) 966-7734
E-mail: mickey@aabh.org
http://www.aabh.org

Association for Behavior Analysis International
550 West Centre Avenue
Suite 1
Portage, MI 49024
Phone: (269) 492-9310
Fax: (269) 492-9316
E-mail: mail@abainternational.org
http://www.abainternational.org

Association for Behavioral and Cognitive Therapies
305 7th Avenue, 16th Floor
New York, NY 10001
Phone: (212) 647-1890
Fax: (212) 647-1865
http://www.abct.org

Association for Death Education and Counseling
111 Deer Lake Road
Suite 100
Deerfield, IL 60015
Phone: (847) 509-0403
Fax: (847) 480-9282
http://www.adec.org

Association for Humanistic Psychology
P.O. Box 1190
14B Beach Road
Tiburon, CA 94920
Phone: (415) 435-1604
E-mail: ahpoffice@aol.com
http://www.ahpweb.org

Association for Prenatal and Perinatal Psychology and Health
P.O. Box 1398
Forestville, CA 95436
Phone: (707) 887-2838
E-mail: apppah@aol.com
http://www.birthpsychology.com

Association of Black Psychologists
P.O. Box 55999
Washington, DC 20040-5999
Phone: (202) 722-0808
Fax: (202) 722-5941
E-mail: abpsi_office@abpsi.org
http://www.abpsi.org

Association of Women Psychiatrists
P.O. Box 570218
Dallas, TX 75357-0218
Phone: (972) 613-0985
Fax: (972) 613-5532
E-mail: info@womenpsych.org
http://www.associationofwomenpsychiatrists.com

Child Neurology Society
1000 West County Road E
Suite 290
St. Paul, MN 55126
Phone: (651) 486-9447
Fax: (651) 486-9436
E-mail: nationaloffice@childneurologysociety.org
http://www.childneurologysociety.org

Child Welfare League of America
2345 Crystal Drive
Suite 250
Arlington, VA 22202
Phone: (703) 412-2400
Fax: (703) 412-2401
http://www.cwla.org

Children's Hospice International
1101 King Street
Suite 360
Alexandria, VA 22314
Phone: (703) 684-0330 *or* (800) 2-4-CHILD
  (242-4453)
E-mail: info@chionline.org
http://www.chionline.org

Clinical Social Work Association
P.O. Box 3740
Arlington, VA 22203
Phone: (703) 522-3866
Fax: (703) 522-9441
http://www.clinicalsocialworkassociation.org

Cognitive Neuroscience Society
c/o Center for Mind and Brain
University of California, Davis
One Shields Avenue
Davis, CA 95616
Phone: (805) 845-6487
Fax: (805) 456-0577
E-mail: cnsinfo@cogneurosociety.org
http://www.cogneurosociety.org

Drug Information Association
800 Enterprise Road
Suite 200
Horsham, PA 19044-3595
Phone: (215) 442-6100
Fax: (215) 442-6199
E-mail: dia@diahome.org
http://www.diahome.org

EEG and Clinical Neuroscience Society (ECNS)
5955 State Bridge Road
Suite 110
Johns Creek, GA 30097
New York, NY 10016
Phone and Fax: (888) 531-5335
http://www.ecnsweb.com

International Psychogeriatric Association
550 Frontage Road
Suite 3759
Northfield, IL 60093
Phone: (847) 501-3310
Fax: (847) 501-3317
E-mail: membership@ipa-online.org
http://www.ipa-online.org

International Society for Mental Health Online
E-mail: ismho@ismho.org
http://www.ismho.org

International Society for the Study of Trauma and Dissociation
8400 Westpark Drive, 2d Floor
McLean, VA 22102
Phone: (703) 610-9037
Fax: (703) 610-0234
E-mail: info@isst-d.org
http://www.isst-d.org

International Society for Traumatic Stress Studies
111 Deer Lake Road
Suite 100
Deerfield, IL 60015
Phone: (847) 480-9028
Fax: (847) 480-9282
E-mail: istss@istss.org
http://www.istss.org

Jean Piaget Society (JPS)
c/o Geoffrey Saxe, President
Graduate School of Education
University of California, Berkeley
4315 Tolman Hall
Berkeley, CA 94720-1670
Phone: (510) 643-6627
E-mail: saxe@socrates.berkeley.edu
http://www.piaget.org

National Association for Children's Behavioral Health (formerly the National Association of Psychiatric Treatment Centers for Children)
1025 Connecticut Avenue, NW
Suite 1012
Washington, DC 20036-3536
Phone: (202) 857-9735
Fax: (202) 362-5145
http://www.nacbh.org

National Association for Home Care and Hospice
228 7th Street, SE
Washington, DC 20003
Phone: (202) 547-7424
Fax: (202) 547-3540
http://www.nahc.org

National Association for Human Development
1424 16th Street, NW
Suite 102
Washington, DC 20036
Phone: (202) 328-2191
Fax: (202) 265-6682

National Association of Cognitive-Behavioral Therapists
P.O. Box 2195
Weirton, WV 26062
Phone: (800) 853-1135
E-mail: nacbt@nacbt.org
http://www.nacbt.org

National Association of Psychiatric Health Systems
701 13th Street, NW
Suite 950
Washington, DC 20004-3903
Phone: (202) 393-6700
Fax: (202) 783-6041
E-mail: naphs@naphs.org
http://www.naphs.org

National Association of School Psychologists
4340 East West Highway
Suite 402
Bethesda, MD 20814
Phone: (301) 657-0270 *or* (866) 331-NASP (6277)
Fax: (301) 657-0275
TTY: (301) 657-4155
http://www.nasponline.org

National Association of Social Workers
750 First Street, NE
Suite 700
Washington, DC 20002-4241
Phone: (202) 408-8600
http://www.naswdc.org

National Association of State Mental Health Program Directors
66 Canal Center Plaza
Suite 302
Alexandria, VA 22314
Phone: (703) 739-9333
Fax: (703) 548-9517
http://www.nasmhpd.org

National Council for Community Behavioral Healthcare
1701 K Street, NW
Suite 400
Washington, DC 20006
Phone: (202) 684-7457
Fax: (202) 684-7472
E-mail: Communications@thenationalcouncil.org
http://www.thenationalcouncil.org

National Federation of Families for Children's Mental Health
c/o Marion Mealing, Administrative Assistant
9605 Medical Center Drive
Rockville, MD 20850
Phone: (240) 403-1901
Fax: (240) 403-1909
E-mail: ffcmh@ffcmh.org
http://www.ffcmh.org

National Hospice and Palliative Care Organization
1731 King Street
Suite 100
Alexandria, VA 22314
Phone: (703) 837-1500
Fax: (703) 837-1233
E-mail: nhpco_info@nhpco.org
http://www.nhpco.org

National Psychological Association for Psychoanalysis
150 West 13th Street
New York, NY 10011-7891
Phone: (212) 924-7440
Fax: (212) 989-7543
E-mail: info@npap.org
http://www.npap.org

Pediatric Development and Behavior Online
E-mail: info@dbpeds.org
http://dbpeds.org

Psi Beta: National Honor Society in Psychology for Community and Junior Colleges
6025 Camino Correr
Anaheim, CA 92807
Phone: (888) PSI-BETA
E-mail: psibeta@psibeta.org
http://www.psibeta.org

Psi Chi: The National Honor Society in Psychology
P.O. Box 709
Chattanooga, TN 37401-0709
Phone: (423) 756-2044
Fax: (877) 774-2443
http://www.psichi.org

Psychonomic Society
1710 Fortview Road
Austin, TX 78704
Phone: (512) 462-2442
Fax: (512) 462-1101
E-mail: psp@psychonomic.org
http://www.psychonomic.org

Reversal Theory Society
c/o Dr. Joanne Thatcher
Department of Sport & Exercise Science
Carwyn James Building - Penglais Campus
University of Wales, Aberystwyth
Ceredigion, Wales SY23 3FD
Phone: 01970 628629
Fax: 01970 628557
E-mail: jet@aber.ac.uk
http://www.reversaltheory.org

Smart Marriages: The Coalition for Marriage, Family and Couples Education
5310 Belt Road, NW
Washington, DC 20015
Phone: (202) 362-3332
Fax: (202) 362-0973
E-mail: cmfce@smartmarriages.com
http://www.smartmarriages.com

Society and Animals Forum (formerly Psychologists for the Ethical Treatment of Animals)
P.O. Box 1297
Washington Grove, MD 20880-1297
Phone and Fax: (301) 963-4751

E-mail: kshapiro@societyandanimalsforum.org
http:// www.psyeta.org

Society for Chaos Theory in Psychology and Life Sciences
c/o Matthijs Koopmans, Ed.D.
525 West 238 Street, Apt. 4A
Bronx, NY 10463
E-mail: mkoopmans@aol.com
http://www.societyforchaostheory.org

Society for Computers in Psychology (SCiP)
E-mail: info@scip.ws
http://home.scip.ws

Society for Consumer Psychology
c/o Dr. Larry D. Compeau, Executive Officer
Box 5795
Snell Hall
Clarkson University School of Business
Potsdam, NY 13699
Fax: (315) 268-3810
E-mail: compeau@clarkson.edu
http://www.myscp.org

Society for Disability Studies
c/o Pratik Patel, Director, Executive Office
The City University of New York
101 West 31st Street, 12th Floor
New York, NY 10001
Phone: (212) 652-2004
Fax: (646) 344-7249
E-mail: pratikp1@gmail.com
http://www.disstudies.org

Society for Gestalt Theory and Its Applications (GTA)
c/o Prof. Hellmuth Metz-Goeckel
Mimosenweg 18, D-44289
Dortmund, Germany
Phone: 49 231 402920
Fax: 49 6451 718556
E-mail: office@gestalttheory.net
http://gestalttheory.net

Society for Judgment and Decision Making
membership information:
c/o Bud Fennema
College of Business
P.O. Box 3061110

Florida State University
Tallahassee, FL 32306-1110
E-mail: fennema@fsu.edu
http://www.sjdm.org

Society for Mathematical Psychology
c/o Richard Golden
University of Texas at Dallas
School of Behavioral and Brain Sciences
GR41, 800 West Campbell Road
Richardson, TX 75080
E-mail: golden@utdallas.edu
http://www.mathpsych.org

Society for Neuroscience
1121 14th Street, NW
Suite 1010
Washington, DC 20005
Phone: (202) 962-4000
Fax: (202) 962-4941
E-mail: info@sfn.org
http://www.sfn.org

Society for Personality and Social Psychology (SPSP)
c/o Christie Marvin, SPSP Office Manager
Department of Psychology
Cornell University
239 Uris Hall
Ithaca, NY 14853
Phone: (607) 254-5416
http://www.spsp.org

Society for Psychophysiological Research
2810 Crossroads Drive, Suite 3800
Madison, WI 53718
Phone: (608) 443-2472
Fax: (608) 443-2474 *or* (608) 443-2478
E-mail: spr@reesgroupinc.com
http://www.sprweb.org

Society for Research in Child Development (SRCD)
2950 South State Street
Suite 401
Ann Arbor, MI 48104
Phone: (734) 926-0600
Fax: (734) 926-0601
E-mail: info@srcd.org
http://www.srcd.org

Society for the Psychological Study of Social Issues (SPSSI)
208 I Street NE
Washington, DC 20002-4340
Phone: (202) 675-6956
Fax: (202) 675-6902
E-mail: spssi@spssi.org
http://www.spssi.org

Society of Behavioral Medicine
555 East Wells Street
Suite 1100
Milwaukee, WI 53202-3823
Phone: (414) 918-3156
Fax: (414) 276-3349
E-mail: info@sbm.org
http://www.sbm.org

Society of Biological Psychiatry
c/o Mayo Clinic Jacksonville
4500 San Pablo Road
Research-Birdsall 310
Jacksonville, FL 32224
Phone: (904) 953-2842
Fax: (904) 953-7117
http://www.sobp.org

Society of Psychologists in Management (SPIM)
Lorraine Rieff and Associates
318 South Halsted Street
Chicago, IL 60661
E-mail: SPIM@lrieff.com
http://www.spim.org

Sufi Psychology Association
9965 Horn Road
Suite C
Sacramento, CA 95827
Phone: (916) 368-5530
Fax: (916) 923-3913
E-mail: sufipsy@comcast.net
http://sufipsychology.org

• **INTERNATIONAL ORGANIZATIONS**

Australian Psychological Society, Ltd.
P.O. Box 38
Flinders Lane VIC 8009 Australia
Phone: (03) 8662 3300 *or* 1800 333 497
Fax: (03) 9663 6177

E-mail: contactus@psychology.org.au
http://www.psychology.org.au

British Psychological Society
St Andrews House
48 Princess Road East
Leicester LE1 7DR UK
Phone: +44 (0)116 254 9568
Fax: +44 (0)116 227 1314
E-mail: enquiries@bps.org.uk
http://www.bps.org.uk

Canadian Psychological Association
141 Laurier Avenue West
Suite 702
Ottawa, Ontario K1P 5J3 Canada
Phone: (888) 472-0657 *or* (613) 237-2144
Fax: (613) 237-1674
E-mail: cpa@cpa.ca
http://www.cpa.ca

Canadian Society for Brain, Behaviour, and Cognitive Science
E-mail: secretary@csbbcs.org
http://www.csbbcs.org

Drug Information Association, China
Room 1177, Block A, Gateway Plaza
No. 18 XiGuangLi, North Road, East Third Ring
ChaoYang District, Beijing, 100027, China
Phone: +86 10 5923 1109
Fax: +86 10 5923 1090
http://diachina.org

Drug Information Association, Europe
Elisabethenanlage 25
Postfach
4002 Basel, Switzerland
Phone: +41 61 225 51 51
Fax: +41 61 225 51 52
E-mail: diaeurope@diaeurope.org
http://diaeurope.org

Drug Information Association (India) Private Limited
Unit 6, Gayatri Commercial Complex
Behind Mittal Industrial Estate
Andheri-Kurla Road
Andheri (East)
Mumbai 400 059, India

Phone: +91 22 67653226
Fax: +91 22 28594543
E-mail: diaindia@diaindia.org
http://diaindia.org

Drug Information Association, Japan
Maruei Building 4F
2-19-9 Iwamoto-cho
Chiyoda-ku Tokyo 101-0032, Japan
Phone: +81 3 5833 8444
Fax: +81 3 5820 8448
E-mail: diajapan@diajapan.org
http://diajapan.org

European Federation of Psychologists'
 Associations
EFPA Head Office
Grasmarkt 105/18
B-1000 Brussels, Belgium
Phone: +32 2 503 49 53
Fax: +32 2 503 30 67
E-mail: headoffice@efpa.be
http://www.efpa.eu

European Federation of Psychology Students'
 Associations
http://www.efpsa.org

European Health Psychology Society
c/o Dr. Manja Vollmann
Fachgruppe Gesundheitspsychologie
Universität Konstanz
78457 Konstanz, Germany
http://www.ehps.net

German Psychological Society
Geschäftsstelle der DGPs
Postfach 42 01 43
D-48068 Münster, Germany
Phone: (0049)(0) 2533/2811520
Fax: (0049)(0) 2533/281144
E-mail: geschaeftsstelle@dgps.de
http://www.dgps.de/en

International Association of Applied Psychology
Fax: 34-91-3510091
E-mail: iaap@psy.ulaval.ca
http://www.iaapsy.org

International Association for Cross-Cultural
 Psychology
http://www.iaccp.org

International Association of Psychosocial
 Rehabilitation Services
601 Global Way
Suite 106
Linthicum, MD 21090
Phone: (410) 789-7054
Fax: (410) 789-7675
E-mail: info@uspra.org
http://www.uspra.org/i4a/pages/index.cfm
 ?pageid=3324

International Committee Against Mental Illness
P.O. Box 1921
Grand Central Station, NY 10163
Phone: (212) 263-6214
Fax: (212) 263-5717
E-mail: rc31@nyu.edu

International Ergonomics Association
Pascale Carayon, Ph.D.
Procter & Gamble Bascom Professor in Total
 Quality Department of Industrial and Systems
 Engineering
Director of the Center for Quality and Productivity
 Improvement
75005 Paris, France
University of Wisconsin-Madison
1515 Engineering Drive, 3126 Engineering Centers
 Building
Madison, WI 53706
Phone: (608) 265-0503 *or* (608) 263-2520
Fax: (608) 263-1425
E-mail: carayon@engr.wisc.edu
http://www.iea.cc

International School Psychology Association
ISPA Central Office
The Chicago School of Professional Psychology
325 North Wells Street
Room 529
Chicago, IL 60654-8158
http://www.ispaweb.org

International Society for Traumatic Stress Studies
60 Revere Drive
Suite 500

Northbrook, IL 60062
Phone: (847) 480-9028
Fax: (847) 480-9282
E-mail: istss@istss.org
http://www.istss.org

International Society of Political Psychology
Moynihan Institute of Global Affairs
346 Eggers Hall
Syracuse University
Syracuse, NY 13244
Phone: (315) 443-4470
Fax: (315) 443-9085
E-mail: ispp@maxwell.syr.edu
http://www.ispp.org

International Society of Sport Psychology (ISSP)
http://www.issponline.org

International Union of Psychological Science
E-mail: web@iupsys.org
http://www.am.org/iupsys

Japanese Psychological Association
5-23-13-7F
Hongo, Bunkyo-ku
Tokyo, 113-0033, Japan
Phone: 81 3 3814 3953
Fax: 81 3 3814 3954
http://www.psych.or.jp/index_e.html

Singapore Psychological Society
93 Toa Payoh Central #05-01
Toa Payoh Central Community Building
Singapore, 319194
E-mail: enquiries@singaporepsychologicalsociety
  .org
http://www.singaporepsychologicalsociety.org

Turkish Psychological Association
Mesrutiyet Cad. 22/12
Kizilay-Ankara, 06640, Turkey
Phone: 90 312 25 67 65
Fax: 90 312 417 40 59
E-mail: bilgi@psikolog.org.tr
http://www.psikolog.org.tr/eng.asp

World Association of Social Psychiatry
656 Romero Canyon Road
Santa Barbara, CA 93108

(805) 969-1376
E-mail: jlcmd@cox.net

World Federation for Mental Health
6564 Loisdale Court
Suite 301
Springfield, VA 22150-1812
Phone: (703) 313-8680
Fax: (703) 313-8683
info@wfmh.com
http://www.wfmh.org

• **SPECIFIC DISORDERS**

American Academy of Sleep Medicine (formerly the American Sleep Disorders Association)
One Westbrook Corporate Center
Suite 920
Westchester, IL 60154
Phone: (708) 492-0930
Fax: (708) 492-0943
E-mail: inquiries@aasmnet.org
http://www.aasmnet.org

Anxiety Disorders Association of America
8730 Georgia Avenue
Suite 600
Silver Spring, MD 20910
Phone: (240) 485-1001
Fax: (240) 485-1035
E-mail: information@adaa.org
http://www.adaa.org

Association for Addiction Professionals
1001 North Fairfax Street
Suite 201
Alexandria, VA 22314
Phone: (800) 548-0497
Fax: (800) 377-1136
E-mail: naadac@naadac.org
http://www.naadac.org

Association for Medical Education and Research in Substance Abuse
125 Whipple Street, 3d Floor
Suite 300
Providence, RI 02908
Phone: (401) 243-8460
Fax: (877) 418-8769
http://www.amersa.org

Brain Injury Association of America
1608 Spring Hill Road
Suite 110
Vienna, VA 22182
Phone: (703) 761-0750
National Brain Injury Information Center:
    (800) 444-6443
Fax: (703) 761-0755
http://www.biausa.org

Child and Adolescent Bipolar Foundation
1000 Skokie Boulevard
Suite 570
Wilmette, IL 60091
E-mail: cabf@bpkids.org
http://bpkids.org

**Children and Adults with Attention Deficit
    Disorders**
8181 Professional Place
Suite 150
Landover, MD 20785
Phone: (800) 233-4050 *or* (301) 306-7070
Fax: (301) 306-7090
http://www.chadd.org

**Coma Recovery Association/Traumatic Brain
    Injury, Inc.**
8300 Republic Airport
Suite 106
Farmingdale, NY 11735
Phone: (631) 756-1826
Fax: (631) 756-1827
E-mail: inquiry@comarecovery.org
http://comarecovery.org

Depression and Bipolar Support Alliance
730 North Franklin Street
Suite 501
Chicago, IL 60654-7225
Phone: (800) 826-3632
Fax: (312) 642-7243
http://www.ndmda.org

**Depression and Related Affective Disorders
    Association**
Meyer 3-181
600 North Wolfe Street
Baltimore, MD 21287-7381
Phone: (202) 955-5800 *or* (410) 955-4647

E-mail: drada@jhmi.edu
http://www.med.jhu.edu/drada

False Memory Syndrome Foundation
1955 Locust Street
Philadelphia, PA 19103-5766
Phone: (215) 940-1040
Fax: (215) 940-1042
E-mail: mail@fmsfonline.org
http://www.fmsfonline.org

Foundation for Depression and Manic Depression
952 5th Avenue
New York, NY 10021
Phone: (212) 772-3400

**International Association of Eating Disorders
    Professionals**
P.O. Box 1295
Pekin, IL 61555-1295
Membership: (800) 800-8126
E-mail: info@iaedp.com
http://www.iaedp.com

**International Foundation for Research and
    Education on Depression**
P.O. Box 17598
Baltimore, MD 21297-1598
Phone: (410) 268-0044
Fax: (443) 782-0739
E-mail: info@ifred.org
http://www.ifred.org

Learning Disabilities Association of America
4156 Library Road
Pittsburgh, PA 15234-1349
Phone: (412) 341-1515
Fax: (412) 344-0224
E-mail: info@LDAAmerica.org
http://www.ldanatl.org

**National Alliance for Research on Schizophrenia
    and Depression**
60 Cutter Mill Road
Suite 404
Great Neck, NY 11021
Main Line: (516) 829-0091
Infoline: (800) 829-8289
Research Grants Program: (516) 829-5576
Fax: (516) 487-6930

E-mail: info@narsad.org
http://www.narsad.org

National Association for Children of Alcoholics
11426 Rockville Pike
Suite 301
Rockville, MD 20852
Phone: (301) 468-0985 *or* (888) 55-4COAS
Fax: (301) 468-0987
E-mail: nacoa@nacoa.org
http://www.nacoa.net

National Association for the Dually Diagnosed
132 Fair Street
Kingston, NY 12401
Phone: (845) 331-4336 *or* (800) 331-5362
Fax: (845) 331-4569
E-mail: info@thenadd.org
http://www.thenadd.org

**National Association of Anorexia Nervosa and
    Associated Disorders**
P.O. Box 7
Highland Park IL 60035
Hotline: (847) 831-3438
Fax: (847) 433-4632
E-mail: anad20@aol.com
http://www.anad.org

National Attention Deficit Disorder Association
P.O. Box 7557
Wilmington, DE 19803-9997

Phone and Fax: (800) 939-1019
E-mail: adda@jmoadmin.com
http://www.add.org

Obsessive-Compulsive Foundation
P.O. Box 961029
Boston, MA 02196
Phone: (617) 973-5801
E-mail: info@ocfoundation.org
http://www.ocfoundation.org

Organization for Bipolar Affective Disorders
1019 - 7 Ave SW
Calgary, Alberta T2P 1A8 Canada
Phone: (403) 263-7408 *or* (866) 263-7408
E-mail: obad@obad.ca
http://www.obad.ca

Schizophrenia Society of Canada
4 Fort Street
Winnipeg, MB R3C1C4 Canada
Phone: (204) 786-1616 *or* (800) 263-5545
Fax: (204) 783-4898
E-mail: info@schizophrenia.ca
http://www.schizophrenia.ca

Tourette's Syndrome Association
42-40 Bell Boulevard
Bayside, NY 11361
Phone: (718) 224-2999
http://www.tsa-usa.org

Support Groups

Aging Network Services
Topaz House 4400 East-West Highway
Suite 907
Bethesda, MD 20814
Phone: (301) 657-4329
Fax: (301) 657-3250
E-mail: ans@AgingNetS.com
http://www.agingnets.com

Agoraphobics in Motion
1719 Crooks Street
Royal Oak, MI 48067

Phone: (248) 547-0400
E-mail: anny@ameritech.net
http://www.aim-hq.org

AIDS Clinical Trials Information Service
P.O. Box 6303
Rockville, MD 20849-6303
Phone: (800) HIV-0440 (448-0440)
Fax: (301) 519-6616
E-mail: ContactUs@AIDSinfo.nih.gov
http://www.aidsinfo.nih.gov

AIDS Health Project
1930 Market Street
San Francisco, CA 94102
Phone: (415) 476-3902
http://www.ucsf-ahp.org

Al-Anon/Alateen Family Group Headquarters, Inc.
1600 Corporate Landing Parkway
Virginia Beach, VA 23454-5617
Phone: (757) 563-1600
E-mail: wso@al-anon.org
http://www.al-anon.alateen.org

Alcoholics Anonymous
P.O. Box 459
New York, NY 10163
Phone: (212) 870-3400
http://www.aa.org

Alliance for Aging Research
2021 K Street, NW
Suite 305
Washington, DC 20006
Phone: (202) 293-2856
Fax: (202) 785-8574
http://www.agingresearch.org

Alzheimer's Association
225 North Michigan Avenue
Floor 17
Chicago, IL 60601-7633
Phone: (800) 272-3900 *or* (312) 335-8700
E-mail: info@alz.org
http://www.alz.org

American Association of Homes and Services for the Aging
2519 Connecticut Avenue, NW
Washington, DC 20008-1520
Phone: (202) 783-2242
Fax: (202) 783-2255
E-mail: info@aahsa.org
http://www.aahsa.org

American Council for Drug Education
164 West 74th Street
New York, NY 10023
Phone: (800) 488-3784
E-mail: acde@phoenixhouse.org
http://www.acde.org

American Federation for Aging Research
55 West 39th Street, 16th Floor
New York, NY 10018
Phone: (212) 703-9977 *or* (888) 582-2327
Fax: (212) 997-0330
E-mail: info@afar.org
http://www.afar.org

American Foundation for Suicide Prevention
120 Wall Street, 22d Floor
New York, NY 10005
Phone: (888) 333-AFSP *or* (212) 363-3500
Fax: (212) 363-6237
E-mail: inquiry@afsp.org
http://www.afsp.org

American Geriatrics Society
Empire State Building
350 5th Avenue
Suite 801
New York, NY 10118
Phone: (212) 308-1414
Fax: (212) 832-8646
E-mail: info@americangeriatrics.org
http://www.americangeriatrics.org

American Professional Society on the Abuse of Children
350 Poplar Avenue
Elmhurst, IL 60126
Phone: (630) 941-1235 *or* (877) 402-7722
Fax: (630) 359-4274
E-mail: apsac@apsac.org
http://www.apsac.org/mc/page.do

American Self-Help Clearinghouse
100 East Hanover Avenue
Suite 202
Cedar Knolls, NJ 07927-2020
Phone: (973) 326-67893
Fax: (973) 326-9467
E-mail: ashc@cybernex.net
http://selfhelpgroups.org

Anti-Stigma Project
1521 South Edgewood Street
Suite C
Baltimore, MD 21227
Phone: (410) 646- 2875 *or* (800) 704-0262
Fax: (410) 646-0264

E-mail: anti-stigma@usa.net
http://www.onourownmd.org/asp.html

**Center for Mental Health Services Knowledge
   Exchange Network**
The Substance Abuse and Mental Health Service
P.O. Box 2345
Rockville, MD 20847-2345
Phone: (877) 726-4727
TTY: (800) 487-4889
Fax: (240) 221-4292
E-mail: SHIN@samhsa.hhs.gov
http://www.samhsa.gov/shin

Center on Addiction and the Family
E-mail: coaf@phoenixhouse.org
http://www.coaf.org

Co-Dependents Anonymous, Inc.
P.O. Box 33577
Phoenix, AZ 85067-3577
E-mail: outreach@coda.org
http://www.codependents.org

Disabled American Veterans
P.O. Box 14301
Cincinnati, OH 45250-0301
Phone: (859) 441-7300
http://www.dav.org

**Dual Recovery Anonymous World Service
   Central Office**
P.O. Box 8107
Prairie Village, Kansas 66208
Phone: (913) 991-2703
E-mail: draws@draonline.org
http://draonline.org

Freedom from Fear
308 Seaview Avenue
Staten Island, NY 10305
Phone: (718) 351-1717
Fax: (718) 980-5022
E-mail: help@freedomfromfear.org
http://www.freedomfromfear.org

**Gamblers Anonymous—International Service
   Office**
P.O. Box 17173
Los Angeles, CA 90017

Phone: (213) 386-8789
Fax: (213) 386-0030
E-mail: isomain@gamblersanonymous.org
http://www.gamblersanonymous.org

Marijuana Anonymous
P.O. Box 2912
Van Nuys, CA 91404
Phone: (800) 766-6779
E-mail: office@marijuana-anonymous.org
http://www.marijuana-anonymous.org

Moderation Management Network, Inc.
22 West 27th Street
New York, NY 10001
E-mail: mm@moderation.org
http://www.moderation.org

Mood Disorders Support Group, Inc.
P.O. Box 30377
New York, NY 10011
Phone: (212) 533-6374
Fax: (212) 675-0218
E-mail: info@mdsg.org
http://www.mdsg.org

Nar-Anon Family Groups
22527 Crenshaw Boulevard
Suite 200B
Torrance, CA 90505 USA
Phone: (310) 534-8688\
http://nar-anon.org

Narcotics Anonymous
P.O. Box 9999
Van Nuys, CA 91409
Phone: (818) 773-9999
Fax: (818) 700-0700
http://www.na.org

National Alliance for the Mentally Ill
Colonial Place Three
2107 Wilson Boulevard
Suite 300
Arlington, VA 22201-3042
Phone: (703) 524-7600
NAMI HelpLine: 1-800-950-NAMI (6264)
Fax: (703) 524-9094
http://www.nami.org

National Clearinghouse for Alcohol and Drug Information
P.O. Box 2345
Rockville, MD 20847-2345
Phone: (800) 729-6686
Fax: (240) 221-4292
http://ncadi.samhsa.gov/help/default.aspx

National Council on Alcoholism and Drug Dependence
244 East 58th Street, 4th Floor
New York, NY 10022
Phone: (212) 269-7797
Hope Line: (800) NCA-CALL
Fax: (212) 269-7510
E-mail: national@ncadd.org
http://ncadd.org

National Council on Child Abuse and Family Violence
1025 Connecticut Avenue, NW, Suite 1000
Washington, DC 20036
Phone: (202) 429-6695
E-mail: info@nccafv.org
http://www.nccafv.org

National Council on Patient Information and Education
4915 Saint Elmo Ave Suite 505
Bethesda MD, 20814-6082
Phone: (301) 656-8565
Fax: (301) 656-4464
E-mail: ncpie@ncpie.info
http://www.talkaboutrx.org

National Empowerment Center
599 Canal Street
Lawrence, MA 01840
Phone: (800) POWER-2-U (769-3728)
Fax: (978) 681-6426
http://www.power2u.org

National Families in Action
2957 Claremont Road
Suite 150
Atlanta, GA 30329
Phone: (404) 248-9676
Fax: (404) 248-1312
E-mail: nfia@nationalfamilies.org
http://www.nationalfamilies.org

National Information Center for Children and Youth with Disabilities
P.O. Box 1492
Washington, DC 20013
Phone: (800) 695-0285
V/TTY: (202) 884-8200
Fax: (202) 884-8441
E-mail: nichcy@aed.org
http://www.nichcy.org

National Institute of Mental Health (NIMH)
6001 Executive Boulevard
Room 8184, MSC 9663
Bethesda, MD 20892-9663
Phone: (301) 443-4513 *or* (866) 615-6464
Fax: (301) 443-4279
E-mail: nimhinfo@nih.gov
http://www.nimh.nih.gov

National Institute on Aging
P.O. Box 8250
Silver Spring, MD 20907
Phone: (800) 438-4380
Fax: (301) 495-3334
http://www.nia.nih.gov/alzheimers

National Legal Support for Elderly People with Mental Disabilities
Bazelon Center for Mental Health Law
1101 15th Street
Suite 1212
Washington, DC 20005
Phone: (202) 467-5730
Fax: (202) 223-0409
http://www.bazelon.org

National Mental Health Association Information Center
2000 North Beauregard Street, 6th Floor
Alexandria, VA 22311
Phone: (800) 969-NMHA
TTY: (800) 433-5959
http://www.nmha.org

National Mental Health Consumers' Self-Help Clearinghouse
1211 Chestnut Street
Suite 1207
Philadelphia, PA 19107
Phone: (800) 553-4539 *or* (215) 751-1810

E-mail: info@mhselfhelp.org
http://www.mhselfhelp.org

National Mental Health Services Knowledge Exchange Network
P.O. Box 42490
Washington, DC 20015
Phone: (800) 789-CMHS (2647)
TTY: (301) 443-9006
E-mail: ken@mentalhealth.org
http://www.mentalhealth.org

National Resource Center on Homelessness and Mental Illness
345 Delaware Avenue
Delmar, NY 12054
Phone: (518) 439-7415
E-mail: pra@prainc.com
http://www.prainc.com

National Self-Help Clearinghouse
c/o CUNY, Graduate School and University Center
365 Fifth Avenue
Suite 3300
New York, NY 10016
Phone: (212) 817-1822
E-mail: info@selfhelpweb.org
http://www.selfhelpweb.org

Phobics Anonymous
P.O. Box 1180
Palm Springs, CA 92263
Phone: (760) 322-2673
http://phobicsanonymous.com

Protection and Advocacy for Individuals with Mental Illness
401 State Street
Schenectady, NY 12305-2397
Phone: (800) 624-4143
http://www.cqc.state.ny.us

Save Our Sons and Daughters (SOSAD)
2441 West Grand Boulevard
Detroit, MI 48208
Phone: (313) 361-5200
Fax: (313) 361-0055

• **HOTLINES**
1-800-488-DRUG
1-800-HEROIN
1-800-RELAPSE
1-800-SUICIDE (784-2433)
1-888-MARIJUANA (627-4582)
Action, Parent, and Teen Support:
   (800) 282-5660
Al-Anon Family Groups: (800) 344-2666
Al-Anon for Families of Alcoholics:
   (800) 344-2666
Al-Anon/Alateen: (800) 356-9996
Alcohol and Drug Abuse Hotline:
   (800) 729-6686
Alcohol and Drug Helpline: (800) 821-4357
Alcohol Hotline: (800) 331-2900
Alcoholics Anonymous: (800) 333-5051
Alzheimer's Disease Education and Referral
   Center: (800) 438-4380
American Association on Intellectual and
   Developmental Disabilities: (800) 424-3688
American Council for Drug Education: (800)
   DRUG-HELP
American Council on Alcoholism:
   (800) 527-5344
American Suicide Foundation: (800) 531-4477
American Trauma Society: (800) 556-7890
America's Crisis Pregnancy Helpline: (800)
   67-BABY-6
Anorexia and Bulimia Crisis: (800) 227-4785
Ask a Nurse: (800) 535-1111
Be Sober Hotline: (800) 237-6237
Child Abuse Hotline: (800) 540-4000 (Los Angeles
   County)
Child Abuse Hotline: (800) 792-5200
   (Massachusetts)
Cocaine Anonymous: (800) 347-8998
Cocaine Hotline: (800) COCAINE (262-2463)
Crisis Intervention Hotline (psychiatric):
   (800) 540-5806
Depression/Alcohol and Drug Addiction Trauma
   Hotline: (800) 544-1177
Depression Awareness Recognition and Treatment
   Helpline: (800) 421-4211
Family Support Network: (800) TLC-0042
Grief Recovery Helpline: (800) 445-4808
National Association for Children of Alcoholics:
   (888) 554-2627
National Center for Victim of Crime:
   (800) FYI-CALL (394-2255)

National Child Abuse Hotline:
(800) 422-4453

National Council on Alcohol and Drug
Dependence HopeLine: (800) 475-HOPE
(4673)

National Council on Problem Gambling:
(800) 522-4700

National Domestic Violence Hotline:
(800) 799-7233; (800) 787-3224 (TDD)

National Drug Information Treatment and
Referral Hotline: (800) 662-HELP (4357)

National Institute on Drug Abuse Hotline:
(800) 662-4357

Obsessive-Compulsive Foundation:
(800) 639-7462

Occupational Therapy Consumer Line:
(800) 668-8255

Panic Disorder InfoLine (NIMH) 800-64-PANIC
(647-2642)

Parental Stress Hotline: (800) 632-8188

Prevent Child Abuse America: (800) CHILDREN
(244-5373)

Prozac Survivors Support Group, Inc.:
(800) 392-0640

Rape and Abuse and Incest National Network:
(800) 656-HOPE

SAFE (Self-Abuse Finally Ends) Alternative
Information Line: (800) DONT-CUT
(366-8288)

Shoplifters Anonymous: (800) 848-9595

Therapist Referral Network: (800) 843-7274

United Way Crisis Helpline: (800) 233-4357

Youth Crisis Hotline: (800) 448-4663

Elizabeth D. Schafer

PHARMACEUTICAL LIST

This appendix is divided into the following sections:

Psychopharmacologic Treatments for Clinical
Depression 2175
Tricyclic Antidepressants (TCAs) 2175
Selective Serotonin Reuptake Inhibitors
(SSRIs or SRIs). 2176
Serotonin-Norepinephrine Reuptake
Inhibitors (SNRIs). 2177
Monoamine Oxidase Inhibitors
(MAOIs) 2177
Miscellaneous (or Atypical)
Antidepressants 2177
Psychopharmacologic Treatments for
Anxiety 2178
Benzodiazepine Anxiolytics 2178
Nonbenzodiazepine Anxiolytics 2179

Psychopharmacologic Treatments for
Mania 2179
Psychopharmacologic Treatments for
Attention Disorders 2180
Psychopharmacologic Treatments for
Sleep Disorders 2181
Psychopharmacologic Treatments for
Dementia 2182
Interaction of Pharmaceutical
Agents 2182
Time Line of Psychotropic Drugs 2185
Sources for Further Study 2185
Web Sites 2186

Psychopharmacologic Treatments for Clinical Depression

Antidepressant medications are grouped into five classes based on their effects on cerebral function:

- Tricyclic antidepressants (TCAs)
- Selective serotonin reuptake inhibitors (SSRIs or SRIs)
- Serotonin-norepinephrine reuptake inhibitors (SNRIs)
- Monoamine oxidase inhibitors (MAOIs)
- Miscellaneous (or atypical) antidepressants

Tricyclic Antidepressants (TCAs). TCAs were introduced into clinical medicine in the late 1950's. Positive features include effectiveness in preventing relapse and recurrence and the ability sometimes to measure blood levels of TCAs to use as guidelines for adjusting dosage. Limitations include side effects (which often can be regulated by lowering dosage) and the fact that a prolonged period of dosage may be required to produce a therapeutic effect.

Antidepressants work by enhancing the function of neurotransmitters. Depression seems to be caused by a highly complex and intricate change in sensitivity of receptors for these neurotransmitters, rather than the quantity of neurotransmitters present in the brain. Two neurotransmitters, norepinephrine and serotonin, are particularly associated with depression, and one or both are affected by almost all antidepressant drugs.

The most frequent side effects are sedation (due to antihistamine properties); orthostatic hypotension (sudden decrease in blood pressure leading to light-headedness or dizziness); and anticholinergic effects (due to a decrease in mucosal moisture production caused by acetylcholine), such as dry mouth, constipation, difficulty urinating, and blurred vision. For older men, the anticholinergic aspect may aggravate the symptoms of an enlarged prostate gland.

TCA Usage

Generic Name	Trade Name	Daily Dosage Range (approx.)	Side Effects
amitriptyline	Elavil	75-300 milligrams	drowsiness, possible blurred vision, urinary hesitation
amoxapine	Asendin	10-300 milligrams	drowsiness, possible blurred vision, dry mouth

(continued)

TCA Usage—*continued*

Generic Name	Trade Name	Daily Dosage Range (approx.)	Side Effects
clomipramine	Anafranil	10-250 milligrams	drowsiness, headache, blurred vision, dry mouth, constipation
desipramine	Norpramin	75-300 milligrams	drowsiness, blurred vision, urinary hesitation
doxepin	Sinequan, Adapin	75-300 milligrams	drowsiness, blurred vision, urinary retention/hesitation
imipramine	Toframil, Aventil	75-300 milligrams	drowsiness, blurred vision, urinary retention/hesitation
nortriptyline	Pamelor	10-100 milligrams	drowsiness, blurred vision, urinary retention/hesitation
protriptyline	Vivactil	5-20 milligrams	drowsiness, blurred vision, urinary retention/hesitation
trimipramine	Surmontil	10-75 milligrams	drowsiness, blurred vision, urinary retention/hesitation

Selective Serotonin Reuptake Inhibitors (SSRIs or SRIs). SSRIs are the most widely used antidepressants in the United States and other parts of the world. They do not cause orthostatic hypotension or anticholinergic side effects and are preferred by some physicians for mild or moderately severe depression, reserving TCAs for the most severe depression. SSRIs are generally more expensive than TCAs. Prozac (fluoextine) was the first SSRI to become available in the United States, and it remains one of the most widely prescribed antidepressants in the world. It has a longer elimination half-life, which means that it can remain effective for a longer period of time, but the side effects also persist longer after discontinuance. Sarafem, another name for Prozac, is marketed as a treatment for symptoms of premenstrual dysphoric disorder (PMDD). Both Zoloft (sertraline) and Luvox (fluvoxamine) have broad therapeutic dosages and relatively few side effects, but upset stomach, bloating, and diarrhea can be common early in treatment. Paxil (paroxetine) tends to be sedating and may cause sporadic constipation, dry mouth, and trouble starting urination. Celexa (citalopram) has a longer half-life and is unique in that it does not have significant interactions with other medications. An isomer of Celexa, Lexapro (escitalopram oxalate), was brought to market, with indications of faster action and reduced side effects in some patients. All SSRIs except citalopram and escitalopram have significant drug interactions with other psychiatric medications as well as with some other medications.

SSRI Usage

Generic Name	Trade Name	Daily Dosage Range (approx.)	Side Effects
citalopram	Celexa	10-40 milligrams	restlessness, insomnia or drowsiness
escitalopram	Lexapro	10-40 milligrams	headache, nausea, insomnia
fluoextine	Prozac, Sarafem	5-40 milligrams, 10-20 milligrams	agitation, nausea, sexual dysfunction
fluvoxamine	Luvox	10-200 milligrams	somulence, nausea, headache, diarrhea
paroxetine	Paxil	5-20 milligrams	nervousness, nausea, sexual dysfunction
sertraline	Zoloft	25-200 milligrams	nausea, diarrhea, sexual dysfunction

Serotonin-Norepinephrine Reuptake Inhibitors (SNRIs). SNRIs are antidepressants that increase the levels of serotonin and norepinephrine by blocking their absorption into the brain. In addition, this class of drugs is also used to treat anxiety disorders, obsessive-compulsive disorder, and attention-deficit hyperactivity disorder (ADHD). There is a warning connected with these drugs that they may worsen the depression of people eighteen to twenty-four years of age, causing suicidal thoughts. Although these drugs are not addictive, stopping them abruptly may cause nausea, dizziness, and lethargy. Gradual discontinuation of the drugs, under a doctor's care, is recommended.

SNRI Usage

Generic name	Trade Name	Daily Dosage Range (approx.)	Side Effects
venlafaxine	Effexor	75-350 milligrams	anxiety, blurred vision, changes in taste
duloxetine	Cymbalta	30-120 milligrams	blurred vision, constipation, sexual dysfunction

Monoamine Oxidase Inhibitors (MAOIs). MAOIs were the first antidepressants prescribed. They were initially discovered (like many psychiatric drugs, by accident) in the 1950's and are now widely used throughout the world. MAOIs work by inhibiting the production of monoamine oxidase, which metabolizes norepinephrine and serotonin in the central nervous system. They can be effective when other drugs are not working, particularly when people are listless and apathetic. Side effects include changes in thyroid function and blood pressure. Sedation or stimulation is not uncommon in older patients. Some commonly prescribed vitamin and mineral supplements, herbal preparations, and pain medications tend to interact with MAOIs. In addition, there may be food interactions, with a synergistic effect on blood pressure that may lead to a potentially fatal stroke or heart attack.

MAOI Usage

Generic Name	Trade Name	Daily Dosage Range (approx.)	Side Effects
phenelzine	Nardil	7.5-30 milligrams	low blood pressure, weight gain, sexual dysfunction
tranylcypromine	Parnate	5-30 milligrams	weight gain, lowered blood pressure, sexual dysfunction

Miscellaneous (or Atypical) Antidepressants. Some of the newer antidepressants have diverse chemical properties and do not fit into standard medication categories. Wellbutrin (bupropion) has a broad dosing range and tends to increase physical energy. It may lead to agitation and insomnia and, in its original form, must be given more than once per day. Serzone (nefazodone) has a broad dosing range and is very sedating, which may lead to daytime drowsiness over a prolonged course of therapy. It has the advantage of not causing hypotension or anticholinergic side effects. Like some SSRIs, it may interfere with enzymes that metabolize other medications, thus increasing their level in the bloodstream. Remon (mirtazapine) is one of the newest antidepressants. It does not cause orthostatic hypotension or have cardiac or anticholinergic side effects. It can function as a mild sedative and is potentially harmful for overweight patients.

Miscellaneous Antidepressant Usage

Generic Name	Trade Name	Daily Dosage Range (approx.)	Side Effects
bupropion	Wellbutrin	75-350 milligrams	possible increase in energy
mirtazapine	Remon	7.5-45 milligrams	very sedating, possible weight gain
nefazodone	Serzone	50-200 milligrams	very sedating, potential drug interactions
trazodone	Desyrel	25-200 milligrams	very sedating, useful as a sleep aid

Psychopharmacologic Treatments for Anxiety

Benzodiazepine Anxiolytics. A variety of medications, especially antidepressants, are used to treat anxiety, but benzodiazepines are still the most frequently prescribed drugs. Generally speaking, benzodiazepines can be divided into two categories based on their elimination half-life, or the time that it takes for the medication to be cleared from the body. The long half-life medications remain in the system for sufficient time to become metabolized in the bloodstream, leading to accumulation in the bloodstream and central nervous system. Short half-life drugs do not accumulate. There are no differences in side effects between short and long half-life benzodiazepines. Benzodiazepine drugs are sedative hypnotics, and their side effects may include a decrease in attention, unsteadiness when large doses are prescribed, and a tendency toward forgetfulness, particularly of recent events. A degree of physiological dependence often develops when a benzodiazepine is taken on a regular basis for more than a few weeks, and a mild withdrawal reaction may occur if the drug is abruptly discontinued. Prolonged usage may lead to a more intense dependency and more severe symptoms such as restlessness, agitation, and flulike discomfort if the medication is discontinued without a gradual reduction in dosage.

Benzodiazepine Anxiolytics Categorized by Half-Life

Long Half-Life	Short Half-Life
diazepam (Valium) 30-100 hours	alprazolam (Xanax) 12-15 hours
chlordiazepoxide (Librium) 50-100 hours	lorazepam (Ativan) 8-12 hours
clonazepam (Klonopin) 18-50 hours	oxazepam (Serax) 8-12 hours
clorazepate (Tranxene) 40-50 hours	

Benzodiazepine Anxiolytics Usage

Generic Name	Trade Name	Daily Dosage Range (approx.)	Side Effects
alprazolam	Xanax	0.25-2 milligrams	drowsiness, dizziness, confusion, dependency
chlordiazepoxide	Librium	10-40 milligrams	drowsiness, dependency, alcohol interaction
clorazepate	Tranxene	3.75-15 milligrams	drowsiness, dizziness, alcohol interaction
diazepam	Valium	2-20 milligrams	drowsiness, dizziness, blurred vision, alcohol interaction, dependency
lorazepam	Ativan	0.25-2 milligrams	drowsiness, alcohol interaction, dependency
oxazepam	Serax	10-45 milligrams	drowsiness, blurred vision, alcohol interaction

Nonbenzodiazepine Anxiolytics. Newer drugs, such as buspirone (Buspar), are part of a different chemical subgroup, the azapirones, and are considered pure anxioselective agents. They do not result in sedation and are less likely to lead to physiological dependence. They do not interact with as many other compounds. Side effects may include dizzi- ness or lightheadedness and nausea, and buspirone takes a longer time to become effective. Hydroxy- zine (Atarax, Vistaril, Marax) is part of the pipera- zine chemical subgroup and is a sedating antihista- mine sometimes used as a medication for anxiety. It is rapidly absorbed and has a half-life of three hours. Its powerful sedating qualities limit its usefulness.

Miscellaneous Anxiolytics Usage

Generic Name	Trade Name	Daily Dosage Range (approx.)	Side Effects
buspirone	Buspar	5-80 milligrams	dizziness, dry mouth, nausea
hydroxyzine	Atarax, Vistaril, Marax	25-100 milligrams	transient drowsiness

---

Psychopharmacologic Treatments for Mania

The alternation of mania and depression is known as bipolar disorder, a condition which tends to in- crease as a person ages such that the normal euthymic (nonsymptomatic) state between episodes may de- crease to the point of nonexistence. Manic states are treated with lithium carbonate (anticonvulsant agents), which functions as a mood stabilizer. For more severe conditions, particularly among elderly patients, antipsychotic medications are utilized, so named for their tendency to cause neurological side effects or extrapyramidal symptoms (EPS). Typical antipsychotics, such as haloperidol (Haldol), have been used since the 1960's. They have a wide range of conventional side effects, such as oversedation and unsteadiness, as well as anticholinergic side ef- fects including dry mouth, constipation, blurred vi- sion, and prostate disorders. EPS include immobile facial features, slowed hand motion, and tremors similar to Parkinson's disease. Over a prolonged period of time, abnormal movements around the mouth and involuntary blinking may occur. Con- sequently, antipsychotics are usually prescribed in very small doses and carefully controlled. Second- generation antipsychotics which do not produce EPS (or only infrequent and mild ones) have begun to replace antipsychotics, but each has individual side effects that affect usage. For bipolar disorders, a combination of mood stabilizers and antipsychotic medications are often used, sometimes in conjunc- tion with antidepressants, requiring a careful coor- dination of the various drugs.

Mood Stabilizers Usage

Generic Name	Trade Name	Daily Dosage Range (approx.)	Side Effects
carbamazepine	Tegretol	50-1,200 milligrams	possible decreased white blood cell count, possible interaction with other medications
divalproex sodium	Depakene, Depakote	125-1,800 milligrams	possible mild weight gain
gabapentin	Neurontin	150-2,000 milligrams	sedation
lamotrigine	Lamictal	12.5-300 milligrams	possible serious rash
lithium	Eskalith, Lithobid	300-2,400 milligrams	possible thirst, increased urination, forgetfulness, and mild tremors
verapamil	Calan, Isoptin, Verelan	120-480 milligrams	possible lower blood pressure

First-Generation Antipsychotics Usage

Generic Name	Trade Name	Daily Dosage Range (approx.)	Side Effects
chlorpromazine	Thorazine	10-800 milligrams	muscle stiffness, tremors, dry mouth, weight gain
fluphenazine	Prolixin	0.25-20 milligrams	muscle stiffness, dry mouth, hypotension
haloperidol	Haldol	0.25-20 milligrams	muscle stiffness, tremors, weight gain, tachycardia
loxapine	Loxitane	10-100 milligrams	mild sedation, dizziness, weight gain, dry mouth
mesoridazine	Serentil	10-200 milligrams	muscle stiffness, dry mouth, mild sedation
molindone	Moban	30-225 milligrams	Hyperactivity, blurred vision, nausea
perphenazine	Trilafon	4-64 milligrams	mild sedation, dry mouth, muscle stiffness, jumpiness
thiothixene	Navane	2-30 milligrams	muscle stiffness, tremors, weight gain
trifluoperazine	Stelazine	2-30 milligrams	muscle stiffness, tremors, weight gain

Second-Generation Antipsychotics Usage

Generic Name	Trade Name	Daily Dosage Range (approx.)	Side Effects
aripiprazole	Abilify	5-20 milligrams	dizziness, drowsiness, headache
clozapine	Clozaril	10-800 milligrams	heavy sedation, anticholinergic effects
olanzapine	Zyprexa	2.5-40 milligrams	mild sedation, mild anticholinergic effects, possible weight gain
quetiapine	Seroquel	25-800 milligrams	possible unsteadiness and orthostatic hypotension
risperidone	Risperdal	0.25-6 milligrams	possible severe EPS in higher doses
ziprasidone	Geodon	10-160 milligrams	possible serious cardiac problems for patients with heart disease

Psychopharmacologic Treatments for Attention Disorders

It has been estimated that 3 to 5 percent of children have some degree of attention-deficient hyperactivity disorder (ADHD), a condition which may continue into adolescence and adulthood. There are three aspects of this disruptive behavior: inattention, hyperactivity, and impulsivity. Methylphenidate (Ritalin) was first used in 1950 to treat hyperactive children and has been joined by the stimulants dextroamphetamine (Dexedrine) and pemoline (Cylert) as effective agents. These drugs alter metabolic activity in the brain, lowering the neurotransmission of dopamine. Serious side effects may include growth retardation related to appetite supression leading to anorexia, impairment of cognitive performance, and (in the case of pemoline) liver toxicity, requiring monitoring every six months. Dextroamphetamine can be fatal if an overdose occurs, and all stimulants can result in insomnia. Because of the latter property, amphetamine-like stimulants can also be used to treat narcolepsy. Ritalin-SR (extended release), Dexedrine-SR, Cylert, methamphetamine hydrochloride (Desoxyn), and modafinil (Provigil) have substantially helped but not cured narcolepsy.

Stimulant Usage

Generic Name	Trade Name	Daily Dosage Range (approx.)	Side Effects
atomoxetine hydrochloride	Strattera	60-120 milligrams	appetite loss, constipation, cough
dexmethylphenidate hydrochloride	Focalin	5-20 milligrams	fever, insomnia, appetite loss
dextroamphetamine	Dexedrine, Dextrostat	5-40 milligrams	hyperactivity, insomnia, headache
dextroamphetamine saccharte/sulfate; amphetamine aspartate/sulfate	Adderal	40-50 milligrams	sleep disturbance, appetite suppression, irritability
methamphetamine hydrochloride	Desoxyn	20-115 milligrams	hyperactivity, insomnia, restlessness
methylphenidate	Ritalin, Metadate, Concerta, Methylin	10-60 milligrams	sleep disorders, appetite suppression, restlessness, irritability
modafinil	Provigil	100-400 milligrams	typical stimulant side effects, but less sympathomemitic
pemoline	Cylert	37.5-112.5 milligrams	hyperactivity, insomnia, hepatitis

Psychopharmacologic Treatments for Sleep Disorders

As people grow older, changes in normal sleep patterns occur frequently, due most fundamentally to age-related alteration in monoamine neurotransmission, as well as to a decrease in melatonin, the primary hormone that regulates sleep cycles. Antidepressants with sedating properties can be helpful in treating sleep disorders, since they affect benzodiazepine receptors in the brain and facilitate neurotransmissions. These drugs decrease the amount of time that it takes to fall asleep and increase the amount of total sleep time. However, steady use may make a patient totally dependent on the drugs and require them to fall asleep. In addition, abruptly discontinuing usage may lead to a rebound reaction resulting in severe insomnia. Benzodiazepine drugs are not physically addictive, and there is no sense of a physical craving, but they also tend toward a degree of mild memory loss and confusion on awakening. In addition, they can be very dangerous when used in conjunction with alcohol. The benzodiazepine drugs in this category are commonly called hypnotics. Zolpidem (Ambien) has fewer side effects, better long-term effectiveness, and less likelihood of dependency than the older hypnotics.

Hypnotics Usage

Generic Name	Trade Name	Daily Dosage Range (approx.)	Side Effects
estazolam	ProSom	0.5-2 milligrams	drowsiness the following day, anxiety and dizziness after effect passes
flurazepam	Dalmane	7.5-30 milligrams	prolonged drowsiness during the day, some withdrawal symptoms, unsteadiness, falls among the elderly
quazepam	Doral	7.5-15 milligrams	possible mild memory loss and confusion

(continued)

Hypnotics Usage—*continued*

Generic Name	Trade Name	Daily Dosage Range (approx.)	Side Effects
temazepam	Restoril	7.5-30 milligrams	strong withdrawal symptoms, mild drowsiness
triazolam	Halcion	0.125-0.25 milligrams	very powerful drug leading to short-term memory loss, rebound insomnia, anxiety
zolpidem	Ambien	5-10 milligrams	fewer side effects than with other hypnotics, some drowsiness possible

Psychopharmacologic Treatments for Dementia

A reduction in memory capability is likely to occur as people age, but there is a distinct difference between age-associated memory impairment (AAMI) and dementia, a general diagnostic term to convey impairment in cognitive functions such as memory, concentration, orientation, and logical reasoning. Alzheimer's disease, a specific form of dementia, involves the production of abnormal proteins. While treatments for dementia are still being developed, donepezil (Aricept) can slow the progression of the disease and improve memory to some extent. Aricept has become the medication of choice due to its lesser side effects for most patients.

Cognitive Enhancer Usage

Generic Name	Trade Name	Daily Dosage Range (approx.)	Side Effects
donepezil	Aricept	5-20 milligrams	mild muscle cramping, nausea
galantamine	Razadyne	4-8 milligrams	abdominal pain, anemia, blood in urine
memantine	Namenda	5-20 milligrams	confusion, constipation, coughing
rivastigmine	Exelon	1.5-3 milligrams	abdominal pain, anxiety, aggression

Interaction of Pharmaceutical Agents

One of the most important considerations in the use of psychiatric drugs is their interaction with medical drugs, an important element in many situations in which more than one pharmacologic agent is required. In addition, psychiatric drugs also may interact to cause problems when treatment requires more than one prescription.

Medical Drugs Interacting with Psychiatric Drugs

Medical Drug	Psychiatric Drug	Interactive Effect
antiarrhythmics	TCAs	possible heart arrhythmias
antibiotics (doxycycline)	carbamazepine	decrease in the antibiotic effect
antibiotics (erythomycin)	nefazodone	increase in the blood level of nefazodone
antibiotics (tetracycline, spectinomycin)	lithium	increase in the effect and side effects of lithium

(continued)

Medical Drugs Interacting with Psychiatric Drugs—*continued*

Medical Drug	Psychiatric Drug	Interactive Effect
bromocriptine	antipsychotics	mutual interference with each other's therapeutic effect
caffeine	Luvox (fluvoxamine)	increased sleepiness, agitation
calcium channel blockers	TCAs	increased sedation, dizziness, dry mouth, urinary retention
cough medicine with dextromethorphan	SSRIs	flushing, sweating, elevated blood pressure
Coumadin (warfarin)	SSRIs, clozapine	increased risk of bleeding
Demerol (meperidine hydrochloride)	MAOIs	increased temperature, risk of death
diabetes medications	MAOIs	decrease in blood glucose levels
	antipsychotics	possible increase in blood glucose levels
digoxin	clozapine	serious cardiac effects
estrogen	imipramine	lethargy, headache, tremor, increase in blood pressure
	TCAs	increased sedation, dizziness, sweating, urinary retention
Hismanal (astemizole), Seldane (terfenadine)	Serzone (nefazodone)	cardiac arrhythmias
	SSRIs	potentially fatal heartbeat irregularity
Inderal (propranolol)	antipsychotics	increased blood level of Inderal, lowered blood pressure
labetalol	imipramine	increased imipramine level, more antidepressant side effects
nonsteroidal anti-inflammatory drugs (NSAIDs)	lithium	increased blood levels and side effects of lithium
prednisone, estrogen	Serzone (nefazodone)	increased steroid blood levels
Propulsid (cisapride)	SSRIs	potentially fatal heartbeat irregularity
quinidine	TCAs	dangerous cardiac arrhythmias, increased sedation
rifampin	antipsychotics	decreased antipsychotic effect
stimulants	MAOIs	increased blood pressure, risk of stroke and heart attack
Tagmet (cimetidine)	TCAs	increased sedation, dizziness, dry mouth, urinary retention
Tegretol (carbamazepine)	TCAs	decreased therapeutic effect
theophylline	Luvox (fluvoxamine)	increased blood pressure, rapid heart rate, shakiness, sweating
Tylenol (acetaminophen)	Luvox (fluvoxamine)	increased Luvox side effects
vasopressors	MAOIs	increased blood pressure, risk of stroke and heart attack

Psychopharmacologic Interaction

Psychiatric Drug	Interacting Drug	Clinical Effect
buproprion	carbamazepine	decreased buproprion effect
	haloperidol	increased haloperidol levels
carbamazepine	benzodiazepine	decrease in clonazepam and alprazolam levels
	lithium	increased dizziness, ataxia
donepezil	carbamazepine	possible decrease in donepezil levels
	nefazodone, fluoxetine	possible increase in donepezil levels, side effects
MAOIs	buspirone	increased blood pressure
	lithium	tardive dyskinesia
	nefazodone	toxic reactions
	SSRIs	hyperserotonergic states
nefazodone	benzodiazepine	enhanced effects
	haloperidol	increased haloperidol levels
neuroleptics	anticholinergics	increased anticholinergic effect
	benzodiazepines	increased sedation, increased risk of respiratory depression
	buproprion	possible increase in haloperidol levels
	carbamazepine	decreased antipsychotic levels
	lithium	possible delirium, possible increased EPS
	MAOIs	hypotension, possible increase in effect of antipsychotics
	nefazadone	possible increase in haloperidol levels
	SSRIs	possible increase in fluoxetine levels
	TCAs	increased sedation, hypotension, possible ventricular arrhythmias, possible risk of seizures
	trazadone	possible increase of hypotension
SSRIs	lithium	fever, increased lithium levels
TCAs	anticholinergics	increased anticholinergic effects
	antipsychotics	possible ventricular arrhythmias, increase in plasma levels, sedation, hypotension, risk of seizures
	benzodiazepines	increased sedation, confusion, impaired motor function
	carbamazepine	decreased TCA levels
	lithium	possible increase in lithium tremor
	MAOIs	increased incidence of mania, increase in TCA toxicity
	SSRIs	significant increase in TCA levels

Time Line of Psychotropic Drugs

- 1930's: Synthetic production of benzodiazepines
- 1948: Serotonin isolated from beef serum
- 1949: Discovery of therapeutic effects of lithium on mania; FDA bans lithium as a result of deaths of patients with cardiac disease
- 1951: Chlorpromazine used to reduce anxiety in surgical patients, suggesting therapeutic implications for neuroleptic agents
- 1952: Chlorpromazine (as Thorazine) used to treat mania; iproniazid identified as a MAOI
- 1955: Molecular structure of chlorpromazine altered, leading to development of antipsychotic agents haloperidol and fluphenazine
- 1957: Halodol developed from haloperidol

- 1958: Tricyclic antidepressants introduced in article in *American Journal of Psychiatry*
- 1960: Benzodiazepines (Valium) developed as effective medications; addictive considerations emerge later
- 1960's: TCAs introduced to treat depression; ban on lithium in the United States lifted
- 1980's: SSRIs (Prozac) developed as antidepressants; antiepileptic drugs carbamazepine and divalproex sodium discovered to have mood-stabilizing properties
- 1990's: Clozapine and risperidone introduced as new form of antipsychotic agents; donepezil (Aricept) introduced as cognitive enhancer

SOURCES FOR FURTHER STUDY

Folks, David G., and Norman L. Keltner. *Psychotropic Drugs*. St. Louis: Mosby-Year Book, 1997. Divided into two parts, an overview of clinical psychopharmacology and a very detailed profile of more than one hundred psychotropic drugs. Designed for the serious student of psychopharmacology but organized so that the layperson can consult it about specific drugs and their properties. The individual profiles are very informative, and the numerous charts, diagrams, illustrations, and indexes complement the text well.

Gorman, Jack M. *The Essential Guide to Psychiatric Drugs*. New York: St. Martin's Press, 1997. Described by experts as "An outstanding book about these drugs for the nonphysican," Gorman's book offers an extensive overview of the discipline and its primary concerns. Presents specific data about the psychotropic drugs and their uses. Includes many tables, detailed discussions about issues and controversies, and sufficient scientific data to assist in an understanding about how psychotropic agents operate.

Hardman, Joel G., and Lee E. Limbird, eds. *Goodman and Gilman's The Pharmacological Basis of Therapeutics*. 10th ed. New York: McGraw-Hill, 2001. A standard reference work in which the contributors attempt to "be reliable in their efforts to provide information that is complete and generally in accord with the standards accepted at the time of publication." The book is directed toward medical students, and chapters 19 and 20 have extensive information about psychopharmacologic agents.

Salzman, Carl. *Psychiatric Medications for Older Adults: The Concise Guide*. New York: Guilford Press, 2001. A comprehensive, very clearly written, and well-organized presentation by the foremost expert in geriatric psychopharmacology. Provides an overview of the entire field of psychotropic drugs. Many charts and tables augment the text, which is accessible to the general reader as well as the health care practitioner.

Schatzberg, Alan F., and Charles B. Nemeroff, eds. *The American Psychiatric Press Textbook of Psychopharmacology*. Washington, D.C.: American Psychiatric Press, 1998. As the prefatory note indicates, the contributors to this volume "have worked to ensure that all information in this book concerning drug dosage, schedules, and routes of administration is accurate as of the time of publication," and the book is "intended to provide background information only." In spite of this cautionary note, this is as reliable a source as a searcher is likely to find. It is thorough, clearly presented, very comprehensive, and unbiased. It includes historical data, numerous diagrams and illustrations, and extensive material about the scientific explorations leading to the development of psychotropic agents. While designed for the professional in the field, it is suitable for consideration by the layperson as well.

Weiden, Peter J., Patricia L. Scheifler, Donald J. Diamond, and Ruth Ross. *Breakthroughs in Antipsychotic Medications: A Guide for Consumers, Families, and Clinicians.* New York: W. W. Norton, 1999. A thorough, informative discussion of the capabilities, advantages, and problems involved in the uses of psychototropic drugs, directed particularly to patients and their friends and families. Detailed information is combined with a directive narrative that introduces and examines the crucial issues of psychiatric approaches to psychotic disorders. An extensive glossary defines many important terms, and a section on resources provides information about support groups, Web sites, volumes on psychopharmacology, individual medications, and journals and newsletters.

WEB SITES

http://www.nami.org
The Web page for the National Alliance for the Mentally Ill, with up-to-date information about treatments for mental disorders.

http://www.cmhc.com/guide/pro22.htm
A Web page of pharmacology references, with basic information about various medications.

http://uhs.bsd.uchicago.edu/dr-bob/tips/tips/html
This Web site is an indexed archive of the psychopharmacology discussion group, with information about the use of medications, including side effects. It is based on clinical experience, rather than research.

Leon Lewis

BIOGRAPHICAL LIST OF PSYCHOLOGISTS

Adler, Alfred (1870-1937). Originally a Freudian psychologist, Adler, by 1911, had broken from Sigmund Freud, resigning as president of the Vienna Psychoanalytic Society when the break became apparent. Adler was known for his work on individual personality and his theory of the creative self. He eschewed environment and heredity as the major governing factors in people's lives. He considered these factors raw materials that individuals can shape as they will.

Albee, George W. (1921-2006). This University of Vermont professor of psychology was primarily interested in social psychology. He sought solutions to mental problems through treatment rooted in social psychology and the value system that was a part of social psychology. He believed that the main causes of mental illness are found in societal factors. Was a leader in developing community psychology.

Allport, Gordon (1897-1967). Allport was well known for his theory of functional autonomy, which disputes Sigmund Freud's notion that adult conduct stems from instincts, desires, and needs that all people share. He resisted classifying people according to such elemental motives. For him, each personality was unique and could not be categorized according to a preconceived set of motivations.

Bandura, Albert (1925-   ). The learning theory advanced by Bandura postulated that people learn largely through realizing what the consequences are of their behavior or of the behavior of others. He advocated observational learning. His social cognitive theory influenced learning theory in the last quarter of the twentieth century.

Beck, Aaron T. (1921-   ). Recognized for his work in cognitive therapy, Beck sought to alter the thinking of depressed patients by encouraging them to assess their problems in alternative ways capable of solution. He also moved his patients toward understanding how their problems might be the result of their own actions or inactions.

The Beck Depression Inventory, a twenty-one-item instrument based on a four-point scale, is used as a quantitative tool for ascertaining the symptoms of depression in adolescents and adults.

Berkowitz, Leonard (1926-   ). A social psychologist, Berkowitz achieved a worldwide reputation as an expert on human aggression, which he defined as an externally elicited drive to harm or injure others. He believed that aggression could be sparked involuntarily by stimuli from the surrounding environment.

Binet, Alfred (1857-1911). A French psychologist, Binet, collaborating with Theodore Simon, devised tests for measuring intelligence, later called intelligence quotient (IQ) tests. Although he originally contended that intelligence was too complex to be reduced to mere numbers, he ultimately accepted the simplified modes of measurement, devised by William Stern and refined by Lewis Terman, that considered IQ to be equal to mental age divided by chronological age and multiplied by one hundred. Terman added the last element so that IQ could be expressed in whole numbers rather than in numbers requiring decimal points.

Blau, Theodore H. (1928-2003). Blau turned his attention to forensic psychology quite early in his career. He was employed by the United States government for many years and was generally acknowledged to be a leading figure in the psychology of addiction. In 1977, he became the first clinician to be elected president of the American Psychological Association. His landmark study was *The Psychologist as Expert Witness* (1984).

Brentano, Franz Clemens (1838-1917). Brentano questioned the theories of the mind espoused by many contemporary psychologists and physicians who were mainly concerned with the brain as a physical entity. He denied the necessity of understanding the physiological mechanisms underlying mental events, contending that experimental psychology was more limited and limiting than many of his colleagues believed because it involves the systematic manipulation of variables, then noting their effect upon other variables. Brentano believed that any study of the mind should emphasize process over a material view of the mind's content.

Breuer, Josef (1842-1925). A noted physician and researcher, Breuer grew close to the young Sigmund Freud, fourteen years his junior. Freud said that while he was still a student preparing for his last examinations in medical school, Breuer applied the methods of psychoanalysis to one of his patients, Anna O., who suffered from hysteria and whom he treated systematically from 1880 to 1882, thereby, in Freud's eyes, inaugurating the field of psychoanalysis.

Bronfenbrenner, Urie (1917-2005). Bronfenbrenner, who was much concerned with behavioral psychology, had a long and productive career as a professor of psychology at Cornell University, where he served in the College of Human Ecology. He is also remembered as the co-founder of the Head Start movement in the United States, a program designed to help learning disadvantaged children improve their academic performance.

Bruner, Jerome (1915-   ). A professor of psychology and educational researcher at New York University, Jerome Bruner was much concerned with the process of education. He advanced a theory of curriculum that had a profound effect on education during the last half of the twentieth century. His ideas, based on categorization, are best articulated in his study, *The Process of Education*, published by the Harvard University Press in 1966.

Cannon, Walter Bradford (1871-1945). A Harvard University professor of physiology, Cannon demonstrated the effects emotions have on the human body. His work led to the mapping of the brain's hypothalamus and limbic systems. Cannon challenged the theory proposed by William James and C. G. Lange that situations caused by certain stimuli produce specific bodily reactions, such as increased heart beat or increases or decreases in blood pressure, pointing out that similar bodily reactions occur in a wide variety of emotional states. He noted that the viscera, with few sensory nerves, are unlikely to perceive changes, contending that autonomic reactions often have relatively long periods of latency.

Cattell, James McKeen (1860-1944). Convinced that applied psychology underlies every aspect of human activity, Cattell was a member of the functionalist school, which demanded that psychology be a practical science. Unlike the structuralists, the functionalists were concerned with the function of the mind rather than with its contents. The approach of Cattell and other functionalists was biological rather than physiological. He was elected president of the American Psychological Association at the age of thirty-five, succeeding William James in that post.

Charcot, Jean-Martin (1825-1893). This French neurologist and professor of anatomical psychology conducted research that linked specific anatomical lesions to various neurological disorders, including amyotrophic lateral sclerosis (ALS), which is commonly referred to as Lou Gehrig's disease. At least fifteen conditions were identified as a result of his research. He had a particular interest in hypnosis and in the roots of hysteria.

Dewey, John (1859-1952). Generally considered the most significant educational philosopher of the twentieth century, Dewey regarded the division of the elements of human reflexes into sensory, brain, and motor processes as inaccurate and misleading. He contended that there is a stream of behavior and that human reflexes are part of a coordinated system that cannot be viewed as anything but a unified whole. Dewey accepted the inevitability of social change but believed that it could be influenced favorably by proper planning. He is considered the father of progressive education.

Dix, Dorothea (1802-1887). While teaching inmates in a Boston prison, Dix concluded that many of the women confined as criminals were really mentally ill. She began a campaign to publicize and improve the treatment of the mentally ill in the United States and later in Europe. When she began her crusade in 1841, only 15 percent of people needing care received it. By 1890, that proportion had increased to 70 percent.

Dollard, John (1900-1980). The frustration-aggression hypothesis of Dollard and his partner Neil Miller departs from the explanations of Sigmund Freud and Konrad Lorenz, which are essentially biological. Miller and Dollard place considerable emphasis on explanations that have to do with social learning and environmental factors. They collaborated on *Frustrations and Aggression* (1963).

Ebbinghaus, Hermann (1850-1909). Ebbinghaus is best remembered for his systematic study of learning and memory, which flew in the face of Wilhelm Wundt's proclamation that the higher mental processes could not be studied experimentally. A rationalist, Ebbinghaus conducted experiments based on learning out-of-context groups of syllables from a pool of 2,300 that he had devised. His chief interests were in such topics as meaning, imagery, and individual differences in cognitive styles.

Egas Moniz, António (1874-1955). Egas Moniz was a Portuguese neurologist, who, aware of C. R. Jacobson's experiments in altering the behavior of chimpanzees by the removal of the frontal lobes of their brains, concluded that such procedures would produce similar results in humans. He was a pioneer in the now largely discredited area of psychosurgery. He was awarded the 1949 Nobel Prize in Physiology or Medicine for his discovery of the therapeutic value of leucotomy in certain psychoses.

Ellis, Albert (1913-2007). As a psychoanalyst and sex therapist, Ellis became disenchanted with the methods of psychoanalysis and sought new means of approaching his patients, which he outlined in *New Approaches to Psychotherapy* (1955). He devised a rational-emotive therapy (RET) which was initially scorned by most of his professional colleagues, many of whom eventually came to see the practical wisdom of this approach. His *Sex Without Guilt* (1958) was widely distributed and influenced much subsequent thinking about sex and sex therapy.

Erikson, Erik H. (1902-1994). In *Childhood and Society* (1950), one of the most influential books on learning theory in the last half of the twentieth century, Erikson defined eight developmental stages through which humans pass as they move from infancy to later adulthood. An understanding of these stages, particularly the first five, which move from infancy to adolescence, substantially affected learning theory in the United States.

Eysenck, Hans (1916-1997). In his theory of personality, Eysenck related the dimensions of introversion/extroversion and neuroticism/stability to the way the nervous system is constituted. He enumerated the characteristics that distinguish behavior therapy from dynamic psychotherapy.

Freud, Anna (1895-1982). The youngest child of Sigmund Freud, Freud became, like her father, a psychoanalyst, dealing exclusively with children. She earned a worldwide reputation as a child psychoanalyst. Following her father's death, she was regarded as the worldwide leader of the Freudian movement in psychology.

Freud, Sigmund (1856-1939). Perhaps the most renowned figure in the field of psychoanalysis, Freud introduced the free-association technique into that field. From his patients' free associations, Freud realized that psychoanalysts have to determine the structure and nature of their patients' unconscious minds. He identified and named the Oedipus complex, which contends that on the unconscious level a male's mother is the object of his sexual desire, thereby setting up his father as a competitor. Freud also identified the id, the ego, and the superego as cornerstones of the human psyche.

Fromm, Erich (1900-1980). In his most renowned book, *Escape from Freedom* (1941), Fromm speculated that freedom is a frightening thing to many people and that when they recognize that they are free, they immediately attempt to affiliate themselves with people or organizations that will reduce or totally eliminate their choices. He concluded that being free places an enormous responsibility upon people, who are often willing to trade freedom for the security of having a structure and direction provided by an external force.

Gilligan, Carol (1936-   ). Gilligan served as chief investigator for a number of studies of the development of girls and women. Her major research interests were in adolescence, moral reasoning, and conflict resolution, with particular emphasis on the contributions women's thinking have made to psychological theory. She pursued her studies because of the lack of attention women and girls received in most psychological research. She uncovered a "deep sense of outrage and despair" over the disconnection women feel because they believe their feelings have been ignored. Her books *In a Different Voice: Psychological Theory and Women's Development* (1982) and *Meet-*

ing at the Crossroads: Women's Psychology And Girls' Development (coauthored with Lyn M. Brown, 1992) have gained widespread recognition among psychologists concerned with matters of gender.

Hall, G. Stanley (1844-1924). A man of diverse talents, Hall was an antistructuralist who embraced the evolutionary theories of Charles Darwin and adapted them to psychology, particularly in his recapitulation theory, which hypothesized that every child from the embryonic stage to maturity recapitulates, first quite rapidly and later more slowly, every stage of development through which the human race has passed from its earliest, prehistoric beginnings. As president of Clark University in Worcester, Massachusetts, for thirty-one years (1888-1919), Hall made the university a major center for the study of psychology in the United States. He was the first person in the United States to call for sex education in public schools.

Horney, Karen (1885-1952). A physician, Horney denied that Sigmund Freud's theories on biological motivation were relevant for the people of her day. For her, social and cultural influences were preeminent. She contended that psychological problems grow out of disturbed human relationships, particularly those between children and their parents. Her essays about the psychology of women are cogent and were compiled in *Feminine Psychology* (1967).

Hull, Clark L. (1884-1952). Hull conducted extensive research that focused on how people learn and also articulated a systematic theory of behavior that was embraced by many of the early behaviorists. He based his research on the scientific laws of behavior. He also investigated the means by which hypnosis takes place. Hull's *Principles of Behavior* (1943) was a highly influential study.

Husserl, Edmund (1859-1938). Husserl contended that the methods employed by researchers in the natural sciences were not wholly appropriate in the study of areas related to psychology and to mental phenomena. He believed that it was incumbent on those studying human mental and emotional processes to understand their underlying mental essences. His phenomenological approach predated both Gestalt and existential psychology, both of which were indebted to Husserl's insights.

James, William (1842-1910). James's ideas sowed early seeds in psychological thought that eventually germinated into the school of functionalism. Wrestling with the implications of German materialism, Charles Darwin's theory of evolution—from which freedom of choice seemed to be absent—and predetermination, James finally, after reading an essay on free will by Charles Renouvier (1815-1903), moved in new directions that led inevitably to the pragmatism for which he is most remembered. His recognition of the importance of stream of consciousness led away from making generalizations about humans and their psychological constituents and led to a theory that emphasized the individuality and instinctuality of humans.

Johnson, Virginia E. (1925-   ). Johnson, along with her partner William H. Masters, was among the leading sexual therapists in the United States. They gathered scientific data relating to sex by means of electroencephalography, electrocardiography, and the use of color monitors. They worked with 694 volunteers photographed in various modes of sexual stimulation, carefully protecting their subjects' identities and privacy. They classified four stages of sexual arousal. Their work, especially *Human Sexual Response* (1966) and *Human Sexual Inadequacy* (1970), helped to spark the sexual revolution of the late 1960's and the 1970's.

Jung, Carl G. (1875-1961). Noted for his word-association research, Jung was essentially Freudian in his formative years as a psychologist, although the two began to part ways philosophically beginning in 1909. He employed Freud's notions of the preconscious and unconscious minds to arrive at the concept of the personal unconscious. This led him to his renowned theory of the collective unconscious that drew on the common experience of people through the ages. Jung contended that predispositions of the human mind are inherited and that in the collective unconscious there exist archetypes, so that at birth the mind is not the blank slate postulated by John Locke (1632-1704), but rather it contains structures inherited from previous spans of human existence.

Kelly, George A. (1905-1967). Notably iconoclastic, Kelly eschewed much of the theoretical psychology of his day, including a great deal of Sigmund

Freud. In dealing with subjects, he concluded that whether a person has a psychological problem or not depends largely on how that person views life. While scientists create theories that help them to predict future events, the general public creates systems constructs to make similar predictions. His two-volume work *The Psychology of Personal Constructs* (1955) explains in great detail how nonscientists create their systems constructs.

Kinsey, Alfred (1894-1956). Kinsey had a distinguished career as a zoologist at Indiana University, where his early work dealt with the life cycle, evolution, geographic distribution, and speciation of the gall wasp. He gained his greatest renown, however, for his extensive studies of human sexual behavior, begun in the late 1930's. They culminated in the publication of his landmark study, *Sexual Behavior in the Human Male* (1948), which was followed by a similar study on the human female in 1953. At the time of his death, he was the founding director of the Institute for Sex Research of Bloomington, Indiana.

Kohlberg, Lawrence (1927-1987). Kohlberg's greatest contribution was his research on the moral development of children and adolescents. Kohlberg ran an extensive longitudinal study in which he recorded the responses of boys aged seven through adolescence to hypothetical moral dilemmas. He concluded that children and adults pass through six identifiable stages in their moral development, which stems from cognitive development. Older children shape their responses on increasingly broad and abstract ethical standards. He detected an evolution from self-interest to more principled, selfless behavior and developed a chronological hierarchy of moral development.

Kraepelin, Emil (1856-1926). Kraepelin's chief contribution to psychology was his formulation of a comprehensive list of mental disorders published in 1883. It was used worldwide for over a century until, in 1952, the *Diagnostic and Statistical Manual of Mental Disorders* (DSM) was published by the American Psychological Association. Kraepelin identified the mental condition of dementia praecox and demonstrated that it was treatable and manageable. He renamed the condition schizophrenia, which means "a splitting of the personality."

Kübler-Ross, Elisabeth (1926-2004). Kübler-Ross, born in Switzerland, gained fame through her writing on matters of death and dying. Her books became popular with lay people who had been forced to cope with the deaths of people who were important to them. Kübler-Ross identified five stages of grieving, although she did not suggest that they occur in the order in which she identified them. She also was a strong advocate of the hospice movement and published over twenty books on death and dying, the most influential of which was *On Death and Dying* (1969).

Lacan, Jacques (1901-1961). Lacan, a French psychoanalyst, was trained as a psychiatrist. In the 1930's and 1940's he worked with psychotic patients. In the 1950's, he began to develop his own version of psychoanalysis, based on the ideas he found in structuralist linguistics and anthropology. He questioned Sigmund Freud's notion of the unconscious. Whereas Freud believed that by bringing the contents of the unconscious into consciousness he could minimize repression and neurosis, Lacan contended that the ego can not replace the unconscious or control it. For Lacan, the ego or "I" self is only an illusion, a product of the unconscious itself, and the unconscious is the center of all being.

Lewin, Kurt (1890-1947). An early apostle of Gestalt psychology, Lewin applied Gestalt principles to such areas as motivation, personality, and particularly group dynamics. For Lewin, many psychologists clung too tenaciously to the notion that the inner determinants of behavior are foremost in shaping human events. This Aristotelian view was contrary to the Galilean view that how organisms behave depends upon the totality of forces acting upon them at any given time. For Lewin, human behavior can be understood only in the light of the many complex, dynamic forces acting upon a person. He viewed groups as physical systems comparable to the brain. He detected an interdependence within members of groups that dynamically affected their functioning.

Maslow, Abraham (1908-1970). Maslow made humanistic psychology a recognized branch of the field. His early experimental work with monkeys led him to conclude that physical strength had less to do with dominance than the inner confidence of animals, although as he matured, he saw little value in studying nonhuman animals.

His emphasis was on studying individuals rather than groups and using subjective reality as the most effect key to understanding human behavior. Maslow's hierarchy of needs led to his concept of self-actualization, for which he is best known.

Masters, William H. (1915-2001). Masters, along with his partner Virginia E. Johnson, was among the leading sexual therapists in the United States. They gathered scientific data relating to sex by means of electroencephalography, electrocardiography, and the use of color monitors. They worked with 694 volunteers photographed in various modes of sexual stimulation, carefully protecting their subjects' identities and privacy. They classified four stages of sexual arousal. Their work, especially *Human Sexual Response* (1966) and *Human Sexual Inadequacy* (1970), helped to spark the sexual revolution of the late 1960's and the 1970's.

May, Rollo (1909-1994). An existentialist psychologist who emphasized the tragic dimensions of human existence, May's pessimistic outlook buttressed the pessimism of many of his readers. In emphasizing the tragic dimensions of human existence, he departs from such influential colleagues as Abraham Maslow, Virginia Satir, and Carl R. Rogers.

Meichenbaum, Donald (1940-   ). Meichenbaum, a founder of the "cognitive revolution" in psychotherapy, advocated the constructivist perspective. Professor of psychology at the University of Waterloo in Ontario, Canada, he has been a prolific writer, researcher, and lecturer. Meichenbaum wrote the influential book *Cognitive Behavior Modification: An Integrative Approach* (1977). His *Clinical Handbook/Treatment Manual for PTSD* (1994) is an impressive summary of information for clinicians and researchers working with persons suffering the effects of traumatic stress.

Menninger, Karl (1893-1990). Dealing psychoanalytically with patients, Menninger claimed that patients' guilt, which can make them seem unworthy in their own eyes, is attributable to the resistance of the superego. Menninger identified acting out as a manifestation of resistance and recognized that when patients go out of their way to please their analysts, they are engaging in what Menninger called "erotization resistance," which he related to the stages of psychosexual development.

Miller, Neal E. (1909-2002). The frustration-aggression hypothesis of Miller and his partner John Dollard departs from the explanations of Sigmund Freud and Konrad Lorenz, which are essentially biological. Miller and Dollard place considerable emphasis on explanations that have to do with social learning and environmental factors. They collaborated on *Frustrations and Aggression* (1963).

Mischel, Walter (1929-   ). Mischel refused to acknowledge that there exist stable characteristics of personality, contending that behavior depends upon specific situations. He questioned the validity of personality inventories and the data obtained from them. For Mischel, the assessment of personality based upon traits is specious because it overgeneralizes. Mischel's most notable works on personality are *Personality and Assessment* (1968) and *Introduction to Personality* (1971, revised 1981).

Murray, Henry A. (1893-1988) Murray had a background in a variety of disciplines, including psychology, chemistry, and biology. He taught at Harvard from 1927 to 1968 and helped to establish the Boston Psychoanalytic Society. He drew his theory of personality from both Freudian and Jungian psychoanalysis, postulating an elaborate system of basic motivational forces. Murray developed the Thematic Apperception Test (TAT), widely used for assessing personality.

Pavlov, Ivan Petrovich (1849-1936). Pavlov gained his reputation for his work on conditioned and unconditioned responses. Using dogs that were fed when a bell sounded, he accustomed the dogs to associating the sound of the bell with food. Once they had made this association, he found that sounding the bell caused them to salivate even though no food was forthcoming. Pavlov was a positivist whose life was centered on his laboratory work. He had a low opinion of psychology not because of its emphasis on consciousness but because of its use of introspection.

Perls, Fritz (1893-1970). Perls developed and popularized Gestalt therapy. In South Africa, where he emigrated from Europe, he established a training institute for psychoanalysis before developing his unique theoretical method, which emphasized a phenomenological and subjective approach to therapy. He noted that people tend to split off experiences (emotions, thoughts, sensations) that are uncomfortable. One goal of his work is to encourage patients to own up to their experience and develop it into a healthy "Gestalt," or whole. Perls's book *Gestalt Therapy Verbatim* (1969) drawn from transcripts of his work, describes his approach.

Piaget, Jean (1896-1980). Piaget was a central figure in the study of human development. His theory of genetic epistemology links the development of intellectual ability to biological maturity and experience. He contended that when an experience fits a child's cognitive structure, assimilation takes place. When such an experience does not fit its cognitive structure, the cognitive structure is adjusted, by a process that Piaget called accommodation, so that it can be assimilated. His stages of intellectual development have been instrumental in teacher education.

Pinel, Philippe (1745-1826). Pinel's book *Philosophy of Madness* (1793) changed the way that many physicians viewed mental illness. Pinel was appalled at the treatment of mental patients, many of whom were chained and abused. He demonstrated that violent behavior among patients who were chained often disappeared when their chains were removed. Pinel also called for a cessation of the blood-letting that was a common means of treatment in his day.

Rogers, Carl R. (1902-1987). Renowned for his client-centered approach to psychotherapy, Rogers outlined his methods in his widely used book, *Client-Centered Therapy: Its Current Practice, Implications, and Theory* (1951). Rogers's nondirective approach was unique and was based on his belief that therapists function most productively when they seek to understand and accept their patients' subjective reality. His complex theory of personality is clearly articulated in *Client-Centered Therapy*.

Rorschach, Hermann (1884-1922). As a small child, Rorschach loved an activity called *Klecksography*, a way of making pictures by using ink blots. This enthusiasm led to his life's work. Undecided about whether to study medicine or art, he finally opted for medicine, but his continuing interest in inkblots caused him to devise a way to use them in exploring the human psyche. Rorschach began showing inkblots to school children, whose reactions he noted and analyzed. After receiving

his medical degree in 1912, he tested three hundred patients and one hundred "normal" people, using inkblots to analyze their unconscious minds. In 1921, he published *Psychodiagnostics: A Diagnostic Test Based on Perception*, which fully described his unique diagnostic method.

Rush, Benjamin (1745-1813). Sometimes referred to as the first psychiatrist in the United States, Rush published *Diseases of the Mind* in 1812. He complained that mentally ill people were treated criminally and urged that their shackles be removed. Such patients should never be put on display for the amusement of others. Despite his revolutionary views, Rush nevertheless accepted bloodletting as a viable treatment for mental disorders, as well as rotating patients to relieve their confused minds and strapping them in tranquilizing chairs in order to calm those who were agitated.

Satir, Virginia (1916-1988). A psychotherapist who emphasized family psychology, Satir did most of her clinical work with families, treating them collectively, rather than dealing with individuals, as many of her colleagues did. Concerned with how change affects organizations, Satir, in her work with the Illinois Psychiatric Institute, an organization she had joined in 1955, did most of her counseling with families rather than individuals.

Seligman, Martin E. P. (1942-   ). A specialist on the psychology of depression, Seligman reached a wide popular audience through his many self-help books. Despite his emphasis on depression, he has been called the father of positive psychology. Director of the University of Pennsylvania's Clinical Training Program, he is more concerned with studying mental wellness rather than mental illness. He is well known for his studies of human happiness and optimal function.

Selye, Hans (1907-1982). Selye demonstrated how environmental stress and anxiety could lead to the release of hormones that, over time, could produce a number of the biochemical and physiological disorders common in industrial societies of the twentieth century. Selye's theory greatly affected popular views of stress. In *The Stress of Life* (1978), Selye reduced the research on stress to terms the general public could understand and appreciate.

Simon, Théodore (1873-1961). In 1904, Simon, an intern in a French institution for mentally retarded children, worked with Alfred Binet to create tests that would quantify intelligence, differentiating intellectually normal children from those who were intellectually deficient. Together, Simon and Binet in 1905 produced the Binet-Simon Scale of Intelligence, which led to the development of a broad range of tests to measure people's intelligence quotient (IQ).

Skinner, B. F. (1904-1990). Skinner's belief that behavior is controlled by environmental reinforcement mechanisms gave him reason to think that understanding such mechanisms can help to solve many of society's problems. In his view, it is more pressing to understand the environment rather than the mind or the inner self. His method was to manipulate environmental factors and note the effect that such alterations had on behavior. His approach has been designated "descriptive behaviorism."

Spencer, Herbert (1820-1903). Spencer applied the concept of evolution to the human mind and to human societies. For him, everything in the universe begins as an undifferentiated whole. Evolution leads to differentiation so that systems become increasingly complex. After Charles Darwin's *On the Origin of Species by Means of Natural Selection* (1859) appeared, Spencer shifted his emphasis from acquired characteristics to natural selection. He coined the term "survival of the fittest," which is widely associated with Darwinian thought.

Stern, William (1871-1938). A German psychologist who introduced the concept of mental age as opposed to chronological age, which led to the quantitative statement of people's intelligence quotients (IQs).

Stumpf, Carl (1848-1936). Stumpf, who studied with and was much influenced by Franz Brentano, stipulated that mental events should be studied holistically and not broken down analytically. Stumpf considered mental phenomena rather than conscious elements the appropriate objects in the study of psychology. This view predated and led to the phenomenological approach that became a major underpinning of the Gestalt psychology that followed.

Sullivan, Harry Stack (1892-1949). An American psychiatrist, Sullivan, along with his teacher William Alanson White (1870-1937), extended Freudian psychoanalysis to the treatment of patients with severe mental disorders, particularly schizophrenia. Sullivan argued that schizophrenics were curable, blaming cultural forces for the condition of many such patients. His writing, especially *Schizophrenia as a Human Process* (1962), greatly altered the views of many psychiatrists.

Terman, Lewis (1877-1956). Working in the field of psychological testing and measurements, Terman abbreviated the term "intelligence quotient" to merely IQ. He modified William Stern's method of measuring IQ by adding one element to it. Once mental age had been divided by chronological age, he multiplied the result by one hundred so that it could be expressed as a whole number rather than as one with a decimal point.

Thorndike, Edward L. (1874-1949). A pioneer in the field of learning theory, Thorndike was also intrigued by and wrote in such fields as verbal behavior, transfer of training, the measurement of sociological events, educational methodology, and comparative psychology. Well known for his theories of the Law of Effect and the Law of Exercise, he subdivided the latter into the Law of Use and the Law of Disuse. The former stated that if an association led to a feeling of satisfaction, it would be strengthened, whereas if it led to an unsatisfying feeling, it would be weakened. He later repudiated these theories. In time the functionalism that he espoused was absorbed into mainstream psychology.

Titchener, Edward (1867-1927). British-born psychologist Titchener spent thirty-five years at Cornell University as director of its psychological laboratory, creating there the largest psychology doctoral program in the United States. Convinced that there was little value in applied psychology, Titchener dogmatically insisted that the field, in order to be truly scientific, must deal with pure knowledge. Despite his close relationship with John B. Watson, Titchener eschewed behaviorism and became the founder of the structuralist school of psychology, which opposed not only behaviorism but such other schools of psychology as functionalism and faculty psychology.

Tolman, Edward C. (1886-1956). A notable behavioral psychologist in the psychological mold of John B. Watson, Tolman spent most of his productive life as a professor of psychology at the University of California at Berkeley. His extensive research often focused on rats in mazes, out of which grew his theory of latent learning, which ran counter to the stimulus-response contentions of the behaviorists. He explained his theories in his most renowned book, *Purposive Behavior in Animals and Man* (1932).

Watson, John B. (1878-1958). A major researcher in animal psychology, Watson was the founder of and the most significant figure in the behaviorist school of psychology. His academic career ended precipitously in 1920 when he was found to be having an adulterous affair with a research assistant. He began to write for the popular press and in 1921 joined the J. Walter Thompson Company, a leading advertising company, of which he became vice president in 1924, remaining with the company for the rest of his working life. Watson continued his interest and writing in psychology and had a significant effect upon the behaviorists who followed him.

Wolpe, Joseph (1933-1997). Wolpe, with his colleague Arnold Lazarus, was considered one of the fathers of behavior therapy. Doing most of his work at Temple University, where he taught, he later moved to the University of California at Los Angeles and to Pepperdine University, where he taught psychology. His book, *The Practice of Behavior Therapy* was highly influential, having gone into four editions by 1991.

Wundt, Wilhelm (1832-1920). One of the most prolific writers in the field of psychology, Wundt held that psychology was a scientific field and that it had become an experimental science. Whereas the other sciences were based on what Wundt termed "mediate experiences," psychology was based on "immediate experiences." He sought to use experimental psychology to discover the basic components of thought and to understand how mental elements combine into complex mental experiences. His method was based largely on introspection, or self-observation and analysis.

Yalom, Irvin D. (1931-   ). Yalom's book *The Theory and Practice of Group Psychotherapy* (1996) outlines the author's approach to group therapy. Yalom eschews having people in group therapy dwell on the past or on events that occurred outside the setting of the therapy. Rather, he encourages patients to identify a problem they are having and then encourage others who have experienced similar problems to enter into a dialogue with them, so that in time everyone in the group will be participating.

Zimbardo, Philip (1933-   ). A researcher in cult psychology, Zimbardo, professor of psychology at Stanford University, has studied James Jones's People's Temple and of such groups as Scientology. He is the originator of the Stanford Prison experiment in which he divides students into two groups, one prisoners, the other their keepers, and has them role play the situation in order to reach understandings and insights in both groups.

R. Baird Shuman

NOTABLE COURT CASES

1843

Rex v. M'Naghten
8 Eng. Rep. 718; 10 Clark & Fin 200, 210 Law Lords
    Council, England
This was the first major appellate case involving a substantive insanity test. Daniel M'Naghten had murdered Prime Minister Robert Peel's private secretary because he had delusions about Peel plotting against him. At trial, nine experts deemed the defendant insane. Lord Chief Justice Nicolas Tindal accepted their expert testimony. Found not guilty by reason of insanity, M'Naghten was institutionalized in Bedlam, then in Broadmoor, where he died. Under the strict M'Naghten Test, a defendant is not criminally responsible if his reasoning at the time of the crime was so defective that he was unable to understand the nature of his act and to distinguish between right and wrong. The rule, with variations, is still used in many American jurisdictions. Under the twentieth century's Durham Rule and Model Penal Code the criteria for insanity are somewhat more lenient.

1881

Chapsky v. Wood
26 Kan. 650 Kansas Supreme Court
After his wife died, Morris A. Chapsky turned over his infant daughter to his deceased wife's sister, Mrs. Wood. For the next five years he took no responsibility for the child's welfare. When Chapsky tried to take back his daughter, Mrs. Wood refused to give her up. On appeal, the Kansas Supreme Court ruled in Wood's favor. Justice Joseph Brewer argued that in a custody dispute under these circumstances, the most important standard was the "best interests" of the child. The decision had broad influence on moving the focus in custody disputes from parental interests to children's interests.

1927

Buck v. Bell
274 U.S. 200 U.S. Supreme Court
The U.S. Supreme Court ruled that involuntary sterilization of the mentally ill for eugenic purposes was constitutional. Carrie Buck of the Virginia Colony for Epileptics and the Feebleminded had undergone sterilization without her consent. Supreme Court Justice Oliver Wendell Holmes, Jr., justified his vote, saying that because Buck was mentally incompetent, she was unsuitable to produce offspring. As a result of this ruling, sterilization laws were enforced in many states and the number of involuntary sterilizations increased despite health risks and moral issues concerning privacy and reproductive freedom. Most people sterilized were either poor or institutionalized. These laws were later overturned.

1954

Brown v. Board of Education of Topeka, Kansas
347 U.S. 483 U.S. Supreme Court
Overruling *Plessy v. Ferguson* (1896), the U.S. Supreme Court held unanimously that the de jure segregation of the public schools violated the Equal Protection Clause of the Fourteenth Amendment. Speaking for the court, Chief Justice Earl Warren argued that segregated schools were inherently unequal and that they produced a feeling of inferiority that had a harmful effect on the psychological and social well-being of minority children. In support of the second proposition, Warren's opinion included the controversial Footnote Eleven, which cited Dr. Kenneth Clark's doll experiment as well as other works by prominent psychologists, psychiatrists, and sociologists. Critics asserted that the scientific inferences of these studies were too uncertain to provide a foundation for such an important legal ruling.

Durham v. U.S.
214 Fed. 2d 862 U.S. Circuit Court of Appeals
   for D.C.

When burglar Monte Durham pleaded not guilty by reason of insanity, the trial judge insisted Durham had to prove that he did not have the mental capacity to know and understand what he was doing at the time of the crime. Durham was found guilty. In an appeal, Judge David L. Bazelon reversed the conviction and formulated the controversial Durham Rule, or "product test," which stated that "an accused is not criminally responsible if his unlawful act was the product of a mental disease or defect." The American Law Institute's (ALI's) Model Penal Code is a compromise between the demanding M'Naghten Test and the more lenient Durham Rule. In 1972, the D.C. Court of Appeals abandoned the Durham Rule in favor of the ALI's criterion of insanity.

1960

Carter v. General Motors Corp. (Chev. Gear & Axle)
361 Michigan 575 Michigan Supreme Court

Schizophrenic James Carter received workers' compensation that he claimed was owed him because of work-related emotional pressures. The Michigan Supreme Court recognized that Carter did not have to cite a specific incident as provoking his inability to work. The court also declared that Carter's schizophrenia prior to employment did not render workers' compensation invalid. Such benefits would not be applicable only if Carter's schizophrenia was no longer present. Carter's legal representation included expert psychological testimony. General Motors did not seek expert evaluation of Carter's psychological state. Michigan laws were subsequently rewritten to prevent employees who were mentally ill prior to their employment from securing workers' compensation from their employers.

Dusky v. U.S.
362 U.S. 402 U.S. Supreme Court

The U.S. Supreme Court affirmed a lower-court ruling that schizophrenic Milton Dusky was competent to stand trial for kidnapping a teenager and helping two other teenagers rape her. He was found guilty and sentenced to forty-five years in prison. In this case, the court defined competency to stand trial as meaning a defendant was capable of communicating with an attorney and could rationally comprehend the facts of the charges against him or her.

1966

Baxstrom v. Herold
383 U.S. 107 U.S. Supreme Court

When prisoner Johnnie K. Baxstrom completed his sentence in a New York Department of Corrections psychiatric hospital, he was supposed to be committed to a civil hospital. The state hospital refused to admit Baxstrom, and he remained in the prison hospital. All transfer requests and legal protests were not considered. The U.S. Supreme Court ruled that Baxstrom had been denied equal protection based on the fact that civilly committed patients were guaranteed the right to a hearing. The court also denounced keeping Baxstrom in prison beyond his sentence.

Rouse v. Cameron, Supt., St. Elizabeth's
373 Fed. 2d 451 U.S. Circuit Court of Appeals for
   D.C.

The plaintiff was committed for four years although the crime of which he was accused had a maximum sentence of one year. Judge David L. Bazelon declared that patients hospitalized based on the plea of not guilty by reason of insanity must be treated or released if they are not dangerous to society. Because of this case, plaintiffs were guaranteed the right to writ of habeas corpus and the precedent was set for mental patients to have the right for appropriate treatment.

1967

Washington v. U.S.
390 Fed. 2d 444 U.S. Circuit Court of Appeals
   for D.C.

Tried for rape, assault, and robbery, Thomas H. Washington pleaded not guilty by reason of insanity but was convicted. Because the defense's psychiatrist said Washington was mentally ill, Washington appealed his verdict. The two prosecution psychiatrists stated that Washington was mentally sound. Judge David L. Bazelon wrote that juries were to decide if an insanity defense was credible and that an expert's testimony would not override the jury's decisions.

1970

In re Lifschutz, M.D., on Habeas Corpus
85 Cal. Rptr. 829 California Supreme Court

When a patient named Joseph Housek sued another person for emotional distress, the defendant subpoenaed records from Housek's psychiatrist, Dr. Joseph E. Lifschutz. Although Lifschutz appeared in court, he declined to testify, stating that doctor-patient interactions were privileged information. Housek had not requested such privacy, and Lifschutz was jailed for contempt of court. The California Supreme Court stated that patients, not their doctors, have the right to exercise privilege. Because Housek revealed information about his treatment, the court had the legal right to Lifschutz's records.

1972

Jackson v. Indiana
406 U.S. 715 U.S. Supreme Court

Theon Jackson, who was accused of burglary, was mentally disabled, deaf, mute, and unable to communicate effectively. The trial court declared him incompetent to stand trial and committed him indefinitely to a mental institution. According to testimony, the state was unprepared to treat his particular problems. He was not found to be legally insane. Jackson's legal representative argued that he had been given a life sentence and petitioned for relief. The U.S. Supreme Court held that the Constitution prohibited an indefinite confinement without any prospects of effective treatment. Therefore, the state had the option of release or treatment designed to achieve competency. In this landmark decision, the Supreme Court put restrictions on the conditions and length of time for the confinement of a person judged incompetent for trial.

Lessard et al. v. Schmidt et al.
349 F. Supp. 1078 U.S. District Court for
    Eastern Wisconsin

Two police officers detained schizophrenic Alberta Lessard, who was recommitted involuntarily to a mental hospital. The court declared that a law that permitted detaining mentally ill people in civil institutions for a maximum of 145 days with no civil rights was unconstitutional. The ruling said that people could be committed for protection and legal procedure for as much time as two weeks prior to a hearing only if their guilt was beyond a reasonable doubt and they posed risks to themselves or others. Specific procedures for committing people were outlined. Mental-health professionals worried that many mentally ill people might not receive the care they needed because of this ruling. The court also stated that psychiatrists were required to inform patients of their Fifth Amendment rights when they questioned them for trials.

1973

Kaimowitz v. Michigan Department of Mental Health
#73-19434-AW, Circuit Court of Wayne City,
    Michigan

Gabe Kaimowitz was an attorney who represented Lewis Smith, who had raped and murdered a woman in 1965. Designated a criminal sexual psychopath, Smith was committed without a trial. By 1972, he consented to participate as a research subject in an experiment studying amygdaloidotomy versus cyproterone treatment at Lafayette Clinic. Kaimowitz argued that the clinic was illegally detaining Smith. The court said that Smith's consent to become a research participant was invalid because he had been denied due process and had not been found guilty in a trial. The court further stated that neither committed patients nor inmates could consent to participating in hazardous experiments.

Seiling v. Eyman, warden, Arizona state prison
478 Fed. 2d 211 U.S. Court of Appeals,
    9th Circuit Arizona

When Gilbert Seiling was charged with assault with a deadly weapon and the intent to commit murder, three psychiatrists concluded that he was insane when he committed the crimes. Two of the psychiatrists determined that Seiling was competent to stand trial. Prior to the trial, Seiling pleaded guilty. Afterward, Seiling said he had not been competent to waive his rights. The appeals court decided that competence to stand trial is not the same as competence to plead guilty.

1974

Wyatt v. Aderholt (Stickney)
503 Fed. 2d 1305 U.S. Court of Appeals, 5th Circuit
    Alabama

When the cigarette-tax income designated for mental-health services was revoked in 1970, Bryce State Hospital in Tuscaloosa, Alabama, fired ninety-nine employees. The hospital's five thousand patients suffered from deprivations caused by lack of sufficient funding. The state appealed a lower-court injunction. Judge Frank M. Johnson, Jr., of the 5th Circuit Court, was the first federal judge to rule that patients who were civilly committed had the constitutional right to receive individual treatment. The Wyatt Committee, the American Psychiatric Association, and the U.S. Department of Justice oversaw Alabama's mental-health services, which were reformed and certified.

1975

O'Connor v. Donaldson
422 U.S. 563 U.S. Supreme Court

Although Kenneth Donaldson had experienced paranoid delusions, psychiatric evaluations never indicated that he was dangerous to others or himself. Nevertheless, he was involuntarily confined in the Florida State Hospital for fifteen years. He refused treatment and unsuccessfully attempted to be released. In a civil suit, he charged that the hospital and its staff, particularly administrator Dr. J. B. O'Connor, were violating his constitutional rights. The U.S. District Court ruled in his favor in 1974. Reaffirming most of this decision, the U.S. Supreme Court declared that a state may not force a non-dangerous person to remain in an institution if he or she is capable of living alone or with the aid of family members or friends. The *Donaldson* ruling is recognized as an important landmark precedent in mental-health law.

1976

Roy v. Hartogs
381 NYS 2d 587 New York Appellate Court

Patient Julie Roy sued therapist Dr. Renatus Hartogs because she claimed she was emotionally damaged by his sexual treatment. Hartogs argued that seduction was not illegal. The court awarded Roy compensatory and punitive damages. An appeals court agreed that Hartogs was guilty of malpractice. That court dropped punitive damages because it declared Hartogs was incompetent, not malicious. When Hartogs sued his insurance com-

pany for not covering his costs, the company argued successfully that Hartogs's treatment method for Roy was not considered professional. A 1976 book by Roy and Lucy Freeman and a 1978 television movie, both titled *Betrayal*, portrayed this case.

Tarasoff v. Regents of University of California
131 Cal. Rptr. 14, 551 P.2d 334 California Supreme Court

After Prosenjit Poddar revealed to a university psychologist that he wanted to murder Tatiana Tarasoff, the therapist alerted authorities. The campus police questioned and released Poddar, who later killed Tarasoff. Tarasoff's parents sued the university for failure to warn Tarasoff of Poddar's threat. A trial court said the university had "no duty" to alert Tarasoff. The California Supreme Court initially stated that "privilege ends where public peril begins" and emphasized the "duty to warn." Because this statement was vague, the state supreme court reheard the case, issuing the decision that a "therapist has an obligation to use reasonable care to protect a potential victim" and has the "duty to protect." This was a landmark decision because it established a new cause for legal action. Many mental-health professionals worried that this decision might interfere with therapist-patient confidentiality and cause liability issues because clinicians could not always detect dangerous patients before they acted violently.

1977

Doe v. Roe & Poe
400 NYS 2d 668 Circuit New York Supreme Court

Psychiatrist Joan Roe and her psychologist husband Peter Poe treated Jane Doe. The couple published a joint autobiography which included information which they said Doe gave oral consent for them to use. Because a New York statute states medical personnel cannot disclose patient information because of implied confidentiality and that oral consent is not sufficient, the court awarded damages to Doe and stopped the book's sale. The defendants could not convince the court of the book's scientific merit to resume sales.

Fasulo & Barberi v. Arafeh
173 Conn. 473 Connecticut Supreme Court

After being committed to the Connecticut Valley

Hospital for thirteen years and twenty-six years, respectively, Ann Fasulo and Marie Barberi filed writs of habeas corpus. Laws at that time stated that for patients to be discharged they either had to prove they were not mentally ill or acquire approval from a hospital superintendent. The Connecticut Supreme Court approved hearings, stating that commitment did not suggest patients were permanently mentally ill and could not recover. The court emphasized Fourteenth Amendment rights and designated any "scheme to set the mentally ill apart" as a possible civil-rights violation.

1979

Addington v. Texas
441 U.S. 418 U.S. Supreme Court

Frank O'Neal Addington was committed to an institution based on an unequivocal "clear and convincing" standard. When he appealed, claiming that commitment should require mental instability "beyond a reasonable doubt," the U.S. Supreme Court unanimously decided that "preponderance of evidence" was insufficient and "beyond a reasonable doubt" too strong. "Clear and convincing" was considered the most appropriate standard for recognizing due-process protection for civil commitments, although the word "unequivocal" was designated as being too strict. "Beyond a reasonable doubt" is valid in several states.

Frendak v. U.S.
408 A.2d 364 U.S. Circuit Court of Appeals for D.C.

Paula Frendak murdered a coworker, fled the country, and was captured. Experts evaluated her during four competency hearings and determined that she was competent to stand trial even though she might be insane. Even though Frendak was ruled insane, she did not want to plead not guilty by reason of insanity. The appeal court determined that a defendant considered mentally competent can decide not to pursue a not guilty by reason of insanity defense. They can choose prison incarceration over hospitalization. The court acknowledged that some crimes might be in protest of laws the defendants consider unfair, such as Martin Luther King, Jr., protesting segregationist laws, and that a not guilty by reason of insanity plea would weaken their objections.

Hawaii Psychiatric Society v. Ariyoshi
481 F. Supp. 1028 U.S. District Court for Hawaii

When Hawaiian legislators approved a law permitting Medicaid officials to search medical records to find incidents of fraud, the Hawaii Psychiatric Society stated that this violated patients' and physicians' privacy. The society's lawsuit sought to protect patients from having to reveal their identities to protest the state's actions. The federal court decided that individuals' privacy was more important than Hawaii detecting fraud. The court allowed government representatives to cite reasons to secure warrants for suspect psychiatric records.

Ibn-Tamas v. U.S.
407 A. 2d 626 U.S. Circuit Court of Appeals for D.C.

Beverly Ibn-Tamas murdered her husband when he beat her while she was pregnant. He had beaten her many times previously and was known to be violent toward women. Ibn-Tamas claimed self-defense. Several witnesses testified that Ibn-Tamas's husband had begged her to spare his life. The judge would not allow expert testimony concerning battered woman syndrome because the victim was not on trial. An appeals court disagreed.

Parham v. J. R. et al.
442 U.S. 584 U.S. Supreme Court

A trial court had said Georgia's lack of a law addressing the release of committed minors, particularly those who had been rehabilitated, was unconstitutional. The U.S. Supreme Court decided that parents or the state acting as a legal guardian could make mental-health decisions based on a child's best interests regardless of the child's protests. The court ordered Georgia to establish posthospital evaluations.

Rogers v. Okin
478 F. Supp. 1342 (D. Mass. 1979)

A Massachusetts federal court ruled that the privacy and freedom of speech rights for committed patients, both voluntarily and involuntarily, also allowed them to refuse to take medication if they were competent to make that choice. Incompetent patients could have guardians choose whether treatment should be administered. Prior to this ruling, mental-health professionals had been allowed to make medication decisions and worried that such patient autonomy might interfere with treatment.

1980

Lipari and Bank of Elkhorn v. Sears, and Sears v. U.S.
497 F. Supp. 185 U.S. District Court Nebraska

An involuntary patient at a Nebraska Veterans Administration Hospital outpatient clinic, Ulysses L. Cribbs, Jr., purchased a shotgun from Sears in September, 1977. The next month, he stopped going to therapy. He murdered Dennis Lipari at an Omaha nightclub in November, 1977. When Ruth Ann Lipari and her bank sued Sears for negligence, that corporation sued the Veterans Administration. A federal district court ruled that the Veterans Administration was not immune and its liability was equivalent to that of a private citizen. The court extended duty in *Tarasoff v. Regents of University of California* (1976) to warn "any foreseeable victim or to that class of victims."

Vitek v. Jones
445 U.S. 480 U.S. Supreme Court

The prisoner Larry D. Jones was transferred without a hearing from a prison mental hospital to a state mental hospital. Both the trial court and the U.S. Supreme Court ruled this action unconstitutional. The Supreme Court emphasized that convicted felons had due-process protection rights and that commitment to a mental hospital involves a "massive curtailment of liberty."

1981

Estelle v. Smith
451 U.S. 454 U.S. Supreme Court

A psychiatrist declared Ernest Benjamin Smith competent to stand trial after his arrest for murder. After a guilty verdict, that psychiatrist testified during sentencing hearings that Smith posed a "danger to society." Smith had not been informed that the same psychiatrist who had examined him pretrial for the defense would later testify for the prosecution. The U.S. Supreme Court unanimously ruled that Smith's Fifth Amendment and his counsel's Sixth Amendment rights had been violated. Without warning that the psychiatrist's expertise would be used by the prosecution, Smith's lawyer had been unable to advise him sufficiently. The justices also thought Smith's due-process rights, guaranteed by the Fourteenth Amendment, had been violated.

Rennie v. Klein
635 Fed. 2d 836 U.S. Court of Appeals, 3d Circuit New Jersey

John Rennie, diagnosed as paranoid, was unwilling to take medication. The court ruled that an independent psychiatrist could treat Rennie and gradually introduce medications into his treatment. The court suggested that medical personnel should follow several steps. First, they should attempt to convince Rennie that medications were needed and encourage him to cooperate. The institution's medical director then should examine Rennie and monitor his treatment weekly. As needed, the medical director could consult an independent psychiatrist to evaluate Rennie.

State of New Jersey v. Hurd
86 NJ 525 New Jersey Supreme Court

After Jane Sell was knifed by an intruder, she initially said her attacker had been a stranger. Later, when she was hypnotized, Sell identified her former husband, Paul Hurd, as the assailant. Her hypnotic identification was questioned because the police officer who had interrogated her suggested Hurd was guilty. The court ruled that hypnotized witnesses must be questioned by trained medical professionals who were independent of legal authorities. Prior to hypnosis, the examining experts must ask the witness to describe events and record all aspects of hypnosis sessions and expert-witness contacts in writing. Hypnotized witnesses can only testify in New Jersey if their hypnosis sessions are limited to the expert and witness participation.

1982

Clities v. State of Iowa D.S.S.
322 NW 2d 917 Iowa Court of Appeals

When he was eleven years old, Timothy Floyd Clities was committed to a state institution because he was mentally disabled. Ten years later, the neuroleptics he received in treatment caused tardive dyskinesia. A court awarded him monetary damages for pain and suffering. The state of Iowa appealed, claiming that the amount was too high and that Clities had given informed consent. The appeals court disagreed, saying that the pharmacy had been poorly managed and citing *Rogers v. Okin* (1979), *Rennie v. Klein* (1981), and *Youngberg v. Romeo* (1982), which addressed medicating and restraining committed patients and securing guardians' consent for mentally incompetent patients.

U.S. v. Hinckley
672 F. 2d 115, 132 (D.C. Cir. 1982)

John Hinckley, Jr., attempted to assassinate President Ronald Reagan in 1981. He was ruled not guilty by reason of insanity. This verdict outraged many Americans. Mental-health professionals responded by saying that the insanity defense either should be abolished or require a stricter standard. Psychiatrists suggested the defense, not the prosecution, should bear the burden of proving defendants' sanity beyond a reasonable doubt. Congress passed an act to shift burden of proof to defense attorneys and also prohibited defendants from claiming they could not control how they behaved because of impulses.

The American Psychiatric Association issued a statement on the insanity defense which outlined how states reacted to the Hinckley verdict. Some state laws were changed to limit insanity defense use. They also created review boards to evaluate people found not guilty by reason of insanity to monitor treatment and determine whether individuals should be released from institutions. Each state and the District of Columbia created distinct insanity statutes. Some use an American Law Institute 1950's insanity defense test which determines the degree to which a person realized his or her behavior was wrong. Other states base their definition on modifications of the M'Naghten case. A few states do not have an insanity defense, and mentally ill defendants ruled guilty are placed in prison.

Youngberg, Supt. Pennhurst State School v. Romeo by his mother
457 U.S. 307 U.S. Supreme Court

Because Nicholas Romeo was mentally disabled and unable to communicate and take care of himself, he suffered injuries at the Pennhurst State School. Distressed about her son's condition, Romeo's mother sued the school's superintendent, claiming that Romeo's Eighth and Fourteenth Amendments rights had been violated. Her complaints included use of unsafe restraints. A trial judge ruled that Romeo's Eighth Amendment right had been violated. An appellate court reversed that decision. The U.S. Supreme Court supported the

appeal decision, declaring that patients have the constitutional right to safe conditions according to medical professionals' decisions, which courts cannot overrule.

1983

Barefoot v. Estelle
463 U.S. 880 U.S. Supreme Court

When murderer Thomas A. Barefoot was convicted in 1978, the American Psychiatric Association filed an amicus brief which stated that psychiatrists are unable to predict whether patients are dangerous. The U.S. Supreme Court declared that, even though such assessments are difficult to determine, they should be undertaken.

Jones v. U.S.
463 U.S. 354 U.S. Supreme Court

Charged with petty larceny in 1975, Michael Jones was committed to St. Elizabeth's Hospital. He was considered competent to stand trial the next year and was found not guilty by reason of insanity. Jones was returned to St. Elizabeth's and sued in 1980 because he was held beyond the one-year sentence for petty larceny. Courts refused to hear Jones's appeals. The U.S. Supreme Court split 5-4, determining that the ruling of not guilty by reason of insanity was sufficient to commit both nonviolent and violent criminals based on a preponderance of the evidence. These criminals are not considered responsible for their actions. The minority wanted clear and convincing proof that committed criminals posed a persistent threat.

People of California v. C. W. Stritzinger
688 P.2d 738 California Supreme Court

A psychologist reported to a law-enforcement officer information divulged during sessions with C. W. Stritzinger and his teenaged stepdaughter, with whom the stepfather had been sexually involved. The psychologist testified about the sessions during the trial against Stritzinger. The stepdaughter became agitated and left the courtroom before testifying. The California Supreme Court stated that psychological sessions involving Stritzinger were privileged information and that medical experts had to verify that the stepdaughter could not testify.

Petersen v. Washington
100 Wash. 2d 1016 Washington Supreme Court

A schizophrenic burglar and drug addict caused an automobile accident with Cynthia E. Petersen within days of his release from a mental hospital. He had stopped taking his medication, which no longer was active in his system at the time of the accident. When the injured Petersen sued the state, the trial court ruled in her favor. The Washington Supreme Court disagreed with the state, which claimed in its appeal that it was not required to warn people when mental patients were released. Citing *Tarasoff v. Regents of University of California*, the supreme court stated that the released patient was a danger to society and should be committed. The justices ruled that plaintiffs did not need expert testimony to prove defendants were hazardous and that state-hospital mental professionals were equally accountable as private psychiatrists to protect the public from patients.

1984

Minnesota v. Andring
342 NW 2d 128 Minnesota Supreme Court

David Andring voluntarily committed himself to a hospital because he sexually molested his stepdaughter and niece. He willingly divulged his crimes to medical personnel and people in his group-therapy sessions. The state of Minnesota subpoenaed Andring's hospital records. The Minnesota Supreme Court declared that medical records and group sessions are confidential and privileged and that only limited information could be released for legal purposes.

U.S. v. Torniero
735 Fed. 2d 725 U.S. Court of Appeals, 2d Circuit New York

When John J. Torniero was charged with transporting $750,000 of stolen jewelry across state lines, he said he had become insane because of compulsive gambling. This plea was not permitted at his trial, and Torniero was declared guilty. He appealed because he said the jury had not heard his compulsive-gambling defense. The court stated that compulsive gambling could not be legally used as a mental illness. The *American Journal of Psychiatry* said that compulsive gambling did not cause people to be unaccountable for their behavior.

1985

Ake v. Oklahoma
470 U.S. 68 U.S. Supreme Court

When Glen Burton Ake was charged with two murder counts, he was initially declared incompetent to stand trial. Medicated with Thorazine, Ake was considered competent within six weeks, but a mental-state opinion was not recorded. Ake pleaded not guilty by reason of insanity. Neither the psychiatrists for the plaintiff nor those for the state testified during the trial regarding Ake's mental state. Convicted, Ake received a death sentence plus one thousand years. His appeals were rejected by the state appeals court. The U.S. Supreme Court ruled that defendants must have access to a psychiatrist to ensure due process.

Commonwealth v. Kobrin
479 NE 2d 674 Massachusetts Supreme Court

The court ruled that patient records cannot be disclosed to grand juries because of psychiatrist-patient privilege but that records for fees paid, appointments scheduled, diagnosis and treatments plans, and somatic therapy could be introduced as evidence.

1986

Colorado v. Connelly
479 U.S. 157 U.S. Supreme Court

Francis Barry Connelly willingly confessed to committing murder. He was read his Miranda rights, then he talked about his crime without an attorney present. Connelly later claimed that he heard voices that forced him to confess. His confession was not permitted into evidence during his trial because authorities said he had involuntarily accepted blame for murder. The Colorado Supreme Court agreed that the confession was involuntary. The U.S. Supreme Court disagreed and stated that involuntary confessions referred to being forced to accept criminal responsibility because of police action, not mental incompetence.

Ford v. Wainwright
477 U.S. 399 U.S. Supreme Court

When Alvin Bernard Ford was convicted and sentenced to death for murder in 1974, he did not enter a plea of insanity. Eight years later, Ford began behaving erratically. A psychiatrist stated Ford was mentally ill and could not comprehend the reason for his execution. Three psychiatrists testified for the state that Ford was competent to undergo execution. The U.S. Supreme Court held that the execution of an insane person violated the prohibition on cruel and unusual punishments in the Eighth Amendment.

1987

Rock v. Arkansas
483 U.S. 44 U.S. Supreme Court

Vickie Lorene Rock was unable to recall shooting her husband. While hypnotized, she remembered the gun discharging without her finger pulling the trigger. An expert testified that the firearm she had held could fire without the trigger being activated. Arkansas courts refused to admit hypnotic testimony. The U.S. Supreme Court admitted hypnosis was not 100 percent accurate but stressed that excluding statements collected during professionally monitored hypnosis was unreasonable. The court said that such exclusion violated the Sixth and Fourteenth Amendments to rights to call witnesses and due process.

1989

Daley v. Koch
51 Fair Employment Practice Cases 1077, 1079
  (2d Circuit 1989)

Both district and appeals courts agreed that the New York City Police Department had not discriminated against Timothy J. Daley when it claimed he had undesirable behaviors based on the California Psychological Inventory and the Minnesota Multiphasic Personality Inventory. Daley claimed the police department treated him as if he were mentally ill.

1990

Maryland v. Craig
497 U.S. 836 U.S. Supreme Court

The operator of a preschool facility, Sandra Ann Craig, was prosecuted for having sexually abused a six-year-old child. At trial, the judge allowed the alleged victim to testify in a one-way closed-circuit television. Although Craig was found guilty, Maryland's high court reversed the decision, insisting

that the procedure violated the confrontation clause of the Sixth Amendment. By a 5-4 vote, however, the U.S. Supreme Court held that the defendant's right to face a witness was not absolute and that the need to protect the psychological welfare of children justified the procedure.

Washington v. Harper
494 U.S. 210 U.S. Supreme Court

An inmate in the Washington prison system, Walter Harper, had a history of violent behavior when not on antipsychotic medication. While at the Washington Department of Corrections Special Offender Center, he was forced to take psychiatric medication against his will. At court, he argued that due-process principles required a judicial hearing before forcing a person to take medication. The American Psychological Association submitted an amicus brief supporting Harper's position. The Supreme Court, however, held that a formal hearing is not required for compulsory medication when a professional psychological evaluation has determined that an inmate with a mental illness is dangerous to the prison community.

1992

Louisiana v. Perry
610 So.2d 746 Louisiana Supreme Court

Michael Perry, a psychotic, killed his parents, two cousins, and a nephew. Against his attorney's advice, he pleaded not guilty. Perry was found guilty and received a death sentence. The U.S. Supreme Court returned Perry's appeal without issuing an opinion. The American Psychiatric Association had wanted the U.S. Supreme Court to rule that insane death-row inmates would instead be subject to life sentences. The Louisiana Supreme Court stated that insane prisoners cannot be executed and that treatment cannot be required in an effort to achieve sufficient sanity for executions.

Menendez v. Superior Court of Los Angeles
834 P.2d 786 California Supreme Court

Dr. L. J. Oziel was the therapist for Erik and Lyle Menendez. They told him that they had murdered their parents and then threatened to kill him, his wife, and his mistress if he revealed the brothers' guilt. Oziel told the intended victims. During the brothers' murder trial, session tapes were introduced as evidence despite the brothers' claims they were privileged information. Citing *People of California v. George Wharton*, the California Supreme Court ruled that privileged material is not confidential after the information has been disclosed. Related therapy sessions are also eligible for court. The court also approved the right of therapists to divulge any warnings made against a criminal's mental-health professional.

Riggins v. Nevada
504 U.S. 127 U.S. Supreme Court

After David Riggins was arrested for murder and robbery, he complained of hearing voices at which point jail psychiatrists treated him with an antipsychotic medication, Mellari. Just before his trial, Riggins asked that the medication be discontinued in order to help him make an insanity defense. His request was denied, and he was found guilty and sentenced to death. The U.S. Supreme Court reversed the conviction, stating that forcing Riggins to take medication for the purposes of a criminal trial violated principles of due process. The Court further held that the state could only require a defendant to take medication upon demonstration that this was the least restrictive alternative for protecting the safety of the defendant or other persons.

1993

Daubert v. Merrell Dow Pharmaceuticals, Inc.
509 U.S. 579 U.S. Supreme Court

When judges made decisions about the admissibility of scientific evidence, the U.S. Supreme Court ruled that they should consider four factors: the testability of the theoretical basis for the evidence, the rates of error associated with the method, whether the method has been subjected to peer review, and whether the method has been generally accepted in the relevant scientific community. This four-pronged text replaced the "general acceptance test" of *Frye v. United States* (1923). In subsequent rulings, the Court clarified that the Daubert test applied broadly to many kinds of expert testimony, including that of mental-health professionals. Daubert hearings are frequently held to determine which expert testimony may be introduced in trials.

Godinez v. Moran
509 U.S. 389 U.S. Supreme Court

After Richard Moran killed three people, two psychiatrists declared him competent to stand trial. He pleaded guilty after discovering that the state of Nevada was asking for the death penalty. Moran appealed after receiving a death sentence. His lawyers then claimed that he was mentally ill, which rendered his guilty plea invalid. In a landmark decision, the U.S. Supreme Court ruled that if a defendant was competent to stand trial, he was automatically competent to plead guilty or waive his right to counsel.

1996

Jaffee v. Redmond
518 U.S. 1 U.S. Supreme Court

In 1991, police officer Mary Lu Redmond shot Ricky Allen, who allegedly was attempting to stab a man with a knife. In a federal suit, the administrator of Allen's estate, Carrie Jaffee, accused Redmond of using excessive force. When Jaffee attempted to acquire the notes from Redmond's counseling sessions with a licensed clinical social worker, Redmond claimed that the notes were protected by a psychotherapist-client privilege. The trial judge rejected the claim and instructed the jury to presume that the notes were unfavorable to the officer. By a 7-2 majority, however, the U.S. Supreme recognized that the relationship was protected. Justice John Paul Stevens observed that congressional legislation of 1975 let the courts determine such evidential rules according to common-law principles and noted that all state laws recognized some form of psychotherapist-client privilege.

U.S. v. Hall
93 F.3d 1337 7th Circuit Court of Appeals

When Larry D. Hall was prosecuted for kidnapping and murder, his attorneys attempted to discredit his confession by arguing that individuals can be coerced into giving false confession. The trial judge refused to allow the expert testimony of psychiatrist Dr. Arthur Traugott and sociologist Dr. Richard Ofshe. The judge explained that such testimony would "add nothing to what the jury would know from common experience." However, the court of appeals ruled that the testimony should have been allowed and voided the conviction. On remand, a federal district court held a Daubert hearing, which concluded that "the science of social psychology, and specifically the use of coercion in confessions, is sufficiently developed in its methods to constitute a reliable body of specialized knowledge."

1997

Kansas v. Hendricks
521 U.S. 346 U.S. Supreme Court

The Kansas Sexually Violent Predator Act allows the indefinite civil confinement of any person likely to commit "predatory acts of sexual violence" because of a "mental abnormality" or "personality disorder." Leroy Hendricks had a long history of sexually abusing children, and a state psychiatrist diagnosed him as suffering from pedophilia, a "mental abnormality" under the act. When Hendricks was released from prison, his attorneys challenged the constitutionality of his involuntary civil commitment, arguing that civil commitment could only be based on a "mental illness." By a 5-4 margin, the Supreme Court upheld the constitutionality of the Kansas statute. Since a civil commitment was not punitive in nature, the Court reasoned that it did not violate the prohibition on double jeopardy. The Court also found that the statute limited confinement to those persons diagnosed to be incapable of controlling their dangerous behavior.

1999

Olmstead v. L. C.
527 U.S. 581 U.S. Supreme Court

Two patients institutionalized for mental disability and schizophrenia, recorded as L. C. and E. W., were not provided with community services that would have allowed them to be released into a community setting. The state of Georgia argued the reason the patients were not provided with proper services was based on insufficient funds, not discrimination. In this landmark ruling on the Americans with Disabilities Act (ADA), the U.S. Supreme Court held that mental illness is a form of disability and that unjustified isolation of a disabled person is a form of discrimination that violates the ADA.

2002

Atkins v. Virginia
536 U.S. 304 U.S. Supreme Court

In 1998, Daryl Atkins was found guilty and sentenced to death for the crimes of armed robbery, kidnapping, and murder. In the penalty phase of the trial, the forensic psychologist for the defense, Evan Nelson, testified that Atkins was "mildly" mentally retarded, with an IQ score of 59, whereas the psychologist for the prosecution, Stanton Samenow, described Atkins as "of average intelligence." Although a 1989 precedent had allowed capital punishment for mentally disabled persons, the Supreme Court voted 6-to-3 to overturn the ruling and decided that the execution of such a person would violate the Eighth Amendment. The Court did not attempt to define the concept of mental retardation. In 2005, a trial jury found that Adkins's IQ had increased to above 70, thereby qualifying him for capital punishment. In 2008, however, his sentence was commuted to life imprisonment because of prosecutorial misconduct.

J. K. v. Eden
No. CIV-91-261-TUC-JMR U.S. District Court
    for Arizona

In 1991, a father sued the state of Arizona because its managed-care system did not provide professionally recommended treatment for his son, who tried to kill himself before being committed. After ten years of discussions, litigants settled this federal class-action lawsuit out of court, initiating the first managed-care state mental-health reform in the United States.

People of New York v. Wise
752 NYS 2d 837, 841 New York Supreme Court

In 1989, Trisha Meili, usually called the "Central Park jogger," was brutally beaten, raped, and left for dead. A large number of young African Americans with criminal records were rounded up. Eventually, Kharey Wise and four other teenagers were prosecuted and found guilty of the crime, even though DNA evidence did not indicate that any of the four had raped Meili. Their convictions were based primarily on four confessions, enhanced by their histories of delinquency. Thirteen years later, however, when DNA evidence pointed to prison inmate Matias Reyes as the murderer, he confessed and claimed that no other person was involved in the crime. Based on Reyes's account, the five earlier convictions were completely voided by the New York Supreme Court in 2002. Publicity about the matter produced great concern about other possible convictions based on false confessions, resulting in many calls for reform. Nevertheless, in 2003, a police panel concluded that the five convicted youths had probably participated in the assault.

2003

Commonwealth of Virginia v. Malvo
63 Va. Cir. 22 Virginia Trial Court

In 2002, seventeen-year-old Lee Boyd Malvo and forty-two-year-old John Allen Mohammad conducted a random killing spree in a large region around Washington, D.C., killing ten people and wounding four others. Malvo's defense attorneys presented an elaborate insanity defense, claiming that he had been brainwashed to the extent that his sense of right and wrong was controlled by Mohammad. Four defense experts testified that Malvo suffered from a "dissociative disorder," substantially eliminating his ability to resist or to understand his actions. The jury rejected the insanity defense, found him guilty of capital murder, and recommended a life sentence without the possibility of parole.

2005

New York v. Kogut
10 Misc 3d 305, 806 NYS 2d 366 Supreme Court of
    Nassau County

In 1985, John Kogut and two other men were arrested for the rape and murder of a sixteen-year-old girl. After Kogut confessed, the three men were found guilty and sentenced to long prison terms. Sixteen years later, DNA tests appeared to exonerate all three men of rape. However, the district attorney decided to retry Kogut for murder largely because of his confession. Kogut claimed the confession has been coerced. When Kogut's lawyers brought in Dr. Saul Kassin, author of a psychological study on false confessions, the prosecution objected. Concluding that Kassin's methodology and analysis were well respected in the field, Judge Victor Ort allowed Kassin to testify. Kogut was acquitted, and the charges against the other two men were dismissed.

Yates v. Texas
171 SW 3d 215 Texas Court of Appeals, First District

In 2002, Andrea Yates was prosecuted for killing her children and entered a plea of not guilty because of insanity. The jury heard a psychiatric interview in which she had expressed delusionary perceptions of wanting to save her children from hell. Although agreeing that Yates was mentally ill, the prosecution argued that she was not legally insane according to Texas law because her behavior indicated that she understood the difference between right and wrong according to the law. She was found guilty and sentenced to life imprisonment. In 2005, the Texas Court of Appeals reversed Yates's conviction because a psychiatrist for the prosecution, Dr. Park Dietz, admitted that part of his testimony in the trial was materially false. He had testified that shortly before Yates killed her children, an episode of the television series *Law and Order* had featured a woman acquitted through an insanity defense after drowning her children. The court concluded that this false information might have influenced the jury. In 2006, Yates's second trial resulted in a verdict of not guilty by reason of insanity. She was then committed to a state mental hospital.

2006

Clark v. Arizona
548 U.S. 735 U.S. Supreme Court

Suffering from paranoid schizophrenia, Eric Clark became convinced that his town had been taken over by aliens. When stopped for a minor offense, he shot and killed a police officer. Despite his delusion, Clark was found competent to stand trial. His attorneys wanted to utilize expert witnesses prepared to testify that Clark's perceptions of reality made it impossible for him to have necessary criminal intent. The trial judge, however, disallowed the testimony, ruling that Arizona law only allows the insanity defense for persons who are unable to distinguish between right and wrong. Clark was found guilty and sentenced to life imprisonment. Upholding the verdict by a 5-4 margin, the Supreme Court endorsed Arizona's insanity law, thereby permitting a restriction on evidence about a defendant's mental condition regarding the issue of insanity.

2007

Panetti v. Quarterman
551 U.S. 930 U.S. Supreme Court

By a 5-4 margin, the Supreme Court overturned the death sentence of Scott Panetti, a convicted murderer who suffered from severe delusions as a result of schizophrenia. In *Ford v. Wainwright* (1986), the Court had ruled that the execution of an insane person violated the Eighth Amendment, but the Court had given almost no direction about the procedures required for determining legal insanity. In *Panetti*, Justice Anthony Kennedy explained that the trial court's hearing had been inadequate because there had been no consideration of psychiatric evidence suggesting that the defendant's delusions may have distorted his sense of reality to the extent that he was incapable of rationally understanding his crime. Kennedy declared it unconstitutional to execute a person who "suffers from a severe, documented mental illness that is the source of gross delusions preventing him from comprehending the meaning and purpose of his punishment."

Taus v. Loftus
40th Cal. 4th 683, 46 Cal. Rptr. 3d 775 California
Supreme Court

In 1997, Dr. David Corwin published a case study about repressed and recovered memories. The study included a video of an unnamed six-year-old girl who claimed to have been sexually abused by her biological father. After psychologist Elizabeth Loftus and an associate published a critical examination of the case, the girl, Nicole Taus, sued the writers and the magazine that published the study for invasion of privacy. The California Supreme Court dismissed all but one of the allegations based on free expression. The Court allowed Taus to sue Loftus for having told a falsehood in order to interview Taus's mother, which was potentially an intrusion into a private matter. Several months later, Loftus agreed to pay a settlement of $7,500, and Taus was ordered to pay $246,000 for the legal expenses of the other defendants.

2008

Indiana v. Edwards
554 U.S. 208 U.S. Supreme Court

Ahmad Edwards was arrested for shooting three people while stealing a pair of shoes. Psychiatric evaluations concluded that he was mentally ill but competent to stand trial. When Edwards insisted on representing himself, his defense was rambling and often incoherent. Found guilty, he appealed with the argument that the lack of a competent defense violated the Sixth Amendment requirement for a fair trial. By a 7-2 vote, the U.S. Supreme Court agreed and overturned the conviction. Although the Court reaffirmed the defendant's right to self-representation when it is a "voluntary and intelligent" choice, the Court insisted that trial judges have the obligation to insist upon other representation when defendants suffer from mental illness to the extent that they are incompetent to conduct trial proceedings by themselves.

Elizabeth D. Schafer; updated by Thomas Tandy Lewis

Indexes

CATEGORY INDEX

Abnormality models· · · · · · · · · · · · CVII
Adolescence· · · · · · · · · · · · · · · · CVII
Adulthood · · · · · · · · · · · · · · · · CVIII
Aging· · · · · · · · · · · · · · · · · · · CVIII
Anxiety disorders · · · · · · · · · · · · · CIX
Attitudes and behavior· · · · · · · · · · · CIX
Behavioral and cognitive models · · · · · · · CX
Behavioral therapies · · · · · · · · · · · · · CX
Biological bases of behavior · · · · · · · · · CX
Childhood· · · · · · · · · · · · · · · · · CXI
Classic analytic themes and issues · · · · · CXI
Cognition · · · · · · · · · · · · · · · · · CXI
Cognitive therapies · · · · · · · · · · · · CXII
Conditioning · · · · · · · · · · · · · · · CXII
Consciousness · · · · · · · · · · · · · · · CXII
Coping · · · · · · · · · · · · · · · · · · CXII
Depression · · · · · · · · · · · · · · · · CXIII
Developmental psychology· · · · · · · · · CXIII
Diagnosis· · · · · · · · · · · · · · · · · CXIV
Emotion · · · · · · · · · · · · · · · · · CXIV
Endocrine system · · · · · · · · · · · · · CXIV
Experimentation · · · · · · · · · · · · · · CXV
Group and family therapies · · · · · · · · CXV
Group processes · · · · · · · · · · · · · · CXV
Humanistic-phenomenological models · · · · CXV
Humanistic therapies · · · · · · · · · · · CXV
Infancy and childhood · · · · · · · · · · CXVI
Intelligence · · · · · · · · · · · · · · · CXVI
Intelligence testing· · · · · · · · · · · · CXVI
Interpersonal relations · · · · · · · · · CXVII
Language · · · · · · · · · · · · · · · · CXVII
Learning · · · · · · · · · · · · · · · · CXVII
Memory · · · · · · · · · · · · · · · · · CXVIII
Men's psychology· · · · · · · · · · · · · CXVIII
Methodology · · · · · · · · · · · · · · · CXVIII
Motivation · · · · · · · · · · · · · · · · CXIX
Multicultural psychology · · · · · · · · · · CXX
Nervous system · · · · · · · · · · · · · · CXX
Organizations and publications· · · · · · · CXX
Origin and definition of psychology · · · · CXX
People · · · · · · · · · · · · · · · · · · CXX
Personality· · · · · · · · · · · · · · · · CXXI
Personality assessment · · · · · · · · · · CXXII
Personality disorders · · · · · · · · · · · CXXII
Prejudice and discrimination · · · · · · · CXXII
Prosocial behavior · · · · · · · · · · · · CXXIII
Psychobiology · · · · · · · · · · · · · · CXXIII
Psychodynamic and neoanalytic
    models · · · · · · · · · · · · · · · CXXIII
Psychopathology · · · · · · · · · · · · · CXXIV
Psychotherapy· · · · · · · · · · · · · · · CXXV
Schizophrenias · · · · · · · · · · · · · · CXXV
Sensation and perception · · · · · · · · · CXXVI
Sexuality · · · · · · · · · · · · · · · · CXXVI
Sleep · · · · · · · · · · · · · · · · · · CXXVI
Social psychology· · · · · · · · · · · · · CXXVI
Stress · · · · · · · · · · · · · · · · · · CXXVII
Testing · · · · · · · · · · · · · · · · · CXXVIII
Thought · · · · · · · · · · · · · · · · · CXXVIII
Treatments· · · · · · · · · · · · · · · · CXXIX
Vision · · · · · · · · · · · · · · · · · · CXXIX
Women's psychology · · · · · · · · · · · CXXIX

ABNORMALITY MODELS

Abnormality: Biomedical models, 6
Abnormality: Legal models, 11
Abnormality: Psychological models, 15
Asperger syndrome, 191
Body dysmorphic disorder, 301
Breuer, Josef, 318
Comorbidity, 439
Dissociative disorders, 609
Ego defense mechanisms, 652

Factitious disorders, 749
Feminist psychotherapy, 772
Forensic psychology, 787
Fromm, Erich, 806
Kraepelin, Emil, 1071
Mental illness: Historical concepts, 1194
Munchausen syndrome and Munchausen syndrome by proxy, 1253
Profiling, 1474
Psychopathology, 1517

S-R theory: Neal E. Miller and John Dollard, 1655
Schizophrenia: Theoretical explanations, 1680

ADOLESCENCE

Adolescence: Cognitive skills, 35
Adolescence: Cross-cultural patterns, 40
Adolescence: Sexuality, 44
Aggression, 74

Anorexia nervosa and bulimia nervosa, 150
Antisocial personality disorder, 161
Asperger syndrome, 191
Attention-deficit hyperactivity disorder (ADHD), 209
Autism, 230
Bilingualism and learning disabilities, 276
Birth order and personality, 295
Blau, Theodore H., 298
Body dysmorphic disorder, 301
Bullying, 324
Child abuse, 358
Children's mental health, 371
Cognitive Abilities Test (CogAT), 391
Cognitive ability: Gender differences, 392
Computer and Internet use and mental health, 446
Conduct disorder, 461
Deception and lying, 545
Development, 576
Developmental disabilities, 580
Dyslexia, 636
Eating disorders, 640
Erikson, Erik H., 710
Family life: Children's issues, 756
Family systems theory, 759
Father-child relationship, 762
Femininity, 770
Games and mental health, 810
Gay, lesbian, bisexual, and transgender mental health, 813
Gilligan, Carol, 851
Hall, G. Stanley, 885
Horney, Karen, 934
Identity crises, 974
Juvenile delinquency, 1059
Masculinity, 1137
Media exposure and mental health, 1142
Mother-child relationship, 1231
Nutrition and mental health, 1300
Oedipus complex, 1322

Parental alienation syndrome, 1349
Pervasive developmental disorders, 1410
Piaget, Jean, 1426
Psychosexual development, 1528
Punishment, 1563
Separation and divorce: Children's issues, 1743
Sibling relationships, 1785
Stepfamilies, 1874
Substance use disorders, 1915
Support groups, 1926
Teenage suicide, 1954
Teenagers' mental health, 1959
Time-out, 1996
Violence by children and teenagers, 2024
Women's psychology: Carol Gilligan, 2059

ADULTHOOD
Ageism, 69
Aggression, 74
Aggression: Reduction and control, 77
Aging: Physical changes, 87
Anger, 142
Antisocial personality disorder, 161
Assisted living, 198
Avoidant personality disorder, 239
Bandura, Albert, 242
Brain damage, 306
Career selection, development, and change, 346
Coaching, 385
Crowd behavior, 525
Defense reactions: Species-specific, 555
Developmental methodologies, 585
Developmental psychology, 589
Domestic violence, 614
Elder abuse, 666
Elders' mental health, 669
Erikson, Erik H., 710
Evolutionary psychology, 715
Family life: Adult issues, 752

Family systems theory, 759
Femininity, 770
Freudian psychology, 801
Gay, lesbian, bisexual, and transgender mental health, 813
Health insurance, 892
Hierarchy of needs, 913
Horney, Karen, 934
Hospice, 935
Identity crises, 974
Jungian psychology, 1055
Juvenile delinquency, 1059
Lorenz, Konrad, 1130
Masculinity, 1137
Media exposure and mental health, 1142
Men's mental health, 1184
Miller, Neal E., and John Dollard, 1210
Nutrition and mental health, 1300
Observational learning and modeling therapy, 1309
Parental alienation syndrome, 1349
Profiling, 1474
Repressed memories, 1628
Road rage, 1643
Separation and divorce: Adult issues, 1740
Sibling relationships, 1785
Sports psychology, 1859
Support groups, 1926
Violence and sexuality in the media, 2020
Violence by children and teenagers, 2024
Women's mental health, 2054
Yalom, Irving, 2084

AGING
Ageism, 69
Aging: Cognitive changes, 81
Aging: Physical changes, 87
Aging: Theories, 91
Alzheimer's disease, 114
Assisted living, 198
Beck Depression Inventory (BDI), 247

Cancer and mental health, 335
Coping: Terminal illness, 504
Death and dying, 541
Dementia, 559
Depression, 566
Developmental psychology, 589
Elder abuse, 666
Elders' mental health, 669
Erikson, Erik H., 710
Family life: Adult issues, 752
Family systems theory, 759
Hospice, 935
Incompetency, 993
Nervous system, 1277
Nutrition and mental health, 1300
Retirement, 1637
Separation and divorce: Adult issues, 1740
Sports psychology, 1859
Suicide, 1920
Support groups, 1926
Yalom, Irving, 2084

ANXIETY DISORDERS

Addictive personality and behaviors, 25
Agoraphobia and panic disorders, 96
Anger, 142
Antianxiety medications, 156
Anxiety disorders, 166
Attitude-behavior consistency, 214
Attitude formation and change, 218
Battered woman syndrome, 243
Beck, Aaron T., 246
Behavior therapy, 252
Body dysmorphic disorder, 301
Brain damage, 306
Breuer, Josef, 318
Caffeine and mental health, 331
Coaching, 385
Cognitive dissonance, 405
Community psychology, 434
Consumer psychology, 479
Coping: Chronic illness, 490
Disaster psychology, 604
Dix, Dorothea, 613

Drug therapies, 631
Ego defense mechanisms, 652
Environmental factors and mental health, 699
Environmental toxicology and mental health, 707
Generalized anxiety disorder, 835
Genetics and mental health, 838
Guilt, 877
Homelessness: Psychological causes and effects, 918
Hope and mental health, 926
Horney, Karen, 934
Impulse control disorders, 984
Kraepelin, Emil, 1071
Lorenz, Konrad, 1130
May, Rollo, 1141
Media psychology, 1146
Men's mental health, 1184
Misbehavior, 1213
Mood stabilizer medications, 1225
Motivation, 1234
Observational learning and modeling therapy, 1309
Obsessive-compulsive disorder, 1317
Oedipus complex, 1322
Panic attacks, 1343
Parental alienation syndrome, 1349
Phobias, 1418
Post-traumatic stress disorder, 1443
Prejudice, 1452
Profiling, 1474
Psychopharmacology, 1523
Psychosurgery, 1537
Religion and psychology, 1618
Religiosity: Measurement, 1623
Road rage, 1643
Self, 1699
Self-perception theory, 1721
Separation anxiety, 1747
Shyness, 1783
Sports psychology, 1859
State-Trait Anxiety Inventory (STAI), 1869

Support groups, 1926
Teenagers' mental health, 1959
Terrorism: Psychological causes and effects, 1968
Tic disorders, 1992
Violence by children and teenagers, 2024
Virtual reality, 2030
Watson, John B., 2046
Women's mental health, 2054

ATTITUDES AND BEHAVIOR

Ageism, 69
Altruism, cooperation, and empathy, 109
Attitude-behavior consistency, 214
Attitude formation and change, 218
Behavior therapy, 252
Collectivism, 427
Cooperation, competition, and negotiation, 483
Cooperative learning, 487
Coping: Social support, 495
Crowd behavior, 525
Factitious disorders, 749
Father-child relationship, 762
Fetishes, 775
Forgiveness, 795
Group decision making, 864
Groups, 872
James, William, 1050
Milgram experiment, 1208
Mood stabilizer medications, 1225
Mother-child relationship, 1231
Multicultural psychology, 1244
Observational learning and modeling therapy, 1309
Parental alienation syndrome, 1349
Philosophy and psychology, 1415
Power, 1448
Prejudice, 1452
Prejudice reduction, 1457
Racism, 1583
Self-efficacy, 1712
Self-help groups, 1719
Sexism, 1753

Sibling relationships, 1785
Social identity theory, 1810
Spirituality and mental health, 1852
Support groups, 1926

BEHAVIORAL AND COGNITIVE MODELS
Abnormality: Psychological models, 15
Aging: Cognitive changes, 81
Anxiety disorders, 166
Artificial intelligence, 184
Beck, Aaron T., 246
Behavior therapy, 252
Behavioral economics, 261
Behaviorism, 269
Bobo doll experiment, 299
Body dysmorphic disorder, 301
Brain damage, 306
Bronfenbrenner, Urie, 322
Cognitive social learning: Walter Mischel, 420
Constructivist psychology, 477
Development, 576
Dewey, John, 593
Dialectical behavior therapy, 602
Forensic psychology, 787
Freudian psychology, 801
Gambling, 808
Hull, Clark L., 937
Inductive thinking, 1001
Jungian psychology, 1055
Kohlberg, Lawrence, 1070
Little Albert experiment, 1117
Maslow, Abraham, 1138
Milgram experiment, 1208
Motivation, 1234
Motivation: Intrinsic and extrinsic, 1238
Nicotine dependence, 1293
Operant conditioning therapies, 1324
Organizational behavior and consulting, 1332
Personal constructs: George A. Kelly, 1382
Piaget, Jean, 1426
Radical behaviorism: B. F. Skinner, 1587

Reinforcement, 1613
Rule-governed behavior, 1650
S-R theory: Neal E. Miller and John Dollard, 1655
Satir, Virginia, 1666
Self-efficacy, 1712
Skinner, B. F., 1792
Skinner box, 1793
Social learning: Albert Bandura, 1815
Stanford prison experiment, 1866
Thorndike, Edward L., 1979
Tolman, Edward C., 1998
Transtheoretical model, 2011
Type A behavior pattern, 2015

BEHAVIORAL THERAPIES
Aversion therapy, 238
Bed-wetting, 248
Behavior therapy, 252
Biofeedback and relaxation, 279
Brief therapy, 320
Cognitive behavior therapy, 396
Constructivist psychology, 477
Coping: Chronic illness, 490
Coping: Strategies, 500
Dialectical behavior therapy, 602
Eysenck, Hans, 743
Implosion, 978
Kraepelin, Emil, 1071
Mental health practitioners, 1190
Observational learning and modeling therapy, 1309
Oedipus complex, 1322
Operant conditioning therapies, 1324
Pain management, 1338
Parental alienation syndrome, 1349
Psychopathology, 1517
Psychotherapy: Children, 1541
Reinforcement, 1613
Self-help groups, 1719
Speech disorders, 1845
Sports psychology, 1859
Support groups, 1926
Systematic desensitization, 1939
Virtual reality, 2030

BIOLOGICAL BASES OF BEHAVIOR
Adrenal gland, 49
Aggression, 74
Bipolar disorder, 283
Birth: Effects on physical development, 290
Brain damage, 306
Brain structure, 312
Cannon, Walter Bradford, 338
Circadian rhythms, 376
Dissociative disorders, 609
Drug therapies, 631
Endocrine system, 690
Endorphins, 695
Environmental factors and mental health, 699
Evolutionary psychology, 715
Fight-or-flight response, 784
Genetics and mental health, 838
Gonads, 852
Hormones and behavior, 928
Hull, Clark L., 937
Inhibitory and excitatory impulses, 1007
James, William, 1050
Learning, 1100
Lobotomy, 1119
Lorenz, Konrad, 1130
Memory: Animal research, 1160
Memory: Physiology, 1169
Motivation, 1234
Nervous system, 1277
Neurons, 1280
Neurotransmitters, 1291
Oedipus complex, 1322
Pain, 1335
Pain management, 1338
Parental alienation syndrome, 1349
Pavlov, Ivan Petrovich, 1367
Pituitary gland, 1429
Prenatal physical development, 1461
Psychobiology, 1495
Psychopharmacology, 1523
Race and intelligence, 1578
Reflexes, 1606
Reticular formation, 1634
Split-brain studies, 1854

Stimulant medications, 1877
Substance use disorders, 1915
Synaptic transmission, 1933
Synesthesia, 1936
Thyroid gland, 1988

CHILDHOOD
Asperger syndrome, 191
Avoidant personality disorder, 239
Bilingualism and learning disabilities, 276
Blau, Theodore H., 298
Bobo doll experiment, 299
Bullying, 324
Children's mental health, 371
Cognitive Abilities Test (CogAT), 391
Computer and Internet use and mental health, 446
Deception and lying, 545
Developmental psychology, 589
Elimination disorders, 674
Family systems theory, 759
Forgiveness, 795
Freudian psychology, 801
Games and mental health, 810
Jungian psychology, 1055
Kohlberg, Lawrence, 1070
Media exposure and mental health, 1142
Pervasive developmental disorders, 1410
Psychopharmacology, 1523
Punishment, 1563
Repressed memories, 1628
Time-out, 1996

CLASSIC ANALYTIC THEMES AND ISSUES
Adler, Alfred, 29
Analytic psychology: Jacques Lacan, 130
Archetypes and the collective unconscious, 176
Death and dying, 541
Deception and lying, 545
Defense mechanisms, 552
Dreams, 623
Ego defense mechanisms, 652

Ego, superego, and id, 664
Fear, 766
Fetishes, 775
Freud, Anna, 799
Freud, Sigmund, 800
Freudian psychology, 801
Gender differences, 817
Guilt, 877
Horney, Karen, 934
Hysteria, 970
Inductive thinking, 1001
Jungian psychology, 1055
Lacan, Jacques, 1076
Oedipus complex, 1322
Penis envy, 1374
Philosophy and psychology, 1415
Power, 1448
Psychoanalysis, 1481
Psychoanalytic psychology and personality: Sigmund Freud, 1491
Psychology: Definition, 1500
Psychosexual development, 1528
Psychotherapy: Historical approaches, 1554
Repressed memories, 1628
Women's psychology: Carol Gilligan, 2059
Women's psychology: Karen Horney, 2064
Women's psychology: Sigmund Freud, 2067

COGNITION
Adolescence: Cognitive skills, 35
Advertising, 52
Aging: Cognitive changes, 81
Albee, George W., 102
Alzheimer's disease, 114
Artificial intelligence, 184
Attention, 205
Automaticity, 234
Bandura, Albert, 242
Beck, Aaron T., 246
Beck Depression Inventory (BDI), 247
Bilingualism, 273
Binet, Alfred, 278

Blau, Theodore H., 298
Bobo doll experiment, 299
Brain damage, 306
Bruner, Jerome, 323
Cognitive Abilities Test (CogAT), 391
Cognitive ability: Gender differences, 392
Cognitive development: Jean Piaget, 401
Cognitive maps, 409
Cognitive psychology, 414
Computer models of cognition, 448
Concept formation, 451
Consciousness, 467
Consciousness: Altered states, 471
Consumer psychology, 479
Coping: Terminal illness, 504
Creativity: Assessment, 517
Decision making, 547
Dementia, 559
Denial, 563
Developmental disabilities, 580
Dewey, John, 593
Dreams, 623
Ebbinghaus, Hermann, 645
Encoding, 687
Evolutionary psychology, 715
Eye movement desensitization and reprocessing, 737
Forgetting and forgetfulness, 791
Gender identity formation, 824
Giftedness, 847
Hallucinations, 886
Hypnosis, 955
Incompetency, 993
Inductive thinking, 1001
Jungian psychology, 1055
Kinesthetic memory, 1064
Kohlberg, Lawrence, 1070
Language, 1077
Law and psychology, 1088
Linguistics, 1111
Lobotomy, 1119
Logic and reasoning, 1121
Long-term memory, 1126
Memory, 1155
Memory: Empirical studies, 1165

Memory: Sensory, 1174
Multiple intelligences, 1246
Neuropsychology, 1284
Neurotransmitters, 1291
Organizational behavior and
    consulting, 1332
Pain management, 1338
Pattern recognition, 1360
Pattern vision, 1364
Pavlov, Ivan Petrovich, 1367
Pervasive developmental
    disorders, 1410
Philosophy and psychology, 1415
Piaget, Jean, 1426
Problem-solving stages, 1467
Problem-solving strategies, 1470
Psychobiology, 1495
Psychosomatic disorders, 1532
Reactive attachment disorder,
    1600
Religion and psychology, 1618
Religiosity: Measurement, 1623
Rosenhan experiment, 1649
Self-efficacy, 1712
Seligman, Martin E. P., 1730
Short-term memory, 1779
Signal detection theory, 1789
Skinner box, 1793
Split-brain studies, 1854
Sports psychology, 1859
Support groups, 1926
Thorndike, Edward L., 1979
Thought: Inferential, 1980
Thought: Study and
    measurement, 1984
Tolman, Edward C., 1998
Virtual reality, 2030
Vision: Brightness and contrast,
    2034
Zimbardo, Philip G., 2086

COGNITIVE THERAPIES
Agoraphobia and panic
    disorders, 96
Beck, Aaron T., 246
Behavior therapy, 252
Blau, Theodore H., 298
Brief therapy, 320
Constructivist psychology, 477
Coping: Chronic illness, 490

Coping: Strategies, 500
Deductive thinking, 551
Dialectical behavior therapy, 602
Ellis, Albert, 676
Eye movement desensitization
    and reprocessing, 737
Mental health practitioners, 1190
Psychotherapy: Children, 1541
Rational emotive therapy, 1595
Reality therapy, 1603
Sports psychology, 1859
Support groups, 1926
Transactional analysis, 2007
Transtheoretical model, 2011
Virtual reality, 2030

CONDITIONING
Behavior therapy, 252
Behaviorism, 269
Bobo doll experiment, 299
Collectivism, 427
Conditioning, 455
Cross-cultural psychology, 523
Culture-bound syndromes, 532
Inductive thinking, 1001
Learning, 1100
Little Albert experiment, 1117
Memory: Animal research, 1160
Milgram experiment, 1208
Motivation, 1234
Motivation: Intrinsic and
    extrinsic, 1238
Multicultural psychology, 1244
Operant conditioning therapies,
    1324
Parental alienation syndrome,
    1349
Pavlov, Ivan Petrovich, 1367
Pavlovian conditioning, 1368
Punishment, 1563
Radical behaviorism: B. F.
    Skinner, 1587
Reinforcement, 1613
Rule-governed behavior, 1650
Skinner box, 1793
Stanford prison experiment,
    1866
Taste aversion, 1945
Time-out, 1996
Tolman, Edward C., 1998

CONSCIOUSNESS
Artificial intelligence, 184
Attention, 205
Automaticity, 234
Brain damage, 306
Circadian rhythms, 376
Consciousness, 467
Consciousness: Altered states,
    471
Coping: Terminal illness, 504
Deductive thinking, 551
Denial, 563
Dewey, John, 593
Dreams, 623
Ecological psychology, 646
Freudian psychology, 801
Hallucinations, 886
Hierarchy of needs, 913
Hypnosis, 955
Inductive thinking, 1001
Insomnia, 1013
James, William, 1050
Jungian psychology, 1055
Meditation and relaxation, 1152
Narcolepsy, 1266
Philosophy and psychology, 1415
Self, 1699
Sleep, 1796
Sleep apnea, 1803
Spirituality and mental health,
    1852

COPING
Aggression, 74
Amnesia and fugue, 126
Anger, 142
Beck Depression Inventory
    (BDI), 247
Biofeedback and relaxation, 279
Cancer and mental health, 335
Coping: Chronic illness, 490
Coping: Social support, 495
Coping: Strategies, 500
Coping: Terminal illness, 504
Crisis intervention, 520
Denial, 563
Disaster psychology, 604
Elders' mental health, 669
Environmental psychology, 702
Forgiveness, 795

Grieving, 861
Health psychology, 895
Hope and mental health, 926
Hospice, 935
Impulse control disorders, 984
Kübler-Ross, Elizabeth, 1072
Media psychology, 1146
Multiple personality, 1250
Pain management, 1338
Parental alienation syndrome, 1349
Religion and psychology, 1618
Religiosity: Measurement, 1623
Satir, Virginia, 1666
Self-help groups, 1719
Seligman, Martin E. P., 1730
Social networks, 1819
Social support and mental health, 1838
Spirituality and mental health, 1852
Stepfamilies, 1874
Stress: Behavioral and psychological responses, 1884
Substance use disorders, 1915
Support groups, 1926

DEPRESSION

Alzheimer's disease, 114
Antidepressant medications, 158
Battered woman syndrome, 243
Beck, Aaron T., 246
Beck Depression Inventory (BDI), 247
Bipolar disorder, 283
Body dysmorphic disorder, 301
Bullying, 324
Cancer and mental health, 335
Children's Depression Inventory (CDI), 369
Circadian rhythms, 376
Coping: Chronic illness, 490
Coping: Terminal illness, 504
Dementia, 559
Depression, 566
Disaster psychology, 604
Drug therapies, 631
Environmental factors and mental health, 699

Environmental toxicology and mental health, 707
Exercise and mental health, 719
Gay, lesbian, bisexual, and transgender mental health, 813
Generalized anxiety disorder, 835
Grieving, 861
Impulse control disorders, 984
Kraepelin, Emil, 1071
Kübler-Ross, Elizabeth, 1072
Lobotomy, 1119
Media psychology, 1146
Men's mental health, 1184
Mood disorders, 1219
Mood stabilizer medications, 1225
Nicotine dependence, 1293
Panic attacks, 1343
Parental alienation syndrome, 1349
Postpartum depression, 1441
Psychopharmacology, 1523
Psychosurgery, 1537
Seasonal affective disorder, 1694
Self-help groups, 1719
Seligman, Martin E. P., 1730
Sexual harassment: Psychological causes and effects, 1767
Social networks, 1819
Social support and mental health, 1838
Suicide, 1920
Support groups, 1926
Teenagers' mental health, 1959
Tic disorders, 1992
Women's mental health, 2054

DEVELOPMENTAL PSYCHOLOGY

Adolescence: Cognitive skills, 35
Adolescence: Cross-cultural patterns, 40
Adolescence: Sexuality, 44
Ageism, 69
Aging: Cognitive changes, 81
Aging: Physical changes, 87
Aging: Theories, 91
Attachment and bonding in infancy and childhood, 201

Binet, Alfred, 278
Birth: Effects on physical development, 290
Birth order and personality, 295
Bronfenbrenner, Urie, 322
Career selection, development, and change, 346
Child abuse, 358
Cognitive ability: Gender differences, 392
Cognitive development: Jean Piaget, 401
Cross-cultural psychology, 523
Death and dying, 541
Denial, 563
Development, 576
Developmental disabilities, 580
Developmental methodologies, 585
Developmental psychology, 589
Elders' mental health, 669
Erikson, Erik H., 710
Family life: Adult issues, 752
Family life: Children's issues, 756
Family systems theory, 759
Father-child relationship, 762
Freud, Anna, 799
Gay, lesbian, bisexual, and transgender mental health, 813
Gender identity formation, 824
Genetics and mental health, 838
Gesell, Arnold, 842
Giftedness, 847
Gilligan, Carol, 851
Hall, G. Stanley, 885
Hierarchy of needs, 913
Identity crises, 974
Juvenile delinquency, 1059
Kinesthetic memory, 1064
Kohlberg, Lawrence, 1070
Mental retardation, 1200
Moral development, 1227
Mother-child relationship, 1231
Motor development, 1240
Multicultural psychology, 1244
Nutrition and mental health, 1300
Oedipus complex, 1322

Parental alienation syndrome, 1349
Parenting styles, 1351
Penis envy, 1374
Pervasive developmental disorders, 1410
Physical development: Environment versus genetics, 1423
Piaget, Jean, 1426
Prenatal physical development, 1461
Psychoanalysis, 1481
Quality of life, 1570
Reactive attachment disorder, 1600
Reflexes in newborns, 1610
Religion and psychology, 1618
Religiosity: Measurement, 1623
Retirement, 1637
Self, 1699
Self-help groups, 1719
Separation and divorce: Adult issues, 1740
Separation and divorce: Children's issues, 1743
Separation anxiety, 1747
Sibling relationships, 1785
Social support and mental health, 1838
Spirituality and mental health, 1852
Stepfamilies, 1874
Stimulant medications, 1877
Systems theories, 1943
Teenage suicide, 1954
Violence by children and teenagers, 2024

DIAGNOSIS
American Psychiatric Association, 120
American Psychological Association, 123
Assessment, 195
Behavioral assessment, 257
Confidentiality, 465
Culture and diagnosis, 531
Diagnosis, 594

Diagnostic and Statistical Manual of Mental Disorders (DSM), 599
Freudian psychology, 801
International Classification of Diseases (ICD), 1037
Jungian psychology, 1055
Mental health parity, 1189
Mental health practitioners, 1190
Mental illness: Historical concepts, 1194
Myers-Briggs Type Indicator (MBTI), 1261
Observational methods, 1314
Psychopathology, 1517
Sampling, 1662
Scientific methods, 1688
Survey research: Questionnaires and interviews, 1929

EMOTION
Affiliation and friendship, 56
Aggression, 74
Altruism, cooperation, and empathy, 109
Anger, 142
Asperger syndrome, 191
Beck Depression Inventory (BDI), 247
Brain damage, 306
Crisis intervention, 520
Defense mechanisms, 552
Denial, 563
Depression, 566
Disaster psychology, 604
Dix, Dorothea, 613
Ego defense mechanisms, 652
Emotional expression, 677
Emotional intelligence, 681
Emotions, 683
Facial feedback, 745
Fight-or-flight response, 784
Forgiveness, 795
Grieving, 861
Guilt, 877
Hierarchy of needs, 913
Hope and mental health, 926
Impulse control disorders, 984
Intimacy, 1044
Introverts and extroverts, 1047
James, William, 1050

Jealousy, 1051
Kraepelin, Emil, 1071
Kübler-Ross, Elizabeth, 1072
Lobotomy, 1119
Love, 1131
Masters, William H., and Virginia E. Johnson, 1139
Media psychology, 1146
Motivation, 1234
Multiple intelligences, 1246
Neurotransmitters, 1291
Oedipus complex, 1322
Pain, 1335
Pain management, 1338
Parental alienation syndrome, 1349
Passive aggression, 1358
Pervasive developmental disorders, 1410
Religion and psychology, 1618
Seligman, Martin E. P., 1730
Shyness, 1783
Sports psychology, 1859
Support groups, 1926
Tic disorders, 1992
Violence by children and teenagers, 2024

ENDOCRINE SYSTEM
Adrenal gland, 49
Aging: Theories, 91
Anger, 142
Circadian rhythms, 376
Emotions, 683
Endocrine system, 690
Exercise and mental health, 719
Fear, 766
Gonads, 852
Hormones and behavior, 928
Imprinting, 980
Lobotomy, 1119
Mood stabilizer medications, 1225
Nervous system, 1277
Neurotransmitters, 1291
Pavlov, Ivan Petrovich, 1367
Pituitary gland, 1429
Psychobiology, 1495
Psychopharmacology, 1523
Psychosurgery, 1537

Sex hormones and motivation, 1750
Sexual behavior patterns, 1757
Thirst, 1977
Thyroid gland, 1988

EXPERIMENTATION
Animal experimentation, 145
Archival data, 180
Behaviorism, 269
Cannon, Walter Bradford, 338
Complex experimental designs, 442
Confidentiality, 465
Data description, 535
Dewey, John, 593
Dialectical behavior therapy, 602
Ebbinghaus, Hermann, 645
Ecological psychology, 646
Experimental psychology, 725
Experimentation: Ethics and participant rights, 728
Experimentation: Independent, dependent, and control variables, 733
Eye movement desensitization and reprocessing, 737
Field experimentation, 777
Milgram experiment, 1208
Placebo effect, 1433
Quasi-experimental designs, 1572
Sampling, 1662
Scientific methods, 1688
Skinner box, 1793
Stanford prison experiment, 1866
Survey research: Questionnaires and interviews, 1929
Virtual reality, 2030
Within-subject experimental designs, 2050

GROUP AND FAMILY THERAPIES
Behavioral family therapy, 265
Children's mental health, 371
Family systems theory, 759
Forgiveness, 795
Group therapy, 868

Intervention, 1043
Oedipus complex, 1322
Parental alienation syndrome, 1349
Psychotherapy: Children, 1541
Satir, Virginia, 1666
Self-help groups, 1719
Social support and mental health, 1838
Strategic family therapy, 1880
Support groups, 1926
Yalom, Irving, 2084

GROUP PROCESSES
Altruism, cooperation, and empathy, 109
Blau, Theodore H., 298
Bystander intervention, 326
Collectivism, 427
Cooperation, competition, and negotiation, 483
Cooperative learning, 487
Coping: Social support, 495
Crisis intervention, 520
Cross-cultural psychology, 523
Crowd behavior, 525
Culture-bound syndromes, 532
Family systems theory, 759
Group decision making, 864
Groups, 872
Industrial and organizational psychology, 1002
Intervention, 1043
Law and psychology, 1088
Lewin, Kurt, 1110
Organizational behavior and consulting, 1332
Parental alienation syndrome, 1349
Power, 1448
Punishment, 1563
Self-help groups, 1719
Social support and mental health, 1838
Spirituality and mental health, 1852
Stanford prison experiment, 1866
Support groups, 1926
Systems theories, 1943

Workplace issues and mental health, 2078
Yalom, Irving, 2084
Zimbardo, Philip G., 2086

HUMANISTIC-PHENOMENOLOGICAL MODELS
Abnormality: Psychological models, 15
Analytic psychology: Jacques Lacan, 130
Ecological psychology, 646
Environmental factors and mental health, 699
Fromm, Erich, 806
Hierarchy of needs, 913
Humanistic psychology, 942
Humanistic trait models: Gordon Allport, 946
Insanity defense, 1011
Kübler-Ross, Elizabeth, 1072
Maslow, Abraham, 1138
May, Rollo, 1141
Personology: Henry A. Murray, 1406
Psychoanalysis, 1481
Qualitative research, 1567
Self-actualization, 1704
Self-efficacy, 1712
Social psychological models: Erich Fromm, 1827
Spirituality and mental health, 1852
Systems theories, 1943

HUMANISTIC THERAPIES
Albee, George W., 102
Exercise and mental health, 719
Forgiveness, 795
Gestalt therapy, 843
Hope and mental health, 926
Humanistic psychology, 942
Intervention, 1043
Kübler-Ross, Elizabeth, 1072
Maslow, Abraham, 1138
May, Rollo, 1141
Nutrition and mental health, 1300
Person-centered therapy, 1377

Play therapy, 1434
Psychoanalysis, 1481
Satir, Virginia, 1666
Self-help groups, 1719
Social support and mental health, 1838
Spirituality and mental health, 1852
Sports psychology, 1859
Transactional analysis, 2007
Transtheoretical model, 2011
Yalom, Irving, 2084

INFANCY AND CHILDHOOD
Antisocial personality disorder, 161
Asperger syndrome, 191
Attachment and bonding in infancy and childhood, 201
Attention-deficit hyperactivity disorder (ADHD), 209
Autism, 230
Bed-wetting, 248
Bilingualism and learning disabilities, 276
Birth: Effects on physical development, 290
Birth order and personality, 295
Bronfenbrenner, Urie, 322
Bruner, Jerome, 323
Child abuse, 358
Childhood disorders, 363
Children's Depression Inventory (CDI), 369
Children's mental health, 371
Conduct disorder, 461
Development, 576
Developmental disabilities, 580
Developmental methodologies, 585
Developmental psychology, 589
Down syndrome, 619
Dyslexia, 636
Elimination disorders, 674
Erikson, Erik H., 710
Family life: Children's issues, 756
Family systems theory, 759
Father-child relationship, 762
Freud, Anna, 799

Freudian psychology, 801
Gender identity formation, 824
Gesell, Arnold, 842
Health insurance, 892
Horney, Karen, 934
Jungian psychology, 1055
Little Albert experiment, 1117
Mental retardation, 1200
Moral development, 1227
Mother-child relationship, 1231
Motor development, 1240
Oedipus complex, 1322
Parental alienation syndrome, 1349
Penis envy, 1374
Pervasive developmental disorders, 1410
Phobias, 1418
Physical development: Environment versus genetics, 1423
Piaget, Jean, 1426
Play therapy, 1434
Prenatal physical development, 1461
Psychotherapy: Children, 1541
Punishment, 1563
Reactive attachment disorder, 1600
Reflexes in newborns, 1610
Schizophrenia: High-risk children, 1675
Separation anxiety, 1747
Sibling relationships, 1785
Speech disorders, 1845
Stanford-Binet test, 1864
Stepfamilies, 1874
Stuttering, 1909
Violence by children and teenagers, 2024
Wechsler Intelligence Scale for Children-Third Edition (WISC-III), 2047

INTELLIGENCE
Aging: Cognitive changes, 81
Artificial intelligence, 184
Asperger syndrome, 191
Bilingualism and learning disabilities, 276

Binet, Alfred, 278
Cognitive Abilities Test (CogAT), 391
Creativity and intelligence, 514
Deductive thinking, 551
Eysenck, Hans, 743
Giftedness, 847
Hierarchy of needs, 913
Incompetency, 993
Inductive thinking, 1001
Intelligence, 1022
Intelligence quotient (IQ), 1027
Intelligence tests, 1028
Memory: Empirical studies, 1165
Mental retardation, 1200
Multiple intelligences, 1246
Pervasive developmental disorders, 1410
Profiling, 1474
Race and intelligence, 1578

INTELLIGENCE TESTING
Ability tests, 1
Bilingualism and learning disabilities, 276
Binet, Alfred, 278
Career and personnel testing, 339
Cognitive Abilities Test (CogAT), 391
College entrance examinations, 431
Confidentiality, 465
Deductive thinking, 551
Eysenck, Hans, 743
General Aptitude Test Battery (GATB), 834
Giftedness, 847
Inductive thinking, 1001
Intelligence, 1022
Intelligence quotient (IQ), 1027
Intelligence tests, 1028
Kuder Occupational Interest Survey (KOIS), 1074
Memory: Empirical studies, 1165
Peabody Individual Achievement Test (PIAT), 1373
Profiling, 1474
Race and intelligence, 1578
Stanford-Binet test, 1864

Strong Interest Inventory (SII), 1902

Testing: Historical perspectives, 1971

Wechsler Intelligence Scale for Children-Third Edition (WISC-III), 2047

INTERPERSONAL RELATIONS

Affiliation and friendship, 56

Affiliation motive, 61

Altruism, cooperation, and empathy, 109

Alzheimer's disease, 114

Attachment and bonding in infancy and childhood, 201

Attraction theories, 222

Battered woman syndrome, 243

Beck Depression Inventory (BDI), 247

Bronfenbrenner, Urie, 322

Coaching, 385

Cooperation, competition, and negotiation, 483

Crisis intervention, 520

Deception and lying, 545

Dementia, 559

Dialectical behavior therapy, 602

Disaster psychology, 604

Emotional expression, 677

Emotional intelligence, 681

Evolutionary psychology, 715

Family systems theory, 759

Forensic psychology, 787

Forgiveness, 795

Gender roles and gender role conflicts, 827

Gilligan, Carol, 851

Hierarchy of needs, 913

Horney, Karen, 934

Impulse control disorders, 984

Intervention, 1043

Intimacy, 1044

Jealousy, 1051

Lewin, Kurt, 1110

Love, 1131

Masters, William H., and Virginia E. Johnson, 1139

Media psychology, 1146

Multiple intelligences, 1246

Nonverbal communication, 1295

Oedipus complex, 1322

Parental alienation syndrome, 1349

Passive aggression, 1358

Penis envy, 1374

Power, 1448

Profiling, 1474

Satir, Virginia, 1666

Self-disclosure, 1708

Sibling relationships, 1785

Social perception, 1823

Social support and mental health, 1838

Stanford prison experiment, 1866

Stepfamilies, 1874

Sullivan, Harry Stack, 1925

Support groups, 1926

Transactional analysis, 2007

Violence by children and teenagers, 2024

Workforce reentry, 2076

Workplace issues and mental health, 2078

LANGUAGE

Aphasias, 171

Artificial intelligence, 184

Asperger syndrome, 191

Bilingualism, 273

Bilingualism and learning disabilities, 276

Brain damage, 306

Children's mental health, 371

Cross-cultural psychology, 523

Culture-bound syndromes, 532

Dyslexia, 636

Freudian psychology, 801

Hierarchy of needs, 913

Jungian psychology, 1055

Kohlberg, Lawrence, 1070

Language, 1077

Linguistics, 1111

Media psychology, 1146

Multicultural psychology, 1244

Multiple intelligences, 1246

Nervous system, 1277

Nonverbal communication, 1295

Pervasive developmental disorders, 1410

Psychobiology, 1495

Qualitative research, 1567

Speech disorders, 1845

Stuttering, 1909

Support groups, 1926

Tic disorders, 1992

Watson, John B., 2046

LEARNING

Ability tests, 1

Aging: Cognitive changes, 81

Artificial intelligence, 184

Asperger syndrome, 191

Beck, Aaron T., 246

Behavior therapy, 252

Behaviorism, 269

Bilingualism and learning disabilities, 276

Bobo doll experiment, 299

Brain structure, 312

Bruner, Jerome, 323

Children's mental health, 371

Cognitive ability: Gender differences, 392

Cognitive maps, 409

Conditioning, 455

Deductive thinking, 551

Defense reactions: Species-specific, 555

Dewey, John, 593

Ebbinghaus, Hermann, 645

Educational psychology, 649

Evolutionary psychology, 715

Games and mental health, 810

Habituation and sensitization, 881

Hull, Clark L., 937

Human resource training and development, 938

Imprinting, 980

Inductive thinking, 1001

Kinesthetic memory, 1064

Learned helplessness, 1097

Learning, 1100

Learning disorders, 1106

Lorenz, Konrad, 1130

Media psychology, 1146

Memory: Animal research, 1160

Memory: Physiology, 1169
Memory storage, 1180
Miller, Neal E., and John Dollard, 1210
Misbehavior, 1213
Motivation, 1234
Motivation: Intrinsic and extrinsic, 1238
Nervous system, 1277
Observational learning and modeling therapy, 1309
Organizational behavior and consulting, 1332
Pavlov, Ivan Petrovich, 1367
Pavlovian conditioning, 1368
Pervasive developmental disorders, 1410
Piaget, Jean, 1426
Psychobiology, 1495
Punishment, 1563
Race and intelligence, 1578
Reinforcement, 1613
Rule-governed behavior, 1650
Self-efficacy, 1712
Seligman, Martin E. P., 1730
Skinner, B. F., 1792
Social learning: Albert Bandura, 1815
Sports psychology, 1859
Stanford-Binet test, 1864
Stimulant medications, 1877
Support groups, 1926
Taste aversion, 1945
Teaching methods, 1949
Thorndike, Edward L., 1979
Tolman, Edward C., 1998
Virtual reality, 2030
Visual system, 2041
Watson, John B., 2046

MEMORY
Aging: Cognitive changes, 81
Alzheimer's disease, 114
Artificial intelligence, 184
Brain damage, 306
Children's mental health, 371
Cognitive maps, 409
Dementia, 559
Ebbinghaus, Hermann, 645
Elders' mental health, 669

Encoding, 687
Eye movement desensitization and reprocessing, 737
Eyewitness testimony, 739
Fetishes, 775
Forgetting and forgetfulness, 791
Freudian psychology, 801
Games and mental health, 810
Hierarchy of needs, 913
Imprinting, 980
Inductive thinking, 1001
Jungian psychology, 1055
Kinesthetic memory, 1064
Little Albert experiment, 1117
Long-term memory, 1126
Memory, 1155
Memory: Animal research, 1160
Memory: Empirical studies, 1165
Memory: Physiology, 1169
Memory: Sensory, 1174
Memory storage, 1180
Motivation, 1234
Multiple intelligences, 1246
Nervous system, 1277
Psychobiology, 1495
Reinforcement, 1613
Repressed memories, 1628
Self-efficacy, 1712
Short-term memory, 1779
Support groups, 1926
Virtual reality, 2030

MEN'S PSYCHOLOGY
Aggression, 74
Aggression: Reduction and control, 77
Anger, 142
Child abuse, 358
Cognitive ability: Gender differences, 392
Couples therapy, 508
Domestic violence, 614
Elder abuse, 666
Family life: Adult issues, 752
Father-child relationship, 762
Fetishes, 775
Gay, lesbian, bisexual, and transgender mental health, 813
Gender differences, 817

Gender identity disorder, 820
Gender identity formation, 824
Gender roles and gender role conflicts, 827
Genetics and mental health, 838
Hope and mental health, 926
Juvenile delinquency, 1059
Masculinity, 1137
Men's mental health, 1184
Mental health parity, 1189
Oedipus complex, 1322
Parenting styles, 1351
Psychosexual development, 1528
Quality of life, 1570
Rape and sexual assault, 1591
Road rage, 1643
Sadism and masochism, 1659
Separation and divorce: Adult issues, 1740
Sexism, 1753
Sexual harassment: Psychological causes and effects, 1767
Sibling relationships, 1785
Sports psychology, 1859
Transvestism, 2013
Violence and sexuality in the media, 2020
Violence by children and teenagers, 2024
Violence: Psychological causes and effects, 2027
Women's psychology: Carol Gilligan, 2059
Women's psychology: Karen Horney, 2064
Women's psychology: Sigmund Freud, 2067

METHODOLOGY
Albee, George W., 102
American Psychiatric Association, 120
American Psychological Association, 123
Animal experimentation, 145
Archival data, 180
Assessment, 195
Beck, Aaron T., 246
Behaviorism, 269
Case study methodologies, 351

Complex experimental designs, 442

Confidentiality, 465

Crisis intervention, 520

Data description, 535

Deductive thinking, 551

Developmental methodologies, 585

Developmental psychology, 589

Diagnosis, 594

Diagnostic and Statistical Manual of Mental Disorders (DSM), 599

Dialectical behavior therapy, 602

Experimental psychology, 725

Experimentation: Ethics and participant rights, 728

Experimentation: Independent, dependent, and control variables, 733

Eysenck, Hans, 743

Field experimentation, 777

Forensic psychology, 787

Freud, Anna, 799

Freudian psychology, 801

Grammar and speech, 856

Hall, G. Stanley, 885

Hypochondriasis, conversion, somatization, and somatoform pain, 960

Hypothesis development and testing, 966

Inductive thinking, 1001

International Classification of Diseases (ICD), 1037

Intervention, 1043

Jungian psychology, 1055

Kinsey, Alfred, 1067

Lewin, Kurt, 1110

Little Albert experiment, 1117

Milgram experiment, 1208

Myers-Briggs Type Indicator (MBTI), 1261

Observational methods, 1314

Philosophy and psychology, 1415

Placebo effect, 1433

Psychoanalysis, 1481

Psychology: Definition, 1500

Psychosurgery, 1537

Qualitative research, 1567

Quasi-experimental designs, 1572

Religiosity: Measurement, 1623

Research ethics, 1630

Rorschach, Hermann, 1646

Rorschach inkblots, 1647

Rosenhan experiment, 1649

Sampling, 1662

Satir, Virginia, 1666

Scientific methods, 1688

Self-help groups, 1719

Signal detection theory, 1789

Skinner box, 1793

Social networks, 1819

Stanford prison experiment, 1866

Statistical significance tests, 1870

Substance Abuse and Mental Health Services Administration (SAMHSA), 1914

Support groups, 1926

Survey research: Questionnaires and interviews, 1929

Systems theories, 1943

Teaching methods, 1949

Virtual reality, 2030

Watson, John B., 2046

Within-subject experimental designs, 2050

MOTIVATION

Achievement motivation, 21

Advertising, 52

Affiliation and friendship, 56

Affiliation motive, 61

Allport, Gordon, 107

Bandura, Albert, 242

Beck Depression Inventory (BDI), 247

Blau, Theodore H., 298

Collectivism, 427

Crowd behavior, 525

Denial, 563

Dix, Dorothea, 613

Drives, 628

Eating disorders, 640

Emotions, 683

Evolutionary psychology, 715

Eysenck, Hans, 743

Field theory: Kurt Lewin, 781

Forensic psychology, 787

Helping, 908

Homosexuality, 922

Horney, Karen, 934

Hull, Clark L., 937

Human resource training and development, 938

Hunger, 950

Hysteria, 970

Incentive motivation, 989

Industrial and organizational psychology, 1002

Instinct theory, 1018

Jealousy, 1051

Learning, 1100

Lorenz, Konrad, 1130

Love, 1131

Masters, William H., and Virginia E. Johnson, 1139

Motivation, 1234

Motivation: Intrinsic and extrinsic, 1238

Obesity, 1304

Optimal arousal theory, 1328

Organizational behavior and consulting, 1332

Parental alienation syndrome, 1349

Pervasive developmental disorders, 1410

Power, 1448

Profiling, 1474

Psychoanalysis, 1481

Punishment, 1563

Reinforcement, 1613

Religion and psychology, 1618

Religiosity: Measurement, 1623

Self-efficacy, 1712

Seligman, Martin E. P., 1730

Sex hormones and motivation, 1750

Sexual behavior patterns, 1757

Sports psychology, 1859

Substance use disorders, 1915

Support groups, 1926

Teaching methods, 1949

Thirst, 1977

Transtheoretical model, 2011

Women's psychology: Carol Gilligan, 2059

Work motivation, 2072

MULTICULTURAL PSYCHOLOGY

African Americans and mental health, 66
Asian Americans/Pacific Islanders and mental health, 188
Bilingualism and learning disabilities, 276
Biracial heritage and mental health, 288
Collectivism, 427
Cross-cultural psychology, 523
Culture and diagnosis, 531
Culture-bound syndromes, 532
Hate crimes: Psychological causes and effects, 890
Latinos and mental health, 1085
Multicultural psychology, 1244
Native Americans/Alaskan Natives and mental health, 1271
Terrorism: Psychological causes and effects, 1968

NERVOUS SYSTEM

Artificial intelligence, 184
Beck, Aaron T., 246
Behaviorism, 269
Brain damage, 306
Brain structure, 312
Caffeine and mental health, 331
Circadian rhythms, 376
Computer and Internet use and mental health, 446
Computer models of cognition, 448
Defense reactions: Species-specific, 555
Drug therapies, 631
Endorphins, 695
Inhibitory and excitatory impulses, 1007
Kinesthetic memory, 1064
Memory: Animal research, 1160
Memory: Physiology, 1169
Mood stabilizer medications, 1225
Neurons, 1280
Neurotransmitters, 1291

Nicotine dependence, 1293
Pain, 1335
Pain management, 1338
Panic attacks, 1343
Parkinson's disease, 1355
Pattern vision, 1364
Psychopharmacology, 1523
Reflexes, 1606
Reticular formation, 1634
Sexual behavior patterns, 1757
Split-brain studies, 1854
Stimulant medications, 1877
Substance use disorders, 1915
Synaptic transmission, 1933
Tic disorders, 1992
Tourette's syndrome, 2003

ORGANIZATIONS AND PUBLICATIONS

American Psychiatric Association, 120
American Psychological Association, 123
Diagnostic and Statistical Manual of Mental Disorders (DSM), 599
Health insurance, 892
Health maintenance organizations, 894
International Classification of Diseases (ICD), 1037
Mental health parity, 1189
National Institute of Mental Health (NIMH), 1270
Organizational behavior and consulting, 1332
Substance Abuse and Mental Health Services Administration (SAMHSA), 1914

ORIGIN AND DEFINITION OF PSYCHOLOGY

American Psychiatric Association, 120
American Psychological Association, 123
Behaviorism, 269
Cognitive psychology, 414
Constructivist psychology, 477
Developmental psychology, 589

Ecological psychology, 646
Ethology, 711
Evolutionary psychology, 715
Forensic psychology, 787
Humanistic psychology, 942
Maslow, Abraham, 1138
Mental illness: Historical concepts, 1194
Multicultural psychology, 1244
National Institute of Mental Health (NIMH), 1270
Neuropsychology, 1284
Philosophy and psychology, 1415
Positive psychology, 1438
Psychoanalytic psychology, 1487
Psychology: Definition, 1500
Psychology: Fields of specialization, 1504
Psychology: History, 1509
Qualitative research, 1567
Structuralism and functionalism, 1904

PEOPLE

Adler, Alfred, 29
Albee, George W., 102
Allport, Gordon, 107
Bandura, Albert, 242
Beck, Aaron T., 246
Binet, Alfred, 278
Blau, Theodore H., 298
Breuer, Josef, 318
Bronfenbrenner, Urie, 322
Bruner, Jerome, 323
Cannon, Walter Bradford, 338
Dewey, John, 593
Dix, Dorothea, 613
Ebbinghaus, Hermann, 645
Ellis, Albert, 676
Erikson, Erik H., 710
Eysenck, Hans, 743
Freud, Anna, 799
Freud, Sigmund, 800
Fromm, Erich, 806
Gesell, Arnold, 842
Gilligan, Carol, 851
Hall, G. Stanley, 885
Horney, Karen, 934
Hull, Clark L., 937
James, William, 1050

Jung, Carl, 1054
Kelly, George A., 1063
Kinsey, Alfred, 1067
Kohlberg, Lawrence, 1070
Kraepelin, Emil, 1071
Kübler-Ross, Elizabeth, 1072
Lacan, Jacques, 1076
Lewin, Kurt, 1110
Lorenz, Konrad, 1130
Maslow, Abraham, 1138
Masters, William H., and Virginia
   E. Johnson, 1139
May, Rollo, 1141
Miller, Neal E., and John Dollard,
   1210
Mischel, Walter, 1218
Murray, Henry A., 1256
Pavlov, Ivan Petrovich, 1367
Piaget, Jean, 1426
Pinel, Philippe, 1428
Rogers, Carl R., 1645
Rorschach, Hermann, 1646
Satir, Virginia, 1666
Seligman, Martin E. P., 1730
Selye, Hans, 1731
Skinner, B. F., 1792
Sullivan, Harry Stack, 1925
Thorndike, Edward L., 1979
Tolman, Edward C., 1998
Watson, John B., 2046
Yalom, Irving, 2084
Zimbardo, Philip G., 2086

PERSONALITY
Achievement motivation, 21
Addictive personality and
   behaviors, 25
Adler, Alfred, 29
Aggression, 74
Allport, Gordon, 107
Analytic psychology: Jacques
   Lacan, 130
Analytical psychology: Carl Jung,
   134
Anger, 142
Antipsychotic medications, 160
Antisocial personality disorder,
   161
Archetypes and the collective
   unconscious, 176

Avoidant personality disorder,
   239
Beck, Aaron T., 246
Behavioral assessment, 257
Birth order and personality, 295
Bobo doll experiment, 299
Borderline personality disorder,
   304
Brain damage, 306
Breuer, Josef, 318
Career and personnel testing,
   339
Clinical interviewing, testing, and
   observation, 381
Codependency, 388
Cognitive social learning: Walter
   Mischel, 420
Comorbidity, 439
Constructivist psychology, 477
Denial, 563
Ego defense mechanisms, 652
Ego psychology: Erik H. Erikson,
   658
Ego, superego, and id, 664
Emotional intelligence, 681
Erikson, Erik H., 710
Existential psychology, 721
Eysenck, Hans, 743
Fear, 766
Field theory: Kurt Lewin, 781
Forensic psychology, 787
Forgiveness, 795
Freud, Sigmund, 800
Fromm, Erich, 806
Gender identity disorder, 820
Helping, 908
Hierarchy of needs, 913
Histrionic personality disorder,
   916
Horney, Karen, 934
Humanistic trait models: Gordon
   Allport, 946
Hysteria, 970
Individual psychology: Alfred
   Adler, 996
Interest inventories, 1033
Introverts and extroverts, 1047
Jung, Carl, 1054
Kelly, George A., 1063
Kleptomania, 1069

Kraepelin, Emil, 1071
Lacan, Jacques, 1076
Media psychology, 1146
Miller, Neal E., and John Dollard,
   1210
Mischel, Walter, 1218
Motivation, 1234
Multiple intelligences, 1246
Multiple personality, 1250
Murray, Henry A., 1256
Myers-Briggs Type Indicator
   (MBTI), 1261
Narcissistic personality disorder,
   1264
Observational learning and
   modeling therapy, 1309
Oedipus complex, 1322
Organizational behavior and
   consulting, 1332
Parental alienation syndrome,
   1349
Passive aggression, 1358
Penis envy, 1374
Personal constructs: George A.
   Kelly, 1382
Personality disorders, 1385
Personality interviewing
   strategies, 1391
Personality: Psychophysiological
   measures, 1394
Personality rating scales, 1399
Personality theory, 1402
Personology: Henry A. Murray,
   1406
Power, 1448
Profiling, 1474
Projection, 1477
Psychoanalysis, 1481
Psychoanalytic psychology and
   personality: Sigmund Freud,
   1491
Psychopathology, 1517
Psychosexual development, 1528
Radical behaviorism: B. F.
   Skinner, 1587
Road rage, 1643
Rorschach, Hermann, 1646
Rorschach inkblots, 1647
S-R theory: Neal E. Miller and
   John Dollard, 1655

Seasonal affective disorder, 1694
Self, 1699
Self-actualization, 1704
Self-efficacy, 1712
Seligman, Martin E. P., 1730
Shyness, 1783
Social learning: Albert Bandura, 1815
Social psychological models: Erich Fromm, 1827
Social psychological models: Karen Horney, 1831
Sociopaths, 1842
Sports psychology, 1859
Stanford prison experiment, 1866
Sullivan, Harry Stack, 1925
Support groups, 1926
Violence by children and teenagers, 2024
Women's psychology: Carol Gilligan, 2059
Women's psychology: Karen Horney, 2064
Women's psychology: Sigmund Freud, 2067
Zimbardo, Philip G., 2086

PERSONALITY ASSESSMENT
Allport, Gordon, 107
Behavioral assessment, 257
Bobo doll experiment, 299
Borderline personality disorder, 304
California Psychological Inventory (CPI), 333
Career and personnel testing, 339
Clinical interviewing, testing, and observation, 381
Confidentiality, 465
Emotional intelligence, 681
Eysenck, Hans, 743
Forensic psychology, 787
Freudian psychology, 801
Inductive thinking, 1001
Interest inventories, 1033
Jung, Carl, 1054
Maslow, Abraham, 1138

Minnesota Multiphasic Personality Inventory (MMPI), 1211
Mischel, Walter, 1218
Myers-Briggs Type Indicator (MBTI), 1261
Personality disorders, 1385
Personality interviewing strategies, 1391
Personality: Psychophysiological measures, 1394
Personality rating scales, 1399
Personality theory, 1402
Profiling, 1474
Rorschach, Hermann, 1646
Rorschach inkblots, 1647
Sociopaths, 1842
State-Trait Anxiety Inventory (STAI), 1869
Thematic Apperception Test (TAT), 1975
Zimbardo, Philip G., 2086

PERSONALITY DISORDERS
Addictive personality and behaviors, 25
Aggression, 74
Antipsychotic medications, 160
Antisocial personality disorder, 161
Avoidant personality disorder, 239
Beck, Aaron T., 246
Borderline personality disorder, 304
Brain damage, 306
Breuer, Josef, 318
Codependency, 388
Comorbidity, 439
Deception and lying, 545
Dialectical behavior therapy, 602
Dissociative disorders, 609
Drug therapies, 631
Ego defense mechanisms, 652
Fetishes, 775
Gambling, 808
Gender identity disorder, 820
Histrionic personality disorder, 916
Horney, Karen, 934

Hysteria, 970
Kleptomania, 1069
Kraepelin, Emil, 1071
Narcissistic personality disorder, 1264
Oedipus complex, 1322
Parental alienation syndrome, 1349
Passive aggression, 1358
Penis envy, 1374
Personality disorders, 1385
Personality interviewing strategies, 1391
Personality: Psychophysiological measures, 1394
Personality rating scales, 1399
Personality theory, 1402
Psychopathology, 1517
Psychopharmacology, 1523
Rorschach, Hermann, 1646
Schizoid personality disorder, 1667
Schizotypal personality disorder, 1685
Seasonal affective disorder, 1694
Sociopaths, 1842
Support groups, 1926
Tic disorders, 1992
Violence by children and teenagers, 2024
Zimbardo, Philip G., 2086

PREJUDICE AND DISCRIMINATION
African Americans and mental health, 66
Ageism, 69
Allport, Gordon, 107
Artificial intelligence, 184
Asian Americans/Pacific Islanders and mental health, 188
Assisted living, 198
Bilingualism and learning disabilities, 276
Biracial heritage and mental health, 288
Bullying, 324
Cognitive ability: Gender differences, 392

Cooperative learning, 487
Coping: Chronic illness, 490
Coping: Social support, 495
Coping: Strategies, 500
Cross-cultural psychology, 523
Culture-bound syndromes, 532
Disaster psychology, 604
Dix, Dorothea, 613
Gay, lesbian, bisexual, and transgender mental health, 813
Gender differences, 817
Gender roles and gender role conflicts, 827
Hate crimes: Psychological causes and effects, 890
Health insurance, 892
Homelessness: Psychological causes and effects, 918
Horney, Karen, 934
Impulse control disorders, 984
Internet psychology, 1039
Latinos and mental health, 1085
Law and psychology, 1088
Learned helplessness, 1097
Learning, 1100
Media psychology, 1146
Multicultural psychology, 1244
Native Americans/Alaskan Natives and mental health, 1271
Parental alienation syndrome, 1349
Piaget, Jean, 1426
Prejudice, 1452
Prejudice reduction, 1457
Problem-solving stages, 1467
Problem-solving strategies, 1470
Racism, 1583
Rosenhan experiment, 1649
Sexism, 1753
Sexual harassment: Psychological causes and effects, 1767
Social identity theory, 1810
Stanford prison experiment, 1866
Support groups, 1926
Teenagers' mental health, 1959
Terrorism: Psychological causes and effects, 1968

Tic disorders, 1992
Transvestism, 2013
Virtual reality, 2030
Workplace issues and mental health, 2078

PROSOCIAL BEHAVIOR

Altruism, cooperation, and empathy, 109
Antisocial personality disorder, 161
Behavior therapy, 252
Bystander intervention, 326
Crisis intervention, 520
Ecological psychology, 646
Evolutionary psychology, 715
Family systems theory, 759
Helping, 908
Kohlberg, Lawrence, 1070
Maslow, Abraham, 1138
Meditation and relaxation, 1152
Observational learning and modeling therapy, 1309
Positive psychology, 1438
Social networks, 1819
Spirituality and mental health, 1852
Support groups, 1926
Workplace issues and mental health, 2078

PSYCHOBIOLOGY

Adrenal gland, 49
Aggression, 74
Aging: Theories, 91
Anger, 142
Birth: Effects on physical development, 290
Brain damage, 306
Brain structure, 312
Cannon, Walter Bradford, 338
Circadian rhythms, 376
Drug therapies, 631
Emotions, 683
Endocrine system, 690
Endorphins, 695
Environmental factors and mental health, 699
Environmental toxicology and mental health, 707

Evolutionary psychology, 715
Fight-or-flight response, 784
Gay, lesbian, bisexual, and transgender mental health, 813
Gonads, 852
Hormones and behavior, 928
Imprinting, 980
Inhibitory and excitatory impulses, 1007
Learning, 1100
Lorenz, Konrad, 1130
Memory: Animal research, 1160
Memory: Physiology, 1169
Nervous system, 1277
Neurons, 1280
Pain, 1335
Pain management, 1338
Pavlov, Ivan Petrovich, 1367
Physical development: Environment versus genetics, 1423
Pituitary gland, 1429
Prenatal physical development, 1461
Psychobiology, 1495
Psychopharmacology, 1523
Psychosurgery, 1537
Race and intelligence, 1578
Reflexes, 1606
Reticular formation, 1634
Sex hormones and motivation, 1750
Sexual behavior patterns, 1757
Split-brain studies, 1854
Stimulant medications, 1877
Substance use disorders, 1915
Synaptic transmission, 1933
Synesthesia, 1936
Thirst, 1977
Thyroid gland, 1988

PSYCHODYNAMIC AND NEOANALYTIC MODELS

Analytic psychology: Jacques Lacan, 130
Analytical psychology: Carl Jung, 134
Analytical psychotherapy, 138
Anxiety disorders, 166

Breuer, Josef, 318
Brief therapy, 320
Denial, 563
Ego defense mechanisms, 652
Ego, superego, and id, 664
Fear, 766
Feminist psychotherapy, 772
Freud, Sigmund, 800
Fromm, Erich, 806
Genetics and mental health, 838
Individual psychology: Alfred
    Adler, 996
Mental health practitioners, 1190
Music, dance, and theater
    therapy, 1257
Penis envy, 1374
Play therapy, 1434
Psychoanalysis, 1481
Psychoanalytic psychology, 1487
Psychoanalytic psychology and
    personality: Sigmund Freud,
    1491
Psychotherapy: Children, 1541
Psychotherapy: Historical
    approaches, 1554
Repressed memories, 1628
Social psychological models:
    Erich Fromm, 1827
Social psychological models:
    Karen Horney, 1831
Spirituality and mental health,
    1852
Sports psychology, 1859
Sullivan, Harry Stack, 1925

PSYCHOPATHOLOGY
Abnormality: Biomedical models,
    6
Abnormality: Legal models, 11
Abnormality: Psychological
    models, 15
Addictive personality and
    behaviors, 25
Aggression, 74
Aging: Cognitive changes, 81
Agoraphobia and panic
    disorders, 96
Albee, George W., 102
Alcohol dependence and abuse,
    103

Alzheimer's disease, 114
Amnesia and fugue, 126
Anorexia nervosa and bulimia
    nervosa, 150
Antianxiety medications, 156
Antidepressant medications, 158
Antisocial personality disorder,
    161
Anxiety disorders, 166
Attention-deficit hyperactivity
    disorder (ADHD), 209
Autism, 230
Avoidant personality disorder,
    239
Battered woman syndrome, 243
Beck, Aaron T., 246
Beck Depression Inventory
    (BDI), 247
Bed-wetting, 248
Bipolar disorder, 283
Body dysmorphic disorder, 301
Borderline personality disorder,
    304
Brain damage, 306
Breuer, Josef, 318
Childhood disorders, 363
Children's Depression Inventory
    (CDI), 369
Codependency, 388
Comorbidity, 439
Conduct disorder, 461
Deception and lying, 545
Dementia, 559
Denial, 563
Depression, 566
*Diagnostic and Statistical Manual of
    Mental Disorders* (DSM), 599
Dialectical behavior therapy,
    602
Dissociative disorders, 609
Domestic violence, 614
Down syndrome, 619
Drug therapies, 631
Eating disorders, 640
Ego defense mechanisms, 652
Elder abuse, 666
Factitious disorders, 749
Fetishes, 775
Grieving, 861
Hallucinations, 886

Histrionic personality disorder,
    916
Homelessness: Psychological
    causes and effects, 918
Hypochondriasis, conversion,
    somatization, and somatoform
    pain, 960
Hysteria, 970
Impulse control disorders, 984
Incompetency, 993
Insanity defense, 1011
*International Classification of
    Diseases* (ICD), 1037
Jung, Carl, 1054
Kleptomania, 1069
Kraepelin, Emil, 1071
Lobotomy, 1119
May, Rollo, 1141
Mental illness: Historical
    concepts, 1194
Minnesota Multiphasic
    Personality Inventory (MMPI),
    1211
Mood disorders, 1219
Mood stabilizer medications,
    1225
Multiple personality, 1250
Munchausen syndrome and
    Munchausen syndrome by
    proxy, 1253
Narcissistic personality disorder,
    1264
Neurotic disorders, 1287
Obsessive-compulsive disorder,
    1317
Oedipus complex, 1322
Panic attacks, 1343
Paranoia, 1346
Parental alienation syndrome,
    1349
Parkinson's disease, 1355
Passive aggression, 1358
Penis envy, 1374
Personality disorders, 1385
Phobias, 1418
Postpartum depression, 1441
Post-traumatic stress disorder,
    1443
Psychopathology, 1517
Psychopharmacology, 1523

Psychosomatic disorders, 1532
Psychotic disorders, 1559
Rape and sexual assault, 1591
Reactive attachment disorder, 1600
Risk assessment, 1641
Rorschach, Hermann, 1646
Schizophrenia: Background, types, and symptoms, 1670
Schizophrenia: High-risk children, 1675
Schizophrenia: Theoretical explanations, 1680
Seasonal affective disorder, 1694
Seligman, Martin E. P., 1730
Separation anxiety, 1747
Sexual dysfunction, 1761
Sexual variants and paraphilias, 1770
Shyness, 1783
Sociopaths, 1842
State-Trait Anxiety Inventory (STAI), 1869
Substance Abuse and Mental Health Services Administration (SAMHSA), 1914
Substance use disorders, 1915
Suicide, 1920
Support groups, 1926
Teenage suicide, 1954
Tourette's syndrome, 2003
Transtheoretical model, 2011
Violence by children and teenagers, 2024

PSYCHOTHERAPY

Abnormality: Psychological models, 15
American Psychiatric Association, 120
Analytical psychotherapy, 138
Anger, 142
Archetypes and the collective unconscious, 176
Aversion therapy, 238
Avoidant personality disorder, 239
Battered woman syndrome, 243

Beck Depression Inventory (BDI), 247
Behavior therapy, 252
Behavioral family therapy, 265
Bipolar disorder, 283
Breuer, Josef, 318
Brief therapy, 320
Cancer and mental health, 335
Cognitive behavior therapy, 396
Confidentiality, 465
Constructivist psychology, 477
Dialectical behavior therapy, 602
Drug therapies, 631
Ecological psychology, 646
Ego defense mechanisms, 652
Ellis, Albert, 676
Eye movement desensitization and reprocessing, 737
Feminist psychotherapy, 772
Forgiveness, 795
Freud, Sigmund, 800
Freudian psychology, 801
Fromm, Erich, 806
Gestalt therapy, 843
Group therapy, 868
Horney, Karen, 934
Hysteria, 970
Implosion, 978
Insanity defense, 1011
Jung, Carl, 1054
Jungian psychology, 1055
Kelly, George A., 1063
Kübler-Ross, Elizabeth, 1072
Lacan, Jacques, 1076
May, Rollo, 1141
Mental health practitioners, 1190
Miller, Neal E., and John Dollard, 1210
Music, dance, and theater therapy, 1257
Observational learning and modeling therapy, 1309
Oedipus complex, 1322
Operant conditioning therapies, 1324
Parental alienation syndrome, 1349
Penis envy, 1374
Person-centered therapy, 1377
Play therapy, 1434

Psychoanalysis, 1481
Psychopharmacology, 1523
Psychotherapy: Children, 1541
Psychotherapy: Effectiveness, 1546
Psychotherapy: Goals and techniques, 1551
Psychotherapy: Historical approaches, 1554
Rational emotive therapy, 1595
Reality therapy, 1603
Repressed memories, 1628
Satir, Virginia, 1666
Shock therapy, 1775
Sociopaths, 1842
Strategic family therapy, 1880
Sullivan, Harry Stack, 1925
Support groups, 1926
Systematic desensitization, 1939
Transactional analysis, 2007
Virtual reality, 2030
Yalom, Irving, 2084

SCHIZOPHRENIAS

Antipsychotic medications, 160
Comorbidity, 439
Coping: Chronic illness, 490
Dissociative disorders, 609
Drug therapies, 631
Genetics and mental health, 838
Homelessness: Psychological causes and effects, 918
Kraepelin, Emil, 1071
Lobotomy, 1119
Nervous system, 1277
Psychopharmacology, 1523
Psychosurgery, 1537
Psychotic disorders, 1559
Schizoid personality disorder, 1667
Schizophrenia: Background, types, and symptoms, 1670
Schizophrenia: High-risk children, 1675
Schizophrenia: Theoretical explanations, 1680
Schizotypal personality disorder, 1685
Sullivan, Harry Stack, 1925
Support groups, 1926

SENSATION AND PERCEPTION

Aging: Cognitive changes, 81
Air rage, 100
Albee, George W., 102
Artificial intelligence, 184
Body dysmorphic disorder, 301
Brain damage, 306
Computer and Internet use and mental health, 446
Defense mechanisms, 552
Depth and motion perception, 572
Dewey, John, 593
Disaster psychology, 604
Emotional intelligence, 681
Eye movement desensitization and reprocessing, 737
Freudian psychology, 801
Hearing, 901
Hormones and behavior, 928
Impulse control disorders, 984
James, William, 1050
Kinesthetic memory, 1064
Little Albert experiment, 1117
Masters, William H., and Virginia E. Johnson, 1139
Media exposure and mental health, 1142
Media psychology, 1146
Nearsightedness and farsightedness, 1273
Nervous system, 1277
Pain, 1335
Pain management, 1338
Pattern recognition, 1360
Pattern vision, 1364
Psychobiology, 1495
Reticular formation, 1634
Road rage, 1643
Sensation and perception, 1732
Senses, 1736
Signal detection theory, 1789
Smell and taste, 1805
Speech perception, 1848
Synesthesia, 1936
Temperature, 1963
Touch and pressure, 1999
Virtual reality, 2030
Vision: Brightness and contrast, 2034
Vision: Color, 2038
Visual system, 2041

SEXUALITY

Adolescence: Sexuality, 44
Breuer, Josef, 318
Coping: Chronic illness, 490
Drug therapies, 631
Femininity, 770
Fetishes, 775
Freud, Sigmund, 800
Freudian psychology, 801
Gay, lesbian, bisexual, and transgender mental health, 813
Gender differences, 817
Gender identity disorder, 820
Gender roles and gender role conflicts, 827
Gonads, 852
Homosexuality, 922
Kinsey, Alfred, 1067
Kohlberg, Lawrence, 1070
Masculinity, 1137
Maslow, Abraham, 1138
Masters, William H., and Virginia E. Johnson, 1139
Men's mental health, 1184
Oedipus complex, 1322
Penis envy, 1374
Psychoanalytic psychology and personality: Sigmund Freud, 1491
Psychosexual development, 1528
Rape and sexual assault, 1591
Repressed memories, 1628
Sadism and masochism, 1659
Sex hormones and motivation, 1750
Sexism, 1753
Sexual behavior patterns, 1757
Sexual dysfunction, 1761
Sexual harassment: Psychological causes and effects, 1767
Sexual variants and paraphilias, 1770
Support groups, 1926
Transvestism, 2013
Violence and sexuality in the media, 2020
Women's mental health, 2054

SLEEP

Caffeine and mental health, 331
Circadian rhythms, 376
Computer and Internet use and mental health, 446
Consciousness, 467
Dreams, 623
Insomnia, 1013
Narcolepsy, 1266
Reticular formation, 1634
Sleep, 1796
Sleep apnea, 1803
Teenagers' mental health, 1959

SOCIAL PSYCHOLOGY

Achievement motivation, 21
Advertising, 52
Affiliation and friendship, 56
Affiliation motive, 61
African Americans and mental health, 66
Ageism, 69
Aggression, 74
Aggression: Reduction and control, 77
Aging: Cognitive changes, 81
Air rage, 100
Albee, George W., 102
Allport, Gordon, 107
Altruism, cooperation, and empathy, 109
Alzheimer's disease, 114
Antisocial personality disorder, 161
Asian Americans/Pacific Islanders and mental health, 188
Asperger syndrome, 191
Attitude-behavior consistency, 214
Attitude formation and change, 218
Attraction theories, 222
Attributional biases, 227
Bandura, Albert, 242

Battered woman syndrome, 243

Beck Depression Inventory (BDI), 247

Behavioral assessment, 257

Biracial heritage and mental health, 288

Blau, Theodore H., 298

Bobo doll experiment, 299

Bronfenbrenner, Urie, 322

Bullying, 324

Bystander intervention, 326

Causal attribution, 354

Child abuse, 358

Coaching, 385

Cognitive dissonance, 405

Cognitive maps, 409

Collectivism, 427

Community psychology, 434

Cooperation, competition, and negotiation, 483

Cooperative learning, 487

Coping: Social support, 495

Coping: Terminal illness, 504

Crisis intervention, 520

Cross-cultural psychology, 523

Crowd behavior, 525

Cultural competence, 529

Culture-bound syndromes, 532

Deception and lying, 545

Dementia, 559

Denial, 563

Dewey, John, 593

Disaster psychology, 604

Domestic violence, 614

Elder abuse, 666

Emotional intelligence, 681

Erikson, Erik H., 710

Evolutionary psychology, 715

Eyewitness testimony, 739

Eysenck, Hans, 743

Facial feedback, 745

Field theory: Kurt Lewin, 781

Forgiveness, 795

Gay, lesbian, bisexual, and transgender mental health, 813

General Aptitude Test Battery (GATB), 834

Group decision making, 864

Groups, 872

Hate crimes: Psychological causes and effects, 890

Help-seeking, 905

Helping, 908

Hierarchy of needs, 913

Horney, Karen, 934

Human resource training and development, 938

Hysteria, 970

Impulse control disorders, 984

Industrial and organizational psychology, 1002

Insanity defense, 1011

Intimacy, 1044

Jealousy, 1051

Kinesthetic memory, 1064

Kraepelin, Emil, 1071

Latinos and mental health, 1085

Law and psychology, 1088

Leadership, 1092

Lewin, Kurt, 1110

Love, 1131

Maslow, Abraham, 1138

Masters, William H., and Virginia E. Johnson, 1139

Media exposure and mental health, 1142

Media psychology, 1146

Milgram experiment, 1208

Moral development, 1227

Motivation, 1234

Motivation: Intrinsic and extrinsic, 1238

Multicultural psychology, 1244

Native Americans/Alaskan Natives and mental health, 1271

Nonverbal communication, 1295

Oedipus complex, 1322

Organizational behavior and consulting, 1332

Parental alienation syndrome, 1349

Penis envy, 1374

Pervasive developmental disorders, 1410

Positive psychology, 1438

Prejudice, 1452

Prejudice reduction, 1457

Profiling, 1474

Punishment, 1563

Quality of life, 1570

Racism, 1583

Rape and sexual assault, 1591

Religion and psychology, 1618

Religiosity: Measurement, 1623

Road rage, 1643

Rosenhan experiment, 1649

Self, 1699

Self-disclosure, 1708

Self-esteem, 1715

Self-perception theory, 1721

Self-presentation, 1725

Sexism, 1753

Sexual harassment: Psychological causes and effects, 1767

Shyness, 1783

Social identity theory, 1810

Social networks, 1819

Social perception, 1823

Social schemata, 1834

Social support and mental health, 1838

Sociopaths, 1842

Spirituality and mental health, 1852

Sports psychology, 1859

Stanford prison experiment, 1866

Stepfamilies, 1874

Support groups, 1926

Terrorism: Psychological causes and effects, 1968

Violence and sexuality in the media, 2020

Violence by children and teenagers, 2024

Violence: Psychological causes and effects, 2027

Virtual reality, 2030

Women's psychology: Carol Gilligan, 2059

Work motivation, 2072

Workforce reentry, 2076

Zimbardo, Philip G., 2086

STRESS

Addictive personality and behaviors, 25

Aggression, 74

Aging: Physical changes, 87
Aging: Theories, 91
Agoraphobia and panic disorders, 96
Air rage, 100
Anger, 142
Behavior therapy, 252
Biofeedback and relaxation, 279
Breuer, Josef, 318
Bullying, 324
Caffeine and mental health, 331
Circadian rhythms, 376
Computer and Internet use and mental health, 446
Coping: Chronic illness, 490
Coping: Social support, 495
Coping: Strategies, 500
Coping: Terminal illness, 504
Death and dying, 541
Denial, 563
Disaster psychology, 604
Drug therapies, 631
Elimination disorders, 674
Environmental factors and mental health, 699
Environmental psychology, 702
Exercise and mental health, 719
Fight-or-flight response, 784
Gay, lesbian, bisexual, and transgender mental health, 813
General adaptation syndrome, 830
Generalized anxiety disorder, 835
Grieving, 861
Health psychology, 895
Impulse control disorders, 984
Kübler-Ross, Elizabeth, 1072
Learned helplessness, 1097
Media psychology, 1146
Meditation and relaxation, 1152
Men's mental health, 1184
Nicotine dependence, 1293
Organizational behavior and consulting, 1332
Pain management, 1338
Panic attacks, 1343
Parental alienation syndrome, 1349
Psychosomatic disorders, 1532

Reactive attachment disorder, 1600
Religion and psychology, 1618
Religiosity: Measurement, 1623
Road rage, 1643
Self-help groups, 1719
Selye, Hans, 1731
Sexual harassment: Psychological causes and effects, 1767
Social networks, 1819
Sports psychology, 1859
Stepfamilies, 1874
Stress: Behavioral and psychological responses, 1884
Stress: Physiological responses, 1890
Stress-related diseases, 1894
Stress: Theories, 1898
Substance use disorders, 1915
Support groups, 1926
Teenagers' mental health, 1959
Tic disorders, 1992
Type A behavior pattern, 2015
Virtual reality, 2030
Workforce reentry, 2076
Workplace issues and mental health, 2078

TESTING
Ability tests, 1
Beck Depression Inventory (BDI), 247
Bilingualism and learning disabilities, 276
Binet, Alfred, 278
California Psychological Inventory (CPI), 333
Career and personnel testing, 339
Career Occupational Preference System (COPS), 344
Children's Depression Inventory (CDI), 369
Clinical interviewing, testing, and observation, 381
Cognitive Abilities Test (CogAT), 391
College entrance examinations, 431
Confidentiality, 465

Creativity: Assessment, 517
General Aptitude Test Battery (GATB), 834
Giftedness, 847
Hull, Clark L., 937
Intelligence tests, 1028
Kuder Occupational Interest Survey (KOIS), 1074
Little Albert experiment, 1117
Milgram experiment, 1208
Minnesota Multiphasic Personality Inventory (MMPI), 1211
Myers-Briggs Type Indicator (MBTI), 1261
Peabody Individual Achievement Test (PIAT), 1373
Placebo effect, 1433
Risk assessment, 1641
Skinner box, 1793
Stanford-Binet test, 1864
Stanford prison experiment, 1866
State-Trait Anxiety Inventory (STAI), 1869
Strong Interest Inventory (SII), 1902
Testing: Historical perspectives, 1971
Thematic Apperception Test (TAT), 1975
Wechsler Intelligence Scale for Children-Third Edition (WISC-III), 2047
Zimbardo, Philip G., 2086

THOUGHT
Aging: Cognitive changes, 81
Alzheimer's disease, 114
Analytic psychology: Jacques Lacan, 130
Bandura, Albert, 242
Beck Depression Inventory (BDI), 247
Behavioral economics, 261
Behaviorism, 269
Brain damage, 306
Brain structure, 312
Cognitive ability: Gender differences, 392

Cognitive psychology, 414
Concept formation, 451
Consciousness, 467
Consumer psychology, 479
Deductive thinking, 551
Dementia, 559
Dreams, 623
Freudian psychology, 801
Inductive thinking, 1001
Jungian psychology, 1055
Lacan, Jacques, 1076
Language, 1077
Linguistics, 1111
Logic and reasoning, 1121
Media psychology, 1146
Nervous system, 1277
Neurotransmitters, 1291
Philosophy and psychology, 1415
Piaget, Jean, 1426
Psychoanalysis, 1481
Psychobiology, 1495
Structuralism and functionalism, 1904
Systems theories, 1943
Thought: Inferential, 1980
Thought: Study and measurement, 1984

TREATMENTS
Adlerian psychotherapy, 30
American Psychiatric Association, 120
Analytical psychotherapy, 138
Antianxiety medications, 156
Antidepressant medications, 158
Antipsychotic medications, 160
Aversion therapy, 238
Behavior therapy, 252
Behavioral family therapy, 265
Biofeedback and relaxation, 279
Bipolar disorder, 283
Brief therapy, 320
Cognitive behavior therapy, 396
Cognitive therapy, 423
Coping: Chronic illness, 490
Coping: Strategies, 500
Couples therapy, 508
Disaster psychology, 604
Drug therapies, 631

Eye movement desensitization and reprocessing, 737
Eysenck, Hans, 743
Feminist psychotherapy, 772
Gestalt therapy, 843
Group therapy, 868
Health insurance, 892
Health maintenance organizations, 894
Hysteria, 970
Implosion, 978
Internet psychology, 1039
Intervention, 1043
Kraepelin, Emil, 1071
Mental health parity, 1189
Mental health practitioners, 1190
Mood stabilizer medications, 1225
Music, dance, and theater therapy, 1257
Nervous system, 1277
Observational learning and modeling therapy, 1309
Operant conditioning therapies, 1324
Pain management, 1338
Parental alienation syndrome, 1349
Person-centered therapy, 1377
Play therapy, 1434
Psychoanalysis, 1481
Psychopathology, 1517
Psychopharmacology, 1523
Psychosurgery, 1537
Psychotherapy: Children, 1541
Psychotherapy: Effectiveness, 1546
Psychotherapy: Goals and techniques, 1551
Psychotherapy: Historical approaches, 1554
Psychotic disorders, 1559
Rational emotive therapy, 1595
Reality therapy, 1603
Reinforcement, 1613
Shock therapy, 1775
Social support and mental health, 1838
Speech disorders, 1845
Sports psychology, 1859

Strategic family therapy, 1880
Substance use disorders, 1915
Support groups, 1926
Systematic desensitization, 1939
Transactional analysis, 2007
Virtual reality, 2030

VISION
Artificial intelligence, 184
Brain damage, 306
Computer and Internet use and mental health, 446
Depth and motion perception, 572
Dewey, John, 593
Eye movement desensitization and reprocessing, 737
Media exposure and mental health, 1142
Nearsightedness and farsightedness, 1273
Nervous system, 1277
Pattern recognition, 1360
Pattern vision, 1364
Psychobiology, 1495
Sensation and perception, 1732
Senses, 1736
Synesthesia, 1936
Vision: Brightness and contrast, 2034
Vision: Color, 2038
Visual system, 2041

WOMEN'S PSYCHOLOGY
Anorexia nervosa and bulimia nervosa, 150
Battered woman syndrome, 243
Child abuse, 358
Codependency, 388
Cognitive ability: Gender differences, 392
Couples therapy, 508
Domestic violence, 614
Eating disorders, 640
Elder abuse, 666
Family life: Adult issues, 752
Femininity, 770
Feminist psychotherapy, 772
Fetishes, 775
Freud, Anna, 799

Gay, lesbian, bisexual, and
    transgender mental health,
    813
Gender differences, 817
Gender identity disorder, 820
Gender identity formation, 824
Gender roles and gender role
    conflicts, 827
Gilligan, Carol, 851
Hope and mental health, 926
Horney, Karen, 934
Hysteria, 970
Mental health parity, 1189

Mother-child relationship, 1231
Obesity, 1304
Oedipus complex, 1322
Parenting styles, 1351
Penis envy, 1374
Postpartum depression, 1441
Psychosexual development,
    1528
Quality of life, 1570
Rape and sexual assault, 1591
Sadism and masochism, 1659
Separation and divorce: Adult
    issues, 1740

Sexism, 1753
Sexual harassment: Psychological
    causes and effects, 1767
Sibling relationships, 1785
Violence: Psychological causes
    and effects, 2027
Women's mental health, 2054
Women's psychology: Carol
    Gilligan, 2059
Women's psychology: Karen
    Horney, 2064
Women's psychology: Sigmund
    Freud, 2067

PERSONAGES INDEX

Ackerman, Nathan, 1542

Adams, Jerome, 1094

Adler, Alfred, 29-30, 996, 1488; aggression, 79; birth order, 297; coping, 500; Sigmund Freud, 803; Karen Horney, 1833; motivation, 64, 1236; self-actualization, 1707

Adler, Norman, 1759

Ahrons, Constance, 1741

Aiken, Lewis, 1030, 1400

Ainsworth, Mary, 203, 1231

Ajzen, Icek, 215

Akil, Huda, 1337

Albee, George W., 102-103

Aldwin, Carolyn, 1886

Alexander, Charles, 1154

Alexander, Franz, 320, 878

Allport, Gordon, 107-109, 340, 947, 1585, 1619; prejudice, 998, 1453, 1457; religion, 1625; self, 1700; stereotypes, 1756

Altman, Irwin, 704-705, 1709

Alzheimer, Alois, 115, 670

Amabile, Teresa, 519

Amato, Paul R., 1745

Amatrude, Catherine, 842

Ambady, Nalini, 686

Ames, Carole, 651

Ames, Louise, 842

Ames, Russell, 651

Amir, Yehuda, 1458

Anastasi, Anne, 1025

Anch, A. Michael, 1017

Anderson, Lynn, 876

Angell, James Rowland, 1907

Anna O., 319, 352, 962, 972, 1489, 1546

Anthony, Albert, 41

Antonovsky, Aaron, 502

Antonucci, Toni, 1823

Anzieu, Marguerite, 133

Apter, Michael J., 1331

Apter, Terri, 753

Arnett, Jeffery J., 976

Aronson, Elliot, 407, 487, 1089

Asch, Solomon, 1825

Aschoff, Jürgen, 377

Aserinsky, Eugene, 1801

Asher, Richard, 1254

Asperger, Hans, 191, 1412

Atkinson, John, 22, 1408

Atkinson, Richard, 689, 1178, 1181, 1779

Auerbach, Stephen M., 1886

Ausubel, David, 652

Axel, Richard, 1809

Axline, Virginia, 1437

Azjen, Icek, 480

Babbie, Earl, 1664

Back, Kurt, 58

Baddeley, Alan, 418, 689, 1156, 1181, 1779

Bahrick, H. P., 83

Bailey, Kent, 1887

Bairstow, Phillip, 1065

Baker, Lester, 153

Baldwin, James Mark, 131

Baltes, Paul, 86

Banaji, Mahzarin R., 83

Bandura, Albert, 242-243, 299, 400, 578, 1217, 1310, 1553, 1712, 1815; cognitive maps, 410; self, 1701

Bangert, Robert, 651

Barclay, J. Richard, 1981

Bard, Philip, 686, 1897

Barker, Roger, 705

Baron, Robert J., 449

Baron-Cohen, Simon, 194

Bartlett, Frederic C., 478, 1157

Barton, Walter E., 122

Bass, Bernard, 1093

Bates, Elizabeth, 1082

Bateson, Gregory, 1681, 1880

Batson, C. Daniel, 110, 1625

Baumeister, Roy, 1701, 1841

Baumrind, Diana, 1351

Beck, Aaron T., 98, 246-247, 397, 424; borderline personality disorder, 306; cognitive distortions, 569; depression, 1837, 1923

Becker, Mark W., 1178

Beecher, Henry K., 1433

Belenky, Mary Field, 394, 1703

Bellak, Leopold, 1478, 1976

Bem, Daryl, 1721

Bem, Sandra, 825, 1354

Benedict, Ruth, 1706

Benedikt, Moritz, 99

Bennett, A. E., 106

Bennett, Susan, 891

Benson, Herbert, 475, 1897

Benzer, Seymour, 378

Berger, Hans, 309

Berkman, Lisa, 1820

Berkowitz, Leonard, 78, 2020

Berlin, Rudolph, 636

Berlyne, D. E., 1329

Berman, Jeffrey, 1544

Bernard, Claude, 833, 951

Berne, Eric, 869, 2007

Bernestein, Ilene, 1947

Berscheid, Ellen, 1133

Bertalanffy, Ludwig von, 759

Bertillon, Jacques, 1038

Bettman, James R., 479

Biederman, Irving, 1361

Binet, Alfred, 1, 278-279, 514, 1027, 1029, 1515, 1865, 1971; sexual fetishism, 776

Bini, Lucino, 1775

Binswanger, Ludwig, 722

Birdwhistell, Ray, 1295

Blackwell, Arshavir, 1082

Blain, Daniel, 122

Blau, Theodore H., 298-299

Blehar, Mary, 1697

Bleuler, Eugen, 1668, 1683

Bloch, Vincent, 1636

Bloom, Benjamin, 847

Bloomfield, Leonard, 860

Blume, Sheila, 987

Boas, Franz, 777, 1581

Bogardus, Emory, 1585

Bogen, Joe, 317

Bolles, Richard N., 348, 1036

Boole, George, 1124

Boring, Edwin, 1022

Bornstein, Marcy, 511
Bornstein, Philip, 511
Boroditsky, Lera, 1082
Borson, Soo, 1947
Bosard, James H. S., 874
Boscolo, Luigi, 1881
Boss, Medard, 722
Bourgondien, Mary Van, 233
Bowen, Murray, 759
Bower, Gordon, 689
Bowlby, John, 201, 862, 1231, 1785
Boyce, Philip, 1695
Boyd-Franklin, Nancy, 761
Braid, James, 959
Brandon, Ruth, 740
Branscombe, Nyla, 1861
Bransford, D., 1981
Bransford, John, 1470
Braswell, Lauren, 212
Bray, James H., 1876
Breland, Keller, 460, 1019
Breland, Marian, 460, 1019
Brentano, Franz Clemens, 1513
Breuer, Josef, 318-320, 352, 962, 1489, 1546; hysteria, 972
Brickman, Philip, 909
Briggs, Isabel Myers, 1262
Broadbent, Donald, 206, 1178
Broca, Paul, 174, 307, 316, 1286, 1511, 1855
Brody, Gene, 1788
Bronfenbrenner, Urie, 83, 322-323, 1578
Brooks, Rodney, 187
Brooks-Gunn, Jeanne, 1701
Broverman, Inge, 817, 1754
Brower, Lincoln, 1947
Browman, Carl P., 1017
Brown, Barbara B., 705
Brown, Paul K., 2040
Brown, Roger, 1182
Brown, Rupert, 1458
Brown, Ryan P., 798
Brown, Stephanie, 1841
Browne, Angela, 243
Brumberg, Joan, 153
Bruner, Jerome, 323, 652, 1362, 1703, 1826
Bruning, Roger, 519

Brunswik, Egon, 705
Brussels, James, 1474
Bryan, James, 1311
Buck, Linda, 1809
Bundey, Sarah, 1201
Buranen, Cheryl, 965
Burckhardt, Gottlieb, 1119
Burkhauser, Richard V., 1640
Burt, Cyril, 1024, 1579
Butler, Charles, 449
Butler, Robert, 69
Buxbaum, Edith, 41
Buys, Christian, 876
Byrne, Donn, 222, 1453

Cacioppo, John, 219
Calkins, Mary W., 108, 1514
Cameron, Judy, 1101
Campbell, D. T., 341
Campbell, David P., 1036
Canady, Herman, 1581
Canevello, Amy, 1841
Cannon, Walter Bradford, 338-339, 686, 785, 833, 1897, 1899; dry mouth hypothesis, 1977
Canter, David, 1476
Caplan, Jeremy, 393
Caplan, Paula, 393
Cardon, Lon R., 1108
Carlsmith, J. M., 406
Carlson, Michael, 909
Carnahan, Thomas, 1868
Carr, Harvey A., 1907
Carskadon, Mary, 1268
Carson, G., 1857
Cartensen, Laura, 1823
Caruso, David R., 682
Carver, Charles S., 493, 502, 898
Casey, Rita, 1544
Castner, Burton, 842
Cattell, James McKeen, 1513, 1908, 1972
Cattell, Raymond B., 3, 342, 1030, 1400
Caudill, Maureen, 449
Cecchin, Gianfranco, 1881
Ceci, S. J., 83
Cerletti, Ugo, 1172, 1775
Cerney, Mary, 1479

Chace, Marian, 1260
Chaffin, Roger, 393
Chaikin, Alan, 1711
Chambless, Dianne, 98
Charcot, Jean-Martin, 17, 514, 916, 972
Charlin, Ventura, 909
Charpentier, Paul, 632
Chemers, Martin, 1095
Cherry, Colin, 207
Chesler, Phyllis, 772
Chodoff, Paul, 916
Chodorow, Nancy, 1702, 2060
Chomsky, Noam, 418, 858, 1080, 1112
Cialdini, Robert, 109, 1727, 1861
Cicirelli, Victor, 1786
Clark, David, 98
Clark, Kenneth, 1453, 1812
Clark, Mamie, 1453, 1813
Clark, Russell, 908
Cleckley, Hervey, 163, 1842
Clinchy, Blythe McVicker, 394
Cloninger, C. Robert, 918
Clore, Gerald, 222
Cobb, Sidney, 495
Coe, W. C., 956
Cohen, Louis, 1089
Cohen, Sheldon, 1820, 1841, 1887
Collins, Nancy, 1840
Comrey, Andrew, 1400
Conture, Edward G., 1910
Cooley, Charles, 1703
Cooper, Joel, 1825
Cornblatt, Barbara, 1679
Costa, P. T., Jr., 1401
Costa, R. R., 1048
Coupe, Patty, 412
Cousins, Norman, 1896
Cowen, Emory, 437
Coyne, James, 569
Craik, Fergus, 1127, 1181
Crawford, Mary, 393
Crespi, Leo P., 990
Crocker, Jennifer, 1459, 1841
Cronbach, Lee, 5
Crowder, Robert G, 83
Csikszentmihalyi, Mihaly, 518, 1440

Curtis, Rebecca, 1825
Custer, Robert, 985
Cytowic, Richard, 1937

DaCosta, Jacob, 99
Dagleish, Tim, 684
Damasio, Antonio, 684, 1702
Darley, John, 86, 326, 527, 967
Darwin, Charles, 678, 683, 767, 1018, 1512, 1581; emotional expression, 745; ethology, 712; nonverbal communication, 1296; sexual selection, 1758
Davidson-Podgorny, Gaye, 1458
Davies, Christie, 740
Davis, Clara, 1946
Davis, Elizabeth, 1381
Davis, Gary, 519
Davis, James H., 865
Davis, Keith, 1824
Davis, Martha, 78
Dawis, René, 340
Dawkins, Richard, 65
Dawson, Geraldine, 233
Dax, Marc, 1857
Deaux, Kay, 1754
DeBono, Edward, 1953
DeFries, John C., 1108
Delk, John, 2037
DeLoache, Judy, 412
Demaree, Robert G., 1401
Dement, William, 1801
De Perczel, Maria, 1923
Derlega, Valerian, 1711
Descartes, René, 1496
Detterman, Douglas, 1023
Deutsch, Diana, 206
Deutsch, J. Anthony, 206
Deutsch, Morton, 483
Devine, Patricia, 1460
DeVito, Joseph, 1296
Dewey, John, 593-594, 651, 1469, 1513, 1907, 1950
Dickson, William, 2075
DiClemente, Carlo, 2011
Diener, Ed, 875
Dilthey, Wilhelm, 1502
Dix, Dorothea, 613-614, 1195, 1556
Dobelle, William H., 2040

Doise, Willem, 1460
Dollard, John, 78, 1210-1211, 1235, 1655
Dombrowski, Stefan, 1465
Donders, Frans C., 1985
Douglas, John, 1594
Dovidio, John, 908
Down, John Langdon, 619, 1202
Down, Reginald, 620
Downing, Leslie, 528
Dowrick, Peter, 1312
Drabman, Ronald, 1996
Dreikurs, Rudolf, 32, 1213
Drozdovitch, V., 1201
Dubois, Rachel, 1458
Dunbar, Flanders, 1532
Duncker, Karl, 1470, 1472
Dunn, Judy, 1787
Dunn, Lloyd M., 1373
Durkheim, Émile, 181, 1820, 1920, 1957
Durkin, M. S., 1202
Dutton, Donald, 243
Duvall, Evelyn Millis, 756
Dweck, Carol, 22
D'Zurilla, Thomas, 398

Earls, F., 906
Easterbrook, J. A., 1330
Ebbinghaus, Hermann, 645-646, 791, 1126, 1168, 1180, 1781, 2053
Eccles, John, 1702
Efran, Michael, 1089
Egas Moniz, António, 307, 1119, 1538
Ehrenfels, Christian von, 1513
Ehrenreich, Barbara, 1137
Eisenberger, Robert, 1101
Ekman, Paul, 685, 1296
Elfenbein, Hilary, 686
Eliason, Grafton, 505
Elkind, David, 38
Ellenberger, Henri, 1558
Elliott, Jane, 1453
Ellis, Albert, 397, 411, 676-677, 1595, 1621, 1833
Ellis, Henry, 1177
Ellis, Thomas, 1923
Epstein, Seymour, 1888

Erikson, Erik H., 40, 176, 659, 710, 752, 974, 1375, 1488, 1515; guilt, 879; personality disorders, 1389; self, 1700
Erlenmeyer-Kimling, L., 1676
Ervin, Frank, 1948
Esdaile, James, 957
Esquirol, Jean-Étienne-Dominique, 1029
Evans, Gary, 1887
Everett, Craig, 1741
Everett, Sandra, 1741
Exline, Julie Juola, 798
Exner, John, 1479, 1647
Eysenck, Hans, 743-744, 1048, 1329, 1400, 1547

Fairbairn, Ronald, 1668
Fairweather, George, 436
Faludi, Susan, 1455
Fanning, Patrick, 78
Fant, Gunnar, 1852
Farberow, Norman, 1922
Faris, Robert, 1820
Farr, William, 1037
Fazio, Russell, 215
Fechner, Gustav, 1400, 1505
Feeney, Brooke, 1840
Felix, Robert H., 1270
Fenz, Walter, 1888
Fernald, Grace, 638
Festinger, Leon, 56, 405, 498, 1724
Fiedler, Fred, 1093
Fillenbaum, Samuel, 2037
Fine, Mark A., 1875
Fischoff, Stuart, 1148
Fishbein, Martin, 215, 480
Fishbein, Sanford, 355
Fisher, Roger, 484
Fisher, Ronald A., 1873
Flavell, John, 37
Fleischman, Edwin, 1096
Flourens, Pierre, 307
Floyd, Frank, 1638
Folkman, Susan, 504, 1886, 1900
Forehand, Rex, 1543
Forsyth, D. R., 1926
Foulkes, David, 625
Francis, Greta, 259

Frank, Jerome D., 1549
Frank, Lawrence, 1480
Franklin, Stan, 185
Franks, Jeffrey J., 1981
Franz, Shepard Ivory, 1512
Freeman, Derek, 43
Freeman, Walter, 1120, 1498, 1538
Fremouw, William, 1923
French, John, 1451
French, Thomas, 320
Freud, Anna, 500, 565, 653, 799-800, 1437, 1490, 1542
Freud, Sigmund, 800-802; aggression, 79; case study methodology, 352; death anxiety, 505; defense mechanisms, 553, 565, 653, 1478; dreams, 625; drives, 629; grieving, 862; guilt, 877; homosexuality, 922; hysteria, 916, 972, 1533; Carl Jung, 1054; masochism, 1660; motivation, 64, 1235; neurosis, 99, 1288; Oedipus complex, 1323; personality theory, 472, 664, 1386, 1395, 1492; phobias, 1418; psychoanalysis, 17, 658, 1481, 1487, 1515, 1546, 1556; psychosexual development, 577, 1228, 1375, 1528; religion, 1618; repression, 1346, 1628; schizophrenia, 1681; self, 1700; women, 2060, 2068
Freudian psychology; anxiety, 167; Karen Horney, 2064
Freund, Kurt, 1774
Fridja, Nico, 683
Friedman, Meyer, 502, 1895, 1901, 2016
Friesen, Wallace, 1296
Frisch, G. R., 987
Frisch, Karl von, 711
Fritsch, Gustav, 307, 316, 1512
Fromm, Erich, 806-807, 879, 1067, 1236, 1827
Frost, Nancy, 5
Fuster, J. M., 1636
Futrell, B. A., 84

Gaertner, Samuel L., 908
Galanter, Eugene, 1732
Galbraith, John Kenneth, 1449
Galinsky, Ellen, 756
Gall, Franz, 1286, 1511
Galt, John M., 121
Galton, Francis, 1025, 1512, 1581, 1864, 1873, 1937, 1972
Garcia, John, 238, 1947
Gardner, Howard, 515, 518, 1025, 1032, 1066, 1246
Gardner, Richard A., 1350, 1742
Garfinkel, Barry, 1922
Garvey, Michael, 1695
Gazzaniga, Michael, 1855
Gélineau, Jean-Baptiste-Édouard, 1267
Gellar, E. Scott, 1644
Gerbner, George, 2020
Gergen, Kenneth, 1703
Gesell, Arnold, 842-843, 1243
Getzsche, P. C., 1434
Gibson, James J., 575, 1361
Gilbert, Daniel, 227
Gilbreth, Frank, 1003
Giles-Sims, Jean, 1876
Gilligan, Carol, 851-852, 1702, 2059, 2071
Gillingham, Anna, 638
Glass, Gene, 1547
Glasser, Barney G., 1568
Glasser, William, 1603
Glover, John, 519
Godden, Duncan, 689
Goffman, Erving, 13, 1728
Gold, Mark, 7
Goldberger, Nancy Rule, 394
Goldfried, Marvin, 258, 398
Goldiamond, Israel, 1325
Goldstein, Alan, 98
Goldstein, Kurt, 64, 1707
Goleman, Daniel, 681
Golgi, Camillo, 1281
Gondolf, Edward, 243
Goodwin, Donald, 964
Gormezano, Isadore, 1608
Gorney, Roderic, 1707
Gorsuch, Richard L., 1625, 1869
Gottman, John M., 509
Gough, Harrison, 333, 341

Gramling, Sandra E., 1886
Graunt, John, 1037
Graves, Robert, 1991
Gray, Laura, 1089
Gredler, Margaret, 652
Greene, David, 735, 1723
Greene, Robert, 1451
Greeno, J. G., 1468
Grice, H. P., 1115
Griffin, John Howard, 779
Griffith, Coleman R., 1862
Grismer, B. A, 84
Groth-Marnat, Gary, 1392
Grundman, Michael, 84
Guidano, Vittorio, 399
Guilford, J. P., 3, 516, 1024, 1400
Guillette, Elizabeth, 708
Gull, William, 1990
Guntrip, Harry, 1668
Gur, Ruben, 964
Gustavson, Carl, 1947
Guze, Samuel, 964

Haan, Norma, 500
Hacker, Frederick J., 1969
Haffner, Debra W, 47
Haggard, E. A., 679
Haley, Jay, 759, 1881
Hall, Calvin, 2070
Hall, David, 968
Hall, G. Stanley, 40, 589, 885-886, 1513, 1581, 1959
Hall, Richard, 8
Hamilton, David L., 1584
Hansen, Jo-Ida, 1036
Hare, Robert, 163
Harlow, Harry, 147, 204, 1389
Harlow, Margaret, 204
Harman, Denham, 92
Harré, Rom, 1703
Harris, Ben, 1118
Harris, John, 1982
Hart, Betty M., 2052
Hart, Roger A., 703
Harter, Susan, 2062
Hartmann, Heinz, 659, 1235
Hathaway, S. R., 341, 1211
Hauri, Peter, 1016
Hayes, Steven C., 1651
Hazan, Cindy, 1134

Hebb, Donald O., 1157, 1163, 1173, 1236, 1286, 1512
Hecht, Michael, 1296
Heft, Harry, 705
Heidegger, Martin, 722
Heider, Fritz, 227, 356, 1824
Heine, Steven, 1714
Helgeson, Vicki S., 59
Heller, Frank, 1095
Heller, Theodore, 1414
Hellmuth, Hug, 1437
Helmholtz, Hermann von, 205, 904, 1274, 1361, 1512, 2036, 2040
Helmreich, Robert, 23
Henderson, Lynne, 1783
Henle, Mary, 1983
Henley, Nancy, 1298
Hering, Ewald, 1512, 2036
Herman, Judith, 243
Herrnstein, Richard, 4, 1578
Herzberg, Frederick, 2075
Hetherington, E. Mavis, 1744
Hewstone, Miles, 1458
Hilgard, Ernest, 475, 956, 958
Hilgard, Josephine, 958, 1340
Hill, Peter C., 1625
Hill, Reuben, 756
Hinshelwood, James, 639
Hitch, Graham, 1181
Hitzig, Eduard, 307, 316, 1512
Hoberman, Harry, 1922
Hobfoll, S. E., 1900
Hobson, J. Allan, 625
Hock, R. A, 84
Hodgkin, Alan, 1010
Hoffer, Abram, 1300
Holland, John L., 339, 346, 1034, 1903
Hollingworth, Leta, 850
Holmes, Thomas, 491, 1889, 1894
Hood, Ralph W., Jr., 1625
Horner, Matina, 1409
Horney, Karen, 934, 1375, 1489, 1700, 1831, 2064, 2069
House, James, 503, 1822
Hovland, Carl, 218
Huarte, Juan, 1031
Hubel, David, 147

Huettel, Scott A., 112
Hull, Clark L., 628, 937, 990, 1235, 1655, 1977
Hunt, Earl B., 5
Hunt, Morton, 85
Hunt, Reed, 1177
Hunter, John, 833
Husserl, Edmund, 723, 945
Hutman, Lucinda, 2036
Huxley, Andrew, 1010
Hyde, Janet Shibley, 393, 1755

Igumnov, S., 1201
Ilg, Frances, 842
Inhelder, Barbel, 36
Inkster, James, 407
Instone, Debra, 1094
Intons-Peterson, Margaret, 1779
Irwin, David E., 1178
Isaacs, F. S., 679
Isaacs, Wayne, 1325
Izard, Carroll, 746

Jack, Demick, 705
Jacklin, Carol, 393
Jackson, Douglas, 342, 1400
Jackson, John Hughlings, 1287, 1858
Jacobs, Gerald A., 1869
Jacobson, Edmund, 280, 1152
Jacobson, Lenore, 1237, 1825
James, William, 1050-1051, 1154, 1512, 1699, 1738, 1760, 1907, 2037; attention, 206; consciousness, 471; education, 651; emotions, 686, 745, 768; memory, 791, 1126, 1779; self-esteem, 1715
Janis, Irving, 866, 1887
Janowsky, David, 51
Jarvis, Eric, 533
Jellen, Hans, 519
Jenkins, C. David, 2016
Jenkins, James, 650
Jensen, Arthur R., 4, 1578
Jewell, Linda, 1005
Johnson, David, 1259, 1952
Johnson, Robert, 528
Johnson, Roger, 1952

Johnson, Virginia E., 1139-1141, 1762, 2071
Johnson, Wendell, 1909
Johnson-Laird, Philip, 1983
Jones, Edward, 1405, 1726, 1824
Jones, James M., 1583
Jones, Mary Cover, 1542, 1940
Jones, R. K., 1856
Jordan, Dale R., 637
Jourard, Sidney, 1709
Julesz, Bela, 574
Jung, Carl, 135, 138, 176, 1054-1055, 1206, 1261, 1707; dreams, 624; introversion and extroversion, 1048; motivation, 64; self, 1700

Kagan, Jerome, 1701, 1783
Kahlbaum, Karl, 1346
Kahn, William A., 79
Kahneman, Daniel, 237, 417, 548, 1824
Kako, Edward, 1077
Kallmann, Franz J., 1682
Kamen, Leslie, 1099
Kamin, Leon, 743, 1582
Kandel, Eric R., 882, 1101, 1159, 1163, 1171, 1609
Kanner, Leo, 230
Kant, Immanuel, 478
Kantor, Martin, 1187
Kaplan, Helen Singer, 1762
Karpman, Benjamin, 165
Kasper, Siegfried, 1695
Kastenbaum, Robert J., 505
Katz, Irwin, 1583
Keel, Pamela, 534
Kelley, Harold, 354, 1824
Kelly, Alison, 828
Kelly, George A., 1063-1064, 1382, 1403
Kendall, Philip, 212
Kendrick, Carol, 1787
Kennedy, Melinda, 70
Kerlinger, Fred, 1391
Kety, Seymour, 1682
Keysers, Christian, 1179
Kierkegaard, Søren, 723
Kilbride, Thomas, 121
Kimble, Gregory A., 1614

Kinsey, Alfred, 90, 814, 925, 1067-1068, 1930
Kirmayer, Lawrence J., 533
Kitayama, Shinobu, 1702
Klasen, Edith, 639
Klein, Donald, 98
Klein, Gary, 1451
Klein, Melanie, 554, 878, 1437
Kleinman, Arthur, 532
Kleitman, Nathaniel, 1801
Klerman, Gerald, 570
Klineberg, Otto, 678
Kluckholm, Richard, 41
Klump, Kelly, 534
Knight, James, 879
Knott, David H., 106
Knox, Robert, 407
Kobasa, Suzanne, 493, 502, 1896, 1900
Koch, August, 165
Koelling, Robert, 1948
Koffka, Kurt, 1513
Kohlberg, Lawrence, 824, 851, 1070-1071, 1228, 1565, 2060
Köhler, Wolfgang, 1473, 1513
Kohut, Heinz, 1700
Kojève, Alexandre, 134
Konopka, Ronald J., 378
Koop, C. Everett, 897
Korchin, Sheldon, 1478
Korner, Anneliese, 1478
Kovacs, Maria, 369
Kovel, Joel, 1583
Kowalski, Robin M., 325
Kraepelin, Emil, 571, 1071-1072, 1196, 1223, 1346, 1517, 1538, 1560, 1673, 1683, 1698
Krafft-Ebing, Richard von, 1659
Kraut, Robert, 747
Kruschwitz, Stanley V., 79
Kübler-Ross, Elisabeth, 335, 505, 543, 863, 1072-1073
Kuder, G. Frederic, 1036
Kulik, James, 651, 1182
Külpe, Oswald, 470
Kunz, George, 1451, 1500
Kurdek, Lawrence A., 1875

L'Abate, Luciano, 1883
LaBerge, Stephen, 624

Lacan, Jacques, 130, 1076-1077
Laing, R. D., 722
Laird, James, 746
Lamplugh, Diane, 79
Landy, David, 1089
Lang, Peter, 169, 1940
Lange, Carl, 686, 746, 768
Langer, Ellen J., 898
Langer, Walter, 1474
Langewisch, M. W., 987
Larson, John, 1644
Lashley, Karl, 307, 1157, 1161, 1173, 1512
Laszlo, Judith, 1065
Latané, Bibb, 326, 527, 967
Latham, Gary, 2074
Lawton, M. Powell, 705
Lazarus, Richard, 491, 500, 504, 1886, 1900
Lazovik, David, 1940
Leary, Mark, 1728, 1841
Leary, Timothy, 888
Le Bon, Gustave, 525, 1756
Lehrman, Daniel, 1759
Lencz, Todd, 1679
Lenneberg, Eric, 859
Lepper, Mark, 735, 1723
Lerner, Harriet Goldhor, 2066
Lesieur, Henry, 985
Levin, Jack, 891
Levine, Robert, 779
Levis, Donald J., 979
Levy, Jere, 1856
Lewin, Kurt, 486, 705, 781, 1110-1111
Lewis, Helen, 879
Lewis, Laurie, 1754
Lewis, Michael, 1701
Liberman, Alvin M., 1851
Licoppe, Christian, 827
Lidz, Theodore, 1681
Likert, Rensis, 1932
Lindemann, Erich, 520, 862
Lindsley, Donald, 1636
Lindzey, Gardner, 948
Linehan, Marsha M., 305, 602, 1389
Linton, Marigold, 1182
Liotti, Gianni, 399
Lippmann, Walter, 1756

Lipsitt, Lewis, 1612
Lochman, John, 79
Locke, Edwin, 2074
Locke, John, 992
Lockhart, Robert, 1127, 1181
Loewald, Hans, 879
Loewi, Otto, 1935
Lofquist, Lloyd, 340
Loftus, Elizabeth F., 82, 416, 740, 968, 1128, 1982
Long, Howard, 1581
Lorenz, Konrad, 711, 981, 1130-1131, 1235
Lorge, Irving, 391
Lovaas, Ivar, 233, 1311
Luchins, Abraham, 1472
Lucy, John, 1082
Lukes, Steven, 1451
Lunneborg, Clifford E., 5
Luria, Aleksandr, 309, 1937
Lushene, Robert, 1869
Lyerly, J. G., 1539
Lykken, David, 163, 1843
Lyons, Henry, 916

McAdams, Dan, 1703
McAllister, Ronald, 777
McBride, K. E., 1858
McCarley, Robert, 625
McCarthy, Diane, 1791
McClelland, David, 22, 1408
McClelland, J. L., 1083
Maccoby, Eleanor, 393
McConahay, John B., 1584
McCrae, P. T., Jr., 1048
McCrae, R. R., 1401
McCullough, Michael E., 796
McDaniels, Carl, 346
McDevitt, Jack, 891
MacDougall, William, 1018, 1513, 1760
McFarland, Sam, 1868
McGaugh, James, 1629
McGinty, D. J., 1636
McGorry, Patrick, 1679
McGregor, Douglas, 945, 1706
Mach, Ernst, 2037
McKay, Matthew, 78
McKinley, J. C., 341, 1211
McKinley, Nita, 393

MacKinnon, Donald, 847
McNally, Richard, 737
McNamara, Timothy, 412
MacNichol, Edward F., 2040
Madanes, Cloe, 1881
Mahler, Margaret, 1700
Maier, Norman R. F., 1472
Maier, Steven F., 1099, 1101
Malan, Daniel, 320
Mann, Horace, 120
Mann, James, 321
Mann, Leon, 527
Mann, Michael, 1449
Maratsos, Michael, 1083
Marcia, James, 976, 1700
Marecek, Jeanne, 2062
Markman, Arthur, 684
Marks, William B., 2040
Markus, Hazel, 1701
Markwardt, Frederick C., 1373
Marland, Sidney P., 848
Martin, Lenny, 747
Martin, Roy, 1465
Maslach, Susan, 1868
Maslow, Abraham, 54, 64, 914,
    944, 1138-1139, 1154, 1236,
    1516, 1700, 1704, 2073
Mason, John, 1899
Masters, William H., 1139-1141,
    1762, 2071
Matheny, Laura, 1083
Matlin, Margaret, 1176
Maultsby, Maxie, 397
May, Rollo, 79, 721, 944, 1141-
    1142, 1449, 1701
Mayer, John, 681
Mayo, Elton, 2075
Mayo, Julia, 906
Mead, George Herbert, 1703,
    1716
Mead, Margaret, 43, 1020
Meadow, Roy, 1255
Medin, Douglas, 684
Mednick, Sarnoff, 1465, 1676
Meehl, Paul, 1686
Meese, Hayden, 1996
Mehrabian, Albert, 1296
Meichenbaum, Donald, 78, 397
Melamed, Barbara, 1312
Melzack, Ronald, 1336, 1339

Menninger, William, 122
Menzel, Emil W., 409
Merikle, Phil, 1175
Merleau-Ponty, Maurice, 724
Merriam, Sharan, 1183
Merrill, Maude, 2
Mesibov, Gary, 233
Mesmer, Franz, 474, 959
Milgram, Stanley, 731, 1208
Miller, George, 1779
Miller, Jean Baker, 2071
Miller, Kim, 1825
Miller, Marian, 1089
Miller, Neal E., 280, 1210-1211,
    1235, 1655
Miller, Norman, 909, 1458
Miller, Thomas, 1548
Milner, Peter, 991
Mineka, Susan, 168
Minuchin, Salvador, 153, 759,
    1544
Mischel, Walter, 420, 824, 1218
Mitchell, Stephen, 879
Mitler, Merrill M., 1017
Monahan, John, 13
Money, John, 1770
Montagu, Ashley, 1578
Montvilo, Robin, 70
Moore, Gary T., 703
Moos, Rudolf, 492
Morgan, C. D., 1256
Morgan, Christiana, 1408
Morganstern, Kenneth P., 979
Morris, Desmond, 1297
Morrison, Frederick, 1177
Mowrer, O. Hobart, 167
Mullainathan, Sendhil, 263
Mullany, Pat, 1475
Mullen, Brian, 527, 874, 1460
Mulley, John C., 1203
Murphy, Debra, 1401
Murray, Charles, 4, 1578
Murray, Henry A., 22, 1256-1257,
    1407, 1975
Mustin, Rachel Hare, 2062
Myers, David G., 1439
Myers, Katharine Cook, 1262

Nakata, Mizuho, 1539
Nansel, Tonja R., 325

Neisser, Ulric, 207, 742, 1175,
    1182, 1516
Nelson, Katherine, 1079
Nerenberg, Arnold, 1644
Neuringer, Allen, 1101, 1105
Newell, Allen, 1125
Nidorf, J. F., 41
Nisbett, Richard, 523, 735, 1339,
    1405, 1722-1723
Nobles, Wade, 1581
Norcross, James, 2011
Nordlie, Johanna, 964
Norenzayan, Ara, 523

Ogbu, John, 1272
Okamura, Amy, 906
Olds, James, 991
Ollendick, Thomas, 259
Olton, David S., 409
Olweus, Dan, 324
Onslow, Mark, 1912
Ord, William, 1990
Ornstein, Robert, 475
Orton, Samuel T., 638, 1108,
    1857
Ortony, Andrew, 684
Osmond, Humphry, 1300
Ostrom, Thomas, 1459
Ostrove, Nancy, 1089
Overmier, J. Bruce, 1099, 1101
Owsley, Cynthia, 2036

Painter, Susan, 243
Paivio, Allen, 411
Palmer, John, 416
Palmore, Erdman, 70
Pargament, Kenneth I., 507, 796,
    1624
Park, Robert, 777
Parker, Gordon, 1695
Parkinson, James, 1355
Parry, Caleb, 1991
Parsons, Frank, 346, 1036
Pask, Gordon, 650
Patterson, Gerald, 266, 1543
Paul, Gordon L., 1941
Pauling, Linus, 1301
Pavlov, Ivan Petrovich, 238, 265,
    269, 456, 1101, 1235, 1367-
    1368, 1608, 1614, 1945

Pearson, Karl, 1873
Peck, Robert, 1639
Pennebaker, James W., 1887
Penrose, Roger, 448
Pepper, Stephen C., 704
Perlmutter, Marion, 90
Perls, Fritz, 843, 869
Perry, William, 394
Person, Ethel, 1450
Pert, Candace, 698
Petersen, Ronald C., 84
Peterson, Lloyd, 1779
Pettigrew, Thomas F., 1453, 1583
Petty, Richard, 219
Phylyshyn, Zenon, 411
Piaget, Jean, 36, 394, 401, 478, 1426-1427; consciousness, 469; development, 40, 578, 1066; intelligence, 1030; language, 1081; moral development, 1227, 1565
Piliavin, Jane Allyn, 109, 908
Pinel, Philippe, 165, 1195, 1428-1429, 1556
Piotrowski, Zygmunt, 627
Pittman, Thane, 1726
Pleck, Joseph, 825
Plomin, Robert, 1426
Plutchik, Robert, 684
Polanyi, Michael, 1702
Poppen, Roger L., 1652
Porter, Natalie, 1755
Power, Mick, 684
Prata, Guiliana, 1881
Premack, David, 459, 1616
Pribram, Karl, 472
Pritchard, James, 165
Prochaska, James O., 2011
Pryor, John, 1459
Puusepp, Ludvig, 1119
Puységur, marquis de, 959

Quay, Herbert, 164
Quinlan, Donald, 1259
Quinn, Joseph F., 1640

Rahe, Richard, 491, 1889, 1894
Ramón y Cajal, Santiago, 1281
Rank, Otto, 803, 1381
Raskin, N. J., 1379

Raven, Bertram, 1451
Rayner, Rosalie, 269, 767, 1118, 1370, 1421, 2046
Rehm, Lynn, 399
Reich, Wilhelm, 1260, 1298
Reicher, Stephen, 527
Reilly, Richard, 259
Reiss, Steven, 1396
Rescorla, Robert, 1609
Ressler, Robert, 1594
Rett, Andreas, 1413
Rice, Robert, 1094
Richardson, Frank, 1703
Rimm, Sylvia, 519
Rips, Lance, 1181
Risley, Todd, 1996
Robins, L. N., 906
Robins, Lee, 162
Rodin, Judith, 898, 1099, 1888
Roethlisberger, Fritz, 2075
Rogers, Carl R., 846, 944, 1377, 1393, 1553, 1557, 1645-1646, 1700, 1705
Rogoff, Barbara, 704
Rorschach, Hermann, 1646-1647
Rosario, Margaret, 48
Rose, Amanda J., 59
Rosenhan, David L., 20, 780, 1199, 1649
Rosenkrantz, Paul, 1754
Rosenman, Ray, 502, 1895, 1901, 2016
Rosenthal, Norman, 1695
Rosenthal, Richard, 985
Rosenthal, Robert, 1237, 1314, 1825
Rosman, Bernice, 153
Ross, Lee, 227
Rothbart, Myron, 1584
Rotter, Julian, 1397
Rozin, Paul, 1946
Rubin, Zick, 58, 225, 1710
Rush, Benjamin, 120, 1195
Rushton, William A. H., 2040
Rutstein, Jeffrey, 355

Saari, Lise, 2052
Sabshin, Melvin, 122
Sacher-Masoch, Leopold von, 1659

Sackheim, Harold, 964
Sacks, Oliver, 1362
Sade, Marquis de, 1659
Sajwaj, Thomas, 1326
Salovey, Peter, 681
Sampson, Edward, 1703
Samuelson, Robert J., 409
Sapir, Edward, 860
Sarbin, T. R., 956
Sartre, Jean-Paul, 724, 1660
Satir, Virginia, 759, 1666-1667
Sattler, Jerome M., 1031
Saunders, Cicely, 505, 935
Scarr, Sandra, 1426, 1581
Schachter, E. P., 976
Schachter, Stanley, 56, 297, 355, 954, 1339
Schacter, Daniel, 791, 793
Scheckenbach, Albert F., 79
Scheier, Michael F., 898
Schildkraut, Joseph, 51
Schlenker, Barry, 1728
Schlossberg, Nancy, 347
Schnarch, David, 1766
Schneider, Kurt, 165
Schneider, Walter, 235
Schoenrade, P., 1625
Schofield, Janet, 1459
Schulsinger, Fini, 1676
Schulz, Leslie Olmstead, 1306
Schwartz, Robert, 953
Scoville, William, 1173, 1781
Sdorow, Lester, 82
Searle, John, 186
Sechenov, Ivan, 1608
Seitz, Jay A., 1065
Sekule, Robert, 2036
Seligman, Martin E. P., 355, 1097, 1101, 1439, 1535, 1730, 1887, 1946
Sells, S. B., 1401, 1983
Selman, Robert, 38
Selvini-Palazzoli, Mara, 1881
Selye, Hans, 830, 863, 1731-1732, 1891, 1894, 1899
Shapiro, Francine, 737
Shaver, Kelly, 228
Shaver, Philip, 1134
Sheehy, Gail, 1206
Sherif, Carolyn, 1460

Sherif, Muzafer, 486, 1460
Sherrington, Charles, 1281, 1291, 1609
Shevrin, Howard, 1289
Shiffrin, Richard, 235, 689, 1178, 1181, 1779
Shisslak, Catherine, 155
Shneidman, Edwin, 1922
Shoben, Edward, 1181
Shockley, William, 4, 1578
Shoda, Yuichi, 1218
Shontz, Franklin, 491
Shore, Cecilia, 1079
Siegal, J. M., 1636
Siegall, Marc, 1005
Sifneos, Peter, 320
Sigall, Harold, 1089
Simmelhag, V., 459
Simon, Herbert, 262, 1125
Simon, Théodore, 1027, 1029, 1865, 1971
Singer, Jerome E., 355
Singleton, Royce, Jr., 777
Skinner, B. F., 265, 270, 458, 1326, 1587, 1651, 1792-1794; language acquisition, 1112; learning, 1102; personality, 1395; reinforcement, 1615; small-n experimental designs, 2053
Skrzypek, George, 164
Slavin, Robert, 488, 651, 1952
Slobin, Dan Isaac, 1080
Smith, Edward, 1181
Smith, Mary, 1547
Smith, Robert, 28
Smith, Stephanie, 356
Smoreda, Zbigniew, 827
Sniezek, Janet A., 866
Snow, Katherine, 1112
Snyder, C. R., 356, 927
Snyder, Mark, 215, 1701
Snyder, Solomon H., 698
Sobel, Nathan, 740
Solman, Robert, 1177
Spearman, Charles, 2, 1024
Spector, Paul E., 78
Spelke, Elizabeth, 523
Spence, Janet, 23
Spencer, Herbert, 1512

Spencer, K. W., 990
Sperling, George, 1175
Sperry, Roger, 317, 1512, 1855
Spiegel, Harold, 958
Spielberger, Charles, 1869, 1885
Spitalnik, Robert, 1996
Spitz, Rene, 565, 1600
Staddon, J. E. R., 459
Stampfl, Thomas G., 979
Stanton, H. E., 958
Starko, Alane, 519
Stein, Barry, 1470
Stephan, Walter G., 1584
Stepper, Sabina, 747
Stern, William, 108, 1027, 1865
Sternberg, Robert, 57, 514, 1023, 1025, 1132
Sternberg, Saul, 1986
Stevens, Albert, 412
Stewart, John, 1089
Stillman, Essie, 638
Stjermsward, Jan, 1337
Stogdill, Ralph, 1096
Stokols, Daniel, 1886
Storms, Philip L, 78
Stott, Clifford, 527
Strack, Fritz, 747
Straits, Bruce, 777
Straits, Margaret, 777
Straus, Murray, 1104
Strauss, Anselm L., 1568
Strentz, Thomas, 1888
Strong, Edward K., Jr., 339, 1036, 1902
Stroop, J. Ridley, 206
Stuart, Richard, 266
Stumpf, Carl, 1513
Sugerman, Roger, 1015
Sullivan, Harry Stack, 1489, 1681, 1700, 1925-1926
Sun, Yongmin, 1746
Sung, B. L., 41
Super, Donald, 347
Sussman, L. K., 906
Sutherland, Grant R., 1203
Sydenham, Thomas, 971
Syme, Leonard, 1820
Symonds, Alexandra, 2065
Szasz, Thomas, 13, 16

Taft, Jessie, 1381
Tajfel, Henri, 525, 1810
Tarnow, Eugen, 527
Tarule, Jill Mattuck, 394
Taylor, C. W., 515
Taylor, Dalmas, 1709
Taylor, Donald, 1458
Taylor, Frederick Winslow, 1003, 1332, 2075
Taylor, Shelley, 1899
Teddie, Charles, 355
Terman, Lewis, 1, 847, 1027, 1029, 1515, 1865, 1972
Test, Mary Ann, 1311
Teten, Howard, 1475
Thoits, Margaret, 1822
Thomas, James, 1325
Thomas, Laura E., 1178
Thompson, Helen, 842
Thompson, Richard F., 1609
Thoresen, Carl E., 796
Thorndike, Edward L., 265, 457, 630, 1101, 1473, 1513, 1587, 1614, 1908, 1979-1980
Thorndike, Robert L., 391
Thurstone, L. L., 3, 1024, 1932
Tinbergen, Nikolaas, 711, 981
Tissot, Simon, 1752
Titchener, Edward, 206, 1512, 1904
Toffler, Alvin, 1449
Tolman, Edward C., 146, 409, 1473, 1713, 1998-1999
Tomer, Adrian, 505
Tomkins, Silvan, 746
Tomm, Karl, 797
Torrance, E. Paul, 518
Torrey, E. Fuller, 8
Tourette, Georges Gilles de la, 2003
Tousignant, James, 968
Treisman, Anne, 207
Trivers, Robert, 713
Troll, Lillian, 1640
Tryon, Robert, 146
Tuckman, Bruce, 873
Tulving, Endel, 83, 688, 1127, 1180
Turing, Allen, 186
Turner, John, 525, 1811

Turner, Ralph, 1717
Turner, Terence, 684
Turvey, Brent, 1476
Tversky, Amos, 417, 548, 1824

Urban, Klaus, 519
Ury, William, 484

Vagg, Peter R., 1869
Vaillant, George E., 655
Van Geert, Paul, 1083
Van Wagnen, William, 317
Vernon, Philip E., 3, 948, 1024
Visher, Emily B., 1876
Visher, John S., 1876
Vogel, Philip, 317
Vroom, Victor, 1095, 2073
Vygotsky, Lev, 652, 1081, 1113

Wagner, Allan, 1609
Wagner, Hugh, 75
Wagner, Rudolph F., 637
Wagner von Jauregg, Julius, 833
Wald, George, 2040
Walker, Alexis, 828
Walker, Lawrence J., 2062
Walker, Lenore, 243, 615
Wall, Patrick, 1336
Wallace, R. K., 475
Walsh, James, 1015, 1557
Walster, Elaine, 223, 1133
Walters, Richard H., 1310, 1818
Wann, Daniel, 1861
Ward, W. S., 957
Warden, Carl J., 629, 990
Watson, Charles, 965

Watson, John B., 269, 417, 468, 1314, 1502, 1514, 1657, 2046-2047; Little Albert study, 238, 266, 352, 767, 1118, 1370, 1421
Watts, James W., 1120, 1498, 1539
Watzlawick, Paul, 1881
Waynbaum, Israel, 748
Weber, Max, 1332
Webster, Ronald L., 1912
Wechsler, David, 1022, 1027, 1029, 2047
Weeks, Gerald, 1883
Wehr, Thomas, 1695
Weiner, Bernard, 22, 354
Weisenberg, T., 1858
Weisz, John, 1544
Wells, Gary, 968
Wernicke, Carl, 174, 1858
Wertheimer, Max, 1513, 1733
Westphal, Alexander, 99
White, Gregory, 355
White, Robert, 500, 1235
Whitehead, George, 356
Whiting, John, 41
Wicker, A. W, 216
Widom, Cathy Spatz, 163
Wiesel, Torsten, 147
Wilkie, William, 481
Wilkins, Arnold, 1183
Will, D. P., 1401
Williams, Carl, 1326
Williams, Carol, 215
Williams, Frank, 518
Williams, George, 651
Williamson, E. G., 1036
Wills, Thomas A., 1841

Wilpert, Bernhard, 1095
Wilson, Edward O., 64, 713
Wilson, Gregory L., 512
Wilson, Laurie, 512
Wilson, Timothy, 1722
Wilson, William, 28
Winnicott, Donald, 776
Wohl, Michael J. A., 798
Wolfe, Montrose, 1996
Wolpe, Joseph, 255, 266, 272, 1371, 1421, 1557, 1940
Woodruff, Robert, 964
Woodworth, Robert S., 1400, 1513, 1908, 1983
Worchel, Stephen, 355
Word, Carl, 1825
Wright, Herbert, 705
Wundt, Wilhelm, 417, 468, 726, 885, 1178, 1512, 1688, 1738, 1904, 1971

Yalom, Irvin D., 723, 871, 2084-2085
Yamada, Jeni, 1082
Yarmey, A. Daniel, 1091
Yetton, Philip, 1095
Young, Thomas, 2040
Yung, Alison, 1679

Zajonc, Robert, 56, 748, 1329
Zanna, Mark, 1825
Zelazo, Philip, 1425
Zettle, Robert D., 1651
Zillmann, Dolf, 1330
Zimbardo, Philip, 1339, 1783, 1866, 2086-2087
Zurif, E. B., 1857
Zyzanski, Stephen, 2016

SUBJECT INDEX

A-B-C theory of personality, 1598
A-B-C (D-E) theory of emotional change, 1598
Ability evaluative system, 651
Ability tests, 1-6, 340, 1507. *See also specific test*
Abnormality; biomedical models, 6-11, 16; legal models, 11-15; psychological models, 15-21
Abuse. *See* Alcohol dependence and abuse; Child abuse; Elder abuse; Spousal abuse
Acceptance, terminal illness, 335, 506, 544
Acculturation; Asian Americans and Pacific Islanders, 188; Latinos, 1086
Acetylcholine, 50, 116, 1009, 1173, 1279, 1292, 1294, 1934
Achievement motivation, 21-25, 991, 1257, 1408
Achievement tests, 340, 394, 1507; interest inventories versus, 1033. *See also specific test*
Ackerman, Nathan, 1542
Acrophobia, 1418
ACT (test), 432
ACTH. *See* Adrenocorticotropic hormone
Activation-synthesis theory, 625
Activation theory of motivation, 1236
Active teaching methods, 1951
Active theories of speech perception, 1850
Activity theory of retirement, 1639
Actor-observer bias, 227, 1824
Acupuncture, 1336
Acute disconnection syndrome, 1855
Adams, Jerome, 1094
Adaptation, 500, 1733, 1827, 2000
Adaptive theory of sleep, 1799
Addiction, 473, 697-698, 958, 986, 991, 1041, 1043, 1189, 1928, 2032; nicotine, 1293-1295; personality and behaviors, 25-29, 1919
Addington v. Texas (1979), 14
ADEA. *See* Age Discrimination in Employment Act (1967)
Adenosine, 1292
ADHD. *See* Attention-deficit hyperactivity disorder
Adjustment; children to divorce, 1744; retirement, 1639
Adler, Alfred, 29-30, 996, 1488; aggression, 79; birth order, 297; coping, 500; Sigmund Freud, 803; Karen Horney, 1833; motivation, 64, 1236; self-actualization, 1707
Adler, Norman, 1759
Adlerian psychotherapy, 30-35
Adolescence, 59, 655, 662, 753, 1718, 1787; cognitive skills, 35-40, 393; cross-cultural patterns, 40-44; eating disorders, 153; gender differences, 2062; homelessness, 921; schizophrenia, 1673; sexuality, 44-48; stepfamilies, 1876
Adrenal gland, 49-52
Adrenaline. *See* Epinephrine
Adrenocorticotropic hormone, 49, 694, 786, 831, 930, 1429, 1891
Adulthood, 976; family issues, 752-755; sibling relationships, 1787; stages of, 662
Advance directives, 541
Advertising, 52-56, 1733, 1982; attitude-behavior consistency, 215, 480
Affiliation, 56-61; motive for, 61-65, 1861
African Americans, 66-69; hate crimes, 891; help-seeking, 906
Age Discrimination in Employment Act (1967), 72, 1638
Ageism, 69-74, 82, 1639
Aggression, 74-77, 462, 855, 987, 1019, 1130, 1187, 1215, 1289, 1431, 2018, 2020; children, 299; reduction and control, 77-81. *See also* Air rage; Bullying; Passive aggression; Road rage
Aging, 83, 88, 791, 932, 1207, 1821, 1921; cognition, 81-87; physical changes, 87-91, 542; theories, 91-95
Agnosia, 114, 1497
Agoraphobia, 96-100, 169, 241, 1343, 1418
Ahrons, Constance, 1741
AI. *See* Artificial intelligence
Aiken, Lewis, 1030, 1400
Ainsworth, Mary, 203, 1231
Air rage, 76, 100-102
Ajzen, Icek, 215
Akil, Huda, 1337
Alaskan Natives, 1271-1273
Albee, George W., 102-103
Alcohol dependence and abuse, 28, 75, 101, 103-107, 439, 697, 1635, 1918; codependency, 388; depression, 567; domestic violence, 616; gender differences, 818; prenatal development, 1466; suicide, 1923; taste aversion, 238, 1948; teenagers, 1961
Alcoholics Anonymous, 28, 105, 1927
Aldwin, Carolyn, 1886
Alexander, Charles, 1154
Alexander, Franz, 320, 878
Alexithymia, 1887
ALI rule, 12
Allport, Gordon, 107-109, 340, 947, 1585, 1619; prejudice, 998, 1453, 1457; religion, 1625; self, 1700; stereotypes, 1756
Altered states; consciousness, 469, 471-477; hallucinations, 887; hypnosis, 956

Alternate personalities, 1251
Altman, Irwin, 704-705, 1709
Altruism, 63, 109-114, 262, 713, 911
Altruistic suicide, 1920, 1957
Alzheimer, Alois, 115, 670
Alzheimer's disease, 71, 84, 114-119, 200, 315, 415, 560, 670, 791, 1164, 1173, 1285, 1935
Amabile, Teresa, 519
Amato, Paul R., 1745
Amatrude, Catherine, 842
Ambady, Nalini, 686
Ambivalence-induced behavior amplification, 1583
American Indians. *See* Native Americans
American Institute of Psychoanalysis, 1833
American Law Institute rule. *See* ALI rule
American Medico-Psychological Association. *See* American Psychiatric Association
American Psychiatric Association, 120-123; *Diagnostic and Statistical Manual of Mental Disorders*, 599; nutrition therapy, 1301
American Psychoanalytic Association, 1484
American Psychological Association, 123-126, 589; certification process, 1191
Americans with Disabilities Act (1990), 584, 2076, 2079
Ames, Carole, 651
Ames, Louise, 842
Ames, Russell, 651
Amir, Yehuda, 1458
Amnesia, 126-130, 1127, 1164, 1169, 1781; brain damage, 309; dissociative, 609; shock therapy, 1777
Amok, 20, 533
Amphetamine psychosis, 1683
Amygdala, 315, 768, 1496
Anal stage, 803, 1493, 1529, 2068
Analogy, 1472

Analytic language acquisition styles, 1079
Analytic psychology; Jacques Lacan, 130-134
Analytical psychology; Carl Jung, 134-138, 1056, 1488
Anastasi, Anne, 1025
Anch, A. Michael, 1017
Anderson, Lynn, 876
Androgyny, 924, 2061
Angell, James Rowland, 1907
Anger, 142-145; terminal illness, 506, 544; Type A behavior pattern, 1901
Anima archetype, 136, 178
Animal experimentation, 145-150, 698, 1100, 1285, 1630; memory, 1160-1165, 1171
Animal Welfare Act (1985), 149
Animals; behavior, 711; emotions, 684
Animus archetype, 136, 178
Anna O., 319, 352, 962, 972, 1489, 1546
Anomic suicide, 1921, 1957
Anorexia nervosa, 150-156, 366, 641, 719, 952, 1259; body dysmorphic disorder versus, 302
Anosodiaphoria, 564
Anosognosia, 308, 564
Anterograde amnesia, 1164, 1781
Anthony, Albert, 41
Antianxiety medications, 156-158, 634, 1527; generalized anxiety disorder, 837
Antidepressants, 158-159, 570, 633, 1221, 1526, 1935; attention-deficit hyperactivity disorder, 211; obsessive-compulsive disorder, 1320; pain management, 1341; panic disorder, 98, 1344; tricyclic, 51, 158, 633; women, 2056
Antipsychotics, 160-161, 635, 1196, 1525, 1562, 1935; body dysmorphic disorder, 303; hallucinations, 887; schizophrenia, 1673, 1683, 2057

Antisocial personality disorder, 161-166, 462, 917, 1387, 1661; sociopathy, 1843
Antonovsky, Aaron, 502
Anton's syndrome, 565
Antonucci, Toni, 1823
Anxiety, 553, 769, 1885; attention-deficit hyperactivity disorder, 211; avoidant personality disorder, 240; existential psychology, 723; Freudian psychology, 653, 802; guilt, 877; impulse control disorders, 985; measurement of, 1869; meditation and relaxation, 1153; modeling therapy, 1312; obsessive-compulsive disorder, 1318; systematic desensitization, 1939
Anxiety disorders, 8, 166-171, 425; caffeine induced, 332; children, 368, 373; drug therapy, 634; gender differences, 818; generalized, 835-837; personality traits, 1396; phobias, 1418; post-traumatic stress disorder, 1444
Anxiety sensitivity, 1396
Anxiety Sensitivity Index, 1396
Anxiolytic. *See* Antianxiety medications
Anzieu, Marguerite, 133
APA. *See* American Psychiatric Association; American Psychological Association
Apgar test, 293, 581
Aphasia, 114, 171-176, 307, 1857; conduction, 309; expressive, 171, 1498
Apperception, 1905, 1975
Applied behavior analysis, 233, 272, 460
Appraisal theory of emotions, 687
Apter, Michael J., 1331
Apter, Terri, 753
Aptitude tests, 340; interest inventories versus, 1033
Arachnophobia, 1418
Archetypes, 136, 176-180, 1055-1056, 1488

Armed Services Vocational Aptitude Battery, 341
Arnett, Jeffery J., 976
Aronson, Elliot, 407, 487, 1089
Arousal, 27, 164, 355, 1328, 1389, 1420, 1635, 1682, 2023; introversion and extroversion, 1048. *See also* Optimal arousal theory
Arousal cost-reward model of helping, 908
Arousal disorders, 1763
Arousal-reduction theory, 109
Articulation disorders, 1845
Artificial intelligence, 184-188, 416, 1473
Asch, Solomon, 1825
Aschoff, Jürgen, 377
Aserinsky, Eugene, 1801
Asher, Richard, 1254
Asian Americans, 188-191; adolescence, 41; help-seeking, 906
Asperger, Hans, 191, 1412
Asperger syndrome, 191-195, 365, 1411
Assessment, 195-198; behavioral, 254, 257-261, 595; coping strategies, 502; developmental disabilties, 581; giftedness, 848; learning disorders, 1109; mental competency, 995; newborns, 293; personality traits, 333, 1391, 1395, 1399, 1647, 1975; post-traumatic stress disorder, 1447; risk, 1641-1643; sociopathy, 1844
Assisted living, 198-201
Association of Medical Superintendents of American Institutions for the Insane. *See* American Psychiatric Association
Association theory, 1156
Association theory of concept formation, 454
Association theory of memory, 793
Athletes, eating disorders, 153, 641

Atkinson, John, 22, 1408
Atkinson, Richard, 689, 1178, 1181, 1779
Atmosphere hypothesis of reasoning, 1123
Attachment, 201-205, 717, 757, 1231; facial expressions, 679; schizophrenia, 1681; separation anxiety, 1749
Attachment disorders, 1601
Attachment theory, 1785
Attention, 205-209; automatic and controlled processes, 234; declines in, 1790; deficits in children of schizophrenics, 1677; misbehavior, 1216; narcissistic personality disorder, 1264
Attention-deficit hyperactivity disorder, 209-214, 366, 373; antisocial personality disorder, 162; drug therapy, 634; stimulants, 1878; Tourette's syndrome, 2005
Attitudes; adolescents toward sex, 47; ageism, 70; cognitive dissonance, 405; consistency with behavior, 214-217, 480; formation and change, 52, 218-222, 1722; jurors, 1090; media violence, 2021, 2023; religiosity, 1624; toward mental illness, 906
Attraction, 56, 1133; theories of, 222-226
Attribution; biases, 227-230, 1584, 1716, 1861; causal, 354-357, 1721, 1824
Attributional style questionnaire, 1097
Auditory model of speech perception, 1852
Auerbach, Stephen M., 1886
Ausubel, David, 652
Authoritarian style of parenting, 1351
Authoritative style of parenting, 1351
Authority, study of, 732, 1209, 1867

Autism, 230-234, 365, 1411; gender differences, 818; modeling therapy, 1311
Autism spectrum disorders, 191, 373, 1669, 2032
Automaticity, 234-237
Automaton conformist personality, 1829
Autonomic nervous system, 1608
Autonomy, functional, 947
Availability heuristic, 1584, 1824
Aversion, sexual, 1763
Aversion therapy, 238-239, 1070; fetishism, 776; paraphilias, 1773
Avoidant attachment, 204
Avoidant personality disorder, 239-241, 1387; schizoid personality disorder versus, 1668
Axel, Richard, 1809
Axline, Virginia, 1437
Azapirones, 157
Azjen, Icek, 480

Babbie, Earl, 1664
Back, Kurt, 58
Baddeley, Alan, 418, 689, 1156, 1181, 1779
Bahrick, H. P, 83
Bailey, Kent, 1887
Bairstow, Phillip, 1065
Bait shyness. *See* Taste aversions
Baker, Lester, 153
Baldwin, James Mark, 131
Baltes, Paul, 86
Baltimore Longitudinal Study of Aging, 90
Banaji, Mahzarin R., 83
Bandura, Albert, 242-243, 299, 400, 578, 1217, 1310, 1553, 1712, 1815; cognitive maps, 410; self, 1701
Bangert, Robert, 651
Barbiturates, 157, 634
Barclay, J. Richard, 1981
Bard, Philip, 686, 1897
Barker, Roger, 705
Baron, Robert J., 449
Baron-Cohen, Simon, 194

Bartlett, Frederic C., 478, 1157
Barton, Walter E., 122
Bass, Bernard, 1093
Bates, Elizabeth, 1082
Bateson, Gregory, 1681, 1880
Batson, C. Daniel, 110, 1625
Battered child syndrome, 361
Battered woman syndrome, 243-245, 615
Baumeister, Roy, 1701, 1841
Baumrind, Diana, 1351
BDD. *See* Body dysmorphic disorder
BDI. *See* Beck Depression Inventory
Beck, Aaron T., 98, 246-247, 397, 424; borderline personality disorder, 306; cognitive distortions, 569; depression, 1837, 1923
Beck Depression Inventory, 246-248, 369
Becker, Mark W., 1178
Bed-wetting, 248-252, 367, 675, 1800
Beecher, Henry K., 1433
Behavior, 420, 943, 998, 1815; animal, 711; antisocial, 461; attitudes, 214, 218; cognitive dissonance, 406; development, 577; endogenous, 558, 713, 1018; environment, 702; exogenous, 558; experimental design, 2050; gender differences, 824; groups, 875; health, 897; hormones, 928-933, 1430; maladaptive, 461, 1324; media violence, 2020; motivation, 989, 2073; religion, 1621; reticular formation, 1634; ritualized, 713, 720; rule-governed, 1589, 1650-1654. *See also* Misbehavior
Behavior modification, 255, 1324-1328; hunger regulation, 953; hypnosis, 958; impulse control disorders, 988; pain management, 1341
Behavior therapy, 252-257, 1521, 1552, 1557; anxiety, 168;

assessment of clients, 260; children, 1542; kleptomania, 1070; obesity, 1308
Behavioral economics, 261-265, 480, 550
Behavioral evidence analysis, 1476
Behavioral insomnia. *See* Persistent psychophysiological insomnia
Behavioral medicine, 1557
Behavioral neuroscience. *See* Psychobiology
Behavioral parent training, 765, 1543
Behavioral Science Unit (BSU), 1475
Behavioral taxonomy, 1314
Behaviorism, 18, 269-273, 713, 1314, 1505, 1514, 2046; aggression, 80; consciousness, 468, 472; emotional expression, 680; field theory versus, 783; instincts, 1019; learning, 651; motivation, 1235; S-R theory, 1657
Behaviorist theories of development, 578
Being-in-the-world, 722
Belenky, Mary Field, 394, 1703
Belief-bias effect, 1123
Bell Curve, The (Herrnstein and Murray), 4
Bellak, Leopold, 1478, 1976
Bem, Daryl, 1721
Bem, Sandra, 825, 1354
Benedict, Ruth, 1706
Benedikt, Moritz, 99
Bennett, A. E., 106
Bennett, Susan, 891
Benson, Herbert, 475, 1897
Benzer, Seymour, 378
Benzodiazepines, 157, 634, 1527
Bereavement, 861
Berger, Hans, 309
Berkman, Lisa, 1820
Berkowitz, Leonard, 78, 2020
Berlin, Rudolph, 636
Berlyne, D. E., 1329
Berman, Jeffrey, 1544

Bernard, Claude, 833, 951
Berne, Eric, 869, 2007
Bernestein, Ilene, 1947
Berscheid, Ellen, 1133
Bertalanffy, Ludwig von, 759
Berthold, Arnold Adolphe, 691
Bertillon, Jacques, 1038
Bettman, James R., 479
Bias, 530; actor-observer, 1824; attribution, 227-230, 1716, 1861; confirmation, 1123; decision making, 549; diagnostic criteria and, 1198; gender differences, 2062; in-group, 1812; intelligence tests, 1580; jurors, 1089; mental health practitioners, 817, 1454; research, 778, 1035, 1314, 1930
Biederman, Irving, 1361
Big Five system of personality, 1048, 1386, 1401, 1404
Bilingualism, 273-276; learning disabilities, 276-278
Binet, Alfred, 1, 278-279, 514, 1027, 1029, 1515, 1865, 1971; sexual fetishism, 776
Binet-Simon test, 1022, 1027, 1029
Binge eating disorder, 152, 643, 951, 1307
Bini, Lucino, 1775
Binswanger, Ludwig, 722
Biofeedback, 279-283, 469, 476; pain management, 1340; stress relief, 747, 832, 1153, 1897
Biogenic approach to psychopathology, 1519
Biopsychiatry, 6
Biopsychology. *See* Psychobiology
Biopsychosocial approach to psychopathology, 1520
Biopsychosocial model of health, 896, 1198, 1533
Bipolar disorder, 50, 283-288, 1072, 1223, 1560; children, 368, 374; depression, 568; drug therapy, 634; elderly, 672; homelessness, 919; impulse control disorders, 985; women, 2057; workplace, 2080

Biracial heritage, 288-290

Birdwhistell, Ray, 1295

Birth, effects on physical development, 290-295

Birth order, 848, 1786; personality, 35, 295-298, 997

Bisexuals, 813-817

Blacks. *See* African Americans

Blackwell, Arshavir, 1082

Blain, Daniel, 122

Blau, Theodore H., 298-299

Blehar, Mary, 1697

Bleuler, Eugen, 1668, 1683

Blindness, 2044; somatoform disorders, 964

Bloch, Vincent, 1636

Bloom, Benjamin, 847

Bloomfield, Leonard, 860

Blume, Sheila, 987

Blumenthal, David R., 911

BMI. *See* Body mass index

Boas, Franz, 777, 1581

Bobo doll experiment, 299-301, 587, 1311, 1816

Body dysmorphic disorder, 301-304, 720, 1306

Body image, 151, 771, 1145, 1306

Body language. *See* Nonverbal communication

Body mass index, 1304

Bogardus, Emory, 1585

Bogen, Joe, 317

Bolles, Richard N., 348, 1036

Bonding, 201-205, 291, 981

Boole, George, 1124

Borderline personality disorder, 304-306, 602, 917, 1387; children, 374

Boring, Edwin, 1022

Bornstein, Marcy, 511

Bornstein, Philip, 511

Boroditsky, Lera, 1082

Borson, Soo, 1947

Bosard, James H. S., 874

Boscolo, Luigi, 1881

Boss, Medard, 722

Bottom-up theories of speech perception, 1850

Boundaries, 760, 1040, 1045

Bourgondien, Mary Van, 233

Bowen, Murray, 759

Bower, Gordon, 689

Bowlby, John, 201, 862, 1231, 1785

Boyce, Philip, 1695

Boyd-Franklin, Nancy, 761

BPD. *See* Borderline personality disorder

Braid, James, 959

Brain; adolescence and, 37; aging and, 83

Brain chemistry, 16; attachment, 1233; drugs, 632; hunger, 951; kleptomania, 1069; pain, 1335; stress, 1890

Brain damage, 306-311, 1284; aphasia, 171; dementia, 559; dyslexia, 637; memory, 791, 1158, 1169, 1183; pattern recognition, 1362; schizophrenia, 1682-1683

Brain structure, 312-318, 448, 1496; aggression, 75; animal experience, 147; euphoria, 1918; gender differences, 826, 856, 923; gender identity, 194; language, 1081; memory, 1127, 1161, 1167; prosocial behavior, 112; stuttering, 1912; Tourette's syndrome, 2005

Brandon, Ruth, 740

Branscombe, Nyla, 1861

Bransford, D., 1981

Bransford, John, 1470

Braswell, Lauren, 212

Bray, James H., 1876

Brazelton Neonatal Behavior Assessment Scale, 293, 1612

Breathing reflex, 1611

Breland, Keller, 460, 1019

Breland, Marian, 460, 1019

Brentano, Franz Clemens, 1513

Breuer, Josef, 318-320, 352, 962, 1489, 1546; hysteria, 972

Brickman, Philip, 909

Brief psychotic disorder, 1560

Brief therapy, 320-321

Briggs, Isabel Myers, 1262

Brightness and contrast, perception of, 2034-2037

Briquet syndrome, 961

British Association of Medical Officers of Lunatic Asylums. *See* Royal Society of Psychiatrists

Broadbent, Donald, 206, 1178

Broca, Paul, 174, 307, 316, 1286, 1511, 1855

Broca's aphasia. *See* Aphasia

Brody, Gene, 1788

Bronfenbrenner, Urie, 83, 322-323, 1578

Brooks, Rodney, 187

Brooks-Gunn, Jeanne, 1701

Broverman, Inge, 817, 1754

Brower, Lincoln, 1947

Browman, Carl P., 1017

Brown, Barbara B., 705

Brown, Paul K., 2040

Brown, Roger, 1182

Brown, Rupert, 1458

Brown, Ryan P., 798

Brown, Stephanie, 1841

Browne, Angela, 243

Brumberg, Joan, 153

Bruner, Jerome, 323, 652, 1362, 1703, 1826

Bruning, Roger, 519

Brunswik, Egon, 705

Brussels, James, 1474

Bryan, James, 1311

Buck, Linda, 1809

Bulimia nervosa, 20, 150-156, 366, 642, 720; culture, 534

Bullying, 324-326; online, 1144

Bundey, Sarah, 1201

Buranen, Cheryl, 965

Burckhardt, Gottlieb, 1119

Burkhauser, Richard V., 1640

Burt, Cyril, 1024, 1579

Butler, Charles, 449

Butler, Robert, 69

Buxbaum, Edith, 41

Buys, Christian, 876

By-product model of homosexuality, 923

Byrne, Donn, 222, 1453

Bystander intervention, 112, 326-330, 527, 967, 1887

Cacioppo, John, 219
Caffeine, 331-332, 1466, 1993
California Psychological Inventory, 333-334, 341
Calkins, Mary W., 108, 1514
Calpain-Fodrin theory, 1171
Cameron, Judy, 1101
Campbell, D. T., 341
Campbell, David P., 1036
Canady, Herman, 1581
Cancer, 94, 335-338, 493, 565; taste aversions, 1947; Type C personality, 1534
Canevello, Amy, 1841
Cannon, Walter Bradford, 338-339, 686, 785, 833, 1897, 1899; dry mouth hypothesis, 1977
Cannon-Bard theory, 686
Canter, David, 1476
Caplan, Jeremy, 393
Caplan, Paula, 393
Carbamazepine, 1227
Cardon, Lon R., 1108
Career; selection, development, and change, 346-350, 1031, 1033, 1035, 1074; testing, 339-344
Career Occupational Preference System, 344-346
Caretaking, 389, 1600
Carlsmith, J. M., 406
Carlson, Michael, 909
Carnahan, Thomas, 1868
Carr, Harvey A., 1907
Carskadon, Mary, 1268
Carson, G., 1857
Cartensen, Laura, 1823
Caruso, David R., 682
Carver, Charles S., 493, 502, 898
Case study methodology, 351-353, 1489, 1568, 1694, 1971; hypothesis testing, 969; psychotherapy, 1546
Casey, Rita, 1544
Castner, Burton, 842
Castration anxiety, 2068
Cataplexy, 1267
Catatonic schizophrenia, 1672
Catecholamines, 50, 1171
Catharsis, 963, 2022

Catholic Psychological Association, 1622
Cattell, James McKeen, 1513, 1908, 1972
Cattell, Raymond B., 3, 342, 1030, 1400
Caudill, Maureen, 449
Cause-effect relationships, 734
CDI. See Children's Depression Inventory
Cecchin, Gianfranco, 1881
Ceci, S. J., 83
Cell phones, excessive use, 1144
Cellular dehydration thirst, 1977
Center for Mental Health Services, 1914
Center for Substance Abuse Prevention, 1914
Center for Substance Abuse Treatment, 1914
Central motive state, 630
Central nervous system, 312, 1278; reflexes, 1611; reticular formation, 1634; stress, 1890; thirst, 1977
Central tendency, measures of, 536
Cerebellum, 313; memory storage, 1064
Cerebral cortex, 307, 312, 1497
Cerletti, Ugo, 1172, 1775
Cerney, Mary, 1479
Chace, Marian, 1260
Chaffin, Roger, 393
Chaikin, Alan, 1711
Chambless, Dianne, 98
Change, stages of, 2011
Character neurosis, 1290
Charcot, Jean-Martin, 17, 514, 916, 972
Charlin, Ventura, 909
Charpentier, Paul, 632
Chastenet, Armand-Marie Jacques. See Puységur, marquis de
Chemers, Martin, 1095
Chemoreceptors, 1805, 2002
Cherry, Colin, 207
Chesler, Phyllis, 772

Chicago school of functionalism, 1907
Child abuse, 358-363; dissociative disorders, 128, 1251; juvenile delinquency, 1061; Munchausen syndrome by proxy, 752, 1255; repressed memories, 1629; stepfamilies, 1876
Child Abuse Prevention and Treatment Act (1974), 358
Child archetype, 179
Childhood disintegrative disorder, 366, 1414
Childhood disorders, 363-369; recognizing, 372
Children, 371-376; aggression, 299; attention-deficit hyperactivity disorder, 210; birth order, 295; cognitive ability, 393, 523; defense mechanisms, 655; development, 576, 803, 842, 1613; family issues, 756-758; gender identity disorder, 822; gender roles, 829, 1755; grieving, 862; homelessness, 921; homosexuality, 924; hunger, 951; learned helplessness, 1098; lying, 546; media exposure, 1142, 2021; obesity, 1305; parenting styles, 1352; personality development, 1492; play therapy, 1435; psychotherapy, 1484, 1541-1546; schizophrenia, 1673, 1675-1680; seasonal affective disorder, 1697; self-perception theory, 1722; sibling relationships, 1786; stepfamilies, 1876; taste aversions, 1946; tic disorders, 1992; Tourette's syndrome, 2003; violence, 2024-2027. See also Juvenile delinquency
Children's Depression Inventory, 369-371
Children's Manifest Anxiety Scale, 259

Chinese room, 186

Chodoff, Paul, 916

Chodorow, Nancy, 1702, 2060

Choice shift, 865

Chomsky, Noam, 418, 858, 1080, 1112

Christian Association for Psychological Studies, 1621

Chronic illness; coping, 490-495; health psychology, 896

Chronotherapy, 1016

Cialdini, Robert, 109, 1727, 1861

Cicirelli, Victor, 1786

Circadian rhythms, 286, 376-381, 473; genetics, 841; hormones, 930; insomnia, 1014; seasonal affective disorder, 1695; sleep, 1796; temperature, 1966

Circle theory of offender behavior, 1476

Civil Rights Act (1964), 343

Civil Rights Act (1991), 835

Clark, David, 98

Clark, Kenneth, 1453, 1812

Clark, Mamie, 1453, 1813

Clark, Russell, 908

Classical conditioning. See Conditioning, classical

Claustrophobia, 1418

Cleckley, Hervey, 163, 1842

Client-centered therapy. See Person-centered therapy

Clinchy, Blythe McVicker, 394

Clinical psychology, 1191, 1506, 1515; interviewing, 1930; George A. Kelly, 1063; origin of, 1509; research, 730

Clock genes, 381

Cloninger, C. Robert, 918

Clore, Gerald, 222

Clozapine, 160

Clozaril. See Clozapine

CMHS. See Center for Mental Health Services

Coaching, 385-388, 1859

Cobb, Sidney, 495

Cocktail party phenomenon, 207

Codependency, 388-390

Co-Dependents Anonymous, 390

Coe, W. C., 956

CogAT. See Cognitive Abilities Test

Cognition, 81, 703, 1230, 1234, 1339, 1519, 1677; restructuring, 256

Cognitive Abilities Test, 391-392

Cognitive ability, 1028; gender differences, 392-396

Cognitive behavior therapy, 256, 396-401; anorexia and bulimia, 154; attention-deficit hyperactivity disorder, 211; body dysmorphic disorder, 303; borderline personality disorder, 306; children, 1543; eating disorders, 643; generalized anxiety disorder, 837; obesity, 1308; pain management, 1341; panic attacks, 1345; separation anxiety, 1749

Cognitive development; adolescence and, 37

Cognitive development theory, 578, 1427; gender identity, 824; language, 1081; Jean Piaget, 401-405

Cognitive dissonance, 219, 405-408, 805, 1237, 1724, 1728

Cognitive distortions, 19, 569

Cognitive impairment, mild, 85

Cognitive maps, 409-413, 415

Cognitive model of panic disorders, 98

Cognitive models of motivation, 2073

Cognitive motivation theory, 410, 1237

Cognitive personality theory, 1403

Cognitive priming theory, 2023

Cognitive psychology, 19, 229, 414-419, 652, 689, 945, 1112, 1157, 1506, 1533, 1984; addiction, 26; logic and reasoning, 1121; origin of, 1509

Cognitive response approach to persuasion, 218

Cognitive science, 184

Cognitive social learning, 420-423

Cognitive stage theory, 36, 40

Cognitive therapy, 397, 423-427, 1521, 1595; anxiety, 169; children, 1543; depression, 570; phobias, 1422

Cohen, Louis, 1089

Cohen, Sheldon, 1820, 1841, 1887

Cohesive family model, 464

Collective unconscious, 135, 139, 176-180, 1055-1056, 1488

Collectivism, 427-430, 523, 686, 1714

Collett-Lester Scale, 505

Collins, Nancy, 1840

Color; perception, 1734, 2038-2041; synesthesia, 1937

Color blindness, 2039, 2044

Columbia school of functionalism, 1908

Commission on Obscenity and Pornography of 1970, 2022

Commitment, 753, 1132

Commitment, civil, 12

Common-enemy strategy, 1460

Communication, 509, 1333, 1435, 1709, 1880, 1982; speech disorders, 173, 364, 1845

Community Mental Health Act (1963), 437, 1199, 1270

Community psychology, 434-438

Comorbidity, 439-442, 596; bipolar disorder, 285; borderline personality disorder, 304; homeless mentally ill, 919; personality disorders, 1388; schizoid personality disorder, 1668

Comparative psychology, 1507

Compensation, after brain damage, 310

Compensatory model of helping, 910

Competence, 420, 1025, 1235; communicative, 275

Competency, mental, 11, 730, 788, 993-996, 1012; confidentiality, 466; death, 541

Competition, 483-487, 555, 1787; relationships, 110

Compulsions, 27, 383, 1318, 1518; computer use, 447

Computers; artificial intelligence, 184; cognition, 415, 448-451, 1125; concept formation, 454; effect on users, 1144; Internet, 446-448; interviewing, 1392; memory, 1065, 1129, 1173; pattern recognition, 1365; problem solving, 1473; research, 182; simulations, 185; testing, 1032, 1974; virtual reality, 2030

Comrey, Andrew, 1400

Concept formation, 451-455

Concrete operational stage, 36, 402, 578, 1427

Conditioned response, 456, 1102, 1368

Conditioned stimulus, 456, 1102, 1368, 1945

Conditioned suppression, 456

Conditioning, classical, 18, 55, 238, 455-461, 1367-1373, 1614; ethology, 713; fetishism, 776; instincts, 1020; language acquisition, 1079; learning, 265, 1101; memory, 1160; motivation, 1235, 1239; phobias, 1419; psychopathology, 1518; reflexes, 269, 1608; substance use disorders, 1917; taste aversion, 1945

Conditioning, operant, 18, 265, 270, 455-461; ethology, 713; language acquisition, 1079; learning, 1102; memory, 1160; substance use disorders, 1917; taste aversion, 1945; therapies, 1324

Conduct disorder, 162, 366, 461-465, 1387, 1542

Confession, 139

Confidentiality, 465-467, 729, 1484, 1630

Conflict, 17, 228, 509, 653, 783, 805, 1741

Conformity, 62, 498, 527; affiliation, 58; discrimination, 1584

Confrontation, in reality therapy, 1603

Congruence, 1378

Connectionism, 186, 1513

Conscience, 877, 879

Consciousness, 467-471, 726, 1905; altered states, 471-477; brain damage, 308; humanistic psychology, 943; William James, 1050; nature of, 1416; transcendental, 1153

Consequences, 1310, 1587

Constructivist psychology, 477-479

Consumer psychology, 479-482, 1507

Contact hypothesis of prejudice reduction, 1458, 1586

Contextualist worldview, 591, 705

Contingency of reinforcement, 1588, 1651

Contingency theory, 1093

Continuous positive airway pressure therapy, 1803

Continuous theory of development, 578

Control; aversive, 1103; disaster psychology, 605; domestic violence, 614; field experimentation, 778; jealousy, 1051; leadership, 1093; learned helplessness, 1098; parenting styles, 1351; perception of, 898. See also Locus of control

Control groups, 734, 1631, 1689

Conture, Edward G., 1910

Conversion, religious, 1618

Conversion disorders, 960-965, 1340, 1536

Conversion therapy, 816

Cooley, Charles, 1703

Cooper, Joel, 1825

Cooperation, 109-114, 483-487, 1787

Cooperative learning, 487-490

Cooperative teaching methods, 1952

Coping; cancer, 336; caregivers, 337; chronic illness, 490-495; depression, 569; disaster psychology, 605; domestic violence, 615; help-seeking versus, 906; self-efficacy, 1714; social support, 495-499; strategies, 280, 500-504, 1832; stress, 1886, 1889; terminal illness, 504-508; trauma, 1446

Coping Orientations to Problems Experienced, 502

Coprolalia, 1993, 2003

Copropraxia, 2004

COPS. See Career Occupational Preference System

Cornblatt, Barbara, 1679

Corollary discharge theory, 575

Correlational studies, 727, 733, 1573, 1691

Cortisol, 49, 1891

Costa, P. T., Jr., 1401

Costa, R. R., 1048

Counterconditioning model of phobias, 1421

Coupe, Patty, 412

Couples therapy, 508-514, 1741; behavioral, 256; domestic violence, 244, 616; reality therapy, 1604

Cousins, Norman, 1896

Cowen, Emory, 437

Coyne, James, 569

CPAP therapy. See Continuous positive airway pressure therapy

CPI. See California Psychological Inventory

Craik, Fergus, 1127, 1181

Crawford, Mary, 393

Creativity, 514-517; assessment, 517-520; birth order, 296; intelligence, 847, 1025; learning, 1105; training, 1953

Crespi, Leo P., 990

Crespi effect, 990

Criminal behavior, 701, 1474; antisocial personality disorder,

162; children and teenagers, 1060, 2024; comorbidity, 441; conduct disorder, 462; hate crimes, 890; rape and sexual assault, 1592; risk assessment, 789, 1641

Criminal psychology, 1506

Crisis intervention, 520-522

Crisis theory of illness, 492

Critical period; brain injury recovery, 1286; imprinting, 980; language acquisition, 859, 1080; physical development, 1424

Crocker, Jennifer, 1459, 1841

Cronbach, Lee, 5

Cross-categorization, 1460

Cross-cultural psychiatry, 532

Cross-cultural psychology, 523-524

Cross-dressing. See Transvestism

Cross-sectional research designs, 586, 591

Crowd behavior, 525-529

Crowder, Robert G, 83

Crying reflex, 1612

Crystallized intelligence, 3, 86, 1028, 1030

CSAP. See Center for Substance Abuse Prevention

CSAT. See Center for Substance Abuse Treatment

Csikszentmihalyi, Mihaly, 518, 1440

Cults, 1619

Cultural competence, 190, 429, 529-530, 1272

Cultural-historical theory of development, 652

Culture; attachment behavior, 204; body dysmorphic disorder, 302; causal attribution, 356; collectivism, 428; diagnosis, 20, 531-532, 597, 601, 1520; eating disorders, 641; emotional expression, 678, 685, 745; family therapy, 761; father-child relationship, 764; gender identity disorder, 822;

grieving, 863; help-seeking, 906; histrionic personality disorder, 917; homosexuality, 814; hunger, 952; intelligence, 4; jealousy, 1052; mental illness and, 1198; midlife crisis, 1207; nonverbal communication, 1297; organizational behavior, 1333; pain, 1339; self, 1702, 1714; terrorism, 1970; transvestism, 2014; women's psychology, 1376, 2064

Culture-bound syndromes, 20, 531-534, 1520

Curtis, Rebecca, 1825

Custer, Robert, 985

Cyberbullying. See Bullying

Cyclothymic disorder, 284, 1223

Cytowic, Richard, 1937

D-sleep, 624, 1798

DaCosta, Jacob, 99

Dagleish, Tim, 684

Damasio, Antonio, 684, 1702

Dance therapy, 1257-1261

Darley, John, 86, 326, 527, 967

Darwin, Charles, 678, 683, 767, 1018, 1512, 1581; emotional expression, 745; ethology, 712; nonverbal communication, 1296; sexual selection, 1758

Data; archival, 180-183; collection, 733, 778, 1929; description, 535-540

Davidson-Podgorny, Gaye, 1458

Davies, Christie, 740

Davis, Clara, 1946

Davis, Elizabeth, 1381

Davis, Gary, 519

Davis, James H., 865

Davis, Keith, 1824

Davis, Martha, 78

Dawis, René, 340

Dawkins, Richard, 65

Dawson, Geraldine, 233

Dax, Marc, 1857

Daydreams, 623

DBT. See Dialectical behavioral therapy

Death, 92, 541-545; attitudes toward, 94, 504, 663; existential psychology, 723; grieving, 862

Deaux, Kay, 1754

DeBono, Edward, 1953

Deception, 545-547; use in experiments, 729, 1631

Decision making, 547-551, 1790, 2073; arousal, 1330; cognitive dissonance, 407; cognitive psychology, 417; competency, 994; consumer psychology, 479; emotions, 684; groups, 864-868; juries, 1089; obsessive-compulsive disorder, 1318; power, 1451

Declarative memory, 1499

Deductive reasoning, 37, 551-552, 1001, 1121, 1981

Defense mechanisms, 17, 500, 552-554, 802, 1492; coping, 492; denial, 564; ego, 652-658; projection, 1478

Defense reactions; species-specific, 555-559

Defining Issues Test, 2061

DeFries, John C., 1108

Deindividuation, 526, 876

Delayed sleep phase syndrome, 378

Delirium, 559, 672, 889

Delirium tremens, 103

Delk, John, 2037

DeLoache, Judy, 412

Delphi techniques, 866

Delusional disorder. See Paranoia

Delusions, 383, 887, 1197, 1559; obsessions versus, 1318; schizophrenia, 1671

Demaree, Robert G., 1401

Dement, William, 1801

Dementia, 559-563, 670; Alzheimer's disease, 117; assisted living, 200; forgetting, 791; music therapy, 1259; Parkinson's disease, 1355; psychosis, 1562

Dementia praecox. See Schizophrenia

Denial, 492, 553, 563-566, 657; terminal illness, 506, 543, 861

Density, 701, 703, 875

Depakote. *See* Valproic acid

Dependent personality disorder, 917, 1387

De Perczel, Maria, 1923

Depersonalization disorder, 127, 610

Depression, 566-572, 1197, 1219, 1519; agoraphobia, 97; Asian Americans and Pacific Islanders, 190; attention-deficit hyperactivity disorder, 211; Aaron T. Beck, 246-247, 1837; bipolar disorder versus, 285; brain structure, 316; causes, 7, 51, 229, 1010, 1535; children, 360, 367, 369, 374; cognition, 82; cognitive behavior therapy, 400; cognitive therapy, 424; dementia versus, 559; drug therapy, 158, 633; elderly, 673; gender differences, 818; Latinos, 1087; learned helplessness, 1097, 1104; men, 1187; Native Americans and Alaskan Natives, 1272; obesity, 1307; pain, 1336, 1340; panic disorder, 97; Parkinson's disease, 1356; personality traits, 1396; seasonal affective disorder, 1695; sexual dysfunction, 1763; shock therapy, 1776; stress, 1887; teenagers, 1955, 1960; terminal illness, 506, 544; women, 774, 2054; workplace, 2080. *See also* Postpartum depression

Derlega, Valerian, 1711

Descartes, René, 1496

Destructive personality, 1828

Detterman, Douglas, 1023

Deutsch, Diana, 206

Deutsch, J. Anthony, 206

Deutsch, Morton, 483

Development, 576-580; career, 347; children, 803, 842, 848, 1435, 1613; language, 1078; linguistics, 1112; parenting styles, 1351; personality, 136, 139; psychoanalysis, 1483; schizophrenia, 1675; stepfamilies, 1875

Development, moral. *See* Moral development

Development, motor. *See* Motor development

Developmental coordination disorder, 1066

Developmental disabilities, 580-584

Developmental Disabilities Act (1984), 583

Developmental Disabilities Assistance and Bill of Rights Act (1990), 580

Developmental Disabilities Services and Facilities Construction Act (1970), 580

Developmental disorders, 1424, 1601; pervasive, 1410-1414

Developmental methodologies, 585-589

Developmental psychology, 589-593, 1506, 1516

Devine, Patricia, 1460

DeVito, Joseph, 1296

Dewey, John, 593-594, 651, 1469, 1513, 1907, 1950

Dhat, 533

Diagnosis, 384, 594-598; constructivist psychology, 478; culture, 531-532; feminist psychotherapy, 773; paraphilias, 1773

Diagnostic and Statistical Manual of Mental Disorders, 531, 595, 599-601

Dialect theory of emotional expressions, 686

Dialectical behavioral therapy, 305, 602-604, 1389

Diathesis-stress model, 21, 285, 305, 1520, 1562, 1681

Dickson, William, 2075

DiClemente, Carlo, 2011

Diener, Ed, 875

Dieting, 151, 641, 953, 958, 1308

Differences model of mental health, 66, 1086

Differential psychology, 1756

Dilthey, Wilhelm, 1502

Disaster psychology, 604-609, 700, 1149, 1444

Disaster Relief Act (1974), 605

Disavowal. *See* Denial

DISC1, 840

Discontinuous theory of development, 578

Discovery learning, 652

Discriminative stimuli, 1588

Discriminative stimulus, 1651

Disease; coping, 492; learned helplessness, 1099; lifestyle, 896; psychiatric symptoms, 7; stress related, 832, 1532, 1888, 1894-1898, 1900; thirst, 1978; Type A behavior pattern, 2015

Disease model of mental disorders, 1195

Disengagement theory of retirement, 1639

Disorganized schizophrenia, 1672

Displacement, 17, 553

Dispositions, types of, 947

Dissociative disorders, 18, 127, 609-612, 972; children, 368

Dissociative fugue, 127

Dissociative identity disorder, 127, 1250-1253, 1562; schizophrenia versus, 1670

Distancing, 426, 506

Distractor recall, 1166

Divorce, 508; adult issues, 1740-1743; children's issues, 1743-1747; men, 1138; parental alienation syndrome, 1349; stepfamilies, 1875

Divorce-stress-adjustment model, 1745

Dix, Dorothea, 613-614, 1195, 1556

Dobelle, William H., 2040

Doise, Willem, 1460

Dollard, John, 78, 1210-1211, 1235, 1655

Dombrowski, Stefan, 1465

Domestic violence, 243, 614-618, 921, 1053, 1098, 1592, 2028
Dominance, 62, 555-556, 1298, 1758
Donders, Frans C., 1985
Dopamine, 50, 633, 809, 991, 1010, 1163, 1280, 1292, 1527; nicotine, 1294; Parkinson's disease, 1357; schizophrenia, 1682-1683
Double-bind theory of schizophrenia, 1681, 1880
Douglas, John, 1594
Dovidio, John, 908
Down, John Langdon, 619, 1202
Down, Reginald, 620
Down syndrome, 579, 619-623, 839, 1201
Downing, Leslie, 528
Dowrick, Peter, 1312
Drabman, Ronald, 1996
Drapetomia, 67
Dreams, 623-627, 1798, 1833; Adlerian psychology, 31; Freudian psychology, 656, 801, 1485, 1493, 2070; Gestalt psychology, 844; Jungian psychology, 137, 140, 176
Dreikurs, Rudolf, 32, 1213
Drive theories, 1977, 2022
Drives, 628-631, 950, 1977; S-R theory, 1655
Drozdovitch, V., 1201
Drug therapy, 631-636; alcohol dependence, 106; bipolar disorder, 287, 1526, 2058; depression, 158, 1526; psychosis, 160, 1196; versus cognitive therapy, 426
DSM. *See Diagnostic and Statistical Manual of Mental Disorders*
DSPS. *See* Delayed sleep phase syndrome
DTB. *See* Dialectical behavioral therapy
Dual code theory, 411
Dual-mode processing models, 219
Dual-task methodology, 236
Dualism, 593, 1416, 1496, 1699

Dubois, Rachel, 1458
Duke Longitudinal Studies, 90
Dunbar, Flanders, 1532
Duncker, Karl, 1470, 1472
Dunn, Judy, 1787
Dunn, Lloyd M., 1373
Durham test, 12, 1012
Durkheim, Émile, 181, 1820, 1920, 1957
Durkin, M. S., 1202
Dutton, Donald, 243
Duty to protect, 466
Duty to warn, 466
Duvall, Evelyn Millis, 756
Dweck, Carol, 22
Dying, 541-545; stages of, 335, 505, 863, 1073
Dynamic play therapy, 1259
Dynamic psychology, 1908
Dynamic system models of language, 1083
Dynorphins, 695
Dyscalculia, 1108
Dysgraphia, 1108
Dyslexia, 636-639, 1065, 1108, 1857
Dyspareunia, 1765
Dyssocial psychopathy, 163
Dysthymic disorder, 285, 1222
D'Zurilla, Thomas, 398

Earls, F., 906
Easterbrook, J. A., 1330
Eating disorders, 150, 640-645, 953; children, 366, 374; gender differences, 818; virtual reality, 2032
Ebbinghaus, Hermann, 645-646, 791, 1126, 1168, 1180, 1781, 2053
Ebbinghaus forgetting curve, 1986
Eccles, John, 1702
Echoic memory, 1176
Echolalia, 232, 2003
École Freudienne de Paris, 134
Ecological model of child abuse, 361
Ecological psychology, 322, 646-649, 705

Ecotherapy, 647
Education, 140, 403, 453, 488, 1239, 1735, 2082; Dorothea Dix, 613; drilling, 236; gender roles, 829; gifted children, 849; humanistic psychology, 945; multiple intelligences, 1249; prejudice, 1455; teaching methods, 1949; virtual reality, 2033
Education for All Handicapped Children Act (1975), 584, 1108
Education of the Handicapped Act Amendments (1986), 584
Educational psychology, 323, 588, 649-652, 1506
Effect, law of, 265, 457, 1101, 1587, 1614, 1980
Efran, Michael, 1089
Egas Moniz, António, 307, 1119, 1538
Ego, 17, 629, 664-666, 802, 1492; analytical psychology, 135, 139
Ego psychology, 658-664, 666, 1485, 1515
Egocentrism, 38, 402
Egoistic suicide, 1920, 1957
Ehrenfels, Christian von, 1513
Ehrenreich, Barbara, 1137
Eidetic memory. *See* Photographic memory
Eisenberger, Robert, 1101
Ekman, Paul, 685, 1296
Elaborative rehearsal, 1126, 1779
Elder abuse, 666-669
Elderly, 200, 667, 669-674, 898, 998; psychosocial development, 663, 754
Electra complex, 877, 1529
Electrical stimulation, 1336
Electroconvulsive therapy. *See* Shock therapy
Electromyography, 1341
Elfenbein, Hilary, 686
Eliason, Grafton, 505
Elimination disorders, 367, 375, 674-676
Elkind, David, 38
Ellenberger, Henri, 1558
Elliott, Jane, 1453

Ellis, Albert, 397, 411, 676-677, 1595, 1621, 1833
Ellis, Henry, 1177
Ellis, Thomas, 1923
Elucidation, 139
EMDR. *See* Eye movement desensitization and reprocessing
Emergent systems, 1702
Emotion-focused coping strategy, 492, 501
Emotional Competence Inventory, 682
Emotional expression, 677-681, 745, 1257, 1296
Emotional instability, 305
Emotional intelligence, 681-683
Emotional support, 1351, 1839
Emotions, 683-687, 716; advertising, 54; arousal, 1330; attachment, 202; cancer, 335; disaster psychology, 605; Freudian psychology, 1493; habituation, 883; intimacy, 1044; memory, 689, 1158; physiology, 1395; social networks, 1823; stress, 832, 1885, 1899; teenagers, 1956; women, 773
Empathy, 109-114, 1380, 1553; projection versus, 1478
Empathy-altruism hypothesis, 110
Employees, 1239, 2074, 2082; training and development, 938-942, 1005
Empty-chair technique, 844
Encoding, 415, 420, 687-690, 739, 792, 1127
Encoding specificity theory, 688
Encopresis, 674
Endocannabinoids, 1292
Endocrine system, 690-695, 929, 1277, 1429
Endorphins, 695-699, 719, 1279, 1891, 1897, 1935
Engineering psychology, 1506
Enkephalins, 695, 1279
Enlightenment model of helping, 910

Entitlement, 1264
Enuresis. *See* Bed-wetting
Environment, 699-702; aggression, 78; antisocial personality disorder, 164; attraction, 222; behavior, 18; child abuse, 360; cognition in elderly, 83; conduct disorder, 463; development, 581, 591, 1423, 1465; intelligence, 2, 1025, 1027, 1578; mental retardation, 1202; obesity, 1307; panic disorder, 98; Parkinson's disease, 1357; personality, 1395; stress, 1892; violence by children and teenagers, 2024
Environmental psychology, 647, 701-707, 1507, 1738
Environmental toxicology, 707-710
Epidemiologic Catchment Area program, 67
Epilepsy, narcolepsy versus, 1267
Epinephrine, 50, 143, 1292, 1294, 2017
Episodic memory, 415, 1127, 1156, 1166, 1180, 1499, 1985
Epstein, Seymour, 1888
Equipotentiality, 85, 307, 1162, 1948
Equity theory, 223
Erikson, Erik H., 40, 176, 659, 710, 752, 974, 1375, 1488, 1515; guilt, 879; personality disorders, 1389; self, 1700
Erlenmeyer-Kimling, L., 1676
Eros, 64, 665, 1487
Erotomanic delusional disorder, 1348
Ervin, Frank, 1948
Escape from freedom, 1828
Esdaile, James, 957
ESP. *See* Extrasensory perception
Esquirol, Jean-Étienne-Dominique, 1029
Estradiol, 853, 1750
Estrogen, 116, 1750
Estrous cycle, 1750, 1759
Ethic of care, 2060

Ethics, 183, 466, 1006, 1973; animal experimentation, 146; experimentation, 728-732, 1209, 1689; media psychology, 1147; research, 592, 1630-1634
Ethnicity, 529; Alzheimer's disease, 115; cooperative learning, 489; domestic violence, 616; help-seeking, 906; obesity, 1305; Parkinson's disease, 1357; testing, 4, 23, 433; Tourette's syndrome, 1994
Ethological theory of attachment, 1231
Ethology, 711-715, 881
Eugenics, 67, 1581
Euphoria, 1916
Eustress, 1731, 1861
Euthanasia, 1922
Evaluation, 195, 651, 938, 1569
Evans, Gary, 1887
Everett, Craig, 1741
Everett, Sandra, 1741
Evolutionary psychology, 224, 715-719
Evolutionary theory of sleep, 1799
Exchange theory, 667, 1926
Excitation-transfer process, 1330
Exercise, 151, 673, 697, 719-721, 1066, 1307, 1897, 1979
Exercise, law of, 1980
Exercises in Divergent Thinking and Divergent Feeling, 518
Exhibitionism, 1592, 1770
Existential guilt, 879
Existential-humanistic school of psychology, 844
Existential psychology, 721-725, 945, 1141, 1708
Exline, Julie Juola, 798
Exner, John, 1479, 1647
Exner Comprehensive System, 1647
Expectancy theory, 23, 228, 420, 548, 991, 1713, 1816, 2073
Experimental design, 1689; between-subject, 2050; complex, 442-446, 1690;

mixed, 1691; quantitative, 351; quasi-experimental, 1572-1577; within-subject, 1690, 2050-2054

Experimental psychology, 725-728, 1507, 1510

Experimentation, 585, 983, 1285, 1689; ethics and participant rights, 728-732, 1630; field, 777-781; independent, dependent, and control variables, 733-736; laboratory versus field, 969. *See also* Animal experimentation

Experiments; Bobo doll, 299-301, 587, 1311, 1816; Harlow, 147, 204, 1389; hunger, 954; Little Albert, 1117-1119; Milgram, 731, 1208-1210; Rosenhan, 20, 780, 1199, 1649-1650; Stanford prison, 1866-1869

Expert systems, 187, 416

Exposure therapy, 255, 979, 1421, 2031

Expressive language acquisition styles, 1079

Externalizing disorders, 1542

Extinction, 1325, 1369, 1655; vicarious, 1312

Extrasensory perception, 1733

Extroversion, 64, 136, 1047-1049, 1330, 1396, 1488

Eye movement desensitization and reprocessing, 737-739

Eyewitness testimony, 416, 739-742, 795, 968, 1091, 1128, 1982

Eysenck, Hans, 743-744, 1048, 1329, 1400, 1547

F-test, 1873

Facial expressions, 679, 1298

Facial feedback, 113, 678, 683, 745-749

Factitious disorders, 368, 749-752, 972, 1254

Facultative homosexuality, 924

Fairbairn, Ronald, 1668

Fairweather, George, 436

Faludi, Susan, 1455

Familial advanced sleep phase syndrome, 378

Family development stage theory, 756

Family interaction theories of schizophrenia, 1681

Family life, 1832; adult issues, 752-755; children's issues, 756-758, 1745; conduct disorder, 464; eating disorders, 153; gender roles, 827; men's role, 1187; socialization, 1213; teenage suicide, 1955

Family stress models, 1875

Family system model of stepfamilies, 1876

Family systems theory, 615, 756, 759-762, 1667, 1785

Family therapy, 869; behavioral, 256, 265-269; children, 1436, 1542; fathers, 765; forgiveness, 798; Gestalt psychology, 845. *See also* Strategic family therapy

Fanning, Patrick, 78

Fant, Gunnar, 1852

Farberow, Norman, 1922

Faris, Robert, 1820

Farr, William, 1037

Farsightedness, 1273-1277, 2044

FASPS. *See* Familial advanced sleep phase syndrome

Fathers, 1353; relationship with child, 131, 762-766

Fazio, Russell, 215

FBI Behavioral Sciences Unit, 790

Fear, 766-770, 1656; advertising, 54; affiliation, 56; cancer, 335; intimacy, 1046; lack of in sociopaths, 1843; modeling therapy, 1312; panic attacks, 96, 1343; stress, 1888; systematic desensitization, 1940; terminal illness, 504

Fear of fear model of panic disorders, 98

Fear Survey Schedule for Children, 259

Feature-comparison model of memory, 1181

Feature integration theory, 207

Fechner, Gustav, 1400, 1505

Feedback, 785, 1715, 1727, 2074

Feeding disorder, 366

Feeney, Brooke, 1840

Felix, Robert H., 1270

Femininity, 770-771, 826, 1754, 2065

Feminist psychology, 615, 1756, 1766, 1833

Feminist psychotherapy, 772-775

Fenz, Walter, 1888

Fernald, Grace, 638

Festinger, Leon, 56, 405, 498, 1724

Fetal alcohol syndrome, 1204

Fetishism, 133, 775-777, 1771

Fiedler, Fred, 1093

Field theory, 705, 781-784, 1111

Fight-or-flight response, 142, 784-787, 1890, 1897, 1899; hormones, 931

Fillenbaum, Samuel, 2037

Fine, Mark A., 1875

Fischoff, Stuart, 1148

Fishbein, Martin, 215, 480

Fishbein, Sanford, 355

Fisher, Roger, 484

Fisher, Ronald A., 1873

Fixation, 1530

Fixed role therapy, 1384

Flashbulb memories, 1182

Flavell, John, 37

Fleischman, Edwin, 1096

Flooding, 98, 255, 738, 1320, 1371, 1446

Flourens, Pierre, 307

Flow (state of mind), 1440

Floyd, Frank, 1638

Fluency disorders, 1845

Fluid intelligence, 3, 86, 1028, 1030

Focal attention, 207

Folk concepts of personality, 333

Folkman, Susan, 504, 1886, 1900

Follicle-stimulating hormone, 1431

Food aversion. *See* Taste aversions

Foot-in-the-door effect, 220, 1722

Forehand, Rex, 1543

Forensic psychology, 298, 787-790, 1088, 1149, 1475
Forgetting, 114, 671, 791-795, 1126, 1628, 1779, 1985, 2053
Forgiveness, 795-799
Formal operational stage, 36, 40, 402, 578, 1427
Forsyth, D. R., 1926
Foss, R. D., 911
Foulkes, David, 625
Fragile X syndrome, 1203
Fragment-completion tasks, 1181
Framing, 263
Francis, Allen J., 1198
Francis, Greta, 259
Frank, Jerome D., 1549
Frank, Lawrence, 1480
Franklin, Stan, 185
Franks, Jeffrey J., 1981
Franz, Shepard Ivory, 1512
Free association, 656, 1393, 1481, 1493, 1557, 1833, 2070; S-R theory, 1657
Free radical theory of aging, 89, 92
Freedom, 723, 943, 1828
Freeman, Derek, 43
Freeman, Walter, 1120, 1498, 1538
Freeman-Watts standard lobotomy, 1120
Fremouw, William, 1923
French, John, 1451
French, Thomas, 320
Frequency distributions, 536
Freud, Anna, 500, 565, 653, 799-800, 1437, 1490, 1542
Freud, Sigmund, 800-802; aggression, 79; case study methodology, 352; death anxiety, 505; defense mechanisms, 553, 565, 653, 1478; dreams, 625; drives, 629; grieving, 862; guilt, 877; homosexuality, 922; hysteria, 916, 972, 1533; Carl Jung, 1054; masochism, 1660; motivation, 64, 1235; neurosis, 99, 1288; Oedipus complex, 1323; personality theory, 472,

664, 1386, 1395, 1492; phobias, 1418; psychoanalysis, 17, 658, 1481, 1487, 1515, 1546, 1556; psychosexual development, 577, 1228, 1375, 1528; religion, 1618; repression, 1346, 1628; schizophrenia, 1681; self, 1700; women, 2060, 2068
Freudian psychology, 801-806, 1403; achievement motivation, 24; Alfred Adler, 999; anxiety, 167; Erich Fromm, 1830; Karen Horney, 934, 2064; Jacques Lacan, 130
Freudian slips, 18
Freund, Kurt, 1774
Fridja, Nico, 683
Friedman, Meyer, 502, 1895, 1901, 2016
Friendship, 56-61
Friesen, Wallace, 1296
Frigidity, 2064
Frisch, G. R., 987
Frisch, Karl von, 711
Fritsch, Gustav, 307, 316, 1512
Fromm, Erich, 806-807, 879, 1067, 1236, 1827
Frontal lobes, 1498
Frost, Nancy, 5
Frotteurism, 1592, 1772
Frustration-aggression hypothesis, 74, 78
FSH. See Follicle-stimulating hormone
Fugue, 126-130, 610
Functional analysis, 423
Functional fixedness, 1472
Functional theory, 1538
Functionalism, 594, 726, 1505, 1513, 1738, 1904-1908
Fundamental attribution error, 227, 524, 1453, 1824, 1861
Fuster, J. M., 1636
Futrell, B. A., 84

GABA. See Gamma-aminobutyric acid
GAD. See Generalized anxiety disorder
Gaertner, Samuel L., 908

Galanter, Eugene, 1732
Galbraith, John Kenneth, 1449
Galinsky, Ellen, 756
Gall, Franz, 1286, 1511
Galt, John M., 121
Galton, Francis, 1025, 1512, 1581, 1864, 1873, 1937, 1972
Galvanic skin response, 282
Gamblers Anonymous, 809
Gambler's fallacy, 1124
Gambling, 238, 808-810, 985
Games, 810-813
Gamma-aminobutyric acid, 633, 1010-1011, 1223, 1279, 1292
Garcia, John, 238, 1947
Gardner, Howard, 515, 518, 1025, 1032, 1066, 1246
Gardner, Richard A., 1350, 1742
Garfinkel, Barry, 1922
Garvey, Michael, 1695
GATB. See General Aptitude Test Battery
Gating mechanism, 1336
Gays, 813-817
Gazzaniga, Michael, 1855
Geese Theatre Company, 1259
Gélineau, Jean-Baptiste-Édouard, 1267
Gellar, E. Scott, 1644
Gender constancy, 825
Gender differences, 717, 817-820, 1185, 1702, 2059, 2061; attention-deficit hyperactivity disorder, 210; attitudes toward sex, 47; birth order, 296; brain structure, 194, 694; cognitive ability, 392-396; color blindness, 2040; cooperation and competition, 23, 486, 1408; depression, 566; dissociative disorders, 611; dyslexia, 637; eating disorders, 640; facial feedback, 679; friendship, 59; hypothyroidism, 1990; jealousy, 1053; kleptomania, 1069; leadership, 1094; learning disorders, 1108; love and attraction, 225, 1134; moral perspective, 851; panic

attacks, 1344; parenting styles, 1353; personality disorders, 162, 305, 1388; retirement, 1640; schizophrenia, 2057; seasonal affective disorder, 1697; sociopathy, 1843; spatial knowledge, 412; stress, 1899; stuttering, 1909; suicide, 1921, 1923, 1954; Tourette's syndrome, 2003; violence by children and teenagers, 2024

Gender dysphoria, 815

Gender identity, 855, 1186; formation, 46, 824-827; sexual orientation versus, 814

Gender identity disorder, 816, 820-823, 825, 925, 2013. *See also* Transsexualism

Gender roles, 46, 827-830; acquisition, 824; analysis, 773; femininity, 770; Japan, 42; men, 1185; sexual harassment, 1768

Gender schema theory, 825

General adaptation syndrome, 144, 280, 787, 830-834, 1731, 1891, 1894, 1899

General Aptitude Test Battery, 341, 834-835

General systems theory, 759

Generalization fallacy, 228

Generalized anxiety disorder, 19, 835-837, 1517

Generativity, 663, 754

Genetic disorders, 1424

Genetic programming theory of aging, 89, 92

Genetic psychology, 1506

Genetics, 7, 16, 838-842, 1520; affiliation, 65; aggression, 77; Alzheimer's disease, 116; antisocial personality disorder, 164; Asperger syndrome, 194; attention-deficit hyperactivity disorder, 211; autism, 232; bed-wetting, 250; bipolar disorder, 285; body dysmorphic disorder, 302; borderline personality disorder, 305; circadian rhythms, 378; color

blindness, 2040, 2044; conduct disorder, 463; depression, 568; development, 577, 581, 591, 1423, 1464; Down syndrome, 620; dyslexia, 1108; eating disorders, 641; homosexuality, 923; imprinting, 980; intelligence, 2, 1025, 1027, 1578; introversion and extroversion, 1048, 1396; language, 1112; memory, 1163; mental retardation, 1202; narcolepsy, 1268; obesity, 1306; panic attacks, 98, 1344; Parkinson's disease, 1357; personality disorders, 1389; personality traits, 1395; pervasive development disorders, 1411; phobias, 1420; research ethics, 1633; schizophrenia, 1674-1675, 1681; schizotypal personality disorder, 1686; stuttering, 1909; substance use disorders, 26, 104, 1916; Tourette's syndrome, 2003

Genital stage, 662, 1493, 1530, 2069

Genuineness, 1380

Gerbner, George, 2020

Gergen, Kenneth, 1703

Geriatrics, 71

Germ theory of disease, 1038

Gerontology, 87

Gerontophobia, 72

Gesell, Arnold, 842-843, 1243

Gestalt psychology, 1503, 1505, 1513

Gestalt therapy, 651, 843-846, 869, 1158

Getzsche, P. C., 1434

Gibson, James J., 575, 1361

GIFT. *See* Group Inventory for Finding Talent

Giftedness, 847-851

Gilbert, Daniel, 227

Gilbreth, Frank, 1003

Giles-Sims, Jean, 1876

Gilligan, Carol, 851-852, 1702, 2059, 2071

Gillingham, Anna, 638

Glass, Gene, 1547

Glasser, Barney G., 1568

Glasser, William, 1603

Global aphasia, 173

Global Assessment of Functioning scale, 385

Glover, John, 519

Glutamate, 1163, 1292

Gluten intolerance, 1302

Goals, 865, 1214, 1377, 1551, 1841; motivation, 1234, 1239, 2074

Godden, Duncan, 689

Goffman, Erving, 13, 1728

Gold, Mark, 7

Goldberger, Nancy Rule, 394

Goldfried, Marvin, 258, 398

Goldiamond, Israel, 1325

Goldstein, Alan, 98

Goldstein, Kurt, 64, 1707

Goleman, Daniel, 681

Golgi, Camillo, 1281

Gonads, 852-856

Gondolf, Edward, 243

Goodness; prosocial behavior and, 911

Goodwin, Donald, 964

Gormezano, Isadore, 1608

Gorney, Roderic, 1707

Gorsuch, Richard L., 1625, 1869

Gottman, John M., 509

Gough, Harrison, 333, 341

Graduated exposure therapy. *See* Systematic desensitization

Gramling, Sandra E., 1886

Grammar, 274, 856-861, 1077

Grandiose delusional disorder, 1348

Grandiosity, 284, 1264

Grasping reflex, 1609, 1612

Graunt, John, 1037

Graves, Robert, 1991

Graves' disease, 1991

Gray, Laura, 1089

Gredler, Margaret, 652

Greene, David, 735, 1723

Greene, Robert, 1451

Greeno, J. G., 1468

Grice, H. P., 1115

Grieving, 861-864, 1741
Griffin, John Howard, 779
Griffith, Coleman R., 1862
Grismer, B. A, 84
Groth-Marnat, Gary, 1392
Grounded theory, 1568
Group dynamics, 871
Group Inventory for Finding Talent, 519
Group processes, 483, 487
Group therapy, 511, 774, 868-872, 953, 2084
Grouping, laws of, 1733
Groups, 872-877; affiliation, 58, 63; bystander effect, 327; decision making, 864-868; guilt, 879; hate crimes, 890; Internet, 1040; membership and social identity, 1811; organizational behavior, 1333; prejudice, 1453, 1458; social identity theory, 1810
Growth spurt, adolescent, 45
Grundman, Michael, 84
Guidano, Vittorio, 399
Guided imagery, 1152
Guilford, J. P., 3, 516, 1024, 1400
Guillette, Elizabeth, 708
Guilt, 877-880, 1445
Gull, William, 1990
Guntrip, Harry, 1668
Gur, Ruben, 964
Gustavson, Carl, 1947
Guze, Samuel, 964

H-Y antigen, 853
Haan, Norma, 500
Habituation, 99, 629, 881-885, 1160, 1315, 1396
Hacker, Frederick J., 1969
Haffner, Debra W, 47
Haggard, E. A., 679
Haley, Jay, 759, 1881
Hall, Calvin, 2070
Hall, David, 968
Hall, G. Stanley, 40, 589, 885-886, 1513, 1581, 1959
Hall, Richard, 8
Hallucinations, 383, 623, 886-889, 1197, 1559; alcoholic,

103; dissociative identity disorder, 1252; schizophrenia, 1671; synesthesia versus, 1937
Hallucinogens, 888
Hamilton, David L., 1584
Hampstead Child Therapy Courses, 800
Hansen, Jo-Ida, 1036
Happiness, 1046, 1439
Haptics. See Touch
Hardiness, 493, 502, 1398, 1535, 1896, 1901
Hare, Robert, 163
Harlow, Harry, 147, 204, 1389
Harlow, Margaret, 204
Harlow experiments, 147, 204, 1389
Harm reduction approaches, 105
Harman, Denham, 92
Harré, Rom, 1703
Harris, Ben, 1118
Harris, John, 1982
Hart, Betty M., 2052
Hart, Roger A., 703
Harter, Susan, 2062
Hartmann, Heinz, 659, 1235
Harvard Group Scale of Hypnotic Susceptibility, Form A, 956
Harvard Negotiation Project, 484
Hate crimes, 890-892, 1969
Hathaway, S. R., 341, 1211
Hauri, Peter, 1016
Hawthorne effect, 778, 1574
Hayes, Steven C., 1651
Hazan, Cindy, 1134
Health insurance. See Insurance, health
Health maintenance organizations, 893-895
Health psychology, 895-900, 1440, 1570
Hearing, 83, 88, 901-905, 1737, 1936
Hebb, Donald O., 1157, 1163, 1173, 1236, 1286, 1512
Hecht, Michael, 1296
Hedonistic theory of motivation, 1236
Heft, Harry, 705
Heidegger, Martin, 722

Heider, Fritz, 227, 356, 1824
Heine, Steven, 1714
Helgeson, Vicki S., 59
Heller, Frank, 1095
Heller, Theodore, 1414
Hellmuth, Hug, 1437
Helmholtz, Hermann von, 205, 904, 1274, 1361, 1512, 2036, 2040
Helmreich, Robert, 23
Help-seeking, 496, 905-908, 1188, 1822, 1962
Helping, 908-913
Helplessness, 34, 90
Hemi-inattention, 1497
Henderson, Lynne, 1783
Henle, Mary, 1983
Henley, Nancy, 1298
Herd defense, 556
Hering, Ewald, 1512, 2036
Herman, Judith, 243
Herrnstein, Richard, 4, 1578
Herzberg, Frederick, 2075
Hetherington, E. Mavis, 1744
Heuristics, 417, 547, 1122, 1468, 1824
Hewstone, Miles, 1458
Hidden observer effect, 956
Hierarchy of needs, 54, 64, 913-916, 944, 1139, 1236, 2073; Henry A. Murray, 1407
Hierarchy of responses, 1655
Hilgard, Ernest, 475, 956, 958
Hilgard, Josephine, 958, 1340
Hill, Peter C., 911, 1625
Hill, Reuben, 756
Hinshelwood, James, 639
Hippocampus, 315, 1162, 1497
Histrionic personality disorder, 916-918, 972, 1387
Hitch, Graham, 1181
Hitzig, Eduard, 307, 316, 1512
HMOs. See Health maintenance organizations
Hoberman, Harry, 1922
Hobfoll, S. E., 1900
Hobson, J. Allan, 625
Hock, R. A, 84
Hodgkin, Alan, 1010
Hoffer, Abram, 1300

Holding therapy, 1602

Holistic approaches, 650, 943, 1079, 1604

Holland, John L., 339, 346, 1034, 1903

Holland reporting system, 1074, 1903

Hollingworth, Leta, 850

Hollins Fluency Program, 1912

Holmes, Thomas, 491, 1889, 1894

Homelessness, 918-922, 1197, 1668, 1673

Homeostasis, 628, 785, 833, 929, 951, 1891, 1965, 1977

Homeostatis, 1279

Homophobia, 925, 1138

Homosexuality, 814, 821, 922-926, 1140, 1751, 1765; aversion therapy, 238; transvestism versus, 2013

Hood, Ralph W., Jr., 1625

Hope, 926-928

Hope Scale, 927

Hopelessness Scale, 1923

Hormic psychology, 1514

Hormone receptors, 49

Hormones, 49, 92, 143, 691, 819, 831, 923, 1429, 1988; behavior, 928-933; postpartum depression, 1442; Type A behavior pattern, 2017

Horner, Matina, 1409

Horney, Karen, 934, 1375, 1489, 1700, 1831, 2064, 2069

Hospice, 199, 505, 542, 935-936

Hostility, 1887, 1901, 2018

Hotlines, 522, 1923, 1957

House, James, 503, 1822

Hovland, Carl, 218

Huarte, Juan, 1031

Hubel, David, 147

Huettel, Scott A., 112

Hull, Clark L., 628, 937, 990, 1235, 1655, 1977

Human Aging Study, 90

Human factors engineering, 1737

Human Genome Project, 90

Human potential movement, 945, 2075

Human resources. *See* Employees

Human validation process model, 760

Humanistic psychology, 18, 26, 915, 942-946, 1506, 1516, 1552, 1704; existential psychology versus, 724; motivation, 1237; origin of, 1509; personality theory, 1395, 1403; play therapy, 1437; psychoanalysis, 807; self, 1700

Humanistic trait models, 24, 946-950

Hunger, 950-955

Hunt, Earl B., 5

Hunt, Morton, 85

Hunt, Reed, 1177

Hunter, John, 833

Hurry sickness, 2017

Husserl, Edmund, 723, 945

Hutman, Lucinda, 2036

Huxley, Andrew, 1010

Hyde, Janet Shibley, 393, 1755

Hydraulic model of motivation, 1236

Hydrocortisone. *See* Cortisol

Hyperopia. *See* Farsightedness

Hyperthermia, 1967

Hyperthyroidism, 1990

Hypnagogic state, 473, 623, 1267, 1796

Hypnopompic state, 473, 623

Hypnosis, 129, 474, 689, 803, 955-960, 1288, 1340, 1555

Hypochondriasis, 960-965, 971, 1536

Hypomania, 284

Hypothalamus, 314, 377, 692, 786, 952, 1269, 1429, 1496

Hypothermia, 1967

Hypotheses, development and testing, 966-970, 1871

Hypothesis-testing theory of concept formation, 454

Hypothyroidism, 1990

Hypovolemic thirst, 1977

Hysteria, 654, 916, 970-973

Hysterical blindness, 964

Hysterical neurosis, 1289

I/O psychology. *See* Industrial and organizational psychology

ICD. See *International Classification of Diseases*

Iconic memory, 1175

Id, 17, 629, 664-666, 802, 1492, 2068

Identity, 66, 289, 876, 1257, 1700, 1810

Identity crises, 40, 974-978

Identity status model, 976

Idiographic psychology, 108

IEP. *See* Individualized Education Plan

Igumnov, S., 1201

Ilg, Frances, 842

Illusory conjunctions, 207

Imagery, 414, 470

Immune system, 89, 94, 116, 1892, 1895

Implicit personality theory, 1825

Implosion, 978-980

Impression management, 1726

Imprinting, 637-638, 980-984

Impulse control disorders, 984-989, 1069; children, 368

Impulses, inhibitory and excitatory, 1007-1011

Impulsivity, 305, 1330

In-groups, 1810

Incentive theory of motivation, 1236

Incest taboo, 131

Individual Family Service Plan, 1109

Individual psychology, 29-30, 297, 996-1000, 1213, 1450, 1488

Individualism, 428, 523, 527, 686

Individualized Education Plan, 583, 1109

Individuals with Disabilities Education Act (1990), 583-584, 1108

Individuation, 137, 176, 1055

Indoleamines, 50

Induced motion, 575

Inductive reasoning, 551, 1001-1002, 1121, 1981

Industrial and organizational psychology, 1002-1007, 1506

Inference; thought, 1122, 1980-1984
Inferiority complex, 29-30, 64, 240, 996, 1488
Influence, 58, 218, 327, 865, 873, 1450, 1785
Information processing, 54, 414, 449, 479, 724, 792, 1025, 1064, 1175, 1234, 1365, 1779, 1855, 1984
Information-processing theory of concept formation, 454
Information-providing teaching methods, 1950
Information retrieval, 411
Information transmission, 1007
Informed consent, 729, 993, 1631
Inhelder, Barbel, 36
Inhibitions, 327, 1817
Initiation rituals. See Rites of passage
Initiative, 661
Inkster, James, 407
Innate language-acquisition device, 1080, 1112
Inquiry-oriented teaching methods, 1950
Insanity defense, 12, 788, 1011-1013
Insanity Defense Reform Act (1984), 14, 1012
Insomnia, 1013-1018
Instinct theory, 1018-1021, 2022
Instincts, 665, 713, 716, 980, 1131, 1760, 2068
Institute for Rational Emotive Therapy, 1599
Institute for Reality Therapy, 1606
Institute for Sexual Research, 1068
Institutional Animal Care and Use Committees, 149
Institutional review board, 729, 1631
Institutionalization, legal requirements, 13
Instone, Debra, 1094
Instrumental conditioning. See Conditioning, operant

Instrumental support, 1839
Insurance, health, 321, 892-894, 906, 936, 1189
Intelligence, 1022-1026; attention-deficit hyperactivity disorder, 210; cognitive theories, 5; creativity, 514-517; dyslexia, 636; genetics, 146; measurement, 2, 1865; race, 67, 743; types, 2, 86
Intelligence quotient, 1, 847, 1022, 1027-1028, 1201, 1865, 2048; racial differences, 1578
Intelligence tests, 1, 36, 279, 340, 1022, 1028-1033, 1427, 1507, 2047; bias, 277; birth order, 295; giftedness, 847; mental retardation, 364. See also specific test
Intelligent tutoring systems, 187
Intentionality, 943
Interactional family therapy, 1881
Interactionism, 1510
Interactionist theories of language, 1081
Interactionist theory, 175
Interest inventories, 343, 1033-1037, 1507, 1902. See also specific inventory
Interference (memory), 740, 792
Intermittent explosive disorder, 987
Intermittent reinforcement, 1617
Internal frame of reference, 1377
Internalizing disorders, 1542
International Center for Genetic Epistemology, 1427
International Classification of Diseases, 531, 595, 599, 1037-1039
International General Medical Society for Psychotherapy, 1055
International Institute of Stress, 1731
International Psychoanalytic Association, 137, 1054, 1484
International Psychoanalytic Societies, 1484

International Statistical Institute, 1038
Internet, 497, 1144, 1720
Internet psychology, 1039-1042
Interpersonal psychology, 1489, 1925
Interpersonal psychotherapy, 570
Interpersonal relationships, 33, 509, 999
Interpersonal skills, 1025
Intervention, 267, 617, 1043-1044, 1061, 1458, 2081; belief congruence, 1458
Interviews, 1391-1392, 1929; clinical, 254, 381-385, 596
Intimacy, 662, 753, 1044-1047, 1052, 1132, 1297, 1709
Intons-Peterson, Margaret, 1779
Intrapersonal models of forgiveness, 797
Intrapersonal pathology, 615
Introjection, 553, 657, 666
Introspection, 417, 1688, 1905
Introversion, 64, 136, 1047-1049, 1396, 1488
Intuition, 1452
Investigative psychology, 1476
IQ. See Intelligence quotient
IRB. See Institutional review board
Irrational beliefs, 169
Irresistible impulse rule, 12, 1012
Irwin, David E., 1178
Isaacs, F. S., 679
Isaacs, Wayne, 1325
Isolation, 657, 662, 753
ITS. See Intelligent tutoring systems
Izard, Carroll, 746

Jack, Demick, 705
Jacklin, Carol, 393
Jackson, Douglas, 342, 1400
Jackson, John Hughlings, 1287, 1858
Jackson v. Indiana (1972), 14
Jacobs, Gerald A., 1869
Jacobson, Edmund, 280, 1152
Jacobson, Lenore, 1237, 1825
James, William, 1050-1051, 1154,

1512, 1699, 1738, 1760, 1907, 2037; attention, 206; consciousness, 471; education, 651; emotions, 686, 745, 768; memory, 791, 1126, 1779; self-esteem, 1715

James-Lange theory, 686, 746, 768

Janis, Irving, 866, 1887

Janowsky, David, 51

Jarvis, Eric, 533

Jealous delusional disorder, 1347

Jealousy, 1051-1054, 1479, 1941

Jellen, Hans, 519

Jenkins, C. David, 2016

Jenkins, James, 650

Jenkins Activity Survey, 2016

Jensen, Arthur R., 4, 1578

Jet lag, 379

Jewell, Linda, 1005

Jigsaw learning, 487

Job analysis, 1005

Job enrichment, 2075

Johnson, David, 1259, 1952

Johnson, Robert, 528

Johnson, Roger, 1952

Johnson, Virginia E., 1139-1141, 1762, 2071

Johnson, Wendell, 1909

Johnson-Laird, Philip, 1983

Jones, Edward, 1405, 1726, 1824

Jones, James M., 1583

Jones, Mary Cover, 1542, 1940

Jones, R. K., 1856

Jordan, Dale R., 637

Jouissance, 132

Jourard, Sidney, 1709

Julesz, Bela, 574

Jung, Carl, 135, 138, 176, 1054-1055, 1206, 1261, 1707; dreams, 624; introversion and extroversion, 1048; motivation, 64; self, 1700

Jungian psychology, 1055-1059

Jurors, psychology of, 1088

Justice system, 740, 788

Juvenile delinquency, 43, 164, 1059-1062, 1642

Juvenile Parkinsonism, 1355

Kagan, Jerome, 1701, 1783

Kahlbaum, Karl, 1346

Kahn, William A., 79

Kahneman, Daniel, 237, 417, 548, 1824

Kako, Edward, 1077

Kallmann, Franz J., 1682

Kamen, Leslie, 1099

Kamin, Leon, 743, 1582

Kandel, Eric R., 882, 1101, 1159, 1163, 1171, 1609

Kanner, Leo, 230

Kant, Immanuel, 478

Kantor, Martin, 1187

Kaplan, Helen Singer, 1762

Karpman, Benjamin, 165

Kasper, Siegfried, 1695

Kastenbaum, Robert J., 505

Katz, Irwin, 1583

Kayak angst, 533

Keel, Pamela, 534

Kelley, Harold, 354, 1824

Kelly, Alison, 828

Kelly, George A., 1063-1064, 1382, 1403

Kendall, Philip, 212

Kendrick, Carol, 1787

Kennedy, Melinda, 70

Kerlinger, Fred, 1391

Kety, Seymour, 1682

Keysers, Christian, 1179

Kibbutzim, 41

Kierkegaard, Søren, 723

Kilbride, Thomas, 121

Kimble, Gregory A., 1614

Kin selection model of homosexuality, 923

Kindling, 286

Kinsey, Alfred, 90, 814, 925, 1067-1068, 1930

Kinship, 63

Kirmayer, Lawrence J., 533

Kitayama, Shinobu, 1702

Klasen, Edith, 639

Klein, Donald, 98

Klein, Gary, 1451

Klein, Melanie, 554, 878, 1437

Kleine-Levin syndrome, 1268

Kleinman, Arthur, 532

Kleitman, Nathaniel, 1801

Kleptomania, 987, 1069-1070

Klerman, Gerald, 570

Klineberg, Otto, 678

Kluckholm, Richard, 41

Klump, Kelly, 534

Knight, James, 879

Knott, David H., 106

Knox, Robert, 407

Kobasa, Suzanne, 493, 502, 1896, 1900

Koch, August, 165

Koelling, Robert, 1948

Koenig, Harold G., 911

Koffka, Kurt, 1513

Kohlberg, Lawrence, 824, 851, 1070-1071, 1228, 1565, 2060

Köhler, Wolfgang, 1473, 1513

Kohut, Heinz, 1700

KOIS. *See* Kuder Occupational Interest Survey

Kojève, Alexandre, 134

Konopka, Ronald J., 378

Koop, C. Everett, 897

Korchin, Sheldon, 1478

Korner, Anneliese, 1478

Koro, 533

Korsakoff syndrome. *See* Wernicke-Korsakoff syndrome

Kovacs, Maria, 369

Kovel, Joel, 1583

Kowalski, Robin M., 325

Kraepelin, Emil, 571, 1071-1072, 1196, 1223, 1346, 1517, 1538, 1560, 1673, 1683, 1698

Krafft-Ebing, Richard von, 1659

Kraut, Robert, 747

Kruschwitz, Stanley V., 79

Kübler-Ross, Elisabeth, 335, 505, 543, 863, 1072-1073

Kuder, G. Frederic, 1036

Kuder Occupational Interest Survey, 341, 1036, 1074-1075

Kulik, James, 651, 1182

Külpe, Oswald, 470

Kunz, George, 1451, 1500

Kurdek, Lawrence A., 1875

L'Abate, Luciano, 1883

LaBerge, Stephen, 624

Lacan, Jacques, 130, 1076-1077

Laing, R. D., 722
Laird, James, 746
Lamplugh, Diane, 79
Landy, David, 1089
Lang, Peter, 169, 1940
Lange, Carl, 686, 746, 768
Langer, Ellen J., 898
Langer, Walter, 1474
Langewisch, M. W., 987
Language, 717, 1077-1084, 1111, 1816, 1856; acquisition, 274, 583, 621, 858; autism, 232; dyslexia, 636; gender stereotypes, 1755; grammar, 857; Jacques Lacan, 130, 1076; B. F. Skinner, 1589; speech perception, 1849
Large numbers, law of, 1871
Larson, John, 1644
Lashley, Karl, 307, 1157, 1161, 1173, 1512
Laszlo, Judith, 1065
Latané, Bibb, 326, 527, 967
Latency stage, 1493, 1530, 2069
Latent learning, 409
Lateral thinking, 1953
Lateralization, 317, 1081, 1855
Latham, Gary, 2074
Latinos, 1085-1088
Law of ____. See ____, law of
Lawton, M. Powell, 705
Lazarus, Richard, 491, 500, 504, 1886, 1900
Lazovik, David, 1940
Lead exposure, 709
Leadership, 874, 1092-1096, 1333, 1755
Learned helplessness, 243, 355, 615, 1097-1100, 1104, 1887
Learned insomnia. See Persistent psychophysiological insomnia
Learned needs theory, 22
Learned variability, 1105
Learning, 649, 1100-1106; associative, 713; conditioning, 456, 689; cooperative, 487-490; emotional intelligence, 682; ethology, 712; gender differences, 824; instrumental avoidance, 1945; memory,

1156, 1160, 1167, 1499, 1781; motivation, 1234; motivation versus, 989; nonassociative, 1160; online, 1041; passive, 1951; performance versus, 409; psychopathology, 1518; rules, 1652; S-R theory, 1655; Edward L. Thorndike, 1979; Edward C. Tolman, 1998. See also Observational learning
Learning disabilities, 277
Learning disorders, 364, 1106-1110
Learning model of persuasion, 218
Learning theory, 265, 615, 1079, 1389, 1418, 1544, 1681, 1738
Leary, Mark, 1728, 1841
Leary, Timothy, 888
Least-preferred coworker scale, 1093
Le Bon, Gustave, 525, 1756
Legal issues, 11-15, 200, 466, 995; battered woman syndrome, 245; child abuse, 358; elder abuse, 668; employee training, 939; experimentation, 729; industrial and organizational psychology, 1006; jury decision making, 1088-1092; media violence, 2022; parental alienation syndrome, 1349; sexual harassment, 1768
Lehrman, Daniel, 1759
Lencz, Todd, 1679
Lenneberg, Eric, 859
Lepper, Mark, 735, 1723
Lerner, Harriet Goldhor, 2066
Lesbians, 813-817
Lesieur, Henry, 985
Lesions, 307
Leukotomy, 307, 1119
Levels-of-analysis model of memory, 1181
Levels-of-processing model of memory, 1127
Levin, Jack, 891
Levine, Robert, 779
Levis, Donald J., 979
Levy, Jere, 1856

Lewin, Kurt, 486, 705, 781, 1110-1111
Lewis, Helen, 879
Lewis, Laurie, 1754
Lewis, Michael, 1701
Lexical decision tasks, 1181
LH. See Luteinizing hormone
Liberman, Alvin M., 1851
Libido, 64, 136, 167, 577, 1375; Carl Jung, 1048
Licoppe, Christian, 827
Lidz, Theodore, 1681
Life scripts, 2008
Life space, 781
Life-span theory, 1375
Light therapy, 1696
Likert, Rensis, 1932
Likert scales, 1399, 1454, 1693, 1932
Limbic system, 315, 1280, 1496, 1539
Lindemann, Erich, 520, 862
Lindsley, Donald, 1636
Lindzey, Gardner, 948
Linehan, Marsha M., 305, 602, 1389
Linguistic determinism. See Sapir-Whorf hypothesis
Linguistic relativity, 858, 1082
Linguistics, 860, 1111-1117
Linton, Marigold, 1182
Liotti, Gianni, 399
Lippmann, Walter, 1756
Lipsitt, Lewis, 1612
Lithium, 51, 634, 1226, 1524
Little Albert study, 238, 266, 269, 352, 767, 1117-1119, 1371, 1421, 2046
Little Hans study, 169, 352, 1421
Lobotomy, 51, 75, 307, 1119-1121, 1196, 1498, 1537
Localizationism, 307
Lochman, John, 79
Locke, Edwin, 2074
Locke, John, 992
Lockhart, Robert, 1127, 1181
Locus of control, 22, 354, 1397, 1535, 1888, 1897, 1900
Lodge concept of prevention programs, 436

Loewald, Hans, 879
Loewi, Otto, 1935
Lofquist, Lloyd, 340
Loftus, Elizabeth F., 82, 416, 740, 968, 1128, 1982
Logic, 36, 82, 227, 261, 1121-1126, 1471. *See also* Deductive reasoning; Inductive reasoning
Long, Howard, 1581
Long-term memory, 82, 415, 688, 792, 1126-1130, 1156, 1165, 1175, 1779, 1985
Longitudinal research designs, 586, 591
Lorenz, Konrad, 711, 981, 1130-1131, 1235
Lorge, Irving, 391
Loss, 861, 1741, 1956
Lovaas, Ivar, 233, 1311
Love, 58, 222, 753, 878, 1046, 1131-1136, 1710
Luchins, Abraham, 1472
Lucy, John, 1082
Lukes, Steven, 1451
Lunneborg, Clifford E., 5
Luria, Aleksandr, 309, 1937
Lushene, Robert, 1869
Luteinizing hormone, 1431
Lyerly, J. G., 1539
Lying, 545-547
Lykken, David, 163, 1843
Lyons, Henry, 916

McAdams, Dan, 1703
McAllister, Ronald, 777
MacArthur Violence Risk Assessment Study, 1642
McBride, K. E., 1858
McCarley, Robert, 625
McCarthy, Diane, 1791
McClelland, David, 22, 1408
McClelland, J. L., 1083
Maccoby, Eleanor, 393
McConahay, John B., 1584
McCrae, P. T., Jr., 1048
McCrae, R. R., 1401
McCullough, Michael E., 796
McDaniels, Carl, 346
McDevitt, Jack, 891

MacDougall, William, 1018, 1513, 1760
McFarland, Sam, 1868
McGaugh, James, 1629
McGinty, D. J., 1636
McGorry, Patrick, 1679
McGregor, Douglas, 945, 1706
Mach, Ernst, 2037
Mach bands, 2037
McKay, Matthew, 78
McKinley, J. C., 341, 1211
McKinley, Nita, 393
MacKinnon, Donald, 847
Mackworth clock, 1790
McNally, Richard, 737
McNamara, Timothy, 412
MacNichol, Edward F., 2040
Macroallocation decisions, 730
Madanes, Cloe, 1881
Madness. *See* Mental illness
Mahler, Margaret, 1700
Maier, Norman R. F., 1472
Maier, Steven F., 1099, 1101
Main effect model of social support, 1841
Maintaining conditions, 253
Maintenance rehearsal, 1779
Maladaptation, 832
Malan, Daniel, 320
Malingering, 749, 972, 1254, 1536
Management, 386, 944, 999, 1095, 1706, 2074, 2079
Management by objectives, 2074
Mania, 51, 1197
Manic-depressive disorder. *See* Bipolar disorder
Mann, Horace, 120
Mann, James, 321
Mann, Leon, 527
Mann, Michael, 1449
MAOIs. *See* Monoamine oxidase inhibitors
Mapping, consistent and varied, 235
Maratsos, Michael, 1083
Marcia, James, 976, 1700
Marecek, Jeanne, 2062
Marital therapy. *See* Couples therapy

Markman, Arthur, 684
Marks, William B., 2040
Markus, Hazel, 1701
Markwardt, Frederick C., 1373
Marland, Sidney P., 848
Marland definition of giftedness, 848
Marriage, 508, 524. *See also* Divorce; Separation; Stepfamilies
Martin, Lenny, 747
Martin, Roy, 1465
Masculine protest, 997
Masculinity, 770, 826, 1137-1138, 1185, 1754
Maslach, Susan, 1868
Maslow, Abraham, 54, 64, 914, 944, 1138-1139, 1154, 1236, 1516, 1700, 1704, 2073
Masochism, 1592, 1659-1662, 1771, 2065
Masochistic personality disorder, 1661
Mason, John, 1899
Mass action, 1162
Masters, William H., 1139-1141, 1762, 2071
Masters and Johnson Institute, 1140
Mastery, 23, 500, 1076, 1952
Maternity blues, 1442
Mathematics disorder, 1107
Matheny, Laura, 1083
Mating behavior, 693
Matlin, Margaret, 1176
Maturity, 46, 250, 655
Maultsby, Maxie, 397
May, Rollo, 79, 721, 944, 1141-1142, 1449, 1701
Mayer, John, 681
Mayer-Salovey-Caruso Emotional Intelligence Test, 682
Mayo, Elton, 2075
Mayo, Julia, 906
MBTI. *See* Myers-Briggs Type Indicator
Mead, George Herbert, 1703, 1716
Mead, Margaret, 43, 1020
Meadow, Roy, 1255

Meaning, 470, 478, 1115, 1296, 1363

Means-ends analysis, 1471

Measurement, 195, 535, 1985

Mechanistic worldview, 590, 704, 711

Mechanoreceptors, 1737, 1999

Méconnaissance, 131

Media; depictions of elderly, 70; depictions of femininity, 770; depictions of masculinity, 1137; mental health practitioners, 1147

Media exposure, 1142-1146

Media psychology, 1146-1151

Media Psychology Research Institute, 1148

Medical model of helping, 910

Medicare, 892, 936

Medin, Douglas, 684

Meditation, 281, 469, 474, 1152-1155

Mednick, Sarnoff, 1465, 1676

Meehl, Paul, 1686

Meese, Hayden, 1996

Mehrabian, Albert, 1296

Meichenbaum, Donald, 78, 397

Melamed, Barbara, 1312

Melatonin, 285, 313, 379, 930, 1695

Melzack, Ronald, 1336, 1339

Memory, 688, 782, 1155-1160, 1471, 1834, 1985; adolescents, 37; animal research, 1160-1165; brain structure, 315, 1497; computers, 450; dementia, 559; Hermann Ebbinghaus, 645; elderly, 84, 671; empirical studies, 1165-1169; kinesthetic, 1064-1067; mutability, 414, 478, 968; physiology, 1169-1174; storage, 1180-1184, 1779. *See also* Amnesia; Eyewitness testimony; Forgetting

Memory, episodic. *See* Episodic memory

Memory, long-term. *See* Long-term memory

Memory, procedural. *See* Procedural memory

Memory, repressed. *See* Repressed memories

Memory, semantic. *See* Semantic memory

Memory, sensory. *See* Sensory memory

Memory, short-term. *See* Short-term memory

Memory, skill. *See* Procedural memory

Memory, state-dependent. *See* State-dependent memory

Memory, working. *See* Short-term memory

Men, 1184-1189; parenting and, 1353

Menarche, 46

Menninger, William, 122

Menopause, 1206, 2055

Mental capacity, 994

Mental disorder; terminology, 1198

Mental Health Parity Act (1996), 893, 895, 1189

Mental Health Parity and Addiction Equity Act (2008), 893, 895, 1189

Mental health practitioners, 1190-1194; bias, 817, 1454; cultural competence, 1272; media, 1147

Mental health services; parity, 893, 1189-1190; trauma, 1445; utilization, 68, 71, 189, 818, 905, 1087, 1185

Mental hospitals, history of, 120, 613, 1195, 1428

Mental illness; functional, 50; historical theories of, 10, 1194-1200; legal issues, 12, 788; organic, 50

Mental Research Institute, 1881

Mental retardation, 364, 581, 619, 1107, 1200-1205

Mental set, 1472

Mental status examinations, 382, 1392

Menzel, Emil W., 409

Mere exposure phenomenon, 223

Merikle, Phil, 1175

Merleau-Ponty, Maurice, 724

Merriam, Sharan, 1183

Merrill, Maude, 2

Mesibov, Gary, 233

Mesmer, Franz, 474, 959

Metabolism, 87, 1989

Metamemory, 415, 469

Metaphor, 132

Metonymy, 132

Meyer, Adolf, 1198

Midbrain, 313

Middle age, 663

Midlife crisis, 136, 141, 977, 1205-1208

Midtown Study, 1453

Milan systemic family therapy, 1881

Milgram, Stanley, 731, 1208

Milgram experiment, 731, 1208-1210

Miller, George, 1779

Miller, Jean Baker, 2071

Miller, Kim, 1825

Miller, Marian, 1089

Miller, Neal E., 280, 1210-1211, 1235, 1655

Miller, Norman, 909, 1458

Miller, Thomas, 1548

Milner, Peter, 991

Mind-body division. *See* Dualism

Mindfulness, 1152

Mineka, Susan, 168

Minimal brain dysfunction, 1259

Minnesota Multiphasic Personality Inventory, 341, 1211-1213

Minority groups. *See* Ethnicity

Minuchin, Salvador, 153, 759, 1544

Mirror stage, 130, 1076

Misbehavior, 1213-1217, 1677, 1745, 1996

Mischel, Walter, 420, 824, 1218

Mitchell, Stephen, 879

Mitler, Merrill M., 1017

MMPI. *See* Minnesota Multiphasic Personality Inventory

M'Naghten test, 11, 788, 1012

Mnemonic techniques, 1128, 1158

Model Penal Code test, 1012

Modeling, 18, 300, 397, 1217, 1656, 1816, 1927

Modeling therapy, 256, 1309-1313

Monahan, John, 13

Money, John, 1770

Mongolism. *See* Down syndrome

Monism, 1496, 1892

Monoamine oxidase inhibitors, 51, 158, 633, 1221, 1526

Monogamy, 1758

Montagu, Ashley, 1578

Montvilo, Robin, 70

Mood, 909, 1560

Mood disorders, 641, 1219-1225, 1442

Mood stabilizers, 634, 1223, 1225-1227, 1526

Moore, Gary T., 703

Moos, Rudolf, 492

Moral development, 613, 851, 1071, 1227-1231, 1435, 1565, 1603, 2059

Moral Judgement Interview, 2061

Moral model of helping, 910

Moral responsibility system, 651

Moral treatment, 1428

Morals; experimentation and, 730

Morgan, C. D., 1256

Morgan, Christiana, 1408

Morganstern, Kenneth P., 979

Moro reflex, 1612

Morphemes, 1077, 1113

Morphine, 695

Morphology, 857, 1077, 1113

Morris, Desmond, 1297

Morrison, Frederick, 1177

Mother archetype, 178

Mother-complex, 178

Mothers, relationship with children, 131, 201, 717, 763, 1231-1234, 2068

Motivation, 109, 320, 549, 804, 1019, 1034, 1234-1238, 1403, 1614, 1619, 1723, 1859; achievement, 21-25, 1257,

1408; incentive and drive, 628, 989-993; intrinsic and extrinsic, 1238-1240; sexual, 1750-1753; theory of, 914, 944; work, 347, 1333, 2072-2076

Motor coordination disorders, 364

Motor development, 192, 313, 1065, 1240-1244, 1677

Motor theory of speech perception, 1851

Mowrer, O. Hobart, 167

Mullainathan, Sendhil, 263

Mullany, Pat, 1475

Mullen, Brian, 527, 874, 1460

Mulley, John C., 1203

Multicultural psychology, 67, 529, 1244-1246

Multigenerational pattern, 760

Multiphasic tests, 1211

Multiple-aptitude tests, 1507

Multiple intelligences, 515, 518, 1025, 1032, 1246-1250

Multiple Neural Network Learning System, 450

Multiple personality. *See* Dissociative identity disorder

Multistore model of memory, 1181

Munchausen syndrome, 750, 972, 1253-1256

Munchausen syndrome by proxy, 751, 1253-1256

Murphy, Debra, 1401

Murray, Charles, 4, 1578

Murray, Henry A., 22, 1256-1257, 1407, 1975

Music therapy, 1257-1261

Mustin, Rachel Hare, 2062

Mutual exclusivity hypothesis of language, 1080

Myers, David G., 1439

Myers, Katharine Cook, 1262

Myers-Briggs Type Indicator, 141, 1261-1263

Myopia. *See* Nearsightedness

Mythomania, 546

Nakata, Mizuho, 1539

Nansel, Tonja R., 325

Narcissistic personality disorder, 33, 917, 1264-1266, 1387

Narcolepsy, 1266-1269

National Aphasia Association, 171

National Center for the Analysis of Violent Crime, 1475

National Hospice and Palliative Care Organization, 935

National Hospice Reimbursement Act (1983), 505

National Institute of Mental Health, 1270-1271

National Mental Health Act (1947), 1270

Native Americans, 1271-1273, 1306

Natural selection, 683, 711, 716, 1018, 1590

Nature-nurture debate, 2, 577, 714, 1025

Nearsightedness, 1273-1277, 2044

Necrophilia, 1773

Needs, 24, 1827; drives versus, 628; primary and secondary, 1407. *See also* Hierarchy of needs

Needs models of motivation, 2073

Negative affect theory, 78

Negative state relief theory, 109

Negotiation, 483-487

Neisser, Ulric, 207, 742, 1175, 1182, 1516

Nelson, Katherine, 1079

NEO Personality Inventory, 1048

Neobehaviorism, 1515

Neo-dissociation theory, 956

Neofunctionalism, 1516

Neologisms, 172

Nerenberg, Arnold, 1644

Nervous system, 785, 929, 1277-1280, 1849, 1934

Neuringer, Allen, 1101, 1105

Neuroactive drugs, 1934

Neurocomputing, 449

Neurodevelopmental therapy, 583

Neuroeconomics, 264

Neuroleptics. *See* Antipsychotics

Neuron theory of the brain, 1281

Neurons, 1007, 1277, 1280-1284, 1499, 1933

Neuropeptides, 1279, 1292

Neurophysiology, 1108, 1366

Neuropsychology, 1157, 1169, 1284-1287, 1503

Neuropsychopharmacology, 1935

Neurosis, 177, 654, 878, 1199, 1530, 1656, 1831, 2069

Neurotic disorders, 1287-1291

Neurotic patient (Lacanian psychology), 133

Neurotic psychopathy, 163

Neurotransmitters, 50, 929, 1008, 1163, 1225, 1291-1293, 1499, 1519, 1776, 1933

New York High-Risk Project, 1676

Newborns, 586, 981; reflexes, 1609-1613

Newell, Allen, 1125

Nicotine dependence, 101, 298, 1293-1295, 1466

Nidorf, J. F., 41

Night blindness, 2043

Night terrors, 624

Nightmares, 624

NIMH. *See* National Institute of Mental Health

Nisbett, Richard, 523, 735, 1339, 1405, 1722-1723

Nobles, Wade, 1581

Nociceptors, 1336, 1737, 2002

Noise pollution, 701

Nonrapid eye movement sleep, 1796

Nonverbal behavior, 844, 1045, 1297

Nonverbal communication, 31, 678, 1295-1300

Noradrenaline. *See* Norepinephrine

Norcross, James, 2011

Nordlie, Johanna, 964

Norenzayan, Ara, 523

Norepinephrine, 50, 568, 633, 1009, 1292, 2017

Normative decision theory, 548

Norms, 215, 259, 395, 498

Nosology, 1198

NREM. *See* Nonrapid eye movement sleep

Nutrition, 233, 673, 1300-1303

Obesity, 153, 640, 1304-1309, 1803

Object permanence, 403

Object relations theory, 554, 666

Objectivity, 727

Observation; clinical, 381-385

Observational learning, 1309-1313, 1816

Observational methods, 254, 258, 585, 1314-1317, 1971

Observer ratings, 1400

Obsessions, 383, 1518

Obsessive-compulsive disorder, 302, 1317-1322, 1388, 1518, 2005, 2080

Obsessive-compulsive personality disorder, 1387

Obsessive neurosis, 1289

Occupation; gender roles, 828

Occupational Information Network, 349

Occupational Outlook Handbook, 349, 1034

Occupational theory, 1034

Oedipus complex, 131, 803, 877, 1322-1323, 1375, 1529, 1681, 2068

Office for the Advancement of Telehealth, 1041

Ogbu, John, 1272

Okamura, Amy, 906

Olds, James, 991

Oliner, Pearl, 911

Oliner, Samuel, 911

Ollendick, Thomas, 259

Olton, David S., 409

Olweus, Dan, 324

Omega-3 fatty acids, 1302

Omission training, 1614

Oneironmancy, 624

O*NET. *See* Occupational Information Network

Onslow, Mark, 1912

Operant chamber. *See* Skinner box

Operant conditioning. *See* Conditioning, operant

Operant conditioning therapies. *See* Behavior modification

Operationism, 727

Opponent process theory of motivation, 883

Oppositional defiant disorder, 162, 366, 462

Optimal arousal theory, 1328-1332

Optimal experience, 1440

Optimism, 493, 502, 898, 1439, 1705

Oral stage, 803, 1493, 1528, 2068

Ord, William, 1990

Organ dialect, 31

Organic lamp theories, 578

Organic theories of schizophrenia, 1681

Organismic theory of personality, 1707

Organismic worldview, 590, 705

Organization (memory), 1167

Organizational behavior modification, 2074

Organizational psychology, 1575

Organizations, 944, 1129, 1451; behavior, 1332-1334

Orgasmic disorders, 1764

Ornstein, Robert, 475

Orton, Samuel T., 638, 1108, 1857

Orton-Gillingham-Stillman method, 638

Ortony, Andrew, 684

Osmond, Humphry, 1300

Osteoporosis, 88

Ostrom, Thomas, 1459

Ostrove, Nancy, 1089

Out-group homogeneity hypothesis of racism, 1584

Out-groups, 1810

Overmier, J. Bruce, 1099, 1101

Owsley, Cynthia, 2036

Oxford Group, 1927

Oxytocin, 932, 1292, 1431

Pacific Islanders, 188-191

Pain, 313, 475, 957, 962, 1335-

1338, 1656, 1916, 1964; management, 25, 505, 695, 1338-1342

Pain, during sexual intercourse. *See* Dyspareunia

Painter, Susan, 243

Paivio, Allen, 411

Palliative medicine, 505, 542, 935

Palmer, John, 416

Palmore, Erdman, 70

Panic attacks, 169, 787, 1343-1346, 1418

Panic disorders, 96-100, 425

Paradoxical procedures, 1882

Paradoxical sleep. *See* Rapid eye movement sleep

Parallel processing, 1986

Paranoia, 133, 1346-1349, 1560

Paranoid personality disorder, 1386

Paranoid schizophrenia, 1672

Paraphasias, 172

Paraphilias, 775, 1592, 1659, 1770-1775, 2014

Parasitism, 555

Parasympathetic nervous system, 785

Paratelic system of arousal, 1331

Parens patriae, 12

Parental alienation syndrome, 1349-1350, 1742

Parental manipulation model of homosexuality, 923

Parenting, 240, 266, 753, 847, 922, 982, 1425; conduct disorder, 464; divorce, 1349, 1745; separation anxiety, 1749; stepfamilies, 1876; stuttering, 1910; styles, 764, 996, 1351-1355; therapeutic, 1602

Pargament, Kenneth I., 507, 796, 1624

Park, Robert, 777

Parker, Gordon, 1695

Parkinson, James, 1355

Parkinson's disease, 560, 1010, 1355-1358, 1935

Parry, Caleb, 1991

Parsons, Frank, 346, 1036

Participant observation, 779

PAS. *See* Parental alienation syndrome

Pask, Gordon, 650

Passion, 1132

Passive aggression, 1358-1360

Passive theories of speech perception, 1850

Pathogenic-pathoplastic model, 532

Pathological lying, 546

Pathophobia, 1418

Pattern recognition, 1360-1363

Pattern vision, 1364-1367

Patterson, Gerald, 266, 1543

Paul, Gordon L., 1941

Paul Wellstone and Pete Domenici Mental Health Parity and Addiction Equity Act. *See* Mental Health Parity and Addiction Equity Act (2008)

Pauling, Linus, 1301

Pavlov, Ivan Petrovich, 238, 265, 269, 456, 1101, 1235, 1367-1368, 1608, 1614, 1945

Pavlovian conditioning. *See* Conditioning, classical

Peabody Individual Achievement Test, 1373-1374

Pearson, Karl, 1873

Peck, Robert, 1639

Pecking order. *See* Dominance

Pedophilia, 925, 1593, 1771

Peer pressure, 41, 62, 826

Penis envy, 565, 804, 1374-1376, 2064, 2068

Pennebaker, James W., 1887

Penrose, Roger, 448

Pepper, Stephen C., 704

Perception, 396, 703, 1732-1736; depth, 572-576, 2043; motion, 572-576; stress, 1894, 1900; threshold of, 1791

Perceptual constancy, 1850

Perceptual vigilance, 1790

Performance, 23, 259, 938, 1329, 1333, 1887; learning versus, 409

Performance-based teaching methods. *See* Active teaching methods

Peripheral nervous system, 1278

Perlmutter, Marion, 90

Perls, Fritz, 843, 869

Permissive style of parenting, 1351

Perry, William, 394

Persecutory delusional disorder, 1347

Persistent psychophysiological insomnia, 1014

Person, Ethel, 1450

Person-centered therapy, 846, 944, 1377-1382, 1393, 1557, 1645, 1706

Person-environment theories, 704

Person-situation debate, 422

Persona archetype, 136

Personal attributions, 227

Personal construct psychology, 420, 1063, 1382-1385

Personal disposition styles, 493

Personal growth, 19, 915, 1377, 1706, 2075

Personal space, 703

Personal unconscious, 135, 139, 1488

Personality; addictive, 25; birth order, 295-298; creativity, 518; environment, 703; Sigmund Freud, 1491-1495; integration of, 663, 755; interviewing strategies, 1391-1394; psychophysiological measures, 1394-1399; rating scales, 340, 1399-1402, 1507, 1975; stress, 502, 1893, 1900

Personality disorders, 161, 916, 1385-1390, 1661

Personality psychology, 1506

Personality Research Form, 342

Personality theory, 1402-1406, 1551; Hermann Rorschach, 1646

Personality traits, 1754; Hans Eysenck, 743; impulse control disorders, 987; jurors, 1090

Personhood, 723

Personology, 1256, 1406-1410

Persuasion, 218, 1090, 1451, 1722

Pert, Candace, 698
Pervasive developmental disorders, 365, 580, 1107, 1410-1414
Perverse patient (Lacanian psychology), 133
Petersen, Ronald C., 84
Peterson, Lloyd, 1779
Pettigrew, Thomas F., 1453, 1583
Petty, Richard, 219
Phallic stage, 654, 803, 922, 1493, 1529, 2068
Pharmacokinetics, 1524
Phasic activity, 1395
Phenomenological therapy, 1377
Phenomenology, 723, 945, 1503, 1568
Phenothiazines, 160
Phenylbutylpiperadines, 160
Phenylketonuria, 1204
Pheochromocytoma, 50
Pheromones, 693, 931, 981, 1431, 1750, 1759
Phi phenomenon, 575, 1513
Philosophy, relation to psychology, 1415-1418, 1509
Phobias, 167, 272, 383, 425, 1102, 1289, 1418-1423, 1886, 1940, 2031; children, 259; weight, 151
Phonemes, 1113, 1849
Phonological loop, 1780
Phonology, 857, 1077, 1113
Photo therapy. See Light therapy
Photographic memory, 1184
Photoreceptors, 2002, 2038
Phrase structure rules, 1114
Phrenology, 1286, 1511
Phylyshyn, Zenon, 411
Physical development; birth, 290-295; environment versus genetics, 1423-1426; prenatal, 620, 1461-1462, 1464-1467
Physical symbol system hypothesis, 186
Physiological psychology, 1506
Piaget, Jean, 36, 394, 401, 478, 1426-1427; consciousness, 469;

development, 40, 578, 1066; intelligence, 1030; language, 1081; moral development, 1227, 1565
PIAT. See Peabody Individual Achievement Test
Pibloktoq, 20, 1520
Pica, 366
Piliavin, Jane Allyn, 109, 908
Pinel, Philippe, 165, 1195, 1428-1429, 1556
Piotrowski, Zygmunt, 627
Pittman, Thane, 1726
Pituitary gland, 314, 692, 1429-1433, 1989
PKU. See Phenylketonuria
Placebo effect, 697, 1279, 1339, 1433-1434, 1690
Plaques, amyloid, 116
Play; fathers and, 1353
Play therapy, 1434-1438, 1542-1543
Pleasure principle, 26, 665, 1235, 1487
Pleck, Joseph, 825
Plomin, Robert, 1426
Plutchik, Robert, 684
Polanyi, Michael, 1702
Political economic theory, 667
Polyandry, 1758
Polygyny, 1758
Polysomnograph, 1803
Poppen, Roger L., 1652
Popular psychology, 1147
Pornography, 2021
Porter, Natalie, 1755
Positive psychology, 1438-1441, 1730
Positive reinforcement, 1325
Positivism, 1511
Post, Stephen G., 911
Postformal thought, 39
Postpartum depression, 1224, 1441-1443, 1991, 2055
Postpartum psychosis, 1442, 2058
Postpartum thyroiditis, 1991
Post-traumatic stress disorder, 243, 605, 624, 737, 1443-1448, 1887, 2028, 2032

Potential, realization of, 1828
Power, 62, 1052, 1216, 1297, 1448-1452, 1726, 1787
Power, Mick, 684
Power distance, 686
PPD. See Postpartum depression
PPOs. See Preferred provider organizations
Practice Directorate, 125
Pragmatics, 1077, 1115
Prata, Guiliana, 1881
Preattentive stage, 207
Preconscious, 472
Predation, 555
Predator-prey interactions, 556
Preferred provider organizations, 893
Prejudice, 530, 783, 998, 1089, 1452-1457, 1583, 1619, 1753, 1813; reduction, 1457-1461
Premack, David, 459, 1616
Premack principle, 1616
Premenstrual dysphoric disorder, 2055
Preoperational stage, 402, 578, 1427
Preparedness, 168, 1948
Presbyopia. See Farsightedness
Pressure, 1407, 1999-2003
Prevention programs, 436
Pribram, Karl, 472
Primacy effect, 1825
Primary Mental Health Project, 437
Primary sex characteristics, 45
Priming, 412, 1181
Primitive reflexes, 1612
Principled negotiation, 484
Principles Concerning the Counseling and Therapy of Women, 775
Prisoner's dilemma, 483
Prisons, drama therapy in, 1259
Pritchard, James, 165
Private logic, 31, 997
Probability, 1663, 1871
Probe recall, 1166
Problem-focused coping strategy, 491, 501

Problem solving, 37, 512, 1025, 1437; stages of, 1467-1470; strategies, 1470-1474
Problem-solving therapy, 398
Procedural memory, 1127, 1499
Prochaska, James O., 2011
Productive love, 1828
Productive work, 1828
Profiling, 789, 1474-1477
Progesterone, 854, 1750
Progressive lateralization hypothesis of learning disorders, 1108
Progressive relaxation, 280, 1152
Project Chronos, 90
Projection, 17, 553, 656, 879, 1477-1481
Projective hypothesis, 1478
Projective techniques, 32
Propinquity, 58
Propositional hypothesis, 411
Proprioception, 1064, 2000
Proprium, 108, 947
Prosocial behavior, 109, 528, 912, 1311
Prospect theory, 263
Prospective memory, 418, 1183
Proxemics, 703
Proximity, 223
Pryor, John, 1459
Pseudodementia, 560
Pseudologia fantastica, 546, 750
Psyche, 135
Psychiatric social workers, 1192
Psychiatrists, 1191
Psychoactive drugs, 469, 473, 888
Psychoanalysis, 656, 801, 868, 1076, 1481-1487, 1542, 2070
Psychoanalytic psychology, 17, 615, 922, 1319, 1487-1491, 1505, 1531; Sigmund Freud, 1491-1495
Psychoanalytic psychotherapy, 1290, 1484
Psychobiology, 460, 691, 1495-1500
Psychodynamic theories of schizophrenia, 1681
Psychodynamic theory of development, 577

Psychodynamic therapies, 1552
Psychogenic amnesia, 127
Psychological distance; Internet communications, 1040
Psychologists, 1191
Psychology; definition of, 1500-1504; fields of specialization, 1504-1509; history, 1509-1517
Psychometrics, 2, 36, 67, 1022, 1623; personality rating scales, 1400
Psychoneuroimmunology, 899, 1895
Psychoneurosis, 1288
Psychopathology, 259, 360, 764, 1141, 1517-1522, 1530; Erich Fromm, 1830; positive psychology versus, 1438
Psychopaths. See Sociopaths
Psychopathy Checklist-Revised, 1844
Psychopharmacology, 632, 1523-1528
Psychophysics, 904
Psychophysiology, 832
Psychosexual development, 659, 922, 1528-1532, 1660, 2068
Psychosexual stages, 1487, 1492
Psychosis, 104, 160, 672, 1199, 1671
Psychosocial development theory, 660, 710, 974, 1488
Psychosomatic disorders, 280, 1532-1537
Psychosomatic medicine, 832, 1893
Psychosurgery, 1498, 1537-1541, 1556
Psychotherapy, 106, 478, 868; analytical, 138-142; children, 1541-1546; effectiveness, 1546-1551; goals and techniques, 1551-1554; historical approaches, 1554-1559; transactional analysis versus, 2007
Psychotic disorders, 284, 1559-1563
Psychotic patient (Lacanian psychology), 133

Psychotropics, 632, 1523; shock therapy versus, 1778
Puberty, 40, 44, 853
Public Interest Directorate, 125
Publications, ethics regarding, 1632
Pulfrich pendulum effect, 2036
Punishment, 271, 407, 459, 879, 1103, 1325, 1563-1566, 1588, 1614; corporal, 1104; negative, 1326; positive, 1326
Puusepp, Ludvig, 1119
Puységur, marquis de, 959
Pyromania, 987

Quality of life, 1570-1572
Quality time, 763
Quay, Herbert, 164
Quest Scale, 1625
Questionnaires, 596, 969, 1693, 1929
Quinlan, Donald, 1259
Quinn, Joseph F., 1640

Race, 288, 433, 1089, 1453, 1812; intelligence, 743, 1578-1582, 1972
Racism, 66, 530, 1583-1587, 1826
Rackets, 2008
RAD. See Reactive attachment disorder
Radical behaviorism, 270, 1587-1591, 1792
Rage, 142
Rahe, Richard, 491, 1889, 1894
Ramón y Cajal, Santiago, 1281
Rank, Otto, 803, 1381
Rape, 614, 1591-1595, 1662, 2021
Rapid eye movement sleep, 313, 380, 473, 624, 1796
Raskin, N. J., 1379
Rational behavior therapy, 397
Rational emotive therapy, 256, 397, 411, 676, 1595-1599
Rationality, 11, 262, 549, 1595
Rationalization, 657
Raven, Bertram, 1451
Rayner, Rosalie, 269, 767, 1118, 1370, 1421, 2046
Reaction formation, 17, 553, 657

Reactive attachment disorder, 367, 1425, 1600-1602
Readiness, law of, 1980
Reading, 1243
Reading disorder, 1107, 1177
Realistic conflict theory of prejudice, 1453
Reality; perception of, 723, 956, 1098
Reality principle, 665, 1235, 1487
Reality therapy, 1603-1606
Reasoned action theory, 215, 480
Reasoning, 316, 1121-1126, 1469, 1471, 1981; adolescence and, 37. *See also* Deductive reasoning; Inductive reasoning
Rebellion, 42
Rebirth archetype, 179
Rebirthing, 1602
Recall, 794, 1166
Re-careering, 348
Reception learning, 652
Receptive aphasia, 172
Reciprocal determinism, 1815
Reciprocal inhibition, 1940
Reciprocity, 223
Recognition (memory), 794, 1166
Recollections, 32
Reconditioning, 1542
Recruiting, 1005
Referential language acquisition styles, 1079
Reflex arc system, 882
Reflexes, 313, 1606-1610; newborns, 293, 1610-1613; sucking, 883
Reframing, 1883
Regression, 17, 656, 1530, 2010
Rehm, Lynn, 399
Reich, Wilhelm, 1260, 1298
Reicher, Stephen, 527
Reilly, Richard, 259
Reinforcement, 18, 258, 271, 280, 1103, 1588, 1613-1618; attraction, 222; bed-wetting, 251; conditioning, 1372; partial, 458, 991; pathological gambling, 809; positive, 1325; prosocial behavior, 111; S-R

theory, 1655; schedules of, 1588; time-out, 1996
Reinforcement-affect model, 222
Reinforcing stimulus, 458, 1588
Reiss, Steven, 1396
Relapsing, 105, 1883
Relational schemata, 1835
Relationships, 222, 511, 760, 874, 1053, 1297, 1439; couples, 509, 1134; digital technology, 60; fathers with children, 131, 762-766; friends, 57; men, 1186; mothers with children, 131, 201, 717, 1231-1234, 2068; parents and children, 753; parents with children, 878, 1489; siblings, 1785-1788; stepparents with stepchildren, 1876; therapist and client, 139, 1552, 1555, 1596, 1645, 1657, 2009; women, 2065
Relaxation, 1152-1155, 1341, 1345, 1420, 1897, 1939
Reliability, 1315
Religion, 507, 891; helping and, 911; psychology, 1618-1623
Religiosity, 1623-1628
Religious Orientation Scale, 1625
REM sleep. *See* Rapid eye movement sleep
Remarriage, 756
Reminiscence therapy, 1183
Repair and restoration theory of sleep, 1798
Repetition compulsion, 132
Repisodic memories, 1182
Representativeness heuristic, 1824
Repressed memories, 475, 793, 1253, 1628-1629
Repression, 17, 99, 167, 553, 654, 679, 793, 802, 1628; S-R theory, 1657
Reproductive behavior, 693, 930
Reproductive Biology Research Foundation, 1140
Rescorla, Robert, 1609
Rescorla-Wagner Model, 457
Research; descriptive, 727, 733, 1930; ethics, 1630-1634;

experimentation versus, 733; factor-analytic, 1024; human development, 585, 591; idiographic, 948; qualitative, 351, 1567-1570; quantitative, 351. *See also* Experimentation; Sampling; Scientific method
Research Center for Group Dynamics, 1111
Residual schizophrenia, 1672
Resiliency, 1535, 1960, 2028
Resistance, 34, 268, 656, 1392, 1551, 1882
Resistant attachment, 204
Resperidal. *See* Resperidone
Resperidone, 160
Response, 989, 1607
Responsibility, 327, 909, 1604
Ressler, Robert, 1594
Restoration, after brain damage, 310
Restraining, 1883
Restricted environmental stimulation therapy, 476
RET. *See* Rational emotive therapy
Reticular formation, 313, 1330, 1634-1637, 1682
Reticular theory of the brain, 1281
Retirement, 198, 263, 754, 1637-1641
Retrieval (memory), 740, 1127, 1159
Retrospective memory, 1183
Rett, Andreas, 1413
Rett syndrome, 365, 1413
Reversibility, 36
Revised Minnesota Paper Form Board Tests, 341
Rewards, 110, 222, 406, 421, 488, 735, 990, 1101
Rhythmic breathing, 281
Rice, Robert, 1094
Richardson, Frank, 1703
Riecken, Henry, 58
Rimm, Sylvia, 519
Rips, Lance, 1181
Risk assessment, 1641-1643
Risley, Todd, 1996

Rites of passage, 41

Riverside Cooperative Learning Project, 488

RMPFBT. *See* Revised Minnesota Paper Form Board Tests

Road rage, 75, 985, 1643-1645

Robins, L. N., 906

Robins, Lee, 162

Rodin, Judith, 898, 1099, 1888

Roethlisberger, Fritz, 2075

Rogers, Carl R., 846, 944, 1377, 1393, 1553, 1557, 1645-1646, 1700, 1705

Rogoff, Barbara, 704

Role Construct Repertory Test, 1384

Role models, 41

Role-playing, 255, 1229, 1258, 2009

Rooting reflex, 1609, 1612

Rorschach, Hermann, 1646-1647

Rorschach inkblots, 340, 1479, 1646-1649

Rosario, Margaret, 48

Rose, Amanda J., 59

Rosenhan, David L., 20, 780, 1199, 1649

Rosenhan experiment, 20, 780, 1199, 1649-1650

Rosenkrantz, Paul, 1754

Rosenman, Ray, 502, 1895, 1901, 2016

Rosenthal, Norman, 1695

Rosenthal, Richard, 985

Rosenthal, Robert, 1237, 1314, 1825

Rosman, Bernice, 153

Ross, Lee, 227

Rothbart, Myron, 1584

Rotter, Julian, 1397

Royal Society of Psychiatrists, 121

Rozin, Paul, 1946

Rubin, Zick, 58, 225, 1710

Rules for decision making, 82, 547, 1297

Rumination, 366

Runner's high, 697

Rush, Benjamin, 120, 1195

Rushton, William A. H., 2040

Rutsein, Jeffrey, 355

S-R theory, 1655-1658

S-sleep, 624, 1796

Saari, Lise, 2052

Sabshin, Melvin, 122

Sacher-Masoch, Leopold von, 1659

Sackheim, Harold, 964

Sacks, Oliver, 1362

Sacrificial care; helping and, 911

SAD. *See* Seasonal affective disorder

Sade, Marquis de, 1659

Sadism, 1593, 1659-1662, 1771

Sadistic personality disorder, 1661

St. John's wort, 159

Sajwaj, Thomas, 1326

Salovey, Peter, 681

SAMHSA. *See* Substance Abuse and Mental Health Services Administration

Sampling, 181, 1662-1666, 1689, 1930

Sampson, Edward, 1703

Samuelson, Robert J., 409

Sapir, Edward, 860

Sapir-Whorf hypothesis, 1082

Sarbin, T. R., 956

Sartre, Jean-Paul, 724, 1660

SAT Reasoning Test, 4, 394, 431, 1973

Satiety, 951

Satir, Virginia, 759, 1666-1667

Satisfaction; decision making, 867

Sattler, Jerome M., 1031

Saunders, Cicely, 505, 935

Scale for Suicide Ideation, 246

Scarr, Sandra, 1426, 1581

SCAT. *See* School and College Ability Test

Schachter, E. P., 976

Schachter, Stanley, 56, 297, 355, 954, 1339

Schacter, Daniel, 791, 793

Scheckenbach, Albert F., 79

Scheier, Michael F., 898

Schemata, 207, 401, 424, 825, 1825

Schildkraut, Joseph, 51

Schizoaffective disorder, 1560

Schizoid personality disorder, 1386, 1667-1670; avoidant personality disorder versus, 241

Schizophrenia, 7, 722, 1072, 1387, 1518, 2080; autism, 230; background, types, and symptoms, 1670-1674; bipolar disorder versus, 284; children, 367, 375; dopamine, 1010, 1280; double-bind theory, 1880; drug therapy, 635; elderly, 672; genetics, 839; hallucinations, 887; high-risk children, 1675-1680; homelessness, 919; nutrition therapy, 1300; paranoia versus, 1347; psychosis, 1560; shock therapy, 1537, 1776; theoretical explanations, 1680-1685; women, 2056

Schizophreniform disorder, 1560

Schizotypal personality disorder, 1387, 1683, 1685-1688

Schlenker, Barry, 1728

Schlossberg, Nancy, 347

Schnarch, David, 1766

Schneider, Kurt, 165

Schneider, Walter, 235

Schoenrade, P., 1625

Schofield, Janet, 1459

School and College Ability Test, 3

School issues, 360, 1747

Schulsinger, Fini, 1676

Schulz, Leslie Olmstead, 1306

Schwartz, Robert, 953

Science Directorate, 125

Scientific management, 1332, 2075

Scientific method, 727, 733, 966, 1503, 1505, 1509, 1688-1694

SCII. *See* Strong-Campbell Interest Inventory

Scoville, William, 1173, 1781

Screening, 595

Scripts, 47, 1834

Sdorow, Lester, 82

SDS. *See* Self-Directed Search

Searle, John, 186

Seasonal affective disorder, 9, 284, 379, 700, 1224, 1694-1699
Sechenov, Ivan, 1608
Second-signal system of conditioning, 1370
Secondary sex characteristics, 45
Seduction theory, 2071
Seitz, Jay A., 1065
Sekule, Robert, 2036
Selective mutism, 367
Selective norepinephrine reuptake inhibitors, 1221
Selective serotonin reuptake inhibitors, 156, 158, 303, 633, 1221, 1526, 1697
Self, 1699-1704
Self-actualization, 19, 30, 64, 915, 943, 1154, 1378, 1704-1708
Self-analysis, 1833
Self archetype, 136
Self-awareness, 844
Self-characterization sketch, 1384
Self-concept, 19, 42, 1377, 1701, 1715, 1727, 1810
Self-condemnation, 1596
Self-confidence, 1909
Self-control, 421
Self-control therapy, 399
Self-definition, 873
Self-Directed Search, 341, 349
Self-direction, 1378
Self-disclosure, 1044, 1708-1712
Self-discovery, 141
Self-efficacy, 1239, 1535, 1701, 1712-1715, 1816
Self-esteem, 25, 31, 54, 360, 996, 1051, 1097, 1378, 1435, 1453, 1715-1719, 1783, 1859
Self-fulfilling prophecies, 1825
Self-generated persuasion, 220
Self-help groups, 507, 1719-1720. See also Support groups
Self-identity, 1045
Self-image, 1296, 1726
Self-inflated personality, 1829
Self-instructional training, 397
Self-interest, 109, 483
Self-knowledge; causal, 1722
Self-medication theories of substance use disorders, 1917

Self-modeling, 1312
Self-monitoring, 215, 254, 258, 426, 1701, 1728
Self-mutilation, 304
Self-perception theory, 219, 1721-1725
Self-presentation, 1725-1729
Self psychology, 1514
Self ratings, 1400
Self-realization, 943, 1056
Self-regulation, 1815
Self-regulatory systems, 421
Self-report questionnaires, 254
Self-report research methods, 585, 1929
Self-schema, 1835
Self-serving bias, 228
Self-socialization, 825
Self-talk, 397
Selfish gene, 65
Seligman, Martin E. P., 355, 1097, 1101, 1439, 1535, 1730, 1887, 1946
Sells, S. B., 1401, 1983
Selman, Robert, 38
Selvini-Palazzoli, Mara, 1881
Selye, Hans, 830, 863, 1731-1732, 1891, 1894, 1899
Semantic differential, 1454
Semantic-encoding hypothesis of synethesia, 1938
Semantic memory, 415, 1127, 1156-1157, 1166, 1180, 1985
Semantic verification tasks, 1181
Semantics, 1077, 1114
Senescence. See Aging
Sensation, 192, 233, 315, 1732-1736
Sense of coherence, 502
Senses, 88, 313, 1736-1740, 1999
Sensitization, 881-885, 1160
Sensorimotor stage, 401, 578, 1427
Sensory deprivation, 476
Sensory integration therapy, 583
Sensory leakage theory of synesthesia, 1937
Sensory memory, 1126, 1156, 1174-1180

Separation; adult issues, 1740-1743; children's issues, 1743-1747
Separation anxiety, 1233, 1747-1750
Separation anxiety disorder, 367
Separation protest, 203
Sequential research designs, 586, 591
Sequential Tests of Educational Progress, 3
Serial learning, 1166
Serial-position effect, 1180
Serial processing, 1986
Serialist learning styles, 650
Serotonin, 50, 568, 633, 809, 1010, 1172, 1220, 1279, 1292
Serotonin-norepinephrine reuptake inhibitors, 156, 159
Set point theory, 952
Seven sins of memory, 793
Sex hormones, 852, 930, 1759; sexual motivation, 1750-1753
Sex-role transcendence, 825
Sex therapy, 1766
Sexism, 1753-1757
Sexual assault, 614, 1591-1595
Sexual behavior, 854, 1140, 1431, 1750; experimentation and, 730; patterns, 1757-1761
Sexual desire disorders, 1763
Sexual dysfunction, 1761-1767
Sexual harassment, 1767-1770
Sexual masochism, 1659
Sexual orientation, 48, 814, 854, 891, 924
Sexual response cycle, 1762
Sexual sadism, 1659
Sexual selection, 1758
Sexual variants, 1770-1775
Sexuality, 72, 76, 90, 1046, 1067, 1289; adolescence, 40, 44-48; media depictions of, 2020-2024
Shadow archetype, 136, 139
Shadowing, 208
Shame, 879
Shaping, 26, 1102
Shapiro, Francine, 737
Shared psychotic disorder, 1560
Shaver, Kelly, 228

Shaver, Philip, 1134
Sheehy, Gail, 1206
Sherif, Carolyn, 1460
Sherif, Muzafer, 486, 1460
Sherrington, Charles, 1281, 1291, 1609
Shevrin, Howard, 1289
Shiffrin, Richard, 235, 689, 1178, 1181, 1779
Shift work, 378
Shisslak, Catherine, 155
Shneidman, Edwin, 1922
Shoben, Edward, 1181
Shock therapy, 51, 75, 1172, 1196, 1222, 1537, 1775-1779
Shockley, William, 4, 1578
Shoda, Yuichi, 1218
Shontz, Franklin, 491
Shore, Cecilia, 1079
Short-term anxiety-provoking psychotherapy, 320
Short-term memory, 82, 415, 418, 688, 1126, 1156, 1165, 1175, 1779-1783, 1985
Short-term psychotherapy. See Brief therapy
Shyness, 1783-1785; Philip Zimbardo, 2087
Siblings, 1052, 1785-1788, 1877
Siegal, J. M., 1636
Siegall, Marc, 1005
Sifneos, Peter, 320
Sigall, Harold, 1089
Sight, 1736
Sign bilingualism, 277
Signal detection theory, 1732, 1789-1792
Signifier and signified, 132
SII. See Strong Interest Inventory
Similarity; attraction, 224
Simmelhag, V., 459
Simon, Herbert, 262, 1125
Simon, Théodore, 1027, 1029, 1865, 1971
Singer, Jerome E., 355
Singleton, Royce, Jr., 777
Situational attributions, 227
Sixteen Personality Factor Questionnaire, 342
Skills training, 512, 1311

Skinner, B. F., 265, 270, 458, 1326, 1587, 1651, 1792-1794; language acquisition, 1112; learning, 1102; personality, 1395; reinforcement, 1615; small-*n* experimental designs, 2053
Skinner box, 1589, 1793-1795
Skrzypek, George, 164
Slavin, Robert, 488, 651, 1952
Sleep, 313, 469, 473, 1267, 1431, 1635, 1796-1802; bed-wetting, 250. See also Dreams; Insomnia
Sleep apnea, 1803-1805
Sleep deprivation, 889
Sleep disorders, 332, 368, 378; homelessness, 920
Sleep mentation, 623
Sleep study. See Polysomnograph
Sleep-wake cycle, 376, 473, 1014
Slobin, Dan Isaac, 1080
Smell, 1176, 1299, 1737, 1805-1810
Smith, Edward, 1181
Smith, Mary, 1547
Smith, Robert, 28
Smith, Stephanie, 356
Smoking, health hazards of, 1294
Smoreda, Zbigniew, 827
Sniezek, Janet A., 866
Snow, Katherine, 1112
SNRIs. See Serotonin-norepinephrine reuptake inhibitors
Snyder, C. R., 356, 927
Snyder, Mark, 215, 1701
Snyder, Solomon H., 698
Sobel, Nathan, 740
Sociability, 1330
Social anxiety disorder, 1520
Social change, 783
Social cognition, 418, 1835
Social cognitive theory. See Social learning theory
Social comparison theory, 56, 498
Social constructionism, 1510, 1516
Social control, 1296
Social convoy model, 1823

Social distance scale, 1585
Social exchange theory, 223
Social facilitation, 1329, 1927
Social-functional interactionist theory, 1081
Social identity theory, 525, 1810-1815, 1859, 1970
Social influence, 1867
Social intelligence, 38
Social interactions, 192, 211, 232, 240, 488, 622, 850, 1039, 1296, 1668, 1846, 2007, 2009
Social interest, 997
Social isolation, 1921; violence by children and teenagers, 2025
Social judgment theory, 219
Social learning theory, 242, 299, 578, 1215, 1419, 1815-1819, 1926, 2022; aggression, 79; elder abuse, 667; homosexuality, 923; Neil Miller and John Dollard, 1210; personality, 1395, 1403; self, 1701, 1713
Social movements, 1456
Social Network Index, 1822
Social networks, 60, 1040, 1819-1823, 1841
Social perception, 1823-1827, 1836
Social phobia, 97, 1418, 1783, 1912
Social power, 1449
Social psychological models, 956; Erich Fromm, 1827-1831; Karen Horney, 1831-1834
Social psychology, 111, 216, 1506
Social Readjustment Rating Scale, 491, 1894
Social schemata, 1834-1838
Social Security Act (1935), 71, 1638
Social support, 90, 569, 876, 1439, 1446, 1626, 1719, 1820, 1838-1842; coping, 492, 495-499, 503; stress, 1899, 1901
Social workers, 1192
Socialization, 42, 111, 1722, 2060
Society and Animals Forum, 148

Society for Individual Psychology, 29

Society for the Scientific Study of Religion, 1622

Society for Traumatic Stress Studies, 1447

Sociobiology, 64, 713, 1927

Socioeconomic status, 23, 67, 162, 616, 1087, 1305, 1453, 2028

Socioemotional selectivity theory, 1823

Sociopaths, 163, 1842-1844

Solman, Robert, 1177

Somatic delusional disorder, 1348

Somatic senses, 2002

Somatic sensory cortex, 2002

Somatic theory, 1538

Somatic therapy, 1521

Somatization, 960-965, 1340

Somatization disorder, 162

Somatoform disorders, 368, 960, 972, 1536

SOMPA. See System of Multicultural Pluralistic Assessment

Sound, generation of, 901

South Oaks Gambling Screen, 809, 987

Spatial memory, 409

Spearman, Charles, 2, 1024

Special education, 582, 639, 1109

Specialization; media psychology, 1148

Species-specific behavior, 1020

Spector, Paul E., 78

Speech, 192, 232, 856-861, 1080, 1672; direct and indirect, 1116

Speech disorders, 1845-1848, 1909

Speech-language pathology, 1847

Speech perception, 1848-1852

Spelke, Elizabeth, 523

Spence, Janet, 23

Spencer, Herbert, 1512

Spencer, K. W., 990

Sperling, George, 1175

Sperry, Roger, 317, 1512, 1855

Spiegel, Harold, 958

Spielberger, Charles, 1869, 1885

Spirituality, 338, 507, 1555, 1852-1854; helping and, 911

Spitalnik, Robert, 1996

Spitz, Rene, 565, 1600

Split attention, 207

Split-brain studies, 308, 317, 1854-1858

Sports psychology, 719, 1859-1864

Spousal abuse, 243, 614, 774

SQ3R method, 1129, 1158

SSRIs. See Selective serotonin reuptake inhibitors

Stability, 22

STAD. See Student teams-achievement divisions

Staddon, J. E. R., 459

Stage model of memory, 1779

Stage theories of family life, 756

Stage theories of language acquisition, 1078

Stages of adulthood, 662, 752

Stages of death, 863

STAI. See State-Trait Anxiety Inventory

Stampfl, Thomas G., 979

Standard deviation, 536

Stanford-Binet test, 1, 340, 847, 1864-1866, 1972

Stanford Hypnotic Susceptibility Scale, Form C, 956

Stanford prison experiment, 1866-1869

Stanton, H. E., 958

Starko, Alane, 519

Startle response, 881, 1612

State-dependent memory, 1128, 1158

State system, 882

State-Trait Anxiety Inventory, 1869-1870, 1885

Statistical significance, 2051

Statistical significance tests, 1870-1874; hypothesis testing, 969

Statistical theory, 1665

Statistics; decision making, 550; inferential, 540

Stein, Barry, 1470

Steiner, Ivan, 865

STEP. See Sequential Tests of Educational Progress

Stepfamilies, 1874-1877; fathers, 763

Stepfamily Association of America, 1876

Stephan, Walter G., 1584

Stepparent/parent involvement or style models, 1875

Stepper, Sabina, 747

Stepping reflex, 1612

Stereotypes, 70, 228, 718, 925, 1459, 1583, 1825, 1834; gender, 772, 817, 825, 827, 1754

Stereotypic movement disorder, 367

Stern, William, 108, 1027, 1865

Sternberg, Robert, 57, 514, 1023, 1025, 1132

Sternberg, Saul, 1986

Steroids, 931

Stevens, Albert, 412

Stewart, John, 1089

Stigma, mental illness, 906

Stillman, Essie, 638

Stimulants, 211, 331, 1877-1880; abuse, 1918

Stimulus, 1607; excitatory or inhibitory, 1008; habituation and sensitization, 881-882

Stimulus antecedents, 258

Stimulus control, 271

Stimulus-discrimination training, 1326

Stimulus-response learning theory, 629

Stimulus-response reflex, 270

Stjermsward, Jan, 1337

Stogdill, Ralph, 1096

Stokols, Daniel, 1886

Storms, Philip L, 78

Stott, Clifford, 527

Strack, Fritz, 747

Straits, Bruce, 777

Straits, Margaret, 777

Strange situation, 203, 1231

Strategic family therapy, 1880-1884

Strategic negotiation, 484

Straus, Murray, 1104

Strauss, Anselm L., 1568

Strentz, Thomas, 1888

Stress, 95, 142, 522, 655, 692, 696, 699, 785, 830, 932, 1335, 1639; behavioral and psychological responses, 1884-1890; Walter Bradford Cannon, 339; depression, 569; dissociative disorders, 127; meditation, 475, 1153; physiological responses, 1890-1894; post-traumatic stress disorder, 1444; reduction of, 280, 495, 719, 1927; theories, 1898-1902

Stress-induced analgesia, 1339

Stress inoculation training, 78, 256, 398

Stress psychology, 832

Stress-related diseases, 832, 1532, 1888, 1894-1898, 1900

Strong, Edward K., Jr., 339, 1036, 1902

Strong-Campbell Interest Inventory, 341

Strong Interest Inventory, 1036, 1902-1904

Strong Vocational Interest Blank, 340

Stroop, J. Ridley, 206

Structural family therapy, 759, 1544

Structural model of personality, 664

Structural psychotherapy, 399

Structuralism, 726, 1505, 1512, 1738, 1904-1908

Structure-of-intellect model, 1024

Stuart, Richard, 266

Student teams-achievement divisions, 488

Stumpf, Carl, 1513

Stuttering, 1845, 1856, 1909-1913

Subject-object distinctions, 131

Subjective expected utility theory, 548

Subjective experience, 468

Sublimation, 17, 554, 657

Subliminal messages, 55

Submission, 1298

Substance Abuse and Mental Health Services Administration, 1914-1915

Substance-induced psychotic disorder, 1561

Substance P, 1279

Substance use disorders, 439, 641, 1390, 1527, 1915-1920; codependency, 388; gender differences, 818; Latinos, 1087; Native Americans and Alaskan Natives, 1272; suicide, 1923, 1956; workplace, 2080. *See also* Alcohol dependence and abuse; nicotine dependence

Subtraction technique of thought measurement, 1985

Success, fear of, 23, 2066

Success identity, 1603

Sucking reflex, 1609, 1612

Sudden infant death syndrome, 1612

Sugerman, Roger, 1015

Suggestibility, 956

Suicidal gestures, 1922

Suicide, 181, 1642, 1820, 1920-1925; Asian Americans and Pacific Islanders, 190; bipolar disorder, 286; borderline personality disorder, 304; depression, 567; gender differences, 818, 1188; teenagers, 1954-1959, 1962

Suicide bombers, 1970

Sullivan, Harry Stack, 1489, 1681, 1700, 1925-1926

Summer depression. *See* Seasonal affective disorder

Sun, Yongmin, 1746

Sung, B. L., 41

Super, Donald, 347

Superego, 17, 664-666, 802, 878, 1492, 1530, 2068

Superstition, 459

Support groups, 337, 390, 562, 1926-1929. *See also* Self-help groups

Suppression, 655

Surgeon General's Scientific Advisory Committee on

Television and Social Behavior of 1972, 2022

Surgery; lobotomy, 1119; obesity, 1307; Parkinson's disease, 1358; sleep apnea, 1804; speech disorders, 1847; Tourette's syndrome, 2004; transsexuals, 1752; vision improvement, 1276, 2044. *See also* Lobotomy; Psychosurgery

Survey research, 596, 1663, 1693; questionnaires and interviews, 1929-1932

Sussman, L. K., 906

Sutherland, Grant R., 1203

SVIB. *See* Strong Vocational Interest Blank

Swallowing reflex, 1612

Swimming reflex, 1612

Sydenham, Thomas, 971

Symbol system hypothesis, 186

Syme, Leonard, 1820

Symonds, Alexandra, 2065

Sympathetic nervous system, 785

Symptom neurosis, 1290

Symptom prescription, 1883

Synaptic transmission, 1933-1936

Synchronicity, 1058

Synergic society, 1706

Synesthesia, 1936-1939

Syntax, 857, 1077, 1114

System of Multicultural Pluralistic Assessment, 277

Systematic desensitization, 239, 255, 266, 272, 1102, 1371, 1446, 1939-1942, 2031; relaxation techniques, 1153

Systematic rational restructuring, 398

Systems theories, 1943-1944, 2067

Syzygy, 178

Szasz, Thomas, 13, 16

T-test, 1872

Taft, Jessie, 1381

Taijin-kyofusho, 533

Tajfel, Henri, 525, 1810

Talk shows, psychologist on, 1147

Talking therapy, 804, 871

Target behavior, 253

Tarnow, Eugen, 527

Tarule, Jill Mattuck, 394

Task-oriented behavior, 22, 651, 1239

Taste, 1737, 1805-1810

Taste aversions, 238, 456, 716, 1020, 1102, 1162, 1945-1949

TAT. *See* Thematic Apperception Test

Tau proteins, 116

Taylor, C. W., 515

Taylor, Dalmas, 1709

Taylor, Donald, 1458

Taylor, Frederick Winslow, 1003, 1332, 2075

Taylor, Shelley, 1899

Teaching methods, 37, 649, 1949-1954

Teams-games-tournament, 488

Teddie, Charles, 355

Teenage suicide, 1921, 1954-1959

Teenagers, 1959-1963; violence, 2024-2027

Tegretol. *See* Carbamazepine

Telehealth, 446

Television violence, effect on viewers, 80, 587, 1143, 1311, 2020

Telic system of arousal, 1331

Temperament, 240

Temperature, 1963-1967

Temperature feedback, 1341

Teratogens, 1204, 1465

Terman, Lewis, 1, 847, 1027, 1029, 1515, 1865, 1972

Terminal illness, coping, 504-508

Territoriality, 557, 703, 930

Terrorism, 1968-1971

Test, Mary Ann, 1311

Test for Creative Thinking and Drawing Production, 519

Testing, 195, 403; career and personnel, 339-344, 349, 1005; clinical, 381-385, 1284, 1392, 1404; college entrance, 431-434; gender differences, 394; historical perspectives, 1515, 1971-1975

Testosterone, 75, 693, 853, 931, 1750

Teten, Howard, 1475

TGT. *See* Teams-games-tournament

Thalamus, 313, 1497

Thanatology, 505, 544

Thanatos, 64, 665, 1487

Theater therapy, 1257-1261

Thematic Apperception Test, 1256, 1408, 1479, 1975-1977

Theory X, 1706

Theory Y, 1706

Thermoreceptors, 1737, 1964, 2002

Third force. *See* Existential psychology

Thirst, 1977-1979

Thoits, Margaret, 1822

Thomas, James, 1325

Thomas, Laura E., 1178

Thompson, Helen, 842

Thompson, Richard F., 1609

Thoresen, Carl E., 796

Thorndike, Edward L., 265, 457, 630, 1101, 1473, 1513, 1587, 1614, 1908, 1979-1980

Thorndike, Robert L., 391

Thought, 315; automatic, 424; divergent, 516-517; inferential, 1980-1984; study and measurement, 1984-1988

Thought disorder, 1519, 1559, 1672

Threat simulation theory, 470

Three-systems approach, 169

THS. *See* Thyroid-stimulating hormone

Thurstone, L. L., 3, 1024, 1932

Thurstone scale, 1454

Thyroid gland, 9, 1988-1992

Thyroid-stimulating hormone, 1430, 1989

Thyrotoxicosis, 1991

Thyroxine, 1989

Tic disorders, 366, 1992-1996, 2003

Ticket to Work and Work Incentives Improvement Act (1999), 2076

Time, 779

Time and motion studies, 1003

Time-limited psychotherapy. *See* Brief therapy

Time loss, 1252

Time-out, 267, 652, 1326, 1996-1998

Tinbergen, Nikolaas, 711, 981

Tip-of-the-tongue phenomenon, 792

Tissot, Simon, 1752

Titchener, Edward, 206, 1512, 1904

Toffler, Alvin, 1449

Token economies, 460, 1325

Tolman, Edward C., 146, 409, 1473, 1713, 1998-1999

Tomer, Adrian, 505

Tomkins, Silvan, 746

Tomm, Karl, 797

Tonic activity, 1395

Top-down theories of speech perception, 1850

Torrance, E. Paul, 518

Torrance Tests of Creative Thinking, 518

Torrey, E. Fuller, 8

Touch, 1176, 1298, 1737, 1999-2003

Tourette, Georges Gilles de la, 2003

Tourette's syndrome, 366, 1993, 2003-2007

Tousignant, James, 968

Tracking, by ability, 38

Training, 395, 938, 1005

Trait anxiety, 1885

Trait factor theory, 346, 1036

Trait theory, 24, 26, 704, 947, 1399

Trance state, 956

Tranquilizers, 51

Transactional analysis, 869, 2007-2011

Transactional model, 491, 501

Transcendental meditation, 1153

Transference, 32, 139, 1288, 1483, 1494, 1553, 1657, 2070

Transformation, 140

Transformational grammar, 1114

Transformational leadership, 1093

Transgendered people, 813-817, 823

Transient insomnia, 1014

Transpersonal therapy, 868

Transsexualism, 825, 924, 1752. *See also* Gender identity disorder

Transtheoretical model, 2011-2013

Transvestic fetishism, 1771

Transvestism, 238, 924, 2013-2015

Trauma, 605, 1443, 1629, 2029; dissociative disorders, 128, 1251

Treatment and Education of Autistic and Related Communication Handicapped Children, 233

Treisman, Anne, 207

Trial and error, 1102, 1467

Trichotillomania, 988

Triiodothyronine, 1989

Triple-response system, 258

Trivers, Robert, 713

Troll, Lillian, 1640

Trust, 660, 1380, 1389

Tryon, Robert, 146

Tuckman, Bruce, 873

Tulving, Endel, 83, 688, 1127, 1180

Turing, Allen, 186

Turing test, 186

Turner, John, 525, 1811

Turner, Ralph, 1717

Turner, Terence, 684

Turvey, Brent, 1476

Tversky, Amos, 417, 548, 1824

Twelve-step programs, 28, 1928; helping and, 911

Twin studies, 840, 1395, 1520, 1896; antisocial personality disorder, 164; cognition, 85; intelligence, 3, 1578; panic disorder, 98; schizophrenia, 1682; schizotypal personality disorder, 1686; Tourette's syndrome, 2006

Two-dimensional circumplex model of stress, 1885

Two-factor theory, 167, 1419, 1615

Two-factor theory of love, 1135

Type A behavior pattern, 503, 899, 1534, 1895, 1901, 2015-2019; physiological responsiveness, 1397

Type B behavior pattern, 2016

Uncertainty avoidance, 686, 1382

Unconditioned response, 55, 456, 1101, 1367-1368, 1946

Unconditioned stimulus, 55, 456, 1101, 1368, 1945

Unconscious, 34, 132, 472, 805, 1487, 1492, 1519, 2068; collective, 135, 139, 176-180, 1055-1056, 1488; personal, 135, 139

Unconscious guilt, 878

Unconscious motivation, 18

Unconscious transference, 740

Underachievement, gifted children, 850

Undifferentiated schizophrenia, 1672

Uninvolved style of parenting, 1352

United States v. Brawner (1972), 12

Urban, Klaus, 519

Urban living, 701

Urine alarm, 251

Ury, William, 484

Utility theory, 262, 548

Vagg, Peter R., 1869

Vaillant, George E., 655

Validity, 197, 1315, 1573

Valproic acid, 1226

Values, 420, 948, 1705; jurors, 1090

Van Geert, Paul, 1083

Van Wagenen, William, 317

Variability, measures of, 538

Variables, 258, 443, 539; between-subject, 1690; dependent and independent, 727, 734, 1573, 1689, 2050; dispositional and situational, 421

Vascular theory of facial efference, 748

Vasopressin, 694, 932, 1430

Verbal behavior, 272

Vernon, Philip E., 3, 948, 1024

ViCAP. *See* Violent Criminal Apprehension Program

Victims, 774, 1592, 1769, 1968

Violence, 527, 1642, 1842; children and teenagers, 2024-2026; gender differences, 819; homelessness, 920; masculinity, 1138, 1187; media depictions of, 1144, 1150, 1311, 2020-2024; psychological causes and effects, 2027-2030

Violent Criminal Apprehension Program, 789

Virtual reality, 979, 1365, 2030-2034

Visher, Emily B., 1876

Visher, John S., 1876

Vision, 315, 1936; aging, 83, 88; brightness and contrast, 2034-2037; color, 2038-2041; pattern recognition, 1361, 1364. *See also* Nearsightedness; Farsightedness

Visual agnosia, 1362

Visual kinesthetic disassociation, 1067

Visual system, 2041-2045

Visuo-spatial sketchpad, 1780

Vogel, Philip, 317

Voice disorders, 1845

Voluntarism, 1512, 1904

Voyeurism, 1592, 1771

Vroom, Victor, 1095, 2073

Vygotsky, Lev, 652, 1081, 1113

Wada test, 1856

Wagner, Allan, 1609

Wagner, Hugh, 75

Wagner, Rudolph F., 637

Wagner von Jauregg, Julius, 833

WAIS. *See* Wechsler Adult Intelligence Scale

Wald, George, 2040

Walker, Alexis, 828

Walker, Lawrence J., 2062

Walker, Lenore, 243, 615
Wall, Patrick, 1336
Wallace, Edwin R., 1198
Wallace, R. K., 475
Walsh, James, 1015, 1557
Walster, Elaine, 223, 1133
Walters, Richard H., 1310, 1818
Wann, Daniel, 1861
Ward, W. S., 957
Warden, Carl J., 629, 990
Watson, Charles, 965
Watson, John B., 269, 417, 468, 1314, 1502, 1514, 1657, 2046-2047; Little Albert study, 238, 266, 352, 767, 1118, 1370, 1421
Watts, James W., 1120, 1498, 1539
Watzlawick, Paul, 1881
Waynbaum, Israel, 748
Ways of Coping Checklist, 502
Weapons effect, 739
Weather, 700, 704
Weber, Max, 1332
Webster, Ronald L., 1912
Wechsler, David, 1022, 1027, 1029, 2047
Wechsler Adult Intelligence Scale, 2, 340, 847
Wechsler Intelligence Scale for Children-Third Edition, 2, 2047-2049
Weeks, Gerald, 1883
Wehr, Thomas, 1695
Weiner, Bernard, 22, 354
Weisenberg, T., 1858
Weisz, John, 1544
Welin Activity Scale, 1822
Well-being, 896, 1046, 1439, 1711, 1821, 1853
Wells, Gary, 968
Wernicke, Carl, 174, 1858
Wernicke-Korsakoff syndrome, 103, 565, 791
Wernicke's aphasia. See Receptive aphasia
Wernicke's area, 1498
Wertheimer, Max, 1513, 1733
Western Collaborative Group Study, 2016

Westphal, Alexander, 99
White, Gregory, 355
White, Robert, 500, 1235
Whitehead, George, 356
Whiting, John, 41
Wicker, A. W, 216
Widom, Cathy Spatz, 163
Wiesel, Torsten, 147
Wilkie, William, 481
Wilkins, Arnold, 1183
Will, D. P., 1401
Williams, Carl, 1326
Williams, Carol, 215
Williams, Frank, 518
Williams, George, 651
Williamson, E. G., 1036
Wills, Thomas A., 1841
Wilpert, Bernhard, 1095
Wilson, Edward O., 64, 713
Wilson, Gregory L., 512
Wilson, Laurie, 512
Wilson, Timothy, 1722
Wilson, William, 28
Winnicott, Donald, 776
Winter depression. See Seasonal affective disorder
WISC-III. See Wechsler Intelligence Scale for Children-Third Edition
Withdrawn personality, 1828
Wohl, Michael J. A., 798
Wolfe, Montrose, 1996
Wolpe, Joseph, 255, 266, 272, 1371, 1421, 1557, 1940
Women, 2054-2059; abuse, 243, 614, 774; eating disorders, 153, 640
Women's psychology; Sigmund Freud, 2067-2072; Carol Gilligan, 2059-2063; Karen Horney, 2064-2067
Wonderlic Personnel Test, 341
Woodruff, Robert, 964
Woodsworth Personal Data Sheet, 340, 1400
Woodworth, Robert S., 1400, 1513, 1908, 1983
Worchel, Stephen, 355
Word, Carl, 1825

Word association, 137
Word-length effect, 1780
Work; elderly, 1638; motivation, 992, 2066, 2072-2076; reentry, 2076-2079
Working backward, 1468, 1471
Working self-concept, 1835
Workplace issues, 78, 345, 489, 1003, 1249, 1393, 1455, 1669, 2078-2083; elderly, 72. See also Sexual harassment
World Health Organization, 1038
WPT. See Wonderlic Personnel Test
Wright, Herbert, 705
Writing, 1243
Writing disorder, 1107
Wundt, Wilhelm, 417, 468, 726, 885, 1178, 1512, 1688, 1738, 1904, 1971
Wyatt v. Stickney (1971), 14

Xenophobia, 1418

Yalom, Irvin D., 723, 871, 2084-2085
Yamada, Jeni, 1082
Yarmey, A. Daniel, 1091
Yerkes-Dodson law, 164, 1328, 1887
Yetton, Philip, 1095
Yoga, 1152
Young, Thomas, 2040
Young-Helmholtz trichromatic theory of color vision, 2040
Yung, Alison, 1679

Zajonc, Robert, 56, 748, 1329
Zanna, Mark, 1825
Zelazo, Philip, 1425
Zen Buddhism, 1152
Zettle, Robert D., 1651
Zillmann, Dolf, 1330
Zimbardo, Philip, 1339, 1783, 1866, 2086-2087
Zoophilia, 1773
Zurif, E. B., 1857
Zyzanski, Stephen, 2016